OXFORD MEDIEVAL TEXTS

General Editors

D. E. GREENWAY   B. F. HARVEY

M. LAPIDGE

THE CHRONICLE OF
JOHN OF WORCESTER

THE CHRONICLE OF
JOHN OF WORCESTER

III

VOLUME III

THE ANNALS FROM 1067 TO 1140

WITH

THE GLOUCESTER INTERPOLATIONS

AND

THE CONTINUATION TO 1141

EDITED AND TRANSLATED BY

P. McGURK

CLARENDON PRESS · OXFORD

1998

Oxford University Press, Great Clarendon Street, Oxford OX2 6DP

Oxford New York

Athens Auckland Bangkok Bogota Bombay
Buenos Aires Calcutta Cape Town Dar es Salaam
Delhi Florence Hong Kong Istanbul Karachi
Kuala Lumpur Madras Madrid Melbourne
Mexico City Nairobi Paris Singapore
Taipei Tokyo Toronto Warsaw
and associated companies in
Berlin Ibadan

Oxford is a trade mark of Oxford University Press

Published in the United States
by Oxford University Press Inc., New York

British Library Cataloguing in Publication Data
Data available

Library of Congress Cataloguing in Publication Data
Data applied for

ISBN 0-19-820702-6

1 3 5 7 9 10 8 6 4 2

Typeset by Joshua Associates Ltd., Oxford
Printed in Great Britain by
Biddles Ltd., Guildford & King's Lynn

PREFACE

THIS volume contains the annals for 1067 to 1140 of the chronicle of John of Worcester. In addition it prints the interpolations a Gloucester chronicler made in John's annals for 1122 to 1140 in the latter's self-styled *chronicula* (Dublin, Trinity College 503) together with the continuation to 1141 which alone survives in this witness. Some of the problems raised by the annals printed here are considered in the introduction to this volume.

As already promised in the preface to vol. ii, vol. i will offer a general introduction, an edition of the episcopal lists, royal genealogies and accounts, and some indication of the contents of the chronicle before 450 and of the Marianan world history on which John's chronicle was based. The supplementary annals prepared by John for the *chronicula* will be edited separately in an appendix to vol. i.

Many obligations are gratefully acknowledged: to Mark Blackburn, Vivien Brown, Charles Burnett, David Dumville, Michael Gullick, Michael Hare, Graham Loud, Simon Keynes, and Christopher Norton for guidance on particular points; to Elizabeth O'Connor for clarifying the arguments in the introduction; and to Michael Winterbottom for making some passages of John more intelligible. As before, Martin Brett was throughout a judicious guide, and read the introduction with great care. My debt to the general editors is as deep as it had been in vol. ii: to Diana Greenway who read the typescript most helpfully; and to Barbara Harvey and Michael Lapidge who scrutinized the proofs vigilantly and beneficially. Christine Butler, Gill Cannell, and Bernard Meehan assisted my study of the John manuscripts in the libraries of Corpus Christi Colleges at Oxford and Cambridge, and of Trinity College, Dublin respectively, and I am grateful to them and to the other librarians and staff there and in the British Library, the Bodleian Library, Oxford, and in Lambeth Palace Library for allowing to examine me their Marianus and John codices. I have been fortunate in being able to use the libraries of the Institute of Historical Research and of Birkbeck College. John Cordy's copy-editing was a salutary and chastening experience, Anne Joshua's transformation of complicated and unclear word-processing files into a well laid-out text miraculous, and Leofranc Holford-Strevens made some helpful suggestions. At the Press Anne Gelling was as before courteous, considerate, and efficient. I can only repeat the hope that the late R. R. Darlington would not have been too disappointed by this further continuation of his work.

9 January 1998   P. MCGURK

CONTENTS

LIST OF PLATES

Reproduced by kind permission of the President and Fellows of
Corpus Christi College, Oxford.

ABBREVIATIONS

AC	*Annales Cambriae*, ed. J. Williams ab Ithel (RS xx; London, 1860)
ANS	*Anglo-Norman Studies: Proceedings of the Battle Conference on Anglo-Norman Studies*, i–xi (1979–89), ed. R. Allen Brown; xii–xvi (1990–4), ed. M. Chibnall; xvii–xviii (1995–6), ed. C. Harper-Bill; continued from 1983 as *Anglo-Norman Studies*
ASC	Anglo-Saxon Chronicle
Ann. Mon.	*Annales Monastici*, ed. H. R. Luard (5 vols., RS xxxvi; London, 1864–9)
Ann. Winchcombe	R. R. Darlington, 'Winchcombe Annals, 1049–1181', in *A Medieval Miscellany for Doris Mary Stenton*, ed. P. M. Barnes and C. F. Slade (Pipe Roll Society, NS xxxviii; London, 1962 for 1960), pp. 111–37
BD	Baudri of Dol, *Historia Jerosolimitana*, in *RHC Occ.*
BHL	*Bibliotheca hagiographica latina antiquae et mediae aetatis* (2 vols., Brussels, 1898–1901)
BL	London, British Library
BS	*Brenhined y Saeson or the Kings of the Saxons*, ed. T. Jones (Cardiff, 1971)
Barlow, *William Rufus*	F. Barlow, *William Rufus* (London, 1983)
Brett, *English Church*	M. Brett, *The English Church under Henry I* (Oxford, 1975)
Brett, 'John of Worcester and his contemporaries'	M. Brett, 'John of Worcester and his contemporaries', in *The Writing of History in the Middle Ages: Essays presented to Richard William Southern*, ed. R. H. C. Davis and J. M. Wallace-Hadrill (Oxford, 1981), pp. 101–26
Brut	*Brut y Tywysogyon or the Chronicle of the Princes*
Her.	*Brut . . . Princes: Red Book of Hergest Version*, ed. T. Jones (Cardiff, 1955)
Pen.	*Brut . . . Princes: Peniarth MS 20 Version*, ed. T. Jones (Cardiff, 1952)
CP	*The Complete Peerage of England, Scotland, Ireland*, by G. E. C. (revd. edn., 13 vols. in 14, London, 1910–59)

Cart. Gloc.	*Historia et cartularium monasterii sancti Petri Glou-cestriae*, ed. W. H. Hart (3 vols., RS xxxiii; London, 1884–93)
Caspar, *Registrum*	E. Caspar (ed.), *Gregorii VII Registrum* (MGH *Epistolae Selectae*, 2nd edn., 1955)
Chibnall, *Empress Matilda*	M. Chibnall, *The Empress Matilda* (Oxford, 1991)
Chronica de Hyda	*Chronica de Hyda*, in *Liber monasterii de Hyda*, ed. E. Edwards (RS xlv; London, 1866)
Chronicles Stephen, etc.	*Chronicles of the Reigns of Stephen, Henry II, and Richard I*, ed. R. Howlett (4 vols., RS lxxxii; London, 1884–9)
Chronicon de Abingdon	*Chronicon monasterii de Abingdon*, ed. J. Stevenson (2 vols., RS ii; London, 1858)
Clark, *Peterborough Chronicle*	C. Clark, *The Peterborough Chronicle 1070–1174* (2nd edn., Oxford, 1970)
Cronne, *Reign of Stephen*	H. A. Cronne, *The Reign of Stephen: Anarchy in England 1135–54* (London, 1970)
Crouch, *Beaumont Twins*	D. Crouch, *The Beaumont Twins: the Roots and Branches of Power in the Twelfth Century* (Cambridge, 1986)
DB	Domesday Book
David, *Robert Curthose*	C. W. David, *Robert Curthose, Duke of Normandy* (Cambridge, Mass., 1920)
Davis, *King Stephen*	R. H. C. Davis, *King Stephen* (3rd edn., London, 1990)
Douglas, *William the Conqueror*	D. C. Douglas, *William the Conqueror* (London, 1964)
EEA	*English Episcopal Acta* (London, 1980–)
EHR	*English Historical Review*
Eadmer, *VA*	Eadmer, *Vita Anselmi*, ed. R. Southern (NMT, 1962, reprinted OMT 1972 and Sandpiper Books 1996)
Eadmer, *HN*	Eadmer, *Historia Novorum in Anglia*, ed. M. Rule (RS lxxxi; London, 1864)
Epis. Lists	The episcopal lists preceding the chronicle of John of Worcester (to be published in vol. i)
Freeman, *Reign of William Rufus*	E. A. Freeman, *The Reign of William Rufus* (2 vols., Oxford, 1882)
GF	*Anonymi Gesta Francorum et aliorum Hierosolymi-tarum*, ed. R. Hill (NMT, 1962)
GFL	*The Letters and Charters of Gilbert Foliot*, ed. A. Morey and C. N. L. Brooke (Cambridge, 1967)
GND	*Gesta Normannorum Ducum of William of Jumièges,*

Orderic Vitalis, and Robert of Torigni, ed. Elisabeth
M. C. Van Houts (2 vols., OMT, 1992–5)

GS   *Gesta Stephani*, ed. K. R. Potter, rev. R. H. C. Davis
(OMT, 1976)

Gaimar   Geffrei Gaimar, *L'Estoire des Engleis*, ed. A. Bell
(Anglo-Norman Texts, xiv–xvi; Oxford, 1960)

Gallia Christiana   *Gallia Christiana* (16 vols., Paris, 1715–1865)

Gervase   *The Historical Works of Gervase of Canterbury*, ed.
W. Stubbs (2 vols., RS lxxiii; London, 1879–80)

Gesta abbatum   *Gesta abbatum monasterii S. Albani* (Matthew Paris
   S. Albani   *et al.*), ed. H. T. Riley (3 vols., RS xxviii; London,
1867–9)

Gesta Guillelmi   *The Gesta Guillelmi of William of Poitiers*, ed.
R. H. C. Davis and M. Chibnall (OMT, 1998)

Gir. Cambr.   *Opera: Giraldi Cambrensis*, ed. J. S. Brewer, J. F.
Dimmock, and G. F. Warner (8 vols., RS xxi;
London, 1861–91)

Green, *Government*   J. Green, *The Government of England under Henry I*
(Cambridge, 1986)

Greenway, *Fasti*   *John Le Neve: Fasti Ecclesiae Anglicanae 1066–1300*
(revd. edn.), i *St Paul's London*; ii *Monastic Cathedrals*; iii *Lincoln*; iv *Salisbury*; v *Chichester*; ed. D. E.
Greenway (London, 1968–96)

HBC   *Handbook of British Chronology*, ed. E. B. Fryde, D. E.
Greenway, and I. Roy (3rd edn., London, 1986)

HC   *Hugh the Chanter: The History of the Church of York
1066–1127*, ed. C. Johnson, rev. M. Brett, C. N. L.
Brooke, and M. Winterbottom (OMT, 1990)

HDE   *Historia Dunelmensis Ecclesiae*, in SD i. 3–160

HH *HA*   *Henry of Huntingdon: Historia Anglorum*, ed. Diana
Greenway (OMT, 1996)

HR   *Historia Regum*, in SD ii. 98–283

Hagenmeyer   H. Hagenmeyer, *Chronologie de la première croisade
(1094–1100)* (Paris, 1902)

Harmer, *Writs*   F. E. Harmer, *Anglo-Saxon Writs* (Manchester,
1952)

Haskins, *Norman*   C. H. Haskins, *Norman Institutions* (Cambridge,
   Institutions   Mass., 1925)

Heads   *The Heads of Religious Houses, England and Wales,
940–1216*, ed. D. Knowles, C. N. L. Brooke, and
V. C. M. London (Cambridge, 1972)

Hoveden   *Chronica Rogerii de Hovedene*, ed. W. Stubbs (4
vols., RS li; London, 1868–71)

JW	John of Worcester
JW, *Chronicle ii*	*The Chronicle of John of Worcester*, ii. *The Annals from 450 to 1066*, ed. R. R. Darlington and P. McGurk (OMT, 1995)
Jaffé	P. Jaffé (ed.), *Regesta Pontificum Romanorum . . . ad annum . . . 1198*, 2nd edn., ed. W. Wattenbach, S. Loewenfeld, F. Kaltenbrunner, and P. Ewald (2 vols., Leipzig, 1885–8)
Kapelle, *Norman Conquest of the North*	William E. Kapelle, *The Norman Conquest of the North: The Region and its Transformation, 1000–1135* (London, 1979)
LE	*Liber Eliensis*, ed. E. O. Blake (Camden 3rd Series, xcii; London, 1962)
LL	J. Gwenogvryn Evans, *The Book of Llandaff: The Text of the Book of Llan Dâv, reproduced from the Gwysaney MS* (Oxford, 1893)
LVD	*Liber Vitae Ecclesie Dunelmensis; nec non obituaria duo ejusdem ecclesiae*, ed. J. Stevenson (Surtees Society xiii; London, 1841)
LVH	*Liber Vitae: Register and Martyrology of New Minster and Hyde Abbey, Winchester*, ed. W. de G. Birch (Hampshire Record Society, 5; London, 1892)
Lanfranc, *Letters*	*The Letters of Lanfranc, Archbishop of Canterbury*, ed. H. Glover and M. Gibson (OMT, 1979)
Lloyd, *History of Wales*	J. E. Lloyd, *History of Wales* (2 vols., 3rd edn., London, 1939)
MGH	Monumenta Germaniae Historica
SS	Scriptores in folio
Marianus	Marianus Scotus, *Chronicon*; bk. iii was printed by G. Waitz, MGH SS v (1884), pp. 481–562
Memorials St Edmund's	*Memorials of St Edmund's Abbey*, ed. T. Arnold (3 vols., RS xcvi; London, 1890–1)
Meyer von Knonau, *Jahrbücher*	G. Meyer von Knonau, *Jahrbücher des deutschen Reiches unter Heinrich IV und Heinrich V* (7 vols., Königliche Akademie der Wissenschaften, Hist. Commission; Leipzig, 1890–1909)
Mon.	W. Dugdale, *Monasticon Anglicanum*, ed. J. Caley, H. Ellis, and B. Bandinel (6 vols. in 8, London, 1817–30)
NMT	Nelson's Medieval Texts
Nicholl, *Thurstan*	D. Nicholl, *Archbishop Thurstan of York (1114–1140)* (York, 1964)
OMT	Oxford Medieval Texts

OV	Orderic Vitalis
OV *HE*	*The Ecclesiastical History of Orderic Vitalis*, ed. M. Chibnall (6 vols., OMT, 1969–80)
PL	*Patrologiae cursus completus, series Latina*, ed. J. P. Migne (221 vols., Paris, 1844–64)
Pipe Roll 31 Henry I	*Pipe Roll, 31 Henry I*, ed. J. Hunter (Record Commission, London, 1833)
Plummer, *Chronicle*	C. Plummer and J. Earle, *Two of the Saxon Chronicles Parallel* (2 vols., Oxford, 1892–9)
Prou, *Recueil*	M. Prou, *Recueil des Actes de Philippe Ier roi de France* (Chartes et Diplômes relatifs à l'Histoire de France; Paris 1908)
Quadripartitus	F. Liebermann, *Quadripartitus, ein englisches Rechtsbuch von 1114* (Halle, 1892)
RHC Occ.	*Recueil des historiens des croisades: historiens occidentaux* i–v (Paris, 1846–1900)
RS	Rolls Series
Raine, *Priory of Hexham*	J. Raine, *The Priory of Hexham* (2 vols., Surtees Society xliv, xlvi; London, 1864–5)
Recueil des historiens de France	*Recueil des historiens des Gaules et de la France*, ed. M. Bouquet *et al.*, new edn. L. Delisle (24 vols., Paris, 1869–1904)
Regesta	*Regesta regum Anglo-Normannorum, 1066–1154*: i. *1066–1100, Regesta Willelmi Conquestoris et Willelmi Rufi*, ed. H. W. C. Davis and R. J. Whitwell; ii. *1100–1135, Regesta Henrici Primi*, ed. C. Johnson and H. A. Cronne; iii. *Regesta Stephani*, ed. H. A. Cronne and R. H. C. Davis (Oxford, 1913–69)
Regesta regum Scottorum	*Regesta regum Scottorum*, i. *Acts of Malcolm IV, King of Scots, 1153–1165*, ed. G. W. S. Barrow (Edinburgh, 1960)
Richter, *Canterbury Professions*	M. Richter, *Canterbury Professions* (Canterbury and York Society lxvii; Torquay, 1973)
SD	*Symeonis monachi opera omnia*, ed. T. Arnold (2 vols., RS lxxv; London, 1888)
Sanders, *English Baronies*	I. J. Sanders, *English Baronies* (Oxford, 1960)
Schmitt, *Anselmi opera omnia*	F. S. Schmitt, ed., *S. Anselmi Opera Omnia*, i (Seckau, 1938); i (repr.)–vi (Edinburgh, 1946–61)
Stubbs, *Select Charters*	W. Stubbs, *Select Charters and other Illustrations of English Constitutional History*, 9th edn., revd. H. W. C. Davis (Oxford, 1913)

Suger, *Vita Ludovici*	Suger, *Vita Ludovici Grossi Regis*, ed. H. Waquet (Paris, 1929)
Torigni, *Chronicle*	*The Chronicle of Robert of Torigni*, in *Chronicles Stephen, etc.* iv
UAG	*Ungedruckte anglo-normannische Geschichtsquellen*, ed. F. Liebermann (Strasbourg, 1879, repr. Ridgwood, NJ, 1966)
VCH	Victoria County History
Vita Lanfranci	Milo, *Vita Lanfranci* in *Lanfranci Opera Omnia*, ed. J. A. Giles (2 vols., London, 1844)
WM	William of Malmesbury
WM *GP*	*Willelmi Malmesbiriensis monachi de gestis pontificum Anglorum libri quinque*, ed. N. E. S. A. Hamilton (RS lii; London, 1870)
WM *GR*	*Willelmi Malmesbiriensis monachi de gestis regum Anglorum libri quinque*, ed. W. Stubbs (2 vols., RS xc; London, 1887–9)
WM *HN*	William of Malmesbury, *Historia novella*, ed. K. R. Potter (NMT, 1955)
WM, *Vita Wulfstani*	*The Vita Wulfstani of William of Malmesbury*, ed. R. R. Darlington (Camden 3rd Series xl; London, 1928)
Wace	*Le Roman de Rou de Wace*, ed. A. J. Holden (3 vols., Société des anciens textes français; Paris, 1970–3)
Watterich	M. Watterich (ed.), *Pontificum Romanorum qui fuerunt inde ab exeunte saeculo ix usque ad finem saeculi xiii vitae ab equalibus conscriptae* (2 vols., Leipzig, 1872)
Whitelock, *ASC*	*The Anglo-Saxon Chronicle: A Revised Translation*, ed. D. Whitelock with D. C. Douglas and S. L. Tucker (London, 1961)
Whitelock, Brett, and Brooke, *Councils and Synods*	D. Whitelock, M. Brett, and C. N. L. Brooke, *Councils and Synods with other Documents relating to the English Church*, i. *A.D. 871–1204* (2 vols., Oxford, 1981)
Worcester Cartulary	*Cartulary of Worcester Cathedral Priory*, ed. R. R. Darlington (Pipe Roll Society lxxvi; London, 1968 for 1962–3)

INTRODUCTION

Both the writers to whom the Worcester chronicle has been attributed are named in the annals for 1067–1140 printed in this volume: the death of Florence of Worcester, 'huius subtili scientia et studiosi laboris industria, preeminet cunctis haec chronicarum chronica', is announced under 1118, and under 1128 and 1138 John is named as the author of two entries.[1] The annals for 1128 to 1140 in the chief working copy of the chronicle (Oxford, Corpus Christi College 157, *siglum* C) seem to have been written in John's hand so that in these annals at least he appears both as compiler and scribe, and his working methods can be examined at close hand.[2] These annals are therefore of particular interest, but the other annals in this volume repay study both for their content and for their evidence of the historical sources available at Worcester in the second quarter of the twelfth century. The first part of this introduction provides a brief description of the manuscripts used in this edition, and this is followed by a second part, an interim assessment of John's sources and working method as seen in the annals for 1067–1140.

The self-styled *chronicula* manuscript, Dublin, Trinity College 503 (*siglum* G), which was largely based on the larger chronicle, was written in John's hand up to the annal 1123. It was then continued mainly by one hand which contributed many additions and interpolations to the chronicle of John. Many of these additions have Gloucester connections, and as they often give information of interest, they are published in this volume. The third part of this introduction considers the additions made by the main scribe in G, and the problems faced by their compiler in grafting them on to John's work. The final section deals with the few pages in the *chronicula* manuscript G which extend John's chronicle beyond its imperfect conclusion in the chief working copy, C, and considers how much of this continuation may have been part of John's original chronicle.

---

[1] See below, pp. 142, 180–2, 244.

[2] For John as scribe see vol. ii, pp. xxix, xxxiv, and Pl. 4.

I. THE MANUSCRIPTS USED IN THIS EDITION

Reference should be made to the full descriptions of the make-up, palaeography, and contents of the John of Worcester chronicle manuscripts in vol. ii, pp. xxi–lix, and the following summaries offer only a brief guide to their date and composition.

1. *Manuscripts of the Chronicle*

There are five complete manuscripts of John of Worcester's chronicle, and four of them are derived, directly or indirectly, from the fifth.

C = Oxford, Corpus Christi College 157

This, the chief manuscript of the chronicle, was the source of all four other copies, and was the only one to continue to 1140 where it now ends imperfectly, and to contain revised annals for 1128 to 1131. It was written at Worcester by three scribes, C^1, C^2, and C^3, all three of whom corrected and added to the text, and transformed a fair copy into a working one. The third scribe has been plausibly identified with John of Worcester, and the date of his final writing here was presumably in or after 1140. C^1 wrote to p. 363 ('exercitus domum' in mid-1101), C^2 from p. 364 ('comitis uero' in mid-1101) to p. 379 l. 35 ('fore promisit' in 1128), and C^3 from p. 379 l. 36 ('De iuramento' in 1128) to the end.

H = Dublin, Trinity College 502

This contains the annals to 1131 with additions to 1138. This is the only witness to the full text of relatively small format. The annals to 1131 were written by one hand probably at Coventry towards the middle of the twelfth century. At a later date a second hand, here called H^2, added some annals from 1132 to 1138 on fos. 260–4. Brett showed that H and the Abingdon witness L were probably copied from a copy of C.[3] In vol. ii, pp. xxxv–xxxvi, it was suggested that E (Evesham, Almonry Museum s. n. fly leaf) was the single-leaf remnant of this copy, but as its annals were confined to parts of 531–2 it is not used in this volume.

---

[3] Brett, 'John of Worcester', pp. 106–7.

L = London, Lambeth Palace Library 42

This contains the annals to 1131, and was written at Abingdon by a late twelfth-century hand. Like H it was copied from a copy of C. It contains some Abingdon interpolations which are here printed in Appendix A.

B = Oxford, Bodleian Library Bodley 297

This contains the annals to 1131. It is a Bury manuscript which was copied directly from C before its final revision by John, and probably before 1143. It has numerous marginal additions, a few interlineations, and many interpolations, some with Bury connections, and these are printed in Appendix B. It was written by two scribes. The first, B[1], wrote pp. 1–344, and was responsible for many of the additions. The second, B[2], wrote pp. 345–423a. Various hands contributed additions, of which B[3], B[4], B[5], and B[6] contributed more than one. Probably another eight contributed one addition each. The two extracts from Jocelin of Brakelond on pp. 423b–425 are in an early thirteenth-century hand.

P = Cambridge, Corpus Christi College 92

This manuscript contains three chronicles, the chronicle of John of Worcester to 1131, the 'Intermediate Compilation' (1132–54), and the Bury chronicle in the Peterborough version from 1152 to 1295. At its opening it is strikingly close to L, and this closeness is confirmed by its copying some of L's Abingdon interpolations, which are printed in Appendix A. But it has indirect connections with C, and this is sometimes demonstrated by its copying of readings that represent two stages in C. The greater part of P (to fo. 174^{v}a l. 15, that is, nearly to the end of the 'Intermediate Compilation' under 1154) was probably written at Abingdon by three later twelfth-century scribes. They were: P[1] (fos. 1–23), P[2] (fos. 24–83^v b l. 38 'coequatur'), P[3] (fos. 83^v b l. 38 'Tibianus'–174). A contemporary later twelfth-century scribe, P[5], contributed some marginal additions. A late thirteenth-century scribe completed the Bury-Peterborough chronicle, probably either at or for Peterborough.

As was stated above, all manuscripts of John's chronicle depend directly or indirectly upon C. All four derivative copies (HLBP) end in 1131, C being the only one of the full Chronicle manuscripts to extend to 1140. H and L are copied from a copy of an early stage of C, though in the later annals in this volume H differs on occasion from L. B is copied directly from a later stage of C than that represented by HL, and P has links both with L and with C.

2. The John of Worcester Chronicula

G = Dublin, Trinity College 503

This manuscript of small format describes itself as a *chronicula* based on the larger *chronica chronicarum*. The greater part of it (to 1123) is written in John of Worcester's hand, but the annals were extended to 1141 and have interpolations with Gloucester connections. There were four scribes: G^I, plausibly John of Worcester (fos. 37^r-113^v l. 23 (1123: 'pro petendo pallio Romam iuit')); G^2 fos. 1^v-36^v, 113^v l. 24 (1123: 'Alexander rex Scottorum . . .')-115^r l. 24 (1125: 'sui abbates'), 116^v l. 17 (1126: 'sicut intrare . . .')-151^v (1141: the end); G^3 on fo. 115^v; and G^4 on fos 116^v (opening of 1126)-116^v l. 17 (1126: 'per uices suas').

3. A Marianus Scotus Manuscript

John used the recension of Marianus Scotus' chronicle represented by London, British Library Cotton Nero C. V

N = London, British Library Cotton Nero C. V

This was written by three hands of probable continental origin of the later eleventh century, and may have been the codex used by Robert of Hereford.[4] It may have been at Worcester for a period in the twelfth century.[5]

---

[4] In vol. ii, p. lxv the hands, which were not described as English, were dated to the early 12th cent. The hands are very likely continental, and an earlier date would make possible the connection with Robert of Hereford who died in 1095.

[5] Michael Gullick has kindly informed me that a title on fo. 3^r dating from the mid-12th cent. is by a hand also responsible for titles in five Hereford manuscripts. Notwithstanding these Hereford connections the addition under 1062 of 'Ordinatio Wlstani episcopi' and 'Ob. Wlstanus et Rodbertus episcopi' could suggest N being at Worcester at some stage.

II. JOHN OF WORCESTER'S CHRONICLE
1067–1140

1. Sources and Working Method

There are some obvious differences in content and approach between many of the annals in this volume and those in the rest of John's chronicle, and these differences are the excuse for offering here an interim assessment of John's sources and working method for the annals 1067–1140 pending a fuller examination in the introduction to vol. i.[6] The later annals in this volume were written down soon after the events described, and their last five years, 1135–40, offer the observations of a contemporary. They include from 1070 onwards a body of conciliar information and material not available to John for events before that date.[7] For most of the period too there survives only one version of the Anglo-Saxon Chronicle (witness E), and consideration of John's use of it is consequently less complex than for the years where more versions survive.[8] Finally, there is a marked contrast between the annals for 1067–1140 and those for 450–1066, since this volume shows the two recensions of John's chronicle ending at two different dates, one at 1131, the other at 1140.

The grafting of many anecdotes on to bare factual annals makes the rewritten annals for 1128–31 strikingly different from those they replaced. Thus the original 1131 annal is made up of some brief entries, that is, of Henry I's crossing over to Normandy, the consecration of Robert de Bethune as bishop of Hereford, the blessing of Abbot Serlo of Cirencester, and, depending on the witnesses, two or four obits. In the rewritten annal for 1131 (which C³ dates 1130 through an error in transcription) these brief entries are swamped by lengthy anecdotal additions, that is, oral witnesses' accounts at Hereford and Brecon of celestial phenomena, the nightmares of Henry I, and the storm on his return crossing from Normandy.[9] C³'s 1131 annal is entirely taken up with the account of Odilia and her father's smelly shirt, and the 1132 annal, except for the report of a comet, is given up to John's personal account of the

---

[6] This examination was promised in vol. ii, p. v.

[7] Take, e.g., the *capitula* for the legatine councils of Westminster of 1125 and 1127: see below, pp. 160–5, 168–73

[8] Plummer, *Chronicle*, i. 200–69, Clark, *Peterborough Chronicle*, pp. 2–60, Whitelock, *ASC*, pp. 146–203.

[9] See below, pp. 198–203.

death of Uhtred, precentor of Worcester Cathedral.[10] John's annals for 1133–8 include portents, visions, and miracles, which seem sometimes to have been assigned rather arbitrarily to particular years, and which make them particularly different in character from most of the annals before 1066.[11]

In the annals before 1131 John depended to a great extent on the Anglo-Saxon Chronicle and Eadmer's *Historia Novorum*, 1087 being an example of one annal almost totally dependent on the first, 1116 another where the derivation from Eadmer was very much more obvious. A glance at the following pages will show that from 1102 to 1122 Eadmer is extensively reproduced, though he was used at an earlier point for alterations to the text, in marginal additions from 1092, and in rewriting over erasures from 1095. Eadmer sometimes seems to replace an entry derived from the Anglo-Saxon Chronicle. The annals for 1095 and 1114, for instance, have Eadmer texts describing respectively the arrival of Bishop Walter of Albano and the exceptional drying up of the river beds of the Medway and Thames, and they were written over erasures: it is very likely that the texts they replaced were renderings of an Anglo-Saxon Chronicle version of these events.[12] The annal for 1108 is made up of entries based on the Chronicle and on Eadmer, though from this point onwards until 1122 the balance of dependence switches to the Canterbury writer.

The Anglo-Saxon Chronicle

In these annals John seems less obviously dependent on a surviving Anglo-Saxon Chronicle text than in the annals before 1067. He always arranges his entries in an annal in calendar sequence when he can, and so often departs from their order in the Anglo-Saxon Chronicle.[13] He also describes many events absent from any surviving vernacular version, and, even when the same episode is covered, John's account is often different. For the period 1067 to 1079 there are two versions of the Anglo-Saxon Chronicle, D and E, which from

---

[10] See below, pp. 202–9.
[11] Miraculous stories are rare and brief in the annals before 1066, the longest being the account of Hermannus Contractus (vol. ii. 497–502), which is a marginal addition in the working copy C, and is absent from the other JW witnesses.
[12] See below, pp. 75–6, 134–5.
[13] John sometimes seems to place an entry in its correct chronological position even when he does not have its exact date, e.g. the death of Henry V under 1125: see below, pp. 158–9.

1057 to 1079, where D ends, drew on a common source. The Peterborough witness E continues to 1155. Its annals to 1131 were written in one hand, and those for 1132–55 were added by a second scribe after 1155 who was rarely able to assign the annals to their proper year.[14] Precursors of E which were made before Peterborough interpolations were added have been assumed to lie behind many twelfth-century historical works such as the Anglo-Saxon Chronicle witness F, the Waverley Annals, Henry of Huntingdon, and William of Malmesbury, and it has been argued that John of Worcester relied on E or a precursor of E for some of his annals.[15]

In the period 1067–79, where two versions survive, D has differences from E, and some of these are shared with John. The hypothesis of a Worcester origin for the compilation of D has been recently revived, and it might be worth looking at some annals where there seems to be an overlap in content between John and D, those for 1067–9.[16] It is well known that D's long annal for 1067 deals with events in that year and in 1068, and that its 1068 annal covered 1068 and 1069. John does not have these inaccurate chronological divisions.[17] He either does not know or ignores the interpolations in D relating to Margaret of Scotland. He gives fuller information for some episodes such as Eadric's revolt (providing an important date), the death of Archbishop Ealdred of York, and the capture of York by the invaders in 1069. Twice he seems to consolidate information. The departure of Harold's mother, Gytha, and other ladies to Flatholme and thence to St Omer, which is placed very late as a

[14] Clark, *Peterborough Chronicle*, pp. xv–xvii, Whitelock, *ASC*, pp. xvi–xvii, also the facsimile edition of E, *The Peterborough Chronicle*, ed. D. Whitelock (Early English Manuscripts in Facsimile iv; Copenhagen, 1954), pp. 14–20.

[15] Whitelock, *ASC*, pp. xvi, xvii, xix, xxi, and in the facsimile edition, *The Peterborough Chronicle*, pp. 26–34.

[16] For D and for the view that Worcester was its place of compilation, see *MS. D*, ed. G. P. Gubbin in *The Anglo-Saxon Chronicle: A Collaborative edition* vi, ed. D. N. Dumville and S. D. Keynes (Woodbridge, 1996), pp. lvi–lxxix, esp. lxv–lxxix. Dr Gubbin declares (on p. lxxix): 'Up to 926 D has long been accepted as a conflation. Now we can add that the conflation was probably done in or near Worcester perhaps around 1060.' On this view, to 1060 or 1069 (the year of the death of its postulated inspirer, Ealdred, archbishop of York) D was compiled and written at Worcester and could have been available to John of Worcester in the writing of his chronicle, though its editor conjectures that after 1069 it 'may have gone to a foundation near Worcester if not in Worcester itself'. It is worth noting that the annals 1066–70 in D were written as a separate stint according to both Ker (N. R. Ker, *Catalogue of Manuscripts containing Anglo-Saxon* (Oxford, 1957), p. 254) and Gubbin (*MS. D*, pp. xiv–xv).

[17] For the differences between John and D under 1067–9 discussed in this paragraph, see the detailed historical commentary on pp. 4–11 below.

separate and independent entry in D's 1067 annal, follows immediately (and possibly appropriately) upon the surrender of Exeter in the same year. In 1068 John has Gospatric leave for Scotland at the same time, and presumably in the same party, as Edgar the Atheling, his mother and sisters, and Mærleswein, whereas D reports Gospatric's departure separately at a much later stage in its 1067 annal. Curiously John does not have any reference to the important entry on events in the North with which D began its 1068 annal, and which it shared with E. These dealt with William I's appointment of Robert as earl in Northumbria, the rebellion against him, and its eventual suppression. This serious omission reduced William's campaigns in the North to only two in 1067–9. John may not have known where to insert this entry in his 1067–9 annals or his exemplar may have been defective at this point. If D had been available at Worcester, the annals for 1067–9 suggest at the very least that John followed it neither slavishly nor exactly, and that he had access to other information.

John seems to derive his description of the Domesday survey not from a text like E's, which he used later in the description of the same survey written in his own hand in the *chronicula*, but from an annal for 1086 added towards the end of the Marianus Scotus chronicle available in England.[18] Taken with John's sometimes markedly different reporting of some events, and his omission of E's report of an earthquake in 1119 which particularly affected Worcestershire and Gloucestershire, the case for John's chronicle relying on a precursor or analogue of E would therefore seem to be weak. Even when the content of John's annal corresponds to that of E, he has important differences, which are sometimes independently supported by other writers like William of Malmesbury and Orderic Vitalis.[19]

[18] For the link between John's 1087 annal and that in the Marianus witness N see W. H. Stevenson, 'A contemporary description of the Domesday Survey', *EHR*, xxii (1907), 72–84, at pp. 77–8. The translation of an E-type version of the Domesday survey also appears in BL Cotton Vitellius C. VIII (printed in *UAG*, pp. 21–2). This codex dates from the third quarter of the 12th cent., and was at Rievaulx in the early 13th cent. (see N. R. Ker, *Medieval Libraries of Great Britain: A List of Surviving Books* (Royal Historical Society Guides and Handbooks, 3; 2nd edn., London, 1964), p. 159). It is largely made up of excerpts from JW and WM, and could well be a mid-12th-cent. Worcester compilation. I am indebted to Michael Gullick for drawing my attention to the reference in Ker, which shows that the Cotton MS was part of BL Royal 6. C. VIII.
[19] An example of overlap with William of Malmesbury is the account of the disturbances at Glastonbury associated with the appointment of Thurstan under 1083

None the less there are many annals in John which are clearly renderings of a text similar to that transmitted by E. Among such are the campaign at Mantes in 1087, the knighting of Henry and the oath of Salisbury in the preceding year, the Scottish successions under 1093 and 1097, the original beginning of John's 1094 annal which is now preserved only in the witness L, the reporting of celestial phenomena under 1104 and 1106, the events of 1106 leading up to the battle of Tinchebrai, the accounts under 1130 of the dedication of Christ Church Canterbury, and the burning of the city of Rochester and the consecration of St Andrew's cathedral there.[20] John's reporting of royal transfretations to 1131 suggests that a vernacular chronicle was consulted at least until that date since they are reported in E and their regular appearance in Henry of Huntingdon to 1133 has rightly been considered as indicating the archdeacon's use of E to that date.[21] John's patchy recording of the meetings of the royal court also demonstrates, as much as their more frequent reporting by Henry, knowledge of an Anglo-Saxon Chronicle, since it is in that text that these meetings are regularly noted.[22] Particular phrases sometimes suggest the translation of a vernacular text. Under 1103, 'sicut ei et rege conuenit', which is surely reminiscent of a phrase like E's 'swa swa him 7 þam cynge gewearð', is placed in the middle of an account of the quarrel between Anselm and Henry I which was based on Eadmer. More tellingly under 1120, the phrase 'ad uelle peractis', an echo of E's 'æfter his willan', is set in the midst of extracts from Eadmer. The use of Eadmer increased to such an extent as the twelfth century opened that traces of an Anglo-Saxon Chronicle connection become fainter, and after borrowing from Eadmer comes to an end with the death of Archbishop Ralph in 1122 it is not easy to find direct links apart from the royal transfretations.

It has just been noted that John seems to have been selective in his recording of the meetings of the royal court. Deliberate rearrangement may in some cases explain other differences between John and his vernacular chronicle. He ends his account, for instance, of the

(see below, pp. 38–40, and of overlap with Orderic Vitalis the Maine campaign of 1098 (see below, pp. 87–8).

[20] See below, pp. 46–7, 44–5, 66–9, 84–5, 68–71, 106–10, and 192–5.

[21] HH *HA*, p. xcii, and for examples see vii. 37, 41 (pp. 477, 489). As far as is known, royal transfretations are regularly reported only in E.

[22] For examples of John's reporting of royal meetings, see below, pp. 90–1, 102–3, and for Henry's see HH *HA*, vii. 23, 34 (pp. 448, 468).

1088 rebellions against the newly established William Rufus with a greatly expanded report of the resistance at Worcester under the miraculous guidance of Bishop Wulfstan. He places the Kentish rebellion first in the annal and the non-Kentish uprisings last, which is the reverse of the order in E, but in so doing he curtails, perhaps through carelessness, the crucial campaigns in Kent on which the survival of William II depended, and thus leaves their outcome uncertain. Appropriately enough E places the conclusion of the Kentish campaign near the end of its annal. Many of John's details in this annal are different from E's, but it is reasonable to assume that his vernacular version did not cut out so important a part of the narrative.[23] Another example of John's possibly deliberate editing of his text is his account of the campaigns in France under 1094. It begins rather like E's but it is then cut rather arbitrarily.[24]

An impression of the differences between John and D and E might be given by tabulating the entries for 1073–9, the last annals shared by the two surviving vernacular chronicles: for details of John's differences from D and E reference should be made to the historical commentary to the text:

1073

D (1074)	E (1073)	JW (1073)
—	—	1. Second lunar cycle (Marianus).
2. William in Maine.	2. William in Maine.	2. William in Maine.
3. Return to England.	3. Return to England.	—

1074

D (1075)	E (1074)	JW (1073)
4. Return to Normandy.	4. Return to Normandy.	—
5. Edgar *cild* reconciled with William.	5. Edgar *cild* reconciled with William.	5. Edgar *cild* reconciled with William.

1075

D (1076)	E (1075)	JW (1074)
—	—	6. Gregory VII (Marianus).
7. Rebellion of the earls.	7. Rebellion of the earls.	7. Rebellion of the earls (with differences).

1076

D (1077)	E (1076)	JW (1075)
8. Death of Cnut.	8. Death of Cnut.	—
9. Execution of Waltheof.	9. Execution of Waltheof.	9. Execution of Waltheof (much fuller).

---

[23] For the whole annal, see below, pp. 48–57.

[24] See below, pp. 72–3.

10. William in Brittany.	10. William in Brittany.	10. William in Brittany. JW (1076) 8. Death of Cnut (added later).
1077 D (1078) 11. Lunar eclipse, various obits. Scottish entry. Wildfire.	E (1077) 11. Agreement between William and Philip I. London burnt down. Two obits.	JW (1077) 11. Robert of Normandy goes to Philip I of France.
1078 Nothing in Anglo-Saxon Chronicle.		JW only has a Marianus entry.
1079 D (1079) 12. Robert goes to Flanders. 13. William and Robert fight.	E (1079) 12. Malcolm's invasion. 13. William and Robert fight at Gerberoi.	JW (1079) 12. Malcolm's invasion. 13. William and Robert fight at Gerberoi (with differences from E).

Some points may be noted here about the above table. First, John appears to be one year behind E in 1074–6. It is just possible that John's exceptional failure to report two transfretations, that is, Anglo-Saxon Chronicle 1073 entry 3 (William I's return to England) and Anglo-Saxon Chronicle entry 4 (William I's crossing over to Normandy), which occur at the very end of 1073 and at the opening of 1074, may have caused the start of a new annal to be overlooked, and consequently the dating of both 1074 entry 5 (the reconciliation between Edgar the atheling and William I) and the annals 1075–6 to be dated one year too early, that is, to 1073, 1074, and 1075 respectively. Second, the death of Cnut seems to be an afterthought in the main John manuscript C, and this might account for a renewed synchronization with the dates in the Anglo-Saxon Chronicle. Third, the entries under 1077 seem to be different in all three chronicles. If John's entry here (on Robert Curthose appealing to King Philip I) has a parallel in D and E it would seem to belong to the 1079 Anglo-Saxon Chronicle account of the war between William I and his son Robert in which Robert was helped by the French king. Fourth, John's entries under 1079 are closer to E than to D. The chronological dislocation under 1073–5 in John and his reporting under 1077 of Robert's appeal to King Philip, which is unknown elsewhere in that year, suggest that John's difficulties may sometimes have been self-inflicted and may not always have originated in the vernacular chronicle texts he was using.

To sum up. John arranged his information in calendar order and this was one obvious difference from D and E. He would seem to have omitted or overlooked some entries which had probably been in his vernacular chronicle, and this oversight may have led him into error. His sources often had more information than either D or E, information which sometimes had the support of other writers. Sometimes even when reporting the same event as D (as with the revolt of Eadric in 1067) or as E (as with the events of 1101) he had different and interesting data. The question of the vernacular chronicles used by John will be examined more fully in the introduction to vol. i. For the moment it can be safely asserted that the chronicle or chronicles used by John sometimes overlapped in content and wording with a precursor and analogue of E and, just possibly, of D.

Eadmer

In the introduction to vol. ii it was noted that the use of Eadmer's *Historia Novorum* in the fair working copy of John's chronicle apparently took place in stages.[25] The first scribe, C^1, who wrote the annals to mid-1101, did not use Eadmer in the body of his text, though he later added some Eadmer passages in the margins.[26] In fact it was the second scribe, C^2, whose stint extended from mid-1101 to mid-1128, who incorporated most of the Eadmer used in John's chronicle into the annals 1102–22, though both he and the third scribe, C^3, used Eadmer when rewriting some text over erasures.[27] There were at least three versions of Eadmer's *Historia Novorum*.[28] The first, only known from a reference in Eadmer's Preface to book V, was in four books and ended with Anselm's death in 1109. Of this no copy survives. The second can be inferred from

[25] See vol. ii, pp. lxxii–lxxiii.

[26] In the section written by C^1 it might be argued that the date of Anselm's consecration under 1093 and the statement under 1097 that Anselm stayed in Gaul before reaching Rome could be based on Eadmer, but the first could easily have come from another source and the second could well be a reasonable inference. It should be noted that C^1's last marginal addition of *capitula* at 1108 gives a text different from that in Eadmer's, and therefore should not have been included, as it was in vol. ii, p. lxxiii, among the marginal additions derived from the Canterbury writer.

[27] See vol. ii, p. lxxiii.

[28] On these see M. Brett, 'A note on the *Historia Novorum* of Eadmer', *Scriptorium*, xxxiii (1979), 56–8.

the single detached leaf in Cambridge, Corpus Christi College 341 and almost certainly was in six books and extended to the death of Archbishop Ralph in 1122. The third, Cambridge Corpus Christi College 452, is Eadmer's autograph copy, and must have been a revision of the second. John probably did not have the first version, but used the second, which would not have been available at Worcester until 1123 at the earliest. Eadmer was presumably not in the exemplar copied by C^1, and the decision to use him in John's chronicle must have been taken therefore sometime between the date of that exemplar and in or after 1131, when the chronicle originally ended. It was suggested above that two Eadmer passages under 1095 and 1114 written over erasures had probably replaced renderings of the Anglo-Saxon chronicle.[29] The preliminary version of John, which did not use Eadmer, must therefore have used other sources, which presumably included the vernacular chronicle for the annals 1102–22.[30] It is surprising that Eadmer was not used for the rewriting of parts of the annals before 1102, particularly those on Lanfranc, and on Anselm's relations with William II, which could have provided some useful information.

As stated above, the injection of Eadmer into the chronicle was gradual. The first annal to use Eadmer in the body of C's text, 1102, has clear contacts with the Anglo-Saxon Chronicle, whilst 1108 is an ingenious mix of the two sources, Eadmer extracts being placed between three separate brief renderings of the vernacular text, and annals 1118–21 are almost totally taken from Eadmer. The first Eadmer quotations in 1102 and 1103 were appropriately enough on ecclesiastical matters, but under 1105 Eadmer is used for a secular event (the turning away of the Norman lords from Duke Robert to Henry I) presumably in preference to a translation from Old English, and this practice is often followed later, for instance 1108 with the measures against false coinage, or 1114 with the drying up of the Medway and the Thames and at Yarmouth.

The capitula *of councils*

Brett showed that John used an early text of Eadmer, of which only a fragment survives.[31] It is possible that other differences between John and the surviving autograph copy of Eadmer's third version can

---

[29] See above, p. xx.
[30] This is incapable of proof, but is a reasonable inference.
[31] Brett, loc. cit.

be accounted for by the use of this early text.[32] This possibility might also account for the absence from the body of John's text of the *capitula* for the council of Westminster of 1102 and the primatial council of London in 1108. Canonical material was certainly used by John. He provides *capitula* for the legatine councils of Westminster in 1125 and 1127.[33] The first scribe of his working copy, C[1], wrote in the margin of p. 367 a version of the primatial council of London in 1108 different from Eadmer's. And if the text of the John witness G, which describes the legatine council of Westminster in 1138, accurately renders a Worcester annal, then he may also have possessed that council's *capitula*. Taken with the extensive investiture dossier provided under 1111 and 1112 and the account of the synod of Meaux of 858 on fos. 58[v]–59[v] of witness G John acquired and used a substantial body of canonical texts.[34]

Additional information in the chronicle of John of Worcester

When appropriate, the historical notes below draw attention to the information in John which is not in the surviving versions of the Anglo-Saxon Chronicle. Some is obviously of local origin. John's own observations or contacts must have been the source of his accounts of recent events such as the celestial phenomena seen at Hereford and Brecon under 1130, the death of the precentor Uhtred under 1132, the account of the miraculous ordeal at Worcester, the fire at Worcester of 1133, the sacking of Worcester in 1139, and the campaigns in and around Worcester and Hereford in 1138–9. Stories of earlier events such as those associated with Bishop Wulfstan under 1088 and 1095, or with Robert of Hereford under 1095, and the thunderstorm at Morville under 1118, must also represent local tradition, and could well have been recorded for the first time in John's chronicle. The balance of the narrative of the rebellions of 1088 was altered to accommodate the events in Worcester of which John was well informed. Other information must have come from local records: the death of Florence of Worcester and the obits of other Worcester monks, episcopal successions and deaths both at Worcester and Hereford; and such records may have included data,

---

[32] Brett suggested that John may have derived the names of Anselm's companions on his journey to Rome in 1103 from an earlier version of Eadmer (Whitelock, Brett, and Brooke, *Councils and Synods*, ii. 658 n. 4). The different order of deposed abbots under 1102 could also have come from such a source.

[33] See below, pp. 160–5 and 168–73.

[34] See below, pp. 118–25 and 130–3, and Brett, 'John of Worcester', p. 123 n. 4.

not just from nearby places like Pershore, Evesham, or Wellesbourne, but also from centres further afield such as Shrewsbury,
Gloucester, Tewkesbury, and Cirencester.[35] Some of John's reporting of northern ecclesiastical events furthermore could well have
come from a local source.[36]

John is sometimes our only extant source for particular dates or
events. William I's legacy to Robert Curthose and Robert's actions
under 1087, the winning over of William Eu, the *seductor maximus*
in 1093, August as the month for Malcolm's invasion in 1095, the
dates for the deaths of Osmund of Salisbury in 1099 and of
Archbishop Thomas of York in 1100, the marriage of Mary and
Eustace under 1101, some details of the reburial of St Cuthbert
under 1104, and the 1132 comet are some examples. Some of these
could have been in John's version of the vernacular chronicle,
others could have a different origin. John often has information,
which, though absent from the Anglo-Saxon Chronicle, is known
elsewhere. His account of the fracas at Glastonbury following
Thurstan's rule in 1083, for instance, shares elements with William
of Malmesbury's account in his *De antiquitate Glastonie Ecclesie*,
though there are important differences between the two.[37] Again the
rebellion of Henry under 1091 was known to Orderic Vitalis as was
the Maine campaign under 1098 which is otherwise omitted by
English chroniclers.[38] That the appointments of Simon to Worcester and of Seffrid to Chichester in 1125 are also found in Henry of
Huntingdon under that year could suggest that both were using
here a common chronicle source.[39]

In addition to the entries from Marianus John had some information of events outside Britain. The date of St Cnut's martyrdom
under 1076 and the raising of his bones in 1098 are not found in the
extant Anglo-Saxon Chronicle. John provides some information
about Henry V under 1115 and 1125 which is not found in other
English sources, and one item, the peace of Neuss, which is even
unknown from continental sources.[40] He also has information about

[35] See below, e.g. pp. 294–7 and 222–7.
[36] e. g. the consecration of Turgot as bishop of St Andrew's (see below, 1109 n. 3,
pp. 118–19).
[37] See below, pp. 38–41.
[38] See below, pp. 58–9 and 86–7.
[39] See below, pp. 158–9, and HH *HA* vii. 35 (p. 472). John's entries for Simon are
much more detailed than the bare record in HH.
[40] See below, pp. 136–7 and 158–9.

papal successions and actions, and some continental ecclesiastical appointments, which is not found in the Anglo-Saxon Chronicle.[41] His accounts of the Crusades must have come from an abbreviated source which had some verbal echoes of the *Gesta Francorum*, but it is perhaps chiefly distinguished by its inaccuracies under 1098.[42] Here as in the brief narrative preceding John's dossier of papal and imperial agreements and oaths under 1111 John must have made use of intractable material.[43]

Gloucester annals

John shares an interest in Gloucester events with the *Cart. Gloc.*, and in some annals their text is identical. The question of the mutual relationship between the two and of the origins of their shared text has been left open by previous scholars.[44] Some of the text of John's annals for 1058, 1100, 1101, 1122, 1130, and 1139 is shared with *Cart. Gloc.*, and, with the exception of the second Gloucester fire in 1122, these Gloucester entries are not in the Anglo-Saxon Chronicle. *Cart. Gloc.* seems to have been compiled at Gloucester by William Frocester *c.*1400, though some of its text is to be found in the surviving extracts from a sixteenth-century copy of a chronicle by Gregory of Caerwent datable to *c.*1300. Comparison of the text suggests that John and *Cart. Gloc.* were derived from a common source. There is one difference which might argue against the direct derivation of *Cart. Gloc.* from John. In the 1122 entry referring to the first fire at Gloucester both use regnal years. Such a dating practice is unusual in the original text of John but more common in

[41] See under 1099, the death of Urban II, and the succession of Paschal II, or under 1138 the consecration of Alberic, the future legate, as bishop of Ostia. Both annals have information not found in any other chronicle source: see below, 1099 n. 6, and 1138 n. 6. Some of this information could not have been taken from the papal lives in William of Malmesbury's edition of the *Liber Pontificalis*.

[42] See below, pp. 82–3, 84–5, and 91–2 for the Council of Clermont (where there are inaccuracies), the captures of Nicaea and Jerusalem, and the battle of Ascalon.

[43] See below, pp. 118–19. As suggested there, this narrative could have been derived from the source or sources which gave John his material on papal and imperial events. John is sometimes wrong in his accounts (e.g. the statement that Wulfstan of Worcester had made a profession of canonical obedience to Archbishop Stigand: see under 1062, vol. ii. 592), but it is not always easy to tell whether the errors were in his sources.

[44] The most recent discussion was by C. N. L. Brooke, 'St Peter of Gloucester and St Cadog of Llancarfan', *The Church and the Welsh Border in the Central Middle Ages*, ed. D. N. Dumville and C. N. L. Brooke (Woodbridge, 1986), pp. 50–94, at 74–9. Brooke makes a strong case for supposing that the Gloucester Chronicle had some early and trustworthy elements. I am grateful to Michael Hare for kindly checking the readings in Gloucester Cathedral Library 34, a manuscript of *Cart. Gloc.* unknown to its editor Hart.

Cart. Gloc.[45] Two other differences might suggest their origin in a common source. In the entries for the fires at Gloucester under both 1101 and 1122 John has errors where *Cart. Gloc.* does not: under 1122 his weekday is wrong, and his date for the 1101 fire under that year differs from that given retrospectively under 1122.[46] Then under 1130 John has one variant and a probably deliberate omission of a phrase present in *Cart. Gloc.*: he has 'senectute' in place of 'infirmitate', and omits 'absque cum sui conuentus consensu' before 'dimissa'. That the Gloucester continuator in G does not have these differences shows that a complete text was available at Gloucester at an early date in the mid-twelfth-century when G was being compiled. Furthermore G's interpolations share three passages with *Cart. Gloc.*[47] There is no evidence that these passages were in John's original chronicle and were later omitted. The further agreement of two of G's interpolations describing Welsh affairs with two entries in Gregory of Caerwent suggests that the latter here borrowed from a source common to the two, which again was presumably available in the mid-twelfth century at Gloucester.[48] John's Gloucester annals could well have been taken therefore from a chronicle available at Gloucester in the twelfth century.

Welsh annals

Worcester showed an expected interest in Wales.[49] Welsh affairs appear in the annals for 1093, 1094 (twice), 1095, 1097, 1098, 1101, 1102, 1111, 1114, 1116 (twice), 1121, and 1137. There are no corresponding entries in the Anglo-Saxon Chronicle for 1093, 1094 (second entry), 1101, 1111, 1116 (twice), and 1137, and the terseness of the vernacular annal for 1098 contrasts with the detail in John's, but Welsh sources have relevant or roughly comparable entries for all except the second entry under 1094, and 1101.[50] It is possible that

---

[45] The difference in the list of participating bishops at the dedication of the Minster under 1100 might also have argued against *Cart. Gloc.*'s derivation from John since there is a gap in the surviving witnesses of *Cart. Gloc.* and John has the missing name. The early recension of John represented by HL omits this name, however.

[46] In witness L the dates are internally consistent.

[47] The death of Abbot William under 1130, and the calling and coming of Gilbert Foliot under 1139: see below, pp. 194–5, 262–5.

[48] See below, pp. 219–23.

[49] This is also true of the annals before 1067, particularly during the reign of Edward the Confessor, see vol. ii. 566, 576–8, 580.

[50] It is true that John sometimes gives information found neither in an English nor in a Welsh source, as, e.g., the betrayal of Gruffyd ap Rhys ap Tewdwr by his wife in 1137,

both the second Welsh entry under 1094 (describing a second campaign of William II in Wales) and the entry under 1101 (describing Robert of Bellême's fortifying of Bridgnorth and Quatford) were the results of John's inferring or of his editing of his text, and may not have been taken directly from his sources.[51] The connections between John and Welsh sources are further strengthened by two readings. Under 1093 John declares that native kings ceased ruling in Wales after the death of Rhys ap Tewdr, and under 1097 that William II's expedition to Wales was his second. Both statements are to be found in Welsh sources. The connection is strengthened by the fact that William II's 1097 Welsh expedition was in fact his third in John, and thus John's 'secundo' must have been due to a mechanical copying of a source. It has been assumed that a Latin text of uncertain date lay behind the Welsh *Brut* texts: at these two points at least, and probably elsewhere in John's annals, there seems to have been contact, directly or indirectly, with this text.[52]

2. *The Annals 1128–40 in the Revised Recension*

These annals will be considered under two heads: their transcription and dating; and their character and content. They were compiled by John himself probably sometime between 1140 and 1143, and were written down by him much more roughly and carelessly and with many more changes of plan than the earlier annals in the chronicle written by the other two scribes, before ending imperfectly in C in the middle of 1140. Their untidiness could suggest that they were an early draft which John was never able to revise and edit properly.

The transcription and dating of the additional annals

Sometime after the succession of Stephen, which is mentioned in his new annal for 1130, John erased the annals 1128–31 and rewrote them so as to accommodate new information for those years. The additional material largely concerned Henry I, including, for instance, an account of the council of London in 1127 (dated 1128 by John), where fealty was sworn to Matilda, the three alarming illustrated visions of Henry I in 1130, and his stormy return from Normandy in

and the miracle associated with the mutilation of the priest Cenred in 1098 (see below, pp. 228–9, 86–7), but there is always a considerable overlap between John and the Welsh annals in all the annals except for 1094 and 1101.

[51] See below, pp. 72–3, 98–101.

[52] J. E. Lloyd, 'The Welsh Chronicles, *Proceedings of the British Academy*, xiv (1928), 369–91 at pp. 379–82.

the same year where the storm was only calmed by a promise to abolish the Danegeld, but there was also other matter such as the sunspots in 1128 and a lengthy German miracle story in 1131.

The edited text below for these years shows that the revised C³ text for 1128–31 differed in details and in dating from the original erased text. C³ must have transcribed the original text before erasure on separate sheets or wax tablets, and he must have made mistakes of omission either in doing this or when incorporating the roughly copied text into his revised and expanded annals in C. There are in particular two striking changes from the original text. He began 1130 at a different point, and he dropped the year 1131 so that entries over the four years from 1128 to 1131 came to be accommodated in three, 1128–30.[53] HLBP (and hence the original text in C) began 1130 with the consecration of Bishop Roger of Coventry on 9 January, C³ with the blessing of Abbot Reginald of Evesham on 27 January. The reason for this difference is simple: at some stage in the transcription John omitted the day (9 January) for the episcopal consecration, and, finding the abbatial blessing on 27 January a reasonably early calendar entry for a new year, began 1130 at this point, leaving Bishop Roger's elevation as its last entry under 1129. Again HLBP open the 1131 annal with Henry I's return to England in June 'sequenti anno', following this with some ecclesiastical preferments dating between 19 June and 30 August. C³, presumably unintentionally, omitted Henry I's return to England, and, in the absence of 'sequenti anno', assigned the ecclesiastical preferments to 1130. In the upper margins of C and of at least two other manuscripts in which he had a hand, Cambridge, University Library Kk. 4. 6, and Oxford, Bodleian Auct. F. 1. 9, John scribbled, sometimes incoherently, notes on the text to be erased or omitted.[54] His transcription of the erased annals for 1128–31 could also have been rushed and imperfect, and could well have caused the different starting point for 1130 and the loss of the original annal number 1131.[55]

[53] See below, pp. 188–9 and 174–97.

[54] See, e.g., vol. ii. 224 nn. d, f, Pl. 1, and below, pp. 190–1.

[55] It could be suggested that John could have used the Worcester copy of C, witness E, which lay behind HL, but it might not have been available for consultation at the time. For E see Vol. ii, pp. xxxv–xxxvi. Henry I's transfretations caused C³ particular difficulties when he rewrote 1128–31 as can be seen in the following table, which shows their appearance in the earlier recension, designated C, and in the final one, C³:

| 1. 1127 | Henry to Normandy | C | C³ |
| 2. 1128 | Henry to Normandy | — | C³ |

C³'s additions to the reconstructed annals 1128–30/31 were added in a block by G immediately after its transcription of C's original annals for those years. This suggests that they were available as a separate group of texts to the scribe of G. It is obviously not possible to establish the form in which C³ acquired them, but it is worth tabulating these additions. The three columns show (i) the year (after revision) to which they were assigned by C³, (ii) their subject, and (iii) any internal evidence for their dating.[56]

1128	1. Oath-taking for Matilda's succession.	28th year of Henry I. Octave of Easter.
	2. Henry I's return to Normandy.	
	3. Sun-spots.	28th year of Henry I. 8 December.
1129	4. An ordeal at Worcester.	25 January.
1130[57]	5. Aerial phenomena in Herefordshire.	17 February.
	6. Visions of Henry I.	30th year of Henry I.
	7. Storm at sea and promise to abolish the Danegeld.	
1131[58]	8. Miracle of Odilia.	Decennovenal year might be 1133.

3.	1129	Henry to England	C		C³
4.	1130	Henry to Normandy	C		—
5.	1131	Henry to England	C	(1130)	—
6.		Henry to Normandy	—	(1130)	C³
7.		Henry to England	—	(1130)	C³

2 was added by C³ after its insertion of the supposed oath-taking of 1128 which required Henry's presence in England in that year. 4 and 5 were probably omitted through errors in transcription, and 6 and 7 added to explain the anecdote of the storm at sea during the return crossing from Normandy which stimulated Henry's vow to abolish Danegeld. A possible lacuna in the account of the oath-taking of 1128 (*recte* ?1127: see below, pp. 178–9). which is shared by both C and G, may have been in the original text, and here John may have copied his text correctly.

[56] The first annal numbers entered between 1130 and 1140 were one or two years too late: see below, pp. xxxvi–xxxvii. John indented the text to the left and right of the first line of an annal for the later rubrication of the Marianan and Dionysian years. These annal numerals would be added mechanically in sequence and mistakes could consequently arise.

[57] Corrected from 1131.

[58] Corrected from 1132.

1132[59]   9. Death of Uhtred of Worcester.   2 April.
           10. Comet.   October.

The regnal years of Henry I were given for entries 1 and 3 under
1128 and for 6 under 1130 and would seem to confirm their dating.[60]
Entry 1, the oath of fealty to Matilda, however, could not have taken
place in 1128, as Henry I, who was present, was in Normandy
throughout the year, and should plausibly be assigned to 1127: its
partial agreement with William of Malmesbury's account of an oath-
taking in 1127 might support such a date.[61] Entry 2, Henry I's return
to Normandy in 1128, might be seen as John's attempt to reconcile
Henry I's presence at the supposed 1128 oath-taking with his known
return from Normandy in 1129.[62] The only other entry with internal
dating is 6 (the visions of Henry I), which is said to have happened in
his thirtieth regnal year and was eventually assigned to 1130.[63] John
probably compiled and wrote his final version of the chronicle
between 1140 and 1143, and it is reasonable to assume that he
could then date fairly accurately events so near in date and close to
home as the death of Uhtred, the miraculous ordeal at Worcester,
and the aerial phenomena in Herefordshire.[64] The one event among
this batch of additions where he or his source was grossly misled was
the attribution of the miraculous experience of Odilia and her father
to 1131 (originally to 1132), as Odilia flourished in the seventh
century.[65]

One consequence of dating the original annals for 1128–31 to
1128–30 remains to be considered. It led at first to an incorrect
dating of the subsequent annals. When John came to incorporate the
aerial phenomena in Herefordshire in his chronicle, he may have
noted their occurrence on 17 February, an appropriately early
calendar date, and originally began 1131 at this point. When,
however, he saw that the visions of Henry I, the entry immediately
following these celestial displays, took place in Henry's thirtieth year,

[59] Corrected from 1133.
[60] In the case of entries 1 and 3 the date given for the octave of Easter (29 April) and the
weekday, Saturday, for December 8 are correct for 1128.
[61] See below, pp. 176–83. In fact G's text of this oath-taking dates it to Henry I's 27th
year and to the indiction appropriate for 1127.
[62] See below, pp. 182–31.
[63] See below, pp. 198–203.
[64] For the dating of the final compilation, see vol. ii, pp. xxxv, lxvii–lxix.
[65] See below, pp. 202–7. As Pertz said (MGH SS xiii. 132), in this annal 'et nomina et
saecula omnino confunduntur'.

he may then have corrected the year to 1130, and thus his chronicle
came to have two such years, the first beginning, as we have seen,
with the blessing of Reginald of Evesham on 27 January, the second
with these Hereford spectacles. John's original dating of the Hereford phenomena to 1131 caused this and subsequent annals at first to
be dated one year too late. A misconception similar to that which led
to the premature dating of the Hereford events may have led John to
assume that the crossing of Stephen to Normandy in March (*recte*
1137) took place at the opening of a new year and to assign it to 1139
to follow his original 1138; and in consequence the original annal
years 1139–42 were all two years too late. These errors were soon
corrected as the following list demonstrates, but their occurrence
shows how mistakes could arise through the same misguided and
conscientious attention to calendar dates which seems to have led
him to begin his 1130 at a different place and to suppress the original
opening of 1131. C³'s annal numbers have been altered, and it is not
always possible to recover the original number, but the probable
original numbers are given in the first column, the altered years in
the second, and an annal's first dated entry in the third.[66]

1131   1130bis Feb. 17: aerial phenomena. The last dated entry
                      under the previous annal was Aug.

1132   1131   Possibly 1131 in the decennovenal cycle mentioned
              at the opening of the annal: a German miracle story
              of Count Norman and his daughter, Odilia.

1133   1132   April 2: the death of Uhtred, precentor of Worcester
              Cathedral.

1134   1133   4 May: fire at London.

1135   1134   No event is dated, though note that the last dated
              entry under the previous annal is a fire at Worcester
              in November. The first entry under 1135/1134 is the
              death of Robert Curthose.

1136   1135   2 December: the death of Henry I.

1137   1136   'After Christmas': the burial of Henry I.

1138   1137   No event is dated, though the last dated entry in the
              previous annal is the holding of Stephen's court at
              Dunstable at Christmas. The first entry under 1138/
              1137 is the death of Abbot Benedict of Tewkesbury.

[66] For the detailed evidence, see below, *s.a.* 1131–40.

1139   1137bis 'After Easter': Stephen crosses to Normandy.

1140   1138   'After Christmas': Stephen captures Bedford castle.

1141   1139   'After Christmas': Archbishop Theobald and other bishops proceed to Rome.

1142   1140   'After Christmas': Stephen proceeds to Reading.

The character and content of John's added annals

At the outset above it was noted how the rewritten annal for 1130 was dominated by narratives and anecdotes. The new annals for 1131–4 were similarly constituted, 1131 being given up to the story of Odilia, 1132–4 being largely made up of anecdotes, that is, 1132 with the account of the death of Uhtred, precentor of Worcester, 1133 with the aerial storm which delayed Henry I's crossing to Normandy, and 1134 with the undated tale of the capture of Christian knights by Saracens in Apulia. The death of Henry I and the succession and consecration of Stephen are the only items in a factual 1135 while the next annal begins with the burial of Henry I at Reading and a comment on the lamentable discord in England and Wales which announced the new reign, and which the siege of Exeter towards the end of the annal illustrates. John knew little about Stephen's stay in Normandy in 1137 beyond the dates of his journeys, and that year is given up for the most part to dreams associated with the death of Abbot Benedict of Tewkesbury, and to stories of miracles at Windsor and Southwell. The annal for 1138, which is much more factual, had two substantial chunks devoted to the take-over of Thuringia by the Saxons and to a miracle at Prüm; 1139 and what C preserves of 1140 is largely narrative, and has John's characteristic staccato awkward style and moralizing asides.

The last three annals give a valuable and informative narrative of English events. Like the *Gesta Stephani* they focus on the west of England, but campaigns closer to home in and around Worcester and Hereford provide detailed information which is not known from other sources. To take 1138 first. This annal covers the whole year from the siege of Bedford 'after Christmas 1137' to the legatine council of Westminster and the arrival of a papal emissary a full year later, and of all narrative sources for the year John has the widest coverage of secular and ecclesiastical events. Between the North-ampton Council on 10 April and the burning of Hereford two months later on 15 June most of the narrative is peculiar to John and fills a gap largely left blank by the other chronicles. From the Bath episode in which Geoffrey Talbot is temporarily the prisoner of the Bishop of Bath to the Scottish incursions which were ended by the battle of the Standard on 22 August there is considerable overlap with the *Gesta Stephani*. One difference between the two is the relative position in the narrative of the warning fiery skies and the Scottish invasion of April–August: in the *Gesta Stephani* the former precedes the latter, whilst John, who, unlike the *Gesta*, reports their dates, reverses their positions.[67] His accounts of the events in the North, though they provide useful additional information, are neither lucid nor internally consistent. Stephen's setting out for Northumbria takes place, as in the *Gesta Stephani*, immediately after the successful siege of Bedford, but in John the Scottish threat is not mentioned, and his reference to the troubles in Northumbria lasting 'fere sex menses' is wrong.[68] His lengthy account of the final campaigns ending with the battle of the Standard and the siege of Wark has some of his characteristic clipped writing, as well as information absent from other sources. John says that King David's invasion (which began around 8 April) was his third, and this shows that, as in the case of one of his Welsh annals, he was copying his source too literally: he had only referred—and, as has just been noted, that was by implication—to one earlier invasion of David's, that which prompted Stephen's northern campaign earlier in the year.

John's annals for 1139 to mid-1140 share many of the same features: a focus largely on events near at home; a chronologically extensive coverage of events, particularly in 1139; a fairly clear chronological framework; the filling up of gaps in the narrative left by other sources, particularly for Stephen's movements; useful information not found elsewhere; compressed awkward writing, most markedly in the description of the siege and sack of Worcester in 1139; asides on Stephen's qualities, on the power of kings, and on the calamities of war; and surprising omissions and clumsy transitions in the narrative.[69] There are fewer ecclesiastical entries than in 1138. John's sources could have been inadequate here: the account of the arrest of the bishops is very skimpy, and the description of a supposed separation of secular and ecclesiastical duties which was decided on immediately after this arrest is mangled, and must be an

---

[67] *GS* 24 (pp. 50–2).   [68] See below, pp. 236–7.
[69] For these see below, pp. xxxix–xl.

oblique reference to the arguments used against the bishops by their opponents such as are mentioned by William of Malmesbury's *Historia Novella*.[70] On the council of Winchester summoned by Henry of Blois John is silent. There is also a serious gap in the account of the ex-empress's movements, since after her landing at Portsmouth and stay at Arundel she disappears from sight.[71]

John contributes many moralizing asides in the later annals of the final recension.[72] Stephen was the first post-Conquest king to be given an epithet by John. John may have thought him 'magnificus' and was certainly well disposed towards him, but his first two appearances in the chronicle are as a perjurer: first among those who betrayed the promise to support Matilda's succession, and second as breaking the undertaking not to collect Danegeld.[73] John recognizes the king's good qualities which render him ineffective. As 'rex pietatis et pacis', he sets his enemies free.[74] By implication his weakness contributes to the disorder which follows the burial of Henry I. The exclamation on the duty of kings under 1139—'rex est pacis, et o utinam rex rigoris iustitie conterens sub pedibus inimicos, et equa lance iudicii decernens omnia, in robore fortitudinis conseruans et corroborans pacis amicos'—comes immediately after the report of the unopposed landing of the ex-empress and the Earl of Gloucester.[75] John applies his favourite metaphor of the empurpled king as a raging lion, full of 'regie maiestatis' to both Henry I and his successor, but where Henry is humiliated in a dream Stephen is undone in reality.[76] John's three separate comments on the savagery of war and fighting men all stand in contrast to the order and security the 'regia maiestas' should provide.[77] It is in these last annals that John personally testifies to the truth of his stories, and contributes doggerel couplets on different occasions.[78] In these few years there are more lengthy miraculous stories than in the rest of the chronicle. However much the chronicle's character changes in these last annals, John retains the calendar framework and still inserts an expected obit like that of Archbishop Thurstan or the less important

[70] WM *HN*, paras. 468, 470 (pp. 26, 28).

[71] This is unless her appearance in G's continuation was in a text G copied from John. See below, pp. xlviii–xlix.

[72] See below, pp. 180–3, 218–19.   [73] See below, pp. 178–83, 202–3.

[74] Under 1138: see below, pp. 242–3.   [75] See below, pp. 268–9.

[76] For Henry I as 'rex purpuratus . . . ut rugitus leonis' see below, pp. 200–1, and for Stephen, pp. 216–17, 278–9.   [77] See below, pp. 217–18, 266–7, 280–1.

[78] e.g. under 1118, 1136, 1138, see below, pp. 142–3, 216–17, 244–5. In the oath-taking of 1127, Henry I is made to speak in hexameters.

account of the bishop of Bangor being persuaded to do homage to Stephen during a truce at Advent 1139 amidst the alarms of war. His accounts are not always clear: the incomplete story of the exploits of Robert fitz Hubert under 1140 makes a confusing episode at times incomprehensible. He omits names and identifies people by their titles.[79] He is clearly blending—as the obits, ecclesiastical preferments, and the Scottish campaigns show—written sources with oral accounts, and the hurried and careless lay-out and script, the frequent changes and erasures making an untidy text messier give the impression of a draft rather than a final or corrected text, though one wonders why John chose to append it to such a fair working copy as C.[80] He shows an interest in aerial phenomena, which is not surprising in itself, but in his references to al-Khwārizmī, his quotations from Walcher of Malvern's *Sententia de dracone* (which was based on Petrus Alfonsi, and where he misunderstands his sources), and his substitution of words based on the *Sententia de dracone* for a dated reference to the 1140 eclipse he seems anxious to demonstrate some recently acquired, though unfortunately misunderstood, knowledge.[81]

A fuller analysis of John's method in these later annals, as in the chronicle as a whole, must await an examination of his contributions to the self-styled *chronicula* and the introduction to vol. i.

III. THE GLOUCESTER INTERPOLATIONS IN G

1. *The Annals in the Hand of the Main Continuator in G*

John stops writing in G on fo. 113[v] l. 23 and in the middle of the annal of 1123. Thereafter one hand (G[2]) continues the annals to 1141 with very brief interruptions by two other hands on fos. 115[v]–116[v], and it is G[2] who is the subject of the following paragraphs.[82] He

---

[79] Thus, Robert, earl of Gloucester is nearly always simply 'comes Glaocestrie', and Earl Waleran 'comes ciuitatis' (of Worcester). The Worcester prior who had a special devotion to the Blessed Virgin, and whose death is foretold to Abbot Benedict of Tewkesbury is not named in witness C (see below, pp. 222–3).

[80] The unruly writing, the frequent erasures, and rewriting in many of John's later annals, the sometimes perplexing paragraph marks indicate changes of plan and working from rough drafts. These aspects of John's procedure in C and in G will be considered in the introduction to vol. i.

[81] See below, pp. 258–9, 210–11, 284–5.

[82] For the scribes in G and their stints, see vol. ii, pp. lxii–lxiii. In so far as their limited contributions allow judgements to be made, G[3] (fo. 115[v]) and G[4] (fos. 116[r]-116[v]) do not differ in their approach to John's text from G[2].

bases his annals on a text close to that which John must have been using, but his approach to this text is quite different from John in his self-styled *chronicula*. In G John excerpted from, and sometimes rewrote, C's annals, but his successor in that manuscript normally copied his text verbatim, especially in the years to 1131, adding information when he could from sources not available at Worcester, some of which had Gloucester concerns.

G²'s additional information is often of great interest, particularly for the early years of Stephen, but G² is sometimes negligent and repetitive, his dates are sometimes wildly out, and he is occasionally internally inconsistent. This edition sets out G's difference from John and its additions, but some brief consideration of G²'s method and use of sources would be helpful. This will be examined under five headings: the annals for 1128–31; G's use of John; the additional information derived from other sources; how he brought the different sources together; and his dating of the annals 1131–40.

The annals for 1128–31

As has been noted above in vol. ii, p. lxiii, G's continuator first copied the annals as represented by HLBP to 1131, and then added in a block the additional annals incorporated by John into his revised annals for these years, assigning them not to separate years, as John came to do, but to the last annal 1131.[83] In this way both the oath-taking (1128 C) and the nightmares of Henry I (1130 C) were placed under 1131, even though these entries are internally dated to Henry I's twenty-eighth (twenty-seventh in G, rightly), and his thirtieth, year respectively.[84] At one point in Henry I's dreams, he realized the difficulty, and added that they occurred in 1130, 'anno precedenti'.[85] The procedure of the G continuator surely suggests that the material which John was to interpolate in C came to him in an undated and undifferentiated block. He either did not receive, or he omitted, the account of the ordeal at Worcester, and, probably deliberately, or just possibly because of omissions in his source, slightly truncated some of the others, dropping verses, for instance, as he was to do elsewhere in his text.[86] The absence of annal years and the assigning of all the material to 1131 could well indicate that he was copying it from a *schedula* or from wax tablets.

[83] See below, p. 196 n. f.   [84] See below, pp. 176, 198.
[85] See below, p. 198.   [86] See below, pp. 190–3, 180–3, 198–9, 216–17.

G²'s use of John

It has just been noted that the G continuator from mid-1123 was faithful to the John text, often reproducing it verbatim. In two cases he preserves the text of John which came to be erased by C³. Under 1139 he records the grant of the shrievalty of Worcester to William Beauchamp, which C³ deleted, and under 1140 he reproduces C's original description of the solar eclipse.[87] Elsewhere he supplies names missing from John, and occasionally tries to make sense of C's text.[88] Sometimes he pads unnecessarily, often he makes careless errors, but his main omissions seem deliberate.[89] The apparently deliberate dropping of the *capitula* of the 1127 and 1128 councils, which are in C, makes tantalizing his slightly fuller account of the 1138 Westminster council, which ends by announcing *capitula* ('sunt autem haec capitula') which he does not give and which were perhaps originally reproduced in the material John was using.[90] With the exception of two passages he either omits or renders impersonally those passages John wrote in the first person.[91] He also cuts most of John's moralizing on the significance of events, and such omissions further reduce the personal character of John's chronicle.[92] Under 1125, G omitted, presumably deliberately, the first of two entries on Simon of Worcester's ordination.[93] There are

---

[87] See below, pp. 276–7, 284–5. It is interesting that C³ under 1140 scribbles the original entry on the solar eclipse in the upper margin whilst the replacement text is rubricated over an erasure.

[88] Thus under 1137 G names the prior of Worcester, Warinus (see below, pp. 222–3), and under 1138 for C³'s shorthand 'Eboracensis' it reads 'Turstinus archiepiscopus Eboracensis' (see below, pp. 240–1). Under 1138 G reads 'Unde iam capi id posse desperans, spe sua frustratus inde discessit' for C³'s terse 'Unde iam desperat capi id posse' (see below, p. 256). It is true that these readings could have been in C³'s source or first draft, which G may have preserved better than C³.

[89] Examples of padding: addition of 'rursus' under 1138 (see below, p. 256), and the addition of 'vir magne religionis' under 1129 (see below, p. 188). Errors include 'statum' for 'stratum' under 1138 (see below, p. 238), 'distans' for 'distante' and 'solutos' for 'solutis' under 1140 (see below, pp. 282, 284).

[90] See below, p. 260.

[91] An example is John's description of his sources for the stories under 1137 (see below, pp. 230–1). The exceptions are John's claim that he had learnt of Henry I's dreams from Grimbald (see below, pp. 200–1) and his account of the death of Uhtred (see below, pp. 206–9).

[92] Examples are found under 1136 (see below, pp. 218–19), and 1131 (see below, pp. 202–3).

[93] For this repetition see below, pp. 158–9. It is, of course, possible that the repetition in C was caused by scribal error, and that G preserved a better text. Whatever the reason, G did not unpick the chronological confusions later in the annal on the enthronement of Simon at Worcester and the blessing of Benedict of Tewkesbury.

other omissions which may not have been intentional. Besides those
due to eyeskip, there are two cases where G's omissions seem
arbitrary.[94] The oath-taking of 1128 (*recte* 1127) is crudely truncated
at the point where the abbot of Bury St Edmunds protested against
the insulting order of precedence, and neither Henry I's reply nor
the final acquiescence of the abbots is recorded: this seems to be a
case where G²'s aversion to John's versifying and moralizing
mutilated the story John had to tell.[95] Again, and as has just been
noted, G's text of the 1138 Westminster council is slightly fuller than
John's in hinting, among other things, at the original presence of a
text of the *capitula*, but episcopal consecrations and the degradation
of abbots are omitted.[96]

The additional information in G²

The bulk of G's additional information is found in the years 1135–
40. G added to the John text numerous dates, particularly of obits,
some factual details, and many important narratives. The first are
scattered through the annals from the date of Abbot Hugh of St
Augustine's death on Palm Sunday 1126 to the fuller information
and dates for the fires at some English cities in 1137.[97] Occasionally
independent sources support the accuracy of these added dates.[98]
The additional small details include the burial of both Richard fitz
Gilbert and Payn fitz John at Gloucester, the death of Abbot Nigel of
Eynsham under 1128, and the reference to William Clito assuming
the monastic habit.[99]

These additional details and narratives can be considered under
various headings. Some supplementary statements apparently ease
the transition between one event and another. Thus G twice adds
statements on the schism to put the ensuing episodes in context.[100]
Others, which will be mentioned below in the next section, try to
explain inconsistencies in dating, as with the arrest of the bishops
under 1138 and 1139. Yet others add details to John's statements:
thus, when John records Thurstan's death, G, besides adding
chronological details, speaks of Thurstan's fostering of monasteries.

---

[94] Examples of eyeskip are the omission of the names of two bishops under 1130 (see
below, p. 192) and the phrase 'et gemmis . . . auro' under 1137 (see below, p. 232).

[95] See below, pp. 180–3.   [96] See below, pp. 260–3.

[97] See below, pp. 168–9, 228–31.

[98] Thus witness L's addition on the death of Vincent of Abingdon supports G's date for
his death (see below, pp. 194–5, 307).

[99] See below, pp. 220–1, 228–9, 186–7.   [100] See below, pp. 188–9, 232–3.

There are under 1127 three additions with a continental interest: two
dealing with events in Flanders, the murder of Charles the Good,
and the actions of Henry I against William Clito, both of which are
echoed in the Anglo-Saxon Chronicle, and the third with the
Invention of St Mathias at Trier, which is not. There are three
important additions which deal with Wales and which share details
with the *Gesta Stephani*. Interestingly enough, the parallels between
the two extend to their both giving the Welsh eruptions a central
place among the troubles occurring immediately after Henry I's
death.[101]

Many of the important additional narratives have a Gloucester
focus. In two entries the compiler had made clear his Gloucester
affiliations: in 1141 he reports a statement made to the annalist by
Miles of Gloucester, and under 1139 he speaks of Gilbert Foliot as
'nostrum domnum' in an entry shared with the annals in the
Gloucester cartulary.[102] The reception of Stephen at Gloucester in
1138, the coming of Gilbert Foliot, and the arrival of the ex-empress
in the city are obvious examples of detailed entries of Gloucester
interest. The important entries after the defection of Miles of
Gloucester and the arrival of the ex-empress presumably also came
from a Gloucester source. Such would have included the movements
of Matilda after her arrival at Arundel, thus plugging a serious gap in
John, and the details of her progress in 1141 from Gloucester to
London and then back to Oxford, the savagery of Philip Gai at Bristol,
and Geoffrey Talbot's stabling of his horses at Hereford cathedral.[103]
But this same source could well have supplied other information
before Miles's defection, such as the arrest of the bishops under 1138
(wrongly), the report of an otherwise unknown siege of Bridgnorth in
the same year, and the fact that Stephen was apparently besieging
Marlborough when the ex-empress landed.[104] G added crucial
information particularly in 1138 and 1139. The narrative it shared
with the *Gesta Stephani* by no means exhausted its contribution.

G^2's merging of its different sources

G sometimes found the merging of its different sources beyond him.
A simple instance is the death of Bishop Godfrey of Bath. John
reports this under 1134, and G has John's entry (though its year here

[101] *GS* 8–12 (pp. 14–24). [102] See below, pp. 298–9, 262–3.
[103] See below, pp. 270–1, 292–9, 248–51, 276–7.
[104] See below, pp. 244–9, 256–7, 268–9.

is 1133) and adds the day (16 August). Under its 1135 annal (which was equivalent to John's 1136) it repeats the obit with its date as part of its separately acquired 'Welsh' annals.[105] Three important events which occurred in 1139 are reported first by G under 1138, using in each case a different text from John's: the arrest of the bishops by Stephen, the defection of Miles of Gloucester, and the death of Bishop Roger of Salisbury.[106] His account of all three is more informative than John's, but rather mindlessly when he reached John's account of them under 1139, he simply reproduced John's words, explaining the repetition of the first and the third very weakly.[107] Under 1139 he says of the arrest of the bishops 'quorum causa scriptus superius est latius propalata que tamen hoc anno constat actitata', and of the death of Bishop Roger in the same year 'cuius obitus anno superiori latius litteris expressus est', clearly not being willing to confront the conflict in his different sources. When he had a group of entries from a 'non-Worcester' source, he could insert them together, as under 1136, where the obits of Abbot Ansger of Reading (27 January) and Bishop Godfrey of Bath (16 August) and the opening of the Gower campaign (1 January) are placed between Stephen's undated Exeter campaign and the death of Archbishop William of Canterbury.[108] Sometimes the inserted date broke up the calendar sequence of an annal: thus under 1128 G's report of the death of Abbot Nigel of Eynsham (9 May) is inserted between the blessing of Abbot Herbert of Shrewsbury (22 July) and the death of William Clito (27 July).[109]

G²'s dating of the annals 1131–40

It was noted above that the annals from 1131 to 1140 in John were first wrongly dated 1132–42 by John.[110] G's annals for 1137–40 start at the same point as John's, but those for 1131–36 do not, and some of its consequent chronological confusions are seen in the following tabulation of the annals of John and G. The table compares the position of entries in an annal, and their dating, in the two manuscripts. Note that C's dates are those after revision.

---

[105] See below, pp. 212–13, 218–19.   [106] See below, pp. 244–9, 252–3, 258–9.

[107] See below, pp. 266–7, 270–1, 278–9. Under 1139 G simply repeated C³'s report of the defection of Miles of Gloucester, which there took place *after*, and not as under 1138 *before*, Matilda's arrival.

[108] See below, pp. 218–19.   [109] See below, pp. 186–7.

[110] See above, pp. xxxvi–xxxvii.

C			G
1132 First entry:	April 2: death of Uhtred of Worcester.		1131 Last entry.
Last entry:	comet of Oct.		1132 First entry.
1133 First entry:	May 14: fire at London.		1132 Second entry.
1134 First entry:	no date: death of Robert Curthose.		1133 First entry.
1135 Only Entries:	Dec. 2: death of Henry I; Dec. 22: coronation of Stephen.		1133 Final entries.
1136 First entry:	'after Christmas': Henry buried.		1134 First entry.
	undated: Stephen's siege of Exeter.		1135 First entry.
—— (Material not in C)			1136 October: battle at Cardigan.
1137 First entries:	March: ecclesiastical obits.		1137 First entries, in slightly different order.
1138 First entry:	succession of Conrad III.		1138 First entry.
1139 First entry:	'after Christmas': Theobald and others go to Rome.		1138 First entry: 'after Christmas': Walter of Gloucester succeeds.
1140 First entry:	'after Christmas': Stephen to Reading.		1140 First entry.

The text of two of G's entries was at variance with their annual dates. Henry I's death is said to have occurred in his thirty-fifth year, which is correct for John's 1135, but obviously not for G's 1133.[111] And the interpolated Welsh wars in G (October 1136) were said to have occurred immediately after Henry I's death, and to be internally consistent should have been assigned to G's 1134 and not 1136.[112] Here G's discrepancies in dating cannot easily be explained. The assigning of Uhtred of Worcester's death to 1131 might, however, be accounted for by supposing that it was copied as part of the block of additional entries John incorporated into the 1128–31 annals, all of which, as was seen above, G attributed to 1131. G opens his 1132 annal with a comet in October. This was the last entry in John's 1131, but it could well have been the first item in a separate batch of annals of Worcester origin which G acquired, and which began a new year in 1132: that the later additions to H began exactly with this comet in 1132 might support this suggestion.[113] G begins his next annal (1133) at the same point as John's 1134, and G could be seen as

[111] See below, pp. 214–15.   [112] See below, pp. 218–19.
[113] See below, pp. 208–9.

trying to keep in step with his own chronology. He does not start a
new annal with the death of Henry I and the coronation of Stephen
(the only entries in C's 1135 annal), but it could well be that their
dates of 2 and 22 December persuaded him not to begin a new year
with December events. He begins his 1134 annal, not at exactly the
same point as C's 1136 (C after all began in mid-sentence) but with
the same event, the burial of Henry I at Reading. These guesses
might offer some explanation for the particular openings of 1132,
1133, and 1134 in G, but the reasons for the divisions of G's annals
at 1135 and 1136 remain elusive. It is curious that it is in these years,
John's 1131–6, that supplementary information is largely absent from
G. G seems to have been faced in these years with material which
was difficult to date, and had no annals of his own from another
source into which it could be dovetailed.[114]

2. Conclusion

On three quires at the opening of G, the main continuator (G²)
copied much of the English material in C's preliminaries, intro-
ducing this with a text not known there entitled 'regalis prosapia
Anglorum'.[115] G² probably added these texts after John had
abandoned his writing of the *chronicula*. How Gloucester and the
continuator acquired G is not known, but as well as G Gloucester
must have obtained, if only on loan, three texts associated with
John's chronicle: a chronicle manuscript containing both the
preliminary texts and a version of the chronicle of at least the
years 1123–31; the material John came to incorporate in his revised

[114] The annals for 1131/2–1138 added at the end of H by its second scribe (which are
shown in the critical apparatus below) do not throw light on the dividing points of G²'s
years. H starts its additions with the October comet of C's 1131 which, as has been noted
above, began G²'s 1132 annal, and ends with Stephen's northern expedition under its
1138. H's additions are selective and are confined to English events or those with a direct
English concern. Its text seems closer to C³'s than to G's, though it has some differences of
date, e.g. it does not give the date for the 1137 York fire, and it has a different date for the
Bath fire in the same year. It begins its 1136, 1137, and 1138 annals at different points
from C and G. Nor do the Winchcombe annals (*Ann. Winchcombe*, p. 112) which 'for 1127
to 1138 inclusive have many points of contact with G', help explain G²'s dating and
division of annals. The cessation of Winchcombe's contact with G in the same year as the
ending of H's continuation seems coincidental, as the final entries in both are different. A
G-type text lay behind the Winchcombe annals for 1127–38 and behind some of the annals
of Gervase (e.g. Gervase, i. 96, 99, 100), and an H²-type lay behind the annals 1132–3 in
the misplaced leaf (fo. 132) in the HR manuscript, Cambridge, Corpus Christi College 139
(John of Hexham 7 (SD ii. 295–6)), but the added annals for 1132–40 of C³ do not seem
to have any descendants. These successor texts do not help unravel G's odd annal
numbers.   [115] See vol. ii, pp. lix–lx, lxii–lxiii.

1128–31 annals, probably on a *schedula* or on wax tablets; and a recension of the added annals from 1131 to at least 1140. The Gloucester compilers found the dating both of the new material for 1128–31, and of the annals 1131–36 very difficult, and it is possible that the texts came to them arranged by paragraphs and separate entries, but not always firmly dated. They added to the Worcester texts many details and dates, which must have come from sources near at hand, and contributed narratives of great interest, some of which had Gloucester concerns, and which were of probable Gloucester origin. They were not always successful in incorporating these new texts and made many elementary errors. The editing behind G²'s work could have been completed not very long after G's *terminus post quem* of 1146 x 1147, and the raw state of G² could also well represent a very early stage in that process.[116] It has long been known that John shares some entries with the annals in the *Cart. Gloc.* The making of G saw Gloucester using extensively the chronicle resources of Worcester.

IV. THE ANNALS 1140–1141 IN THE CONTINUATION IN G

C³ ends imperfectly near the end of the Robert fitz Hubert episode.[117] This G completes and then continues with an important account of the campaigns in 1140 and 1141 before it also ends imperfectly in the middle of the negotiations for the exchange of King Stephen and the earl of Gloucester.[118] It is impossible to distinguish in this continuation the contributions of John and the Gloucester compiler. After all if C had not survived and G was our sole surviving witness for the John text to 1140 it would not have been easy to identify G's interpolations besides its obviously misplaced entries on the arrest of the bishops or on the defection of Miles of Gloucester.[119]

Two passages in the continuation suggest that there was at least at the outset a continued mix of John and Gloucester. The episode on the effects of a violent storm at Wellesbourne, a township expressly said to be one mile from an estate of the Worcester bishopric, was probably in John's original continuation.[120] Conversely, the reported

---

[116] For the *terminus post quem* and G's date, see vol. ii, pp. lxii–lxiv.
[117] See below, pp. 288–9.
[118] See below, pp. 304–5.
[119] See below, pp. 244–9, 252–3.
[120] See below, pp. 294–7.

remarks of Miles of Gloucester on his essential support of the empress must surely have been written down in the Gloucester circle.[121] Beyond that it is not easy to proceed. John has rightly been regarded as partial to Stephen, and G as sympathetic to the opposing forces, but neither was an uncritical supporter. Some of G's interpolations before 1140 describe in horror the savagery and destruction of the empress's allies, just as John criticizes some of Stephen's actions.[122] For these reasons the description of Stephen's defeat at Lincoln as the just judgement of God could quite as well be John's as G's.[123] Nor is it easy to distinguish John and G stylistically since G's interpolations before C's imperfect ending in 1140 are too short for convincing analysis. Certainly nothing which G contributes is as awkward and staccato as some of John's writing, and the absence of these traits from the continuation might have suggested that this was mostly the work of Gloucester. But not all John's writing is jerky before 1140, and so stylistic arguments cannot take the question very far. The absence from the continuation of John's characteristic comments on the fate of kings and on the vagaries of life need only mean that G dropped these remarks as he had apparently done in his copying of earlier passages of John.[124] Two small usages might offer faint clues. With one debatable exception John uses 'emensa' to describe the passing of a feast, thus 'emensa festiuitate Pascha', whereas G on the only two occasions when a word is required in its interpolations uses the more usual 'peracta'.[125] In the continuation the word is only required once, and it is interesting that 'peractis' is used.[126] And in the pre-1140 chronicle, Robert, earl of Gloucester, is described by John as 'comes Glaocestrense', by G as 'comes Bricstowense'.[127] At first in the continuation Robert is described as earl of Gloucester and he only appears as earl of Bristol from p. 298 onwards. These leads could be used to suggest that John had originally completed the Robert fitz Hubert story and may have continued the chronicle to the Lincoln defeat of Stephen and his capture and imprisonment, perhaps adding as a postscript the Wellesbourne storm ('his diebus horrendum quid in Wigornensi contigit diocesi, quod relatu iudicauimus'); and that G continued the account of the empress's triumphs at some point after Stephen's

---

[121] See below, pp. 298–9.
[123] See below, pp. 292–3.
[125] See below, pp. 262–3, 242–3.
[127] See below, pp. 248–9, 252–3, 286–7.

[122] See below, pp. 270–1, 218–19.
[124] See below, pp. 218–19, 286–7.
[126] See below, pp. 294–5.

imprisonment, inserting at the appropriate chronological point John's concluding episode of Wellesbourne. It must always be remembered, however, that the continuation in G could have been made up of the same mixture of Worcester and Gloucester annals as its pre-1140 text.

V. THIS EDITION

In C a new annal began with a Marianan year on the left of a line, followed immediately by an imperial year, with the Dionysian year on the right. Within each annal an English annal is usually distinguished from Marianus' by a large initial. C^3 omits the imperial years. In this edition, at the beginning of each annal, Dionysian, imperial, and Marianan years are placed in that order, and Marianan and English annals, and Roman imperial successions are given separate paragraphs. C^2 and C^3's use of paragraph marks and C^3's rubrication of text are indicated in the critical apparatus. C^2 and C^3's capitalization and rubrication of names and dates, and interlineations and marginal additions later than the twelfth century, have not been noted.

Italic in the text indicates quotation. The marginal page numbers are those of MS C.

Conventions

Anglo-Saxon Æ and æ and Ð ð and þ are printed as they appear in John of Worcester's text.

E *caudata* (ę) has been rendered as E.

Capital U and V are printed as V, Uu as W, and lower case u and v as u.

Pl. 1. Oxford, Corpus Christi College 157, p. 382: the first nightmare of Henry I. Scale 1:1.47. Scribe C³ (John) wrote the text. The illustrations from the Corpus manuscript are reproduced by kind permission of the President and Fellows of Corpus Christi College, Oxford.

Pl. 2. Oxford, Corpus Christi College 157, p. 382: the second nightmare of Henry I. Scale 1:1.47

Pl 3. Oxford, Corpus Christi College 157, p. 383: the third nightmare of Henry I. Scale 1:1.49.

Pl. 4. Oxford, Corpus Christi College 157, p. 383: Henry I in a storm at sea. Scale 1:1.63.

THE CHRONICLE OF
JOHN OF WORCESTER
1067–1140
WITH THE GLOUCESTER
INTERPOLATIONS AND THE
CONTINUATION TO 1141

SIGLA

John of Worcester

C   Oxford, Corpus Christi College 157
H   Dublin, Trinity College 502
L   London, Lambeth Palace 42
B   Oxford, Bodleian Library Bodley 297
P   Cambridge, Corpus Christi College 92
G   Dublin, Trinity College 503

Marianus Scotus

N   London, British Library Cotton Nero C. V

In the apparatus G is shown in parentheses as it includes passages and readings sometimes independent of John of Worcester; N is shown in parentheses because, although its text represents the Mainz edition of Marianus used by John, it was probably not his exemplar.

⟨ ⟩ indicate an editorial addition to the base MS C; and to L and B in Appendices A and B respectively.

CHRONICON
IOHANNIS WIGORNENSIS

[1067] (.xi.) 1099 Adueniente Quadragesima rex Willelmus Nortmanniam repetiit, ducens secum Dorubernensem archiepiscopum Stigandum, Gleastoniensem abbatem Agelnothum, clitonem Eadgarum, comites Eduuinum et Morkarum, Waltheouum Siuuardi ducis filium, nobilem satrapam Agelnothum Cantuuariensem, et multos alios de primatibus Anglie: fratremque suum Odonem Baiocensem episcopum, et Willelmum filium Osberni, quem in Herefordensi prouincia comitem constituerat, Anglie custodes relinquens, castella per loca firmari precepit.[1] Wlfuuius Dorkecestrensis episcopus decessit Wintonie, sed sepultus est Dorkecestre.[2] Eo tempore extitit quidam prepotens minister, Edricus, cognomento Siluaticus, filius Alfrici, fratris Edrici Streone, cuius terram, quia se dedere regi dedignabatur, Herefordenses castellani, et Ricardus filius Scrob, frequenter uastauerunt, sed quotienscunque super eum irruerant, multos e suis militibus et scutariis perdiderunt. Iccirco asscitis sibi in auxilium regibus Walanorum Blethgento, uidelicet, et Riuuatlo,[a] idem uir Edricus, circa Assumptionem sancte Marie,

p. 346 Herefordensem | prouinciam usque ad pontem amnis Lucge deuastauit, ingentemque predam reduxit.[3] Post hec, hieme imminente, rex Willelmus de Normannia Angliam rediit, et Anglis importabile tributum imposuit.[4] Dein in Domnaniam hostiliter profectus, ciuitatem Execeastram, quam ciues et nonnulli Anglici ministri contra illum retinebant, obsedit, et cito infregit. Gytha uero

[a] Riuuado H, Riwado L, Riuuardo P

---

[1] JW is close to ASC D which dates William's return impossibly to the spring of 1066. E is much briefer. JW identifies sees, family relationships and William fitz Osbern's earldom; and adds Æthelnoth, the Kentish *satrap* to D's list of those accompanying William abroad, in this being followed by OV *HE* iv (ii. 196). Æthelnoth has been plausibly identified with the important landowner 'Alnod cild' in DB. A recent list of his DB holdings is found in Peter A. Clarke, *The English Nobility under Edward the Confessor* (Oxford, 1994), pp. 237–8. ASC reports the fire at Christ Church, Canterbury. William fitz Osbern had been Duke William's steward in Normandy, and was one of the most important landowners in central Normandy and in England after the Conquest.
[2] ASC D has this without naming the place where Wulfwig died.

THE CHRONICLE OF
JOHN OF WORCESTER

[1067] During Lent William went back to Normandy, taking with him Stigand, archbishop of Canterbury, Æthelnoth, abbot of Glastonbury, Edgar the atheling, earls Edwin and Morkar, Waltheof, son of Earl Siward, the noble Kentish 'governor' Æthelnoth, and many other leading Englishmen. He left as guardians of England his brother Odo, bishop of Bayeux, and William fitz Osbern, whom he had made earl in Herefordshire. He ordered that castles be strengthened in various places.[1] Wulfwig, bishop of Dorchester, died at Winchester but was buried at Dorchester.[2] At that time there lived a powerful thegn Eadric, called *Silvaticus*, son of Ælfric, brother of Eadric Streona. The Hereford castle garrison as well as Richard, son of Scrob, frequently laid waste his land, which he had refused to hand over to the king, but whenever they attacked him they lost many of their knights and soldiers. Thereupon, about the time of the Assumption [15 August], Eadric, calling on the help of the kings of the Welsh, Bleddyn and Rhiwallon, laid waste Herefordshire up to the bridge over the river Lugg, and brought back great spoil.[3] After this, as winter approached, William returned to England from Normandy and imposed an unbearable tax upon the English.[4] Then invading Devon, he laid siege to, and quickly broke into, Exeter which the citizens and a few English thegns held against him.

---

[3] ASC D's brief undated sentence on Eadric *Cild* is placed after William's return from Normandy on 6 Dec. ASC does not have: Eadric's parentage and identifying name (OV *HE* iv (ii. 194) also calls him *siluaticus* and *nepos* of Eadric Streona); the description of him as 'prepotens minister'; his failure to surrender his estates; the ravaging of these lands; the date, 15 Aug., on which he laid waste Hereford; and the last sentence on the success gained with his Welsh allies (who had already appeared *s.a.* 1063: see vol. ii. 592). Eadric is among those added by OV to William of Poitiers's list of those Englishmen who submitted to William at Barking in Jan. 1067, a submission omitted by ASC and JW (*Gesta Guillelmi*, ii. 34 (p. 162)). Eadric 'Salvage' had landholdings in Shropshire (DB Shropshire, see *Domesday Book seu Liber Censualis Wilhelmi Primi Regis Angliae*, ed. Abraham Farley (2 vols., London, 1783), i, fos. 253ᵛ, 256, 256ᵛ, 258), and Herefordshire (DB Herefordshire, ibid., i, fo. 183ᵛ). Eadric, and possibly his descendants, held land in 1086: see Ann Williams, *The English and the Norman Conquest* (Woodbridge, 1995), pp. 92–3.
[4] ASC DE date William's return to Dec. 6, and D mentions the tribute and William causing the ravaging of all that was overrun. Presumably this tax was collected soon after William's return. ASC E describes William's distribution of land on his return.

comitissa, scilicet, mater Haroldi regis Anglorum, ac soror Suani regis Danorum, cum multis de ciuitate fugiens euasit, et Flandriam petiit: ciues autem dextris acceptis regi se dedebant.[5] [b]Siwardus .xix. Hrofensis episcopus obiit.[b 6]

[1068] (.xii.) 1090 *Duo pape in Roma facti sunt, id est episcopus Parmensis qui expulsus est, et episcopus de Luca qui papa permansit.*[1]

Post pasca comitissa Mahtilda de Normannia uenit Angliam, quam die Pentecostes Aldredus Eboracensis archiepiscopus consecrauit in reginam.[2] Post hec Marlesuein, et Gospatric, et quique Northumbrane gentis nobiliores, regis austeritatem deuitantes, et ne sicut alii in custodiam mitterentur formidantes, sumptis secum clitone Eadgaro, et matre sua Agatha, duabusque sororibus suis Margareta et Cristina, nauigio Scottiam adierunt, ibidemque, regis Scottorum Malcolmi pace, hiemem exegerunt.[3] Rex autem Willelmus cum exercitu suo Snotingaham[a] uenit, ubi castello firmato Eboracum perrexit, ibidemque duobus castellis firmatis, quingentos milites in eis posuit, et in ciuitate Lindicolina aliisque locis castella firmari precepit.[4] Dum hec agerentur, Haroldi regis filii, Goduuinus, Eadmundus, Magnus, de Hibernia redeuntes, in Sumersetania applicuerunt; quibus Eadnothus, qui fuit Haroldi regis stallarius, occurrit cum exercitu, et cum eis proelio commisso, cum multis aliis

[b–b] *add. by* ?C[3] *at line end*
[a] Stnotingaham *CB*

[5] In ASC D a long interpolation on Margaret of Scotland separates an 18–day siege of Exeter (which could not have occurred in 1067) from Gytha's exile (after her long stay in Flatholme) to St Omer (for JW's 'Flanders'). OV *HE* iv (ii. 224) also does not link Gytha's flight to France to the Exeter siege. D mentions the loss of a great part of William's army before Exeter, and distinguishes between those who surrendered Exeter to William (after he had made promises) and the thegns who betrayed them ('for þan þa þegenas heom geswicon hæfdon'), and JW's distinction between *cives* and *Anglici ministri* might echo this distinction. JW adds Gytha's relationship to Swein Estrithson (who was, however, her nephew, not her brother), and where D has 'manegra godra manna' JW has simply 'multi'. OV's different account of the siege (*HE* iv (ii. 210–14)) is in some ways more elaborate. It says that William forgave Exeter its rebellion (apparently confirmed, as J. H. Round, *Feudal England* (London, 1895), pp. 446–50, suggested, by DB's demonstration that Exeter's obligations were not altered), and that he built and garrisoned a castle there.
[6] This addition is misplaced, like so many episcopal successions added to the earlier annals (see vol. ii, e.g. *s.a.* 1005, 1015). Siward died in 1075: see Greenway, *Fasti*, ii. 75.
[1] Marianus. The popes were Honorius (II) (1061–4), the antipope, and Alexander II (1061–73).
[2] This agrees with ASC D 1067 which also reported William spending Easter at Winchester. D's date for Easter (23 Mar.) shows that the year is 1068.

The countess Gytha, mother of Harold, king of the English, and sister of Swein, king of the Danes, escaped with many in flight from the city and went to Flanders. Then the citizens accepted pledges and gave themselves up to the king.[5] Siward, the nineteenth bishop of Rochester, died.[6]

[1068] Two popes were elected in Rome. One, the bishop of Parma, was driven out. The second, the bishop of Lucca, remained pope.[1]

After Easter, the countess Matilda came from Normandy to England, and the archbishop of York consecrated her queen on Whit Sunday [11 May].[2] After this Mærleswein and Gospatric and the more nobly-born among the Northumbrians, in order to avoid the king's harsh rule, and fearful of being imprisoned like so many others, sailed to Scotland with the atheling Edgar, his mother Agatha, his two sisters, Margaret and Christina, and there spent the winter under the protection of Malcolm, king of the Scots.[3] The king now came with his army to Nottingham, and, strengthening the castle there, arrived in York. There he strengthened two castles, and garrisoned them with 500 knights. He also ordered castles to be set up at Lincoln and at other places.[4] Whilst this was happening, the sons of King Harold, Godwine, Edmund, and Magnus, returning from Ireland, landed in Somerset. Eadnoth, who had been King Harold's staller, opposed them with an army, and, engaging them in battle, he was slain with many others. Harold's sons, having gained

---

[3] There are three main differences from ASC D 1067. JW places the exile of Edgar and his companions in its probably correct chronological sequence, reversing D's recording of this exile (in the summer of 1067) before the coronation of Matilda (at Whitsun 1067). JW consolidates Gospatric's exile (mentioned in D much later under 1067, though without a precise date) with Edgar's. The reasons 'regis austeritatem . . . formidantes' JW gives for the exile contrast with D's simple statement: 'Eadgar cild for út'. Mærleswein, the sheriff of Lincoln, had remained in office until his exile (*Regesta* i. 8). OV *HE* iv (ii. 214–18) provides some of the background to this exile and to William's first expedition to the North, including the rebellions and subsequent submission of Edwin and Morkar, which are omitted by ASC and JW.

[4] Close to ASC D 1067, E being different, though JW does not have D's clear inference that William had come north to meet a threatened challenge to his authority, which must have occurred in the summer of 1068, and at least after Matilda's coronation. 'Quingentos milites in eis posuit' is not in ASC. OV *HE* iv (ii. 218) says that one castle (on the site of the present Clifford's Tower) was built on this expedition, and a second early in 1069 after the Northumbrian uprising. ASC and JW are silent both about the control of Northumbria beyond the Tees in 1067–8 by successively Copsige, Osulf, and Gospatric, which is described in *HR* (SD ii. 198–9), and about the rebellions elsewhere in England in 1068, which are mentioned in OV *HE* iv (ii. 228).

occisus est: illi uero potiti uictoria de Domnania et Cornubia preda rapta non modica, in Hiberniam redierunt.[5]

[**1069**] (.xiii.) 1091   *Marianus post .x. annos sue inclusionis in Fulda, iussione episcopi Mogontini et abbatis Fuldensis, .iii. non. April., feria .vi., ante Palmas Mogontiam uenit.*[1]

⟨D⟩uo Haroldi filii, circa Natiuitatem Iohannis Baptiste, denuo .lxiiii. nauibus de Hibernia uenientes, in ostio fluminis Tau applicuerunt, et cum Breona Brytonico comite graue prelium commiserunt; quo confecto, unde uenerant redierunt.[2]

Marianus *.vi. id. Iulii, feria .vi., in natali sanctorum .vii. Fratrum, in eadem urbeᵃ iuxta monasterium principale includitur.*[3]

Ante Natiuitatem sancte Marie, Suani regis Danorum filii, Haroldus, Canutus, et patruus eorum Esbernus comes, et comes Turkillus, .cc. et .xl. nauibus de Danemarcia uenientes, in ostio Humbre fluminis applicuerunt, ubi eis clito Eadgarus, comes Waltheofus, et Marlesuein, multique alii, cum classe quam congregauerant, occurrerunt.[4] De quorum aduentu Eboracensis archiepiscopus Aldredus ualde tristis effectus, in magnam incidit infirmitatem, et .x. anno sui archiepiscopatus, .iii. id. Sept. feria .vi., ut Deum rogauerat, uitam finiuit, et in ecclesia sancti Petri est sepultus.[5] Octauo post hunc die, scilicet .xiii. kal. Octob., sabbato, Normanni qui castella custodiebant, timentes ne domus, que prope castella erant, adiumenta Danis ad implendas fossas castellorum essent, igne eas succendere coeperunt; qui nimis excrescens, totam ciuitatem inuasit, monasteriumque sancti Petri cum ipsa consumpsit.

ᵃ *om.* HL

[5] This landing is in ASC D 1067 with some differences. D does not name Harold's sons. (Gaimar ll. 5401–2 names the first two, and adds Tostig, son of Swein). D speaks of the sons coming with 'mid scyphere' and of a first landing at the mouth of the Avon and an abortive attack on Bristol, but has no equivalent for JW's 'illi uero . . .non modica', and does not identify Eadnoth as King Harold's staller. He had been a staller of Edward the Confessor: see Harmer, *Writs*, no. 85. He is addressed in King William's writ for Bath abbey (*Regesta* i. 7). On his DB holdings, see Clarke, *English Nobility under Edward the Confessor*, pp. 281–3.

[1] Marianus.

[2] ASC D does not have a separate annal for 1069, and places a slightly wordier account of the return of Harold's sons *s.a.* 1068 'to þam middan sumera'. Their landing is 'unwærlice', and Count Brian comes upon them 'unwær'. OV *HE* iv (ii. 224) describes the support given them by Diarmait mac Máel na mBó, king of Leinster, and by Irish princes, their landing at Exeter with 66 ships, and adds William Gualdi to the leaders of the force which defeated them.

victory, took much booty from Devon and Cornwall, and went back
to Ireland.[5]

[1069] After being enclosed in a cell for ten years in Fulda, at the
command of the bishop of Mainz and of the abbot of Fulda,
Marianus came to Mainz on 3 April, the Friday before Palm
Sunday.[1]

Two of Harold's sons, about the time of the feast of St John the
Baptist [24 June], came again from Ireland with sixty-four ships,
landed at the mouth of the river Taw, and fought a great battle with
Brian, a Breton earl. After it was over, they returned whence they
had come.[2]

On Friday, 10 July, on the feast-day of the Seven Holy Brothers,
Marianus was enclosed in a cell in the same city near the chief
monastery.[3]

Before the Nativity of St Mary [8 September], Harold and Cnut,
the sons of Swein, king of the Danes, and their uncle earl Osbeorn,
and earl Thorkell came with 240 ships from Denmark and landed at
the mouth of the Humber. There the atheling Edgar, earl Waltheof,
and Mærleswein and many others joined them with the fleet they
had assembled.[4] Much affected with distress at their arrival,
Ealdred, archbishop of York, became very ill, and died, as he had
entreated God, on Friday, 11 September, in the tenth year of his
archiepiscopate, and was buried in the church of St Peter.[5] Eight
days later, that is on Saturday, 19 September, the Norman garrison
in York began setting fire to the houses near the castle as they
feared that they might be of use to the Danes in filling up the
castle's ditch. The fire spread too far, encroached on the whole city
and burned it together with the monastery of St Peter. This was

---

[3] Marianus.

[4] Either deliberately or because of a defective exemplar, JW omits the important events
under ASC DE 1068, that is, the appointment and murder of Earl Robert in Northumbria
and William's punitive expedition north in early 1069. ASC D 1068 dates the arrival of
Swein Estrithson's three (unnamed) sons and the two earls with 240 ships soon after the
death of Ealdred of York, which like JW it dates to 11 Sept. (Gaimar, ll. 4344–5 names
three sons of Swein.) E 1069 speaks only of Swein's sons and of Osbeorn coming with 300
ships between 15 Aug. and 8 Sept. and does not mention Ealdred's death. OV *HE* iv (ii.
224–6) describes the Danish fleet's earlier coastal attacks on Kent and East Anglia.
'Patruus eorum' has no equivalent in ASC. D (supported here by *HR* 153 (SD ii. 187))
identifies Gospatric and 'the Northumbrians' among JW's 'multi alii'.

[5] ASC D 1068 records and dates Archbishop Ealdred's death and burial without linking
his death to the arrival of the Danes, see above, 1069 n. 4.

Sed hoc ultione diuina citissime in eis uindicatum est grauissime.[6]
Nam priusquam tota ciuitas esset combusta, Danica classis superuenit, feria .ii., et castellis eodem die fractis, et plus tribus milibus ex
Normannis trucidatis, Willelmo Malet cum sua coniuge et duobus
liberis, aliisque perpaucis, uite reseruatis, naues cum innumeris
repetiere manubiis.[7] Quod ubi regi innotuit Willelmo, exercitu mox
congregato, in Northymbriam efferato properauit animo, eamque per
totam hiemem deuastare, hominesque trucidare, et multa mala non
cessabat agere. Interea nuntiis ad Danicum comitem Esbernum
missis, spopondit se clanculo daturum illi non modice summam
p. 347 pecunie et permissurum | licenter exercitui suo uictum sibi circa
ripas maris rapere, ea tamen interposita conditione, ut sine pugna
discederet peracta hieme. Ille autem auri argentique nimis auidus,
non sine magno dedecore sui petitis concessit. Normannis Angliam
uastantibus, in Northymbria et quibusdam aliis prouinciis anno
precedenti, sed presenti et subsequenti fere per totam Angliam,
maxime per Northymbriam et per contiguas illi prouincias, adeo
fames preualuit, ut homines equinam, caninam, cattinam, et carnem
comederent humanam.[8]

[1070] (.xiiii.) 1092 Willelmi Herefordensis[a] comitis et quorundam
aliorum consilio, tempore Quadragesimali, rex Willelmus monasteria
totius Anglie perscrutari, et pecuniam, quam ditiores Angli, propter
illius austeritatem et depopulationem, in eis deposuerant, auferri et
in erarium suum iussit deferri.[1] Concilium magnum in octauis Pasce[b]
Wintonie celebratum est, iubente et presente rege Willelmo, domno
Alexandro papa consentiente, et per suos legatos Hearmenfredum
Sedunensem episcopum, et presbiteros Iohannem et Petrum, cardinales sedis apostolice, suam auctoritatem exhibente. In quo concilio
Stigandus Dorubernie archiepiscopus degradatur tribus ex causis,
scilicet, quia episcopatum Wintonie cum archiepiscopatu iniuste

---

[a] Herefordensi *HL*   [b] .iii. id. Apr. *add. (G)*

[6] ASC D 1068 gives no date for its bare recording of the burning of York and of St
Peter by the Normans, which is not in E. OV's account (*HE* iv (ii. 226–8)) makes no
reference to this fire, but speaks of the garrison emerging to attack the besiegers and
engaging them within the city walls.
[7] ASC D 1068 E do not date the storming of York. JW's 'more than three thousand' is
'many hundreds' in ASC which has no equivalent for 'Willelmo Malet . . .reseruatis' nor
for the implication that the disasters were due to divine vengeance. OV *HE* iv (ii. 222)
mentions William Malet as castellan at an earlier stage. ASC D speaks of only one castle
being stormed.

quickly followed by heavy divine vengeance.[6] For before the whole city had been burnt, the Danish fleet arrived on Monday and on the same day destroyed the castles, slew more than 3000 Normans, sparing William Malet with his wife and two children, and very few others, and returned to their ships with an immense plunder.[7] When William learned of this, he immediately assembled an army, and hastened angrily to Northumbria, devastated it for the whole winter, killing men and ceaselessly inflicting many calamities. In the mean time, he sent messengers to the Danish earl Osbeorn, and secretly promised him a large sum of money and permission for his army to forage freely along the coasts on condition that he would leave without fighting a battle at the end of winter. Osbeorn, who was exceeding greedy for gold and silver, agreed to William's proposal—to his great disgrace. The Normans had devastated England (that is, Northumbria as well as other shires) in the previous year, but in this and in the following year they laid waste almost all England, (though particularly in Northumbria and in its adjacent provinces) and famine so prevailed that men ate the flesh of horses, dogs, cats and human beings.[8]

[1070] During Lent, King William, on the advice of William, earl of Hereford, and of some others, ordered that the monasteries all over England be searched and that the wealth which the richer English had deposited in them, because of his ravaging and violence, be seized and taken to his treasury.[1] A great council was held at Winchester, in the octave of Easter [11 April], at the command and in the presence of King William, with the consent of Pope Alexander whose authority was represented by his legates Ermenfrid, bishop of Sion, and John and Peter, cardinal priests of the apostolic see. In this council Stigand, archbishop of Canterbury, was deposed for three reasons: that he unlawfully held the bishopric

---

[8] ASC D 1068 E speak here of William's devastation but only in Northumbria and in this year. The bribery of Osbeorn (found also in WM *GR* iii. 261 (ii. 319)) is not in ASC which also does not have JW's description of the consequences of the famine, which is confirmed for Northumbria 'between York and Durham' by *HR* 154 (SD ii. 188). OV *HE* iv (ii. 228, 230–6), which here, as earlier, could have been based on the lost section of William of Poitiers, *Gesta Guillelmi*, provides more details of the devastation of the North and of William's itinerary during the campaign.

[1] ASC D 1071 E are more succinct about this plundering, E alone dating it to the spring, and do not refer to William's counsellors. *Chronicon de Abingdon* i. 486 describes the attentions at Abingdon of the sheriff of Berkshire, which may have been connected with this spoliation.

possidebat; et quia, uiuente archiepiscopo Rotberto, non solum
archiepiscopatum sumpsit, sed etiam eius pallio, quod Cantuuarie
remansit, dum ui iniuste ab Anglia pulsus est, in missarum cele-
bratione aliquandiu usus est; et post a Benedicto, quem sancta
Romana ecclesia excommunicauit, ᶜeo quod pecuniis sedem aposto-
licamᶜ inuasit, pallium accepit. Eius quoque frater Agelmarus East
Anglorum episcopus est degradatus. Abbates etiam aliqui ibi degra-
dati sunt, operam dante rege ut quamplures ex Anglis suo honore
priuarentur, in quorum locum sue gentis personas subrogaret, ob
confirmationem scilicet sui quod nouiter adquisierat regni.ᵈ Hinc et
nonnullos, tam episcopos quam abbates, quos nulla euidenti causa
nec concilia nec leges seculi damnabant, suis honoribus priuauit, et
usque ad finem uite custodie mancipatos detinuit, suspitione, ut
diximus, tantum inductus noui regni. In hoc itaque consilio, dum
ceteri trepidi, utpote regis agnoscentes animum, ne suis honoribus
priuarentur timerent, uenerandus uir Wulstanus, Wigornensis episcopus, possessiones quamplures sui episcopatus ab Aldredo arciepiscopo,ᵉ dum a Wigornensi ecclesia ad Eboracensem transferretur,
sua potentia retentos, qui tunc eo defuncto in regiam potestatem
deuenerant, constanter proclamabat, expetebat, iustitiamque inde
fieri tam ab ipsis qui concilio preerant, quam a rege flagitabat. At
quia Eboracensis ecclesia, non habens pastorem qui pro ea loqueretur, muta erat, iudicatum est ut ipsa querela sic remaneret
quousque, arciepiscopo ibi constituto qui ecclesiam defenderet,
dum esset qui eius querele responderet, ex obiectis et responsis
posset euidentius ac iustius iudicium fieri. Sicque tunc ea querela ad
tempus remansit.² Die autem Pentecostes rex apud Windesoram
uenerando Baiocensi canonico Thome Eboracensis ecclesie arciepiscopatum, et Walcelino suo capellano Wintoniensis ecclesie dedit
presulatum; cuius iussu mox in crastino predictus Sedunensis
episcopus Armenfridus sinodum tenuit, Iohanne et Petro prefatis

ᶜ⁻ᶜ *over erasure* C   ᵈ *H marginal addition* In hoc concilio degradatur est de sede
episcopali Leofwinus et reuersus ad abbatiam suam scilicet Coventr' unde prius assumptus
fuerat   ᵉ ut leo confidens et absque terrore solus *add. (G)*

² The summons printed in Whitelock, Brett, and Brooke, *Councils and Synods*, ii. 568,
shows that the council was to be held on 7 Apr. John was probably the cardinal-priest of S.
Maria in Trastevere, and Peter the cardinal-priest of St Chrysogonus. On this legatine
council of Winchester, see Whitelock, Brett, and Brooke, *Councils and Synods*, ii. 565, 569–
70, which notes that the *Vita Lanfranci* and OV *HE* confused this council with that at
Windsor. For the possible dependence of these on a lost account of William of Poitiers, see

of Winchester together with the archbishopric; that, in the lifetime
of Archbishop Robert, he not only seized the archbishopric, but had
for some time used, during mass, Robert's pallium, which the latter
left at Canterbury when he was unjustly driven from England by
force; and that afterwards he had received the pallium from
Benedict, whom the holy Roman see excommunicated because he
had simoniacally invaded the apostolic chair. His brother Æthelmær,
bishop of the East Angles, was also removed from his office. Some
abbots were also deposed there, the king striving to deprive so many
Englishmen of their offices. In their place he would appoint men of
his own race and strengthen his position in the newly acquired
kingdom. He stripped of their offices many bishops and abbots who
had not been condemned for any obvious cause, whether of conciliar
or secular law. He kept them in prison for life simply on suspicion (as
we have said) of being opposed to the new kingdom. In this synod
also, while others, aware of the king's resolve, were afraid of losing
their honours, the venerable Wulfstan, bishop of Worcester, was
fearless and asked for many lands of his see which had been
retained by Archbishop Ealdred when he was transferred from
the church of Worcester to York, which had, on his death, come
under royal control. Wulfstan demanded that justice be done both
by those who were at the council and by the king. Because the
church of York, in the absence of a pastor who could speak on its
behalf, was unable to respond, it was decided that the dispute be
held over until the appointment of an archbishop who could defend
her, when there would be someone who could answer Wulfstan's
plea and a clearer and fairer judgement could be made of arguments
and counter arguments. And so that dispute was held over for the
moment.[2] On Whit-Sunday [23 May] the king at Windsor gave the
archbishopric of York to the venerable Thomas, canon of Bayeux,
and the bishopric of Winchester to his chaplain Walkelin. At the
king's command on the following day, the above-mentioned Ermenfrid, bishop of Sion, held a synod, and the aforesaid cardinals John

OV *HE* ii, pp. xxxii–xxxiv. There were vacancies, possibly through deposition, at the
following abbeys: Bath, Canterbury, St Augustine's, and St Albans (*Heads*, pp. 28, 36, 66).
An abbreviated form of the canons attributed to this council is printed in Whitelock, Brett,
and Brooke, *Councils and Synods*, ii. 574–6. On York's claims over Worcester and on the
lands disputed between York and Worcester, see WM *Vita Wulfstani*, pp. xxv–xxxi. No
other source says that these matters were raised at this council. Whitelock, Brett, and
Brooke, *Councils and Synods*, ii. 565, 573–4, notes that the grounds for Stigand's deposition
are echoed in the profession of Remigius, bishop of Dorchester to Lanfranc.

cardinalibus Romam reuersis. In qua sinodo Agelricus Suth Saxonum pontifex non canonice degradatur, quem rex sine culpa mox apud Mearlesbeorge in custodiam posuit:

[HL]	[C³BP]
abbates etiam degradati sunt quamplures. Quibus degradatis, rex suis capellanis Arfasto Orientalium Anglorum presulatum et Stigando Suthsaxonum dedit episcopatum.	ᶠabbates etiam quamplures degradantur. Quibus degradatis, rex suis capellanis, Arfasto East Anglorum, et Stigando Suð-Saxonum dedit episcopatum; qui Stigandus mutauit sedem in Cicestram diocesis sue ciuitatem.³

Nonnullis etiam Normannicis monachis dedit abbatias. Et quia Dorubernensisᵍ archipresul depositus et Eboracensis erat defunctus, iussu regis, in octauis Pentecostes ab eodem Armenfrido Sedunensi episcopo sedis apostolico legato, ordinatus est Walcelinus.ᶠʰ⁴ Imminente autem festiuitate sancti Iohannis Baptiste, comes Esbernus, cum classe que in Humbre flumine hiemauerat, Danemarciam adiit; sed frater suus, rex Danorum Suanus, illum, propter pecuniam, quam contra uoluntatem Danorum a rege Willelmo acceperat, exlegauit.⁵ Vir strenuissimus Edricus, cognomento Siluaticus, cuius supra meminimus, cum rege Willelmo pacificatur.⁶ Post hec, rex accito de Normannia Landfranco Cathomensi abbati, genere Longobardo, uiro undecunque doctissimo, omnium liberalium artium diuinarumque simul ac secularium litterarum scientia peritissimo, consiliis quoque ac gubernatione rerum mundialium eque prudentissimo, | die Assumptionis sancte Marie arciepiscopum constituit Cantuuariensis ecclesie, et in festiuitate sancti Iohannis Baptiste die dominica, arciepiscopum consecrari fecit Cantuuarie. Consecratus est autem ab episcopis Gisone Wyllensi, et a Walterio Herefordensi, qui ambo Rome a Nicolao papa ordinati sunt, ⁱquando Aldredus

p. 348

ᶠ⁻ᶠ over erasure C³   ᵍDorubernie C   ʰ 1070ᵐ incorporated here B   ⁱ⁻ⁱ over erasure by C³. In the upper mg. a scrawl by C³: quando Aldredus . . .consecrationi

³ WM GP ii. 96 (p. 205).
⁴ On the legatine council of Windsor, for which JW is the 'sole direct evidence', see Whitelock, Brett, and Brooke, Councils and Synods, ii. 577. The deposition of Bishop Æthelric of Selsey is mentioned in Pope Alexander II's letter to William of late 1071 (ibid., ii. 579–80). Æthelsige of St Augustine's, Canterbury, Ecgfrith of St Albans and Godric of Winchcombe could be among the abbots removed from office to be succeeded by Scotland, Frederick, and Galandus; see Heads, pp. 36, 66, and 79.
⁵ WM GR iii. 261 (ii. 319) also records Osbeorn's exile, which is not in ASC. ASC E 1070 reports the following events which are not in JW: Swein Estrithson's arrival with a

and Peter returned to Rome. At this synod Æthelric, bishop of the South Saxons, was uncanonically deposed. The king soon after kept him under guard at Marlborough even though he was guiltless.

Many abbots were there deposed. When they had been deposed, the king gave the bishoprics of the East Angles and of the South Saxons to his chaplains Arfast and Stigand respectively.	Many abbots were there deposed. The king gave the bishoprics of the East Angles and of the South Saxons to his chaplains, Arfast and Stigand respectively. Stigand changed the site of his see to the city of his bishopric, Chichester.[3]

William gave abbeys to many Norman monks. Since the archbishop of Canterbury was deposed and that of York dead, Walkelin, at the king's command, was ordained on the octave of Whit-Sunday [30 May] by the same Ermenfrid, bishop of Sion, and legate of the apostolic see.[4] On the approach of the feast of St John the Baptist [24 June], earl Osbeorn went to Denmark with the fleet which had wintered in the Humber, but his brother Swein, king of the Danes, exiled him because he had received money from King William against the wishes of the Danes.[5] The valiant Eadric called *Silvaticus*, whom we have mentioned above, was reconciled with King William.[6] After this the king summoned from Normandy Lanfranc, abbot of Caen, a Lombard by birth, a man learned in all things, skilled both in the liberal arts, and in sacred and secular letters, most prudent both in his counsels and in his management of earthly affairs, and on the Assumption of St Mary [15 August] the king made him archbishop of Canterbury, and on Sunday, the feast of John the Baptist [29 August], he had him consecrated archbishop of Canterbury. He was consecrated by Giso, bishop of Wells, and Walter, bishop of Hereford. They had both been ordained in Rome by Pope Nicholas when

fleet in the Humber which proceeded to the Thames 'the following summer' before returning to Denmark, after William and Swein had agreed terms; Osbeorn and Bishop Christian of Aarhus' arrival at Ely; in great detail the attack by the Danes and Hereward on Peterborough. ASC D 1070 refers briefly to a Danish fleet (presumably Swein's) staying in the Thames for two nights before returning to Denmark; and to the plundering of Peterborough.

[6] This is not recorded elsewhere under 1070, though OV *HE* iv (ii. 194) had dated a reconciliation to 1067 (see above, 1067 n. 3). OV *HE* iv (ii. 228–9) had spoken of Eadric assisting Welshmen and the men of Chester in an attack on Shrewsbury in 1068. Presumably Eadric had continued in rebellion since 1067. That he and his family retained land is suggested by Williams, *English and the Norman Conquest* (above, 1067 n. 3), pp. 92–3.

Eboracensium archiepiscopus pallium suscepit; uitabant enim a Stigando, qui tunc arciepiscopatui Dorubernie presidebat, ordinari, quia illum nouerant non canonice pallium suscepisse.[7] Herimannus etiam

[HL]	[C³BP]
Searesbyriensis episcopus	episcopus, qui iam presulatus sedem *a Scireburna transtul*erat *Salesberiam*,[8]

cum*ⁱ* quibusdam aliis, eius interfuit consecrationi. Deinde Landfrancus Thomam Eboracensem consecrauit episcopum.[9] His gestis, reuerendi Wlstani, Wigornensis episcopi, mota est iterum querela, episcopo iam consecrato Thoma, qui pro Eboracensi loqueretur ecclesia; et in concilio, in loco qui uocatur Pedreda celebrato, coram rege ac Dorubernie arciepiscopo Landfranco, et episcopis, abbatibus, comitibus, et primatibus totius Anglie, Dei gratia adminiculante, est terminata. Cunctis siquidem machinamentis non ueritate stipatis, quibus Thomas eiusque fautores Wigornensem ecclesiam deprimere, et Eboracensi ecclesie subicere, ancillamque facere modis omnibus satagebant, iusto Dei iudicio ac scriptis euidentissimis detritis, et penitus annichilatis, non solum uir Dei Wlstanus proclamatas et expetitas possessiones recepit, sed et suam ecclesiam, Deo donante ac *ʲ*rege concedente, ea libertate liberam suscepit, qua primi fundatores eius, sanctus rex Athelredus, Osherus Huuiciorum subregulus, ceterique Merciorum reges, Kenredus, Athelbaldus, Offa, Kenulfus, eorumque successores, Eadwardus senior, Athelstanus, Eadmundus et Edredus, Eadgarus ipsam liberauerant.[10] *Ægelwinus* Dunholmi episcopus *ab hominibus regis* Willelmi *capitur*, et in carcerem truditur: *ubi, dum ex nimia cordis* dolore *comedere nollet, fame* et *dolore moritur.*[11] Siwardo Hrofensi episcopo defuncto, Arnostus Beccensis monachus et Arnosto Gundulfus,

ʲ⁻ʲ written by C³ partly on line over erasure and extending into mg.

---

[7] Whitelock, Brett, and Brooke, *Councils and Synods*, ii. 585 n. 3, points out that *Intrauit* (Lanfranc's account of the preliminaries to the council of 1072) implies that Walter of Hereford was absent. ASC A 1070 records Lanfranc's consecration at Canterbury on 29 Aug., but JW seems the only source for the date of his election and investiture.

[8] WM *GP* ii. 83 (p. 183).

[9] Thomas was consecrated in late 1070 or very early in 1071. ASC A records the consecration under 1070. JW does not hint here at Lanfranc's contentious demand for a profession of obedience from Thomas, which was refused when Thomas went to

Ealdred, archbishop of York, received the pallium. They avoided ordination by Stigand who was then archbishop of Canterbury because they knew he had received the pallium uncanonically.[7] Hereman, already

bishop of Salisbury,	bishop, who had already transferred the see from Sherborne to Salisbury,[8]

with some others attended the consecration. Then Lanfranc consecrated Thomas bishop of York.[9] When these things had been done, the claim of the revered Wulfstan, bishop of Worcester, was again raised as Thomas who had been consecrated bishop would speak on behalf of the church of York, and it was settled, with the aid of God's guidance, at a council held at the place called *Pedreda* before the king, Lanfranc, archbishop of Canterbury, and the bishops, abbots, earls, and leading men of all England. All the machinations, none founded in the truth, by which Thomas and his abettors tried by all means to lower the church of Worcester, subject it to the church of York, and make it its handmaiden were quashed and destroyed completely by the fair judgement of God and the clearest evidence of the documents. Not only did the man of God Wulfstan receive the lands he had asked for and sought but he recovered that freedom which the first founders, Æthelred, king and saint, Oshere, sub-king of the Hwicce, and the other Mercian kings, Cenred, Æthelbald, Offa, and Cenwulf, and their successors Edward the Elder, Æthelstan, Edward, Eadred and Edgar had conferred on Worcester.[10] Æthelwine, bishop of Durham, was seized by King William's men and thrown into prison, where, after refusing all food in his great anguish, he died of hunger and grief.[11] On the death of Siward, bishop of Rochester, Arnost, a monk of Bec, succeeded, and in

Canterbury for consecration in 1070, and accepted, but only for Lanfranc's lifetime, before this consecration.

[10] This 'council' or meeting on the Parret (which could not have met before Thomas's consecration in late 1070 or early 1071) is also mentioned in WM *Vita Wulfstani*, p. 26, and discussed there on pp. xxix–xxxi, where it is suggested that it was presumably held at North Petherton or South Petherton, which were royal manors on the Parret. The texts of JW and WM *Vita Wulfstani* are printed and translated in R. C. Van Caenegem, *English Lawsuits from William I to Richard I* (2 vols., Selden Society, vols. cvi–cvii; London, 1990–1), i. no. 3 (pp. 3–5).

[11] *HDE* iii. xvii (SD i. 105). This addition is misplaced since Æthelwine was imprisoned in 1071, see *s.a.*

eiusdem ecclesie monachus, successit.[k][12] Comes Flandrensium Baldwinus iunior[l] obiit.[j][13]

[C³B]

[m]*In ciuitate* Wintonia est *monasterium quod rex Ælfredus quondam edificaverat et Grimbaldo quodam Flandrensi suadente, in eo canonicos posuit, sed* sanctus *Æthelwoldus, expulsis* clericis, *monachos* ibidem constituit. Est aliud monasterium *sanctimonialium* quibus idem *Æthelwoldus Ælfðrytham uirginem* abbatissam preposuit. In eadem diocesi *sunt .iii.* cenobia *Certesie, Rumesie, Wærewælle.* Hoc monasterium *Ælfryth, uxor regis* Eadgari, *compuncta priuigni sui nece, edificau*it *in honore sancte Crucis.* In *Rume*sie *ia*cent sancta *Merewynna* et sancta *Ælfleda.*[m][14]

[1071] (.xv.) 1093 [a]*Ab Heinrico* imperatore *clericus quidam, Karolus nomine, comparauit episcopatum urbis Constantie. Quapropter Sigifrido episcopo Mogontino concilium faciente coram prefato rege idem clericus et episcopatum perdidit et non longe post etiam uitam.*[1] ⟨C⟩omes Frisie Rodbrihtus fratruelem suum Arnulfum Flandrie comitem in loco qui dicitur Cassel in bello occidit et eius comitatum optinuit.[2]

[b]Landfrancus et Thomas Romam iuerunt, et ab Alexandro papa pallium susceperunt.[b][3] Comites Eduuinus et Morkarus, quia rex Willelmus eos in custodiam ponere uoluit, latenter e curia eius fugerunt, et aliquandiu contra illum rebellauerunt. Verum ubi

---

[k] *interlin.* C³   [l] *interlin.* C³   [m–m] *written in mg. next to 1070* C³, *incorporated in text at 1070*[h] B, *om.* HLP

[a] *For B's addition here, see Appendix B*   [b–b] *For B's substituted text, see Appendix B*

---

[12] Siward did not die until 1075: see Greenway, *Fasti,* ii. 75.

[13] Baldwin VI (1067–70) died on 16 July (*Chronicon S. Amandi Elnonensis,* in *Recueil des historiens de France,* xi. 345). ASC D (1071) E records in addition Arnulf's accession.

[14] WM *GP* ii. 78 (pp. 173–5). It is not clear why this marginal entry was placed here.

[1] Marianus. Henry invested Charles on 2 Feb. 1070, and the synod of Mainz was held in Aug. 1071 (Meyer von Knonau, *Jahrbücher,* ii. 1–2, 81–3).

turn Gundulf. a monk of the same church, succeeded.[12] Baldwin
the younger, count of Flanders, died.[13]

> In the city of Winchester
> there is a monastery which
> King Alfred formerly built,
> and, on the entreaty of Grimbald
> the Fleming, settled canons in it,
> but holy Æthelwold expelled
> them and established monks
> there. There is also a convent
> of nuns over which the same
> Æthelwold set as abbess the
> virgin Ælthfryth. In that diocese
> there are three monasteries,
> Chertsey, Romsey and Wherwell.
> Chertsey Ælthfryth, wife of
> King Edgar, stirred by the
> death of her stepson, built in
> honour of the Holy Cross. In
> Romsey lie the bodies of St
> Mærwynn and St Ælflæd.[14]

[1071] A certain cleric, Charles by name, bought the bishopric of the
city of Constance from Emperor Henry. On account of this a council
was summoned by Siegfried, bishop of Mainz, before the same king,
and the same cleric lost his see and shortly afterwards his life.[1]
Robert, count of Frisia, slew in battle his younger brother Arnulf,
count of Flanders, at the place called Cassel, and seized his county.[2]
Lanfranc and Thomas went to Rome and received the pallium
from Pope Alexander.[3] Earls Edwin and Morkar fled secretly from
the king's household because he wanted to place them in custody,
and they rebelled against him for some time. When they saw that

---

[2] ASC D 1071 E 1070 speaks of Arnulf's guardian William fitz Osbern and many
thousands as well as Arnulf being slain and of King Philip of France being put to flight at
an unnamed battle. The battle took place on Monday, 21 Feb. according to Lambert of
Saint-Omer (MGH SS v. 66), on 22 Feb. on the evidence of the foundation charter of St
Peter's, Cassel (see C. Verlinden, *Robert I le Frison* (Antwerp–Paris, 1935), pp. 65–6); and
on Sunday, 20 Feb. according to OV (*GND* vii. (25) (ii. 146), *HE* iv (ii. 282)) and Torigni
(*GND* vii. 14 (ii. 224)).
  [3] ASC A 1070 mentions Lanfranc's and Thomas's visit. The archbishops were certainly
in Rome in Oct. 1071 (Jaffé 4692; Hermann the Archdeacon, *Miracula S. Eadmundi* 38,
(*UAG*, pp. 249–50)).

quod ceperunt, sibi non prospere cessisse uiderunt, Eduuinus regem
Scottorum Malcolmum adire decreuit; sed in ipso itinere a suis
insidias perpessus occiditur. Morkarus uero, et Aegeluuinus, Dunholmensis episcopus, et Siuuardus, cognomento Barn, et Here-
uuardus uir strenuissimus, cum multis aliis, Heli insulam nauigio
petierunt, in ea hiemare uolentes. Sed hoc audito, rex cum butse-
carlis in orientali plaga insule omnem illis exitum obstruxit, et
pontem in occidentali duum miliariorum longum fieri iussit. At
illi, ubi se uiderunt sic esse conclusos, repugnare desistebant; et
omnes, excepto Hereuuardo uiro strenuissimo, qui per paludes cum
paucis euasit, regi se dedebant; qui mox episcopum Aegeluuinum
Abbandoniam missum in custodiam posuit, ubi in ipsa hieme uitam
finiuit. Comitem uero ceterosque per Angliam diuisos, partim
custodie mancipauit, partim manibus truncatis uel oculis erutis,
abire permisit.[c 4]

[1072] (.xvi.) 1094 Post Assumptionem sancte Marie rex Anglorum
Willelmus, habens in comitatu suo Edricum, cognomento Siluati-
cum, cum nauali et equestri exercitu Scottiam profectus est, ut eam
sue dicioni subiugaret; cui rex Scottorum Malcolmus, in loco qui
dicitur Abernithici, occurrit, et homo suus deuenit.[1]

*Sigifridus episcopus Mogontinus .v. id. Sept., die dominico, quasi causa
orationis, in Galatiam ad sanctum Iacobum perrexit. Cum autem
monasterium Cluniacum intrasset, seculum relinquens, ibi perstitit, sed
cum mercennarii Mogontinum comparare uellent episcopatum Sigifridus
precipiente sibi abbate per obedientiam quam ei uel sancto Benedicto
debebat ad sedem suam rediit.*[2]

Aegelricus, quondam Dunholmensis episcopus, apud West-
p. 349 monasterium, quo rex Willelmus illum miserat custodiendum |

[c] *For L's addition, see Appendix A*

---

[4] JW is quite close to ASC D 1072 E. ASC does not report Edwin and Morkar's fears
('quia rex . . . uoluit'), Edwin's decision to visit Malcolm, the rebels' intention of wintering
on Ely, and the length of William's bridge at Ely; and it does not describe the various fates
of the prisoners. JW does not have ASC E's (1070) account of the events in Peterborough
and Ely which provide the context for the arrival of Morkar and others at Ely; here under
1071 it has no equivalent for ASC's reference to the aimless wanderings in woods and
moors of Edwin and Morkar; and it does not have ASC's reference to William's capture of
ships and weapons. Siward Barn was an important landowner (see C. R. Hart, 'Hereward
"the Wake" and his companions' in id, *The Danelaw* (London 1992), pp. 640–4), who had
joined the English rebels supporting the Danish invasion of 1070 (OV *HE* iv (ii. 226), *HR*
(SD ii. 190)). Gaimar's account (ll. 5451–97, 5693–5704) confirms the roles of Morkar,

their undertaking had ended unsuccessfully, Edwin decided to go to Malcolm, king of the Scots, but on his journey he was ambushed by his followers and slain. Morkar indeed, Æthelwine, bishop of Durham, and Siward, called Barn, and the most vigorous Hereward with many others sailed to the island of Ely, intending to spend the winter there. But, on learning of this, the king with his buscarls, blocked all exits to the eastern shore of the island, and ordered a two-mile-long bridge to be built on the western shore. Seeing that they were surrounded, the rebels stopped resisting and surrendered to the king, except for the valiant Hereward who fled with a few men through the fens. William immediately sent Bishop Æthelwine to Abingdon and placed him in custody, and there the bishop ended his life that same winter. Of the earl and the others scattered about England, some he imprisoned, some he allowed to go free after their hands had been cut off or their eyes gouged out.[4]

[1072] After the Assumption of St Mary [15 August], William, king of the English, accompanied by Eadric called *Silvaticus*, set out with a navy and a land army to Scotland in order to bring it under his control. Malcolm, king of the Scots, met him at the place called Abernethy and became his man.[1]

On Sunday, 9 September, Siegfried, bishop of Mainz, set out for the tomb of St James in Galicia for prayer. After entering the monastery at Cluny, he left the world and remained there. But since greedy men were hoping to purchase the Mainz bishopric, Siegfried, at the command of the abbot, returned to his see bound by the obedience he owed his abbot and to St Benedict.[2]

On Monday, 15 October, Æthelric, formerly bishop of Durham, died at Westminster where King William had sent him to be

Æthelwine, and Siward Barn (making them meet at Upwell or Outwell in Norfolk), William's offensive actions by sea and his assault across a bridge, and the imprisonment of Æthelwine and Morkar, though it also contributes a long account of Hereward. *LE*, pp. 173–6, 179–88, also has much on Hereward, and the confusions in its narrative are discussed ibid. pp. lv–lvii. OV *HE* iv (ii. 258) says little about the Ely revolt, but reports that Edwin was killed by Normans after being betrayed by his servants, and comments that the imprisonment of Morkar was unjust. *HR* 158 (SD ii. 195) adds to its copying of JW the information that Æthelwine and Siward returned from Scotland by ship. JW like ASC E dates Æthelwine's death to the winter.

[1] ASC D 1073 E reports this expedition without dating it and without mentioning Eadric or Abernethy. Gaimar (l. 5711) mentions Abernethy. *HDE* (SD i. 106) says that William reached Durham on the way back by 1 Nov. 1072.

[2] Marianus. Siegfried reached Cluny on 23 Sept., but was back in Mainz by 6 Dec. 1072 (Meyer von Knonau, *Jahrbücher*, ii. 168–9).

idibus Octobris, feria secunda, uita decessit.[3] *a*Successit Ægelwino in episcopatum Dunholmensem Walcerus, genere Lotharingus.*a*[4]

[**1073**] (.xvii.) 1095 *In hoc anno omnia iuxta cursum solis et lune habentur sicut in anno .xv. Tiberii in quo baptizatus est Dominus, id est dies baptismatis .viii. idus Ianuarii, die dominico Epiphanie, et secunda feria initium ieiunii eius .xl. diebus. A baptismate itaque Domini in anno .xv. Tiberii huc usque duo magni cicli hoc est mille .lxiiii. anni.*[1]

Rex Anglorum Willelmus ciuitatem que uocatur Cinomannis, et prouinciam ad illam pertinentem, maxime Anglorum adiutorio, quos de Anglia secum duxerat, sibi subiugauit.[2] Clito Eadgarus de Scottia per Angliam uenit in Normanniam, et cum rege se repacificauit.[3]

[**1074**] (.xviii.) 1096 *Hiltibrandus, qui et Gregorius, Romanus archidiaconus papa est electus et factus. Iste papa sinodo celebrata ex decreto sancti Petri apostoli et sancti Clementis aliorumque sanctorum patrum, et banno interdixit clericis maxime diuino ministerio consecratis uxores habere uel cum mulieribus habitare, nisi quas Nicena synodus uel alii canones exceperunt. Decreuit quoque sub sententia sancti Petri ut cum Simone Mago dampnaretur non solum emptor et uenditor cuiuscunque officii, ut puta, episcopatus, abbatie, prepositure, decanie uel decimationis ecclesie sed et quicunque consentiret eis. Dominus enim dixit: gratis accepistis, gratis date.*[1] *De predicta synodo duo episcopi missi sunt a papa ad regem Romanum Heinricum cum matre ipsius imperatrice Agnete*

---

a–a add. by C² at line end

[3] ASC D 1073 E record Æthelric's death on 15 Oct. and his burial in St Nicholas' Chapel, Westminster after recapitulating his earlier history. Æthelric was bishop of Durham from *c.*1041 to 1056. His resignation and retirement to Peterborough had been recorded *s.a.* 1056 (see vol. ii. 580).

[4] Information based on *HDE* iii. xviii (SD i. 105). Æthelwine's death in the winter of 1071–2 had been recorded in the previous annal, and erroneously in an adddition by C² under 1070 (see above, 1070 n. 11).

[1] Cf. Luke 3: 1. JW's source, Marianus, refers to the two great cycles of 532 years each. The first started in AD 9, the 15th year of Tiberius Caesar. The Epiphany was on Sunday in 1073.

[2] This campaign is in ASC D 1074 E, which describe the damage caused by the English. JW's 'maxime Anglorum adiutorio' could echo ASC's emphasis on the central English role in this destructive campaign. OV *HE* iv (ii. 306–8) has a fuller account.

[3] Corresponds to ASC D 1075 (*recte* 1074) E 1074. JW's 1073 annal begins with ASC E's first entry under 1073 (the Maine campaign; see above, 1073 n. 2) and ends with E's second entry under 1074 (Edgar's reconciliation with William). The intervening entries in ASC, which record William's return to England in 1073 and his crossing to Normandy in 1074, are not in JW, and this omission could have led him to date the reconciliation with

confined.[3] Walcher, a Lotharingian by birth, succeeded Æthelwine to the see of Durham.[4]

[1073] In this year everything in the course of the sun and moon was as it had been in the fifteenth year of Tiberius when the Lord was baptized. Thus the day of His baptism, the Epiphany, was on Sunday, 6 January, and the beginning of His forty-day fast was on a Monday. From the baptism of the Lord in the fifteenth year of Emperor Tiberius up to this day are two great cycles, making a total of 1064 years.[1]

William, king of the English, subdued the city called Le Mans and the province attached to it, being greatly helped by the English he had brought with him from England.[2] After passing through England, the atheling Edgar came to Normandy from Scotland, passing through England, and was reconciled with the king.[3]

[1074] Hildebrand, also known as Gregory, an archdeacon at Rome, was elected and made pope. At a synod held by this pope and based on the decrees of St Peter the apostle, of St Clement, and of other fathers, the pope banned clerics specifically consecrated to the Holy ministry from having wives and from living with women except for those which the Nicaean synod and other canons had allowed. He also decreed, as with the judgement of St Peter in the case of Simon Magus, that not only the purchaser and vendor of whatever ecclesiastical office, that is, bishopric, abbacy, priorate, diaconate, or any church tithe, should be condemned but also whoever consented to this. For the Lord said: freely you have received, freely give.[1] From the aforesaid synod two bishops were sent by the pope to Henry, the Roman king, and his mother, Empress Agnes,

Edgar and subsequent events under 1074 and 1075, and possibly 1077, one year too early. ASC D's fuller account of the reconciliation says that Edgar went first to Scotland from Flanders on 8 July, and received letters from Philip I before making peace with William in Normandy. R. Latouche, *Histoire du Comté du Maine pendant le Xᵉ et le XIᵉ siècle* (Paris, 1910), p. 38 n. 7, and Douglas, *William the Conqueror*, p. 229 n. 3, noted that William confirmed grants in Maine to Saint-Pierre de Solesmes (*Cartulaire des Abbayes de Saint-Pierre la Couture et de Saint-Pierre de Solesmes* (Le Mans, 1881), nos. viii–ix (pp. 10–13)) and to Saint-Vincent of Le Mans (*Cartulaire de l'abbaye de Saint-Vincent du Mans* (2 vols.; Mamers-le Mans, 1886–1913), i. 177 (cols. 107–8)) at Bonneville-sur-Touques, apparently early in 1073 (for Saint-Pierre de Solesmes on 30 Mar., but for Saint-Vincent du Mans earlier on a Sunday in mid-Lent) and that could suggest that he had jurisdiction over Maine by that time. It is just possible that the grants simply anticipated William's reconquest of Maine later that year.

[1] Cf. Matt. 10: 8.

ob hoc scilicet ut decreta pape roborata perficerentur. Ipsique duo episcopi noluerunt esse in Pasca cum rege in ciuitate Babenberg, ne aliquam societatem haberent cum Herimanno eiusdem urbis episcopo qui episcopatum emit et in illo Pasca regi seruiuit.[2]

[3]Herefordensis comes Rogerus, filius Willelmi eiusdem page comitis, East Anglorum comiti Rodulfo, contra preceptum regis Willelmi, sororem suam coniugem tradidit, nuptiasque per magnificas cum plurima multitudine optimatum in Grantebrycgensi prouincia, in loco qui Yxninga dicitur, celebrantes, magnam coniurationem, plurimis assentientibus, contra regem Willelmum ibi fecerunt;[4] comitemque Waltheofum suis insidiis preuentum, secum coniurare compulerunt. Qui mox ut potuit, Landfrancum Dorubernensem archiepiscopum adiit, penitentiamque *ᵃab eoᵃ* pro facto licet non sponte sacramento accepit, eiusque consilio regem Willelmum in Normannia degentem petiit, eique rem ex ordine gestam pandens, illius misericordie ultro se dedit.[5] Verum illi supra memorati coniurationis principes, ceptis operam daturi, sua castella repetiere, rebellationemque adoriri omni conatu cum suis fautoribus coepere.[6] Sed Herefordensi comiti, ne, Sabrina transuadato, Rodulfo comiti ad locum destinatum cum suo exercitu occurreret, restitit Wlstanus Wigornensis episcopus cum magna militari manu, et Aegeluuius Eoueshamnensis abbas cum suis, asscitis sibi in adiutorium Vrsone uiceomite Wigorne, et Waltero de Laceio, cum copiis suis, et cetera multitudine plebis.[7] At uero Rodulfo comiti prope Grantebrycgeiam castrametanti, Odo Baiocensis episcopus, frater regis, et Gosfridus Constantiensis episcopus, congregata magna copia, tam Anglorum quam Normannorum, ad bellum parati occurrerunt.[8] Ipse autem

ᵃ⁻ᵃ *om.* L

---

[2] Marianus. Gregory VII was elected on 22 Apr. 1073, the Roman council was held in Mar. 1074, and the papal legates were Gerald of Ostia and Hubert of Palestrina. Marianus seems to be the only source to report the legates' refusal to enter Bamberg at Easter 1074: see Meyer von Knonau, *Jahrbücher*, ii. 377.

[3] The rebellion is in ASC D 1076 (*recte* 1075) E 1075 with the important differences shown. Roger of Breteuil, earl of Hereford, was the second son of William fitz Osbern: see *CP* vi. 449–50. Ralph of Gaël, the son of Ralph the Staller, was earl of Norfolk and Suffolk, and held Breton estates: see *CP* ix. 571–4.

[4] In ASC the king is said to have arranged the marriage, which it locates at Norwich. Lanfranc's letters to Earl Roger of Hereford (Lanfranc, *Letters*, nos. 31–3, pp. 118–22) do not refer to the marriage being prohibited. OV *HE* iv (ii. 316) refers to William of Warenne and Richard of Bienfait summoning the rebels to the king's court.

[5] Waltheof's early regret and his appeal to Lanfranc are not in ASC. D alone speaks of his visit to William. WM *GR* iii. 265 (ii. 313–14) describes Waltheof's visit to

to enforce the decrees given force by the pope. The same bishops were not willing to spend Easter with the king in the city of Bamberg so as not to be associated in any way with Hermann, bishop of the same see, who had bought the bishopric and was keeping Easter with the king in that same city.[2]

[3]Roger, earl of Hereford, son of William, earl of the same county, gave his sister in marriage to Ralph, earl of the East Angles, in contravention of King William's orders. Celebrating a splendid wedding with many of the chief men of Cambridgeshire in the place called Exning, they formed there a large conspiracy against King William with the agreement of many.[4] They forced Earl Waltheof, who had been trapped by their wiles, to join the plot. As soon as he could, Waltheof went to Lanfranc, archbishop of Canterbury, and received absolution from him for the oath into which he had entered unwillingly, and on Lanfranc's advice, he went straightaway to King William in Normandy. Relating the whole business from beginning to end, he gave himself up to William's mercy.[5] In order to carry out the plan which they had hatched, the said leaders of the conspiracy returned to their castles, and began with every effort and with their followers to activate the rebellion.[6] But Wulfstan, bishop of Worcester, with a great force and Æthelwig, abbot of Evesham, with his, and with the assistance of Urse, sheriff of Worcester, and Walter de Lacy with huge forces and a great multitude of people, prepared to oppose the earl of Hereford's crossing of the Severn and his meeting with Earl Ralph and his army at the agreed place.[7] When Earl Ralph had encamped near Cambridge Odo, bishop of Bayeux, the king's brother, and Geoffrey, bishop of Coutances, assembled a large force of English and Normans and prepared for battle.[8] Earl Ralph, seeing that his plans had

---

William in Normandy on Lanfranc's advice. According to OV *HE* iv (ii. 314), Waltheof refused to participate in the conspiracy, which he had promised not to reveal, however.

[6] ASC speaks of the Bretons being lured to the rebels and of an appeal to the Danes.

[7] Here JW is much more specific about the suppression of Earl Roger's rebellion. ASC D speaks only generally of matters turning out to Roger's great harm ('ac hit wearð heom seolfan to mycclan hearme'), and E of his being thwarted ('ac he wærð gelet').

[8] OV *HE* iv (ii. 316) names William of Warenne and Richard of Clare as the leaders in a battle at *Fagaduna* while Lanfranc in his letters to William I (Lanfranc, *Letters*, nos. 34–5 (pp. 124–6)) names Geoffrey of Coutances, William of Warenne, and Robert Malet among the leaders later before Norwich, and reports the surrender of Norwich castle. In the first letter (Lanfranc, *Letters*, no. 34 (p. 124)) he had reported the flight of Earl Ralph after the battle. ASC does not record the battle.

suos conatus infirmari cernens, multitudinem resistentium ueritus, ad Northuuic clanculo refugit, et castello sue coniugi militibusque suis commendato, ascensa naui de Anglia ⁹ad minorem Brytanniam fugit: quem fugientem aduersarii illius insecuti, omnes quos de suis comprehendere poterant uel interemerunt, uel diuersis modis debilitauerunt.⁹ Dein principes castellum tamdiu obsederunt, quoad pace data permissu regis, comitisse cum suis exire de Anglia liceret. His gestis, rex autumnali tempore de Normannia rediens, comitem Rogerum in custodia posuit; comitem etiam Waltheofum, licet ab eo misericordiam expetierat, custodie tradidit.¹⁰ Edgitha, regis Haroldi germana, quondam Anglorum regina, Decembri mense ᵇ.xiiii. kal. Ian.ᵇ decessit Wintonie; cuius corpus regis iussu Lundoniam delatum, iuxta corpus domini sui regis Eaduuardi honorifice est in Westmonasterio tumulatum; ubi rex proxima Natiuitate Domini curiam suam tenuit, et ex eis qui contra illum ceruicem erexerant, de Anglia quosdam exlegauit, quosdam erutis oculis, uel manibus p. 350 truncatis, deturpauit.¹¹ | Comites uero Waltheofum et Rogerum, iudiciali sententia dampnatos, artiori custodie mancipauit.¹²

[1075] (.xix.) 1097 *Dum clerici magis eligerent anathemati subiacere quam uxoribus carere, Hiltibrandus papa, ut per alios si posset eos castigaret, precepit ut nullus audiret missam coniugati presbiteri sic: 'Gregorius papa, qui et Hiltibrandus, seruorum Dei seruus, per totum Italicum regnum et Teutonicum debitam sancto Petro obedientiam exhibentibus apostolicam benedictionem. Si qui sunt presbiteri, diaconi, subdiaconi, qui iacent in crimine fornicationis, interdicimus eis ex parte omnipotentis Dei et auctoritate sancti Petri introitum ecclesie usque dum peniteant et emendent. Si qui autem in peccato suo perseuerare maluerint, nullus uestrum officium eorum auscultare presumat quia benedictio illorum uertitur in maledictionem et oratio in peccatum, testante Domino per prophetam: maledicam, inquit, benedictionibus uestris.'*¹

Comes Waltheofus, iussu regis Willelmi, extra ciuitatem Wintoniam ductus, indigne et crudeliter securi decapitatur, et in eodem

---

ᵇ⁻ᵇ *interlin.* C³, *om.* HLBP

⁹⁻⁹ Not in ASC.
¹⁰ ASC DE do not date William's return to England, but mention the arrival of a Danish fleet, D describing its ravages in York. OV *HE* iv (ii. 316) had spoken of Earl Ralph visiting Denmark after escaping from Norwich, and HH *HA* vi. 34 (p. 398) of his wishing to return with the Danish fleet.
¹¹ ASC D 1076 (*recte* 1075) E 1075 record both Edith's death and William's punishment

been balked, and, fearing the size of the forces opposing him, fled in
secret to Norwich. He entrusted the castle to his wife and his
knights, embarked on a ship, and fled from England [9]to Brittany.
His enemies pursued him as he fled and either put to death or
mutilated in various ways all those they were able to capture.[9] The
magnates besieged the castle for some time until the king granted a
peace which allowed the countess and her followers to leave England.
After this the king returned from Normandy in the autumn. He
imprisoned Earl Roger and placed in custody Earl Waltheof even
though he had sought mercy from him.[10] Edith, sister to King
Harold, and formerly queen of the English, died at Winchester on 19
December. Her body was carried at the king's command to London
and was buried honourably at Westminster next to the tomb of her
husband, King Edward. The following Christmas, the king held his
court at Westminster, and of those who had raised their heads against
him, some he exiled from England, and others he disgraced by
gouging out their eyes or cutting off their hands.[11] He kept in closer
confinement the earls Waltheof and Roger who had been judicially
condemned.[12]

[1075] As clerks would rather be anathematized than set aside their
wives, Pope Hildebrand tried, if he could, to punish them through
others, and decreed that no one should attend the mass of a priest
who was married, thus: 'Pope Gregory, also known as Hildebrand,
servant of the servants of God, sends an apostolic blessing to those in
the Italian and German kingdom who showed the obedience due to
St Peter. On behalf of Almighty God and with St Peter's authority,
we bar priests, deacons, and sub-deacons who wallow in the guilt of
fornication from admission to church until they have done penance
and made amends. No one of you should dare to attend their divine
services if they persist in sin since their benediction will change to a
curse and their prayer into sin, as the Lord testifies through the
prophet, saying "I will curse your benediction" '.[1]

On King William's orders, Earl Waltheof was led out of the city of
Winchester, unworthily and cruelly beheaded with an axe, and there

of the rebels (described as those Bretons present at the wedding feast) at the Christmas
court.
    [12] Not in ASC D 1076 (*recte* 1075) E 1075. OV *HE* iv (ii. 318) describes Roger's
imprisonment and forfeiture after judgement by the law of the Normans.

    [1] Cf. Mal. 2: 2. JW's source, Marianus, could be referring to a council held at Rome,
24-8 Feb. 1075.

loco terra obruitur: sed processu temporis, Deo sic ordinante, corpus eius de terra leuatur, et magno cum honore Cruland deportatur, et in ecclesia honorifice tumulatur. Hic cum adhuc temporali frueretur uita, arta positus in custodia, ea que gesserat inique incessanter defleuit et amarissime, uigiliis, orationibus, ieiuniis, et elemosinis Deum studuit placare. Cuius memoriam uoluerunt homines in terra delere, sed creditur uere illum cum sanctis in celo gaudere, predicto arcipresule pie memorie Landfranco, a quo, confessione facta, penitentiam acceperat, fideliter attestante; qui et imposti criminis, supradicte scilicet coniurationis, illum immunem affirmabat esse, et que in ceteris commisisset, ut uerum Christianum, penitentialibus lacrimis defleuisse; seque felicem fore si, post exitum uite, illius felici potiretur requie.[2] Post hec mare transito, rex in minorem Brytanniam suam mouit expeditionem, et castellum Rauulfi comitis, quod Dol nominatur, tamdiu obsedit donec Francorum rex Philippus illum inde fugaret.[3]

[1076] (.xxi.) 1098 [a]Rex Danorum Suanus bene litteris imbutus obiit, cui filius suus Haroldus successit.[1]

[1077] (.xxii.) 1099 *In concilio .xxiiii. episcoporum, abbatum, multorumque clericorum in Wormatia[a] mense Martio facto, agente Heinrico rege, ipso presente, decretum est ut iussa siue decreta Hiltibrandi pape quisque paruipenderet uel contempneret, et ut nequaquam ultra papa esset. Papa autem predictus regem cum suis sequacibus seu consentaniis in quadragesima excommunicauit tribus ex causis: prima ob infamiam peccatorum suorum; secunda propter unitatem suam cum simoniacis; tertia propter distributionem ecclesie inter papam et alios. Inde quasi*

[a] preceded by two and a half blank lines, one of which has traces of erasure C
[a] Wormatia ex Wormatio CB

---

[2] ASC D 1077 E 1076 simply record Waltheof's execution at Winchester (D on May 31), and his later burial at Crowland. OV's full account (*HE* iv (ii. 320–2)) does not mention Lanfranc's testimony. Van Caenegem, *English Lawsuits from William I to Richard I* (above, 1070, n. 10), i, no. 7 (pp. 16–22) prints and translates the texts covering Earl Waltheof's execution.

[3] ASC D 1077 E 1076 do not identify Dol's defender, but speak of William's heavy losses, which OV *HE* iv (ii. 352) valued at 15,000 pounds sterling. *Annales dites de Renaud*, in *Recueil d'annales angevines et vendômoises*, ed. L. Halphen (Collection de textes pour servir à l'étude de l'histoire; Paris, 1903), p. 88 date the siege to Sept. 1076. A charter in Prou, *Recueil*, no. lxxxiv (p. 220), mentions a siege taking place on 14 Oct. 1076. A *Chronicon Britannicum* (*Recueil des historiens de France*, xi. 413) says that Geoffrey Granon

at the same spot thrown into the earth. Later, God so ordaining matters, his body was taken out of the earth, carried with great reverence to Crowland, and buried there with honour. When he was still alive and held in close confinement, he would weep endlessly and bitterly for those wrongs he had done, and he strove to please God with vigils, prayers, fastings, and alms. Men wanted to blot out his memory on earth, but in truth it is to be believed that he is worshipped with the saints in heaven. The aforementioned Archbishop Lanfranc of pious memory faithfully bears witness to this. For Waltheof had made his confession to him, and did penance, and Lanfranc affirmed that Waltheof was innocent of the crime imputed to him, that is of the aforesaid conspiracy, that whatever sins he had committed he had washed away (as a true Christian) with penitential tears, and that Lanfranc would be pleased to enjoy, at the end of life, Waltheof's happy repose.[2] After this the king crossed the channel, invaded Brittany, and besieged Earl Ralph's castle of Dol for some time until Philip, the French king, forced him to retreat from there.[3]

[1076] Swein, the Danish king, well instructed in letters, died and was succeeded by his son Harold.[1]

[1077] At the command and in the presence of King Henry a council of twenty-four bishops, of abbots, and many clergymen was held in March at Worms. It was decreed that all the commands and decretals of Pope Hildebrand were of nothing and were to be condemned, and that he was no longer to be pope. The aforesaid pope in Lent excommunicated the king and his followers and confederates for three reasons: first, because of their infamous sins; second, because of their common front with simoniacs; third, because of the division

---

joined Earl Ralph in fighting Count Hoel. William acted in close association with Count Hoel. OV *HE* iv (ii. 350–2) has an account of the siege.

   [1] ASC D 1077 (*recte* 1076) E 1076 do not mention Swein's learning. In this annal, unlike in the latter part of 1073, and in 1074 and 1075, JW's year agrees with ASC. The tradition that Cnut became studious is found in Saxo Grammaticus, *Saxonis Gesta Danorum*, ed. J. Olrik and H. Ræder (2 vols., Copenhagen, 1931–57), i. 311. Danish sources date Cnut's death to 1074, and Ælnoth's *Historia Sancti Canuti*, c. iii in *Vitæ Sanctorum Danorum*, ed. M. C. Gertz (3 vols., Copenhagen, 1908–12), i. 60–1, to 28 Apr. in that year, but his death was not known to Gregory VII when writing to him in Apr. 1075. The evidence is tabulated in *Scriptores Rerum Danicarum*, ed J. Langebek (9 vols., Copenhagen, 1772–1878), iii. 339 n. l, and some of it discussed in E. Christiansen, *Saxo Grammaticus Danorum Regum Heroum Historia*, British Archaeological Reports International Series 84, 118 (i, ii; Oxford, 1980–1), i. 236–7.

iusta ex causa primates regni regi quasi excommunicato contradicunt eumque[b] *de regno proicere temptant.*[1]

Rotbertus, Willelmi regis primogenitus, eo quod Normanniam, quam sibi ante aduentum ipsius in Angliam, coram Philippo rege Francorum dederat, possidere non licebat, Franciam adiit, et auxilio Philippi regis, in Normannia magnam frequenter predam agebat, uillas comburebat, homines perimebat, et patri suo non paruam molestiam et anxietatem inferebat.[2]

[**1078**] (.xxii.) 1100 *Heinricus rex et Hiltibrandus papa conuenientes in mense Martio in Longobardia, inuicem pacificantur, sed falso ut postea claruit. Conuenientes interim Sueui et Saxones et Welf, dux Bauuariorum, et episcopi de Saxonia septem aliique numero quinque, id est Patauiensis, Salzburgensis, Wirziburgensis, Wormatiensis et Mogontinus, Ruodolfum regem Sueuorum in Foracheim super se regem constituunt, et in Quadragesima Mogontie in regem unguunt, Alpesque contra regem* p. 351 *Heinricum muniunt. Quo cognito, Heinricus rex | Radisponam per Aquileiam post Pasca uenit, et contra Rodolfum cum exercitu festinauit. Rodolfo uero cedente fuga, Heinricus Sueuiam depredando inuasit. Eodemque anno, iuxta Renum inter Mogontiam et Wormatiam Heinricus et Rodolfus conuenerunt, sine pugna tamen discesserunt. Anno Coloniensis episcopus obiit.*[1]

[**1079**] (.xxiii.) 1101 *Heinricus rex iterum Sueuiam uenit, non cessans depredari, et castella frangere.*[1]

Rex Scottorum Malcolmus, post Assumptionem sancte Marie, Northymbriam usque ad magnum flumen Tine deuastauit, multos occidit, plures captiuauit, et cum preda magna rediit.[2] Rex Willelmus

[b] eum *HL*

---

[1] Marianus. The synod of Worms was held on 24 Jan. 1076 (Meyer von Knonau, *Jahrbücher*, ii. 613-15), and the papal letter sent after the Lenten synod of Feb. is printed in Caspar, *Registrum* iii. 10a (p. 270).

[2] ASC does not refer here to Robert's campaign against his father, which must have started after 13 Sept. 1077 when Robert was present at the dedication of St Stephen's, Caen (see L. Musset, *Les Actes de Guillaume le Conquérant et de la reine Mathilde pour les abbayes caennaises* (Mémoire de la Société des Antiquaires de Normandie, xxxvii; Caen, 1967), pp. 14-15, 58), and which ended with the siege of Gerberoi. For Robert's rebellion see David, *Robert Curthose*, pp. 12-18. The occasion for Robert's withdrawal, William's refusal to let Robert rule in Normandy, as he had earlier promised with King Philip's consent, is in ASC D 1079, though JW, like OV *HE* iv (ii. 356), v (iii. 98, 112), vii (iv. 92), dates the promise before Hastings. The most recent discussions of this grant are R. H. C. Davis, 'William of Jumièges, Robert Curthose and the Norman Succession', *EHR* xcv (1980), 597-606, and *GND* i. 137-8. JW ignores the obits in ASC D (1078) E (1077), D's

of the church between the pope and others. For these just reasons the prelates of the realm opposed the king as an excommunicate, and tried to expel him from the kingdom.[1]

Robert, the eldest of William's sons, had not been allowed to take possession of Normandy, which William had given him, in the presence of the French king, Philip, before his coming to England. For this reason he went to France, and, with the help of King Philip, ravaged in Normandy far and often, burnt townships, killed people, and caused his father much trouble and worry.[2]

[1078] King Henry and Pope Hildebrand met in Lombardy in March, and came to a peaceful agreement, which was later proved illusory. In the mean time the Swabians and the Saxons, Welf, the Bavarian duke, seven Saxon bishops, and five from outside Saxony, that is, the bishops of Passau, Salzburg, Würzburg, Worms and Mainz, set up Rudolf, king of the Swabians, as king over them at Forcheim, anointed him king at Mainz during Lent, and fortified the Alpine passes against Henry. When he had learnt of this, Henry after Easter passed through Aquileia, reached Regensburg, and rushed against Rudolf with an army. Rudolf retreated and Henry invaded and ravaged Swabia. In the same year Henry and Rudolf assembled by the Rhine between Mainz and Worms, but left without engaging in battle. Anno, bishop of Cologne, died.[1]

[1079] King Henry again invaded Swabia, ravaging ceaselessly, and destroying castles.[1]

Malcolm, the Scottish king, after the feast of the Assumption [15 August], laid Northumbria waste as far as the Tyne, killed many people, took captive many more, and returned home with a great booty.[2] King William whilst he was campaigning against his son

lunar eclipse, E's fire in London, and the temporary agreement it records between William and Philip.

[1] Marianus. Note that neither version of ASC records anything under 1078. The reconciliation was effected at Canossa in Jan. 1077, and the election of Rudolf of Swabia at Forcheim in Mar. 1077 (Meyer von Knonau, *Jahrbücher*, ii. 764, 783–5).

[1] Marianus. This entry is at the end of the 1078 annal in the Vatican Marianus witness and refers to battles later in that year. In the Marianus witness N it is found, as in JW, under 1079. The battle of Meleichstadt was fought on 7 Aug. 1078 (Meyer von Knonau, *Jahrbücher*, iii. 138–40).

[2] This is close to ASC E. This invasion could have been timed to coincide with William's preoccupations in Normandy.

filio suo Rotberto, ante castellum Gerbothret, quod ei rex Philippus prestiterat, dum pugnam intulerit, ab ipso uulneratus in brachio, de suo deiectus*a* est emissario: sed mox ut illum per uocem cognouisset, festinus descendit, ac illum suum caballum ascendere iussit, et sic abire permisit. Ille autem, multis suorum occisis nonnullisque captis, ac filio suo Willelmo cum multis aliis uulnerato, fugam iniit.[3] Venerandus uir Rotbertus, qui per ministerium reuerentissimi Wigornensis episcopi Wlstani gradum presbiteratus suscepit, a Landfranco arcipresule Dorubernie, ad Herefordensem ecclesiam, .iiii. *b*kal. Ianuarii, die dominica,*b* episcopus ordinatur Cantuuarie.[4]

[1080] (.xxiiii.) 1102 Dunholmensis episcopus Walcerus, genere Lotharingus, in loco qui dicitur Ad Caput Capree, .ii. idus Maii, feria .v., a Northymbrensibus est occisus, in ultionem necis Liulfi, nobilis generosique ministri. Hic itaque uir late per Angliam possessiones multas ex hereditario iure possedit; sed quia ubique*a* locorum Normanni incessanter ea tempestate operam dabant sue feritati, cum suis omnibus ad Dunholme se contulit, quia sanctum Cuthberhtum corde sincero dilexit, quippe cui idem sanctus, ut ipsemet Aldredo Eboracensi arciepiscopo, et aliis uiris religiosis narrare consueuerat, et dormienti et uigilanti persepe apparuit, et que fieri uoluit ut suo fideli amatori, reuelauit. Sub cuius pace, nunc in oppido, nunc in suis possessionibus, quas illis in partibus habuerat, longo tempore deguit. Cuius aduentus episcopo Walcero non extitit ingratus, quia eidem sancto ualde deuotus extiterat in omnibus. Iccirco ab ipso in tantum diligebatur, ut absque illius consilio maiores secularium negotiorum causas nullatenus agere uellet aut disponere. Ob quam rem suus capellanus Leobuuinus, quem in tantum exaltauerat ut et in episcopatu et in comitatu fere nil sine illius arbitrio agitaretur, inuidie stimulis succensus, et propter suam potentiam tedis superbie nimis inflatus, se contra predictum uirum arroganter erexit, quapropter nonnulla eius iudicia atque consilia floccipendebat, omnibusque modis annullare sudabat. Frequenter etiam coram episcopo, non sine minis, cum eo litigans, illum uerbis probrosis sepius ad iracundiam prouocabat. Quadam itaque

a eiectus *L*, eiectus *from* deiectus *P*   *b–b* *over erasure* C[3]

a ubi *HL*

---

[3] Closer to ASC E than to a defective D. E mentions William's engagement near Gerberoi and the wounding of the two Williams, father and son, though D speaks of William I being wounded in the hand. JW contributes the story of Robert's recognition of

Robert before the castle of Gerberoi (which King Philip had given Robert), was wounded in the arm by him, and forced off his horse. As soon as Robert recognized William's voice, he quickly dismounted, and ordered his father to mount his horse, and in this way allowed him to leave. William then retreated, after many of his men had been slain, and some had been taken prisoner, and his son William and many others wounded.[3] The revered Robert, who had been ordained priest by the most reverend Bishop Wulfstan of Worcester, was consecrated bishop of Hereford by Lanfranc, archbishop of Canterbury, on Sunday, 29 December, at Canterbury.[4]

[1080] Bishop Walcher of Durham, who was a Lotharingian, was killed by the Northumbrians on Thursday, 14 May, at Gateshead, in revenge for the death of the noble and benevolent thegn, Liulf. Liulf had many hereditary estates throughout England, but because the Normans were then ceaselessly rampaging everywhere, he retired to Durham with all his followers, because of his true love for St Cuthbert. He used to tell Archbishop Ealdred of York and many other religious men that the saint would often appear to him when he was either asleep or awake, and reveal to him, as his true devotee, what he wished done. For a long time Liulf lived, both in the town, and on the estates he owned in those parts, under Cuthbert's protection. Liulf's arrival in Durham was not unwelcome to Bishop Walcher, who was greatly and completely devoted to the same saint. Walcher's respect for Liulf was such that he would not carry out or complete any important secular matter without his advice. Walcher's chaplain, Leobwine, whom he had so raised up that hardly anything in the bishopric or county was decided without his consent, was roused by envy, and was excessively puffed up with pride at his own power. He opposed Liulf with great arrogance, valued his opinions and counsels as nothing, and strove in every way to render them void. Often he would, in front of the bishop, argue threateningly with him, and frequently stir Liulf to anger by scornful words. One day when Liulf had been asked by the bishop for his

his father. ASC D is defective from this point. OV *HE* v (iii. 108–10) reports that William began the siege of Gerberoi after Christmas and that it lasted for three weeks. An authentic charter of Philip I and William in favour of St Quentin, Beauvais issued during the siege of Gerberoi in Jan. 1079 (Prou, *Recueil*, no. xciv) shows that the two kings must have come to terms by then, perhaps after William had been wounded, but that Norman rebels were still in Gerberoi.

[4] JW is the earliest extant source for this.

die, cum idem uir Liulfus ab episcopo uocatus ad consilium, legalia queque et recta decerneret,[b] obstinatius ei Leobuuinus obstitit, et loquelis illum contumeliosis exacerbauit. Sed quia ille respondit ei durius solito, de placiti loco discessit ilico, et euocans ad se Gilebertum, cui presul, quia suus propinquus extitit, comitatum Northymbrensium sub se regendum commiserat, ut se uindicaret obnixe rogauit, et Liulfum quam citius posset morti tradere maturaret. Ille autem confestim iniquis petitionibus adquiescens suis, et episcopi et eiusdem Leobuuini militibus in unum coadunatis, ad uillam ubi tunc Liulfus morabatur, nocte quadam perrexit, ac illum cum sua familia fere tota in domo propria iniuste peremit. Quo cognito, grauiter antistes ex corde suspirauit intimo, et capitio de capite extracto et in terram proiecto, Leobuuino, qui tunc presens aderat, tristis dixit continuo: 'Tuis, Leobuuine, factionibus dolosis acta sunt hec, et insiliis stolidissimis, iccirco uolo te scire pro certo quia et me et te omnemque familiam meam tue lingue peremisti gladio.' Hoc dicto, in castellum se proripuit festinato, confestimque nuntiis per Northymbriam missis, omnibus nuntiari curauit, se necis Liulfi conscium non fuisse, quin potius eius occisorem Gilebertum omnesque socios ipsius de Northymbria penitus exlegasse, ac paratum fore semetipsum purgare secundum iudicium pontificale. Dein, missis intercurrentibus, ille parentesque occisorum, pace ad inuicem data et accepta, locum et diem quo conuenire interque se pacem

p. 352 firmiorem | facere possent, statuere. Quo adueniente, loco constituto in unum conuenere, uerum cum illis episcopus sub diuo noluit placitare, sed in ecclesiam que ibi erat, cum suis clericis ac honorabilioribus militibus intrauit, et consilio habito, semel et iterum de suis quos uoluit, pro pace facienda, foras ad eos misit. At illi nequaquam petitis adquiescebant, quia Liulfum illius iussione peremptum fuisse pro certo credebant. Nam Gilebertum eiusque socios, nocte post necem propinqui sui proxima, non solum in domum suam Leobuuinus familiariter et amicabiliter suscepit, uerum etiam episcopus ipse illum, ut prius, in suam gratiam familiamque recepit.[c] Unde omnes, qui parte antistitis foris inuenti fuerant, primitus occiderunt, paucis fuga reseruatis. Quo uiso, ut hostium furori satisfaceret, propinquum suum, prefatum Gilebertum, cuius anima

    [b] discerneret L   [c] over erasure C

advice, and had decided on whatever was just and right, Leobwine opposed him pigheadedly, and exasperated him with insulting remarks. But because Liulf had answered him with a greater vehemence than usual, Leobwine left the court and summoned Gilbert, a man to whom the bishop, who was his kinsman, had entrusted the administration of the county placed under his control. Leobwine clearly asked Gilbert to avenge him and kill Liulf as soon as possible. Gilbert willingly agreed to Leobwine's evil request, and gathering together the bishop's and Leobwine's knights, went one night to the township where Liulf was staying, and unjustly killed him in his residence with nearly all his household. On learning of this, Bishop Walcher sighed heavily and deeply, and, pulling his hood off his head, and casting it on the ground, mournfully said directly to Leobwine, who was then present: 'This has been done, Leobwine, by your heinous actions and most foolish counsels, and I want you to know for certain that you have, by the sword of your tongue, slain both yourself and me and all my household.' Saying this, he quickly shut himself up in the castle, and straightaway sent messengers throughout Northumbria, to make it known generally that he had not been privy to Liulf's murder, that he had outlawed from Northumbria Gilbert, his murderer, and all his accomplices, and that he was ready to clear himself according to the mode of trial for a bishop. Then, through the exchange of messengers between himself and the kin of those who had been slain, a truce between them was pledged and agreed, and they decided on a place and a date for a meeting when a more binding agreement could be reached. At the appointed time, they met together at the agreed place, but the bishop was unwilling to plead with them in the open air, and he went into a nearby church with his clergy and the more worthy of his knights. Taking counsel, he sent out again and again to them specially chosen followers to discuss the making of peace. They would in no way agree to his proposals since they believed for certain that Liulf has been killed on his orders for not only had Leobwine received Gilbert and his associates (the very night after the murder of Walcher's kinsman) with friendly familiarity into his household, but the bishop also had received him into his residence with the same favour as before. They therefore first massacred all of the bishop's party who were outside, a few saving themselves in flight. When Walcher saw this, he ordered his kinsman, the aforesaid Gilbert (whose life was demanded), to go out of the church in order to satisfy his enemies'

querebatur, presul de ecclesia iussit exire, quem egredientem milites
repugnaturi e uestigio sunt secuti, sed mox ab hostibus undique
gladiis et lanceis appetiti, in momento sunt perempti, duobus tamen
Anglicis ministris propter consanguinitatem pepercerunt. Leofuui-
num*d* quoque Dunholmensem decanum, quia sepius episcopo aduersus illos multa dederat insilia, et clericos alios, statim, ut egressi sunt,
occiderunt. Episcopus autem, ut intellexit illorum furorem nulla
ratione iri mitigatum quiuisse, nisi caput et auctor totius illius
calamitatis occideretur Leobuuinus, rogauit illum egredi foras, sed
cum penitus ut egrederetur ab illo extorquere nequiret ad ecclesie
ianuas ipsemet accessit, ibique uitam concedi poposcit. Quibus
renuentibus, caput sue clamidis limbo cooperiens, foras exiuit, et
mox inimicorum gladiis percussus occubuit. Deinde Leobuuinum
egredi iusserunt. Quo nolente, ecclesie tecto parietibusque ignem
imposuere. At ille potius ustulatione quam occisione uitam eligens
finire, flammas aliquandiu sustulit, sed cum semiustus esset, exiliuit,
et frustim concisus nequitie sue penas exoluendo miser interiit. Ob
quorum detestande necis uindictam, rex Willelmus eodem anno
deuastauit Northymbriam.[1]

*Heinricus rex Hiltibrandum papam in Pentecosten Mogontie decernit
deponendum, et Wigbertum Rauenne urbis episcopum in natale sancti
Iohannis Baptiste pro eo facit*e *papam. Ruodolfus rex Saxonum bello
occiditur apud Merseburg, ubi*f *et sepultus est idus*g *Octob. Mogontia
ciuitas magnum terre motum k. Dec. sensit, et sequenti anno ex magna
parte incendio conflagrauit cum principali monasterio et aliis tribus.*
h*Heinricus rex hostiliter Romam aduersus papam adiit oppugnans eam
non tamen intrauit.*h 2

---

d Leobfuuinum *H*   *e* fecit *HL*   *f* ibi *HL*   *g* idibus *HL*
h–h *written over erasure by* C² *when rewriting and adding the entry s.a. 1081*

[1] JW's account of Walcher's murder is the fullest of surviving sources. *HDE* iii. 23–4
(SD i. 113–14, 116–17) is briefer and vaguer than JW. It gives the general grounds for
criticism of Walcher, but provides neither the immediate background to the murder nor
the names found in JW. *HR* (SD ii. 209) glosses its borrowing from JW by naming Liulf's
wife and her kin, *HDE* iii. 23 (SD i. 115) says one Waltheof was the bishop's murderer, and
HR 159 (SD ii. 197–8) mentions an Eadulf 'cognomento Rus' (a grandson of the Gospatric
slain in 1064) among those involved in the murder. No other source mentions Leofwine,
the English dean. WM's account (in nearly the same words in both *GR* iii. 271 (ii. 330–1)
and *GP* iii. 132 (pp. 271–2)) must have been using the same story as JW. HH *HA* vii. 34

fury. In a moment they killed both Gilbert as he emerged and the knights who were following closely to defend him were slain by their enemies with lance and sword, except for two English thegns because of their consanguinity. They also killed Leofwine, a dean of Durham, because he often counselled the bishop against them, and other clergy as soon as they emerged. The bishop now understood that their anger could in no way be assuaged unless Leobwine, the chief author of all the debacle, was killed, and he ordered him to go out. Walcher was wholly unable to persuade him to venture out, and he himself went to the door of the church, and asked there that his life be spared. This request was refused, and Walcher, covering his head with the hem of his cloak, went out, and immediately fell, struck by his enemies' swords. Then they ordered Leobwine to emerge. As he was unwilling they set fire to the roof and walls of the church. Leobwine preferring death by fire than by the sword, suffered the flames for some time, but when he was half-burnt, he rushed out, and cut to pieces, died a wretched death, paying the penalty for his iniquity. King William laid waste Northumbria the same year to avenge the appalling death of these men.[1]

On Whit-Sunday [31 May] at Mainz, King Henry decreed the deposition of Pope Hildebrand, and on the feast of St John the Baptist [24 June] made Wibert, bishop of Ravenna, pope in his place. King Rudolf, king of the Saxons, was slain at Merseburg in battle, and was buried there on 15 October. The city of Mainz felt an earthquake on 1 December, and the following year with its chief monastery and three others was ravaged by fire. King Henry approached Rome against the pope with hostile intent, but however he did not go into Rome.[2]

(pp. 398–400) whilst relying on E's brief account of the murder, locates it at a Tyneside *placitum*. JW and *HDE* alone identify the place of the murder as Gateshead.

[2] Marianus. The last sentence, which is under 1081 in the witness N, could have been under that annal in JW before the addition of 1081 n. a. The council of Mainz was held on 31 May (Meyer von Knonau, *Jahrbücher*, iii. 279), Wibert was elected anti-pope at the council of Brixen on 25 June (ibid., iii. 293–4), and Rudolf died of wounds received at the battle of the Elster (ibid., iii. 644–52). A fire occurred at Mainz, but not an earthquake, in July 1081 (ibid., iii. 416 n. 124). Henry was at Verona on 4 Apr. 1081 and camped outside Rome for 14 days after Pentecost (ibid., iii. 353, 391–3).

[**1081**] (.xxv.) 1103   ^{ab}*Willelmus abbas monasterii sancti Vincentii martyris a rege* Willelmo *electus, Dunholmensem episcopatum suscepit, et non. Ian. ab archiepiscopo Thoma* consecratus est.^{b 1}

[**1082**] (.xxvi.) 1104   *Prima paschalis luna toto orbi .iiii. non. April. apparuit cum prima esse deberet .ii. non. April. Multis homicidi*is *et predation*ibus *inter Heinricum regem et Hiltibrandum papam* actis *in nocte Palmarum multi sunt occisi.*[1]

Rex Willelmus fratrem suum Odonem, Baiocensem episcopum, Normannie in custodiam posuit.[2]

[**1083**] (.xxv.) 1103   ^a*Heinricus urbem Rome infregit et cepit. Wigbertum in sede apostolica constituit. Hiltibrandus uero Beneuentum adiit ubi usque ad obitum suum deguit. Heinricus autem in Teutonicam patriam rediit.*[1]

Seditio nefanda inter monachos et indigne nominandum abbatem Turstanum Glaestonie facta est, quem rex Willelmus de monasterio Cadomi, nulla prudentia instructum, eidem loco abbatem prefecerat. Hic *inter cetera* stultitie sue opera, *Gregorianum cantum aspernatus, monachos cepit compellere, ut, illo relicto, cuiusdam Willelmi Fescamnensis cantum discerent et cantarent. Quod* dum *egre accip*erent, *quippe qui iam tam in hoc quam in* cetero *ecclesiastico officio secundum morem Romane ecclesie insenuerant,* subito, armata militari manu, illis ignorantibus, *quadam die* in *capitulum* irruit, *monachos* nimio terrore *fugientes* in ecclesiam *ad altare* usque persequitur, *iaculis*que et *sagittis* cruces et *imagines* ac feretra sanctorum manus militaris *trans*figens, *unum* etiam monachum *sacrum*^b *amplexantem altare lancea trans*uerberans, interemit; *alium ad altaris crepidinem sagittis confossum* necauit; ceteri uero, *necessita*te *compulsi,* scamnis et candelabris ecclesie fortiter se defendentes, licet *grauiter* uulnerati, milites omnes retro chorum abegerunt; sicque factum est, ut duo occisi, *quattuordecim*

---

^a *For B's two additions here, see Appendix B*   ^{b–b} *written partly over erasure by* C²
^a *starts on second line of 1083, the first line being blank* C   ^b *om.* HL

---

[1] *HDE* iv. 1 (SD i. 119) has 'tertio nonas Ianuarii' as the date of consecration, a date repeated in *De iniusta vexatione Willelmi episcopi* i (SD i. 170). *HR* (SD ii. 211), apparently copying from JW, has '.iv. nonas Ian.' As Greenway, *Fasti* ii. 29 notes, 3 Jan. was a Sunday in 1081. The text erased here (see 1081 n. *b*) could have been ASC's report of William's expedition to Wales.

[1] Marianus, who could have been referring to Henry IV's second siege of Rome during Lent 1082 (Meyer von Knonau, *Jahrbücher*, iii. 437 n. 7).

[1081] William, abbot of St Vincent Martyr, was chosen by King William, received the see of Durham, and was consecrated on 5 January by Archbishop Thomas.[1]

[1082] The first Easter moon appeared throughout the world on 2 April when the first should have been on 4 April. Many murders and plunderings took place because of the struggles between King Henry and Pope Hildebrand, and on Palm Sunday [16 April] many were slain.[1]

King William placed his brother Odo, bishop of Bayeux, in custody in Normandy.[2]

[1083] Henry broke into and occupied Rome. He set Wibert on the apostolic throne. Hildebrand went to Benevento, where he stayed until he died. Then Henry returned to the German homeland.[1]

A shocking conflict took place at Glastonbury between the monks and Abbot Thurstan, who was not worthy to be nominated to that office, and whom, although he was a man of little wisdom, William had, from the monastery of Caen, set up there as abbot. Among his other acts of folly, he tried to force the monks to abandon the Gregorian chant, which he despised, so that, when it had been given up, they would learn to sing the chant of one William of Fécamp. When the monks would with difficulty accept the new chant since they had been accustomed for a long time, in accordance with the practice of the Roman church, to the old chant and to other ecclesiastical offices, he suddenly burst into the chapter house, when they were least expecting it, with a band of armed knights. He pursued the monks who fled in absolute terror into the church and up to the altar. The band of knights struck the crosses and images and shrines of the saints with spears and arrows, even speared to death a monk as he clung to the holy altar, and slew another pierced with arrows at the foot of the altar. The others of necessity defended themselves vigorously with the benches and candlesticks of the church and, although seriously wounded, drove the knights from the choir. Thus it happened that two

---

² ASC E. OV *HE* vii. 8 (iv. 40–5) gives a dramatized account of the trial of Odo.

¹ Marianus. The pope was at Benevento on 6 Jan. 1083 (Meyer von Knonau, *Jahrbücher*, iii. 470–1), Henry entered Rome on 3 June (ibid., iii. 474–5), and Wibert was crowned pope on 28 June (ibid., iii. 488).

*uulne*rati ex monachis, nonnulli etiam de militibus sauciati existerent.
p. 353 | Hinc moto iudicio, *dum maxima abbatis esse culpa patuit*, rex
eundem abbatem summouit, et in *monasterio* suo in Normannia
posuit. *De monachis uero quamplures per episcopatus et abbatias, iussu
regis, custodiendi disperguntur.* Cuius post mortem, *idem* abbas iterum
abbatiam suam *a filio* eius rege *Willelmo quingentis libris argenti* emit
et *per* ecclesie *possessiones aliquot annis peruagatus, longe ab ipso*
monasterio, *ut dignus erat, misere uitam finiuit.*[2] Regina Mahtilda
*.iiii. non. Nou., feria .v., discessit in Normannia, et Cadomi est
sepulta.*[c 3]

[1084] (.xxviii.) 1106 Apostolicus papa Hiltibrandus in extremis suis
ad se uocauit unum de .xii. cardinalibus, quem multum diligebat, et
confessus est omnipotenti Deo et sancto Petro ac toti[a] ecclesie, ualde
se peccasse in pastorali cura, que ei ad regendum erat commissa,
suadenteque diabolo contra humanum genus odium et iram incitasse.
Postea uero sententiam, que in orbem terrarum effusa est, pro
augmento[b] Christianitatis se cepisse dicebat. Tunc demum misit
predictum confessorem suum ad imperatorem et ad totam ecclesiam
ut optarent illi indulgentiam, quia finem uite sue aspiciebat, et tam
cito induebat se angelicam uestem, et dimisit ac dissoluit uincula
bannorum omnium suorum imperatori et omni populo christiano,
uiuis et defunctis, clericis ac laicis, et iussit eos abire de domo
Theoderici, et amicos Heinrici ascendere, teste Mogontino archiepiscopo nec multo post obiit.[c 1]

Rex Anglorum Willelmus de unaquaque hida per Angliam sex
solidos accepit.[2]

[c–c] *slightly smaller script extending into mg.* B

[a] totius *HL*   [b] augmentato *HL*   [c] *For the addition in LP, see Appendix A.* P[5]
wrote the addition in the mg. with guiding signes

[2] The italicized words are shared with WM, *De antiquitate Glastonie ecclesie*, printed in
Adami de Domerham Historia de rebus gestis Glastoniensibus, ed. T. Hearne (Oxford, 1727),
i. 114–16, which dates Thurstan's appointment to 1082. The incident is also described in
ASC, which, however, does not give the information JW shares with WM (e. g. that
Thurstan was from Caen or the occasion for the dispute), which gives the number of dead
monks as 3 and of wounded as 18, and which has no report on the incident's aftermath.
ASC shows that some archers fired on the altar from an upper floor, but the distinction it
possibly makes between the 'cyrcc' into which the monks took refuge, and the 'mynster'
into which the knights broke, may be difficult to follow as are the exact movements of the
knights in the incident. JW is earlier than WM, but the way in which the latter's account
centres on the miracle of the wounded crucifix could suggest that WM did not borrow
directly from JW but from a common source. The much briefer accounts in WM *GR* iii.

monks were slain and fourteen wounded, and some knights were wounded. At a judicial investigation it was clear that the abbot was most to blame, and the king summoned that abbot and sent him back to his monastery in Normandy. At the royal command, many of the monks were distributed and confined among various bishoprics and abbeys. After William I's death, the same abbot again purchased the abbey from his son William for 500 silver pounds and, wandering for some years among the church estates, he ended his life wretchedly, as was fitting, far from the same monastery.[2] Queen Matilda died in Normandy on Thursday, 2 November, and was buried at Caen.[3]

[1084] The apostolic pope Hildebrand when he was dying summoned one of the twelve cardinals, whom he much loved, and confessed to Almighty God, St Peter, and the whole church that he had truly sinned in the pastoral care which had been entrusted to his governance, and that, at the devil's prompting, he had stirred up hatred and anger against mankind. Afterwards he said that he had enforced the judicial sentence, which was effective throughout the world, for the benefit of Christianity. Then at last he sent the aforesaid confessor to the emperor and to the whole church that they might forgive him, for he was waiting for the end of life and would quickly put on angelic clothes. He set aside and cancelled all his bans against the emperor and all the Christian people, living and dead, clerical and lay, and ordered them to go out of the house of Theoderic and go up to Henry's friends. The archbishop of Mainz, who died soon after, testifies to this account.[1]

King William collected six shillings from every hide in the whole of England.[2]

270 (ii. 329–30) and *GP* ii. 91 (p. 197) and OV *HE* iv (ii. 270) clearly go back to this common source though OV adds Thurstan's robbing and starving of the monks to the reasons for their hatred.

[3] In reporting Matilda's death, ASC E refers neither to Normandy nor Caen. OV *HE* vii. 9 (iv. 44–7) describes her burial and gives her epitaph.

[1] The text of the letter referred to in this annal is found at the opening of N on fo. 1ᵛ, inscribed 'Teste Mogontino archiepiscopo', and quite separate from the Marianus chronicle. It was printed from N in H. E. J. Cowdrey, *The Age of Desiderius: Monte Cassino, the Papacy and the Normans in the Eleventh and Early Twelfth Centuries* (Oxford, 1983), p. 250. Gregory died at Salerno on 25 May 1084, and Wernher was archbishop of Mainz from 1084 to 1088. On Marianus' account see Meyer von Knonau, *Jahrbücher*, iv. 60 n. 105.

[2] This is close to ASC E 1083 (*recte* 1084). E's dating the levy to 'after Christmas' could have led JW to assign it to 1084.

[1085] (.xxviiii.) 1107 *Heinricus rex Saxones bello uicit patriam optinuit, eosque sibi iurare, et obsequi coegit, sed postquam exercitum dimisit, Saxones occulte coeperunt congregari aduersus imperatorem Heinricum, dolo uolentes eum occidere. Ille autem dolo comperto, declinauit insidias eorum egrediendo de illa prouincia.*[1]

[a]Eximie uir probitatis et uenerationis, Persorensis abbas Eadmundus, .xvii. kal. Iul., die dominica, in bona senectute decessit, et a uenerabili Glauuornensi abbate Serlone sepultus est honorifice. Cui successit Glauuornensis monachus Turstanus.[a][2] Eodem anno rex Danorum Canutus, cum classe ualida, et auxilio soceri sui Rotberti, Flandrensis comitis, in Angliam uenire paratus erat. Vnde rex Willelmus, de tota Gallia solidariis, pedonibus, et sagittariis multis milibus conductis, et nonnullis de Normannia sumptis, autumnali tempore Angliam rediit, et eis per totum regnum diuisis, episcopis, abbatibus, comitibus, baronibus, uicecomitibus, ac regiis prepositis uictum prebere mandauit.[3] Sed ubi cognouit suos inimicos impeditos fuisse, partem exercitus remisit, partem secum per totam hiemem retinuit, et in Natiuitate Domini curiam suam Glauuorne tenuit, ubi tribus suis capellanis, Mauricio scilicet Lundoniensem, Willelmo Theodfordensem, Rotberto Castrensem dedit presulatum.[4]

[1086] (.xxx.) 1108 *Heinricus rex iuxta Wirzburgum Sueuis et Saxonibus bello congressus et quorundam suorum perfidorum, in ipso conflictu se ad hostes conuertentium, presidio desertus, a quodam etiam collaterali suo in uertice ense percussus dedit se cum paucis in fugam. Hostes uero insecuti usque ad urbem predictam ceperunt eam, et episcopum Alberonem ab Heinrico ob perfidiam expulsum ibidem restituerunt, expulso Mainardo episcopo ibidem ab Heinrico constituto. Paulo post Heinricus eandem urbem congregato exercitu obsedit et cepit, episcopoque Alberoni, quia suus erat patrinus, concessit, ut remaneret sibi fidelis et episcopus urbis. Illo*

[a-a] *om.* H

[1] Marianus. This refers presumably to Henry IV's Jan. campaign.
[2] The entry in *Ann. Winchcombe*, p. 118, is based on JW. 15 June is the commemoration day for Edmund in a late entry added to a calendar in the Wulfstan Collectar (printed in I. Atkins, 'The church of Worcester from the eighth to the twelfth century, part ii', *Antiquaries Journal*, xx (1940), 29–31, at p. 30).
[3] ASC E, which is close, gives both the threatened Danish invasion and William's defensive preparations. E speaks of William's wasting the coastal areas and of the billeting being proportionate to land resources, but does not date William's actions to the autumn, though this date could have been inferred from William's retention of mercenaries for the whole winter. ASC has 'mannon' for JW's different categories from 'episcopis' to 'regiis prepositis'. OV *HE* vii. 11 (iv. 52–3) refers to Cnut's naval preparations and appears to link

[1085] King Henry overcame the Saxons in war, took over their land, and made them swear allegiance and obedience to him, but after he dismissed his army, the Saxons began secretly to gather together against the emperor Henry, wanting to kill him through guile. He, however, discovered their plot, and, avoiding their ambushes, emerged from that province.[1]

Edmund, the abbot of Pershore, a man of rare virtue and godliness, died at a good age on Sunday, 15 June, and was buried honourably by the revered abbot Serlo of Gloucester. The Gloucester monk Thurstan succeeded him.[2] In the same year Cnut, the Danish king, prepared to come to England with a strong fleet and with the help of his father-in-law, Robert, count of Flanders. For this reason William took into his pay from the whole of Gaul many thousand paid troops, footsoldiers, and archers, collecting some also from Normandy, and returned to England in the autumn. He spread them throughout the whole kingdom, and ordered bishops, abbots, earls, barons, sheriffs, and royal officers to supply them with provisions.[3] When he learnt that his enemies had been frustrated, he dismissed part of the army, and kept part with him all winter. He held his court at Christmas at Gloucester where he gave bishoprics to three of his chaplains, that is, London to Maurice, Thetford to William, Chester to Robert.[4]

[1086] King Henry fought a battle against the Swabians and Saxons near Würzburg. He was deprived of the support of some of his treacherous followers, who went over to the enemy during the battle, and struck on the head by a sword by one of the followers by his side, he fled with a few men. The enemy followed in pursuit up to the above-mentioned town ·which they took, and restored Bishop Adalbero, who had been expelled thence by Henry for his treachery, and drove out Meginhard who had been appointed there by Henry. A little later Henry assembled an army, besieged and took the same town, and allowed Bishop Adalbero, since he was his godfather, to remain as his follower and as the town's bishop. Adalbero was

---

these to William's making a record of the 'milicia Anglici regni'. The relationship between the apparently equitable billeting of this army and the Domesday inquest and the oath of Salisbury in the next annal has been much discussed, e. g. *Domesday Monachorum of Christ Church Canterbury*, ed. D. C. Douglas (London, 1944), pp. 26–7.

   [4] ASC E is close, though it distinguishes between the five-day royal court and a three-day synod, where the three elections took place.

autem nolente Heinrico subesse. Heinricus quia nimium pius erat liberum illum permisit abire.[1]

*Wil*lelmus *rex fecit describi om*nem *Angl*iam, quantum terre quisque baronum suorum *pos*sidebat, quot feudatos milites, quot carrucas, quot uillanos, quot animalia, immo quantum uiue pecunie quisque possidebat in omni regno suo, *a ma*ximo *usque ad minim*um, et quantum reditus queque possessio *redd*ere *po*terat: *et uexata est terra multis cladibus inde procedentibus.*[2] Et in ebdomada Pentecostes, suum filium Heinricum, apud Westmonasterium, ubi curiam suam tenuit, armis militaribus honorauit.[3] Nec multo post mandauit ut archiepiscopi, episcopi, abbates, comites, barones, uicecomites, cum suis militibus, die kalendarum Augustarum sibi occurrerent Searesbyrie, quo cum uenissent, milites illorum sibi fidelitatem contra omnes homines iurare coegit.[4] Eo tempore, clito Eadgarus, licentia a rege impetrata, cum .cc. militibus mare transiit, et Apuliam adiit. Cuius germana, uirgo Cristina, monasterium, quod Rumesia nuncupatur, intrauit, et uestem sanctimonialis | habitus suscepit.[5] Eodem anno animalium pestis, et magna extitit aeris intemperies.[6]

p. 354

[1087] (.xxxi.) 1109 [a]Hoc anno, primo febribus, deinde fame quamplures mortui sunt.[1] Interea uorax flamma consumpsit omnes ferme principales ciuitates Anglie, ecclesiam quoque sancti Pauli apostoli cum maiore et meliori parte Lundonie.[2] Dani suum domnum regem Canutum, .vi. id. Iul., sabbato, in quadam ecclesia martirizauerunt.[3] Cicestrensis episcopus Stigandus, abbas sancti Augustini Scotlandus,[b] abbas Bathoniensis Alsius, et abbas

[a] For B¹'s addition in lower mg. with signe, see Appendix B   [b] Scolandus HL

[1] Marianus. This is the last Marianus entry in N. Henry was defeated at Pleichfeld on 11 Aug. 1086, and retook Würzburg not long afterwards in the same year. Adalbero was bishop 1045–90, and Meginhard took up the appointment in 1084 (Meyer von Knonau, *Jahrbücher*, iv. 125–32).
[2] The account of the Domesday survey in ASC E 1085 (*recte* 1086) is fuller, and JW's account shares words with the annal added to the Marianus witness N; see W. H. Stevenson, 'A contemporary description of the Domesday Survey', *EHR* xxii (1907), 72–84. Both G and the probably Worcester compilation, BL Cotton Vitellius C. VIII, are closely based on ASC E's account, though with some additional information. The Cotton MS dates from the third quarter of the 12th cent. and was at Rievaulx in the early 13th cent., but, made up as it is of excerpts from WM and JW, it could have been compiled at Worcester in the mid-12th cent.
[3] As in ASC E 1085 (*recte* 1086).
[4] Again close to ASC E 1085 (*recte* 1086). JW's 'archiepiscopi . . . cum suis militibus' presumably corresponds to ASC's 'ealle þa landsittende men þe ahtes wæron ofer eall Engleland'.

however, unwilling to submit to Henry and Henry allowed him to go free because of his great piety.[1]

King William had a record of the whole of England made: that is how much land each of his barons possessed, how many enfeoffed knights, how many carucates, villeins, beasts, indeed how much livestock each man owned in his whole kingdom, from the greatest to the lowest, and how much each estate was able to render; and the country was vexed with the disasters which proceeded from this survey.[2] In the week of Whitsun [24-31 May], he honoured his son Henry with knighthood at Westminster, where he was holding his court.[3] Shortly afterwards he ordered his archbishops, bishops, abbots, earls, barons, sheriffs with their knights to meet him on 1 August at Salisbury. When they had come, he made their knights swear allegiance to him against all others.[4] At that time the atheling Edgar, having asked the king's permission, crossed the sea with 200 knights and went to Apulia. His sister, the virgin, Christina, entered the monastery called Romsey, and took the veil.[5] In the same year there was murrain among cattle and much unseasonable weather.[6]

[1087] In this year many perished at first through fevers and later through hunger.[1] In the course of the year raging fire destroyed almost all the chief English cities as well as the church of St Paul and the greater and best part of London.[2] The Danes martyred their king, Cnut, on Saturday, 10 July in a church.[3] Stigand, bishop of Chichester, Scotland, abbot of St Augustine's, Ælfsige, abbot of

---

[5] ASC E 1085 (recte 1086) simply records Edgar's departure from court, attributing it to William's failure to honour him, as well as Christina's taking the veil at Romsey. JW is the only source which mentions Edgar's departure to Apulia with 200 men.

[6] ASC E 1085 (recte 1086) is wordier and refers to a failed harvest.

[1] ASC E 1086 (recte 1087) is more eloquent on the fevers and famine, moralizes on the reasons for the disasters, and comments on William's harshness which added taxes and tolls to the natural calamities.

[2] ASC E 1086 (recte 1087) records these fires 'before autumn', the derivative Waverley Annals (Ann. Mon. ii. 196) also report them, whilst the Winchester Annals (Ann. Mon. ii. 35) simply mention the fire at St Paul's.

[3] Near the end of its annal, ASC E 1086 (recte 1087) records Cnut's martyrdom without dating it. Cnut was slain at Odense, and his death is commemorated on 10 July in the calendar of Odense's mother house, Evesham (Oxford, Bodleian Library, Barlow 41, fo. 161; see F. Wormald, English Benedictine Kalendars after AD 1100 (2 vols., Henry Bradshaw Society 77, 81; 1939-46), ii. 23, 33). For a discussion of the alternative years of 1086 and 1087 for Cnut's death, see Scriptores Rerum Danicarum (above, 1076 n. 1), iii. 371 n. u. The earliest extant evidence for the date of Cnut's death, the Tabula Othiniensis, is printed in Vitæ Sanctorum Danorum (above, 1076 n. 1), i. 60-1.

Persorensis Turstanus decesserunt.[4] Ante Assumptionem sancte
Marie rex Willelmus in Franciam cum exercitu uenit, et oppidum
quod Mathantum nuncupatur, et omnes ecclesias in eo sitas, duosque
reclusos, igne succendit, indeque in Normanniam rediit, sed in ipso
reditu dirus uiscerum dolor illum apprehendit, et magis ac magis de
die in diem grauabat.[5] Cum autem ingrauescente[c] egritudine diem
sibi mortis imminere sensisset, fratrem suum, Odonem Baiocensem
episcopum, comites Morkarum et Rogerum, Siuuardum, cognomento Barn, et Wlnothum regis Haroldi germanum, quem a pueritia
tenuerat in custodia, et omnes quos uel in Anglia uel in Normannia
custodie manciparat, laxauit.[6] Dein filio suo Willelmo regnum
tradidit Anglie, et Rotberto, filio suo primogenito, qui tunc exulabat
in Francia, comitatum concessit Normannie, et sic, celesti munitus
uiatico, postquam .xx. annis, mensibus .x., et .xxviii. diebus, genti
Anglorum prefuit, .v. iduum Septembrium, die ⟨. . .⟩,[d] regnum cum
uita perdidit, et Cadomi, in ecclesia sancti Stephani Protomartyris,
quam ipse a fundamentis construxerat bonisque ditauerat, sepultus
requiescit.[7] Willelmus autem filius eius Angliam festinato adiit,
ducens secum Wlnothum et Morkarum, sed mox ut Wintoniam
uenit, illos, ut prius fuerant, custodie mancipauit, et .vi. kal. Octob.,
die dominico, in Westmonasterio, a Landfranco, Dorubernie archiepiscopo, in regem consecratus est.[8] Dein Wintoniam rediens,
thesauros sui patris, ut ipse iusserat, per Angliam diuisit, scilicet
quibusdam principalibus ecclesiis .x., quibusdam .vi. marcas auri,
quibusdam minus, ecclesiis etiam in ciuitatibus uel uillis suis per
singulas denarios .lx. dari, cruces, altaria, scrinia, textos, candelabra,
situlas, fistulas, ac ornamenta uaria gemmis, auro, argento, lapidi-
busque pretiosis redimita, per ecclesias digniores ac monasteria iussit
diuidi.[9] Eius quoque germanus Rotbertus in Normanniam reuersus,
thesauros quos inuenerat monasteriis, ecclesiis, pauperibus, pro

[c] ingrauascente CH(G)   [d] blank space here though sign of erasure C, Iouis interlin. B

[4] ASC E 1086 (recte 1087) gives these obits near the annal's end, though it does not name the abbots.
[5] This is close to ASC E 1086 (recte 1087), which makes it clear that William's campaign was against King Philip.
[6] The names of those released are not in ASC E, which speaks in general of all in captivity under his jurisdiction being set free.
[7] ASC E 1086 (recte 1087) has a long assessment of William from which JW may have extracted the basic facts of death, burial, and succession, whilst contributing the regnal length.

Bath, and Thurstan, abbot of Pershore, died.[4] King William came to
France with an army before the Assumption of St Mary [15 August],
and having burnt the town called Mantes with all its churches, and
two recluses, returned thence to Normandy. On his return fierce
intestinal pains afflicted him, and he got worse from day to day.[5]
When, as his illness worsened, he felt the day of death approaching,
he set free his brother, Odo, bishop of Bayeux, earls Morkar and
Roger, Siward called Barn, and Wulfnoth, King Harold's brother
(whom he had kept in custody since childhood), as well as all he had
kept imprisoned either in England or in Normandy.[6] Then he
handed the English kingdom over to William, and granted the
Norman duchy to Robert, his first-born son, who was then exiled
in France. In this way, fortified by the holy viaticum, he abandoned
both life and kingdom on Thursday, 9 September, after ruling the
English for twenty years, ten months, and twenty-eight days. He was
laid to rest and buried at Caen, in the church of St Stephen, the first
martyr, which he himself had built from its foundations, and
endowed with gifts.[7] William his son went thereupon in haste to
England, taking with him Wulfnoth and Morkar, though as soon as
he reached Winchester, he placed them under guard, as they had
been before. He was consecrated king by Lanfranc, archbishop of
Canterbury, at Westminster on Sunday, 26 September.[8] He then went
back to Winchester, and distributed throughout England his father's
treasure in accordance with his orders, that is, ten gold marks to
some of the chief churches, six to some others, to some others less,
sixty pennies to the churches in the towns and townships. He
ordered crosses, altars, reliquaries, Gospel books, candlesticks, holy
water stoups, eucharistic straws, and various ornaments encrusted
with gems, gold, silver, and precious stones to be distributed to the
larger churches and monasteries.[9] His brother Robert returned to
Normandy, and also generously distributed the treasure which he

[8] This is presumably based on ASC E 1086 (*recte* 1087), which also mentions a general
submission to William, but which does not refer to the imprisonment of Wulfnoth and
Morkar at Winchester.
[9] ASC E 1086 (*recte* 1087) reports the distribution of William's treasure. It also refers to
gifts to the poor, but has no equivalent for 'quibusdam minus', and does not refer to the
liturgical objects given to churches and monasteries. WM *GR* iv. 283 (ii. 338) describes the
gifts thus: 'monasteriis aurum, ecclesiis agrestibus solidos quinque argenti, unicuique pago
centum libras viritim egenis dividendas'. JW appears to render 'ælcen cyrcean uppeland' by
'ecclesiis etiam in ciuitatibus uel uillis suis'. OV *HE* vii. 14–viii. 1 (iv. 78–120) describes the
events in this annal fully, but gives no specific details about the distribution of William's
treasure.

anima patris sui, largiter diuisit. Et Vlfum, Haroldi quondam regis Anglorum filium, Dunechaldumque, regis Scottorum Malcolmi filium, a custodia laxatos, et armis militaribus honoratos, abire permisit.[10]

[1088] (.xxxii.) 1110   [1]Hoc anno inter primates Anglie magna orta est discordia, pars etenim nobiliorum Normannorum fauebat regi Willelmo, sed minima. Pars uero altera fauebat Rotberto comiti Normannorum, et maxima, cupiens hunc sibi assciscere in regnum, fratrem uero aut fratri tradere uiuum, aut regno priuare peremptum. Huius execrande rei principes extiterunt Odo episcopus Baiocensis, qui et erat comes Cantuuariensis, Rotbertus etiam frater eius, comes Moritunensis, et hic uterque frater fuerat Willelmi regis senioris, sed tantum de matre. Intererat etiam predicto consilio cum Rotberto, nepote suo, comite Northymbrie, Gosfridus episcopus Constantiensis,[a] Rogerus comes Scrobbesbyriensis, quod etiam erat peius, Willelmus episcopus Dunholmensis, ea quoque tempestate rex predictus illius,[b] ut ueri consiliarii, fruebatur prudentia, bene enim sapiebat, eiusque consiliis totius Anglie tractabatur respublica.[2] Hi erant quorum maiorum terrenarum diuitiarum in regno pollebat gloria. Commilitonum etiam, et consodalium coniurationis eis indies crescebat abundantia. Execrabile autem hoc factum clam tractauerunt in Quadragesima quod cito in palam prorumpi posset post Pasca, nam a regali se subtrahentes curia, munierunt castella, ferrum, flammam, predas, necem excitauerunt in patria.[3]   [4]Ecce factum execrabile, ecce bellum, et *plusquam ciuile*. Pugnabant enim parentes in filios, fratres in germanos, amici pridem in cognatos, ignoti in extraneos.[4] Interea predictus episcopus Baiocensis, munita Roueceastra, misit Normanniam, exortans comitem Rotbertum cito uenire in

---

[a] Constantiensis *ex* Constantinensis C   [b] *interlin.* C

[10] There is no parallel in ASC or any other independent source for the last two sentences here.

[1] JW's account of this rebellion differs from ASC's (1087, *recte* 1088), and from those in other sources, in details, in the customary identification of offices and family relationships, in style, and in the arrangement of the narrative. JW reverses ASC's sequence of campaigns, placing those in Kent first, and those in Worcester last. This rearrangement caused the decisive Kentish campaign to be severely truncated, probably through an error by the compiler or by a scribe. Unusually *HR* 170 (SD ii. 214–15) does not copy JW fully, but begins with the first sentences of JW, then seems to turn to the account in the JW *chronicula* G, before apparently depending on ASC for much of the rest of its 1088 annal. For a recent discussion of the 1088 rebellion, see Barlow, *William Rufus*, pp. 70–85.

found to monasteries and churches and to the poor for the repose of his father's soul. He freed from captivity Ulf, son of Harold, once king of the English, and Duncan, son of Malcolm, king of the Scots, knighted them, and allowed them to leave.[10]

[1088]   [1]This year there was great dissension among the chief men of England, and indeed only a small part of the Norman nobility supported King William. Most were in favour of Robert, the Norman duke, and wished to bring him to the kingdom and either hand William alive to him, or deprive him of his kingdom through death. The leaders of this execrable plot were Odo, bishop of Bayeux, who was also earl of Kent, Robert, his brother, count of Mortain, both brothers of King William I, but only through their mother. Other conspirators were Geoffrey, bishop of Coutances, with his nephew, Robert, earl of Northumbria, Roger, earl of Shrewsbury, and what is worst of all, William, bishop of Durham. At this time the king (who knew him well) relied on Bishop William's wisdom as a true counsellor, and the affairs of all England were managed by his advice.[2] Their vast landed wealth made them pre-eminent in England. The number of comrades-in-arms, and of fellow conspirators grew daily. This cursed plot was secretly planned during Lent, and quickly came out into the open after Easter, when the conspirators left the king's court, fortified castles, and stirred up fire and sword, plunderings, and death over the whole country.[3] [4]This was war, a cursed affair, and what was worse a civil war! Fathers fought against sons, brothers against brothers, friends against their kinsmen, strangers against strangers.[4] The bishop of Bayeux fortified Rochester, and sent messengers to Normandy to urge Duke Robert to come

[2] Robert of Mortain (Odo's half-brother) is not mentioned by ASC, and JW further adds here to the list of chief plotters Robert of Mowbray (whom he identifies as earl of Northumbria; WM *GR* iv. 306 (ii. 360) calls him 'comes Humbrensium'). ASC mentions Mowbray as assisting Bishop Geoffrey of Coutances in the campaigns from Bristol, but is silent on their relationship (which is given by WM *GR* iv. 306 (ii. 360)). On Robert of Mowbray, see Brian Golding, 'Robert of Mowbray', *ANS* xiii (1991), 119–44, and *CP* ix. 705–6. Like WM *GR* iv. 306 (ii. 360), JW identifies William, not Odo, as the well-trusted bishop. On this identification, see Barlow, *William Rufus*, p. 61 n. 35.

[3] OV says the rebellion started after Christmas 1087 (*HE* viii. 2 (iv. 124)), and for evidence that it was already under way by 12 Mar., see Barlow, *William Rufus*, p. 75. JW's reference to the plotting taking place in Lent is also in ASC, though he alone speaks of the rebels leaving court, presumably at Easter.

[4-4] One of JW's more rhetorical passages with, as Michael Winterbottom informs me, echoes of Lucan, *De bello civili* i. 1–7.

Angliam, nuntians ei rem gestam, affirmans paratum sibi regnum, et si sibi non desisteret, paratam et coronam. Rumore autem percussus insolito, comes exultat, amicis nuntiat, quasi iam de uictoria securus p. 355 triumphat, plures ad^c predam incitat. Odoni episcopo, | patruo suo, auxiliarios in Angliam legat, se quantotius, congregato maiori exercitu, secuturum affirmat.[5] Missi a comite Rotberto uenerunt in Angliam, ab Odone episcopo ad custodiendum receperunt Roueceastram, et horum ut primates Eustatius iunior, comes Bononie, et Rotbertus de Bellesmo gerebant curam.[6] Huius uero rei ut ad aures regis peruenit notitia, insolito turbatur molestia, iure autem regio, militari, ut impiger, fretus audacia, mittit legatos, uocat quos sibi credit fidos, uadit Lundoniam, belli tractaturus negotia, expeditionis prouisurus necessaria.[7] Congregato uero quantum ad presens poterat Normannorum, sed tamen maxime Anglorum, equestri et pedestri, licet mediocri, exercitu, statuens leges, promittens fautoribus omnia bona, fretus Dei clementia, qua maior⟨em⟩ hostium esse audiebat multitudinem, tendere disposuit Roueceastram. Relatum enim erat ei, ibi esse episcopum Odonem cum omnibus suis, et cohortem ultramarinam. Hinc signa mouens, ceptumque aggrediens iter, Tunebrycgiam, cui preerat Gilebertus filius Ricardi, contrarium sibi inuenit: obsedit, in biduo expugnauit, uulneratum Gilebertum cum castello ad deditionem coegit.[8] Fama uolans dicti peruenit Odonis ad aures, et cum sociis inito consilio, relinquens Roueceastram, cum paucis adiit castrum fratris sui Rotberti Moritunensis comitis, quod Peuenesea dicitur, fratremque reperiens, eum ut se teneat hortatur, pollicens se securos ibi posse esse, et dum rex ad expugnandam Roueceastram intenderet, comitem Normannie cum magno exercitu uenturum, seque suosque liberaturum, et magna fautoribus suis dando premia, regnum accepturum.[9] Rex igitur,

---

^{c} om. HL

[5] Odo's optimistic appeal to Robert and Robert's exultant reaction, emphatically expressed, are not in ASC. In ASC Robert's despatch of (unnamed) followers succeeds, and does not precede, William's defensive preparations. ASC reports the interception at sea of some of Duke Robert's men.

[6] JW makes it clear that Eustace the Younger and Robert of Bellême were among those whom Duke Robert had despatched to Kent. ASC simply notes the presence at Rochester of Eustace and three sons of Roger of Montgomery, Robert of Bellême presumably among them. For Robert de Bellême, see Kathleen Thompson, 'Robert of Bellême reconsidered', *ANS* xiii (1991), 263–86. For Gilbert fitz Richard, see *CP* iii. 242–3. His father was Richard of Tonbridge, son of Gilbert, count of Brionne. Eustace the Younger could be Eustace II or III: for the conflicting evidence, see J. C. Andressohn, *The Ancestry and Life of Godfrey of Bouillon* (Bloomington, Ind., 1947), pp. 24–5.

quickly to England, to report what had already been done, and to assure him of both crown and of kingdom, if he did not tarry. Excited by this unexpected news, the Duke exults and tells his friends almost as though he had already gained his victory, and incites many to share the spoil. He sends forces to England, and assures his uncle, Bishop Odo, that he would himself follow as soon as he had been able to assemble a larger army.[5] The troops sent by Duke Robert arrived in England, led by the noble leaders Eustace the Younger, count of Boulogne, and Robert of Bellême, and were dispatched by Bishop Odo to garrison Rochester.[6] When the king heard this news, he was unusually troubled, but confident in his royal rights and his energetic military valour. He sent envoys, summoned those he believed he could rely on, and went to London to prepare for the affairs of war and to provide the provisions needed for an army.[7] He gathered together an army of horsemen and footsoldiers, although of moderate size, made up principally of Englishmen and of as many Normans as he could find. He made laws, promised bountiful rewards to his supporters, and, placing his trust in God's mercy, for he knew that the enemy had a larger force, prepared to march on Rochester. He had learnt that it was there that Bishop Odo was with all his forces, and with the cross-Channel contingent. He set his army on the move, advanced on the planned march, and found Tonbridge, which was commanded by Gilbert fitz Richard, held against him. He besieged it, and stormed it in two days, forcing the wounded Gilbert to yield with his castle.[8] The news of Tonbridge's capture reached Odo, and, consulting his companions, he left Rochester, and went with a few men to Pevensey, the castle of his brother, Robert, count of Mortain. Finding his brother there, he encouraged him to hold out, assuring him that they would be secure, and that, whilst the king meant to invest Rochester, the Norman duke would arrive with a large army, would set them and their possessions free, and would become king, generously rewarding his supporters.[9]

---

[7] London is not mentioned in ASC.

[8] In ASC William's supporters are exclusively English. William's promises are reported in ASC, *HR* 170 (SD ii. 215), and WM *GR* iv. 306 (ii. 361). JW names Tonbridge's defender (like HH *HA* vii. 1 (p. 414)), reports his being wounded, and records the siege's duration.

[9] ASC does not mention here that Robert of Mortain held Pevensey nor that Robert's arrival was expected. HH *HA* vii. 1 (p. 412) incorrectly says that Pevensey was held by Roger, count of Mortain. ASC does not report the presence of an overseas contingent at Rochester.

expugnata Tunebrycgia, et ab incolis fidelitate accepta, relicto propter uulnus Gileberto, et castello in custodia locato, iturus ut disposuerat Roueceastram, audiuit patruum inde recessisse et Peuenesea adisse. Inito itaque salubri consilio, illum eo usque cum exercitu persequitur, sperans se belli citius finem assecuturum, si ante triumphare posset de principibus malorum predictorum. Accelerat, machinas parat, patruum utrumque obsidet; locus erat munitissimus: ad expugnationem in dies laborat.[10] Interim circumquaque per Angliam tempestas seuit bellica: Rofenses Cantuuariensibus et Lundoniensibus cedes inferunt et incendia; Lanfrancus enim archiepiscopus, et pene omnes optimates eiusdem prouincie erant cum rege.[11] Rogerus fautor Rotberti erat in castello suo Arundello, comitis predicti opperiens aduentum.[12] Gosfridus episcopus Constantiensis, in castello Brycstoua, socium coniurationis et perfidie habebat secum nepotem suum Rotbertum de Mulbraio, uirum gnarum militie, qui congregato exercitu inuasit Bathoniam, ciuitatem regiam, igne succendit eam, et illa depredata transiuit in Wiltusciram, uillasque depopulans, multorumque hominum strage facta, tandem adiit Giuelceastram, obsedit, et expugnare disposuit. Pugnant exterius spe capti prede et amore uictorie, repugnant intrinsecus acriter pro se suorumque salute. Tandem inter utrumque necessitatis uicit causa, repulsus et tristis recedit Rotbertus priuatus uictoria.[13] Willelmus de Owe Glauuornensem inuadit comitatum, regiam uillam depredatur Beorchelaum, per totam ferro et flamma grande perpetrat malum.[14] [d]Dum autem hec interim circumquaque perpetrantur mala, Bernardus de Nouo Mercatu, Rogerius de Laceio, qui iam super regem inuaserat Herefordam, Rauulfus de Mortuo Mari, coniurationis socii, cum hominibus comitis Rogeri de Scrobbesbyria, congregato magno Anglorum, Normannorum, et Walensium exercitu, Wigornensem irruperunt in prouinciam, affirmantes se igne crematuros ipsam ciuitatem Wigreceastram, spoliaturos Dei et sancte Marie ecclesiam, grandem de regis incolis fidelibus sumpturos uindictam. His auditis, uir magne pietatis et columbine simplicitatis, Deo populoque quem

---

[d] For B's addition here, see Appendix B

[10] Another example of JW's style in this annal. JW omits the rest of the decisive Kentish campaign.

[11] Earlier in the annal, ASC, as an introduction to the Kentish campaigns, records Odo's plundering raids from Rochester (without referring to London).

[12] ASC nowhere mentions Arundel. WM *GR* iv. 306 (ii. 361–2) speaks of William detaching Roger of Montgomery from the rebels, and OV *HE* viii. 2 (iv. 126–9) shows that Roger was nominally besieging Rochester with the king.

The king then, having taken Tonbridge, and accepted its inhabitants' fealty, left Gilbert, because of his wounds, under guard in the castle. When he was about to set out for Rochester, as he had originally planned, he learnt that his uncle had departed thence and had gone to Pevensey. Taking sound advice, he followed Odo there with his army, hoping to bring the war more quickly to an end by triumphing over, if possible, the authors of the discord which has been described. He hastened forward, prepared his siege engines, and besieged his two uncles. Pevensey was strongly fortified and he spent a long time in investing it.[10] In the mean time war raged over all England. The garrison of Rochester carried fire and sword on the men of Canterbury and London, for Archbishop Lanfranc and almost all the shire's leaders were with the king.[11] Robert's ally, Roger, was in his castle at Arundel, waiting for the coming of the Norman duke.[12] Geoffrey, bishop of Coutances, holding Bristol castle with his nephew and accomplice in the treasonable conspiracy, Robert of Mowbray, a skilled soldier, put together an army, attacked, set fire to, and plundered the royal city of Bath, and passing through Wiltshire, sacking townships and slaughtering a multitude, he at last reached and besieged Gloucester, and prepared its assault. The besiegers were emboldened by hope of booty and passion for victory while the besieged fought back fiercely defending both themselves and their possessions. In the end those driven by their needs triumphed, and Robert withdrew sadly, deprived of victory.[13] William of Eu attacked Gloucestershire, devastating the royal township of Berkeley, and did much harm, ravaging everywhere by fire and sword.[14] While these evils were being committed everywhere, Bernard of Neufmarché, Roger de Lacy, who had just attacked Hereford against the king, and Ralph Mortimer, their fellow conspirators, with the men of Earl Roger of Shrewsbury, brought together a large army of English, Normans, and Welsh, broke into Worcestershire, intending to burn down the city of Worcester, to despoil the church of God and St Mary, and to wreak heavy vengeance on the local supporters of the king. When he learnt this, the bishop of Worcester, Wulfstan, a man of great piety and dove-like simplicity, cherished in every way by

[13] ASC does not record the crossing into Wiltshire at Ilchester, nor Robert of Montgomery's failure to gain a complete victory.
[14] ASC does not mention William of Eu and attributes the devastation of Berkeley ('eall Beorclea hyrnesse hi awæston') to Bishop Geoffrey and Robert of Mowbray. William, count of Eu, a considerable landowner in 1086, succeeded his father, count of Brionne, when he died c.1090: see CP v. 153–4.

regebat in omnibus amabilis, regi, ut terreno domno, per omnia
fidelis, pater reuerendus Wlstanus, Wigornensis episcopus, magna
turbatur molestia, sed Dei respirans misericordia, iam quodammodo
alter Moyses parat se uiriliter staturus pro populo et ciuitate sua.
Hostes ad debellandum parant arma, ipse pro imminenti periculo
fundit precamina, exortans subditos ne desperent de Deo, qui non
pugnat gladio neque hasta. Normanni interim ineuntes consilium,
rogant ipsum episcopum ut ab ecclesia transiret in castellum, tutiores
se affirmantes de eius presentia, si maius incumberet periculum:
diligebant enim ualde eum. Ipse autem, ut erat mire mansuetudinis,
et pro regis fidelitate, et pro eorum dilectione, petitioni eorum
adquieuit. Interea audenter in arma se parat episcopalis familia:
conueniunt castellani et omnis ciuium turma, occurrere se affirmant
hostibus ex altera parte Sabrine fluminis, si hoc eis pontificis
annueret licentia. Parati igitur et armis instructi, ipsum ad castellum
p. 356 | euntem habent obuiam, quam optabant requirunt licentiam; quibus
libenter annuens, 'Ite,' inquit, 'filii, ite in pace, ite securi, cum Dei et
nostra benedictione. Confidens ego in Domino, spondeo uobis, non
hodie nocebit uobis gladius, non quicquam infortunii, non quicquam
aduersarius. State in regis fidelitate, uiriliter agentes pro populi
urbisque salute.' His dictis, alacres pontem reparatum transeunt,
hostes de longinquo accelerantes conspiciunt; inter quos magna belli
iam feruebat insania, contumaciter enim episcopi contempnentes
mandata, in terram ipsius posuerunt incendia. Quo audito, episcopus
ingenti concutitur dolore, uidens debilitari res ecclesie, acceptoque
inde consilio, graui eos, ab omnibus qui circumaderant coactus,
percussit anathemate. Res miranda, et Dei uirtus et uiri bonitas
nimis in hoc predicanda, nam statim hostes, ut sparsi uagabantur per
agros, tanta membrorum percutiuntur debilitate, tanta exteriori
oculorum attenuantur cecitate, ut uix arma ualerent ferre, nec
socios agnoscere, nec eos discernere qui eis oberant ex aduersi
parte. Illos fallebat cecitatis ignorantia, nostros confortabat Dei et
episcopalis benedictionis confidentia. Sic illi insensati nec sciebant
capere fugam, nec alicuius defensionis querebant uiam, sed Dei nutu
dati in reprobum sensum,[15] facili cedebant manibus inimicorum.
Ceduntur pedites, capiuntur milites, cum Normannis tam Angli
quam Walenses, ceteris uero uix debili elapsis fuga. Regis fideles

---

[15] Cf. Rom. 1: 28.

God and by the people over whom he ruled, utterly faithful to the
king, his earthly lord, was very troubled, but drawing on God's
compassion, like a second Moses, got ready to defend vigorously his
flock and his city. The enemy prepared to do battle, and he poured
out prayers in the face of the approaching peril, urging his people not
to despair of God, who relied neither on the sword or the spear. The
Normans now taking counsel, asked Wulfstan to move from the
church to the castle, declaring that they would feel safer with him
there, if a greater danger threatened for they were very much
attached to him. He agreed to their request because he was of a
wonderful sweetness, and because of his loyalty to the king and of his
love for his flock. Meanwhile the episcopal household boldly got
ready for war. The garrison and all the citizens came together,
declaring that, if the bishop were to allow them, they would fight the
enemy on the other side of the Severn. They took up their arms and
prepared for battle, and met him as he was going to the castle, and
asked his permission. He gave it gladly, saying, 'Go, go forth in
peace, my sons, go forth assured by God's blessing and by mine.
With trust in God, I assure you that this day the sword will not hurt
you, nor will any adversity nor any adversary. Remain firm in your
loyalty to the king, fight vigorously for the citizens of Worcester.'
When he had said this, they eagerly crossed the bridge which had
been repaired and saw the enemy hurrying from afar. The madness
of war had already affected them for in disobedience to the bishop's
commands, they fired their own estates. The bishop was much
pained when he learnt of this, seeing the depletion of the church's
lands, and, taking counsel, and under pressure from all around him,
he pronounced a weighty anathema. A wonder followed which
testified at the same time to a miracle of God and to the goodness
of Wulfstan, for straightaway the enemy, as they spread out across
the fields, were seized with such pain in their limbs and affected
by such a blindness that they lost the strength to carry arms or to
recognize their companions and distinguish them from their
opponents. While blindness beguiled them, the blessing of God
and of the bishop invigorated our men. Senseless, they knew not
how to flee nor how to defend themselves, but, in accordance with
God's judgement, given up to the feelings of reprobates,[15] they fell
easily into their enemy's hands. The footsoldiers were killed, the
knights, Normans and English as well as Welsh, were captured,
the rest barely escaped in a wretched flight. The king's followers

cum pontificis familia, exultantes in gaudio, sine ulla diminutione suorum, redeunt ad propria: gratias Deo referunt de rerum ecclesie incolumitate, gratias episcopo referunt de consilii eius salubritate.[e][16]

[1089] (.xxxiii.) 1111   Dorubernensis arciepiscopus Lanfrancus, ix. kal. Iunii, feria .v., obiit. Eodem anno .iii. id. Aug., sabbato, circa horam diei tertiam, terre motus permaximus extitit per Angliam.[1]

[1090] (.xxxiiii.) 1112   Rex Anglorum Wilelmus iunior, fratri suo Rotberto Normanniam adimere et sue dicioni cupiens subicere, primo castellum Walteri de sancto Walarico, et castellum Odonis de Albamarno,[a] deinde alia sibi conduxit castella, et in eis milites, ut Normanniam deuastarent, posuit. Qua re uisa, et suorum infidelitate cognita, comes Rotbertus, legatis ad regem Francorum Philippum, domnum suum, missis, illum in Normanniam uenire fecit, unumque de castellis, in quo milites fratris sui fuerunt, ipse et rex obsederunt. Quod cum regi Wilelmo nuntiatum esset, non modica pecunie quantitate regi Philippo occulte transmissa, ut obsidione dimissa, domum rediret, flagitauit et impetrauit.[1]

[1091] (.xxxv.) 1113   [C³B]
                                        [a]Iohannes successor Gise Wyllensis
                                        episcopi natione Turonicus, non
                                        scientia sed usu medicus, an-
                                        nuente rege, presulatus sedem
                                        de Wælle transtulit Bathoniam.[a][1]
Mense Februario[2] rex Wilelmus iunior Normanniam petiit, ut eam

[e] For B⁴'s lower marginal (with signe) addition here, see appendix B
[a] Albarmario HL
[a-a] mg. next to opening of 1091 C³, incorporated here B, om. HLP

[16] The account in ASC (which does not name the rebels' leaders though it says 500 of their forces were captured in the end) and in the other sources is much sketchier. It is followed by references to other rebellions in England omitted by JW such as those of Roger Bigod, earl of Norfolk, at Norwich, of Hugh of Grandmesnil, castellan of Leicester, which are both in ASC, and which were added by the JW witness B.

[1] ASC E has this information (without the date for Lanfranc's death and the hour for the earthquake) though it reports an unusually late harvest. A. J. Macdonald, Lanfranc (Oxford, 1926), p. 280 n. 4, showed that Gervase (ii. 370) gave the correct date of 28 May 1089, and that this is confirmed by other evidence.

[1] JW is more succinct than ASC in describing this campaign. ASC does not name the castellans at St Valéry and Aumale, though the latter was held in 1090 by Stephen, the son of Odo, count of Champagne. The castle unsuccessfully besieged by King Philip is

with the bishop's household rejoiced greatly, returned home without any losses. They thanked God for the safe protection of the church's possessions, and thanked Wulfstan for his beneficial counsel.[16]

[1089] Lanfranc, archbishop of Canterbury, died on Thursday, 24 May. In the same year there was a big earthquake over all England on Saturday, 11 August, at about the third hour.[1]

[1090] King William the Younger wanted to take Normandy from his brother Robert and subject it to his rule. Before ravaging Normandy, he took over by agreement and garrisoned first the castle of Walter of St Valéry and that of Odo of Aumale, and later other castles. Duke Robert, seeing this and recognizing his followers' infidelity, sent envoys to his lord, Philip, the French king, caused him to come to Normandy, and together with Philip he besieged one of the castles defended by his brother's knights. On learning of this, William secretly dispatched a large sum of money to Philip, and earnestly sought and accomplished Philip's abandonment of the siege and his return home.[1]

[1091]   John, who originated from Tours, succeeded Giso as bishop of Wells. He practised as a doctor, though he had not been trained as one, and he moved the see from Wells to Bath with the king's permission.[1]

In February,[2] King William the Younger went to Normandy to take

unknown. De controuersia Guillelmi, Rotomagensis archiepiscopi in Gallia Christiana, xi, col. 18, refers to a siege of La Ferté-en-Bray which is not known from other sources. William's plotting against Robert in Normandy might quite well have started in 1089; see OV HE viii. 9 (iv. 179–80). Perhaps ironically ASC says that Philip's abandonment of Robert was 'for his lufan oððe for his mycele gersuma'. For these events, see Barlow, William Rufus, pp. 273–6.

[1] WM GP ii. 90 (p. 194) says the transfer had been considered by John during William I's lifetime, although John did not become bishop until 1088. Regesta i. 315, dated 27 Jan. 1091, confirms the grant of the abbey of Bath to John. The grant seems to have been made originally before 24 May 1089 if the interlineation in the charter referring to Lanfranc's advocacy of the transfer is to be trusted.

[2] William was at Dover on 27 Jan. (Regesta i. 315). ASC dates his expedition to 2 Feb., and OV HE viii. 16 (iv. 236) to within a week of the death on 23 Jan. of Gerard, bishop of Séez, or just possibly, as Chibnall notes, within a week of his burial.

fratri suo Rotberto abriperet, sed dum ibi moraretur, pax inter illos
ea conuentione facta est, ut comes regi comitatum de Owe,
Fescamnense cenobium, abbatiam in Monte Sancti Michaelis
sitam, et Keresburh, et castella que a se defecerant, bono animo
concederet; Cinomannicam uero prouinciam, et castella que tunc in
Normannia comiti reluctabantur, illius dominio rex subiugaret;
omnibus etiam Normannis terras quas in Anglia ob fidelitatem
comitis perdiderant, redderet, et tantum terre in Anglia quantum
conuentionis inter eos fuerat comiti daret. Ad hec etiam inter se
constituerunt, ut si comes absque filio legali matrimonio genito
moreretur, heres eius esset rex, modoque per omnia simili, si regi
contigisset mori, heres illius fieret comes. Hanc conuentionem .xii.
ex regis, et .xii., ex parte comitis, barones iuramento firmauerunt.[3]
Interim germanus illorum Heinricus Montem Sancti Michaelis,
ipsius loci monachis quibusdam illum adiuuantibus, cum omnibus
militibus quos habere potuit, intrauit, regisque terram uastauit, et
eius homines quosdam captiuauit, quosdam expoliauit. Eapropter rex
et comes, exercitu congregato, per totam Quadragesimam, montem
obsederunt, et frequenter cum eo proelium commiserunt, et homines
et equos nonnullos perdiderunt. At rex cum obsidionis diutine
pertesus fuisset, impacatus recessit,[4] et non multo post Eadgarum
clitonem honore, quem ei comes dederat, priuauit, et de Normannia
expulit.[5] Interea mense Maio rex Scottorum Malcolmus cum magno
exercitu Northymbriam inuasit; si prouentus successisset, ulterius
processurus, et uim Anglie incolis illaturus. Noluit Deus; ideo ab
incepto est impeditus: attamen antequam redisset, eius exercitus de
Northymbria secum non modicam predam abduxit.[6] Quo rex audito,
cum fratre suo Rotberto rediit Angliam mense Augusto, nec multo
post, cum classe non modica et equestri exercitu, Scottiam profectus
p. 357 est, ut regem Scottorum Malcolmum debellaret, | sed priusquam

---

[3] JW's terms of the agreement are very close to those in ASC though he identifies
Fécamp as a monastery and adds Mont Saint-Michel to William's acquisitions. OV *HE*
viii. 16 (iv. 236) locates the agreement at Rouen, speaks of William's great gifts to Robert,
and mentions the lands of Gerard of Gouvray and of Ralph of Conches among those
granted to William by the duke. Torigni (*GND* viii. 3 (ii. 204–6)) claims that the
agreement was reached with the help of Philip I. ASC asserts that the agreement was 'syððan
litle hwile stode'. On the terms, see David, *Robert Curthose*, pp. 60–2, and Barlow, *William
Rufus*, pp. 281–4.
[4] Henry's rebellion is not in ASC, and both OV *HE* viii. 18 (iv. 250–3) and WM *GR* iv.
308–10 (ii. 363–5) describe the siege of Mont Saint-Michel, which OV says lasted two
weeks about the middle of Lent. Neither speak of William unilaterally abandoning the
siege, which OV says was ended by the granting of Henry's request for a safe-conduct,

the duchy out of his brother Robert's hands. While he was there, peace was made between them. Under its terms the duke would with good will surrender to the king the county of Eu, the abbey of Fécamp, the abbey at Mont Saint-Michel, Cherbourg, and the castles which had abandoned the duke, and the king would subdue to the duke's rule the county of Maine, and those castles in Normandy which were resisting the duke; he would restore to all those Normans the English lands which they had lost because of their loyalty to the duke, and would give to the duke as many English lands as had been mutually agreed between them. They further agreed that the king would inherit if the duke died without a legitimate male heir, and likewise, the duke would be William's heir if the king should die without leaving a son. This treaty was ratified by the oaths of twelve barons on the king's side, and of twelve on the duke's.[3] Meanwhile their brother Henry occupied Mont Saint-Michel with all the knights he had been able to find, some of the monks there assisting him. He ravaged the king's lands, captured some of his men, and despoiled others. For this reason the king and the duke assembled a force, and during the whole of Lent, they besieged the Mount, and often fought against Henry, losing both horses and men. William grew weary of the long siege, and departed unappeased.[4] Not long afterwards William deprived the atheling Edgar of the honour, which the duke had given him, and expelled him from Normandy.[5] Meanwhile in May Malcolm, the Scottish king, invaded Northumbria with a large army, with the intention of proceeding further and of terrorizing the English if he were successful. God did not allow this. He was frustrated in his aim, but before he returned home his army came away with much plunder from Northumbria.[6] When the king learnt of this, he returned to England with his brother Robert in August, and a little later with a large fleet and army, he made for Scotland to do battle with Malcolm; but before he reached Scotland, almost all his fleet was

though WM, here supported by Wace iii. 9595–612 (ii. 242–3), speaks of differences between the besiegers caused by Robert's chivalrous and generous attitude to the besieged. The Winchester Annals (*Ann. Mon.* ii. 36) speak of the ending of the siege (Henry 'ipse vero sponte vel non montem reddidit') and of William returning to England.

  [5] ASC says Edgar's exile in mid-Lent was the result of the treaty, and here names Scotland as his place of exile.

  [6] ASC does not date Malcolm's invasion. The repulse of his forces is apparently confirmed by the miraculous flight described in *De miraculis et translationibus S. Cuthberti* c. 10 (SD ii. 340). For this invasion and the English counter-attack, see Barlow, *William Rufus*, pp. 288–95.

illuc peruenisset, paucis diebus ante festiuitatem sancti Michaelis fere tota demersa est classis, multique de equestri exercitu eius fame et frigore perierunt, cui rex Malcolmus cum exercitu in prouincia Loidis occurrit. Quod uidens comes Rotbertus, clitonem Eadgarum quem rex de Normannia expulerat, et tunc cum rege Scottorum degebat, ad se accersiuit: cuius auxilio fretus, pacem inter reges fecit, ea conditione, ut Willelmo, sicut patri suo obediuit, Malcolmus obediret; et Malcolmo .xii. uillas, quas in Anglia sub patre illius habuerat, Wilelmus redderet, et .xii. marcas auri singulis annis daret. Sed pax inter eos facta non multo tempore durauit. Ipsum etiam Eadgarum cum rege Willelmo comes pacificauit.[7] Idibus Octobris, feria quarta, turrim Wincelcumbensis ecclesie uehemens ictus fulminis concutiens, parietem iuxta culmen ample perforauit, unamque de trabibus discidit, caputque imaginis Christi fortiter percussum in terram deiecit, et crus eius dextrum fregit. Imago etiam sancte Marie, que[b] iuxta crucem stabat, ictu percussa ad terram decidit. Magnus deinde fumus cum nimio fetore subsecutus, totam ecclesiam repleuit, et tamdiu durauit, quoad loci illius monachi cum aqua benedicta et incensu, et reliquiis sanctorum, officinas monasterii psalmos decantando circumirent. Nec minus .xvi. kal. Nou., feria .vi., turbo ueniens ab Affrico perualidus, Lundonie plusquam sexcentas domus et ecclesias quamplures concutiendo diuerberauit. In ecclesiam quoque sancte Marie que dicitur ad Arcum irruens, in ea duos occidit homines, et tectum cum tignis in altum leuans, et huc illucque diu per aera ferens, tandem sex de tignis, eo ordine quo tecto prius infixa erant, tam alte in terram defixit, ut de quibusdam eorum septima, de quibusdam uero octaua pars appareret; erant enim .xxvii. uel .xxviii. pedum longitudinis.[8] Post hec rex de Northymbria per Merciam in West Saxoniam rediit, et secum fere usque ad Natiuitatem Domini comitem retinuit, sed conuentionem inter eos factam illi persoluere noluit. Quod comes grauiter ferens, .x. kal. Ianuariarium

___
[b] qui HL

___
[7] OV HE viii. 16 (iv. 236) supports JW's dating of the brothers' return to England when he speaks of William staying in Normandy until 1 Aug. JW alone mentions the losses suffered by the mounted force, though it is surprising that cold could cause these losses 'before Michaelmas'. OV HE viii. 22 (iv. 268–70) is badly informed here and telescopes 'the events of two years in a few weeks'. William of St Calais entered Durham on this outward expedition, apparently on 11 Sept. (HR 172 (SD ii. 218), De iniusta Vexatione (SD i. 195)). JW has differences from ASC: ASC does not date either Malcolm's invasion or William's return to England, and mentions neither the losses of

sunk a few days before the feast of St Michael [29 September], and many of his mounted force perished from hunger and cold. King Malcolm opposed William with an army in Lothian. Duke Robert saw this, and summoned the atheling Edgar, whom the king had expelled from Normandy, and who was then staying with the Scottish king. Through Edgar's help, he achieved peace between the kings, on condition that Malcolm would do fealty to William, as he had done to his father, and that William would return to Malcolm the twelve townships, which he had possessed in England at the time of William I, and would pay him annually twelve golden marks. The peace, however, between them did not last for long. The duke also reconciled Edgar with King William.[7] On Wednesday, 15 October, lightning violently struck the tower of the church of Winchcombe, making a large breach in the wall near the top, and splitting one of the beams, threw the head of Christ on the crucifix violently to the ground, and broke Christ's right leg. The statue of St Mary standing by the cross, was also forcefully cast to the ground. A dense smoke followed by a fetid stench filled all the church for a long time, until the monks of Winchcombe with holy water and incense, and relics of the saints, processed round the monastic buildings, singing psalms. Moreover, on Friday, 16 October, a very powerful whirlwind from the south-west shook and destroyed more than 600 houses and many churches in London. Raging through the church of St Mary-le-Bow, it killed two men, raised up and carried through the air for some time its roof and timbers until six of the beams, in the same order in which they had previously held the roof in position, were sunk so deeply into the earth that there was visible the seventh part of some, and the eighth part of others. They were twenty-seven or twenty-eight feet long.[8] After this the king returned to Wessex from Northumbria passing through Mercia, and kept the duke with him until Christmas. He was not willing to implement the treaty they had agreed. The duke was much displeased, and returned to Normandy

the land army, nor the grant to Malcolm of 12 estates, and does not record the promised annual payment. WM *GR* iv. 311 (ii. 165) says that a Welsh expedition preceded the Scottish.

[8] The storms at London and Winchcombe are reported by WM *GR* iv. 323 (ii. 374–5) with very similar details, though the wind at London is said to be from the south-east, and the number of affected beams and their measurements at the St Mary-le-Bow fire differ. The Margam and Bermondsey Annals' (*Ann. Mon.* i. 5, iii. 427) report on the London and Winchcombe disasters is taken from WM, and the Wykes (*Ann. Mon.* iv. 12), Rouen, and Bury annals (*UAG* pp. 46, 130) mention those at London.

die, cum clitone Eadgaro Normanniam repetiit.⁹ *ᶜErant duo, ut in Anglia ferebatur, qui dicebantur Romani pontifices, a se inuicem discordantes, et ecclesiam Dei inter se diuisam post se trahentes: Vrbanus scilicet, qui primum uocatus Odo fuerat episcopus Ostiensis, et Clemens, qui Wibertus appellatus fuerat arciepiscopus Rauennensis. Que res, ut de aliis mundi partibus sileamus, per plures annos ecclesiam Anglie in tantum occupauit, ut ex quo Gregorius, qui et Hildebrandus, defunctus fuit, nulli loco pape usque ad hoc tempus subdi uel obedire uoluerit. Sed Vrbanum, pro uicario beati Petri, Italia Galliaque iam receperat.ᶜ ¹⁰*

[**1092**] (.xxxvi.) 1114 Ciuitas Lundonia maxima ex parte incendio conflagrauit.¹ Osmundus, Searesbyriensis episcopus, ecclesiam, quam Searesbyrie in castello construxerat, cum adiutorio episcoporum Walcelini Wintoniensis et Iohannis Bathoniensis, nonis Aprilis, feria .ii., dedicauit.² Antistes etiam Remigius, qui, licentia regis Wilelmi senioris, episcopalem sedem de Dorkeceastreᵃ mutauerat ad Lindicolinam, constructam in ea ecclesiam pontificali cathedre dignam dedicare uolebat, quia sibi diem mortis imminere sentiebat, sed Thomas Eboracensis arciepiscopus illi contradicendo resistebat, affirmans eam in sua parrochia esse constructam. At rex Wilelmus iunior, pro pecunia, quam ei Remigius dederat, fere totius Anglie episcopis mandauit, ut, in unum conuenientes, septenis idibus Maii, ecclesiam dedicarent, sed biduo ante diem statutum, occulto Dei iudicio, ipse episcopus Remigius migrauit e seculo, et ecclesie per hoc remansit dedicatio.³ His actis, rex in Northymbriam profectus, ciuitatem que Brytannice Cairleu, Latine Legubaliaᵇ uocatur, restaurauit, et in ea castellum edificauit. Hec enim ciuitas, ut illis in partibus alie nonnulle, a Danis paganis ante .cc. annos diruta, et usque ad id tempus mansit deserta.⁴

ᶜ⁻ᶜ *written by C¹ at the end of 1091 and into the mg.*

ᵃ ke *in* Dorkeceastre *erased C*   ᵇ u *interlin. above* e *C*

---

⁹ The essential details are in ASC E which, however, records Robert and Edgar embarking in the Isle of Wight.

¹⁰ Eadmer, *HN* i (p. 52). Urban II (1088–99), Clement III, antipope (1080; 1084–1100). In Eadmer, this passage appears before the meeting of Anselm and the king at Gillingham in 1095, and it is not clear why C¹ should have added this extract at this point.

¹ This fire is not reported elsewhere.

² The year of the dedication is confirmed by WM *GR* iv. 325 (ii. 375) and by *The Chronicle of Holyrood*, ed. M. O. Anderson (Scottish History Society, 3rd series, vol. xxx; Edinburgh, 1938), p. 111 and n. 2, and the Waverley Annals (*Ann. Mon.* ii. 202). The last

with the atheling Edgar on 23 December.[9] As it was reported in England, there were at this time two so-called Roman popes in conflict with each other, who dragged the church into division with them. One was Urban who, previously called Odo, had been bishop of Ostia; the other was Clemens, who, as Wibert, had been archbishop of Ravenna. This affair so troubled the English church for many years—to say nothing about the other parts of the world—that from the death of Gregory (also known as Hildebrand), it would up to the present neither recognize nor obey any pope. Italy and France had long recognized Urban as the vicar of Peter.[10]

[1092] Most of London was consumed by fire.[1] On Monday, 5 April, Osmund, bishop of Salisbury, assisted by Walkelin, bishop of Winchester, and John, bishop of Bath, dedicated the church which he had built in Salisbury castle.[2] Bishop Remigius, who had moved the see from Dorchester to Lincoln with King William the Elder's permission, wanted to build and dedicate there a church worthy of a bishopric because he felt the day of his death approaching; but Thomas, archbishop of York, opposed him, saying that the church was in his own diocese. King William the Younger, in return for some money given him by Bishop Remigius, summoned almost all the English bishops to assemble on 9 May and to dedicate the church. Two days before the agreed date Bishop Remigius was, by the mysterious judgement of God, taken from this world, and for this reason the church's dedication was put off.[3] After this the king went to Northumbria, restored the city which is in British called Cairleu, and in Latin Legubalia, and built a castle there. This city, like some others in that region, had been destroyed by the Danes 200 years earlier, and had remained deserted to that time.[4]

two, which have an identical annal, say that seven bishops took part in the dedication. JW alone contributes the day.

[3] WM *GP* (p. 313), HH *HA* vii. 2 (p. 416), *HC* (pp. 14–16) all agree that Remigius died the day before the cathedral's dedication, which JW (alone among chronicles) dates 9 May. For evidence of Remigius' death on 8 or 6 May, see Greenway, *Fasti* iii. 1. *HC* (pp. 14–15) refers to a claim made by Archbishop Thomas of York that Remigius had bought the see from William Rufus.

[4] The sole entry under 1092 in ASC E speaks of a local ruler Dolfin being expelled and of William's garrisoning of the castle of Carlisle and of the settlement of the area with peasants from the south. For the disputed identification of Dolfin as Gospatric's son, see Kapelle, *Norman Conquest of the North*, pp. 151–2. The last recapitulatory remark is similar to those found in the accounts of the kingdoms prefixed to JW's chronicle and to be published in vol. i.

[**1093**] (.xxxvii.) 1114 *a*Rex Wilelmus iunior, in regia uilla que uocatur Aluuuestan, uehementi percussus infirmitate, ciuitatem Glauuornam festinanter adiit, ibique per totam Quadragesimam languosus iacuit. Qui cum se putaret cito moriturum, ut ei sui barones suggesserunt, uitam suam corrigere, ecclesias non amplius uendere, nec ad censum ponere, sed illas regia tueri potestate, irrectas leges destruere, ac rectas statuere Deo promisit. Insuper Anselmo Beccensi abbati, qui tunc in Anglia morabatur, Dorubernensem archiepiscopatum, et cancellario suo Rotberto, cognomento Bloet, Lindicolinensem*b* dedit presulatum, *c*.ii. no. Mar.*c d*Sed Anselmo nil de archiepiscopatu, preter id quod rex illi dari iusserat, accipere licebat, quoad tributum, quod post Landfranci obitum singulis annis inde acceperat, persolueretur.*d*1 Res, Walanorum rex, in ipsa ebdomada Pascali, iuxta castellum quod Brecehenieau nominatur, in pugna occisus est. Ab illo die regnare in Walonia reges desiere.2 Rex Scottorum Malcolmus, die festiuitatis sancti p. 358 Bartho|lomei Apostoli, regi Wilelmo iuniori, ut prius per legatos inter eos statutum fuerat, in ciuitate Glauuorna occurrit, ut, sicut quidam primatum Anglie uoluerunt, pace redintegrata, stabilis inter eos amicitia firmaretur, sed impacati ab inuicem discesserunt. Nam Malcolmum uidere aut cum eo colloqui, pre nimia superbia et potentia, Wilelmus despexit, insuper etiam illum ut, secundum iudicium tantum suorum baronum, in curia sua rectitudinem ei faceret, constringere uoluit, sed id agere, nisi in regnorum suorum confiniis, ubi reges Scottorum erant soliti rectitudinem facere regibus Anglorum, et secundum iudicium primatum utriusque regni, nullo modo Malcolmus uoluit.3 Post hec in sole signum apparuit ualde mirabile,4 et comes Scrobbesbyriensis Rogerus, et Wido abbas monasterii sancti Augustini, et Paulus abbas monasterii

---

a For the lower marginal (with signe) addition here in B by a scribe not found elsewhere, see Appendix B   *b* 1093*c* add. here P   *c–c* interlin. CB, om. HL, incorporated at 1093*b* P   *d–d* For B's substituted text, see Appendix B

1 JW differs from ASC in naming Alveston as the place where William was first taken ill, in explicitly dating his illness to the whole of Lent, in attributing William's change of heart to the magnates' advice, and in describing the restriction placed on Anselm's revenues. ASC speaks of William granting land to many monasteries and of the fragility of his promises. Barlow, *William Rufus*, p. 300 n. 166, notes three possible grants made in this year: *Regesta* i. 339 (to St Peter's, Gloucester), 351 (to St Augustine's, Canterbury), and 407 (to the canons of Lincoln). Eadmer, *HN* i (pp. 30–7), gives a full account of Anselm's investiture, which took place on 6 Mar., the date given by the addition to C.
2 This is Rhys ap Tewdwr, king of Deheubarth, on whom see Robert S. Badcock, 'Rhys

[1093] King William the Younger was taken seriously ill at the royal township of Alveston, and rushed to Gloucester, where he remained sick during the whole of Lent [2 March–16 April]. Thinking that he would die soon, he vowed before God, following his barons' counsel, to reform his way of life, never again to sell or tax churches, but to guard them with royal power, to annul unjust laws, and establish just ones. In addition, on 5 March he gave the archbishopric of Canterbury to Anselm, the abbot of Bec, who was then in England, and the bishopric of Lincoln to his chancellor Robert called Bloet. But Anselm was not allowed to receive anything from the archbishopric over and above what the king had ordered should be assigned to him until the annual tribute, which William had received since Lanfranc's death, had been paid.[1] Rhys, king of the Welsh, was killed in battle in Easter Week [17–23 April] near the castle of Brecknock. From that day kings ceased to rule in Wales.[2] On the feast of St Bartholomew the apostle [24 August], Malcolm, the Scottish king, by a prior arrangement made between envoys, met King William the Younger, at Gloucester, so that, in accordance with the wishes of the chief men of the English, peace could be restored, and a firm friendship established between them; but they separated without any agreement. William, through excessive pride and insolence, refused to see and talk to Malcolm. Furthermore he wanted to force Malcolm to do homage to him at his court in accordance with the judgement of his barons, whereas Malcolm would do homage only on the frontier of their kingdoms where Scottish kings had done in the past, and in accordance with the judgement of the chief men of both realms.[3] After this a marvellous sign appeared in the sun,[4] and Roger, earl of Shrewsbury, Guy, abbot of St Augustine's, and Paul, abbot of St

---

ap Tewdwr, king of Deheubarth', *ANS* xvi (1994), 21–35. *AC* (p. 29), *Brut* Pen. (p. 19), Her. (pp. 32–3), and BS (pp. 84–5) date his death to 1091 (*recte* 1093), the Brut texts speaking of the kingdom of the Britons coming to an end and of the Normans living in Brycheiniog being responsible.

[3] Malcolm's unsuccessful meeting with William at Gloucester is common to ASC and JW, but there are significant differences between the two. ASC says that William summoned Malcolm, that he gave him hostages, including the atheling Edgar 'æfter', that Malcolm, though escorted to Gloucester with great honour, was neither received by William nor granted the promised terms. JW says that the two met on 24 Aug. and that William's pride and insolence, and his insistence on homage being performed not, as Malcolm claimed was the custom, on the frontiers of the two kingdoms, but at his own court, were the causes of the rupture. For a discussion of Malcolm's possible grievances, see Barlow, *William Rufus*, pp. 310–16.

[4] WM *GR* iv. 326 (ii. 375–6) and other chronicles (e. g. Margam (*Ann. Mon.* i. 5)) report floods and storms, but JW's solar phenomenon is peculiar to him.

sancti Albani decesserunt.[5] Decessit etiam eodem anno uir magne strenuitatis Flandrensis comes Rodbrihtus, cui successit primogenitus filius eius Rotbertus.[6] Rex Scottorum Malcolmus, et primogenitus filius suus Eaduuardus, cum multis aliis, in Northymbria, die festiuitatis sancti Bricii, a militibus Rotberti Northymbrorum comitis occisi sunt.[7] Quorum morte cognita, regina Scottorum Margareta tanta affecta est tristitia, ut subito magnam incideret infirmitatem. Nec mora, presbiteris ad se accersitis, ecclesiam intrauit, eisque sua peccata confessa, oleo se perungui, celestique muniri uiatico fecit, Deum assiduis et precibus intentissimis exorans, ut in hac erumnosa uita diutius illam uiuere non permitteret. Nec multo tardius exaudita est. Nam post tres dies occisionis regis, soluta carnis uinculis, ut creditur, ad gaudia transiuit eterne salutis. Quippe dum uiueret, pietatis, iustitie, pacis, et caritatis cultrix extitit deuota, frequens in orationibus, corpus uigiliis et ieiuniis macerauit, ecclesias et monasteria ditauit, seruos et ancillas Dei dilexit et honorauit, esurientibus panem frangebat, nudos uestiebat, omnibus peregrinis ad se uenientibus hospitia, uestimenta, et alimenta prebebat, et Deum tota mente diligebat.[8] Qua mortua Dufenaldum, regis Malcolmi fratrem, Scotti sibi in regem elegerunt, et omnes Anglos qui de curia regis extiterunt, de Scottia expulerunt. Quibus auditis, filius regis Malcolmi, Dunechan, regem Willelmum, cui tunc militauit, ut ei regnum sui patris concederet, petiit, et impetrauit, illique fidelitatem iurauit, et sic ad Scottiam cum multitudine Anglorum ac Normannorum properauit, et patruum suum Dufenaldum ᵉde regnoᵉ expulit, et in loco eius regnauit. Deinde nonnulli Scottorum in unum congregati, homines illius pene omnes peremerunt, ipse uero cum paucis uix

---

ᵉ⁻ᵉ om. HL

---

[5] Roger of Montgomery, earl of Shrewsbury, died on 27 July (OV *HE* viii. 25 (iv. 302), v. 14 (iii. 148)), and in the last reference the year is identified as the sixth after William I's death. This is usually taken as 1094 (*CP* xi. 687 n. d) on the evidence both of ASC 1094, where his second son, Hugh, is described as earl of Shropshire, and of the grant printed by H. E. Craster, 'A contemporary record of the episcopacy of Ranulf Flambard', *Archeologia Aeliana*, 4th series, vii (1930), 36, which is witnessed by Earl Roger at Gloucester, and is dated there to Christmas 1093. Robert Bloet, who witnesses that charter, seems to have been nominated to Lincoln in the spring of 1093, and the charter could have been issued at the Gloucester spring court. The reference in the Waverley Annals (*Ann. Mon.* ii. 204) to the death of Earl Roger in 1094 could be a simple inference from the description in ASC of Hugh as earl, and JW's 1093 for Roger's death could be acceptable. *Heads*, p. 36, gives JW as the only extant source for the year of Abbot Guy of St Augustine's death, which seems to have been commemorated on 9 Aug.; and, p. 66, shows that the year of Paul of St

Alban's, died.[5] In the same year the energetic count of Flanders, Robert, died, and his first-born son, Robert, succeeded him.[6] Malcolm, king of the Scots, and his first-born son Edward, were slain with many others on St Brice's day [13 November] by the knights of Robert, earl of Northumbria.[7] Queen Margaret was so saddened by the news of their death that she suddenly became gravely ill. Immediately, summoning priests, she went into church, confessed her sins to them, and caused herself to be anointed with oil, and to be strengthened by the holy viaticum. She asked God earnestly and intensely that she should not stay much longer in this grievous world. Not much later her prayers were answered. Three days after the king's death, she passed over to the eternal joys of salvation, so it is to be believed, shaking off the chains of the flesh. When she was alive, she devoted herself to piety, justice, peace, and charity, often chastening her body with vigils and fasts, enriching churches and monasteries, loving and honouring the servants and handmaidens of the Lord, breaking bread for the hungry, clothing the naked, furnishing lodgings, clothes, and food for those strangers coming to her, and loving God with all her spirit.[8] On her death the Scots chose Donald Bane, King Malcolm's brother, as their king, and expelled from Scotland all the English at the royal court. On learning of this, Duncan, King Malcolm's son, who was in King William's service, successfully obtained from him the grant of his father's kingdom, swore fealty to William, moved swiftly to Scotland with a multitude of English and Normans, expelled his uncle Donald Bane from the kingdom, and ruled in his place. At length many Scots gathered together and slew almost all his followers, he barely

Alban's death is confirmed by the St Alban's source, *Gesta abbatum S. Albani*, ed. H. T. Riley (3 vols., RS 28; 1867–9), i. 64.

[6] Robert the Frisian 1070–93. He died on 13 Oct. (C. Verlinden, *Robert Ier le Frison* (Antwerp–Paris, 1935), p. 166).

[7] ASC has a fuller account of the death of Malcolm: it says his invasion was foolish and improper, and that he was killed by Morel of Bamburgh, the steward of Robert of Northumbria. OV *HE* viii. 22 (iv. 270) describes Morel as Robert's nephew. *HR* (SD ii. 221–2) locates the place of battle near the river Alne, and the burial of Malcolm at Tynemouth (as WM *GR* iii. 250 (ii. 309) does also). WM *GR* says that Malcolm's body was recently ('nuper') removed to Dunfermline. Gaimar ll. 6115–17 adds Geoffrede Lilevant to Malcolm's killers, and says that 3000 Scots were slaughtered. JW dates the slaying to 13 Nov., a day also given in the Margam annals (*Ann. Mon.* i. 5–6).

[8] JW's account is much fuller than that in ASC E, and dates Margaret's death. WM *GR* iv. 311 (ii. 366) has a similar account of Margaret's reactions to the deaths of her husband and son, but there are no verbal parallels. ASC describes Donald Bane as Duncan's kinsman (mæg) here, but as his paternal uncle (fædera) under 1094.

euasit. Verumtamen post hec illum regnare permiserunt, ea ratione, ut amplius in Scottiam nec Anglos nec Normannos introduceret, sibique militare sineret.⁹ Conuenientibus ferme totius Anglie episcopis, in quibus Thomas Eboracensis arciepiscopus primatum tenebat, Anselmum, Beccensem abbatem, pridie nonarum Decembrium consecrauerunt antistitem.ᶠ ¹⁰ Eodem anno Willelmus comesᵍ de Ouue, auri ingenti uictus auiditate, et promissi honoris captus magnitudine, a naturali domno suo Rotberto, Normannorum comite, cui fidelitatem iurauerat, defecit, et in Angliam ad regem Willelmum ueniens, illius se dominio, ut seductor maximus, subiugauit.¹¹

[1094] (.xxxviii.) 1116

[HLP]

ᵃComes Normannorum Rotbertus fratri suo regi Willelmo iuniori per legatos mandauit pacem quam inter se firmauerant se non diutius seruaturum. Insuper illum uocauit periurum et perfidum nisi conuentionem inter illos in Normannia factam esset ei persoluturus. Ob hanc causam rex circa k. Feb. Heastsingam adiit, et dum ibi moraretur ecclesiam de Bello dedicari fecit. ᵇVbi etiam Herebertum Theotfordensem episcopum pastorali baculo priuauit, latenter enim Vrbanum papam adire et ab eo pro episcopatu quem sibi

[C³BP]

ᶜArfasto prius *Wilelmi comitis* et *post Willelmi regis capellano,* processu uero temporis Theodfordensi episcopo, iam de medio facto, ᵈeiusque successore Willelmo,ᵈ *Hereberhtus,* qui *cognom*inabatur *Losinga ars adulationis* nuper ei egerat, *ex priore* Fescamni *et ex abbate Ramesie,* empto presulatu, Theodfordensis ecclesie factus est episcopus, *patre suo Rotberto eiusdem cognominis in abbatiam Wintonie intruso. Veruntamen erroneum impetum iuuentutis aboleuit penitentia, Romam profectus senioribus annis, ubi loci*

ᶠ For B's addition in text here, see Appendix B   ᵍ interlin. C

ᵃ⁻ᵃ add. in mg. by P⁵ with signe pointing to 1094ᶠ   ᵇ⁻ᵇ om. now but probably erased by H which now has: Hoc anno uenerabilis Herbertus Theofordensis episcopus a Roma cum benedictione apostolica rediit et a Willelmo rege impetrauit ut sedes episcopalis in Norwicensi ecclesia firmaretur, ubi ipse Christi iuuante gratia pulcherrimam congregationem monachorum ad honorem sancte Trinitatis adunauit   ᶜ⁻ᶜ written over erasure by C³; note that in P the sequence of texts is 1094ᶜ up to 1094ᶠ where the marginal addition 1094ᵃ was to be inserted, after which the remainder of the text of 1094ᶜ follows ᵈ⁻ᵈ marginal addition with signes C³

⁹ The details of the Scottish succession are close to ASC E's account. Where JW has 'cui tunc militauit' ASC says Duncan had been a hostage at William's court. ASC makes

escaping, with only a few. Nevertheless, afterwards they allowed him to reign over them on condition that he would no longer bring English or Normans into Scotland and allow them to serve him.[9] Almost all the English bishops, among whom Thomas, archbishop of York, was chief, consecrated as bishop Anselm, abbot of Bec, on 4 December.[10] In the same year William, count of Eu, bought over by his great greed of gold, and the promise of great honours, abandoned his natural lord, Robert, the Norman duke, to whom he had sworn fealty, came to King William in England, and, prince of traitors, placed himself under the king's lordship.[11]

[1094]

Robert, duke of the Normans, told his brother King William the Younger through envoys that he would no longer keep the peace which they had both agreed. Furthermore he called him faithless and deceitful unless he discharged fully the terms of the agreement they had made in Normandy. It was for this reason that about 1 February the king went to Hastings, and whilst there, he dedicated the church at Battle. He deprived Herbert, bishop of Thetford, of a pastoral staff, for Herbert had wanted clandestinely to go to Pope Urban to ask absolution for the bishopric

After the deaths of Herfast, formerly chaplain of Earl William, and later of King William, and in the course of time bishop of Thetford, and of his successor, William, Herbert known as Losinga (for he had recently acted as a flatterer of him), prior of Fécamp and abbot of Ramsey, bought the episcopacy, became bishop of Thetford, and intruded his father Robert, also Losinga, into the abbacy of Winchester. Nevertheless penance absolved his youthful unrighteous action. Setting out for Rome in later years, he there put aside his simoniacal staff and ring, which he was thought

clear William's agreement to Duncan's expedition. Scottish king lists give Donald Bane a reign of 6 months, which would date his defeat to May 1094 (see e.g. M. O. Anderson, *Kings and Kingship in Early Scotland* (Edinburgh, 1980), p. 276: Regnal list F). For an improbable hypothesis on the brevity of Donald Bane's reign, see Kapelle, *Norman Conquest of the North*, pp. 154, 274-5 (n. 130).

   [10] ASC does not give this date which is in Eadmer, *HN* i (p. 42). For the conflicting accounts of Thomas's attitude at the consecration of Anselm as archbishop of Canterbury, see *HC*, pp. xxxix, 26-8, and Eadmer, *HN* i (pp. 42-3).

   [11] William of Eu's father, Robert, count of Eu, had supported William on his intervention in Normandy in 1090-1. The purchase of William's allegiance and the description of him as 'seductor maximus' are not known elsewhere.

et abbatia quam patri suo Rotberto ab ipso rege Willelmo
mille libris emerat absolutionem
querere uoluerit.^{b} Dein media
.xl. rex^a Normanniam petiit ad
fratris colloquium sub pace statuta uenit sed impacatus ab eo
recessit. Denuo in campo martii
conuenere, ubi illi qui sacramentis inter illos pacem con-
firmauere regi omnem culpam
imposuere. At ille culpam nec
agnoscere conuentionem uoluit
persoluere. Iccirco nimis irati
discesserunt impacati.^{1}

simonicum baculum et anulum
deponens, indulgentia clementis-
sime sedis iterum recipere meruit.
Domum uero reuersus, sedem
episcopalem transportauit ad
insignem mercimoniis et populorum
frequentia uicum nomine
Northwic, ibique monachorum
congregationem instituit.^{c} ^{e}Rex
Willelmus Hæstingam adiit,
ibidemque ecclesiam de Bello
dedicare fecit, ^{f}et post^f
Normanniam petit ad fratris
colloquium sub statuta pace
uenit, sed impacatus ab eo
recessit.^{2}

Comes quidem Rotomagum perrexit. Rex^g ad Owe rediit, et in illo

p. 359 resedit, solidarios undique conduxit,^{e} | aurum, argentum, terras, quibusdam primatum Normannie dedit, quibusdam promisit, ut a germano suo Rotberto deficerent et se cum castellis sue dicioni subicerent, quibus ad uelle suum paratis, per castella, uel que prius habuerat, uel que tunc conduxerat, suos milites distribuit.^{3} Interea castellum quod Bures uocatur expugnauit, comitis milites in illo captos partim in Angliam custodiendos misit, partim in Normannia custodie mancipauit, et fratrem suum multis modis uexans, exheredare laborauit.^{4} At ille necessitate compulsus, domnum suum, regem Francorum Philippum, cum exercitu Normanniam adduxit,

---

$^{e-e}$ written over erasure in C by hand not found elsewhere $^{f-f}$ erased to make way for
signe marking the insertion of marginal addition 1094^a by P^5 ^{g} Rex vero HL

^{1} JW's original text, which is now only preserved in witness L and in *HR* 175 (SD ii. 223–4), is close to ASC E with some variants such as its locating the meeting place for the negotiations at the *Campus Martius* at Rouen and its substituting the vague 'circa Kal. Feb.' for ASC's 2 Feb. as the date of William's stay at Hastings. JW provides reasons for William's deprivation of Herbert Losinga's staff as well as the story of Herbert's purchase of the bishopric of Thetford for himself and of the abbacy of Hyde for his father. Herbert was present at the Christmas court 1093 (*Regesta* i. 338), and was back in office by Apr. 1095 (*Memorials St Edmund's*, i. 87). William could have deprived him of his staff when he learnt of his intended unsanctioned departure for Rome, possibly early in 1094. *EEA* iv. p. xxix, considers it probable that the deprivation took place before, not after, Henry's visit to the pope. Herbert's reputation for simony prompted the verses reported by WM in *GR* iv. 338 (ii. 385–6). Battle was dedicated on 11 Feb. (*The Chronicle of Battle Abbey*, ed E. Searle (OMT, 1980), pp. 96–7), and William crossed over in mid-Lent (ASC and JW).

he had bought for himself for £1,000 from King William as well as the abbacy for his father. At length in the middle of Lent the king went to Normandy to confer with his brother on the terms of the agreement but he left him without coming to terms. Finally in the *Campus Martis* they met. There those who confirmed on oath the peace between them put all the blame on the king. But he would neither accept the blame nor implement the agreement. Thereupon they departed angry and unreconciled.[1]

worthy of receiving again through the indulgence of that most merciful see. Then on his return home he moved the episcopal see to Norwich, that famous centre of trade and general resort, and there he established a community of monks. King William went to Hastings and there he dedicated the church at Battle. Then he crossed to Normandy and met his brother to discuss the peace, but he left him without being reconciled.[2]

The duke now reached Rouen. The king returned to Eu, and staying there, he collected mercenaries from everywhere, and to some of the chief men of Normandy he gave, and to others he promised, gold, silver, and land so that they would defect from his brother Robert and place themselves and their castles under his jurisdiction. When they were prepared to do what he asked, he distributed his soldiers through the castles he formerly held or which he now had acquired.[3] Meanwhile he stormed the castle of Bures, sent some of the duke's knights captured there to be held in England, and held others prisoner in Normandy, and harassing his brother in many ways, strove to disinherit him.[4] Forced by extreme need, Robert brought his lord, Philip, the French king, with an army into Normandy.

David, *Robert Curthose*, p. 84 n. 214, comments that 'if by "mid-Lent" an exact day is designated, it was probably Sunday, 19 Mar.'. Freeman, *Reign of William Rufus*, i. 461 n. 3 asked whether the *Campus Martius* could be the 'Champ de Mars; outside the east of Rouen'. The place where the brothers met is not recorded. *Heads*, p. 82, notes that *Regesta* i. 315 shows Robert Losinga in office on 27 Jan. 1091.
  [2] WM *GP* ii. 74 (pp. 150–1). The WM text, on which the revised JW text is based, leaves out the deprivation of the pastoral staff, and H's final version (after a passage which was almost certainly like that originally in JW, and which is still preserved in L, had been erased) omits both Herbert's simony and the loss of his staff.
  [3] Robert's arrival at Rouen, William's at Eu, and William's military and financial preparations are not in ASC.
  [4] This is in ASC E though William's retention of some captives in Normandy is only implied there, and there is no equivalent for the final clause ('fratrem suum . . . laborauit').

sed rex Argentinum castellum obsedit, et ipso die obsessionis, .dcc. milites regis cum bis totidem scutariis, et castellanis omnibus qui intus erant, sine sanguinis effusione cepit, captosque in custodia tamdiu custodire mandauit, donec quisque se redimeret, et post hec in Franciam rediit. Comes uero Rotbertus castellum quod Holm nuncupatur obsedit, donec Wilelmus Peuerel, et .dccc. homines, qui id defendebant, illi se dederent.[5] Quod cum regi innotuerit, nuntiis in Angliam missis, .xx. milia pedonum in Normanniam sibi iussit in auxilium mitti. Quibus ut mare transirent, Heastinge congregatis, pecuniam que data fuerat eis ad uictum, Rannulfus Passeflambardus precepto regis abstulit, scilicet, unicuique decem solidos, et eos domum repedare mandauit, pecuniam uero regi transmisit.[6] Interea graui et assiduo tributo, hominumque mortalitate, presenti et anno sequenti, tota uexabatur Anglia.[7] Ad hec etiam primitus North Walani, deinceps West Walani et Suth Walani, seruitutis iugo, quo diu premebantur, excusso, et ceruice erecta, libertatem sibi uindicare laborabant. Vnde collecta multitudine, castella, que in West Walania firmata erant, frangebant, et in Castrensi, Scrobbesbyriensi, et Herefordensi prouincia frequenter uillas cremabant, predas agebant, et multos ex Anglis et Normannis interficiebant. Fregerunt et castellum in Meuania insula, eamque sue dicioni subiciebant.[8] Interim Scotti regem suum Dunechan, et cum eo[h] nonnullos, suasu et hortatu Dufenaldi, per insidias peremerunt, et illum sibi regem rursus constituerunt.[9] Post hec rex Wilelmus .iiii. kal. Ianuarii Angliam rediit, et ut Walanos debellaret, mox exercitum in Waloniam duxit, ibique homines et equos perdidit multos.[10]

---

[h] ea *CHP*

---

[5] In ASC E Robert (with King Philip's assistance) initiates both campaigns, and Roger of Poitiers is the castellan captured at Argentan; it speaks of both sides burning each other's villages and capturing people; and it does not mention either the 1400 *scutarii* captured at Argentan, or Philip's initiative in keeping the Argentan prisoners under guard and in returning home after that or the defence of Le Houlme by William Peverel and 800 men. Barlow, *William Rufus*, p. 333 n. 293, defends the identification of Le Houlme with Briouze, the *caput* of Philip of Briouze's honour.
[6] Again close to ASC though neither the ferry port of Hastings nor Ranulf Flambard are mentioned in ASC. As with the events in Kent in 1088, JW appears to cut the campaign short: he does not mention the further activity in Normandy nor Henry's actions against Robert in 1095.
[7] This is not in ASC E. *GR* iv. 327 (ii. 376) speaks of the tribute collected for the Norman campaign leading to famine and mortality. Eadmer, *HN* i (p. 52), claims that the immense tribute collected served little purpose.

Philip besieged the castle of Argentan, and on the very first day of the siege, he took captive without the spilling of blood 700 royal knights and 1400 squires, as well as all the garrison in the castle. He ordered those who had been captured to he held in custody until each had paid their ransom, and then he returned to France. Duke Robert besieged the castle of *Houlme* until William Peverel and the 800 men defending it yielded to him.[5] When the king learnt of this, he sent messengers to England, and ordered that 20,000 foot soldiers be sent to his aid in Normandy. When they had assembled at Hastings before crossing the sea, Ranulf Flambard on the king's instructions took the money which had been given them for their keep, that is, ten shillings for each man, and commanded them to return home, and sent the money to the king.[6] Meanwhile all England was oppressed by heavy and persistent taxation, and a mortality of men, both in this, and in the following, year.[7] In addition first the North Welsh, then the West and South Welsh, shaking off the yoke of slavery, which they had long endured, and holding their heads up high, sought to recover their liberty. Assembling a multitude of men, they razed the castles which had been built in West Wales, and often ravaged townships in Cheshire, Shropshire and Herefordshire, taking booty, and killing many of the English and Normans. They demolished the castle on Anglesey, and reduced the island to their control.[8] At the same time the Scots, on the advice and goading of Donald Bane, ambushed and slew their king Duncan, and many with him, and again set Donald Bane as king over them.[9] After this King William on 29 December went back to England and led an army into Wales in order to fight the Welsh, and there lost many men and horses.[10]

---

[8] ASC E is much briefer. JW distinguishes between the Welsh of different regions, and mentions the castles in West Wales, the places where booty is seized, and the castle of Anglesey. ASC adds the successful resistance by Hugh, earl of Shrewsbury, to one of these incursions. WM *GR* iv. 327 (ii. 376) describes Welsh advances in Chester, Shropshire and Anglesey. *Brut* Pen. (p. 19) and Her. (pp. 34–5) *s.a.* 1092 (*recte* 1094) has a general reference to Welsh success, and Pen. has a specific reference to Cadwgan ap Bleddon's resistance and advance. *AC* (year not clear) speaks of the Britons throwing off the yoke and advancing against the French. For the context, see Lloyd, *History of Wales*, ii. 403–4.

[9] This is in ASC E which describes Donald Bane as Duncan's paternal uncle. An inserted folio (fo. 13) in the Chronicle of Melrose names the Mormaer of Mearns as Duncan's assassin.

[10] ASC E 1095 does not mention William's Welsh expedition, but says that he was at Wissant on 25–8 Dec. 1094 and returned to England after 28 Dec. This expedition is not recorded elsewhere.

[1095] (.xxxix.) 1117   ^{ab}Vir uenerabilis et ualde admirabilis uite, Wlstanus, episcopus sancte Wigornensis ecclesie, ab adolescentia diuinis mancipatus seruitiis, post multos sancti sudoris agones, quibus pro gloria regni celestis adipiscenda magna mentis deuotione et humilitate sedulus Deo seruiuit intentissime, die mensis Ianuarii octauo decimo noctis septimi Sabbati, hora mediante septima, migrauit e seculo, ^canno a primo seculi die, certa scripture ratione diuine, .v. milia .ccxcix., ^cnoni magni anni quingentesimo uigesimo nono, noni uero magni anni ab initio seculi quadringentesimo septuagesimo sexto, ^ca passione Domini secundum euangelium millesimo octogesimo quarto, ^ciuxta chronicam Bede millesimo sexagesimo sexto, ^csecundum Dionisium millesimo sexagesimo primo, ^cab aduentu Anglorum in Brytanniam septingentesimo quadragesimo quinto, ^cab aduentu sancti Augustini quadringentesimo nonagesimo octauo, ^ca transitu sancti Oswaldi archipresulis centesimo tertio, ^cundecimi magni paschalis cycli tricesimo secundo, ^cdecimi uero a capite mundi quingentesimo decimo, ^csecundi solaris cycli quarto, ^cbissextilis cycli tertio, ^csecundi decennouenalis cycli tertio decimo, ^csecundi lunaris cycli decimo, ^cendecadis quinto, ^cindictionalis cycli tertio, ^clustro sue etatis octauo decimo, ^csui uero pontificatus septimi lustri anno tertio. Miroque modo ^dipsa sui^d transitus hora, suo quem specialiter dilexerat amico, Rotberto, Herefordensi episcopo, in oppido quod Criccelad uocatur, in uisione apparuit, illique ad se tumulandum Wigornam properare mandauit. Anulum etiam cum quo pontificalem susceperat benedictionem, neminem Deus passus est digito extrahere, ne post mortem uir sanctus suos uideretur fallere, quibus predixerat sepissime, nec illum uita comite se uelle perdere, nec etiam sepulture sue die.[1] Pridie non. Aprilis, in nocte p. 360 uise sunt stelle | quasi de celo cadere.[2] Walterus, Albinensis episcopus, sancte Romane ecclesie legatus, *ab ^eVrbano papa^e missus*, ante Pasca *uenit Angliam*, pallium pro quo rex Willelmus anno precedenti miserat, illi ^fdeferens, *quod iuxta condictum die dominica, que erat .iiii. idus Iun.* ab eodem *Cantwariam super altare Saluatoris*

---

^a *For B's marginal addition here (with guiding signe) by a scribe not found elsewhere, see Appendix B*   ^b *For B's lower marginal addition here (with guiding signes) by a scribe not found elsewhere, see Appendix B*   ^c *capitals are used for each initial of the dates C* ^{d-d} ipso die *HL*   ^{e-e} *written over erasure C*²   ^{f-f} *written over erasure C*²

---

[1] ASC does not record Wulfstan's death which was commemorated at Worcester on 20 Jan. WM *Vita Wulfstani*, pp. 61, 67, gives the day as Saturday, 19 Jan. 'paulo post mediam noctem'. As noted in *Vita Wulfstani*, p. xliii n. 1, Saturday in 1095 was 20 Jan. and the

[1095] The revered and admirable Wulfstan, bishop of the holy church of Worcester, from adolescence devoted to godly service, after making many strenuous and holy efforts to serve God assiduously with great reverence and humility of spirit in the hope of attaining the glories of the heavenly kingdom, died on the night of the seventh day of the week, 18 January, about the middle of the seventh hour, in the 5299th year from the day of Creation, following the undoubted calculation of holy scripture, the 529th year of the ninth great cycle, the 476th year of the ninth cycle from the beginning of the world, the 1084th year from the Passion of Our Lord on the Gospel reckoning, the 1066th year according to Bede's chronicle, the 1061st year according to Dionysius, the 745th year from the coming of the English, the 498th year from the coming of St Augustine, the 103rd year from the death of Archbishop Oswald, the 32nd year of the eleventh great paschal cycle, the 510th year of the tenth cycle since the beginning of the world, the fourth year of the second solar cycle, the third year of the bissextile cycle, the thirteenth year of the second decennovenal cycle, the tenth year of the second lunar cycle, the fifth of the hendecad [eleven-year period], the third indiction, the eighteenth lustre [five-year period] of his life, the third year of the seventh lustre of his pontificate. In the very hour of his death, he miraculously appeared at the town called Cricklade in a vision to Robert, bishop of Hereford, a friend to whom he was particularly attached, and commanded him to hasten to Worcester to bury him. God did not allow anyone to pull off from his finger the ring with which he had received episcopal consecration so that the holy man should not mislead his people in death since he had very often predicted that he would never lose it either whilst alive or even on the day of his burial.[1] On 4 April, stars appeared in the night falling, as it were, from the sky.[2] Walter, bishop of Albano, legate of the holy Roman see, sent by Pope Urban, came to England before Easter, bearing with him the pallium which King William had sent for the year before. He placed it, as agreed, on the altar of the Saviour at Canterbury on Sunday, 10 June. It was taken up by

weekdays given in *Vita Wulfstani*, p. 61, and here by JW were therefore wrong. JW's characteristically elaborate dating system is not internally consistent since 745 years from the coming of the English gives 1195 not 1095. WM *Vita Wulfstani*, pp. 62–3, reports Robert's vision of Wulfstan and the tale of the immovable ring, and locates it at the royal court, which was presumably held at Cricklade.

[2] ASC is slightly fuller on these falling stars. It dates them 'to the eve' (3 Apr.) 'of St Ambrose'.

delatum, ab Anselmo assumptum est, atque ab omnibus pro reuerentia sancti Petri suppliciter deosculatum.[f] [3] Vir magne religionis, Herefordensis episcopus Rotbertus, .vi. kal. Iul., feria .iii. obiit. Huic predictus Wigornensis episcopus Wlstanus, tricesimo die postquam de hoc seculo migrauit, denuo in uisione apparuit, eumque pro sui negligentia et ignauia acriter corripuit, ammonuitque ut tam de sue uite quam sibi subiectorum emendatione, quam uigilantissime posset, studeret, quod si faceret, dicebat eum omnium peccaminum a Deo posse ueniam cito promereri, adiunxitque quod non diu in cathedra qua tunc sedebat, sedem haberet, sed secum, si uigilantior esse uellet, coram Deo conuiuari deberet. Fuerant enim hi ambo patres nimia karitate in Dei dilectione, et ad se inuicem coniuncti, ideoque credi fas est, ipsum qui prius de hoc seculo ad Deum migrauit, sollicitudinem egisse sui dilectissimi, quem in hoc seculo reliquit, et ut quam citius simul ante Deum gauderent operam dedisse.[4] [5]Northymbrensis comes Rotbertus de Mulbrei et Willelmus de Ouue, cum multis aliis, regem Willelmum regno uitaque priuare, et filium amite illius, Stephanum de Albamarno, conati sunt regem constituere, sed frustra, nam ea re cognita, rex exercitum de tota Anglia congregato, castellum predicti comitis Rotberti, ad ostium Tine fluminis situm, per duos menses obsedit, et interim, quadam munitiuncula expugnata, ferme omnes meliores comitis milites cepit, et in custodiam posuit, dein obsessum castellum expugnauit, et fratrem comitis, et equites, quos intus inueniebat, custodie tradidit.[6] Post hec ante Bebbanbyrig, id est, urbem Bebbe regine, in quam comes fugerat, castellum firmauit, idque Malueisin nominauit, et in illo militibus positis, in Suthymbriam rediit. Post cuius discessum, comiti Rotberto uigiles Noui Castelli promisere in id se permissuros illum intrare, si ueniret occulte. Ille autem letus effectus, quadam nocte cum .xxx. militibus ut id peragere exiuit. Quo cognito, equites qui castellum custodiebant illum insequentes, eius exitum custodibus

---

[3] Eadmer, *HN* ii (pp. 68, 72–3). JW's original text was presumably like ASC's, which dates Bishop Walter's arrival 'towards Easter' (25 Mar.) and his handing of the pallium to Anselm 'on Whitsunday' (13 May). JW's reference to William having requested the pallium in the previous year is paralleled neither in ASC nor in Eadmer. Eadmer, *HN* ii (p. 69), says that Walter arrived 'nonnullis diebus ante Pentecosten' (13 May), a more likely date than ASC's 'towards 25 Mar.' (see Eadmer, *VA* xvi (p. 87 n. 2), but his date of 10 June for Anselm's receiving the pallium (which JW borrows) is a fortnight too late (ibid.)

[4] Neither in his *GP* nor in his *Vita Wulfstani* does WM record this second vision, which was probably derived from local sources.

[5] JW's account of the rebellion of Robert of Mowbray is close to ASC with the differences shown. They differ widely on the antecedents and aims of the rebellion, ASC

Anselm and humbly kissed by all out of reverence for St Peter.[3] The most devout Bishop Robert of Hereford died on Tuesday, 26 June. Bishop Wulfstan of Worcester, thirty days after his own death, appeared again to Robert in a vision, sharply reproved him for his negligence and idleness, and admonished him to apply himself as vigilantly as possible in the correction of his own life and those of his flock. He said that if he did this he might quickly gain pardon from God for all his sins, and added that he would not have the episcopal chair on which he now sat for much longer, but that, if he were more vigilant, he would feast with him before God. These two fathers had such great affection in their love for God, and were so attached to each other that it is to be believed that he who first departed this world to God, would show full solicitude for his most cherished friend left behind in this world, and would seek that they might both rejoice before God as soon as possible.[4] [5]Robert de Mowbray, earl of Northumbria, and William of Eu with many others attempted to deprive King William of his life and of his kingdom, and to set up as king the son of his aunt, Stephen of Aumale. They did so in vain, for as soon as the plan was known, the king assembled an army from all England, and besieged the said Earl Robert's castle at the mouth of the Tyne for two months. During this time he reduced a small fort, took captive nearly all the earl's best knights, and put them in custody. At length he stormed the besieged castle, and placed in captivity the earl's brother, and the horsemen he found inside the castle.[6] After this he built a castle before Bamburgh that is, the city of Queen Bebba, to which the earl had fled. This castle he called *Malveisin*, and, garrisoning it, he returned to Southumbria. After William's departure, those who guarded Newcastle promised Earl Robert that they would admit him if he came secretly. Robert was glad at the offer, and at night he went out with thirty knights to do this. When they discovered this the knights watching over the castle pursued him, and informed the garrison of Newcastle through

saying that Robert's failure to attend the court meetings at Winchester and Windsor precipitated William's expedition against him, but it does not give the conspirators' aims nor number William of Eu among them at this point. On Robert of Mowbray, see above, 1088 n. 2. For the hostile Durham view, see *De miraculis et translationibus Sancti Cuthberti* c. xiii (SD ii. 345–6).

[6] The details of the sieges and capture of strongpoints and men are particularly close to ASC. 'Munitiuncula' (for ASC's 'fæsten') is presumably the Morpeth guarded by William of Merlay which Gaimar (ll. 6144–50) mentions. JW contributes the duration of the siege of Tynemouth. Barlow, *William Rufus*, p. 351, argues that there was no castle at Tynemouth and that ASC and JW were both referring to Newcastle.

Noui Castelli per nuntios intimauerunt. Quod ille nesciens, die Dominica temptauit peragere cepta, sed nequiuit, deprehensus enim erat. Eapropter ad monasterium sancti Osuuini regis et martyris fugit, ubi sexto die obsessionis sue grauiter in crure est uulneratus, dum suis aduersariis repugnaret, quorum multi perempti, multi sunt uulnerati, de suis quoque nonnulli uulnerati, omnes sunt capti, ille uero in ecclesiam fugit, de qua extractus, in custodiam est positus.[7] Interea Walenses castellum Muntgumri fregerunt, et Hugonis Scrobbesbyrie comitis homines in illo nonnullos occiderunt. Vnde rex iratus, expeditionem cito mandauit, et post festiuitatem sancti Michaelis exercitum in Waloniam duxit, ibique homines et equos quamplures perdidit.[8] Qui inde reuersus, comitem Rotbertum ad Bebbanbyrig duci et eius oculos erui iussit, nisi uxor illius ac propinquus eius Moreal castrum redderent. Qua necessitate compulsi, castellum reddiderunt. Comes autem forti custodie mancipandus ad Windlesoram est ductus, Moreal uero facte traditionis causam regi detexit.[9]

[C³B]

[g]In Wigornensi pago, in diocesi predicti Wlstani episcopi est monasterium quod dicitur *Eouesham*, a sancto *Ecgwino*, .iii. *Wigorn*ensi *presule*, olim constructum.[10]

De Perscora.

Est et aliud quod Perscore uocatur ab Oswaldo ministro et propinquo regis Merciorum, sancti Æthelredi, in honore sancti Petri constructum. Et hoc usque ad nostra tempora. Nunc autem in nomine Dei

---

[g-g] *add. in mg. by C³ on p. 360, om. HLP*

[7] ASC is much briefer, relating Robert's escape from Bamburgh towards Tynemouth, and his being attacked, wounded, and captured by the garrison of the 'New Castle'. The treachery of the 'vigiles' of the 'New Castle', the alerting of the 'custodes' of the same castle to Robert's escape from Bamburgh, the number of Robert's knightly companions, and the duration of the siege of the monastery at Tynemouth are JW's contributions. JW seems to distinguish a 'nouum castellum' (presumably Newcastle) from a 'castellum' (which was perhaps *Malveisin* or just possibly Bamburgh). In ASC Robert flees to Tynemouth, in JW to the monastery of Tynemouth. Van Caenegem, *English Lawsuits*

messengers of his flight. Robert did not know this and tried on Sunday to carry out the plan, but in vain for he was intercepted. He therefore fled to the monastery of St Oswine king and martyr. There on the sixth day of the siege he was seriously wounded in the leg while resisting his enemies, of whom many were slain and many wounded. Several of his own men also were wounded, and all were taken captive. He himself fled to the church, from which he was taken out and placed under guard.[7] Meantime the Welsh stormed the castle of Montgomery, and there slew many of Earl Hugh of Shrewsbury's men. This angered the king, he quickly mounted an expeditionary force, and after the feast of St Michael [29 September] led an army into Wales, there losing many men and horses.[8] When William had returned from Wales, he ordered Earl Robert to be taken to Bamburgh and his eyes to be put out unless his wife and her kinsman, Moreal, surrendered the castle. Forced by extreme need, they yielded the castle up. The earl was led to Windsor and closely confined, Moreal disclosing the source of the treason to the king.[9]

In the Worcester region, in the diocese of the said Bishop Wulfstan, there is a monastery called Evesham which was formerly built by St Ecgwine, the third bishop of Worcester.[10]

Concerning Pershore.

There is another monastery called Pershore which was founded in honour of St Peter by Oswald, the thegn and kinsman of St Æthelred, the Mercian king. It survives to this day,

---

from William I to Richard I (above, 1070 n. 10), i. no. 143 (pp. 113–17), printed and translated the texts dealing with this revolt and the subsequent trials.

[8] ASC in addition mentions the assembly of William's army at Snowdon on Nov. 1 after striking deep into Wales, and Welsh evasive tactics in the face of William's attack. The phrase describing William's losses repeats almost exactly that at the end of JW's 1094 annal, and there is nothing comparable in ASC. *AC* (year indeterminate) and *Brut* Pen. (pp. 19–20) and Her. (pp. 34–5) 1093 (*recte* 1095) refer to William's unsuccessful expedition in mid-autumn; BS 1097 (*recte* 1095) (pp. 88–9) has a more elaborate text without a specific date. See Lloyd, *History of Wales*, ii. 405–6.

[9] JW is more succinct than ASC here. ASC reports William's proclamation summoning all landholders to his next court.   [10] WM *GP* iv. 160 (p. 296).

genitricis Marie dedicatum constat.

De Malvernia.

Increuit etiam nostris temporibus[h] *in eadem prouincia Malvernense monasterium quod* nobis *per antifrasin uidetur sortitum esse uocabulum. Non enim ibi male sed bene et pulch*re *religio uernat, ubi ad immortale⟨m⟩ spem[i] ⟨et⟩ commodum mortalium rerum penuria monachos trahit et animat.*[11]

De Gloecestra.

In eadem diocesi in Glaornensi prouincia est monasterium Glaucestre dictum quod Osric minister et propinquus regis Æthelredi et frater prefati Oswaldi fundauit.

De Wincelcumbe.

Est et *monasterium Wincelcumbe* nominatum *in eodem pago* situm.[12]

De Teodekesberie.

Monasterium etiam quod *Teo*de*kesberie* dicitur eadem in prouincia habetur. Quod Teodocus quidam nomine quondam construxit a quo idem locus ut sic uocaretur nomen accepit. Quod etiam processu temporis *Rotbertus, filius Haimonis, fauore suo prouexit nec facile memoratu quantum exaltauit.* In quo uidelicet cenobio consilio domni Wlstani Wigornensis episcopi Wintoniensis monachus

---

[h] *MS D of WM (GP) has* temporibus   [i] semper *CB*

and is now dedicated to the name of the Mother of God.

Concerning Malvern.

In our day the monastery of Malvern was added in the same Mercian province. Its name appears to us to be the opposite of what it is. For in that place a good and beautiful (not evil) religious life springs up where the dearth of earthly goods tugs and inspires the monks towards eternal and beneficial hope.[11]

Concerning Gloucester.

In the same diocese in Gloucestershire is the monastery of Gloucester which the thegn Osric, a kinsman of King Æthelred, and brother of the said Oswald founded.

Concerning Winchcombe.

There is a monastery called Winchcombe in the same province.[12]

Concerning Tewkesbury.

In the same province there is also a monastery called Tewkesbury. A certain Theodocus built it some time ago. The place took its name from him. In the course of time Robert fitz Haimo enlarged it with his bounty and it is not easy to relate how much he raised it up. In this monastery, on the lord Bishop Wulfstan of Worcester's advice, the Winchester monk Gerald,

[11] WM *GP* iv. 158 (p. 296).
[12] WM *GP* iv. 156 (p. 294).

Geroldus eiusdem ecclesie abbas
monachos qui erant *apud Crone-*
*burg*am^*j* locauit. *Teodekesberia*
dicitur quasi Theotokesberia, id
est Dei genitricis curia.^*g* 13

[1096] (.xl.) 1118   Dunholmensis episcopus Willelmus apud Windlesoram, in curia regis, kal. Ian., feria .iii.,^*a* obiit, sed Dunholmi est
sepultus.[1] Octauis Epiphanie apud Searesbyriam celebrato concilio,
Willelmi de Ouue in duellio uicti oculos eruere et testiculos
abscidere, et dapiferum illius Wilelmum de Alderi,^*b* filium amite
illius, traditionis conscium, iussit rex suspendi, comitem uero
Odonem de Campania, predicti scilicet Stephani^*c* patrem, Philippum
Rogeri Scrobbesbyriensis comitis filium, et quosdam alios traditionis
participes, in custodiam posuit.[2] Vrbanus papa uenit in Galliam, et
apud Clarum Montem, Quadragesimali tempore, sinodo celebrata,
ad Turcos, Sarracenos, Turcopolos, aliosque paganos debellandos,
p. 361   Ierusalem profi|cisci hortatus est Christianos. Cuius hortatu, mox in
ipsa sinodo comes sancti Egidii Raimundus, et cum eo multi alii,
cruce Christi signati, peregrinationem se pro Deo subituros, et quod
suaserat peracturos spoponderunt. Quibus auditis, de Italia, Ger-
mania, Gallia, Anglia, ceteri Christiani ad eandem profectionem
certatim se parauere, quorum duces et primates extitere Podiensis
episcopus,^*d* Ostiensis episcopus^*e* cum aliis episcopis quampluribus,
Petrus monachus, Hugo Magnus, Philippi regis Francorum germanus, dux Lothariensis Godefridus, Carnotensis comes Stephanus,
Normannorum comes Rotbertus, Flandrensis comes Rotbertus, duo
germani Godefridi ducis, Bononiensis comes Eustatius et Balduuinus, predictus comes Raimundus, Beomundus Rotberti Wiscardi
filius.[3] Samson Wigornensis episcopus ab Anselmo Dorubernie

---

^*j* Craneburnan *B*

^*a* *over erasure* C, .iiii. *HP*   ^*b* Aldari *HL*   ^*c* om. *HL*   ^*d* *gap (in C an*
erasure) after episcopus *CBHL*   ^*e* *big gap after* episcopus *CBHL*

---

[13] WM *GP* iv. 157 (p. 295).

[1] This agrees with ASC, which, however, does not record William's burial place. *HDE*
iv. 10 (i. 134) and *HR* (SD ii. 226) give 2 Jan. as his day of death, the former giving a long
account of his death and burial. See Greenway, *Fasti* ii. 29.

[2] These punishments are in ASC. ASC describes William of Eu as the king's kinsman
('mæg') and names Geoffrey Barnard, his accuser and conqueror in the duel. JW's
'Stephani patrem' is a different relationship from ASC's 'þæs cynges aðum'. Philip of
Shrewsbury is not named in ASC, which speaks in general of 'others being taken to

> abbot of the same church, placed
> the monks who were at Cran-
> borne. The name of Tewkesbury
> is almost *Theotokesberia*, that is
> the court of the Mother of
> God.[13]

[1096] William, bishop of Durham, died at the royal court at
Windsor on Tuesday, 1 January, but was buried at Durham.[1] In the
octave of the Epiphany [13 January], at the council held at Salisbury,
the king ordered William of Eu who had been defeated in a duel to
have his eyes put out and to be castrated, and his steward, William of
Aldrie, the son of his aunt, and privy to his treason, to be hanged. He
also imprisoned Odo, count of Champagne, father of the said
Stephen, Philip, son of Roger, earl of Shrewsbury, and other
accomplices in the treason.[2] Pope Urban came to Gaul and held a
council at Clermont during Lent and urged Christians to set out for
Jerusalem to fight the Turks, Saracens, Turcopoles and other
heathen. In response to his exhortation, directly in the same council,
Raymond, count of St Giles, and many others, taking the cross of
Christ, promised to undertake the *peregrinatio* for God and to do what
the pope asked. On this news other Christians in Italy, Germany,
France, and England began to vie with each other in their prepara-
tions. Among their leaders were the bishop of Le Puy, the bishop of
Ostia with many other bishops, Peter the monk, Hugh the Great,
brother of Philip, the French king, Duke Godfrey of Lorraine,
Stephen, count of Chartres, Robert, the duke of Normandy,
Robert, count of Flanders, the two brothers of Duke Godfrey,
Eustace, count of Boulogne, and Baldwin, the said Count Raymond,
Bohemond, son of Robert Guiscard.[3] Samson, bishop of Worcester,

London and mutilated there'. WM *GR* iv. 319 (ii. 372) and *Chronica de Hyda*, pp. 301–2,
attest William of Aldrie's blamelessness. OV *HE* viii. 23 (iv. 284) suggests that William's
sentence was instigated by Hugh, earl of Chester, because of William's infidelity to his
wife, Hugh's sister.

  [3] ASC refers to the crusading movement in general terms. It is difficult to establish
JW's sources for his crusading annals, but there are some errors here. The council of
Clermont took place in Nov. 1095, and the source of JW's error in dating it to Lent 1096 is
unknown. JW's inclusion of Turcopoles among the Crusaders' adversaries, and of a bishop
of Ostia (presumably Odo II) and other bishops among the departing crusaders, is not
supported elsewhere. These bishops apart, JW's list of crusaders agrees with that in other
sources, e.g. OV *HE* ix. 3 (v. 30–7), though additional names are also found elsewhere.
Raymond of St Giles sent envoys to the council, but did not attend himself (Hagenmeyer,
pp. 10–11).

arciepiscopo, Lundonie, in ecclesia sancti Pauli .xvii. kal. Iul., dominica die, consecratur.[4] Post hec comes Nortmannorum Rotbertus, cum
Ierusalem proficisci cum aliis animo proponeret, nuntiis in Angliam
missis, germanum suum regem Wilelmum petiit, ut, inter se pace
redintegrata, illi .x. milia marcas argenti prestaret, et ab eo Normanniam in uadimonium acciperet, qui mox petitioni eius satisfacere
gestiens, indixit maioribus Anglie, ut quisque illorum pro posse sibi
pecuniam festinanter accommodaret. Iccirco episcopi, abbates,
abbatisse, aurea et argentea ecclesie ornamenta fregerunt, comites,
barones, uicecomites, suos milites et uillanos spoliauerunt, et regi non
modicam summam auri et argenti detulerunt. Ille autem mense
Septembri mare transiit, pacem cum germano fecit, .vi. milia .dclxvi.
libras illi prestitit, et ab eo Normannia in uadimonium accepit.[5]

[1097] (.xli.) 1119 Rex Anglorum Willelmus Quadragesimali tempore Angliam rediit, et post Pasca cum equestri et pedestri exercitu
secundo profectus est in Waloniam, ut omnes masculini sexus
internitioni daret, at de eis uix aliquem capere aut interimere
potuit, sed de suis nonnullos, et equos perdidit multos.[1] Post hec
clitonem Eadgarum ad Scottiam cum exercitu misit, ut in ea
consobrinum suum Eadgarum, Malcolmi regis filium, patruo suo
Dufenaldo, qui regnum inuaserat, expulso, regem constitueret.[2]
Christiani ceperunt Niceam ciuitatem .xiii. kal. Iul. sabbato.[3] Stella
que cometis dicitur, .iii. kal. Octob. per .xv. dies apparuit. Nonnulli

---

[4] Eadmer, *HN* ii (p. 74), says Samson was ordained priest on 7 June, and bishop the next day. 8 June, like JW's 15, was a Sunday in 1096.

[5] In a single sentence ASC speaks very generally of the reconciliation between king and duke after the exchange of Normandy for an unspecified sum of money. It does not say how it was raised nor that William went to Normandy in Sept. (*Regesta* i. 377, 377a indicate William's presence at Hastings in Sept. before the crossing, and OV *HE* x. 4 (v. 208) confirms the month.) Eadmer, *HN* ii (pp. 74–5), and Hugh of Flavigny, *Chronicon* ii (MGH SS viii. 475), say the bargain was to last 3 years, Torigni (*GND* viii. 7 (ii. 211)) for as long as Robert was away, and OV *HE* ix. 3, x. 4, x. 12 (v. 26–7, 208–9, 278–81) says William was to hold Normandy for 5 years. The final meeting between king and duke took place at Rouen (OV *HE* x. 8 (v. 22)). Eadmer, *HN* ii (pp. 74–5) in general, and WM *GP* v. 271 (p. 432), specifically in relation to Jumièges, graphically describe the exactions from churches to raise the money. ASC reports Robert and his followers spending the winter in Apulia.

[1] ASC dates William's return to Easter eve, which can barely be reconciled with JW's 'quadragesimale tempore'. JW seems to render only part of the beginning of ASC's fuller account of William's invasion of Wales, which says he remained there 'between mid-summer and nearly Aug.'. JW's 'post pascha' seems confirmed by the chronology implied by Eadmer, *HN* ii (p. 77), which dates a Welsh campaign to the early part of 1097. JW's date could be based, however, on a hasty reading of ASC, which says that William began

was consecrated in London, at the church of St Paul's, on Sunday, 15 June, by Anselm, archbishop of Canterbury.[4] After this, when Duke Robert of Normandy had decided to set out with others to Jerusalem, he sent envoys to England, to ask his brother King William that they should both re-establish peace and that he would lend him 10,000 silver marks in return for Normandy in pledge. William straightaway strove to meet his request and asked the greater men of England all to furnish him with money quickly and as far as their resources allowed. Thereupon bishops, abbots, abbesses broke up their gold and silver ornaments, earls, barons, sheriffs despoiled their knights and villeins, and gave the king a large sum of gold and silver. In September, William crossed the channel, made peace with his brother, advanced him 6,666 pounds, and received Normandy from him in pledge.[5]

[1097] William, king of the English, returned to England during Lent, and after Easter [5 April] set out a second time for Wales with an army of horse and foot with the intention of killing all the male population; but he was barely able to capture or kill anyone, but lost many men and horses.[1] After this he sent the atheling Edgar to Scotland with an army in order to establish his cousin, Edgar, son of King Malcolm, as king after expelling the kingdom's usurper, Donald Bane, this Edgar's uncle.[2] The Christians took Nicaea on Saturday, 19 June.[3] The star called a comet appeared on 29 September for fifteen days. Many claimed that they had seen at

his invasion after his Easter court at Windsor. Barlow, *William Rufus*, p. 370, like Freeman before him (*Reign of William Rufus*, ii. 110–11), resolves the discrepancy in dating by postulating two campaigns. Welsh sources (*AC* 1097, *Brut* Pen. (p. 20), Her. (pp. 36–7), and BS, pp. 88–9) speak of only one expedition in 1097, which *AC*, Pen., and Her. describe as William's second, his first being that of 1095. Such a description could lie behind JW's 'secundo', though JW has two earlier expeditions in 1094 and 1095 whereas all the Welsh sources record only one (see above 1095 n. 8). It is probable therefore that William campaigned only once in Wales in 1097. ASC 1096 had reported an unsuccessful Welsh expedition led by the 'chief men in this country'.

   [2] ASC places this at the end of annal 1097, and dates the invasion to 'after Michaelmas'. Two writs, apparently issued during William's campaign in Northumbria in 1095, seem to confirm a grant made by Edgar as king of Scotland then. As pointed out years ago by Raine, it is possible that 'Edgar assumed the title of king of Scotland and paid homage to William soon after Duncan's death' (*Facsimiles of English Writs to AD 1100*, ed. T. A. M. Bishop and P. Chaplais (Oxford, 1957), pl. viiia, no. 9). See also the discussion of this grant in A. A. M. Duncan, 'The earliest Scottish charters', *Scottish Historical Review* xxxvii (1958), 103–35, at pp. 103–18. Donald Bane is assigned three years for his second reign in Scottish King Lists (see M. O. Anderson, *Kings and Kingship in Early Scotland* (Edinburgh, 1980), p. 75). ASC dates his return to 1094.

   [3] 19 June was a Friday in 1097.

signum mirabile et quasi ardens, in modum crucis, eo tempore se uidisse in celo affirmabant.[4] Mox inter regem et Dorubernensem archiepiscopum Anselmum orta dissensione, quia ex quo archipresul effectus est, synodum tenere et praua, que per Angliam pullulauerant, non licuit corrigere. Mare transiit, et ad tempus in Gallia mansit, et post ad papam Vrbanum Romam perrexit.[5] Rex autem, circa festiuitatem sancti Andree, de Anglia Nortmanniam profectus est.[6] Eximie uir religionis, monasterii sancti Eadmundi abbas, Balduuinus, genere Gallus,[a] artis medicine bene peritus, .iiii.[b] kal. Ian., feria .iii.,[c] in bona senectute decessit, et in medio choro principalis ecclesie sepultus requiescit.[d][7]

[1098] (.xlii.) 1020   Wintoniensis episcopus Walcelinus, .iii. non. Ianuarii, die Dominica, obiit.[1] Et abbas monasterii sancti Petri de Burh, Turoldus, et abbas Noui Monasterii, Rotbertus, obierunt.[2] Estatis tempore rex Anglorum Willelmus iunior ciuitatem que Cinomannis uocatur, magnamque partem illius prouincie per uim sue dicioni subegit.[3] Interea comites Hugo de Legeceastra,[a] et Hugo de Scrobbesbyria Meuaniam insulam, que consuete uocitatur Anglesege, cum exercitu adierunt, et multos Walanorum quos in ea ceperant occiderunt, quosdam uero, manibus uel pedibus truncatis, testiculisque abscisis, excecauerunt. Quendam etiam prouecte etatis presbiterum, nomine Cenredum, a quo Walani in iis que agebant consilium accipiebant, de ecclesia extraxerunt, et eius testiculis abscisis et uno oculo eruto, linguam illius absciderunt, sed die tertia, miseratione diuina illi reddita est loquela. Eo tempore rex Norreganorum Magnus, filius regis Olaui, filii regis Haroldi

[a] *For B's marginal addition here by a hand not found elsewhere, see Appendix B*   [b] .ii. *interlin. over* .ii. *C,* .ii. *HL (G)*   [c] .iii. *C (over erasure) BP,* .vi. *HL (G)*   [d] *For the addition in L and by* P[5] *(in the mg.), see Appendix A*

[a] Ceastra *HL*

[4] Sources differ on the starting date of this comet: 1 Oct. (JW, WM *GR* iv. 328 (ii. 376), Bermondsey Annals (*Ann. Mon.* iii. 429)), 2 Oct. (Margam Annals (*Ann. Mon.* i. 6)), 4 Oct. (ASC, Waverley Annals (*Ann. Mon.* ii. 206)), and 5 Oct. (Plympton Annals (*UAG*, p. 26)); and on its duration: 1 week or so (ASC, Waverley), 15 days (JW, WM, Bermondsey, Margam). ASC, WM, Waverley and Margam describe its nocturnal progress through the sky, but none refer to a celestial burning cross.
[5] ASC describes the reasons for Anselm's discontent differently, and says simply that he went 'overseas'. Eadmer, *HN* ii (pp. 78–97), is very much fuller and shows that Anselm left on 8 Nov. 1097 and did not reach Rome until Apr. 1098.
[6] ASC dates William's departure to 11 Nov., and laments on the damage caused by his

that time a wondrous sign in the sky, apparently on fire and in the shape of a cross.[4] There arose immediately dissension between the king and Anselm, archbishop of Canterbury, because from the time he had become archbishop he had not been allowed to hold a synod nor to correct the evil practices which had multiplied in England. Anselm crossed the sea, remained a while in France, and afterwards went to Pope Urban in Rome.[5] The king himself set out for Normandy from England on the feast of St Andrew [29 November].[6] Baldwin, a most devout man, abbot of the monastery of St Edmund, in origin from France, well skilled in medicine, died at a great age, on Tuesday, 29 December, and lies buried in the middle of the choir of the main church.[7]

[1098] Walkelin, bishop of Winchester, died on Sunday, 3 January.[1] Thurold, abbot of Peterborough, and Robert, abbot of Hyde, also died.[2] In the summer William the Younger, the English king, by force reduced the city of Le Mans and most of its province to his rule.[3] Meanwhile Hugh, earl of Leicester, and Hugh, earl of Shrews- bury, with an armed force invaded the Mevanian island, which is usually called Anglesey, and killed many Welshmen taken prisoner there, blinding some, cutting off their hands and arms, and castrating them. They seized from his church a priest of advanced years, Cenred by name, to whom the Welsh turned for advice with their plans, castrated him, putting out one eye, and cutting off his tongue, but by God's mercy, speech was restored to him three days later. At that time Magnus, king of the Norwegians, son of king Olaf, himself

household, and on the year made severe by bad weather, calamitous taxes, and the burden of public works at London.

[7] The original weekday was correct for 31 Dec. 1098, but C[3]'s Tuesday is correct for the revised day of death, 29 Dec. 1097, a date confirmed by London BL Harl. 743 fo. 1 (printed *Mon.* iii. 155; see *Heads*, p. 32). ASC's date (1098 (*recte* 1097)) is 'about Christmastime', but it does not mention Baldwin's origins, his medical experience or his burial place.

[1] ASC 1098 (*recte* 1097) dates the death to 'about Christmastime'. Greenway, *Fasti* ii. 85 notes that Winchester obits confirm JW's 3 Jan. as the day of death. 3 Jan. was a Saturday in 1098.

[2] ASC gives Turold's death in this year but JW is the only source for Robert Losinga's death in 1098 (see *Heads*, p. 82).

[3] OV *HE* x. 8 (v. 244–6) reports the capture of Le Mans by William in the third week of July, a date which 'agrees approximately with the St Aubin Annals' statement that Fulk le Rechin's rule, which began in Le Mans on 1 May, lasted for 3 months' (OV *HE* v. 245 n. 5). See Barlow, *William Rufus*, pp. 376–91 for William's campaigns in the Vexin and Maine in 1098. JW's brief notice here is the only known English reference to them.

Haruagri, Orcadas et Meuanias insulas cum suo adiecisset imperio, paucis nauibus aduectus illuc uenit. At cum ad terram rates appellere uellet, comes Hugo de Scrobbesbyria, multis armatis militibus in ipsa maris ripa illi occurrit, et, ut fertur, mox ab ipso rege sagitta percussus, die .vii. quo crudelitatem in prefatum exercuerat presbiterum interiit.[4] Antiochia ciuitas a Christianis .iii. non. Iunii, | feria .iiii., capta est, in qua, paucis diebus transactis, *lancea* qua mundi *Saluator in crucis pendens patibulo uulneratus fuit*, Andrea apostolo, sanctorum mitissimo, reuelante, in *ecclesia* sancti *Petri apostoli inuen*ta est. Cuius inuentione Christiani animati, .iiii. kal. Iul., feria .ii., secum illam deferentes, de ciuitate exierunt, et cum paganis prelio commisso, *Curbaram princip*em *militie Soldani Persie*, et *Turcos, Arabes, Sarracenos, Publicanos, Azimatos, Persas, Agulanos, et alias multas gentes* in ore gladii fugantes, multis milibus ex eis occisis, Dei uirtute plenam uictoriam habuerunt.[5] Splendor insolitus per totam fere noctem, .v. kal. Octob., emicuit.[6] Eodem anno ossa regis et martiris Canuti de tumulo leuata, in scrinio honorifice sunt collocata.[7][b] *Rogerius dux Apulie, adunato grandi exercitu, Capuanam ciuitatem a sua ditione resilientem obsedit.*[8] Vrbanus papa comitante secum Dorubernensi arciepiscopo Anselmo, ut illi mandarat, ad *concili*um *quod apud Barum kal. Octob. celebrar*i *constitui*t, proficiscitur, *in quo concilio plurima de fide catholica* ab apostolico diserta sunt *facunda ratione.*[c] *Vbi etiam mota questio*ne *ex parte Grecorum, euangelica auctoritate probare uolentium Spiritum Sanctum processionem non habere nisi tantum a patre*, prefatus *Anselmus sic*ut *de negotio tractauit, disseruit, absoluit, ut in ipso conuentu nemo existeret, qui non inde sibi satisfactum consentiret.*[b][9]

[b-b] *written in left mg. by C¹ with signes*   [c] *oratione HL*

---

[4] ASC simply records the killing of Earl Hugh of Shrewsbury at Anglesey 'fram utwikingan' and Robert of Bellême's succession to Hugh. The miracle of 'Cenred' the priest seems to be JW's own contribution, though the reference in Gir. Cambr. vi. 129 (*Itin.* ii. 7) to Earl Hugh's using the church at Llandyfrydog as a kennel for his dogs, if not directly related, reports retribution striking Hugh 'infra mensem'. Welsh sources confirm some of the events reported: the arrival of Vikings in Anglesey (*AC s.a.* 1098 and *Brut s.a.* 1096 (*recte* 1098)); refer to the invasion by Magnus 'king of Germany' (Pen. p. 21, Her. pp. 36–7; 'king of Norway' in BS, pp. 90–1); the counter attack of the two Hughs (*AC*); and the slaying of Earl Hugh of Shrewsbury (*AC* version C, *Brut* Her. p. 37, BS, pp. 90–1). See discussion in Lloyd, *History of Wales*, ii. 408–10. OV *HE* x. 6 (v. 222–4) and WM *GR* iv. 329 (ii. 376) give slightly discordant accounts of Hugh's campaigns, though WM clearly shares some details with JW. Magnus Barefoot was king of Norway 1093–1103. His father was Harold Hardrada, not Harold Fairhair.

son of Harold Fairhair, added the Orkneys and the Mevanian islands
to his rule, and came there with a few ships. When he tried to beach
his ships, Hugh, earl of Shrewsbury, met him on that same shore
with many armed troops, and, as it is reported, struck by an arrow
from the king's own bow, died seven days after he had barbarously
treated the said priest.[4] The city of Antioch was captured by the
Christians on Thursday, 3 June. There the lance by which the
Saviour of the world hanging on the cross was wounded, was
found in the church of St Peter the apostle, through the revelation
of St Andrew, the most merciful of saints. Strengthened by this
discovery, the Christians, carrying it with them on Monday, 28 June,
went out from the city, and engaged the heathen in battle, and by a
divine miracle gained a complete victory, putting to flight at sword
point Kerbogha, prince of the Persian Sultan's troops, and Turks,
Arabs, Saracens, Paulicians, Azymites, Persians, Agulani, and many
other peoples, and killing many thousands of them.[5] There was an
unusual light in the sky through all the night on 27 September.[6] In
the same year the bones of the king and martyr Cnut were raised
from their tomb, and placed with honour in a shrine.[7] Roger, duke of
Apulia, assembled a large army, and besieged the city of Capua,
which resisted his rule.[8] Pope Urban, accompanied by Anselm,
archbishop of Canterbury, as he had commanded, set out for the
council at Bari which he had fixed for 1 October. There was much
eloquent discussion by the apostolic pope of the catholic faith. The
question was raised by the Greeks who wanted to prove on the
authority of the Gospels that the Holy Spirit proceeded from the
Father alone. The said Anselm debated the question, expounded it,
and brought it to a conclusion in such a way that everyone present at
the council was satisfied upon the point.[9]

[5] *GF*, pp. 59, 65 and 49, which could have been the ultimate source of the italicized
words. JW, like OV *HE* ix. 9 (v. 92–3) and BD (*RHC Occ.* iv. 58), wrongly gives Wednesday
(not Thursday) as the weekday for the capture of Antioch.

[6] ASC and following it the Waverley Annals (*Ann. Mon.* ii. 207), date the celestial
phenomenon to 'before Michaelmas', and mention the taxes and rain which made 1098
oppressive.

[7] The elevation of Cnut's bones to a shrine took place 8 years and 9 months after his
martyrdom: see Ælnoth, *Historia Sancti Canuti*, in *Vitæ Sanctorum Danorum* (above, 1076
n. 1), i. 133–4. This is not in ASC.

[8] Eadmer, *HN* ii (p. 97). This campaign took place in the summer of 1098 (Meyer von
Knonau, *Jahrbücher*, v. 41).

[9] Eadmer, *HN* ii (pp. 104, 106). The council of Bari took place from 3 to 10 Oct. (Meyer
von Knonau, *Jahrbücher*, v. 53–5).

[**1099**] (.xliii.) 1121   *ª Vrbanus papa .iii. ebdomada Pasce, magnum concilium* tenuit Rome, *in quo recisis reciden*dis, *et statutis* statuendis *in aduersarios sancte ecclesie, excommunicationis sententiam* in *omnes laicos inuestituras ecclesiarum dantes, et omnes easdem inuestituras de manibus illorum accipientes, nec*non *omnes in officium sic dati honoris huiusmodi consecrantes, cum toto concilio papa intorsit. Eos* quoque *anathematis uinculo colligauit, qui pro ecclesiasticis honoribus laicorum hominum homines fiunt, dicens, nimis execrabile uideri,* ut *manus que in tantam eminentiam excreuer*ant, *ut quod nulli angelorum concessum est, Deum cuncta creantem suo* signaculo *creent, et eundem ipsum pro redemptione et salute totius mundi, summi Dei patris optutibus offerant, in hanc* ignorantiam *detrud*antur, *ut ancille fiant earum manuum que die ac nocte obscenis* contactibus *inquinantur,* siue *rapinis ac iniuste sanguinum effusioni addicte commaculantur. 'Fiat, fiat,'* ab omnibus est clamatum, *et in his concilium consummatum. Post* hec arciepiscopus *Lugdunum* perrexit.*ª* [1]

Rex Anglorum Willelmus iunior in Angliam de Normannia rediit, et festiuitate Pentecostes Lundonie curiam suam tenuit, ac Rannulfo, quem negotiorum totius regni exactorem constituerat, Dunholmensem episcopatum dedit, quem Thomas, Eboracensis arciepiscopus, ibi mox consecrauit.[2] Idus Iulii, feria quinta, Ierusalem a Christianis capta est, et post hec .xi. kal. Aug., eadem feria, Lothariensis dux Godefridus ab omni exercitu in regem est electus.[3] Vrbanus papa, .iiii. kal. Aug., feria .v., obiit.[4] Christiani cum Amirauisso principe militie, et secundo in potestate totius regni regis Babylonie, ante ciuitatem Ascalonam, pridie idus Aug., eadem feria, bellum habentes maximum, Christo largiente, potiti sunt uictoria.[5] Pascalis, uir uenerandus, qui ab Hiltibrando papa presbiter fuerat ordinatus, a Romano populo idus Aug., electus, die sequenti, id est, .xix. kal. Sept., feria prima, in papam est consecratus.[6] *ᵇ*Tertio non. Nou.,*ᵇ*

ª⁻ª written in left mg. near opening of 1099 with signes C¹   *ᵇ⁻ᵇ written in right mg.*
and over erasure at the beginning of the next line ?C¹

---

[1] Eadmer, *HN* ii (pp. 111, 114).
[2] ASC says that the meeting (at Whitsuntide) was held at the new Westminster Hall for the first time (as does HH *HA* vii. 21 (pp. 444–6)). *HDE* First Continuation (SD i. 138) and *HR* 181 (SD ii. 230), and not ASC, say that Archbishop Thomas consecrated Ranulf at St Paul's London on 5 June.
[3] 15 and 22 July were Fridays (not Thursdays) in 1099.

[1099] Pope Urban held a great council at Rome in the third week after Easter [24–30 April]. In it some decrees were repealed, and new ones established against the church's enemies. The pope with the council's unanimous agreement declared excommunicate all laymen who gave investitures of churches, all those who received such investitures at their hands, and all who consecrated to the office of any preferment given in this way. He further excommunicated all who did homage to laymen for their ecclesiastical office, declaring it to be execrable that hands which had been so honoured as to be able to form God, creator of all things (a power granted to no angel), and which could offer the very God for the redemption and salvation of all for the contemplation of God the Father, should be debased to such infamy as to become enslaved to hands which are polluted day and night by filthy contacts or soiled by the unjust spilling of blood and by rapine. 'So be it, so be it,' all acclaimed, and with this the council ended. After this the archbishop went to Lyons.[1]

King William the Younger returned from Normandy to England, and held his court at London at Whitsun [29 May]. He gave the bishopric of Durham to Ranulf, whom he had made the executor of all the kingdom's business. Thomas, archbishop of York, consecrated him there.[2] On Thursday, 15 July, Jerusalem was captured by the Christians, and after this on Thursday, 22 July, Godfrey, duke of Lorraine, was chosen king by the whole army.[3] Pope Urban died on Thursday, 29 July.[4] The Christians fought a big battle with *Amirauisus*, second in power in the kingdom of the king of Babylon, and leader of the army, before the city of Ascalon on Thursday, 12 August, and by Christ's bounty gained a victory.[5] The venerable Paschal, who had been ordained priest by Pope Hildebrand, was elected by the Roman people on 13 August, and was consecrated pope the next day, that is, Sunday, 14 August.[6] On 3 November, the

---

[4] As sometimes elsewhere JW gives the wrong weekday: 29 July was a Friday in 1099.

[5] The victory at Ascalon is described in all crusading sources, but none accurately describes al-Afḍal Shāhānshāh, son of Badr al-Jamālī, vizier of Egypt, as 'secundo in potestate'. 'Admirauisus' is used in other sources, e.g. OV *HE* ix. 16 (v. 176). The Dictionary of Medieval Latin from British Sources tentatively suggests its origin in the Arabic term for a military commander, 'amir aj–juyūsh'.

[6] JW is the sole chronicle source for this information which is confirmed by Paschal II's letter to Hugh of Cluny (*PL* clxiii. 31) and Peter of Pisa's life (Watterich, ii. 1–2).

mare litus egreditur, et uillas et homines quamplures, boues et oues innumeras demersit.[7] Osmundus, Searesbyriensis episcopus, .iii. non. Dec., feria vi., obiit.[8]

[1100] (.xliiii.) 1122 Clemens papa, qui et Wibertus obiit.[1] ⟨I⟩dibus *Iulii, die dominica, ecclesia, quam uenerande memorie abbas Serlo a fundamentis construxerat Glauuorne, ab episcopis Samsone Wigornensi, Gundulfo Hrofensi, ᵃGerardo Herefordensi,ᵃ et Herueao Bancornensi, dedicata est magno cum honore.*[2] Deinde .iiii. non. Aug., feria .v., indictione .viii., rex Anglorum Willelmus iunior, dum in Noua Foresta, que lingua Anglorum Ytene nuncupatur, uenatu fuisset occupatus, a quodam Franco, Waltero, cognomento Tirello, sagitta incaute directa percussus, uitam finiuit, et Wintoniam delatus, in Veteri Monasterio, in ecclesia sancti Petri est tumulatus. Nec mirum, ut populi rumor affirmat, hanc proculdubio magnam Dei uirtutem esse et uindictam. Antiquis enim temporibus, Eaduuardi scilicet regis, et aliorum Anglie regum predecessorum eius, eadem regio incolis Dei cultoribus et ecclesiis nitebat uberrime, sed, iussu regis Wilelmi senioris, hominibus fugatis, domibus semirutis, ecclesiis destructis, terra ferarum tantum colebatur habitatione, et inde, ut creditur, causa erat infortunii. Nam et antea eiusdem Wilelmi iunioris germanus, Ricardus, in eadem foresta multo ante perierat, et paulo ante suus fratruelis, Ricardus, comitis scilicet Normannorum Rotberti filius, dum et ipse in uenatu fuisset, a suo milite sagitta percussus interiit. In loco quo rex occubuit, priscis temporibus ecclesia fuerat constructa, sed patris sui tempore, ut prediximus, erat diruta.[3] Eiusdem regis tempore, ut ex parte pretitulatum est, in sole, luna et stellis multa fiebant signa, mare quoque litus persepe egrediebatur, et homines et animalia summersit, uillas et domus quamplures subuertit; in pago qui Barrucscire nominatur, ante occisionem illius, sanguis de fonte tribus septimanis emanauit, multis etiam Normannis diabolus in horribili specie se frequenter

---

ᵃ⁻ᵃ om. HL

[7] Floods are reported in ASC and in the Rouen, Margam, and Bermondsey Annals (*UAG*, p. 47, *Ann. Mon.* i. 6, iii. 429) and WM *GR* iv. 330 (ii. 376), and, with the exception of the first two, are localized on the Thames. ASC, and following it the Waverley Annals (*Ann. Mon.* ii. 208), record the appearance of a new moon on the same day (ASC: 11 Nov.).
[8] ASC says that Osmund died in Advent, and Greenway, *Fasti* iv. 2 notes Salisbury evidence which assigns Osmund's death to 4 (not 3) Dec.
[1] Clement died on 8 Sept. at Civita Castellano.
[2] The italicized words are shared with *Cart. Gloc.* i. 12, though JW adds the name of

sea flooded the shore, and drowned many men and innumerable cattle and sheep.[7] Osmund, bishop of Salisbury, died on Friday, 3 December.[8]

[1100] Pope Clement, also known as Wibert, died.[1] On Sunday, 15 July, the church at Gloucester, which Abbot Serlo of revered memory had built from the foundations, was dedicated with great honour by bishops Samson of Worcester, Gundulf of Rochester, Gerard of Hereford, and Hervey of Bangor.[2] On Thursday, 2 August, in the eighth indiction, King William the Younger was hunting in the New Forest, which is called in the English tongue *Ytene*, and ended his life, struck by an arrow carelessly fired by a Frenchman, Walter surnamed Tirel. He was carried to Winchester, and buried in the church of St Peter in the Old Minster. It is not surprising that, as common report has it, this showed without doubt the powerful and miraculous vengeance of God. In times past, that is, in those of King Edward, and of his other predecessors as English kings, that area was fruitfully planted with churches and with people who worshipped the Lord, but, on King William the Elder's command, men were expelled, homes were cast down, the land was made habitable only for wild beasts, and this is credibly the reason for this accident. For some time before, Richard, brother of William the Younger, had died in the same forest, and a little before that, his nephew Richard, son of Duke Robert of Normandy, whilst himself hunting in the forest, died struck by an arrow fired by his knight. In the place where the king fell, in former times a church had been built, but in his father's time, as we have said, it was destroyed.[3] In the time of the same king, as we have already partly reported, there were many signs in the sun, moon, and stars, the sea flooded the shore, drowned men and beasts, destroying townships and houses; in Berkshire for three weeks before his death blood bubbled out of a spring, the devil often appeared in a horrible guise to many Normans in the woods, and spoke at length to

Bishop Gerard of Hereford to those present, as does Gregory of Caerwent (BL Cotton Vespasian A. V, fo. 196ᵛ). In the Gloucester chronicle manuscripts there is a gap after Gundulf of Rochester. Michael Hare kindly checked the readings in Gloucester Cathedral Library 34, the Gloucester Cartulary witness not used by Hart for the edition in *Cart. Gloc.*

[3] Unlike ASC JW names the forest and the hunter who slew William 'incaute', refers to the earlier deaths in the forest of the two Richards, that is, William's brother and his nephew, and associates all 3 deaths with the destruction caused by the making of the New Forest. WM *GR* iii. 275, iv. 332–3 (ii. 332–3, 377–8) and OV *HE* v. 11 (iii. 114), x. 14–15 (v. 282–94) have many of the same ingredients.

in siluis ostendens, plura cum eis de rege et Rannulfo et quibusdam
aliis locutus est.⁴ Nec mirum, nam illorum tempore fere omnis
legum siluit iustitia, causisque sub iustitio positis sola in principibus
imperabat pecunia. Denique eadem tempestate, nonnullis regis
uoluntati magis quam iustitie obedientibus, Rannulfus contra ius
ecclesiaticum, et sui gradus ordinem, presbiter enim erat, ad censum
primitus abbatias, dehinc episcopatus, quorum patres a uita dis-

p. 363 cesserant nouiter, accepit a rege, et inde singulis annis, | illi persoluit
non modicam summam pecunie. Cuius astutia et calliditas tam
uehemens extitit, et paruo tempore adeo excreuit, ut placitatorem
ac totius regni exactorem rex illum constitueret. Qui tanta potestate
adepta, ubique locorum per Angliam ditiores ac locupletiores
quosdam, rerum terrarumque ablatione, multauit, pauperiores
autem graui iniustoque tributo incessanter oppressit, multisque
modis, et ante episcopatum et in episcopatu, maiores et minores
communiter afflixit, et hoc usque ad regis eiusdem obitum, nam eo
die quo occisus periit, Dorubernensem archiepiscopatum, Wintoniensem et Searesbyriensem presulatus in sua manu tenuit.ᵇ⁵
Regnauit idem rex .xiii. annis minus .xxxviii. diebus, cui successit
iunior frater suus Henricus, et mox non. Augusti, die dominico, in
Westmonasterio a Mauricio, Lundoniensi episcopo, in regem est
consecratus, ᶜsed a Thoma Eboracensi coronaturᶜ. Quiᵈ consecrationis sue die sanctam Dei ecclesiam, que fratris sui tempore uendita et
ad firmam erat posita, liberam fecit, ac omnes malas consuetudines et
iniustas exactiones, quibus regnum Anglie iniuste opprimebatur,
abstulit, pacem firmam in toto regno suo posuit et teneri precepit,
legem regis Eaduuardi omnibus in commune reddidit, cum illis
emendationibus quibus pater suus illam emendauit. Sed forestas
quas ille constituit et habuit in manu sua retinuit.ᵉ⁶ Nec multo post
Dunholmensem episcopum Rannulfum Lundonie in Turri custodie
mancipauit, et Dorubernensem arciepiscopum Anselmum de Gallia

ᵇ For L's addition, see Appendix A   ᶜ⁻ᶜ add. by C³ mostly in left mg., sed being over
an erasure, om. HL   ᵈ qui in right mg. now, probably originally erased to make way for
sed in 1100ᶜ C   ᵉ For B¹'s addition in the lower mg. (with signes), see Appendix B

⁴ ASC, the Plympton Annals (UAG, p. 26) and the Winchester Annals (Ann. Mon. ii.
40) speak of blood bubbling in Berkshire, Winchester naming the place, Finchampstead.
The portent and the story of the appearance of the devil are also found in WM GR iv. 331
(ii. 376) and in the Margam Annals (Ann. Mon. i. 7). The blood is said to have spurted for
15 days (Margam) or for 4 weeks (Winchester). Blood is reported bubbling s.a. 1098 in the
Waverley and Bury Annals (Ann. Mon. iii. 207, UAG, p. 130), and s.a. 1099 in the

them concerning King William, Ranulf, and many others.[4] Nor is it to be wondered at, for in their time all justice in law was silent, and money alone commanded the judges in all cases brought before them. At that time many obeyed the king's wishes rather than justice, and Ranulf, acting against canon law and against the rules of his calling, for he was a priest, received from the king for sale first the abbeys, then the bishoprics, whose incumbents had recently died, and from them paid out to the king each year a large sum of money. So strong was his cunning and acumen that in a brief spell he grew in influence and the king made him judge and revenue collector for the whole kingdom. Raised to such powers, he mulcted some of the wealthier and well-endowed men throughout the kingdom, and took away their possessions and lands, he ceaselessly afflicted the poorer with severe and unjust taxes, and, in many ways, both before, and after, he became bishop, he oppressed equally the great and the small. This was the case up to the king's death, for on the day he was slain and died, Ranulf held in his hands the archbishopric of Canterbury, and the bishoprics of Winchester and Salisbury.[5] William reigned thirteen years less thirty-eight days. His younger brother Henry succeeded him, and was consecrated king by Maurice, bishop of London, on Sunday, 5 August, at Westminster, though he was crowned by Thomas of York. On the day of his anointing, he freed the church of God, which in his brother's day was put up for sale and farm, and he removed all the evil customs and unjust exactions by which the English kingdom had wrongly been oppressed. He established a firm peace throughout the kingdom, and ordered its maintenance. He restored the law of King Edward to all in common, with the changes his father had made. However, he kept in his hands the forests which his father had established and held.[6] A little later he placed under custody in the Tower of London Ranulf, bishop of Durham, and recalled Anselm, archbishop of

Bermondsey Annals (*Ann. Mon.* iii. 429). See the discussion of William's death in Barlow, *William Rufus*, pp. 420–32.

[5] ASC does not associate Ranulf Flambard so clearly with royal injustice and misrule. WM in both *GP* iii. 134 (p. 274) and in *GR* iv. 314 (ii. 368–9) is eloquent on the subject. JW does not have ASC's character sketch of William. ASC says that William II (not Ranulf) kept the three bishoprics named in his hands.

[6] The royal consecration and two general coronation promises are in ASC, though JW's words are based on the coronation charter (Stubbs, *Select Charters*, pp. 117–19), and they add the reference to the Forest laws. WM *GP* iii. 116 (p. 258) might have been the source for the information that Archbishop Thomas crowned Henry, which was added later in the JW MS C.

reuocauit.[7] Interea ab Ierusalem domum redierunt comites Rotbertus Flandrensis et Eustatius Bononiensis primitus, dein Normannorum comes Rotbertus cum uxore, quam sibi in Sicilia desponsauerat, repatriauit.[f 8] Interim rex Anglorum Henricus maiores natu Anglie congregauit Lundonie, et regis Scottorum Malcolmi et Margarete regine filiam, Mahtildem nomine, in coniugem accepit, quam Dorubernensis archiepiscopus Anselmus, dominica, die festiuitatis sancti Martini, reginam consecrauit et coronauit.[9] Venerande memorie, et uir religionis eximie, affabilis, omnibusque amabilis, Eboracensis arciepiscopus Thomas, .xiiii. kal. Dec., die dominica, ex hac uita decessit Eboraci, cui successit Herefordensis episcopus Gerardus.[10]

[1101] (.xlv.) 1123 Dunholmensis episcopus Rannulfus, post Natiuitatem Domini, de custodia magna calliditate euasit, mare transiit, Nortmannorum comitem Rotbertum adiit, eique suasit, ut Angliam hostiliter adiret.[1] Nec minus perplures huius terre principes, missis ad eum legatis, rogauerunt ut Angliam festinato ueniret, coronam et regnum illi promittentes.[a 2] Ciuitas Glauorna, cum principali monasterio, et aliis, [b].viii. idus[b] Iunii,[c] feria quinta, incendio conflagrauit.[3] Comes Nortmannorum Rotbertus, equitum, sagittariorum, et peditum, non paruam congregans multitudinem in loco, qui Nortmannica lingua dicitur Vltresport, naues coadunauit. Quibus rex cognitis, buzecarlis precepit mare custodire, et obseruare ne quis de partibus Nortmannie fines adiret Anglie. Ipse uero,

---

[f] For L's addition here, see Appendix A

[a] For B's addition here, see Appendix B   [b–b] .xi. k. L   [c] Ian. H

[7] ASC reports that both Ranulf's arrest and Anselm's recall ('before Michaelmas') took place on the advice of Henry's advisers. Eadmer, *HN* ii (p. 119) dates Anselm's arrival at Dover on 23 Sept.

[8] ASC reports the three crusading princes' return and describes Robert's reception in Normandy 'in the autumn' ('mense Augusto', HH *HA* vii. 22 (p. 448); 'September', OV *HE* x. 17 (v. 300)). Robert's marriage to Sybil of Conversano (which is not in ASC) is described by OV *HE* x. 12 (v. 278), Torigni, *GND* vii. 14 (ii. 222) and Wace (iii. 10302–6 (ii. 287)), and mentioned by WM *GR* iv. 389 (iv. 461).

[9] ASC reports both marriage and coronation and calls the queen Maud.

[10] ASC does not date Thomas's death nor name his successor. *HC*, pp. 20–1, confirms JW's date for Thomas's death and reports the translation of Gerard to York at Epiphany 1101. *Cart. Gloc.* i. 12 reports Thomas's death on 18 Nov. more briefly.

[1] Ranulf's escape, which is described in some detail in OV *HE* x. 19 (v. 32), is dated to 2 Feb. by ASC, and 3 Feb. by the continuator of *HDE* (SD i. 138), and in BL Cotton Caligula A. VIII, a condensed version of *HR* (printed in *EHR* lxxxviii (1973), 334). Ranulf's role in instigating Duke Robert's invasion, which ASC places together with his

Canterbury, from France.[7] In the mean time first counts Robert of Flanders and Eustace of Boulogne returned home from Jerusalem, and then Duke Robert of Normandy came home with his wife, whom he had married in Sicily.[8] At the same time King Henry of England assembled the greater men of England to London, and he took as wife Matilda, daughter of Malcolm, king of the Scots, and Queen Margaret. Archbishop Anselm of Canterbury consecrated and crowned her queen on Sunday, the feast of St Martin [11 November].[9] Archbishop Thomas of York of revered memory and a man of great piety, affable and beloved by all, died at York on Sunday, 18 November to be succeeded by Gerard, bishop of Hereford.[10]

[1101] After Christmas, Ranulf, bishop of Durham, cunningly escaped from prison, crossed the sea, went to Duke Robert of the Normans, and persuaded him to invade England.[1] Many of the nobles of England also sent envoys to him and asked him to hasten to England, where they promised him both crown and kingdom.[2] The city of Gloucester with the chief monastery as well as others was consumed by fire on Thursday, 6 June.[3] Duke Robert of Normandy raised a large force of horsemen, archers, and footsoldiers in the place which is called in the Norman tongue *Ultresport* [Tréport] and assembled his ships. When the king learnt of this, he ordered his buscarls to guard the sea, and see that no one approached England

escape at the end of its annal (after the invasion), presumably led JW to reverse the order of ASC's annal. Both Eadmer, *HN* iii (p. 120), and Henry's letter to Anselm between 5 Aug. and 23 Sept. (Epist. 212 (Schmitt, *Anselmi opera omnia*, iv. 109)) show that Henry I had clearly been anxious about Robert's reactions quite soon after his English coronation. ASC says Ranulf escaped from the Tower of London.

[2] Whilst other English sources emphasize Duke Robert's English ambitions and his threatened invasion (ASC and HH *HA* vii. 23 (p. 448) soon after Easter (ASC) or at Whitsuntide (Eadmer, *HN* iii (p. 127)), JW gives the English magnates a more active role in encouraging the duke. OV *HE* x. 19 (v. 306–20) gives the fullest account. On this civil war, see David, *Robert Curthose*, pp. 127–37 and C. W. Hollister, 'The Anglo-Norman Civil War of 1101', *EHR* lxxxviii (1973), 315–34, repr. in id, *Monarchy, Magnates and Institutions in the Anglo-Norman World* (London, 1986), pp. 77–96.

[3] The chronicles date the fire to 1102 (*Cart. Gloc.*, i. 12, the Margam, Tewkesbury, and Winchester Annals (*Ann. Mon.* i. 7, 44, ii. 41), Gregory of Caerwent (BL Cotton Vespasian A. V, fo. 196ᵛ)), where it is described as Henry I's 3rd year; and Margam gives the day as 20 May and Gregory of Caerwent as 22 May. JW *s.a.* 1122 (see below, 1122 n. 1) dates the fire to Thursday, 22 May, in the 1st year of Henry I (presumably 1101), though 22 May was a Wednesday in 1101 and a Thursday in 1102. JW's 6 June here was a Thursday in 1101. The JW witnesses HL or their exemplar have tried to correct JW's calendar date.

innumerabili exercitu congregato de tota Anglia, non longe ab
Heastinga castra posuit in SutSaxonia; autumabat enim pro certo
fratrem suum illis in partibus naue appulsurum. At ille, consilio
Rannulfi episcopi, quosdam de regis buzsecarlis adeo rerum diuersarum promissionibus fregit, ut, fidelitate quam regi debebant
postposita, ad se transfugerent, et sibi ad Angliam duces existerent.
Paratis igitur omnibus, cum exercitu nauim conscendit et circa ad
uincula sancti Petri, in loco qui Portesmuth dicitur, appulit, statimque uersus Wintoniam exercitum mouens, apto in loco castra posuit.[4]
Cuius aduentu cognito, quidam de primoribus Anglie mox ad eum,
ut ante proposuerant, transfugere, quidam uero cum rege ficta mente
remansere, sed episcopi, milites gregarii, et Angli animo constanti
cum illo perstitere, unanimiter ad pugnam parati cum ipso descen-
dere. Verum sapientiores utriusque partis, habito inter se salubri
consilio, pacem inter fratres ea ratione composuere, ut .iii. mille
marcas, [d]id est .ii. milia libras[d] argenti, singulis annis rex persolueret
comiti, et omnibus suos pristinos honores, quos in Anglia pro comitis
fidelitate perdiderant, restitueret gratuito, et cunctis, quibus honores
in Nortmannia causa regis fuerant ablati, comes redderet absque
p. 364 pretio. Quibus pacatis, regis exercitus domum, | comitis uero pars in
Normanniam rediit, pars in Anglia secum remansit.[5] Filius Eustatii
senioris, comitis Bononiensium, Godefridus rex Ierosolimorum, qui
prepotens extiterat dux Lothariensium, diem clausit ultimum, et in
ecclesia Golgothana sepultus requiescit. Cuius post obitum, Christiani, unanimi consilio, eius germanum sibi in regem elegerunt
Balduuinum.[6] Arcem quam in occidentali Sabrine fluminis plaga,

[d-d] interlin. CB, om. P

[4] Possibly Warnford, Hants, if Hollister's identification of 'riuaria de Walmesforda/o' in
BL Cotton Caligula A. VI fo. 41 (Hollister, 'The Anglo-Norman Civil War of 1101', p. 334)
is right.
[5] For a discussion of Robert's invasion, see Hollister, 'The Anglo-Norman Civil War of
1101', pp. 315–34. News of Robert's threatened invasion, which was to a great extent planned
by Ranulf (ASC, JW, possibly HH HA vii. 23 (p. 450), OV HE x. 19 (v. 310)) reached Henry
soon after Easter (ASC) and certainly by the Whitsun (9 June) court (Eadmer, HN iii (pp. 126–
7)). Henry took defensive measures in mid-summer (ASC), camping at Pevensey (ASC) or at
Hastings (JW), and calling up his subjects (Eadmer). JW alone names Robert's port of
embarkation, Tréport. Robert's landing at Portsmouth is dated 20 July by ASC and the
Caligula version of HR, before 1 Aug. (HH HA), Aug. (WM GR v. 395 (ii. 471)) or the autumn
(OV HE x. 19 (v. 314)). That Ranulf took part in the invasion is clear from the Winchester
Annals (Ann. Mon. ii. 41) and the continuator of HDE (SD i. 138), and that he circumvented
Henry's defensive preparations, which is explicitly stated by JW, may be implicit in Anselm's
reference to Ranulf being the lord of sea pirates (Epist. 214 (Schmitt, Anselmi opera omnia, iv.
113) and might be glancingly referred to in 'the connivance of traitors' of OV HE x. 19 (v. 314).

from Normandy. King Henry himself gathered together a massive force from all England; and camped not far from Hastings in Sussex; for he was sure that his brother would land in that region. Robert, on the advice of Bishop Ranulf, so won over some of the buscarls with different promises, that they abandoned the fidelity owed their king, came over to him, and became his pilots to England. Having got everything ready, he set sail with his army, landed at Portsmouth about the feast of St Peter ad Vincula [1 August], marched his army straightaway to Winchester, and camped at a suitable spot.[4] On learning of his arrival, some leading men among the English, redeeming an earlier promise, immediately went over to him, others remained, though with dubious commitment, with the king. The bishops, the ordinary soldiers, and the English stood resolutely with him, all prepared to do battle on his side. The wiser heads on both sides had sensible discussions with each other, and drew up a peace between the two brothers on condition that the king would pay the duke every year 3000 marks, that is 2000 silver pounds, and would freely restore to all the duke's followers their former honours which they had lost in England through their allegiance to the duke, and that the count would freely give back the honours in Normandy taken from all who had been faithful to the king. Peace being confirmed, the royal army returned home, part of the duke's force returned to Normandy, and part stayed with him in England.[5] Godfrey, king of Jerusalem, previously the powerful duke of Lorraine, son of Eustace the Elder, count of Boulogne, died and lies buried in the church of Golgotha. On his death the Christians unanimously chose his brother Baldwin as king.[6] Robert of Bellême,

BL Cotton Caligula A. VIII, fo. 41, describes both Henry's movements from Pevensey and those of Robert after camping at Warnford (Wace iii. 10319–75 (ii. 268–70) who confirms the general movements of both without mentioning either Pevensey or Warnford), the preliminary agreement between Henry and Robert at Alton (here confirmed by Wace iii. 10343, 10363 (ii. 268, 269)) and the final solemn ratification of the treaty at Winchester. ASC adds to the agreement (which it says was witnessed by 12 men on each side) the restoration of lands held forcibly by William in Normandy, of lands in England lost because of Duke Robert, and of Count Eustace's lands in England, and each brother's right of succession to the other's land in the event of death. ASC reports that Robert's men caused much damage in England, but it omits much which is in JW: Robert's assembly of his army at Tréport; Ranulf's part in persuading the seamen to desert Henry; Robert's camping in a suitable spot on his way to Winchester; the mixed reaction of the English leaders to Robert's landing; and the continued support of Henry by the bishops, the rank and file soldiers, and the English.

[6] WM *GR* iv. 373–4 (ii. 434), who relies on Fulcher of Chartres, gives this death and succession, but correctly dates Godfrey's death to 18 July 1000 after a reign of one year. OV *HE* x. 12 (v. 268–9) says that Godfrey reigned for three years, which could agree with JW's incorrect date for his death.

in loco qui Brycge dicitur lingua Saxonica, Agelfleda Merciorum
domina quondam construxerat, fratre suo Eaduuardo seniore
regnante, Scrobbesbyriensis comes Rotbertus de Beleasmo, Rocgeri
comitis filius, contra regem Heinricum, ut exitus rei probauit, muro
lato et alto, summoque restaurare cepit. Cepit etiam in Walonia
edificare aliam, in loco qui Carocloue dicitur.[7]

[1102] (.xlvi.) 1124   [a]Supradictus comes Rotbertus de Beleasmo,
qui comitatum etiam Pontiuensis pagi rexit eo tempore, ac in
Normannia castella possedit quamplurima, ciuitatem Scrobbesbyr-
iam, et castellum in ea situm, castella quoque Arundel et Tychyll,[b]
alimentis, machinis, armis, militibus, ac peditibus contra regem
Heinricum firmiter muniuit. Muros quoque ac turres castellorum,
uidelicet Brycge et Carocloue, die noctuque laborando et operando,
perficere modis omnibus festinauit. Walanos etiam suos homines, ut
promptiores sibique fideliores ac paratiores essent ad id perficiendum quod uolebat, honoribus, terris, equis, armis incitauit, uariisque
donis largiter donauit. Sed conatus illius et opera nimis cito sunt
impedita, insidiis enim et conatibus eius per certa indicia detectis,
publicum hostem rex illum pronuntiauit. Iccirco mox Walanis et
Normannis, quot tunc habere potuit, in unum congregatis, ipse et
suus germanus Arnoldus partem Steaffordensis page uastauerunt, ac
inde iumenta et animalia multa, hominesque nonnullos in Waloniam
abduxerunt. At rex sine dilatione castellum eius Arundel primitus
obsedit, et castellis ante illud firmatis, recessit. Deinde Rotbertum,
Lindicoline ciuitatis episcopum, cum parte exercitus Tychyll[b] obsi-
dere iussit. Ille autem Brcyge cum exercitu pene totius Anglie
obsedit, machinas ibi construere et castellum firmare cepit. Interim
Walanos, in quibus fiduciam magnam Rotbertus habuerat, ut iura-
menta que illi iurauerant irrita fierent, et ab illo penitus deficerent, in
illumque consurgerent, donis modicis facile corrupit. Infra .xxx. dies
ciuitate omnibusque castellis redditis, inimicum suum Rotbertum
superauit, et ignominiose de Anglia expulit, germanus quoque illius

[a] Two marginal additions in H in a late 12th-c. hand, the first near the opening of 1102: (i)
Ciclus .xix. .iii., (ii) (some lines below) In hoc anno .xiiii. kl. Maii, indictione .x.,
pontificatus autem domni Paschalis .ii. pape anno tertio, translata est sedes episcopalis
de Cestria apud Couentriam   [b] Tykenhyll B

[7] OV HE xi. 3 (vi. 22) refers to Robert's castle building at Bridgnorth, and on xi. 3 (vi.
20) says that Henry I had had Robert's activities closely watched for a whole year. JW's
chronicle source could have referred to the completion of the castles at Bridgnorth and

earl of Shrewsbury, son of Earl Roger, began to strengthen with a high and thick wall the fort on the western bank of the Severn, at the place called in the Saxon tongue *Brycge*. This had been built by the lady of the Mercians, Ægelfleda, when her brother Edward the Elder was king, and Robert built it, as events were to show, against King Henry. He also began to build another strongpoint in Wales at Carreghofa.[7]

[1102] The said Count Robert of Bellême, who then ruled the county of Ponthieu, and had many castles in Normandy, strongly fortified against King Henry the city of Shrewsbury and the castle there, as well as the castles of Arundel and Tickhill, supplying them with provisions, siege engines, arms, knights, and footsoldiers. He further rushed, by all possible means and by carrying out the work day and night, to complete the walls and towers of the castles of Bridgnorth and Carreghofa. He encouraged his Welsh followers with honours, lands, horses, and arms so that they would carry out his plans more faithfully and eagerly, and showered them with many gifts. His effort and labours were too speedily cut short, for the king proclaimed him a public enemy on clear proof of his plots and designs. He therefore brought together immediately as many of his Welsh and Norman followers as he then could, and with his brother Arnold laid waste part of Staffordshire, and took away to Wales many oxen and beasts, and some men. Without delay the king first besieged Arundel castle, and then withdrew after having set up castles in front of it. The king then ordered Robert, bishop of Lincoln, with part of the army, to besiege Tickhill. He himself with almost all the army of England laid siege to Bridgnorth, and there built siege engines and a strong castle. In the meanwhile he easily won over by small gifts the Welsh, in whom Robert placed great trust, so that they broke the promises which they had sworn to him, and, completely deserting him, rose up against him. Within thirty days the city and all the castles had surrendered, Henry had triumphed over his enemy Robert, had expelled him with ignominy from England, and had similarly sentenced his brother Arnold also

Carreghofa in 1102, and he may have inferred that the enterprise began earlier in 1101. The construction of a castle at Carreghofa was against the Welsh and is not mentioned elsewhere. For the meaning of *Brycge*, see J. F. A. Mason and P. Barker, 'The Norman castle at Quatford', *Trans. Shropshire Archaeological Society*, lvii (1961–4), 37–46.

Arnoldum paulo post, pro sua perfidia, simili sorte dampnauit.¹ Post
hec, in festiuitate sancti Michaelis, rex fuit Lundonie apud Westmonasterium, et cum eo omnes principes regni sui, ecclesiastici et
secularis ordinis, ubi *duos de clericis suisᶜ duobus episcopatibus inuestiuit,
Rogerium uidelicet cancellarium episcopatu Særesbyriensi, et Rogerium
larderarium suum pontificatu Herefordensi.* Vbi etiam Anselmus arciepiscopus tenuit magnum concilium de his que ad Christianitatem
pertinent, *considentibus secum arciepiscopo Eboracensi Gerardo, Maur-
icioᵈ Lundoniensi, Willelmo electo episcopo Wintoniensi, Rotberto episcopo Lincoliensi, Samsone Wigornensi, Rotberto Cestrensi, Iohanne
Bathoniensi, Hereberto Norðwicensi, Radulfo Cicestrensi, Gundulfo
Hrofensi, Herueo Bangorensi, et duobusᵉ inuestitis,* Rogerioᶠ et Rogerio.ᵍ
*Osbernus autem episcopus Exoniensis, infirmitate detentus, interesse non
potuit. In hoc concilio* ʰplures abbates, Francigeni et Angli, sunt
depositi, et honoribus priuati, quos iniuste adquisierunt, aut in eis
inhoneste uixerunt, scilicet, *Wido Persorensis, Aldwinus Ramesiensis,
et* ⁱille *de Tæuestoce,ⁱ Haimo de Cernel,* et ille de *Micelenei, Ægelricus
de Middel\tune, Godricus de Burh, Ricardus de Heli, Rotbertus de
sancto Eadmundo.*ʰ² ʲ*Prefatus Rogerius Herefordensi ecclesie episcopus
electus, Lundonie infirmitate percussus, mortuus est, et cancellarius
regine, Reignelmus nomine, loco illius pari inuestitura subrogatus est.*³
ᵏRex Anglorum Heinricus Mariam, regine sororem, Eustatio, Bononiensium comiti, nuptum tradidit.ᵏ⁴

p. 365

[1103] (.xlvii.) 1125   Magna discordia facta est inter regem Heinricum et Anselmum arciepiscopum, eo quod arciepiscopus nollet

ᶜ *om.* HL   ᵈ episcopo *add.* B   ᵉ duobus nouiter B   ᶠ Rogerio scilicet
Serberiensi B   ᵍ Rogerio Herefordensi B   ʰ⁻ʰ *For B's substituted text, see
Appendix* B   ⁱ⁻ⁱ Wimundus Tauestokensis HL   ʲ *For B⁴'s addition in the lower
mg. of pp. 406–7 with appropriate signes de renuoi, see Appendix* B   ᵏ⁻ᵏ *add. at line-end
and extending into mg.* C

---

¹ ASC's account of a campaign begun shortly after 6 Apr. and completed by 9 Sept. is
much briefer, and only JW's sentence on the siege of Arundel overlaps slightly with
ASC, which does not have much of JW's information under this annal. JW has much
more in common with Orderic's narrative (*HE* xi. 3 (vi. 20–30)), which in part is
supported by *Brut* Pen. pp. 22–5, Her. pp. 42–5, BS pp. 94–7 *s.a.* 1100 (*recte* 1102),
though JW's sentence on Robert's preparations is peculiar to him. JW alone says that
Robert and his allies ravaged Staffordshire and that Robert Bloet, bishop of Lincoln, led
the force against Tickhill (Blyth in OV *HE* and *Brut*), though OV says that Henry took
Tickhill. JW's period of less than 30 days, if it refers to the siege of Bridgnorth seems
confirmed by OV's statement that the siege lasted 3 weeks (xi. 3 (vi. 24)). See the
discussion of the chronology of these campaigns set against the charter evidence in C. W.
Hollister, 'The Campaign of 1102 against Robert of Bellême,' *Studies in Medieval history*

for his treachery.[1] After this on St Michael's feast day [29 September] the king was at London in Westminster, and with him were all the kingdom's magnates, both churchmen and laymen. There he invested two of his clergy with two bishoprics, that is, Roger the chancellor with the bishopric of Salisbury, and Roger his larderer with that of Hereford. Archbishop Anselm held a great council in that place concerning the Christian faith, and there sat with him Archbishop Gerard of York, Maurice, bishop of London, William, bishop-elect of Winchester, Bishop Robert of Lincoln, Samson of Worcester, Robert of Chester, John of Bath, Herbert of Norwich, Ralph of Chichester, Gundulf of Rochester, Hervey of Bangor, and the two newly-invested bishops, the two Rogers. Osbern, bishop of Exeter, was unable to attend through illness. In this council many abbots, both French and English, were deposed, and deprived of the honours, which they had unjustly acquired or in which they had lived dishonestly, that is, Guy of Pershore, Aldwin of Ramsey, the abbot of Tavistock, Haimo of Cerne, the abbot of Muchelney, Æthelric of Milton, Godric of Peterborough, Richard of Ely, Robert of Bury St Edmund's.[2] The said Roger, bishop-elect of Hereford, fell ill at London and died, and the queen's chancellor, Reinhelm, was substituted for him and was invested as he had been.[3] King Henry of England gave Mary, the queen's sister, in marriage to Eustace, count of Boulogne.[4]

[1103] Great discord arose between King Henry and Archbishop Anselm because the archbishop would neither agree to royal

presented to R. Allen Brown, ed. C. Harper-Bill, C. Holdsworth, and J. L. Nelson (Woodbridge, 1989), pp. 193–202.

[2] Eadmer, HN iii (pp. 141–2). The phrases on the royal court at Westminster, on Anselm's holding a council, and on the reasons for the deposing of abbots are clearly based on ASC. The order of JW's list of deposed abbots is different from the text of the canons reproduced by Eadmer, which distinguishes between the first six in the list deposed for simony, and the last three pro sua quisque causa. Wimund was the (unnamed) abbot of Tavistock—he is named in the JW witnesses HL and Eadmer—but the name of the abbot of Muchelney is unknown. For the identification of these deposed abbots, and the reasons for their deposition, see Whitelock, Brett, and Brooke, Councils and Synods, ii. 668–9. The long and varied canons of this council, which are found in the JW MS B, are printed from Eadmer ibid., ii. 674–9. The council is discussed there (ibid. ii. 668–9) and in Brett, English Church, pp. 76–9.

[3] Eadmer, HN iii (p. 144). WM GP iv. 166 (p. 303) reports Roger the Larderer's death 'infra .viii. dies' after his election (at the Michaelmas court). Reinhelm could have been invested with the see of Hereford after Christmas 1102, perhaps at the Christmas court. Regesta ii. 613, dated 25 Dec. [1102], is witnessed by Rainald (possibly a mistake for Reinhelm), the queen's chancellor.

[4] This marginal addition appears to be the only early source for this marriage.

consentire ut rex daret inuestituras ecclesiarum, neque consecrare, neque communicare iis quibus rex iam dederat ecclesias, quia apostolicus sibi et omnibus hoc interdixerat. Unde *rex precepit Gerardo*, arciepiscopo *Eboracensi*, quatinus consecraret episcopos, quibus ipse rex dederat inuestituras, scilicet, Willelmum Giffardum, et Rogerum, qui fuit capellanus eius, cui iam dederat Searesbyriensem ecclesiam. Gerardus preceptum regis suscepit, sed Willelmus, causa iustitie, illud et benedictionem archiepiscopi Gerardi spreuit. Quare regis iudicio *suis omnibus expoliatus, eliminatur a regno*, ceteri uero inconsecrati remanserunt. Reignelmus autem paulo ante episcopatum Herefordensem regi reddidit, quia intellexit se Deum offendisse in hoc, quod de manu laici alicuius inuestituram ecclesie suscepisset.[1] Post hec rex tenuit curiam suam in Pasca Wintonie.[2] Anselmus arciepiscopus, post multas iniurias et diuersas contumelias quas passus est, rogatus a rege perrexit Romam, .v. kal. Mai, sicut ei et regi conuenit, habens in comitatu Willelmum Wintoniensi ecclesie electum antistitem, et abbates de abbatia*a* depositos, Ricardum Eliensem et Aldwinum abbatem*b* Ramesensem.[3] Rotbertus comes Normannie uenit in Angliam loqui cum fratre suo, et antequam redisset de Anglia pardonauit ter mille marcas argenti, quas rex sibi omni anno per conuentionem debuit.[4] In prouincia etiam, que nominatur Bearrucscire in loco qui dicitur Heamstede, uisus est a multis sanguis effluere de terra. Eodem anno .iii. idus Aug., magna intemperies uenti facta est, que tantum dampnum fecit in fructibus terre per Angliam, quantum qui tunc uixerunt, retroactis temporibus, nunquam uiderunt.[5]

[1104] (.xlviii.) 1126   Venerandi abbates, Walterus Eoueshamnensis, .xiii. kal. Feb. et Serlo Gloecestrensis .iiii. non. Mar. obierunt.[1] Rex

---

a abbatiam *L*   *b* om. *HL*

---

[1] Eadmer, *HN* iii (pp. 145–6) where this dispute is discussed. Unusually JW, while conveying the substance of Eadmer, does so mostly in his own words.
[2] The last sentence clearly translates ASC, which also mentions William Giffard's departure from England.
[3] The phrase 'sicut ei et regi conuenit' is based on ASC ('swa swa him 7 þam cynge gewearð'), but JW's account of the quarrel is related to that in Eadmer, *HN* iii (pp. 144–9). JW differs in two details: 27 Apr. is Eadmer's date for Anselm's arrival, not at Rome, but at Wissant, and Eadmer does not name Anselm's companions on the journey. Evidence confirming Richard and William's journey to Rome is discussed in Brett, *English Church*, p. 235 n. 6, and Whitelock, Brett, and Brooke, *Councils and Synods*, ii. 658 n. 4, raises the possibility that JW derived the names of Anselm's companions from an earlier version of Eadmer. Brett (ibid., p. 658 n. 3) has shown that Anselm had reached Rome by 10 Nov.

investitures nor would he consecrate, or communicate with, those to whom the king had given churches since the apostolic pope had forbidden this to him and to all others. The king then ordered Gerard, archbishop of York, to consecrate the bishops he had invested, namely, William Giffard, and Roger, who was his chaplain, to whom he had already given the see of Salisbury. Gerard acceded to the king's request, but William, deferring to right principles, refused both that order and the archbishop's blessing. Henry ordered the confiscation of all William possessed and he was banished from the kingdom, and the others remained unconsecrated. A little earlier Reinhelm returned the bishopric of Hereford to the king for he understood that he had offended God by receiving the church from a layman's hands.[1] After this the king held his Easter [29 March] court at Winchester.[2] Archbishop Anselm, after suffering many slights and various injustices, set out for Rome, at the king's orders, and as agreed with the king, on 27 April, in the company of William, bishop-elect of Winchester, and Richard of Ely and Aldwin of Ramsey, abbots who had been deposed from their posts.[3] Duke Robert of Normandy came to England to confer with his brother, and before his return from England, he released the king from the payment of 3000 silver marks, which William had agreed to pay him annually.[4] In Berkshire at Finchampstead blood was seen by many to spurt from the earth. In the same year, on 3 August, there was a violent storm, which did more damage to the fruits of the earth throughout England than anyone living then had seen in former times.[5]

[1104] Two revered abbots died: Walter of Evesham on 20 January, and Serlo of Gloucester on 4 March.[1] King Henry of England held

---

[4] Clearly based on ASC. OV *HE* xi. 2 (vi. 12) claims that Robert Curthose crossed to England to intercede with Henry on William of Warenne's behalf, and that William's approach to Robert was made in 1102. OV *HE* places Robert Curthose's visit before, not after, the rebellion of Robert of Bellême. OV *HE* xi. 2 (vi. 14) and WM *GR* v. 395 (ii. 472) imply that the queen persuaded Robert to renounce his pension. Wace iii. 10653–706 (ii. 280–2) makes the queen's intervention a central part of the episode.

[5] The spurting of blood is also reported in ASC, in the Waverley, Rouen, and Bury Annals (*Ann. Mon.* ii. 210, *UAG*, pp. 47, 131) and by HH *HA* vii. 24 (pp. 450–2). The tempest on 11 Aug. reported by JW and Waverley was presumably derived from ASC, which adds a customary lament on a year made calamitous by taxes, cattle, plague, and ruined crops.

[1] JW is the only source for Walter of Evesham's death (*Heads*, p. 47). *Heads*, p. 52 gives 24 Feb. and 3 Mar. as the alternative dates for Serlo of Gloucester's death.

Anglorum Heinricus tenuit curiam suam apud Westmonasterium in Pentecosten.² Tertia feria, id est, .vii. idus Iun., quattuor circuli uisi sunt circa solem albi coloris, circa horam .vi., quisque circulus sub alio, quasi essent picti. Mirati sunt omnes qui tunc uiderunt, quia nunquam amplius talia uisa sunt ab aliquo illorum.³ Willelmus comes de Moreteon exheredatus est de tota terra sua quam habuit in Anglia.⁴ Non facile potest narrari miseria quam sustinuit isto tempore terra Anglorum propter exactiones regias.⁵ ᵃCorpus sancti Cuthberti episcopi, ob quorundam incredulitatem abbatum, pontificante Rannulfo episcopo, ostensum est, et a Rodulfo Saiense abbate, postmodum Hrofensi episcopo, et a fratribus Dunholmensis ecclesie, cum capite sancti Oswaldi regis et martyris, sanctique Bede, multorum sanctorum reliquiis, certo indicio incorruptum inuentum est,ᵃ presente Alexandro comite, Eadgari regis Scottorum fratre, postea rege. Hic quia tam sancte rei sibi licuit interesse, datis ᵇquamplurimis marcis auri et argenti,ᵇ parari fecit scrinium, in quo sanctum corpus, nouis indutum uestimentis, honorifice est reconditum.⁶

[1105] (.xlix.) 1127 Rex Anglorum Henricus transiuit mare. *Omnes autem pene* Normannorum maiores, ad *eius* aduentum, spreto comite, domno suo, et fide quam ei debebant, in aurum et argentum regis, quod ipse de Anglia illuc portauerat, cucurrerunt, eique *castra, munitasque* ciuitates et urbes tradiderunt.¹ Ille uero Baius, cum ecclesia sancte Marie, que intus erat, combussit, et Cathum fratri suo abstulit, et post Angliam rediit, quia Normanniam sibi totam subiugare nequiuerat, ut copiosiori pecunia fretus, rediens anno sequenti, quod residuum erat, exheredato fratre suo, sibi subiceret.² Comes

---

ᵃ⁻ᵃ *written partly over erasure, partly extending into mg., and announced by a paragraph mark* C²   ᵇ⁻ᵇ *written over erasure* C²

² This court is reported in ASC as well as the other courts (at Christmas and Easter), which are as usual omitted by JW.
³ This is from ASC. The description in the Waverley Annals (*Ann. Mon.* ii. 211) is also based on ASC. These celestial phenomena are reported in HH *HA* vii. 24 (p. 452), and under 1103 in the St Augustine, and the apparently derivative Chichester Annals (*UAG* pp. 76, 93). The Margam Annals (*Ann. Mon.* i. 8) describe the same phenomena differently.
⁴ ASC is much fuller, giving reasons for this confiscation, which it places after the agreement between Duke Robert and Robert of Bellême, William's visit to Normandy, and Robert of Bellême's departure from England.
⁵ ASC is close though it is fuller and places the entry at the end of the annal. It says that William fled England and worked against Henry. William of Mortain, the son of the Conqueror's half-brother, Robert, count of Mortain, was one of the great landholders of

his court at Westminster at Whitsun [5 June].[2] On Tuesday, 7 June, four white circles were seen around the sun at the sixth hour, one inside the other as though they had been painted. Everyone marvelled as such a spectacle had never before been seen by anyone.[3] William, count of Mortain, was disinherited from all his English lands.[4] It is not easy to describe the miseries England suffered as a result of the king's exactions at that time.[5] Because some abbots were sceptical, St Cuthbert's body was uncovered during Bishop Ranulf's episcopacy, together with the head of St Oswald king and martyr, and the relics of Bede, and many other saints. It was found clearly to be uncorrupted by Ralph, abbot of Séez, later bishop of Rochester, and the monks of Durham in the presence of Earl Alexander, brother of Edgar, king of the Scots, and himself afterwards king. As he had been allowed to attend so holy an occasion, he gave very many marks of gold and silver, and had a shrine made, in which the holy body, again dressed in new vestments, was reburied with honour.[6]

[1105] King Henry of England crossed the channel. On his arrival, almost all the Norman nobles abandoned their duke and lord, and the fealty owed to him, and rushed over to the gold and silver the king had brought with him, and handed castles over to him, and fortified cities and towns.[1] Henry set fire to Bayeux with the church of St Mary therein, took Caen from his brother, and then returned to England. He had been unable to subjugate all Normandy to his control, and equipped with more money, he would return next year to subjugate what was left and disinherit his brother.[2] William, count

England; see *CP* iii. 428–9. William's alliance with Robert of Bellême in Normandy is mentioned by OV *HE* xi. 10 (vi. 58) and WM *GR* v. 397 (ii. 473–4).
    [6] The *Capitula de miraculis et translationibus Sancti Cuthberti* c. vii (SD i. 247–61) seems to be the earliest account of this translation, though there are no verbal borrowings or echoes here. JW's reference (in part apparently over an erasure) to Alexander's sponsoring of the shrine is found neither in *HR* iii (ii. 236) nor in Hoveden (i. 162). Hoveden adds the archbishop of Canterbury to the list of those present.
    [1] Eadmer, *HN* iii (p. 165).
    [2] ASC and the other brief accounts of this expedition (OV *HE* xi. 11 (vi. 60–1, 78–81), WM *GR* v. 398 (ii. 474–5), HH *HA* vii. 25 (pp. 452–4)) are different from JW's. OV *HE* dates Henry's crossing to Normandy to Holy Week (3–9 Apr.). ASC dates this crossing to the spring, and his return to England to the autumn. The purchase of Norman support, which JW derived from Eadmer, is mentioned by HH *HA* in connection with the capture of Caen. WM, OV *HE* and *Quadripartitus*, p. 87, mention the firing of Bayeux, WM also specifying its chief church. JW's anticipation of the events of 1106 is not in ASC. For this campaign, see David, *Robert Curthose*, pp. 161–9.

Willelmus de Moreteon, ubicunque potuit, nocuit rebus et homini-
p. 366 bus regis, propter honorem suum, quem perdiderat in Anglia.³ |

[1106] (.l.) 1128 Rotbertus comes Normannie uenit in Angliam, ut
loqueretur fratri suo Henrico regi, quem inuenit apud Northamtun.
Tunc comes quesiuit ab eo ut redderet sibi ea que acceperat super
eum in Normannia, cui rex omnia contradixit. Quare comes iratus
recessit, et mare transiuit.¹ In prima autem septimana .xl., .vi. feria,
.xiiii. kl. Martii, in uespera, ostensa est quedam insolita stella, et per
.xxv.ᵃ dies, eodem modo eademque hora, uisa est lucere inter
austrum et occidentem. Parua enim uisa est et obscura, sed splendor,
qui de ea exiuit, ualde erat clarus, et quasi ingens trabes de orientali
et aquilonali parte claritas ingessit se in eandem stellam. Quidam
dixerunt se plures insolitas stellas eo tempore uidisse. In Cena autem
Domini nocte uise sunt due lune, paulo ante diem, una in oriente,
altera in occidente, et utraque plena, et erat eo die .xiiii. luna.² Quo
anno facta est nimis execrabilis contentio inter imperatorem de
Alamannia et filium eius.³ Rex Anglorum Henricus, ante Augustum
mensem transiuit mare, uadens in Normanniam, cui fere omnes
primi Normannorum se dederunt, exceptis Rotberto de Beleasmo,
Willelmo de Moreteon, et paucis aliis, qui se tenebant cum comite
Rotberto.⁴

Romanorum .xcvi. Heinricus .iiii.ᵇ obiit, cui filius suus Heinricus
succedens regnauit annis .xviiii.⁵

Rex Anglorum Heinricus, *in Assumptione sancte Marie, Beccum
uenit*, ubi *ipse et* Anselmus archiepiscopus in unum *conuenerunt,* ᶜ*et
tandem omnia que in diuersa traxerant pacem et concordiam inuenerunt.*ᶜ⁶ Non multo post idem arciepiscopus, iussu et rogatu regis,
Angliam rediit. Congregato exercitu, rex ad quoddam castrum
comitis de Moretoin, quod uocatur Tenercebrei, perrexit, et obsedit
illud. Interim dum ibi moraretur, uenit comes Rotbertus, frater regis,

ᵃ .xxv. *from* .xxi. C   ᵇ *written over erasure* C   ᶜ⁻ᶜ *written in mg.* B¹

³ This is close to ASC.
¹ This is close to ASC. HH *HA* vii. 25 (p. 452) says that Robert came 'amicabiliter', and
departed 'iratus'. In his letter to Anselm Henry reported that Robert had gone away in a
good humour (Epist. 396 in Schmitt, *Anselmi opera omnia*, v. 340). The dating of *Regesta* ii.
736 to 1106 1–7 Feb.(?) depends on ASC's dating Henry's stay at Northampton to 'before
spring'.
² The description of the comets and the two moons is very close to that in ASC. The
comet is also described fully, but with different details, in the Margam Annals (*Ann. Mon.*
i. 9), and is mentioned by both OV *HE* xi. 12 (vi. 68) and the Winchester Annals (*Ann.
Mon.* ii. 42); whilst the two moons are reported in the Rouen (*UAG*, p. 47) and

of Mortain, did as much hurt as he could to the king's men and possessions in revenge for the loss of his English lands.[3]

[1106] Duke Robert of Normandy came to England to confer with his brother King Henry, whom he found at Northampton. The duke then asked for the return of what Henry had taken from him in Normandy, but the king refused all his requests. The duke left in anger, and crossed the channel.[1] On Friday, 16 February, in the first week of Lent, a strange star appeared in the evening, and shone in the same shape and at the same time between the south and the west for twenty-five days. It seemed small and dark, but the lustre which shone from it was extremely bright, and darts of light, like huge beams, flashed into the same star from east and the north. Many said that they saw several unusual stars at the same time. On the night of Maundy Thursday [22 March], two moons were seen, a little before dawn, one in the east and the other in the west, and both were full, for this moon was fourteen days old.[2] In this year there arose a truly violent dispute between the German emperor and his son.[3] King Henry of England crossed the sea before August and went into Normandy, where almost all the leading Normans went over to him except Robert of Bellême, William of Mortain and a few others, who held firm with Duke Robert.[4]

Henry IV, the ninety-sixth emperor of the Romans, died. His son Henry succeeded him and reigned nineteen years.[5]

King Henry of the English came to Bec on the feast of the Assumption [15 August]. There he conferred with Archbishop Anselm, and they made peace and came to an agreement on all the matters which divided them.[6] Not long afterwards, the archbishop, on the king's orders, returned to England. Henry brought together an army, reached Tinchebrai, the castle of the count of Mortain, and besieged it. While he was detained there, Duke Robert, the king's

Bermondsey Annals (*Ann. Mon.* iii. 430). In ASC the comet lasts for several hours ('lange stunde þæræfter') and in Margam, and Winchester for 24 days, where C originally read 21 (like OV).

[3] This sentence like the later one on the imperial succession was probably based on ASC: see below, 1106 n. 5.

[4] This is very close to ASC, which is followed by HH *HA* vii. 25 (pp. 452–4). ASC had mentioned at the opening of 1106 Robert of Bellême's departure 'in hostile fashion' to Normandy from the 1105 Christmas court.

[5] This was based on the last sentence in ASC's annal, but its location here could suggest that JW was able to place it in its correct chronological position since Henry IV, deposed on 31 Dec. 1105, died on 7 Aug. 1106.

[6] Eadmer, *HN* iii (pp. 182–3). The next sentence is also based on *HN* iii (p. 183).

super eum cum exercitu suo in uigilia sancti Michaelis, et cum eo
Rotbertus de Beleasm, et comes *d*Willelmus de Moreteon*d* sed ius et
uictoria facta est regis. Ibi captus est Rotbertus comes Normannie, et
comes Willelmus de Moreteon, et *e*Rotbertus de Stutauilla.*e* Rotbertus autem de Beleasm in fugam uersus est. Willelmus Crispinus
captus,*f* et plures alii cum eo. His ita gestis, rex subegit sibi totam
Normanniam, et secundum suam uoluntatem dictauit, et hoc per
litteras Anselmo arciepiscopo indicauit.[7]

[1107] (.i.) 1129 Eadgarus rex Scottorum .viii. idus Ian.*a* obiit, cui
Alexander*b* frater suus successit.[1] *Normannia sub regia pace disposita,
duce*que Normannorum *Rotberto,* et *comite Moritonii* Willelmo*c* *in
Angliam sub captione premissis, rex ipse* ante *Pasca in regnum suum
reuersus est.*[2] *In kal. Aug. conuentus* omnium *episcoporum, abbatum, et
procerum regni Lundonie in palatio regis factus est, et per tres dies,
absente Anselmo* arciepiscopo, *inter regem et episcopos satis actum de
ecclesiarum inuestituris, quibusdam ad hoc nitentibus ut rex eas faceret
more patris et fratris sui, non iuxta preceptum*d* et obedientiam apostolici.
Nam papa* Pascalis *in sententia que* exinde *promulgata fuerat firmus
stans, concesserat hominia que papa Vrbanus eque ut inuestituras
interdixerat, ac per hoc regem sibi de inuestituris consentaneum fecerat.
Dehinc, presente Anselmo, astante multitudine, annuit rex et statuit, ut ab
eo tempore in reliquum, nunquam per dationem baculi pastoralis uel anuli
quisquam* de *episcopatu aut abbatia per regem uel quamlibet laicam
manum in Anglia inuestiretur, concedente quoque Anselmo, ut nullus in
prelationem electus pro hominio quod regi faceret, consecratione suscepti
honoris priuaretur.*[3] *Gerardus* Eboracensis arciepiscopus *sua manu
imposita manui Anselmi, ut ipse uolebat, interposita fide sua, pollicitus
est, se eandem subiectionem et obedientiam* | *ipsi et successoribus eius in*

p. 367

d–d written over erasure C   *e–e* written over erasure C   *f* captus est H
a Iun. L   *b* Alex- *of* Alexander *over erasure* C   *c* Rotberto CLP
d over erasure C

[7] This is extremely close to ASC. ASC adds Edgar the Atheling to those captured, as
well as the despatch of Duke Robert, William, count of Mortain, and Robert of
Estouteville to England. The reference to Henry's letter to Anselm was probably based
on Eadmer, *HN* iii (p. 184) where it is included. OV *HE* xi. 20 (vi. 84–90) has a fuller
account of the battle, which confirms some of the detail added in HH *HA* vii. 25 (pp. 452–
4). For the alternative dates of 27 and 29 Sept. for the battle, see Chibnall in OV *HE* xi. 20
(vi. 89 n. 4).

[1] This is probably taken from ASC, which, however, like HH *HA* vii. 26 (p. 456), speaks
of Alexander succeeding with Henry I's permission. JW's apparent derivatives, *HR* iii. 187
(SD ii. 238), Hoveden (i. 164), and the Melrose Chronicle (*The Chronicle of Melrose from*

brother, came upon him on the eve of St Michael's day [28 September], accompanied by Robert of Bellême and William, count of Mortain, but justice and victory were with the king. Duke Robert of Normandy, William, count of Mortain, Robert de Stuteville were taken prisoner. Robert of Bellême fled. William Crispin was captured, and many others with him. After this battle the king subjugated all Normandy, and ruled as he willed, and let Archbishop Anselm know by letter.[7]

[1107] Edgar, king of the Scots, died on 6 January and was succeeded by his brother Alexander.[1] Peace had been restored in Normandy under the king, and Duke Robert of Normandy and William, count of Mortain, had been sent on to England under guard, and the king himself returned to his own kingdom before Easter.[2] On 1 August a council of all the bishops, abbots, and magnates of the kingdom was held in the royal palace in London. In Anselm's absence the subject of ecclesiastical investitures was fully discussed between king and bishops for three days. Some urged the king to proceed as his father and brother had done and to ignore the apostolic command and refuse to obey it. Pope Paschal while standing firm on the decree which had been pronounced on this matter, allowed homages which Pope Urban before him had forbidden as much as investitures, and through it had gained the royal consent on the question of investitures. Afterwards in Anselm's presence and in front of a crowd of people, King Henry agreed and declared that from that time onwards no one in England should be invested with a bishopric or abbey by the king or any layman. In return Anselm agreed that no one elected to office should be deprived of consecration to his office if he had already done homage.[3] Gerard, archbishop of York, placed his hand in Anselm's, as he had wanted, and promised, pledging his fidelity, that he would show to him and his successors in the archiepiscopate the same

---

the Cottonian Manuscript Faustina B. IX in the British Museum: a Complete Facsimile, introd. by A. O. and M. O. Anderson (London, 1936), p. 31) date Edgar's death to 8 (not 6) Jan., a day confirmed by *LVD* (p. 140).

[2] Eadmer, *HN* iv (p. 184). ASC records Henry's control of Normandy, and return thence 'in spring'. Under 1106 (see above, 1106 n. 7) it had recorded the despatch of Duke Robert and Count William to England.

[3] Eadmer, *HN* iv (p. 186). This council is mentioned in ASC as one where the king disposed of episcopal and abbatial vacancies without reference to the main agreement on investitures.

arciepiscopatu exhibiturum, quam Herefordensi ecclesie ab eo sacrandus episcopus *illi promiserat. Willelmus Wintoniensi, Rogerus Searesbyriensi,[e] Reignelmus Herefordensi,[e] Willelmus Execestrensi,[e] et Vrbanus Clamorgatensi[e] ecclesie, que in* Walonia *est, electi episcopi, simul Cantuuariam uenerunt, et in die dominica, que fuit .iii. idus Aug., pariter ab Anselmo consecrati sunt, ministrantibus sibi in hoc officio suffraganeis ipsius sedis, Gerardo,* scilicet, *arciepiscopo Eboracensi, Rotberto Lincoliensi, Iohanne Bathoniensi, Hereberto Northwicensi, Rotberto Cestrensi,[f] Radulfo Cicestrensi, Rannulfo Dunholmensi.*[4] Nullus certe fuit tunc temporis qui meminisset retroactis temporibus tot simul pastores electos et ordinatos in Anglia, nisi regis Eadwardi senioris tempore, quando Pleigmundus archiepiscopus .vii. episcopos .vii. ecclesiis in una die ordinauit.[g][5] Hoc etiam anno Mauricius Lundoniensis episcopus, Ricardus Eliensis abbas, Rotbertus abbas de sancto Eadmundo, Milo Crispin, Rotberto filius Haimonis, Rogerus Bicod, Ricardus de Retuers, regis consiliatores, uita decesserunt.[h][6]

[1108] (.ii.) 1130   [a]Hrofensis ecclesie episcopus Gundulfus obiit non. Mar.[1] Rex Anglorum Heinricus pacem firmam legemque talem constituit, ut si quis in furtu uel latrocinio deprehensus fuisset, suspenderetur. *Monetam quoque corruptam et falsam sub tanta animaduersione corrigi statuit, ut nullus qui posset deprehendi falsos denarios facere, aliqua redemptione quin oculos et inferiores corporis partes perderet, iuuari ualeret. Et quoniam sepissime dum denarii eligebantur, flectebantur, rumpebantur, respuebantur, statuit, ut nullus denarius uel obolus,* quos et rotundos esse instituit, aut etiam

---

[e] s *originally at end of place-name, but erased* C   [f] Couentrensi H   [g] H *addition here:* in presentis concilii conuentu, Alduuino Ramesiensis apostolico iussu, restituta est abbatia quam Rome sibi iniuria subtractam conquestus est. Venerabilis etiam Cantuariensis ecclesie prior Arnulfus ibi de Burh abbas eligitur; *for* B[1]*'s addition here, see Appendix B*   [h] *For* ?B[1]*'s mutilated addition here, see Appendix B;* 1108[e] *add. here* P

[a–a] *placed at* 1108[m] HL

---

[4] Eadmer, *HN* iv (p. 187). See comments on this council in Whitelock, Brett, and Brooke, *Councils and Synods*, ii. 689–91. ASC refers to the numerous consecrations but omits the compromise agreement between Archbishop Gerard and Anselm.

[5] The reference to Plegmund echoes JW's recording *s.a.* 909 (see above, vol. ii. 362–3 and n. 5) of his supposed consecration of seven bishops on one day.

[6] The first three obits are in ASC. Greenway, *Fasti* i. 1, shows that Canterbury and Jumièges obituaries date Bishop Maurice's death to Sept. 1107. ASC and JW alone record the deaths of Robert II of Bury and Richard of Ely. The JW MS B's addition is the earliest evidence for the day (16 Sept.) of Robert's death (*Heads*, p. 32), and an Ely obit gives 16

submission and obedience as he had promised when he had been consecrated bishop of Hereford by him. William of Winchester, Roger of Salisbury, Reinhelm of Hereford, William of Exeter, and Urban of the see of Glamorgan in Wales were elected bishops, and all came together to Canterbury. On Sunday, 11 August, they were all consecrated by Anselm, who was assisted in this ceremony by the suffragans of his see, Gerard, archbishop of York, Robert of Lincoln, John of Bath, Herbert of Norwich, Robert of Chester, Ralph of Chichester, Ranulf of Durham.[4] No one could remember at that time the simultaneous election and consecration of so many pastors in England since the reign of Edward the Elder when Archbishop Plegmund ordained seven bishops to seven sees on one day.[5] This year Bishop Maurice of London, Abbot Richard of Ely, Abbot Robert of Bury St Edmund's, Miles Crispin, Robert son of Haimo, Roger Bigod, Richard Redvers, who were royal counsellors, died.[6]

[1108] Gundulf, bishop of Rochester, died on 7 March.[1] King Henry of England established a strict peace by legislating that anyone caught thieving or robbing should be hanged. He also decreed that spoiled or false coinage should be reformed with such severe force that anyone caught making forged pennies should be blinded and lose his lower limbs without the option of saving himself by a money payment. Furthermore since very often pennies when selected were found to be bent or broken and so rejected, he decreed that no penny or halfpenny (which he also ordained should be round), and no farthing should be whole. This

June for the day of Richard's death (*Heads*, p. 45). Miles Crispin of Wallingford, a landholder in Oxfordshire, Berkshire, and Buckinghamshire, a benefactor of Abingdon, a witness of many charters of Henry I, is known to have been sick in the 7th year of Henry I (*Chronicon de Abingdon*, ii. 97), and was buried at Montebourg in Normandy (OV *HE* xi. 32 (vi. 146 n. 2)). Roger Bigod, royal steward, sheriff of Norfolk, died on 10 Sept. 1107, and was buried at the Cluniac priory of Thetford, which he had founded (OV *HE* xi. 32 (vi. 147 n. 4)). Richard de Reviers, a justiciar of Devon and the Isle of Wight, was also buried at Thetford (OV *HE* xi. 32 (vi. 144–6)). Robert fitz Hamon, son of Hamon the steward, conqueror of Glamorgan, received the honour of Gloucester from William II, and founded Tewkesbury abbey. He was grievously wounded at the siege of Falaise (WM *GR* v. 398 (ii. 475)) and his death is recorded Mar. 1107 in late Tewkesbury annals, BL Cotton Cleopatra C. III, fo. 212 (*Mon.* i. 60). The information added by the JW witnesss H on Aldwin's restoration to Ramsey and on Ernulf's election to Peterborough is confirmed elsewhere (see *Heads*, pp. 62, 60).

[1] The earlier *Vita Gundulfi* printed in *The Life of Gundulf, Bishop of Rochester*, ed. R. M. Thomson (Toronto Medieval Texts, vii; Toronto, 1977), c. 47 (pp. 68–9) gives the time of his death as after Vespers, 8 Mar. 1108. Greenway, *Fasti* ii. 76, gives the evidence for 8 and 9 Mar. as the days of his commemoration.

quadrans, *integer esset. Ex quo facto magnum bonum toti regno creatum est,* quia ipse *rex hec in secularibus ad releuendas terre erumnas agebat.*[a][2] [b]Gerardus Eboracensis arciepiscopus obiit, pro quo Thomas, [c]predecessoris sui Thome fratruelis,[c] eligitur.[d][3]

[e]*Hec sunt statuta de archidiaconibus, presbiteris, diaconibus, subdiaconibus, et canonicis in quocunque gradu constitutis,* que anno Dominice incarnationis .mcviii., *statuerunt Anselmus arciepiscopus Cantuuariensis, et Thomas electus arciepiscopus Eboracensis cum eo, omnesque[f] alii Anglie episcopi, in presentia gloriosi[g] regis Heinrici, assensu baronum suorum:*

'*Statutum est ut presbiteri, diaconi, subdiaconi caste uiuant, et feminas in domibus suis non habeant, preter proxima consanguinitate sibi iunctas, secundum hoc quod sancta Nicena synodus definiuit.*

Illi uero presbiteri, diaconi, subdiaconi, qui post interdictum Lundoniensis concilii feminas suas tenuerunt, uel alias duxerunt, si amplius missam celebrare uoluerint, eas a se omnino sic facient alienas, ut nec ille in domos eorum, nec ipsi in domos[h] earum intrent, sed neque in aliqua domo scienter conueniant, neque huiusmodi[i] femine in territorio ecclesie habitent. Si autem propter aliquam honestam causam eas colloqui oporteat, cum duobus legitimis testibus extra domum colloquantur.

Si uero in .ii. aut in[j] .iii, legitimis testibus, uel publica parrochianorum fama, aliquis eorum accusatus fuerit quod hoc statutum uiolauerit, purgabit se adiunctis secum ordinis sui[k] idoneis testibus, .vi. si presbiter, .iiii. si diaconus, .ii. si subdiaconus fuerit. Cui autem hec purgatio defecerit, ut transgressor sacri statuti iudicabitur.

Illi autem presbiteri qui, diuini altaris et sacrorum ordinum contemptores, preelegerint cum mulieribus habitare, a diuino officio remoti, omnique[l] ecclesiastico beneficio priuati, extra chorum ponantur, infames

---

[b] *paragraph mark here* C   [c-c] *om.* HL   [d] *1108*[n] *placed here* B
[e-e] *written in right mg. by* C¹, *incorporated at 1107*[h] P   [f] omnibusque HL
[g] *om.* HL   [h] domus CBP   [i] huiusmodo CB   [j] *om.* L   [k] *om.*
HL   [l] omnisque HL

---

² Eadmer, *HN* iv (p. 193), from whom the general statement on the hanging of thieves and robbers and the peace of Henry I must have been deduced. That coins should not be 'integer' was presumably a reference to the deliberate snicking of coins before circulation. This passage has been most recently discussed by M. Blackburn, 'Coinage and currency under Henry I: a review', *ANS* xiii (1991), 49–81, at pp. 62–4, who reported that numismatic evidence confirmed both Eadmer's statement on Henry I's deliberate snicking of coins and JW's reference to the issue of a halfpenny. 'A few coins of type 6 [of Henry I's coinage] and all those of types 7–12 have a deliberate cut extending a quarter or third of the way across the coin, the purpose presumably being to show that it was not plated with a

was of great benefit to the whole kingdom, the king acting to relieve the sufferings of the land in secular matters.[2] Gerard, archbishop of York, died, and Thomas, nephew of Gerard's predecessor, Thomas, was chosen in his place.[3]

These are the decrees concerning archdeacons, priests, deacons, subdeacons, and canons of whatever grade, which in the year of the Lord 1108, Anselm, archbishop of Canterbury, together with Thomas, archbishop-elect of York, and all the other English bishops, established in the glorious King Henry's presence and with the nobles' assent:

'It is decreed that priests, deacons and subdeacons live chastely, that they do not have women in their households, save those closely related to them in consanguinity, in accordance with the order of the Council of Nicaea.

Those priests, deacons, subdeacons, who, after the London Council's prohibition, keep their women, or marry others, are, if they wish to celebrate mass any more, not only to put them away completely and treat them as strangers so that the women are not to come to their houses nor are they into the women's, but further they are also never to meet them knowingly in any other house nor are any such women to live on the lands of the church. If, moreover, there is a good reason for them to converse with each other, then they should meet out of doors in the presence of two legitimate witnesses.

If on the testimony of two or three lawful witnesses, or the parishioners' common report, any clerk should be accused of violation of this canon, he is to purge himself by the oaths of competent witnesses of his own order, six, if he is a priest, four, if he is a deacon, two, if a subdeacon. The person unable to clear himself in this way shall be adjudged to have contravened the holy canons.

Those priests who choose to live with women, without respect for God's altar and their holy orders, are to be removed from their divine ministry, deprived of ecclesiastical benefices, turned outside the

base core.' Halfpennies seem to have been issued during the currency of type 5 or early in type 6, continuing possibly into the following issue, type 9.

[3] *HC* (pp. 24–5) dates Gerard's death to 21 May after 7 years and about 5 months as archbishop, being succeeded 6 days later by Thomas, the king's chaplain. ASC (which also reports Thomas II's succession) simply says that he died before Whitsun (24 May). *HC* also describes Thomas II as Thomas I's nephew, which is confirmed by the statements of Eadmer, *HN* iv (p. 208), and WM *GP* iii. 118 (p. 260) that he was the son of Samson, bishop of Worcester.

pronuntiati. Qui uero rebellis et contemptor feminam non reliquerit, et missam celebrare presumpserit, uocatus ad satisfactionem, si neglexerit .viii. die excommunicetur.

*Eadem sententia arcidiacon*os *et canonicos omnes complectitur, et de mulieribus relinquendis, et de uitanda earum conuersatione, et de districtione censure, si statuta transgressi fuerint.*

*Iurabunt archidiacon*i *omnes quod pecuniam non accipient pro toleranda transgressione huius statuti, nec tolerabunt presbiteros, quos scient feminas habere,* missam *cantare, uel uicarios habere. Similiter decani* facient. *Qui uero arcidiaconus uel decanus hec iurare noluerit, arcidiaconatum uel decaniam perdet.*

Presbiteri uero, qui relictis mulieribus Deo et sacris altaribus seruire elegerint, .xl. dies ab officio cessantes, pro se interim uicarios habebunt, iniuncta eis penitentia, secundum hoc quod episcopis eorum uisum fuerit.'[em 4]

[n]Philippus rex Francorum obiit, cui Ludowicus filius suus successit. Rex Anglorum Heinricus mare transiit.[5] Anselmus arciepiscopus, ut rex *rogau*erat, *Ricardum Lundoniensi ecclesie electum pontificem, in capella sua apud Paggaham consecrauit, ministrantibus ei in hoc officio Willelmo episcopo Wintoniensi, Rogero Sear*esbyriensi, *Radulfo Cicestrensi, et Willelmo Execestrensi, accepta prius ab eo* consueta *professione de obedientia et subiectione sua. Post hec Cantuuariam uenit, et Radulfum* Saiensem *abbat*em, *uir*um *religios*um, pro Gundulfo, ad *Hrofens*em *ecclesi*am, *.iii. idus Aug,.* episcopum consecrauit, *ministrantibus sibi in hoc* officio *Willelmo episcopo Wintoniensi, Radulfo Cicestrensi, et Ricardo Lundoniensi. Qui Ricardus, antecessorum suorum more, honorauit ipso die matrem suam ecclesiam Cantuuariensem honesto munere.*[n 6]

[1109] (.iii.) 1131 Dorubernensis arciepiscopus *Anselmus .xi. k. Mai.* feria .iiii., [a]*Cantuuarie* obiit,[a] *et sequenti die que fuit Cena Domini honorifice sepe*litur.[1] Rex Anglorum Heinricus circa Rogationes Angliam rediit, et curiam suam apud Westmonasterium in

[m] *1108*[a] *placed here HL*   [n–n] *placed at 1108*[d] *B*

[a–a] obiit Cantuuarie *HL*

---

[4] Primatial Council of London, printed with full apparatus and discussion in Whitelock, Brett, and Brooke, *Councils and Synods*, ii. 694–702. There it is shown that JW's marginal addition of the canons belongs to a different family from that in Eadmer, *HN* iv (pp. 192–5). It 'could be a reissue on royal authority when the king interested himself in the enforcement of these canons after Anselm's death'.

chancel, and declared infamous sinners. Whoever deliberately and contumaciously keeps his wife, and presumes to celebrate mass, shall be called to make amends, and, if he fails to do so shall after eight days, be excommunicated.

This decree on putting women aside, on avoiding contact with them, and on the penalties imposed if it is contravened shall apply to all archdeacons and canons.

All archdeacons shall swear that they shall not receive a bribe for the contravention of this decree and that they shall not allow priests to say mass or to appoint deputies if they know them to have wives. A dean should do likewise. An archdeacon or dean unwilling to swear this shall lose his archdeaconry or deanery.

Priests who choose to put aside their wives and to serve God and the holy altars shall suspend their duties for forty days. During this time they shall have vicars to perform them, and shall do penance as prescribed by the bishop.'[4]

Philip, the French king, died and was succeeded by his son Louis. King Henry of England crossed overseas.[5] Archbishop Anselm, as requested by the king, consecrated Richard, bishop-elect of London, in his chapel at Pagham, having first received from him the customary profession of obedience and submission. William bishop of Winchester, Roger of Salisbury, Ralph of Chichester, and William of Exeter assisted Anselm at this consecration. After this Anselm came to Canterbury, and on 11 August consecrated Ralph, abbot of Séez, a religious man, to the see of Rochester in Gundulf's place, being assisted by William, bishop of Winchester, Ralph of Chichester, and Richard of London. On the same day this Richard, following the precedence of his predecessors, honoured his mother, the church of Canterbury, with a generous present.[6]

[1109] Anselm, archbishop of Canterbury, died there on Wednesday, 21 April, and was buried with honour the following day, which was Maundy Thursday.[1] Henry, king of England, returned to England at the Rogation days [31 May, 1–2 June], and held his court at

---

[5] The French royal succession, with an incorrect date, 5 Aug., for Philip's death, and Henry's crossing the sea ('before Aug.') are in ASC followed by a report of the struggles between the French and English kings. Philip I died on 29 or 30 July (see Prou, *Recueil* pp. xxxiv–xxxviii).

[6] Eadmer, *HN* iv (pp. 196–8). Eadmer dates Ralph d'Escures' consecration to 26 July.

[1] Eadmer, *HN* iv (p. 206). ASC records Anselm's death (wrongly on 22 Mar.) at the end of the annal.

Pentecosten tenuit.² Thomas Eboracensis*b* ecclesie arciepiscopus electus, a Ricardo Lundoniensi episcopo, .v. kl. Iul. Lundonie consecratur, et post*c* ab Vlrio cardinali pallium, quod sibi papa miserat, in k. Aug., die dominica, Eboraci suscepit, et ipso eodem die Turgodum, Dunholmensem priorem, ad episcopatum sancti Andree de Scottia, qui dicitur Cenrimunt, consecrauit.³ Eodem anno rex abbatiam Eliensem ad episcopalem mutauit sedem, et Herueum, Bancornensem episcopum, eidem ecclesie prefecit.⁴ *Stella cometa mense Dec. uisa est circa lacteum circulum, crinem in australem celi dirigens plagam.*^d⁵

[1110] (.iiii.) 1132   Rex Anglorum Heinricus filiam suam Heinrico regi Teutonicorum dedit in coniugem.¹ Eodem anno diuersa per p. 368 Angliam signa monstrata sunt. | Terremotus Scrobbesbyrie factus est maximus. Fluuius qui Trenta dicitur, apud Snotingaham, a mane usque ad horam diei tertiam, spatio unius miliarii, exsiccatus*a* est, ita ut homines sicco uestigio per alueum incederent. Stella cometa .vi. idus Iunii apparuit, et ^b per tres*b* ebdomadas uisa est lucere.²

[1111] (.v.) 1133   Heinricus rex Theutonicorum Romam uenit, Pascalem papam cepit, et in custodiam posuit, sed postmodum ad pontem uie Salarie, ubi Pascalem festiuitatem in campo cele-brauerunt, pacem cum eo fecit.¹

b Eboracensi *CL*   *c interlin. C*   ^d 1111^pp *placed here B*

a exiccatus *CB*   ^b-b *possibly over erasure H*

---

² ASC dates Henry's return to 'before Whitsuntide' (13 June) and mentions the Westminster court (which was presumably held at Whitsun (Eadmer, *HN* iv (p. 207)), where arrangements for Matilda's marriage to Henry V were completed.

³ The consecration of Thomas II at London on 27 June is reported by Eadmer, *HN* iv (p. 210), who also reports (p. 211) Cardinal Odalric giving him the pallium in York at some time after 27 June. *HC* (p. 50) reports Thomas II's return to York, and his consecration of Turgot as bishop of St Andrew's on the day Odalric gave him the pallium. JW's 'kal. Aug.' was a Sunday in 1109 which is a more likely day for the consecration than the 30 July of *HR* 189 (SD ii. 241). The latter's '.iii. kal.' could be a misreading of JW's 'in kal.'

⁴ JW emphasizes royal initiative in the creation of the new see, which is implied in Anselm's letter to Paschal II (included in Eadmer, *HN* iv (pp. 195–6)). Henry in *Regesta* ii. 119 of 17 Oct. 1109 creates the see, but Eadmer, *HN* iv (pp. 195–6), shows that the creation was discusssed at least as early as the Whitsun court of 1108. *LE*, pp. 245 ff., and the correspondence printed in Schmitt, *Anselmi opera omnia*, v. 441, 457–60, give the background to the foundation and to Hervey's translation. Eadmer, *HN* iv (p. 211), records Bishop Hervey's translation.

⁵ Eadmer, *HN* iv (p. 212). A different comet is recorded under 1110 in some chronicles.

¹ ASC, OV *HE* xi. 38 (vi. 166), HH *HA* vii. 27 (p. 456) and the Winchester Annals

Westminster at Whitsun [13 June].[2] Thomas, archbishop-elect of
York, was consecrated by Richard, bishop of London, on 27 June at
London, and afterwards at York, on Sunday, 1 August he received
the pallium. which the pope had sent, from Cardinal Ulric, and on
the same day, he consecrated Turgot, prior of Durham, to the see of
St Andrew's of Scotland, which is called Cenrimont.[3] In this year the
king changed Ely from an abbey to a bishopric, and appointed
Hervey, bishop of Bangor, over that see.[4] In December a comet was
seen near the Milky Way, its tail extending to the northern part of
the sky.[5]

[1110] Henry, king of England, gave his daughter in marriage to
Henry, the King of the Germans.[1] In the same year amazing things
occurred all over England. At Shrewsbury there was a large earthquake. At Nottingham, from dawn right up to the third hour, a mile
of the Trent dried up so that men walked along its channel dryshod.
A comet appeared on 8 June and was visible for three weeks.[2]

[1111] On his arrival in Rome, Henry, king of the Germans, seized
and imprisoned Pope Paschal, but later came to an agreement with
him at the bridge of the *Via Salaria*, where they celebrated Easter
[2 April] in the open.[1]

(*Ann. Mon.* ii. 43) report Henry's giving of his daughter in marriage to Henry V, OV under
1109. ASC and HH describe the taxes raised to pay for Matilda's dowry. For the
background to the marriage negotiations, see K. Leyser, 'England and the empire in the
twelfth century', *Transactions of the Royal Historical Society*, 5th ser., x (1960), 61–83, rep.
in id., *Medieval Germany and its Neighbours 900–1250* (London, 1982), pp. 191–213.
  [2] A comet is reported in ASC, in HH *HA* vii. 27 (pp. 456–8) and in the Winchester,
Waverley, Bermondsey, Rouen (in June 1110 in the last two and in ASC), and in the Bury
Annals (*Ann. Mon.* ii. 43, 215, iii. 431, *UAG*, pp. 47, 131); the disappearance of the moon
on 5 May is noted in ASC, and tempests in ASC and in the Winchester and Waverley
annals. The drying up of the Trent is described under 1108 in the Tewkesbury, and under
1110 in the Burton Annals (*Ann. Mon.* i. 44, 186). The earthquake in Shrewsbury is not
recorded elsewhere. In addition ASC records four obits and the Count of Anjou's
succession to Maine.
  [1] Soon after celebrating Christmas 1110 at Florence, Henry V advanced on Rome, and
an agreement was reached on 4 Feb. at S. Maria in Turri between papal and royal legates,
which was confirmed by Henry at Sutri. Paschal was seized on the evening of 12 Feb., and,
after two months of captivity, by the treaty of Ponte Mammolo on 11 Apr., he conceded
investiture by ring and staff and promised to abstain from any future excommunication of
the king. As Easter was on 2 Apr., JW has antedated the peace between Henry and Paschal.
Henry was crowned on 13 Apr. The so-called *Annales Romani* (MGH *Leges* iv. 1,
Constitutiones, i, no. 99 (p. 147)) refer to the writing down of the 11 Apr. agreements
and meetings 'in eodem campo qui Septem Fratrum dicitur' and to crossing 'iuxta pontem

*^a*Hoc autem modo reconciliatio inter regem et domnum papam facta est. Et hoc est iuramentum regis.

'*Ego Heinricus rex* liberos *dimittam, .iiii. ^buel .v. feria proxima,^b domnum papam, et episcopos, et cardinales, et omnes captiuos et obsides, qui pro eo uel cum eo capti sunt, securos perduci faciam intra portas Transtiberine ciuitatis, nec ulterius capiam aut capi permittam. Eos qui in fidelitate domni pape Pascalis permanent, et populo Romano, et Transtiberine et insule* ciuitatis*^c pacem et securitatem seruabo, tam per me quam meos, et in personis et in rebus, qui pacem mihi seruauerint. Domnum papam Pascalem fideliter adiuuabo ut papatum quiete et secure teneat: patrimonia et possessiones Romane ecclesie, que abstuli, restituam, cuncta* que *habere debet more antecessorum meorum recuperare et tenere adiuuabo bona fide, et domno pape Pascali obediam,^d saluo honore regni et imperii, sicut catholici imperatores catholicis pontificibus Romanis. ^eHec omnia obseruabo bona fide, sine fraude et malo ingenio.^e Et isti sunt iuratores ex parte ipsius regis, Fredericus^f Coloniensis archiepiscopus, Gebehardus Tridentius episcopus,^g ^hBurchardus ⁱMonasteriensis episcopus,^{ih} Bruno Spirensis episcopus,^j Albertus cancellarius, comes Herimannus, Fredericus comes palatinus, ^kBerengarius comes,^k Fredericus comes, Bonefacius marchio, Albertus comes de Blandriaco, Fredericus comes, Godefridus comes, Warnerius marcio.'¹²*

^mConventio secunda inter papam et regem.^m

'*Domnus papa Pascalis,ⁿ concedet domno regi Heinrico et regno eius, et priuilegio suo sub anathemate confirmabit et corroborabit, episcopo uel abbate libere electo sine symonia, assensu regis, quod domnus rex* eum

---

^a *in the investiture documents in 1111 and 1112 some variants of the two possibly related texts,* BL Harl. 633 *(=* Harl.*) and* WM (GR) *are shown*   ^{b–b} feria proxima *over erasure with* pascha *interlin.* B   ^c ciuitati WM (GR)   ^d obedientiam HL   ^{e–e} *om.* (G) WM(GR)   ^f Freothericus HL   ^g Berengarius comes *add.* Harl.   ^{h–h} *om.* WM GR   ^{i–i} comes Harl   ^j *om.* B, Berengarius comes *add.* WM (GR)   ^{k–k} *om.* Harl. WM (GR)   ^l *over erasure* C   ^{m–m} *om.* HL   ⁿ Pascalis centesimus .lvi. H

Salarium Tyberis fluuio', but the context of these references is quite different from JW's mention of the *Via Salaria* at the opening of this annal. On the *Annales Romani*, see U.-R. Blumenthal, '*Patrimonia* and *regalia* in 1111', *Law, Church, and Society: Essays in Honor of Stephan Kuttner*, eds. K. Pennington and R. Somerville (Philadelphia, Pa, 1977), 9–20. In his narrative background to these documents, WM acknowledged a debt in his account to a lost work by the Irish ecclesiastic David.

² MGH *Leges* iv. 1, *Constitutiones*, i, nos. 95–6 (pp. 144–6). JW's text has the siglum C4 in the MGH edition. That JW's text of these two documents and of those under 1111 n. 4 (the mutual oaths of Henry V and Paschal II), 1111 n. 5 (the 'pravilegium' of 1111), and 1112 n. 1 (the Acts of the 1112 Lateran Council) was taken from William of Malmesbury's edition of the *Liber Pontificalis* was demonstrated by R. M. Thomson, 'William of

These are the terms of the reconciliation between Pope and king. This is the king's promise:

'On Thursday or Friday next, I, King Henry, will set free the lord Pope, the bishops, cardinals, and all prisoners and hostages, seized either because they stood by him or were with him, will give them safe conduct within the walls of Trastevere, and never again arrest them, or allow them to be arrested. For myself and mine I will keep peace and safeguard those in allegiance with the lord Pope Paschal who will observe peace with me, whether the Roman people or the people of Trastevere or of the Tiber island, both their persons and goods. I will faithfully help Pope Paschal to hold his office both peacefully and securely. I will restore the patrimony and possessions of the Roman church which I have usurped. I will faithfully help her recover and keep, as my ancestors have done, all which was rightfully hers. I will obey the lord pope Paschal, saving the rights of crown and empire, as catholic emperors have obeyed the catholic Roman pontiffs, and will keep all these promises in good faith without deceit or trickery. These are the oath-takers on the king's side: Frederick, archbishop of Cologne, Gebhard, bishop of Trent, Burchard, bishop of Münster, Brun, bishop of Speyer, Albert, chancellor, Count Hermann, Frederick, count palatine, Count Berengar, Count Frederick, Marquis Boniface, Albert, count of Biandrate, Count Frederick, Count Godfrey, Marquis Werner.'[2]

This is the second agreement between pope and king.

'The lord Pope Paschal grants to the lord King Henry and his kingdom, and confirms and sanctions under the sentence of anathema this privilege, that a bishop or abbot should be freely elected

Malmesbury's edition of the *Liber Pontificalis*, *Archivum Historiae Pontificae*, xvii (1978), 93–112 (reprinted in id., *William of Malmesbury* (Woodbridge, 1987), pp. 119–38 at 134). The Worcester copy of this edition, Cambridge, University Library Kk. 4. 6, omits these documents because they had already been included in a 'magna Cronica', as an explanatory note makes clear: 'Quapropter Henricus, filius superioris Henrici, qui Hildebrandum expulerat, in ecclesia sancti Petri papam cepit et sacramentum ab eo exegit, quod in magna Cronica descripsimus. Epistolas etiam illius alibi descriptas, quoniam ad alias tendimus, rescribere omittimus.' The other surviving copy of William's edition, BL Harl. 633, fos. 62ᵛ-63ᵛ, preserves these documents, but its text and that which WM gives in his *GR* as well as John's text 'all derive independently from their source, but are more closely related to each other than any is to the other English copies of the texts' examined by Brett (Brett, 'John of Worcester and his contemporaries', p. 116 n. 3). JW obtained neither the narratives under IIII n. I and IIII n. 6 nor his text of the IIII 'conventio' (IIII n. 3) from William's edition. On the Lateran Council of III2, see U.-R. Blumenthal, 'Opposition to Paschal II: some comments on the Lateran Council of III2', *Annuarium Historiae Conciliorum*, x (1978), 82–98.

anulo et uirga inuestiat. Episcopus autem uel abbas a rege *inuestitus, libere accipiat consecrationem ab* episcopo *ad quem pertinuerit. Si quis uero a clero et populo eligatur, nisi a rege inuestiatur, a nemine consecretur. Et arciepiscopi et episcopi libertatem habeant consecrandi a rege inuestitos. Super his* etiam *domnus papa Pascalis non inquietabit regem Heinricum, nec eius regnum et imperium.*³

^oHoc sacramentum est ex parte papa.^o

'*Domnus papa Pascalis non inquietabit domnum regem Heinricum, nec eius* imperium uel *regnum, de inuestitura episcopatuum* uel *abbatiarum, neque de iniuria sibi illata et suis,*^p *neque*^q *aliquod malum reddet sibi uel alicui persone pro hac causa, et penitus in personam regis Heinrici nunquam anathema ponet. Nec remanebit in domno papa, quin coronet eum, sicut in ordine continetur. Et regnum et imperium officii sui auxilio eum tenere adiuuabit pro posse suo. Et* hoc^r *adimplebit domnus papa sine fraude et malo ingenio.*⁴ *Hec sunt nomina illorum episcoporum et cardinalium qui, precepto domni pape Pascalis, priuilegium*^s *et amicitiam* ^t*sacramento confirmauerunt domno imperatori Heinrico:*^t *Petrus Portuensis episcopus, Centius Sabiniensis episcopus, Rotbertus cardinalis sancti Eusebii, Bonifacius cardinalis sancti Marci, Anastasius cardinalis sancti Clementis, Gregorius cardinalis sanctorum*^u *apostolorum Petri et Pauli, item Gregorius cardinalis sancti Grisogoni, Iohannes cardinalis sancte Potentiane, Risus cardinalis sancti Laurentii, Rainerus cardinalis sanctorum Marcellini et Petri, Vitalis cardinalis sancte Balbine, Duu*zo *cardinalis sancti Martini,*^v *Teodbaldus cardinalis Iohannis et Pauli, Iohannes diaconus*^w sancte Marie in Schola Greca.'^{x 5}

^yIstud est priuilegium domni pape, quod fecit imperatori de inuestituris episcopatuum.^y

'*Pascalis episcopus, seruus seruorum Dei, karissimo in Christo filio* ^z*Heinrico, glorioso Teutonicorum regi,*^z *et per Dei omnipotentis | gratiam Romanorum imperatori augusto,*^{aa} *salutem et apostolicam benedictionem. Regnum uestrum sancte Romane ecclesie singulariter*^{bb} *coherere, dispositio*

p. 369

---

^{o–o} om. HL   ^p in persona et bonis add. Harl. WM (GR)   ^q follows gap with possible erasure C   ^r haec Harl. WM (GR)   ^s sacramento add. Harl. ^{t–t} domno imperatori Heinrico confirmauerunt Harl., domno imperatori Henrico sacramento confirmauerunt WM (GR)   ^u om. Harl. WM (GR)   ^v Marci Harl. WM (GR)   ^w decanus Harl. WM (GR)   ^x Leo decanus sancti Vitalis, Albo decanus Sergii et Bacchi add. Harl. WM (GR)   ^{y–y} om. HL   ^{z–z} om. WM (GR)   ^{aa} Henrico add. WM (GR)   ^{bb} om. WM (GR)

---

³ MGH *Leges* iv. 1, *Constitutiones*, i, no. 91 (p. 142). As noted above (IIII n. 2) this document was found neither in WM's edition of the *Liber Pontificalis* nor in his *GR*.

without simony, and with royal consent, and that the lord king should invest him with ring and staff. The bishop or abbot invested by the king should be consecrated freely by the bishop to whom the right belongs. He who is freely elected by clergy and people should not be consecrated unless invested by the king. And archbishops and bishops should be free to consecrate those invested by the king. In all these matters the lord pope Paschal should not disquiet King Henry nor his kingdom and empire.'[3]

This is the oath made by the pope:

'The lord pope Paschal shall not harm the lord king Henry nor his kingdom nor empire in the investiture of bishops and abbots, nor for any wrongs done to him and to his. Nor will he do any evil either to him or to any other person for that reason. Nor will he ever pronounce the sentence of excommunication on the person of King Henry. Nor will the pope fail to crown the King in accordance with the coronation *ordo*. With all his strength and with the authority of his office, the pope will help the king maintain his kingdom and empire. The lord pope will carry out all these things without deceit or trickery.[4] These are the bishops and cardinals, who, at the lord pope Paschal's command, have confirmed on oath this privilege and alliance to the lord emperor Henry: Peter, bishop of Porto, Crescentius, bishop of Sabina, Robert, cardinal of St Eusebius, Boniface, cardinal of St Mark, Anastasius, cardinal of St Clement, Gregory, cardinal of the Holy Apostles Peter and Paul, then Gregory, cardinal of St Chrysogonus, John, cardinal of St Pudentiana, Risus, cardinal of St Laurence, Rainer, cardinal of SS Marcellinus and Peter, Vitalis, cardinal of St Balbina, Divizo, cardinal of St Martin, Theobald, cardinal of John and Paul, John, deacon of St Mary in the Greek compound [Cosmedin].'[5]

This is the privilege the lord Pope Paschal made for the emperor concerning investitures:

'Paschal, bishop, servant of the servants of God, to the most beloved son in Christ, Henry, the glorious king of the Germans, and by the grace of almighty God august emperor of the Romans, greetings and apostolic blessing. God's providence has decided that there be a specially close bond between your kingdom and the holy

---

[4] MGH *Leges* iv. 1, *Constitutiones*, i, no. 92 (pp. 142–3). Like WM *GR* v. 420–9 (ii. 498–504), JW provides the documents arising out of the treaty.
[5] MGH *Leges* iv. 1, *Constitutiones*, i, no. 93 (p. 143).

diuina constituit. Predecessores uestri, probitatis cum*^{cc} prudentie amplioris gratia, Romane urbis coronam et imperium consecuti sunt. Ad cuius uidelicet corone et imperii dignitatem tuam quoque personam, fili karissime Heinrice, per nostri sacerdotii ministerium maiestas diuina prouexit. Illam igitur dignitatis prerogatiuam, quam predecessores nostri uestris predecessoribus, catholicis imperatoribus, concesserunt, et priuilegiorum paginis confirmauerunt, nos quoque dilectioni tue concedimus, et presentis priuilegii pagina confirmamus, ut regni tui episcopis uel^{dd} abbatibus, libere, preter uiolentiam et symoniam electis inuestituram uirge et anuli conferas. Post inuestitutionem uero, canonice consecrationem accipiat^{ee} ab episcopo, ad quem pertinuerit. Si quis autem a clero et populo, preter tuum assensum, electus fuerit, nisi a te inuestiatur, a nemine consecretur.^{ff} Sane episcopi uel arciepiscopi libertatem habeant a te inuestitos episcopos uel abbates canonice consecrandi. Predecessores enim uestri ecclesias regni sui tantis regalium suorum beneficiis ampliarunt, ut regnum ipsum^{gg} episcoporum maxime^{hh} uel abbatum prediis oporteat communiri, et populares dissensiones, que in electionibusⁱⁱ sepe contingunt, regali oporteat maiestate compesci. Quam ob rem prudentie et potestatiue cure^{jj} debes* sollicitius imminere, ut Romane ecclesie celsitudo^{kk} et ceterarum salus, prestante domno, beneficiis et seruitiis conseruetur. Si qua igitur ecclesiastica* uel^{ll} *secularis^{mm} persona hanc nostre concessionis paginamⁿⁿ temerario ausu* peruertere^{oo} *temptauerit, anathematis uinculo, nisi resipuerit, innodetur, honoris* quoque *ac dignitatis* sue *periculum patiatur. Obseruantes autem misericordia diuina custodiat, et personam potestatemque tuam ad honorem suum et gloriam feliciter imperare concedat.'*

His conuentionibus et iuramentis inter domnum papam et regem, in Pascali festiuitate, facta est concordia. Deinde Romam idus April. rex uenit, quem papa in ecclesia sancti Petri, missam celebrans, in imperatorem consecrauit, et ei suisque omnibus absolutionem fecit, et omnem iniuriam sibi factam condonauit.[6]

Rex Anglorum Heinricus Flandrenses qui Norðymbriam incolebant, cum tota suppellictili sua, in Waloniam transtulit, et terram,

---

^{cc} et *Harl. WM (GR)*   ^{dd} et *Harl.*   ^{ee} accipiant *WM (GR)*   ^{ff} exceptis nimirum illis qui uel in archiepiscoporum uel in Romani pontificis solent dispositione consistere *add. WM (GR)*   ^{gg} maxime *add. WM(GR)*   ^{hh} om. *WM(GR)*   ⁱⁱ electione *Harl.*, electis omnibus *WM (GR)*   ^{jj} cura *WM (GR)*   ^{kk} magnitudo *WM (GR)*   ^{ll} om. *Harl.*   ^{mm} secularisue *Harl.*   ⁿⁿ sciens, contra eum *add. Harl. WM (GR)*   ^{oo} uenire *Harl. WM(GR)*

---

⁶ MGH *Leges* iv. 1, *Constitutiones*, i, no. 96 (pp. 144–5). As before JW assumes that the peace between Henry V and Paschal II took place at Easter (2 Apr.) whereas it occurred on

Roman church. Your predecessors, by virtue of their uprightness and their more ample worth, received the crown and empire of the city of Rome. To the dignity of this crown and empire the divine majesty has raised you also, most beloved son Henry, through the office of our priesthood. Therefore we also grant to you, beloved, and confirm through the text of this privilege, the prerogative of honour, which our predecessors granted and confirmed by written privileges to your precursors, the catholic emperors, so that you may freely confer staff and ring on the bishops and abbots of your kingdom, except for those elected by force or simoniacally. After such investiture they may receive, in accordance with the canons, consecration from the bishop to whom that right belongs. If any be elected by the clergy and people without your assent, they will be consecrated by none unless they have been invested by you. Bishops and archbishops should certainly have the right to consecrate in accordance with the canons bishops or abbots who have been invested by you. For your predecessors endowed the churches of your kingdom with so many grants from your royal domain that it is particularly appropriate that the kingdom itself should be strengthened by the resources of bishoprics and abbeys, and that popular dissensions, which often occur during elections, should be put down by the royal majesty. For this reason you should, with the help of God, watch solicitously with prudence and potent care so that the eminence of the Roman church and the health of the other churches be preserved by grants and services. If therefore any ecclesiastical or lay person should try with foolish rashness to pervert the terms of this concession, he is to be bound by the chain of anathema, unless he repent, and in addition suffer the endangering of his honour and dignity. May the divine mercy protect those who respect it and may it allow you and your power to rule happily to His honour and glory.'

Peace was made during Easter [2 April] between the lord pope and the king by these agreements and oaths. At length on 13 April, the king came to Rome. The pope, whilst celebrating mass, consecrated him emperor in the church of St Peter, gave absolution to him and to all his followers, and forgave him the injuries which had been done to him.[6]

Henry, king of the English, removed to Wales some Flemings, who were living in Northumbria, together with all their chattels, and

11 Apr. Henry was crowned on 13 Apr. JW repeats here the reference to Henry V's coming to Rome.

que Ros nominatur, incolere precepit.[7] Nouum etiam monasterium, quod infra murum Wintonie erat, agente Willelmo Wintoniensi episcopo, rex extra murum construi iussit, et non multo post mare transiit.[8] Hoc anno hyemps asperrima, fames ualida, mortalitas hominum, pestis animalium, agrestium simul et domesticorum, stragesque auium extitit permaxima.[9]

[C³B]

[pp]*Heli stagnensium insularum maxima ab anguillarum copia ita dicta. Ibi sancta Ætheldrytha prima monasterium constituit ancillarum Dei, cui successit Sexburh soror eius, uxor Erconberti regis Cantuuariorum et mater sancte uirginis Ercongote. Illique successit altera filia eius Ermenhilda, uxor Wlferi regis Merciorum et mater sancte Wereburge uirginis. He tres ibidem abbatisse fuerunt usque ad Danorum tempora, qui, habitatricibus effugatis, habitacula subruerunt. Sed post ibi canonici constituti sunt. Quorum unus procacior ceteris ad uirginis incorruptionem certius explorandam accessit, et per foramen quod ictus claui[qq] effecerat,*

[pp–pp] *add. mg. C³, incorporated at 1109[d] B*   [qq] Dani *WM (GP)*

---

[7] The settlement of Flemings in Rhos is reported in *Brut* Pen. p. 27, Her. pp. 52–3 and BS pp. 104–5 under 1105 (*recte* 1108) and in *AC* under 1107, and mentioned in WM *GR* i. 477, OV *HE* xiii. 16 (vi. 442–3) *s.a.* 1134, and Gir. Cambr. *Itinerarium* (i.11 (vi. 83–4)), though the Northumbrian origins of these Flemish settlers seems peculiar to JW. One of the leaders of these settlers, a 'prince' Wizo, came directly from Flanders, and had settled in Deugleddyf before the death of Wilfrid, the last native bishop of Wales, in 1112: see *Worcester Cartulary*, pp. xxxi–xxxii, nos. 252–6. See also the discussion in I. W. Rowlands, 'The making of the March: aspects of the Norman settlement of Dyfed', *ANS* iii (1980), 142–57, at pp. 147, 148. The evidence for the settlement of Flemings in northern England is scarce. Turgis Brundis and Michael le Fleming are the only ones known from this period, and only two place names in Cumberland may indicate the presence of Flemings (*Place Names of Cumberland* (3 parts, English Place Name Society, xxi–xxii; Cambridge, 1950–2) i. 240–1, ii. 286, iii. xxxii). G. W. S. Barrow, 'The beginnings of medieval feudalism,' *The Kingdom of the Scots: Government, Church and Society from the Eleventh*

made them settle in the district which is called Rhos.[7] The king ordered the Hyde monastery, which was built within the walls of Winchester, to be built outside them under the supervision of William, bishop of Winchester, and shortly afterwards he crossed the sea.[8] This year there was a very harsh winter, a serious famine, mortality of men, disease among animals, both wild and domestic, and a very great destruction of birds.[9]

Ely, which is principally made up of marshy islands, is so called from the abundance of eels. There St Æthelthryth first established a monastery for female servants of God. Seaxburg, her sister, the wife of Earconberht, king of the people of Kent, and mother of the holy virgin, Earcongota, succeeded her. Another daughter of hers, Eormenhild, wife of Wulfhere, king of the Mercians, and mother of the holy virgin Werburg succeeded her. These were the three abbesses up to the time of the Danes, who put to flight the residents and destroyed the houses. But afterwards canons were established there. One of these, more forward than the rest, came to test more surely the incorruption of the virgin, and, inserting a candle fixed on a stick into the hole made by the

to the Fourteenth Century (London, 1973), pp. 289–90, drew attention to the parallels between the names of some Flemings settled in Clydesdale and in Pembroke.

    [8] The Winchester Annals (Ann. Mon. ii. 43) date the move of the New Minster to Hyde to 1110. ASC reports Henry's crossing to Normandy in Aug. to deal with frontier problems.

    [9] ASC and the Waverley, Bermondsey, and Rouen (with reference to Normandy) Annals (Ann. Mon. ii. 214, iii. 431, UAG, p. 47) report a severe winter and consequently poor harvest, and a plague of cattle (Bermondsey only), but not the great loss of birds. In addition ASC refers to frontier warfare between Henry and the Count of Anjou and the succession in Flanders.

p. 369

appositam uirge candelam immit-
tens curiositate oculorum omnia
rimari. Mox summitate uirge fissa
pannos, quibus sacrum corpus
inuoluebatur, ad se trahere conari.
Iamque partem attraxerat, cum
uirgo, indignata nudum corpus a
nebulone posse uideri, pannum
introrsus uiolenter retraxit, adeo
ut illum contranitentem terra supi-
num dederit.^{rr} ^{10} | Brihtnothus ab
Æthelwoldo Wintoniensi epis-
copo abbas Heli constitutus.
Corpus sancte Wihtburge uirginis
sororis sancte Ætheldryðe quod ad
hoc tempus in rure ignobili
iacuerat, ad Eliense cenobium
transtulit. De cuius corporis
incorruptione cum qui⟨bus⟩dam
dubitarent, tempore Ricardi abbatis, cum transferrentur corpora
sanctarum ipsam penitus ultra
mammas detexere. Visaque est
toto corpore integra dormienti
similior quam mortue. Puluillo
serico ad caput apposito, uelo et
totis uestibus integra nouitate reni-
tentibus. Serena facie, roseo rubore
suauis, dentibus candidis, labiis
paululum reductis papillis admodum paruulis. Habuit hoc cenobium abbates usque ad nonum
annum Heinrici regis. Tunc quia
Lincoliensis episcopatus nimium
protendebatur, consilium habitum

^{rr} elideret WM (GP)

^{10} WM GP iv. 183 (pp. 323–4).

force of a nail, to scrutinize everything with his enquiring eyes. Then holding with the tip of the stick the cloth with which the holy body was wrapped, he tried to pull it towards him. He had already pulled a bit when the virgin seeing that her body might be exposed by the scoundrel, suddenly pulled it back with force so that the earth rendered him as he resisted unconscious.[10] Brihtnoth was appointed abbot of Ely by Æthelwold, bishop of Winchester. The body of St Wihtburg the virgin, the sister of St Æthelthryth, which had lain in an ignoble place he translated to the monastery of Ely. As some doubted the incorruption of her body, at the time of Abbot Richard, when the bodies of the saints were being transferred, they completely uncovered Æthelthryth above her breasts. And it was seen that her whole body was preserved, more as if she was asleep than dead. There was a pillow of silk placed at her head, her veil and vestments gleaming as though they were brand new. Her face was serene, of a sweet rosy hue, her teeth white, her lips slightly pulled in, her breasts still small. Up to the ninth year of King Henry there were abbots at the monastery. Then, it was decided because the diocese of Lincoln was too

est ut apud Heli constitueretur episcopus haberetque pagum Grantebryggensem. Intrusus *est* ibi contra leges canonum *Herueus Bancornensis episcopus. Est enim Bancor monasterium in ipsis Walis tot habitatoribus plenum ut, sicut Beda refert, si in .vii. partes diuideretur, non minus queque portio quam .ccc. homines haberet.* In Heliensi parrochia *est Thorneie cenobium.*^{pp ss 11}

[1112] (.vi.)^a 1134   ^b*Actio concilii contra heresim de inuestitura.*^b
^c*Anno pontificatus domni pape Pascalis Secundi .xiii.,* ^d*indictione .v.,*^d *mense Martio, .xv. k. April., celebratum est concilium Rome, Lateranis, in basilica Constantiniana. In quo*^e *cum domnus papa*^f *resedisset cum arciepiscopis, et episcopis, et cardinalibus, et uaria multitudine clericorum et laicorum, ultima die concilii, facta coram omnibus professione catholice fidei, ne quis de fide ipsius dubitaret, dixit: 'Amplector omnem diuinam scripturam, scilicet,*^g *ueteris* ac *noui Testamenti, legem a Moyse scriptam et a sanctis prophetis. Amplector .iiii. euangelia, .vii. canonicas epistolas, epistolas gloriosi doctoris beati Pauli apostoli, sanctos canones Apostolorum, .iiii. concilia uniuersalia sicut .iiii. euangelia, Nicenum, Ephesinum, Constantinopolitanum, Calcedonense ⟨et⟩*^h *Antiocenum concilium, et decreta sanctorum patrum Romanorum pontificum, et precipue decreta domni mei pape Gregorii .vii., et beate memorie pape Vrbani. Que ipsi laudauerunt, laudo, que ipsi*ⁱ *tenuerunt, teneo, que confirmauerunt, confirmo, que dampnauerunt, dampno, que repulerunt, repello, que interdixerunt, interdico, que prohibuerunt, prohibeo in omnibus et per*
p. 370 *omnia, et in his semper perse|uerabo.' Quibus expletis, surrexit pro omnibus Girardus Engolismensis episcopus, legatus in Aquitania, et communi assensu domni pape*^j *Pascalis totiusque concilii, coram omnibus legit hanc scripturam:*

^{ss} et Caeteriht sanctimoniales *add. B*²

^a *om. C*   ^{b-b} *om. HL*   ^c Anno ab incarnatione Domini millesimo centesimo duodecimo, indictione quinta *add. here Harl. WM (GR)*   ^{d-d} *om. here Harl. WM (GR)*   ^e qua *WM (GR)*   ^f Paschalis *add. here Harl. WM (GR)*   ^g *om. WM (GR)*   ^h *followed by paragraph mark C,* praeterea *WM (GR)*   ⁱ *om. WM (GR)*   ^j *om. Harl.*

extensive that there should be set
up a bishop at Ely who should
control the region of Cambridge.
Against canon law Hervey,
bishop of Bangor, was brought
in. Bangor was the monastery
among the same Welsh which
was filled with so many inmates
that (as Bede relates) if it were
divided into seven parts, each
would not have fewer than 300
men. In the diocese of Ely there
is a monastery at Thorney.[11]

[1112] The acts of the council against the investiture heresy.

In the thirteenth year of Pope Paschal II, in the fifth indiction, in
March, on the 18th, there was held a council at Rome in the Lateran
in the Constantinian basilica. In this after the Pope had sat down
together with archbishops and cardinals and bishops and a mixed
assembly of clergy and laity, on the last day of the council, the pope
made profession of the catholic faith before all so that no one should
question his commitment. He said: 'I embrace all Holy Scripture,
that is, the Old and New Testament, the law written down by Moses
and the holy prophets. I embrace the four Gospels, the seven
canonical epistles, the epistles of the splendid teacher, blessed Paul
the Apostle, the sacred canons of the Apostles, the four councils
universal like the four Gospels, that is, those of Nicaea, Ephesus,
Constantinople, and Chalcedon, the council of Antioch, the decrees
of the holy fathers, the Roman popes, especially those decrees of my
lord Pope Gregory VII and of Pope Urban of blessed memory. What
they have praised I praise, what they held I hold, what they
confirmed I confirm, what they have condemned I condemn, what
they rejected I reject, what they prohibited I prohibit in all things
and through all, and in these matters I shall always persevere.' After
these words had been spoken, Gerard, bishop of Angoulême, legate
in Aquitaine, and with the general assent of Pope Paschal and the
whole council, read out this text:

[11] WM *GP* iv. 184 (pp. 324–6). Chatteris (Cambs.) is the convent B has added to its text.

'Priuilegium illud quod non est priuilegium, sed uere debet dici prauilegium, pro liberatione captiuorum et ecclesie, a domno Pascali papa per uiolentiam regis Heinrici extortum, nos omnes, in hoc sancto concilio cum domno papa congregati canonica censura et ecclesiastica auctoritate, iudicio sancti Spiritus, dampnamus, et irritum esse iudicamus, atque omnino quassamus, *et, ne quid auctoritatis et effi⟨ca⟩citatis habeat, penitus excommunicamus. Et hoc ideo dampnatum est, quia in eo prauilegio continetur, quod electus canonice a clero et populo a nemine consecretur, nisi prius a rege inuestiatur, quod est contra Spiritum Sanctum et canonicam institutionem.' Perlecta uero hac carta, acclamatum est*[k] *ab uniuerso concilio: 'Amen, amen, fiat, fiat.'*

*Arciepiscopi, qui cum suis suffrageneis interfuerunt, hi sunt: Iohannes patriarcha Veneticus, Se*mies *Capuanus, Landulfus Beneuentanus, Amalphitanus, Regitanus, Hidrontinus, Brundu*lsinus,[l] Capsanus, *Girontinus, et Greci, Rosanus, et archiepiscopus sancte Seuerine, episcopi uero, Centius Sa*uinensis, *Petrus Portuensis, Leo Ostiensis, Cono Prenestinus, Girardus Engolis*mus,[m] Galo *Leonensis, legatus pro Bituricensi et Viennensi*[n] *arciepiscopis, Rogerus W*lturnensis, *Gaufridus Senensis, Rolandus Populoniensis,*[o] *Gregorius Terracinensis, Willelmus Troianus,*[p] Gibinus[q] *Siracusanus, legatus pro omnibus Siculis, et alii fere .c. episcopi. ⟨Bruno⟩*[r] *Sig*uinus[s] *et Iohannes Tusculanus episcopi,*[t] *cum essent Rome illa die, concilio non interfuerunt, qui postea lecta dampnatione prauilegii consen*suerunt *et laudauerunt.*[1]

Samson .xxv. Wigornensis episcopus, .iii. non. Mai., die dominica, obiit.[2] Rex Anglorum Heinricus comitem Rotbertum de Beleasmo in Kæresburga mense Octobri in custodia posuit.[3]

[1113] (.vii.) 1135 Ciuitas Wigorna, cum principali ecclesia, et omnibus aliis, et castello, .xiii. kal. Iul., feria .v., igne cremata est. De monachis unus monasterio utillimus, cum duobus seruientibus, et .xv. de ciuibus, igne combusti sunt.[1] Rex Anglorum Heinricus, mense

---

[k] *om.* WM (GR)   [l] Brundisinus WM (GR)   [m] Engolismensis *Harl.* WM (GR)   [n] Viennensis WM (GR)   [o] Populonensis *Harl.* WM (GR)   [p] *from* Tronianus *Harl.*   [q] Willelmus *Harl.* WM(GR)   [r] *om. Harl.* WM (GR)   [s] Siwinus *Harl.* WM (GR)   [t] episcopus *Harl.* WM(GR)

[1] MGH *Leges* iv. 1, *Constitutiones* i, no. 399 (pp. 570–3) where JW's text is given the numeral 6. WM *GR* v. 426–7 (ii. 502–4) provides some background to the document.

[2] JW seems to be the only extant source for the date of Samson's death: see Greenway, *Fasti* ii. 99.

[3] ASC reports Henry's remaining in Normandy all year on account of warfare against King Philip and the count of Anjou. Robert of Bellême's undated arrest (though not his

'All of us here assembled in this holy council with the lord Pope condemn, with canonical censure and ecclesiastical authority, and by the judgement of the Holy Spirit, that privilege, which is not a privilege, but ought in truth to be called a depraved privilege, which was extorted by the force of King Henry from the lord Pope Paschal in return for the freeing of prisoners and of the church. We judge it to be invalid, we utterly suppress it, and we totally condemn it lest it have any authority or effectiveness. That which is contained in this depraved privilege is condemned, namely that a person elected canonically by clergy and people should be consecrated by no one unless he has first been invested by the king, which is against the Holy Spirit and canon law.' This document was read out and was acclaimed by the universal council: 'Amen, amen, let it be, let it be!'

The archbishops who attended with their suffragans were as follows: John, the patriarch of Venice, Sennes of Capua, Landulf of Benevento, and those of Amalfi, Reggio, Otranto, Brindisi, Conza, *Gyrontinus*, and of the Greeks, there were Rossano and the archbishop of St Severinus. The bishops were: Crescentius of Sabina, Peter of Porto, Leo of Ostia, Cono of Preneste, Gerard of Angoulême, Walo of St Pol de Leon, the legate for the archbishops of Bourges and Vienne, Roger of Volterra, Geoffrey of Siena, Roland of Pisa, Gregory of Terracina, William of Troia, Gibinus of Siracuse, legate for all the Sicilies, and about another one hundred bishops. ⟨Bruno⟩ of Segni and John the bishop of Tusculum, although they were at Rome on that day, were not present at the council. They supported and praised the condemnation of the depraved privilege, when they had read it later.[1]

Samson, twenty-fifth bishop of Worcester, died on Sunday, 5 May.[2] Henry, king of the English, placed Robert of Bellême under arrest in Cherbourg in October.[3]

[1113] The city of Worcester with its principal church and many others as well as the castle was consumed by fire on Thursday, 19 June. One of the monks, who had rendered many services to the monastery, with two servants and fifteen citizens, perished in the flames.[1] Henry,

confinement at Cherbourg) is reported among other actions of Henry in Normandy. In addition ASC reports a good harvest and a severe pestilence.

[1] The fire is noted by the Reading and St Augustine Annals (*UAG*, pp. 10, 76) while the Worcester Annals (*Ann. Mon.* iv. 375) record the death of one monk and 20 others in the fire. WM *GP* iv. 149 (pp. 288–9) mentions a cathedral fire some years after Wulfstan's death from which his shrine was miraculously preserved.

Iulio, Angliam rediit, et comitem Rotbertum de Beleasmo, de Normannia ductum, apud Werham in artissima custodia posuit.[2] *a*Viri probitatis eximie, domnus prior Thomas, et Colemannus, sancte Marie Wigornensis ecclesie nobiles cenobite, .iiii. non. Octob., sabbato, modum fecerunt huic uite.

> Communi sorti, soluentes debita morti,
> Gaudia summa petant, ubi summa pace quiescant:
> Cum sanctis leta contemplando sine meta.*a*

Teoulfus, regis capellanus, .v. k. Ian., die dominica, Wigornensem episcopatum apud Windleshoram suscepit.[3]

[1114] (.viii.) 1136 Heinrico, Romanorum imperatori, Mahtildis, filia regis Anglorum Heinrici, .viii. idus Ian., Mogontie desponsata, et in imperatricem est consecrata.[1]

Thomas Eboracensis arciepiscopus .vi. k. Martii, feria .iii. obiit.[2] *Hrofensis episcopus Radulfus, .vi. k. Mai, die dominica, ad archiepiscopatum Cantuuariensem apud Windleshoram* eligitur.[3] Ciuitas Cicestra cum principali monasterio, per culpam incurie, .iii. non. Mai., feria .iii., flammis absumpta est.[4] Turstanus regis capellanus ad Eboracensem arciepiscopatum, die Assumptionis sancte Marie, eligitur Wintonie.[5] Arnulfus abbas de Burh ad Hrofensem ecclesiam eligitur episcopus.[6] Rex Anglorum Heinricus, postquam exercitum in Waloniam duxit, ante festiuitatem sancti Michaelis mare transiit.[7] *Fluuius Medewege uocatus, per nonnulla miliarii .vi. idus Octob., ita a se defecit, ut in medio alueo sui etiam paruissime naues ob penuriam aque*

---

a–a om. L

[2] ASC E has the events in this sentence in reverse order, dating Robert's incarceration at Wareham to the summer, and Henry I's return 'soon after' that. HH *HA* vii. 28 (p. 458) and WM *GR* v. 398 (ii. 475) also record Robert's imprisonment.

[3] JW is the earliest extant source for these obits, which are repeated (without the day being given) in the *Ann. Winchcombe* (p. 123) and in the Worcester Annals (*Ann. Mon.* iv. 375). The latter describe Coleman as 'capellanus beatus Wulfstani'. For the date of Theulf's succession to Worcester, see Greenway, *Fasti* ii. 99.

[1] Matilda was formally married to Henry V at Worms in Jan. 1114 and had been crowned queen at Mainz on 25 July 1113. See OV *HE* v. 200 n. 2. The sources are listed in Meyer von Knonau, *Jahrbücher*, vi. 285 n. 1. WM *GR* v. 420 (ii. 498) reports Matilda's marriage before Henry V's expedition to Italy in 1111. This is not reported by ASC. From now on ASC often has information which is not in JW.

[2] *HC* (p. 54) gives 19 Feb. for the day of Thomas II's death, 'a date which is internally inconsistent' (see *HC*, p. 54 n. 2). Brett there notes that J. Leland, *Itinerary* (ed. L. Toulmin Smith, v (London, 1910), p. 135) appears to give '1113 .v. idus Mart.' from an

king of the English, came back to England in the month of July, and placed Earl Robert of Bellême, whom he had brought back from Normandy, in the closest confinement at Wareham.[2] Prior Thomas and Coleman, two men of great virtue, noble monks of the church of St Mary at Worcester, made an end to this life on Saturday, 4 October.

Paying their debt to death, a fate all share,
May they seek the highest joys and rest there in perfect peace:
With the saints they look on joys without end.

Theulf, the royal chaplain, became bishop of Worcester on Sunday, 28 December at Windsor.[3]

[1114] Henry, the emperor of the Romans, was married to Matilda, daughter of Henry, king of the English, on 6 January, at Mainz, and she was crowned empress.[1]

Thomas, archbishop of York, died on Tuesday, 24 February.[2] Ralph, bishop of Rochester, was elected archbishop of Canterbury at Windsor on Sunday, 26 April.[3] The city of Chichester with its chief church was consumed by fire on Tuesday, 5 May, through carelessness.[4] Thurstan, the royal chaplain, was elected archbishop of York at Winchester on the feast of the Assumption [15 August].[5] Ernulf, abbot of Peterborough, was chosen bishop of Rochester.[6] Henry, king of the English, after leading his army to Wales, crossed the sea before the feast of St Michael [29 September].[7] The river, which is called the Medway, became so shallow for some miles on 10 October that in the middle of the channel even the smallest ships

inscription from the tomb, and that if Leland had misread '.v. kal. Mart.' as '.v. idus Mart.' then JW's date could be confirmed. Thomas's death is recorded by ASC (H dating it to 17 Feb.).
    [3] Eadmer, *HN* v (pp. 222–3) records the date and the place of Ralph d'Escures's postulation, while ASC E simply notes Henry's appointment of Ralph.
    [4] The Chichester fire is recorded in ASC H, and in the Chichester (*UAG*, p. 94) and Winchester Annals (*Ann. Mon.* ii. 44), an addition to the latter confirming JW's day.
    [5] The place and date for Thurstan's election is confirmed by Richard of Hexham (Raine, *Priory of Hexham*, i. 57). *HC* (pp. 54, 56) implies that Thurstan was elected on the day of the Assumption. The succession of Thurstan is in ASC EH.
    [6] Eadmer, *HN* v (p. 225) gives this election (which is recorded in ASC EH) in more detail. It took place at Canterbury on 28 Sept. Eadmer also reports Ernulf's consecration on 10 Oct.
    [7] The Welsh expedition (which was against Gruffydd ap Cynan) 'at midsummer' and the crossing to Normandy 'in September' are in ASC E (H omitting the Norman crossing). *Brut* Pen. p. 7, Her. pp. 78–9 and BS pp. 120–3 under 1111 (*recte* 1114) speak of Henry moving against the men of Gwynedd and above all to Powys. *AC s.a.* 1114 reports briefly his invasion of Wales and his coming to a castle.

elabi aliquatenus minime possent. ᵃTamisia nichilominus eidem illa die defectui patuit, nam inter pontem et regiam turrim, sub ponte etiam in tantum fluminis ipsius aqua diminuta est, ut non solum equis, sed et innumera hominum et puerorum multitudo illud pedibus transuaderent, aqua uix genua eorum attingente. Durauit autem hic aque defectus a medio noctis precedentis usque in profundas tenebras noctis subsequentis. Similem quoque aquarum defectum ipso die apud Gernemutham, et in
p. 371 *aliis locis per Angliam, certo relatu contigisse didicimus.ᵃ ⁸ |*

[**1115**] (.ix.) 1137   ᵃHoc anno hiemps extitit asperrima, ita ut omnes fere per Angliam pontes glacie frangerentur.¹ Imperator Heinricus, postquam Coloniam diu obsedit, et multos suorum campestri prelio perdidit, pacem apud ciuitatem Nussam iuramento fecit.² Radulfus, Dorubernensis archiepiscopus, ab Anselmo, sancte Romane ecclesie legato, *.v. kl. Iulii, die dominica, pallium su*scepit Cantwarie ubi fuere congregati episcopi totius Anglie. Ipsoque die magno cum honore consecratus est Teoulfus, Wigornensis ecclesie episcopus.³ Wilfridus episcopus de sancto Dauid in Walonia obiit: usque ad illum episcopi extitere Brytonici.⁴ In octauis Apostolorum magnum concilium a Cono, Romane ecclesie cardinali, Catalaunis celebratum est, in quo excommunicauit episcopos qui concilio non interfuere, quosdam etiam degradauit, et plurimos abbates baculis priuatos deposuit de sedibus, ecclesiasticum illis interdicens officium.⁵ Rex Anglorum Heinricus mediante Iulio mense Angliam rediit.⁶ *Bernardus regine* cancellarius, ad ecclesiam *sancti Dauid in Wal*onia, *.xiiii.ᵇ kal. Octobris sabbato*, presul eligitur, ᶜ*et eodem die ad gradum presbiteratus a Wentano pontifice Willelmo apud Suthwercam*

ᵃ⁻ᵃ *partly written over erasure and partly on extra lines ruled at the bottom of the page* C
ᵃ *For B's addition here, see Appendix B*   ᵇ .xiii. HL   ᶜ⁻ᶜ *written over erasure and extending into mgs.* C³

⁸ Eadmer, *HN* v (pp. 225–6), who dates the low tide to 10 Oct. The drying up of the Thames is reported in ASC E and in the Margam, Winchester, Waverley, Bermondsey, Osney, and Worcester Annals (*Ann. Mon.* i. 9, ii. 44, 215, iii. 432, iv. 16, 376), the Margam Annals dating it to 10 Oct., and Winchester to 'luna octaua'. The drying up of the Medway and of water at Yarmouth is not reported outside Eadmer, who does not mention the strong winds described by ASC. C's original entry could have corresponded to ASC's.

¹ ASC records this winter and a consequential plague of cattle, as do the derivative Waverley annals (*Ann. Mon.* ii. 215). The Winchester, Osney, and Worcester Annals (*Ann. Mon.* ii. 44, iv. 16, 376) like JW only mention the severe winter, the first and third recording its duration of nine and eleven weeks respectively.

² Three events of 1114, Henry V's siege of Cologne, his defeat at Andernach, and an otherwise unrecorded peace at Neuss, are brought together by JW here: see Meyer von Knonau, *Jahrbücher*, vi. 301 n. 25, 306 n. 33.

could not keep afloat for the want of water. On the same day the Thames suffered the same want, for between the bridge and the royal tower the water below the bridge had so diminished that a countless number of men and even boys could wade across it, not only on horseback, but also on foot, the water scarcely reaching their knees. This lack of water lasted from the middle of the preceding night to the darkest shadows of the following night. We have it on trust-worthy authority that a similar lack of water happened at Yarmouth and at other places.[8]

[1115] This winter was extremely severe so that nearly all the bridges in England were broken by the ice.[1] Emperor Henry, after besieging Cologne, and losing many men in a pitched battle, made a peace confirmed by oaths at Neuss.[2] Ralph, archbishop of Canter-bury, received the pallium from Anselm, legate of the holy Roman see, on Sunday, 27 June, at Canterbury, where the bishops from all England were gathered. On the same day, Theulf, bishop of the church of Worcester, was consecrated with great honour.[3] Wilfrid, bishop of St David's, died in Wales. Before him all the bishops had been Welsh.[4] In the octave of the feast of the Apostles [6 July], a well-attended council was held at Châlons by Cono, cardinal of the Roman church. At it he excommunicated those bishops who had not attended the council, he deposed some, and deprived many abbots of their staffs, deposed them from their seats, and prohibited them from fulfilling their ecclesiastical offices.[5] Henry, king of the English, returned to England in mid-July.[6] Bernard, the queen's chancellor, was elected bishop of the church of St David's in Wales on Saturday, 18 September. On the same day he was promoted to the priesthood

---

[3] See Eadmer, *HN* v (pp. 229–30), for both the assumption of the pallium and Theulf's consecration immediately afterwards. Eadmer names six bishops present on this occasion: JW's 'episcopi Anglie totius' could be an inference. ASC records, without giving a date, Archbishop Ralph's receiving the pallium ceremoniously at Canterbury.

[4] The year of death is confirmed by *AC* (MSS BC) and by *Brut* Pen. pp. 39, 166, Her. pp. 82–3 and BS pp. 124–5 under 1112 (*recte* 1115), but Wilfrid is called Geffrei or Jeffre in these sources. Lloyd, *History of Wales*, ii. 451 notes that Gir. Cambr.'s (vi. 105) statement that his successor was 'primus Francorum' of the St David's bishops supports Wilfrid's Welsh origins. *Brut* makes it clear that the appointment of Wilfrid's successor, Bernard, a 'Norman', was against the wishes of the British clergy.

[5] Neither Eadmer, *HN* v (p. 234), nor WM *GR* i. 69 (p. 129) name and date the Council of Châlons–sur-Marne, though the legate Bishop Cono of Palestrina's suspension of Norman bishops and abbots who failed to attend an unnamed council is reported by Eadmer and by WM *GP* i. 68 (p. 129).

[6] ASC reports Henry's return to England in July after ensuring that the Norman nobles had sworn oaths of allegiance to his son, William.

promotus est, *in crastino*, presente *regina, consecra*tur episcopus apud Westmonasterium a Radulfo arciepiscopo.[7] Regnelmus, Herefordensis episcopus,[c] [de].vi. kal. Nov.,[e] obiit,[d] pro quo Gausfridus, regis capellanus, eligitur. *Radulfus* Dorubernensis *archiepiscopus,* A*rnulfum* ad H*rofens*em [f]et Gaus*fridu*m ad ecclesiam *Herefordens*em[f] die sancti Stephani, episcopos ordinauit *Cantwarie.*[8]

[1116] (.x.) 1138 Griffinus filius Res uerno tempore Walonie predam egit, et castella incendit, quoniam rex Anglie Heinricus [a]particulam de terra patris sui ei dare[a] noluit.[1] *Conuentio* optimatum et baronum *totius* Anglie *apud Selesberiam .xiiii.*[b] *k. Aprilis, fact*a est, qui in presentia *regis Heinrici* homagium filio suo Willelmo fecerunt, et fidelitatem ei iurauerunt. [c]*Habita est ibi causa de querela, que inter arciepiscopum Cantuuar*iensem Radulfum *et electum pontificem Eboracensem* Turstanum *per integrum annum uersata fuerat. Hic electus, cum ab ipso pontifice moneretur, ut ecclesie Cantwariensi faceret quod debebat, et benedictionem suam ecclesiastico more susciperet, respondit*: et bene*dictionem quidem se libenter suscipere uelle, sed professionem quam exigebat nulla ratione facturum. Rex autem Heinricus, ubi aduertit Turstanus in sua peruicacia stare, aperte protestatus est illum, aut morem antecessorum suorum, tam in professione facienda, quam et in aliis dignitati ecclesie Cantwariensis ex antiquo iure competentibus executurum, aut episcopatu Eboracensi cum benedictione funditus cariturum. His auditis, ille sui cordis consilio impremeditatius credens, renuntiauit pontificatui, spondens regi et archiepiscopo se dum uiueret illum non reclamaturum, nec aliquam calumniam[d] inde moturum, quicunque substitutus[e] fuisset.*[c] [2] Owinus rex Walanorum occiditur,[3] et rex Anglorum Heinricus mare transiit, comitante secum Turstano

[d-d] *written over erasure* C[3]   [e-e] circa festiuitatem omnium sanctorum *HLBP HR* (SD ii. 249)   [f-f] *om.* H

[a-a] *written over erasure* C[2]   [b] .xiii. B   [c-c] *written over erasure* C[2] [d] calunniam C   [e] subsecutus *HL*

---

[7] Eadmer, *HN* v (pp. 235–6) which says that Bernard, 'quidam capellanus regine', was consecrated on 19 Sept., the day after his ordination as a priest. For discussion see Whitelock, Brett, and Brooke, *Councils and Synods,* ii. 709–10, where it is noted (p. 709 n. 3) that JW's description of Bernard as the queen's chancellor is accurate, and (p. 710 n. 3) that JW follows an early version of *HN.*

[8] *EEA* v, p. xxxvi n. 61 notes that 28 Oct. is the day of Reinhelm's death in Oxford, Bodl. Rawlinson B. 328, fo. 43. Eadmer, *HN* v (p. 237) is JW's source for the consecration of Geoffrey and Ernulf on 26 Dec., though neither Eadmer nor WM *GP* iv. 168 (p. 304) identify Geoffrey as the king's chaplain.

[1] *Brut* Pen. pp. 40–5, Her. pp. 86–95 and BS pp. 126–35 under 1113 (*recte* 1116) give the

at Southwark by William, bishop of Winchester, and on the morrow, in the presence of the queen, he was consecrated bishop at Westminster by Archbishop Ralph.[7] Reinhelm, bishop of Hereford, died on 27 October, and Geoffrey, the royal chaplain, was chosen in his place. Ralph, archbishop of Canterbury, ordained Ernulf bishop of Rochester and Geoffrey bishop of Hereford at Canterbury on St Stephen's day [26 December].[8]

[1116] In the spring, Gruffydd, son of Rhys, took much booty in Wales, and burnt castles because Henry, king of the English, was not willing to give him a portion of his father's land.[1] An assembly of the leading men and barons of all England was held at Salisbury on 19 March, and they did homage, in the presence of the king, to his son William, and promised him fealty. The dissension which had been carried on for a whole year between Ralph, archbishop of Canterbury, and Thurstan, bishop-elect of York, was brought before the council. The archbishop-elect, when he was admonished by Archbishop Ralph that he should make the submission which was due to the church of Canterbury, and that he should receive Canterbury's blessing according to the canons, replied that he would freely receive the blessing but that he would not in any way make the submission which was demanded. King Henry therefore, seeing that Thurstan persisted in his obstinacy, openly declared that he should either follow the custom of his predecessors both in making the profession and in doing other things pertaining by ancient right to the church of Canterbury or totally lose the bishopric of York with his blessing. When he had heard these things, Thurstan, trusting the hasty counsels of his heart, renounced the pontificate, promising the king and the archbishop that he would never claim it as long as he lived and would never demand it whoever might be appointed in his stead.[2] Owen, king of the Welsh, was slain,[3] and Henry, king of the English, crossed the sea, accompanied by

fullest account of Gruffydd ap Rhys ap Tewdwr's attempt to recover his inheritance: see Lloyd, *History of Wales*, ii. 433–5. *AC* (version C) *s.a.* 1116 gives more information than JW. ASC does not report Gruffydd's attempt.

[2] Eadmer, *HN* v (pp. 237–8), JW witness B alone having Eadmer's '.xiii. kal. Apr.' As noted above, *s.a.* 1115 n. 6, ASC had recorded the swearing of allegiance to William in the previous year by the leading men in Normandy. For the York–Canterbury dispute, see discussion in Nicholl, *Thurstan*, pp. 52–7. *HC* pp. 62–80, covers this dispute.

[3] Owain ap Cadwgan ap Bledddyn's death (which is not in ASC) is described in *Brut* Pen. p. 45, Her. pp. 98–9 and BS pp. 134–5 under 1113 (*recte* 1116) and recorded in *AC s.a.* 1116.

electo Eboracensi arciepiscopo, *sperante se reuestituram sui pontificatus recuperaturum*, et ex regio iussu *benedictionem ab arciepiscopo sine exactione professionis* adepturum. *Circa mensem Aug. reuersus a Roma Anselmus*, qui pallium arciepiscopo Cantuuarie*ᶠ* Roma detulerat, *uenit Normanniam ad regem Heinricum, litteras apostolici deferens, que* illi *uices apostolicas in Anglia administrare concedebant. Quod regno Anglie breui innotuit.* Vnde *communi consilio* regine et nobilium quorumlibet Anglie, Cantuuariensis archiepiscopus Radulfus, emensa festiuitate Natiuitatis sancte Marie transiit, *regem* adiit, illumque *Rotomagi* consistentem *repperit*, et *cum* ipso *de negotiis pro quibus uenerat, iuxta rerum ordinem, diligent*er *agens, ad consilium eius Romani itineris uiam ingreditur.*⁴

[**1117**] (.xi.) 1139

[CB]

*ᵃ*Luna*ᵇ* per longa spatia noctis apparuit sanguineam et postea obscurata est ualde et in nocte sequente .xvi. kl. Ian. celum totum quasi ardentem uisum est.*ᵃ* ¹

Secundum regis Heinrici preceptum, apud Cirenceastre nouum opus est inceptum.² Apud Lumbardiam, magno terremotu facto, et, ut testati sunt qui nouere, .xl. dierum spatio durante, plurima domorum edificia corruere, et, quod uisu dictuque constat mirabile, uilla quedam pergrandis mota est repente de statu proprio, iamque ab omnibus in longe remoto consistere cernitur loco. Mediolani, dum

p. 372 patricie dignitatis uiri, de republica tractantes, | sub una resident turri, auribus omnium uox foras insonuit, unum ex illis nomine uocans, et festinato exire rogans. Quo tardante, persona quedam coram apparuit, que uocatum uirum ut egrederetur prece optinuit. Exeunte illo, turris repente cecidit et omnes qui ibidem aderant casu

---

ᶠ Cantuarie *followed by an erasure* C

ᵃ⁻ᵃ add. mg. by hand not found elsewhere in C   *ᵇ* lunam C

---

⁴ Eadmer, *HN* v (pp. 238–9). In its sole 1116 entry to overlap with JW, ASC dates Henry's crossing overseas to 'after Easter', and Eadmer's (p. 238) reference to Thurstan's following Henry across the sea could lie behind JW's 'comitante secum Turstano'. See Nicholl, *Thurstan*, pp. 52–7, for some discussion. Eadmer makes it clear (pp. 238–9) that Archbishop Ralph crossed the channel after the arrival in Normandy about Aug. of Abbot

Thurstan, archbishop-elect of York, who hoped that he would recover the investiture of his bishopric, and that, by the king's command, he might receive the blessing from the Canterbury archbishop without having to make profession to him. In August, Anselm, returning from Rome (he had borne the pallium for the archbishop of Canterbury from Rome), came to King Henry in Normandy. He bore a letter from the pope giving him the powers of legate in England. This was made clear to the kingdom of the English in the letter. Whence by the common assent of the queen and some leading men of England, Ralph, archbishop of Canterbury, after the feast of the Nativity of St Mary [8 September], crossed the sea and went to the king. He found him residing at Rouen, and carefully consulting Henry item by item on the business which had brought him there, on his advice set out for Rome.[4]

[1117]

For a long part of the night the moon appeared bloody, and afterwards it was placed in great darkness. And the following night, 17 December, the whole sky seemed to be ablaze.[1]

In accordance with the command of King Henry, a new building was begun at Cirencester.[2] In Lombardy there was a great earthquake, and, as is reliably testified, it lasted for forty days, many dwellings were destroyed, and what is marvellous to see and to relate, a large villa was suddenly taken from its original site, and may now be seen by all standing in a distant spot. At Milan, while men of patrician rank were sitting in a tower discussing matters of state, a voice outside was heard by all who were there, calling one of them by name and commanding him to hasten outside. As this person lingered, a form appeared before them, and by coaxing managed to get the summoned man to go out. When he had gone out, the tower suddenly collapsed and in its wretched fall buried all who were

Anselm, the papal legate, and that the archbishop was laid low by a severe carbuncle at La Ferté-Fremel for a month before going on to Rome, but JW's date 'after 8 Sept.' for the crossing is his own.

[1] ASC (of which JW seems a partial rendering), the St Augustine (*UAG*, p. 77) and Bermondsey Annals (*Ann. Mon.* ii. 432) record a bloody moon which in ASC is later eclipsed on 11 Dec., and followed the next night by a red sky.

[2] JW seems to be the only extant source for this building.

miserabili oppressit.*c 3* Rotbertus Stæffordensis*d* episcopus obiit, et Gilebertus abbas Westmonasterii *e*.viii. idus Decembris.*e 4*

[1118] (.xii.) 1140 *Sacre memorie Pascalis papa .xiiii. kal. Febr. defungitur et loco eius Iohannes quidam Gaite natus substitutus, et mutato nomine Gelasius est nuncupatus.* Hic *in monasterio Montis Cassini ab infantia monachus nutritus et adultus, in ministerio uenerabilium apostolicorum Desiderii, Vrbani et Pascalis assiduus fuerat, cancellarii officio functus. Rex uero Teutonicus, qui et Romanus imperator, audito papam huic uite decessisse, Romam aduolat et Bracarensem episcopum, iam anno preterito ab eodem papa Beneuenti excommunicatum, cedente ab urbe Gelasio, papam instituit, et ex* Mauricio*a Gregorium nominat.*[1] Mahthildis regina Anglorum *apud Westmonasterium, Kal. Maii,* *b*feria .iiii.*b*, obiit, *et in ipso monasterio decenter sepulta* est.[2] *Plures Normannorum quam regi Henrico iurauerant fidelitatem postposuerunt, et* ad *regem Francie Ludowicum principesque eius, aduersarios scilicet ipsius*c *naturalis domni sui, non ueriti iustitiam, se transtulerunt.*[3] *Prefatus papa Gelasius per mare Burgundiam uenit, et aduentus eius mox Gallie toti innotuit.*[4] Non. Iulii obiit Domnus Florentius Wigornensis monachus. Huius subtili scientia et studiosi laboris industria preeminet cunctis hec chronicarum chronica.

*d*Corpus terra tegit, spiritus astra petat;
Quo cernendo Deum cum sanctis regnet in euum, Amen.*d 5*

---

c For addition in L and by P[5] *(lower mg.), see Appendix A*   *d* Coventrensis HL   *e–e interlin. above* Westmonasterii *C*[2], *incorporated BP, om.* HL
a over erasure C[3], Burdino *HR (SD ii. 251)*   *b–b interlin. C*[2], *om.* HL
c om. HL   *d–d rubricated C*

---

[3] ASC records a great earthquake in Lombardy on 3 Jan., but JW's account is fuller and does not seem paralleled in any other known source. The eyewitness account by Landulph Junior (*Landulphi Iunioris sive de sancto Paulo, Historia Mediolanensis*, ed. C. Castiglione, in L. A. Muratori, *Rerum Italicarum Scriptores* v: iii (Bologna, 1934), cc. 43–4, (pp. 27–8)) does not mention the tower incident though it describes the Archbishop of Milan holding a church council in the open because of the earthquake. Earthquakes in Italy are reported elsewhere (e. g. Ekkehard, *Chronici universalis pars altera a. 1106–1125* (MGH SS vi. 252–3)) as well as others elsewhere in Europe (e. g. at Rheims (Annals of St Denis at Rheims, MGH SS xiii. 83), at Liège (MGH SS vi. 253)).
[4] HBC gives 1 Sept. 1117 as the day of Bishop Robert de Limesey's obit, presumably on the evidence of Thomas of Chesterfield (*Anglia Sacra*, i. 434). Bishop Robert's obit is not in ASC. The obit of Gilbert Crispin is 6 Dec. 1114 (*Flete's History of Westminster Abbey*, ed. J. Armitage Robinson (Cambridge, 1909), p. 87), but 6 Dec. 1117 in ASC E or the Winchester Annals (*Ann. Mon.* ii. 45) and 6 Dec. 1118 in the Thorney Annals (BL Cotton

within it.[3] Robert, bishop of Stafford, and Gilbert, abbot of Westminster, died on 6 December.[4]

[1118] Pope Paschal of holy memory died on 19 January and John of Gaeta took his place. He changed his name to Gelasius. From his boyhood he had been brought up as a monk at Monte Cassino, and as an adult he served diligently as chancellor the venerable popes Desiderius, Urban and Paschal. When the German king, who was also the Roman emperor, learnt of the pope's death, he hastened to Rome, and, as Gelasius had retreated from Rome, installed as pope the bishop of Braga, who had been excommunicated by Paschal at Benevento in the previous year, and who changed his name from Maurice to Gregory.[1] The English queen, Matilda, died at Westminster on Wednesday, 1 May, and was fittingly buried in the monastery there.[2] Many Normans renounced the fealty they had sworn to King Henry, and went over, in defiance of true justice, to the enemies of their natural lord, the French king Louis and his magnates.[3] The aforesaid Pope Gelasius crossed to Burgundy by sea, and his arrival was straightaway known to the whole of Gaul.[4] On 7 July, the Worcester monk Florence died. His meticulous learning and scholarly labours have made this chronicle of chronicles outstanding among all others.

His body is covered by earth, his soul searches the skies.
There in the sight of God may he reign among the saints
    for ever. Amen.[5]

Nero C. VII fo. 81ᵛ), see *Heads*, p. 77. *Flete's History* . . ., p. 142, shows that 1114 is certainly wrong.

[1] Eadmer, *HN* v (p. 246). 'Burdino' was Eadmer's reading for 'Mauricio', as indeed it was in *HR* 195 (SD ii. 251). Paschal II died on 21 Feb. ASC reports the death of Paschal II and the succession of Gelasius without dates at the end of 1118. The pope Desiderius mentioned by JW had been abbot of Monte Cassino, and took the name of Victor (II).

[2] Eadmer, *HN* v (p. 248). Matilda's death on 1 May (a Wednesday in 1118) and her burial at Westminster are reported by ASC.

[3] Eadmer, *HN* v (p. 248). HH *HA* vii. 29 (p. 460) speaks of the desertion of many of Henry's *proceres* in 1117, as does ASC under 1118. Both put the betrayal clearly in the context of Henry's struggles against the French king and the counts of Anjou and Flanders, and report the wounding of Count Baldwin of Flanders. OV *HE* xii. 1 (vi. 188–9) names some who rebelled against Henry at unspecified dates.

[4] Eadmer, *HN* v (p. 248), which shows that Gelasius was at Rheims in mid-Lent 1118.

[5] The death of Florence in 1118 is one of the arguments against his authorship of the chronicle.

Ecclesia apud Momerfeld a Gosfrido Herefordensi episcopo dedicata, omnes qui ad dedicationem uenerant, domum redibant. Verum post aeris serenitatem que prius extiterat maxima, repente cum tonitruo orta est tempestas nimia, qua perculsi quidam in itinere, dum loco in quem deuenerant cedere non ualerent, subsistebant. Erant numero .v., tres uiri et .ii. femine, quarum *e*una, ictu*e* fulmineo percussa, occubuit; altera uero ab umbilico usque ad pedum uestigia misere percussa et ignita, decidit, uiris dumtaxat uix uite reseruatis. Quinque etiam caballi illorum *f* fulmine percussi, interierunt.[6]

[1119] (.xiii.) 1141   Gelasius papa obiit, *aet Cluniaci sepultus est,a* cui successit *Guido Viennensis* episcopus qui alio *nomine* Calixtus nominatus est.[1] Gosfridus Herefordensis episcopus .iii. non. Feb. obiit,*b* et Herebertus Norðwicensis .xi. kal. August.[2] Orto bello inter regem Anglorum Heinricum et regem Francorum Ludowicum et comitem Andegauensium et comitem Flandrensium, ipse rex Heinricus, inito oportunitatis consilio, anticipauit pacem facere cum comite Andegauensi, accepta filia eius in uxorem filio suo Willelmo, quem iam heredem totius regni sui constituerat. Comes idem Andegauensis Ierosolimam adiit. Post hec rex Heinricus, consilio optimatum suorum, fecit pacem cum rege Francorum, in qua pace accepit Willelmus filius eius Normanniam, a predicto rege Francorum tenendam. Cum suis etiam optimatibus qui iniuste et infideliter ab eo recesserant, et cum comite Flandrensi fecit rex pacem.[3] Terremotus in pluribus locis per Angliam factus est .iiii. k. Octob., die dominica, circa horam diei tertiam.[4] *Calixtus papa instituit generale concilium Remis, .xiii. Kal. Nou., ad quod concilium factus est*

e–e written over erasure C²   *f written with elongated letters possibly over erasure ?C³*

a–a interlin. C²   *b For B's interlineated addition here, see Appendix B*

[6] The consecration of the church at Morville (Shropshire) is not recorded elsewhere. This could be local evidence for the lightning and thunder in Epiphany week reported by ASC, though its chronological location at the end of JW's annal might suggest a date after Florence's death on 7 July.

[1] Calixtus II (1119–24). JW, with its interlineated addition on Gelasius' burial at Cluny, is here close to ASC, and while the italicized words here are in Eadmer, *HN* v (p. 249), they could also be a translation of ASC. ASC does not give Calixtus's original name.

[2] *HR* 197 (SD ii. 254) gives 2 Feb. (not 3 Feb.) for Geoffrey's death, and *EEA*, vii, p. xxxvi n. 65, reports the obit in Oxford, Bodleian Library Rawlinson B. 328, fo. 4ᵛ as 4 Feb. JW's date for Herbert Losinga's death (22 July) is confirmed by *First Register of Norwich Cathedral*, ed. H. W. Saunders (Norfolk Record Society, xi; 1939), pp. 56–7: see Greenway, *Fasti* ii. 55.

All who had attended the dedication of the church at Morville by Geoffrey, bishop of Hereford, made their way home. Suddenly a violent thunderstorm began where there had been strikingly calm skies, and some were overtaken by it as they travelled, and, unable to move away, stayed where they were. There were five in all, three men and two women. One of the women fell, struck down by lightning. The other also fell, shaken and scorched most pitifully from the navel to the soles of her feet. The men only just escaped with their lives. Their five horses perished, hit by lightning.[6]

[1119] Pope Gelasius died and was buried at Cluny. He was succeeded by Guy, bishop of Vienne, who was called Calixtus.[1] Geoffrey, bishop of Hereford, died on 3 February, and Herbert, bishop of Norwich, on 22 July.[2] War began between the English king Henry, and Louis, the French king, the count of Anjou and the count of Flanders. King Henry, initiating an advantageous plan, made a separate peace with the count of Anjou, receiving the count's daughter as bride for his son William, whom he had already made heir to all his kingdom. This count of Anjou went to Jerusalem. Afterwards, on the advice of his chief men, King Henry made a peace with the French king by which his son William received Normandy, to be held of the aforesaid French king. He also came to terms both with those magnates who had unjustly and faithlessly deserted him, and with the count of Flanders.[3] There was an earthquake in many places in England at about the third hour of the day, on Sunday, 28 September.[4] Pope Calixtus held a general council at Rheims on 20 October, and this was attended by a diverse

[3] JW's account of Henry's actions in France is different from that in ASC. ASC 1118 had already referred to the triple alliance against Henry; under 1119 it reports the defeat of the French king (presumably at the battle of Brémule on 20 Aug.), the return to Henry's allegiance of some of the disaffected Norman magnates, and then, at two separate places in the annal, the marriage alliance with Anjou and Charles the Good's succession to Count Baldwin of Flanders; and under 1120 Henry's peace with the French king and the counts of Flanders and Ponthieu, and his subsequent reconciliation with his disaffected subjects. The 'French' entries are consolidated in JW, which refers neither to the battle nor to the Flemish succession, but contributes William's homage to the French king. JW does not have the count of Anjou's pilgrimage to Jerusalem, which is reported by ASC. OV *HE* xii. 18 (vi. 234–42), Suger, *Vita Ludovici*, xxvi (pp. 196–8), HH *HA* vii. 31 (pp. 463–5), and *Chronica de Hyda*, pp. 316–17 are much fuller on the battle of Brémule.

[4] ASC records this earthquake on 28 Sept., and the Margam Annals (*Ann. Mon.* i. 10) on 29 Sept., neither chronicle specifying the hour, but ASC stresses that it was felt most strongly in Worcestershire and Gloucestershire, which could argue for JW's ignorance or deliberate omission of a version of ASC like E here.

*multiplex arciepiscoporum, episcoporum, abbatum et principum diuer-
sarum prouinciarum concursus, cum numerosa clericorum ac plebium
multitudine.* Episcopi*c* *Anglie qui tunc temporis in Normannia cum*
rege *degebant, Willelmus uidelicet Exoniensis, Rannulfus Dunholmensis,
Bernardus Menewensis et Vrbanus Glammorgatensis et insuper episcopi et
abbates Normannie, ab* ipso *rege Anglorum Heinrico ad ipsum concilium
directi sunt.* Radulfus archiepiscopus *Cantuuari*e pre infirmitate non
potuit interesse. *Turstanus, electus Eboracensis arciepiscopus, a rege
licentiam petens illuc eundi,* tandem optinuit, ea tamen *interposita fide,*
p. 373 ut *benedictionem episcopalem a* papa n*ulla ratione sua\dente susciperet.
Tali sponsione ligatus iter arripuit, et ad papam uenit*; et mox, *posthabita
sponsione, Romanos in causam suam largitatis officio transtulit, et per eos
ut a papa episcopus* consecraretur *sua manu cooperante impetrauit.
Consecratus est* autem *in pontificatum Eboracensem,* et *consecrationi* eius
*plures e Gallia episcopi ad iussum pape inter*fuere. *Episcopi uero Anglie
nondum ad concilium uenerant,* qui ubi quod factum est cognouere,
regi nuntiauere. Commotus in furorem ille, *Turstano et suis interdixit
in Angliam et Normanniam redire, in omnemque locum dominationis
sue.*[5]

[1120] (.xiiii.) 1142 *Radulfus* archiepiscopus Cantuuariensis, *.ii.
non. Ian.,* feria *.i., Angliam reuertitur* et *.ii. non. Apr.,* dominica die,
apud Westmonasterium consecrauit *in pontificatum Pangornensis ecclesie*
quendam *clericu*m uenerandum, *Dauid* nomine, *electu*m *a principe
Griffino, clero et populo Walie.* Cuius *consecrationi interfuere Ricardus
episcopus Lundoniensis, Rotbertus Lincoliensis, Rogerius Særesbyriensis,
Vrbanus Glammorgatensis.*[1] Rex Anglorum Heinricus, omnibus prospere et ad uelle peractis, *a Normannia in Angliam* redit, quem
Willelmus filius eius *sequi gestiens, nauem ingreditur, copiosa nobilium,
militum, puerorum, ac feminarum multitudine comitatus.* Hi *portu maris
euecti, miraque aeris serenitate freti freto illapsi, in modico nauis qua
uehebantur rupem incurrens euersa est, et omnes qui in ea residebant,
excepto rustico uno et ipso, ut ferebatur, nec nomine digno, qui mira Dei
gratia uiuus euasit, marinis fluctibus sunt absorpti.* Quorum nobilissimi

---

c uero *add.* HL

---

[5] Eadmer, *HN* v (pp. 255–8). Both the council of Rheims and the Thurstan episode are in ASC, which, however, dates the council to 18 Oct. The year to which JW assigns both could have been derived from Eadmer. *HC,* pp. 118–23, has a fuller account of the episode.

[1] Eadmer, *HN* v (pp. 259–60), which gave JW the year and which also says that Henry I

assembly of archbishops, bishops, abbots, and princes of various provinces, and a great host of the clergy and people. The English bishops at that time in Normandy with the king, that is, William of Exeter, Ranulf of Durham, Bernard of St David's, and Urban of Glamorgan, as well as the bishops and abbots of Normandy were sent to this council by the English king, Henry. Ralph, archbishop of Canterbury, could not attend because of illness. Thurstan, archbishop-elect of York, at last obtained from the king the permission to attend which he had sought on promising, however, that he would on no account receive consecration from the pope. Bound by this pledge, he set out on his journey, and came to the pope. Straightaway setting aside his promise, he bribed some Romans over to his cause, and through them asked the pope to consecrate him bishop with his own hands. He was then ordained to the see of York, and many bishops from Gaul attended his consecration at the pope's request. The English bishops had not yet come to the council, but they informed the king when they learnt what had happened. Henry, was roused to anger, and forbade Thurstan and his men to return to England or Normandy or any place in his realms.[5]

[1120] Ralph, archbishop of Canterbury, returned to England on Monday, 4 January, and, at Westminster on Sunday, 4 April, consecrated to the see of Bangor the respected clerk David, who had been chosen by Prince Gruffydd and the Welsh clergy and people. Richard, bishop of London, Robert, bishop of Lincoln, Roger, bishop of Salisbury, and Urban, bishop of Glamorgan, attended this consecration.[1] After successfully carrying out all his aims, Henry, the English king, returned to England from Normandy. His son William, intending to follow, embarked in the company of a large crowd of nobles, knights, young men, and women. They left the harbour, set out for sea, relying on the extremely calm weather, and, shortly afterwards, the ship in which they were travelling hit a rock and was overturned, and all who were in it were swallowed by the waves, save for one villein, who, it was said, was not worthy of being named, and who survived by the wonderful mercy of God. Those of

consented to the election, and gives a text of the petition of the consecration. The Worcester Annals (*Ann. Mon.* iv. 377) say David was a Welshman, but for the description of David as a Scot, see *Episcopal Acts and Cognate Documents relating to Welsh Dioceses, 1066–1272*, ed. J. Conway Davies (2 vols., Historical Society of the Church in Wales; Cardiff, 1948–53), i. 100.

fuerunt hi, Willelmus *regis filius,*[a] Ricardus frater eius, Ricardus comes Cestrensis, Othuel frater eius,[b] Gausfridus Riddel, Walterus de Euerci, Gosfridus Herefordensis arcidiaconus, filia regis comitissa de Perceio, neptis regis comitissa de Cestra, et alii quamplurimi quos breuitatis causa preterimus.[c] *Que res* et regis prospero nauigio Angliam uenientis, et omnium qui audiebant, *mentes exterruit atque turbauit, et de occultis iusti Dei iudiciis in admirationem concussit.*[2]

[1121] (.xv.) 1143   *Rex* Anglorum Heinricus, *legalis coniugii olim nexu solutus, ne quid ulterius inhonestum committeret, consilio Radulfi Cantuuariorum pontificis et principum regni, quos omnes in Epiphania Domini sub uno Lundonie congregauit, decreuit sibi in uxorem Atheleidem,*[a] *filiam Godefridi ducis Lotharingie, puellam uirginem decore modesti uultus decenter insignitam. Directi sunt nuntii, et futuram regni dominam summo cum honore* de transmarinis partibus *ad curiam regis* adduxerunt.[1] *Inter hec electi sunt ad regimen ecclesiarum iamdudum uiduatarum clerici duo, assumpti de capella regis, Ricardus scilicet qui regii sigilli sub cancellario custos erat, et Rotbertus qui et ipse domno regi in cura*[b] *panum ac potus strenue ministrare solebat. Horum prior Herefordensi, sequens* uero *Cestrensi*[c] *ecclesie prelatus est. Herebertus quoque abbatie Westmonasterii monachus, ipsius loci abbas constitu*itur.[d] *Ricardus, .vii. idus Ian.,* feria .vi., *electus, .xvii. kal. Feb.,* feria .i., *apud Lamhetham*[e] *consecra*tus est in episcopum a Radulfo Cantuuariensi arciepiscopo, *cooperantibus* sibi *episcopis Ricardo Lundoniensi, Rotberto Lincoliensi, Arnulfo Rofensi, Vrbano Glammorgatensi, Bernardo Sancti*[f] *Dauid.*[2] Puella predicta, in regni domnam electa, .iiii. kal. Feb., [g]sabbato,[h] regi desponsatur a Willelmo Wintoniensi episcopo, iubente Rawlfo[i] Cantuarie arciepiscopo, et crastino die, .iii. kal.

[a–a] filius regis *HL*   [b] Willelmus Bigod *add. HL*   [c] *Two verses of lament add.* in the outer mg. by P[5]

[a] Adhelizam *interlin. above* Atheleidem C[3], Atheleidam *H*, Athelizam *B*, Adhelizam *P*. Verses are added in the outer mg. by P[5] on Queen Adelaide   [b] curia *HL*   [c] Couentrensi *HL*   [d] *For L's addition here, see Appendix A*   [e] Lambytham *H*, Lambitham *L*   [f] de Sancto *HL*   [g–g] om. *P*   [h] interlin. C[2]   [i] Radulfo *HL*

---

[2] Eadmer, *HN* v (pp. 288–9). ASC names JW's first four drowned companions, and dates Henry's return to 'before Advent' (28 Nov.). WM *GR* v. 419 (p. 497) does not mention Geoffrey Ridel, Walter de Everci, or Geoffrey the archdeacon. OV *HE* xii. 26 (vi. 304–5) has a fuller list, but omits Walter and the archdeacon Geoffrey; Wace iii. 10190–202 (ii. 263) names a Rouen butcher and a noble lord as the sole survivors. Other accounts include *HR* (SD ii. 259) and HH *HA* vii. 32 (p. 466). Othuer was the illegitimate son of

the highest rank were William, the king's son, his brother Richard, Richard, earl of Chester, his brother Othuer, Geoffrey Ridel, Walter of Everci, Geoffrey, archdeacon of Hereford, the countess of Perche, the king's daughter, the countess of Chester, the king's niece, and many others who are omitted for the sake of brevity. This news shocked and distressed the king, who had reached England after a safe journey, and all who heard it, and struck them all in awe at the hidden judgements of a just God.[2]

[1121] Henry, the king of the English, had been a widower for some time, and there was concern that he should not lead a depraved life any longer. On the advice of Ralph, the Canterbury pontiff, and of the kingdom's magnates, who assembled together at London on the Epiphany [6 January], Henry decided to marry Adelaide, daughter of Duke Godfrey of Lorraine, a maiden of great beauty and modesty. Envoys were dispatched, who brought the future queen from overseas to the king's court with great honour.[1] In the mean time, two clerks from the royal chapel were chosen to fill sees which had been vacant for a long time, that is, Richard, keeper of the king's seal under the chancellor, and Robert, the royal household's steward, who was energetically in charge of providing food and drink. Richard was preferred to Hereford, Robert to Chester. Herbert also, a monk of Westminster, was made abbot of that monastery. Richard was chosen on Friday, 7 January, and was consecrated bishop on Sunday, 16 January, at Lambeth by Ralph, archbishop of Canterbury, with the assistance of bishops Richard of London, Robert of Lincoln, Ernulf of Rochester, Urban of Glamorgan, Bernard of St David's.[2] On Saturday, 29 January, the aforesaid maiden, the queen-elect, was married to the king by William, bishop of Winchester at the command of Archbishop Ralph of Canterbury, and the following

Earl Hugh of Chester. Geoffrey Ridel was a prominent justiciar and king's servant. Matilda, the illegitimate daughter of Henry I, married Rotrou, count of Perche, son of Geoffrey, count of Mortagne. Richard, earl of Chester, married Matilda, daughter of Stephen, count of Blois, and Adelaide, William I's daughter.

   [1] Eadmer, *HN* vi (p. 290). ASC and HH *HA* vii. 33 (pp. 466–8) refer to a Christmas meeting of the court at Brampton (a royal manor near Huntingdon) at which Theobald, count of Blois, was present.
   [2] Eadmer, *HN* vi (pp. 290–1). *HR* 200 (SD ii. 259) reports Richard de Sigillo's election at Windsor a few days before Candlemas 1121. 16 Jan. was a Saturday in 1121. The year of Abbot Herbert's succession to Westminster is discussed in *Flete's History of Westminster Abbey*, ed. Robinson, p. 88, and confirmed by *Regesta* ii. 1301 (see *Heads*, p. 77).

Feb.,^{g} ab eodem arcipresule regina consecratur et coronatur.^{3} *Post hec idem pontifex cum rege Abbandoniam ueniens, .iii. idus Martii, die dominica, sacrauit supramemoratum Rotbertum ad episcopatum Cestrensis^j ecclesie,* astantibus *et cooperantibus huic sacramento Willelmo Wentano episcopo, Willelmo Exoniensi, Vrbano et Bernardo episcopis Walensibus.* Paucis *diebus elapsis, electus est quidam de regis capella, Eouerardus nomine, ad episcopatum Northwicensis ecclesie* et a Radulfo Cantwariensi pontifice, *.ii. idus Iun., sacratur Cantuuarie, conuenientibus pro hoc ipso Arnulfo Rofensi episcopo, Ricardo Herefordensi, et*
p. 374 Rotberto Couentrensi.^{4} *Calixtus papa, uiribus undecunque collectis,* | *supramemoratum Mauricium, cognomento Burdinum, quem uocatum Gregorium in sede apostolica imperator cum suis fautoribus constituerat, cepit, eumque, suis omnibus spoliatum, monasterio, ut monachus esset, contumeliose intrusit.*^{5} Rex Anglorum Heinricus super Walenses exercitum duxit, et acceptis obsidibus ab eis, totam Waliam sue dicioni subegit.^{6} *Clericus quidam,* natione Hiberniensis, *nomine Gregorius, a rege Hibernie, clero et populo* in episcopatum *Dubline ciuitatis electus,* Angliam uenit, antiquo pro more ordinandus ab arciepiscopo Cantwarie, Anglorum primate. Quem ex precepto eiusdem arcipresulis, Rogerius Særesbyriensis episcopus apud castellum suum quod uocatur Diuisio, .xi. kal. Octob., sabbato, *ad diaconatus et ad presbiteratus promouit gradum.* Ordinatus est autem episcopus, *.vi. non. Oct.,* feria .i., *apud Lamhetham* a Radulfo Cantwariorum pontifice, eiusque *consecrationi interfuere episcopi* Ricardus Lundoniensis, *Rogerius Særesbyriensis, Rotbertus Lincoliensis,* Eouerardus Northwicensis *et Dauid Bangornensis.*^{7} ⟨P⟩rincipalis ecclesia Teodekesbyrie ab episcopis Teowlfo Wigornensi, Ricardo Herefordensi, Vrbano Glammorgatensi^k et a prefato Gregorio Dublinensi, .viiii. kal. Novemb., feria .ii., consecrata est summo cum honore.^{8}

---

^{j} Couantrensis *H*, Couentrensis *L* ^{k} Glammorgartensi *CB*

---

^{3} ASC, HH *HA* vii. 33 (pp. 466–8) and *HR* 200 (SD ii. 259) report the marriage taking place at Windsor (ASC dating it to 'before Candlemas', and the Bermondsey Annals (*Ann. Mon.* iii. 433) to 3 Feb.). Neither Eadmer, *HN* vi (p. 293), nor WM *GP* i. 71 (p. 132 n. 3) gives dates for the marriage and coronation. Eadmer, *HN* vi (pp. 292–3), was presumably JW's source for William of Winchester celebrating the wedding at Ralph's command, and for Ralph's anointing the queen the day before. Where JW obtained his exact dates is not known.
^{4} Eadmer, *HN* vi (pp. 293–4).
^{5} Eadmer, *HN* vi (p. 294).

day, 30 January, she was consecrated and crowned queen by the same archbishop.[3] The archbishop then accompanied the king to Abingdon where he consecrated this Robert to the see of Chester on Sunday, 13 March, in the presence and with the assistance of William, bishop of Winchester, William of Exeter, and the Welsh bishops Urban and Bernard. Some days later, Everard, a member of the royal chapel, was elected bishop of Norwich, and was consecrated by Ralph, archbishop of Canterbury, on 12 June, at Canterbury, in the presence of Ernulf, bishop of Rochester, Richard of Hereford, and Robert of Coventry.[4] Pope Calixtus collected a force from all sides, arrested the aforementioned Maurice, called Burdinus, whom the emperor and his supporters had set up as Pope Gregory, and, taking away all his possessions, humiliatingly thrust him into a monastery. He had earlier been a monk.[5] Henry, the English king, led an army against the Welsh, took hostages from them, and subjected all Wales to his rule.[6] A certain Irish clerk called Gregory was elected by the Irish king, clergy, and people to the see of Dublin and came to England to be ordained according to established custom by the English primate, the archbishop of Canterbury. On the archbishop's orders Bishop Roger of Salisbury conferred on him the orders of the diaconate and priesthood on Saturday, 21 September, at his castle of Devizes. Ralph, archbishop of Canterbury, with the assistance of Bishops Richard of London, Roger of Salisbury, Robert of Lincoln, Everard of Norwich and David of Bangor consecrated Gregory bishop at Lambeth on Sunday, 2 October.[7] The chief church at Tewkesbury was consecrated with great ceremony on Monday, 24 October, by bishops Theulf of Worcester, Richard of Hereford, Urban of Glamorgan and the said Gregory of Dublin.[8]

---

[6] See Lloyd, *History of Wales*, ii. 465. ASC, followed by HH *HA* vii. 33 (p. 468) says that this expedition took place in the summer. *HR* 202 (SD ii. 263) reports that it was provoked by attacks against Cheshire. *AC s.a.* 1121 records Henry's expedition (without a date) against the men of Powys and their buying peace with 10,000 cattle. *Brut* Pen. pp. 47–8, Her. pp. 104–9 and BS pp. 138–41 under 1118 (*recte* 1121) record Maredudd ap Bleddyn purchasing peace by paying a fine of 10,000 cattle. JW alone mentions hostages.

[7] Eadmer, *HN* vi (pp. 297–8). Eadmer dated Gréne's ordination as deacon and priest to the Ember Days of September (21, 23, 24 Sept.): JW's Saturday was 24 Sept. JW adds Bishops Richard of London and Everard of Norwich to Eadmer's list of three bishops participating in his consecration as bishop.

[8] The Tewkesbury Annals (*Ann. Mon.* i. 45) date the consecration by Bishop Theulf and '4' bishops to 23 Oct., which was a Sunday in 1121.

[1122] (.xvi.) 1144   *Ciuitas Glaworna cum principali monasterio* .vii. *idus Mar., feria .iiii., denuo conflagrauit incendio, anno regni regis Anglorum Heinrici .xxii.; siquidem* primo *quo regnare cepit anno, .xi. kal. Iunii, feria .v., combusta est primo.*[1] Dorubernensis archiepiscopus .xxxv.,*ᵃ Radulfus .xiii*i.*ᵇ kal. Nou.*, feria .v., *Cantwarie* uita decessit.[2] ᶜIohannes Bathoniensis episcopus .iiii. Kl. *ᵈ*Ianuarii obiit*ᵈ*

[C³BP]

qui adhuc uita comite *ab Heinrico rege .d. libris argenti totam* urbem Bathoniensem *mercatus* est.ᶜ³

[1123]ᵃ (.xvii.) 1145   Rotbertus .xviii. Lincoliensis episcopus, mense Ianuario, dum apud Wudestoke, equo sedens, cum rege Heinrico colloquium haberet, subito decidere cepit et ommutuit.ᵇ Deportatus ad hospitium, morte improuisa obiit.[1] Rannulfus quoque, regis cancellarius, miserabili obitu uita decessit.[2] ᶜVir eximieᶜ religionis, Willelmus canonicus Sancte Osgithe de Cicc, ad archiepiscopatum Cantuuariensem, Glaorne, ubi in Purificatione Sancte Marie rex tenuit curiam suam, eligitur, et a Willelmo Wintoniensi episcopo, pluribus cooperantibus episcopis, .xiiii. kal. Martii, Cantuuarie consecratur episcopus.[3] Quo annuente, datus est ipso Quadragesimali tempore Lindicoline ciuitatis episcopatus Alexandro Særesbyriensi archidiacono.[4] Postea idem archiepiscopus Willelmus, comitantibus secum Turstino Eboracensi archipontifice, Bernardo episcopo de Sancto Dauid, Sigefrido Glæstoniensi abbate, Anselmo

---

ᵃ .xxv. HL   ᵇ .xiii. HL   ᶜ⁻ᶜ *written on last line of annal in small script extending into the mg., and then interlin. on the next line* C   ᵈ⁻ᵈ obiit Ian. H

ᵃ 1113 (G)   ᵇ *verses on Bishop Robert add. by* P⁵ *in the outer mg.*   ᶜ⁻ᶜ *over erasure* C

---

[1] ASC, *Cart. Gloc.* i. 14–15 (which shares the italicized words with JW) and Gregory of Caerwent (BL Cotton Vespasian A. V, fo. 197ʳ) date the fire to 8 Mar., which was, unlike JW's date, a Wednesday in 1122. The Margam Annals (*Ann. Mon.* i. 10) date it 7 Mar. 1121, while the Tewkesbury Annals (*Ann. Mon.* i. 45) have it under 1122 (without a calendar date). With the exception of ASC, the chronicles refer here to an earlier fire which they had reported under 1101 (see above, 1101 n. 3). *Cart. Gloc.* (i. 15) had reported this earlier fire under 1102 (against JW's 6 June 1101) but here dates it to the third year of Henry I, presumably therefore to 22 May 1103, though this was a Friday in that year. ASC alone describes the fire's effect on the monastery in 1122.
[2] Although HL's 19 Oct. is supported by a late entry in a Canterbury annal (*UAG*, p. 78), most sources (ASC, Eadmer *HN* vi (p. 302) (which might be the source of the italicized words), OV *HE* xi. 31 (vi. 318–19), WM *GP* i. 71 (p. 132) and obits) have 20 Oct.: see Greenway, *Fasti* ii. 3. Eadmer concludes *HN* with Ralph's death.

[1122] The city of Gloucester and its chief monastery was again destroyed by fire on Wednesday, 9 March, in the twenty-second year of Henry, the king of the English. It had first been burnt down in the first year of Henry's reign on Thursday, 22 May.[1] Ralph, the thirty-fifth archbishop of Canterbury, died there on Thursday, 19 October.[2] John, bishop of Bath, died on 29 December.

> During his lifetime he had bought the city of Bath from King Henry for 500 pounds of silver.[3]

[1123] In January at Woodstock, Robert, the eighteenth bishop of Lincoln, was riding, and conversing with King Henry, when he fell suddenly and was struck dumb. He was carried to some lodgings, and died unexpectedly.[1] The king's chancellor, Ranulf, also came to a wretched end.[2] William, the most pious canon of St Osyth's, Chich, was elected to the archbishopric of Canterbury at Gloucester where the king was holding his court on the Feast of the Purification [2 February]. He was consecrated at Canterbury on 16 February by Bishop William of Winchester assisted by many other bishops.[3] With William's agreement the see of Lincoln was given during the same Lenten season to Alexander, the archdeacon of Salisbury.[4] Later, accompanied by Archbishop Thurstan of York, Bishop Bernard of St David's, Abbot Seffrid of Glastonbury and also Abbot Anselm of St

[3] *HR* 205 (SD ii. 268) dates John's death to 26 Dec. The italicized words in C[3]'s text are from WM *GP* ii. 90 (p. 194). HBC has 26 x 30 Dec. 1122. JW has 29 Dec.

[1] ASC, WM *GP* iv. 175 (p. 313), and HH *HA* viii, *De contemptu mundi* 2 (p. 588), give an account of Robert Bloet's death, which ASC and HH *HA* vii. 34 (p. 470) date to 10 Jan.

[2] HH *HA* vii. 34 (p. 470) has an account of Ranulf's death, which took place 'a few days after' his fall from a horse at Christmastime at Berkhampstead. Green, *Government*, pp. 28, 160, 179 n., discusses Ranulf's career and the estate at Berkhampstead.

[3] ASC covers the election discussions at the Candlemas Gloucester council, and refers to the disagreements caused by the choice of William of Corbeil, reporting at a later point in the annal the latter's consecration. HH *HA* vii. 35 (p. 470) speaks simply of Henry giving William of Corbeil Canterbury at Candlemas. Of the sources dating William's consecration, some Canterbury sources (*UAG*, pp. 5, 78) give 18 Feb., a Sunday in 1123. JW has 16, *HR* 206 (SD ii. 269) 25, and Gervase, *Actus pontificum* (Gervase, ii. 380) 19 Feb. Whitelock, Brett, and Brooke, *Councils and Synods*, ii. 726-7 outlines the background to this disputed election.

[4] An Alexander the Archdeacon (who could be JW's Salisbury archdeacon) witnesses *Regesta* ii. 1301, which is dated to 1121 (after 5 Aug.). ASC (followed by HH *HA* vii. 35 (p. 470)) says that Alexander, whom it describes as a clerk and as Bishop Roger of Salisbury's nephew, was elected at Winchester during the king's stay there 'at Eastertide' (HH at 'Pascha').

quoque abbate de Sancto Eadmundo, pro petendo pallio Romam iuit.[d][5] Alexander rex Scottorum, .vii. kal. Maii, obiit.[6] Rex Anglorum Heinricus, emensa festiuitate Pentecostes, mare transiit.[7] Archiepiscopus Cantuuariensis Willelmus, suscepto pallio a papa Calixto, et Turstinus Eboracensis archipresul cum sociis, Roma redeuntes, ad regem in Normannia morantem uenerunt; et non multo post archiepiscopus Willelmus Angliam redit et Alexandrum Lincoliensi ecclesie, .xi. kal. Augusti, Cantuarie, Godefridum uero cancellarium regine, .vii. kal. Sept., in ecclesia Sancti Pauli Apostoli Lundonie consecrauit episcopum Bathoniensi ecclesie.[8] Teowlfus .xxvi. Wigornensis ecclesie antistes, .xiii. kal. Nou., Sabbato, apud Hamtun uillam suam obiit.[9] [e]Rotbertus abbas Teodekesbyriensis ecclesie, .vi. idus Dec., uita decessit.[10] [f]Alexandro regi Scottorum successit David frater eius.[ef][11]

[C[3]BP[3]]
[g]In Suthsaxonia in *diocesi* Cicestrensi *sunt duo cenobia e nouo facta. Sancti Martini de Bello quod rex Willelmus* senior *fundauit et prouexit in loco ubi Angliam debella*uit. *Altare ecclesie est in loco ubi Haroldi pro patrie caritate occisi cadauer examine repertum est. Sancti Pancratii de Læwes quod auctore Willelmo comiti de Warenna, Lanzo quidam Cluniacensis*

[d] *JW's hand stopped here* G   [e–e] *om.* H   [f–f] *om.* L   [g–g] *written in the mg. next to 1123* C[3]P[3]

[5] William set out on 13 Mar. (Canterbury Easter table annals in BL Cotton Caligula A. XV, printed in *UAG*, p. 5). To the members of William's embassy ASC, which dates William's departure to the spring, adds John, archdeacon of Canterbury, and Giffard, the king's chaplain, and makes it clear that Thurstan reached Rome before William. *HR* 208 (SD ii. 272) and *HC* (p. 188) agree that Thurstan reached Rome first, three days before, according to ASC and one apparently corrupt reading in *HC* (p. 188 and n. 2); a few days previously, according to *HR*; and six months earlier, according to *HC*.
[6] No other source dates Alexander's death to 1123, though JW's day, 25 Apr., is supported by *LVD* (p. 150) and for 1124 by the Holyrood (*A Scottish Chronicle known as the Chronicle of Holyrood*, ed. M. O. Anderson, Scottish History Society (Edinburgh, 1938), p. 116 s.a. 1124) and Melrose chronicles (*The Chronicle of Melrose from Cottonian Manuscript Faustina B. IX in the British Museum: a Complete Facsimile*, introd. by A. O. and M. O. Anderson (London, 1936), p. 32). ASC gives 23, and *HR* 210 (SD ii. 275) 26 Apr. 1124. OV *HE* viii. 22 (iv. 277) gives 1125 like Torigni (*Chronicles Stephen, etc.* iv. 111).
[7] ASC, HH *HA* vii. 35 (pp. 470–2) and *HR* (SD ii. 273) report Henry's crossing to

Edmund's, the same Archbishop William journeyed to Rome to collect the pallium.[5] Alexander, king of the Scots, died on 25 April.[6] After Pentecost [3 June], Henry, the English king, crossed the channel.[7] After receiving the pallium from Pope Calixtus, Archbishop William of Canterbury with Archbishop Thurstan and their other companions came back from Rome and went to the king who was in Normandy. Soon afterwards Archbishop William returned to England and consecrated Alexander bishop of Lincoln on 22 July at Canterbury, and Godfrey, the king's chancellor, bishop of Bath on 26 August at St Paul's, London.[8] Theulf, the twenty-sixth bishop of Worcester, died at Hampton, his township, on Saturday, 20 October.[9] Abbot Robert of Tewkesbury, died on 8 December.[10] The Scottish king Alexander was succeeded by his brother David.[11]

In the diocese of Chichester in Sussex two new monasteries have been founded. First St Martin at Battle which King William the Elder founded and erected at the site of his battle in England. The church's altar was placed where the body of Harold (slain for the love of his country) was found. Then there was St Pancras of Lewes established by William, earl of Warenne, with

Normandy (the first two dating it close to Whitsun, *HR* precisely to 11 June) and his campaigns there, including the siege of Pont Audemer. *HR*'s account of the siege (Nov., Dec. 1123) is full and supplements that in OV *HE* xii. 34 (vi. 332–6).

[8] ASC does not refer to William and Thurstan's return from Rome and their stay in Normandy. JW seems to be the sole extant source for the two archbishops' stay in Normandy and for the dates of the consecrations of Bishops Alexander of Norwich and Godfrey of Bath, though Gervase, *Actus pontificum* (Gervase, ii. 380), confirms their locations.

[9] JW alone provides the day of Theulf's death. His death was the second since 1122 to throw open an election to an episcopal chapter. This is discussed by D. L. Bethell, 'English monks and episcopal elections in the 1120s', *EHR* lxxxiv (1969), 673–98, where Eadmer's letter to Prior Nicholas of Worcester which it occasioned is printed at pp. 697–8. Hampton could have been either one of the Hamptons near Leominster or Hampton Lucy in Warwickshire.

[10] *Heads*, p. 73, notes an obit for 24 Dec. in Cambridge, University Library Gg. 3. 21, fos. 5–9ᵛ. The Tewkesbury Annals (*Ann. Mon.* 1. 45) place Robert's death and that of Bishop Theulf (see above, 1123 n. 9) under 1124.

[11] The chronicles listed above under 1123 n. 6 report this succession a year later, in 1124.

monachus in summe religionis
cacumine locauit.*gh* 12

[1124] (.xviii.) 1146*ª*   *b*Radulfus*c* Cicestrensis episcopus successor Willelmi, succes-
soris Stigandi, uite modum fecit.*b1*
Arnulfus .xxiii. Hrofensis episcopus, mense Martio obiit.² Waler-
annus*d* comes de Mellant, in ebdomada Dominice Passionis, a
militibus regis Heinrici in Normannia captus, cum pluribus in
artam custodiam Rotomagi detruditur.³ *e*Gosfridus, abbas Noui Monasterii, Wintonie obiit.*e* ⁴ Reuerendus prior Wigornensis ecclesie,
Nicolaus nomine, .viii. kal. Iulii, feria .iii., obiit.

p. 375   *f*Gaudeat in celo qui miserante Deo.*f* ⁵ |

Willelmus Cantuuariensis archiepiscopus, ut rex mandarat, mare
transiit.⁶ *g*Kalixtus papa obiit, cui Honorius, Ostiensis episcopus,
successit.*g* ⁷

[1125] (.xix.) 1147*ª* Monetarii per Angliam cum falsa moneta
capti, truncatis dextris manibus et abscisis inferioribus corporis
partibus, regis ferale subeunt edictum.*b* Mutatione postmodum
monete, cara facta sunt omnia. Hinc preualida fames oborta,
plurimam multitudinem hominum morte tenus affligit.¹ *cd*Eximie
religionis et probitatis uiri,*d* Symon cancellarius regina, et Sigefridus

---

h *1124b incorporated here* B

ª partly erased (G)   *b–b written in the mg. next to 1124* C³, *next to 1123–24* P³,
incorporated at 1123h B   *c Luffa interlin.* CB   *d Galeranus over erasure* C, *om.*
HLP   *e–e om.* H   *f–f rubricated* C   *g–g add. at line end and extending into
the mg.* C³

ª .m. of .mcxlvii. alone survived an erasure (G)   *b uel iudicium interlin.* CB
(G)   *c paragraph mark* C   *d–d om.* H

---

¹² WM *GP* ii. 97–8 (p. 207).
¹ The Chichester Annals (*UAG*, p. 94) assign Ralph Luffa's death to 14 Dec. 1123. It is
possible that JW's marginal addition may have been intended for 1123, which is the year in
HR 209 (SD ii. 275).
² ASC and a Canterbury obit (see Greenway, *Fasti* ii. 76) give Ernulf's obit as 15 Mar.
1124.
³ ASC under 1123 and 1124 and OV *HE* xii. 34, 39 (vi. 332–6, 346–50, 356) both give
fuller accounts of the unsuccessful rebellion of Waleran, count of Meulan, and other
named leaders, and of its suppression. The beginnings of Waleran's campaign of 1124
(starting with the raid against royal forces at Vatteville-on-the-Seine) is dated 25 Mar. by
ASC and OV *HE* xiiii. 39 (vi. 352). The battle near Bourgthéroulde where Waleran was
captured took place on 26 Mar. (OV *HE* xii. 39 (vi. 348) and Torigni (*GND* ii. 234–6)).
For this rebellion see Crouch, *Beaumont Twins*, pp. 13–24.

the Cluniac monk Lanzo as its abbot.[12]

[1124]   Ralph, bishop of Chichester, successor to William, who was Stigand's successor, died.[1] Ernulf, the twenty-third bishop of Rochester, died in March.[2] Waleran, count of Meulan, was taken prisoner with many others by King Henry's army in Normandy in Passion week [30 March– 5 April], and held under close custody in Rouen.[3] Geoffrey [I], abbot of New Minster, died at Winchester.[4] The revered prior of Worcester, Nicholas, died on Tuesday, 24 June.

May he rejoice in heaven through the mercy of God![5]

The archbishop of Canterbury, William, crossed overseas at the royal command.[6] Pope Calixtus died and was succeeded by Honorius, bishop of Ostia.[7]

[1125] By the savage command of the king, moneyers throughout England, taken with counterfeit money, had their right hands and their lower limbs amputated. Afterwards when coins were changed, everything became dearer, and a severe famine arose which reduced a multitude even to death.[1] Two men of great piety and virtue, Simon, the queen's chancellor, and Seffrid, abbot of Glastonbury,

---

[4] JW is the only extant source for the date of Geoffrey I's death (see *Heads*, p. 82).

[5] JW is the only known source for the date of Prior Nicholas's death (see *Heads*, p. 83).

[6] William witnesses charters in Normandy Jan.-Mar. 1125 (*Regesta* ii. 1424–5). His visit to Normandy may have been connected with the arrival there of the legate John of Crema, and the appointment of new prelates (*HC* (pp. 202–4)). Under 1125 both JW and ASC report William conducting John to England from Normandy.

[7] Honorius II (1124–30). This succession, with 14 Dec. for Calixtus II's death, is in ASC. *HC* (p. 202) has this information, dating Calixtus's death to 'Advent' (30 Nov.–23 Dec.).

[1] ASC and other chronicles (Tewkesbury, Worcester, Winchester, *Ann. Mon.* i. 45, iv. 377, ii. 47) report Henry's actions against moneyers, ASC commenting on the consequences of their dishonesty. The Margam Annals (*Ann. Mon.* i. 11) mention (like JW) the particular punishments of moneyers, giving the number mutilated as 93, and the Winchester Annals (*Ann. Mon.* ii. 47) noted that three moneyers, among many, escaped mutilation at Winchester. WM *GR* v. 399, 411 (ii. 476, 487) and *GP* v. 278 (p. 442) both comment on Henry's tough actions. It is possible that JW's comment on the consequences of the drive against counterfeit money could be his interpretation of ASC's reference to the consequences of the moneyers' dishonesty. This purge of moneyers is discussed by M. Blackburn, 'Coinage and currency under Henry I: a review', *ANS* xiii (1991), 49–81, at pp. 64–8, where it is reported that Type 14 of Henry I showed the sharpest drop in the number of moneyers.

abbas Glestonie, in episcopos eliguntur Normannie; Symon quidem ad episcopatum Wigornensem, Sigefridus*e* ad Cicestrensem.² *f*Vir non modice prudentie duorum episcoporum Wigornensium, Samsonis uidelicet et Teowulfi, archidiaconus, Hugo nomine, .xii. kal. Aprilis obiit.*f3* Pascali festiuitate emensa, Symon et Sigefridus, electi episcopi cum archiepiscopis Willelmo et Turstino et cardinali Romano Iohanne uocabulo, Angliam uenere: et Sigefridus apud Lamhythe,*g* .ii. idus April., a Willelmo archiepiscopo ordinatur antistes Cicestrensi ecclesie,*h* eiusque ordinationi interfuerunt Romanus cardinalis, Turstinus Eboracensis archiepiscopus, Eouerardus Norðwicensis, Ricardus Herefordensis, Bernardus Sancti*i* Dauid, Dauid Pangornensis, Vrbanus Glammorgatensis et Iohannes Hrofensis electus episcopus. Symon electus presul Wigornensis, .viii. idus Maii, die uidelicet Ascensionis Dominice, a clero et a populo cum festiua processione suscipitur Wigorne, *j*et .x. kal. Iunii a Willelmo archiepiscopo Dorubernie presbiter ordinatur Cantuuarie.*j4* Imperator Heinricus obiit et sepultus est Spira, ubi et auus eius.

Romanorum .xcviii. Hlotharius*k* regnauit annis .xii.*l5*

Symon electus Wigornensis episcopus, comitante*m* Godefrido Bathoniensi episcopo, Cantwariam uenit, et a Willelmo Cantuuariensi archiepiscopo, sabbato ebdomade*n* Pentecostes presbyter ordinatur, et crastino cum magno honore sancte matri Wigornensi ecclesie presul consecratur, cum quo Iohannes Cantwariensis archidiaconus ad ecclesiam Hrofensem episcopus ordinatur. Quorum consecrationi interfuere Ricardus Herefordensis episcopus,*o* Dauid Pangornensis, Godefridus Bathoniensis, Sigefridus Cicestrensis. Symon Wigorniam ad sui presulatus sedem ueniens, maxima populi confluente multitudine, cum honorifica processione denuo suscipitur, inthronizatur, laus Summe Trinitati in illo

---

e Saffridus *H*   *f-f* om. *H*   *g* Lambytham *H*, Lambhithe *L*   *h* om. *H*   *i* de sancto *HL*   *j-j* om. *(G)*   *k* Hlotharius *interlin. above* Leodegarius *C*³, Leodegarius *HL*   *l* .xii. *add. in blank space* *C*³, om. *HL BP (G), though HL (G) leave a blank space for a number, later hand in B has added* .xii. menses iii. *in mg.* *m* comit- *written in elongated letters over erasure* *C*   *n* *over erasure* *C*   *o* *interlin.* *C*, om. *H*

---

² HH *HA* vii. 35 (p. 472) notes these choices, calling Simon the queen's cleric. Two sentences later JW makes it clear that these men were chosen by the king when he was in Normandy as stated explicitly at this point by HH.

were elected bishops in Normandy, Simon to Worcester and Seffrid to Chichester.[2] Hugh, a man of great moderation and archdeacon to two Worcester bishops, Samson and Theulf, died on 21 March.[3] After Easter [29 March] the bishops-elect, Simon and Seffrid, came to England with archbishops William and Thurstan and the Roman cardinal John. Seffrid was ordained bishop of Chichester at Lambeth on 12 April by Archbishop William of Canterbury with the Roman cardinal in attendance, and Archbishop Thurstan of York, Everard of Norwich, Richard of Hereford, Bernard of St David's, David of Bangor, Urban of Glamorgan, and John, bishop-elect of Rochester. Simon, bishop-elect of Worcester, was welcomed into Worcester by the clergy and people in a joyous procession, on 8 May, Ascension Day, and was ordained priest at Canterbury on 23 May by Archbishop William of that see.[4] The emperor Henry died, and was buried at Speyer where his grandfather was also buried.

Lothar, the ninety-eighth emperor of the Romans, ruled twelve years.[5]

Simon, bishop-elect of Worcester, accompanied by Bishop Godfrey of Bath, came to Canterbury, was ordained priest on the Saturday of Pentecost [23 May], and consecrated with due ceremony the next day to St Mary's see at Worcester at the same time as John, the Canterbury archdeacon, was ordained to the see of Rochester. Bishop Richard of Hereford, David of Bangor, Godfrey of Bath and Seffrid of Chichester were present at their consecration. Simon came to his see at Worcester, being again escorted with great honour in procession by a vast crowd, was enthroned and concelebrated a mass

[3] *Worcester Cartulary*, pp. lxiii–lxvi, notes that the Worcester bishopric was divided into two archdeaconries from Bishop Samson's time, but that the evidence for division into two territorial archdeaconries is from the 1140s: see also Greenway, *Fasti* ii. 104–5.

[4] John of Crema arrived in England at Lent (ASC and *HC* p. 204) and at the time of these consecrations (Gervase, *Actus pontificum* (Gervase ii. 381)), celebrating the Easter (29 Mar.) High Mass at Canterbury (ASC and Gervase), but JW is alone in naming the bishops-elect and Thurstan among those accompanying the legate to England and in giving the date (12 Apr.) of, and the names of those present at, Seffrid's consecration. Simon's ordination as priest is repeated by JW later in the same annal though the second reference is fuller (see below, 1125 n. 6). JW's date here for Simon's ordination seems to be wrong: Ascension day was 7, not 8, May in 1125. JW claims that Simon was twice received at Worcester, once as bishop-elect on 7/8 May, and later as bishop.

[5] Henry V died at Utrecht on 23 May (Meyer von Knonau, *Jahrbücher*, vii. 322–4). Lothar III (1125–38) was still reigning when the earlier versions of JW MS C which lay behind HL and B were transcribed.

concelebratur.[6] Eodem die, id est .ix. kal. Iun., Dei seruus et in tota domu sua fidelis amicus, Benedictus nomine, anno preterito de priore electus abbas Teodekesbyriensi[p] ecclesie, ibidem a puero nutritus in monachico habitu et processu temporis concessu domni Wlstani presulis, a quo omnes ecclesiasticos ordines iamdudum susceperat, in pace et dilectione unus de cenobitis Wigornensibus effectus, ab eodem nouo presule Simone nouus abbas consecratur Wigornensi ecclesie; cuius consecrationi interfuere processionales susceptores eiusdem presulis, Ricardus Herefordensis, Godefridus Bathoniensis, Dauid Pangornensis episcopi, et parrochiani sui, abbates Wido Persorensis, Willelmus Glaucestrensis, Godefridus Wincelcumbensis et, pro abbate suo infirmitate depresso, domnus prior Eoueshamnensis Dominicus, prior etiam Maluernensis domnus Walcerus, illi inquam de quibus illud psalmographi potest pronuntiari: Emittit Deus fontes in conuallibus, et totum processionale agmen quod antistiti obuiam processerat.[7]

Celebrata est synodus Lundonie in ecclesia beati apostolorum principis apud Westmonasterium mense Septembrio, nona die p. 376 eiusdem mensis, id est .v. idus Septemb., ubi | post multarum discussionem causarum promulgata sunt hec[q] capitula et ab omnibus confirmata, numero .xvii. Prefuit autem huic synodo Iohannes de Crema, sancte et apostolice ecclesie de titulo Sancti Grisogoni presbiter cardinalis et domni pape Honorii in Angliam legatus, cum Willelmo Cantuuariensi et Turstino Eboracensi archiepiscopis et cum episcopis diuersarum prouinciarum numero .xx. et abbatibus circiter .xl., et cum innumera cleri et populi multitudine.[r] Sunt autem hec capitula:

[s]Primum capitulum.[s] Sanctorum patrum uestigiis inherentes, quenquam in ecclesia per pecuniam ordinari auctoritate apostolica prohibemus.

[p] *corrected from* Teodecesbyriensi *C* [q] *erased (G)* [r] *C's text om. from here to 1125*[x] *(G)* [s–s] *om. HL*

[6] The Sunday after Pentecost when Simon's episcopal consecration took place was Trinity Sunday, 24 May in 1125. JW seems to be the earliest extant source for the details of the episcopal consecrations of Simon and John to Worcester and Rochester respectively. The date of Simon's reception as bishop at Worcester is uncertain. It could not have been Trinity Sunday, in spite of the references to the concelebratory mass being in praise of the Trinity, and to the blessing of Benedict as abbot of Tewkesbury, 'eodem die, .ix. kal. Iun.', that is, 24 May or Trinity Sunday. JW, who had referred twice, presumably unintentionally, to Simon's ordination as priest, may have stumbled again at this point and the reference to

in praise of the Trinity.[6] The same day, 24 May, Benedict, a loving and faithful servant of God in his household, who had the previous year, when he was prior, been chosen as abbot of Tewkesbury, was consecrated as the new abbot by Simon, the new bishop of Worcester. Since his boyhood he had been a monk there, and had in due course and by the permission of Bishop Wulfstan long ago received all ecclesiastical ordinations, and in peace and love become a monk at Worcester. At Benedict's consecration the following escorted the same bishop in procession: Bishops Richard of Hereford, Godfrey of Bath, David of Bangor, the fellow abbots of the same diocese Guy of Pershore, William of Gloucester, Godfrey of Winchcombe, Prior Dominic of Evesham in place of his sick abbot, and Prior Walcher of Malvern. To these the words of the Psalmist might be applied: He sendeth out the fountains into the valleys. The whole processional column proceeded to meet the bishop.[7]

On the ninth day of September, that is, on the fifth of the Ides of that month, a synod was held in London in the church of the blessed prince of the apostles in Westminster. After a discussion of various matters, these seventeen canons were published and confirmed by all. Present at the synod were John of Crema, cardinal priest of the holy apostolic *titulus* church of St Chrysogonus, and Pope Honorius' legate in England, the Archbishops William of Canterbury and Thurstan of York, twenty bishops from various dioceses, about forty abbots, and a great gathering of clergy and people. These are the canons:

First canon. Following in the footsteps of the Holy Fathers, we forbid by apostolic authority the sale of any church office.

the concelebration 'laus summe Trinitatis' could have been attached in his draft to the mass on 24 May when Simon and John were consecrated.

[7] Ps. 103: 10. *Heads*, p. 73, suggests that JW is the only extant source for Benedict's blessing as abbot. The Tewkesbury Annals (*Ann. Mon.* i. 45) simply record Benedict's succession *s.a.* 1124 in the year before Simon's consecration as bishop. For Benedict's blessing to have taken place on 24 May, the day of Simon's consecration, it must have taken place at Canterbury. This is unlikely and JW was probably in error in dating it to that day: it probably took place on a now unknown day, that of the reception and enthronement of Bishop Simon at Worcester. The repetition of the report of Simon's ordination as priest, the uncertain date of Simon's enthronement, and the erroneous date for Benedict's blessing suggests that JW (or the scribe C²) had difficulty in inserting material from some rough notes on these events in their proper places: perhaps the insertion of Henry V's death and the succession of Lothar at the appropriate point in the calendar caused some confusion.

II.*¹* Interdicimus etiam pro chrismate, pro oleo, pro baptismate, pro penitentia, pro uisitatione infirmorum seu unctione, pro communione corporis Christi, pro sepultura, nullum omnino pretium exigatur.

III. Statuimus preterea et apostolica auctoritate decernimus, ut in consecrationibus episcoporum, uel abbatum benedictionibus, seu in dedicationibus ecclesiarum, non cappa, non tapete, non manutergium, non baccilia, et nihil omnino per uiolentiam nisi sponte oblatum fuerit, penitus exigatur.

IIII. Nullus abbas, nullus prior, nullus omnino monachus uel clericus, ecclesiam, siue decimam, seu quelibet beneficia ecclesiastica, de dono laici, sine proprii episcopi auctoritate et assensu, suscipiat. Quod si presumptum fuerit, irrita erit donatio huiuscemodi et ipse canonice ultioni subiacebit.

V. Sancimus preterea ne quis ecclesiam sibi siue prebendam paterna uendicet hereditate aut successori sibi in aliquo ecclesiastico constituat beneficio. Quod si presumptum fuerit, nullas uires habere permittimus, dicentes cum psalmista, Deus meus, pone illos ut rotam, et sicut dixerunt, Hereditate possideamus sanctuarium Dei.⁸

VI. Adicientes quoque statuimus ut clerici, qui ecclesias seu beneficia habent ecclesiarum, et ordinari, quo liberius uiuant,*ᵘ* subterfugiunt, cum ab episcopis inuitati fuerint, si ad ordines promoueri contempserint, ecclesiis simul et beneficiis earum priuentur.

VII. Nullus in decanum, nullus in priorem, nisi presbiter, nullus in archidiaconum nisi diaconus, promoueatur.

VIII. Nullus in presbyterum, nullus in diaconum, nisi ad certum titulum ordinetur. Qui uero absolute fuerit ordinatus, sumpta careat dignitate.

VIIII. Nullus abbas, nullus omnino clericus uel laicus, quenquam per ecclesiam in ecclesia ordinatum absque proprii episcopi iudicio, presumat eicere. Qui autem secus facere presumpserit, excommunicationi subiacebit.

X. Nullus episcoporum alterius presumat parrochianum ordinare aut iudicare; unusquisque enim suo domno stat aut cadit; nec tenetur aliquis sententia non a suo iudice prolata.

XI. Nemo excommunicatum alterius presumat in communione suscipere. Quod si scienter fecerit, et ipse communione careat Christiana.

ᵗ numerals of all canons om. HL   *ᵘ* uiuunt H, corrected from uiuunt L

II. We prohibit utterly the exaction of any money for the chrism, oil, baptism, penance, the visitation or anointing of the sick, the communion with Christ's body, and burial.

III. Furthermore we ordain and decree by apostolic authority, that in the consecration of bishops, the blessing of abbots, and the dedication of churches, copes, tappets, maniples, ewers, and anything else are not to be exacted by force but are to be offered voluntarily.

IV. No abbot, prior, monk, or clerk of any kind should receive a church or tithe or any ecclesiastical benefice from a layman's hands unless with the bishop's authority and agreement. Should anyone presume to do this, the gift will be void and the beneficiary subject to canonical sanction.

V. Furthermore we forbid anyone to inherit a church or prebend and to bequeath an ecclesiastical benefice to a successor. Should anyone presume to do this, we declare it to have no force, for as the Psalmist said, My God, make them like unto a wheel, and as they say, let us possess the house of God as an inheritance.[8]

VI. Furthermore we also decree that clerks holding churches or ecclesiastical benefices, who avoid ordination (in order to live with less restraint) and who show contempt for proceeding to ordination after being invited to do so by their bishop, should be deprived of their churches and benefices.

VII. No one who is not a priest should be promoted to the office of dean or prior. No one not a deacon should be promoted to the archdiaconate.

VIII. No one should be ordained as priest or deacon without a fixed charge. Whoever is ordained unconditionally should lose his office.

IX. No abbot, clerk, or layman should dare to expel any person ecclesiastically ordained to a church without the sentence of his own bishop. He who presumes to do otherwise should be subject to excommunication.

X. No bishop should presume to ordain or judge someone belonging to another diocese. Every person should stand or fall by the judgement of his own bishop. Nor should he be bound by a sentence not pronounced by his own judge.

XI. No one should presume to receive into communion someone excommunicated in another diocese. If he does so knowingly he too is to be deprived of Christian communion.

---

[8] Ps. 82: 13, 14.

XII. Precipimus etiam ne uni persone duo archidiaconatus uel diuersi ordinis tribuantur honores.

XIII. Presbyteris, diaconibus, subdiaconibus, canonicis, uxorum, concubinarum, et omnino omnium feminarum contubernia auctoritate apostolica inhibemus; preter matrem, sororem, amitam, siue illas mulieres que omni careant suspicione. Qui huius decreti uiolator extiterit, confessus uel conuictus, ruinam proprii ordinis patiatur.

XIIII. Vsura et turpe lucrum clericis omnimodis prohibemus. Qui uero super crimine tali confessus fuerit aut^v conuictus, a gradu proprio deiciatur.

p. 377 XV. Sortilogos, ariolos, et au|guria queque sectantes eisque consentientes, excommunicari precipimus, perpetuaque notamus infamia.

XVI. Inter consanguineos seu affinitate coniunctos, usque ad septimam^w generationem matrimonia contrahi prohibemus. Si qui uero taliter coniuncti fuerint, separentur.

XVII. Interdicimus etiam ut uiri proprias uxores de consanguinitate impetentes, et testes quos adducunt non suscipiantur, sed prisca patrum seruetur auctoritas: Placet uobis? Placet. Placet uobis? Placet. Placet uobis? Placet.[9]

^{x}Idem cardinalis, relicta Anglia, Normanniam uadit, ac demum reuertitur Romam. Willelmus quoque archiepiscopus, considerans ecclesiam regni Anglorum in ecclesie Cantuuariensis humiliatione graui scandalo consternatam, transit et ipse mare Romam iturus, rebus que non eque processerant, ne pari exorbitatione amplius procederent, opem pro posse laturus. Venit ergo Romam et ab Honorio summo pontifice qui Calixto successerat honorifice susceptus est; cui idem apostolicus uices suas in Anglia et Scottia commisit et apostolice sedis legatum constituit.[10]

[1126] (.i.)^{a}1148 Rex Anglorum Heinricus, Angliam reuersus, in Natiuitate Domini curiam suam in castro quod Windleshora uocatur

^{v} uel L ^{w} space left blank CBL, no space H, septimam add. B², .vii. P
^{x} (G) resumed its copying of C³'s text here

^{a} .xxvi. P. P⁵ noted in the mg. that the imperial regnal years of its exemplar were defective at this point and that English regnal years would have to be used

⁹ This legatine council of Westminster is discussed, and its canons printed (using JW as the base text) in Whitelock, Brett, and Brooke, Councils and Synods, ii. 733–41. It is reported by ASC as taking place on the Nativity of St Mary (8 Sept.).

XII. We forbid that any one person should hold two archdeaconries or honours of any other kind.

XIII. We forbid by apostolic authority priests, deacons, subdeacons, and canons from living with wives, concubines, or any women unless these be mothers, sisters, aunts, or other women free from all suspicion. He who breaks this decree should, on confession and conviction, endure the loss of his order.

XIV. We forbid usury and filthy lucre to all sorts of clerks. He who either confesses, or is convicted of such an offence, should be deprived of his own office.

XV. We command that sorcerers, fortune-tellers, and divinators of any kind be excommunicated and we brand them with perpetual infamy.

XVI. We prohibit marriages between those linked through consanguinity or affinity up to the seventh generation. If any contract such marriages, they are to be separated.

XVII. We forbid the acceptance of the testimony of men accusing their own wives of consanguinity or of the witnesses whom they bring forward in their support. Let the authority of the Fathers of old be preserved. Does this please you? It does. Does it please you? It does. Does it please you? It does.[9]

The cardinal left England for Normandy and returned to Rome. Archbishop William also, who thought that the church of the English realm had been much offended through the humiliation of the Canterbury see, crossed overseas to go to Rome and to gain what he could in the affair which had proceeded inequitably and to prevent it from getting worse. He came to Rome and was received with honour by Pope Honorius, successor to Calixtus. The pope entrusted England and Scotland to him as vicar and appointed him legate of the apostolic see.[10]

[1126] Henry, king of the English, returned to England and held his court at Christmas with great magnificence at Windsor castle. To it

---

[10] The legate and Archbishop William began their journey to Rome together (*HC* (p. 208), cf. ASC) soon after 29 Sept. (ASC). ASC reports that they were accompanied by Archbishop Thurstan, Bishops Alexander of Lincoln and John of Glasgow, and Abbot Geoffrey of St Albans. For William's legatine commission which is not reported in ASC, see Whitelock, Brett, and Brooke, *Councils and Synods*, ii. 741–3. It is worth noting that many of the events reported *s.a.* 1126 in ASC are not noted by JW, whose 1126 begins with Henry's undated return to England and his Christmas court (see below, 1126 n. 1).

diuiti apparatu celebrauit, et illuc totius regni nobilitatem sua sanctione adunauit. Vbi cum Eborace episcopus, in equalitate archiepiscopi Cantuuariensis, regem uellet coronare, exemplo antecessorum suorum, iudicio omnium repulsus est, et ad eum coronam regni nihil pertinere, una omnium sententia concorditer promulgauit. Lator insuper crucis quam in regis capella se coram fecit deferri, extra capellam cum cruce eiectus est: iudicio enim episcoporum et quorunque prudentium ecclesiasticas leges scientium probatum est ac roboratum, nulli metropolite extra diocesim suam crucem facere[b] ferre ante se.[1]

Finitis diebus festiuioribus, rex ac tota que confluxerat dignitas regni Lundoniam uadit, ibique ad iussum regis, Willelmus archiepiscopus et ecclesie Romane legatus, ceterique Anglice regionis episcopi omnes, cum principibus terre ipsius, fide et sacramento spoponderunt filie regis se totum regnum Anglorum illi contra omnes defensuros, si patrem suum superuiueret, nisi de legali coniugio filium qui sibi succederet, adhuc ante obitum suum procrearet. Ipsa siquidem, defuncto imperatore Heinrico qui eam per plures annos in matrimonio tenuerat, absque liberis, ad patrem suum reuersa, circa illum excellenti, sicut decebat, honore fulciebatur. Rex igitur, Willelmo filio suo sicut olim descripsimus ex hac uita subtracto, alium qui regni heres legitime existeret necdum susceperat, et ea re in filiam suam, sororem scilicet Willelmi, conditione qua diximus, regni iura transferebat.[2] Ipse etiam rex, *consilio baronum* suorum, *concessit Cantuuariensi ecclesie et Willelmo archiepiscopo et omnibus successoribus eius custodiam* et *constabulationem castelli Hrofi semper in posterum possidendam: et in eodem castello munitionem uel turrim quam uoluerint sibi faciant, et in perpetuum habeant et custodiant; et milites qui custodie eiusdem castelli deputati fuerint, intrent et exeant per uices suas sicut intrare et exire debuerint, et de eodem castello ei securitatem faciant.*[3] [c]Rotbertus, cognomento

---

[b] licere *(G)*   [c] *paragraph mark C*

---

[1] Henry returned to England around 11 Sept. 1126 (*HR* 213 (SD ii. 281); cf. ASC 'between 8 and 29 Sept. 1126', HH *HA* vii. 37 (pp. 474–6) 'about 29 September', WM *HN* 451 (p. 3) and *HC* (pp. 216–7) 'September'), and this council was therefore held at Christmas 1126, even though JW makes it the first event of 1126; the subsequent events in this annal, if JW has placed them in calendar order, should probably therefore be assigned to 1127. *HC*'s account (pp. 216–18) differs in giving the Canterbury archbishop the initiative in raising the issues of coronation and of the carrying of the cross, in not mentioning the universal opposition to Thurstan's stand, in giving the king the key role in

he had summoned all the nobility of the kingdom. When the York bishop, claiming equality with the archbishop of Canterbury, wished to place the crown on the king's head, as his predecessors had done, this was turned down by everyone, and it was unanimously agreed that nothing to do with the crown was his business. The bearer of the cross which Thurstan had caused to be carried before him in the king's chapel was thrown out of the chapel with the cross, for it was affirmed and confirmed by the judgement of the bishops and of those skilled in church law that a metropolitan should not, outside his own province, have his cross carried before him.[1]

Soon after Christmas, the king and all the assembled nobility went to London. There, at the king's command, Archbishop William, legate of the Roman see, and all the other bishops of England, together with its chief men, swore fealty to the king's daughter, promising, if she survived her father, to defend the English realm on her behalf against all unless a son, born from a legitimate union before Henry's death, should succeed him. On the death of the emperor Henry, her husband for many years, Matilda had come home without any offspring, and there dwelt in the court in the greatest state, as was appropriate. The king, therefore, after the already-described loss of his son, William, had transferred the rights to the crown to his daughter on the condition just mentioned because he had as yet no legitimate heir to the kingdom.[2] Henry also, on his nobles' advice, entrusted to the church of Canterbury, to William, the archbishop, and to all his successors the custody and constabulary of Rochester castle in perpetuity: that he should be free to erect fortification or tower in the same castle, that he should hold and guard it for ever; and that the garrison chosen to guard the castle should be free to go in and come out whenever it pleased, and that it should defend the castle on his behalf.[3] Robert Pecche,

---

the outcome of the dispute, and in raising the issue of Thurstan's dispute with the bishop of Glasgow.

[2] ASC (Christmas 1126), HR 213 (SD ii. 281) (1 Jan. 1128), and WM HN 451–2 (pp. 3–5) (Christmas in Henry's 27th year) describe this oath. HR and WM both agree that the oath was sworn at London. While ASC later in the 1127 annal reports that the oath was exacted at the Christmas Windsor court, it does make it clear that the king was at London between Christmas and Candlemas.

[3] Regesta ii. 1475, appendix no. clxxxviii. Brett noted (English Church, p. 71 n. 3) JW's copying of the charter, apparently issued at Winchester on 29 Apr. according to two transcripts. ASC says Henry went to Winchester after Candlemas.

Peccatum, Couentrensis*^d* episcopus, uita decessit et Couentreie sepultus quiescit. Hugo abbas Sancti Augustini*^e* obiit.⁴

[1127] (.ii.) 1149 Willelmus Dorubernensis archiepiscopus congregauit generale concilium omnium episcoporum et abbatum et quarunque religiosarum personarum totius Anglie apud monaster-

p. 378 ium Sancti Petri, in occidentali parte Lundonie situm. | Cui concilio presedit ipse sicut archiepiscopus Cantuuariensis et legatus apostolice sedis, considentibus secum, Willelmo *^a*episcopo Wintoniensi,*^a* Rogerio Særesberiensi, Willelmo Execestrensi, *^b*Herueo Eliensi, Alexandro Lincoliensi,*^b* Eouerardo Norðuicensi, Seifredo Cicestrensi, *^c*Ricardo Herefordensi, Godefrido Bathoniensi, Iohanne Hrofensi,*^c* Bernardo de Sancto Dauid Walensi, Urbano Glamorgatensi *^d*seu Landauensi,*^d* Dauid Pangornensi. *^e*Ricardus Lundoniensis et Robertus Cestrensis*^f* iam obierant, nec aliquis in sedem illorum eo usque successerat. Turstanus autem Eboracensis archiepiscopus, directis nuntiis ac litteris, rationabili causa ostendit se conuentui ipso adesse*^g* non potuisse. Rannulfus uero Dunholmensis episcopus, eo tendens, infirmitate correptus est, nec iter ceptum perficere potuit, sicut prior ecclesie et clerici quos illuc direxerat sub testimonio ueritatis attestati sunt. Wigornensis autem episcopus Symon ad parentes suos trans mare iuerat, et nondum reuersus erat. Confluxerant quoque illuc magne multitudines*^h* clericorum, laicorum, tam diuitum quam mediocrum, et factus est conuentus grandis et inestimabilis. *ⁱ*Sedit autem tribus diebus, id est, .iii. idus Maii et die sequenti, tertioque post hunc qui fuit .xvii. kal. Iun. Acta sunt ibi de negotiis secularibus nonnulla, quedam quidem determinata, quedam dilata, quedam uero, propter nimium estuantis turbe tumultum, ab audientia iudicantium profligata. *^j*Que autem communi episcoporum consensu in ipso concilio decreta sunt et statuta, sicut illic publice recitata sunt et suscepta, in hoc opere placuit annotare. Sunt igitur hec:

I.*^k* *Ecclesias et ecclesiastica beneficia seu quoslibet ecclesiasticos honores uendi uel emi, auctoritate beati Petri apostolorum principis et nostra, omnino prohibemus. Qui uero hoc preceptum uiolasse conuictus fuerit,*

---

^d Conuentrensis C   *^e* dominica die Passionis Domini subito paralisus percussus add. (G)

^{a–a} Wintoniensi episcopo HL (G)   *^{b–b}* Alexandro Lincoliensi, Herueo Eliensi H
^{c–c} om. (G)   *^{d–d}* om. H   *^e* paragraph mark here C   *^f* Conuentrensis HL (G)
^g interesse (G)   *^h* multitudinis HL   *ⁱ* paragraph mark here C   *^j* JW's
capitula text om. from this point (G)   *^k* all the canon numerals om. HL

bishop of Coventry, died and was buried there. Hugh, abbot of St Augustine's, died.[4]

[1127] William, archbishop of Canterbury, summoned a general council of all the bishops, abbots, and other religious from all over England, to the monastery of St Peter's in the west of London [Westminster]. William, as archbishop of Canterbury and papal legate, presided over the council. There were present with him the bishops William of Winchester, Roger of Salisbury, William of Exeter, Hervey of Ely, Alexander of Lincoln, Everard of Norwich, Seffrid of Chichester, Richard of Hereford, Godfrey of Bath, John of Rochester, Bernard of the Welsh see of St David's, Urban of Glamorgan or Llandaff, David of Bangor. Richard of London and Robert of Chester were dead, and no one had as yet succeeded them. Through messengers and by means of letters, Thurstan, archbishop of York, explained the reasonable grounds for his absence. Ranulf, bishop of Durham, fell sick on the road, and was unable to complete his journey, as the prior of Durham and the clerks he had sent to Westminster solemnly attested. Simon, bishop of Worcester, had gone overseas to visit his kinsmen, and had not yet returned. There flocked great crowds of clergy and lay people, both rich and poor, and a great and impressive council took place. It sat for three days, that is, 13 May and the day following, and then the third day after this, which was 16 May. A few secular matters were discussed, some were resolved, some deferred, and others indeed, on account of the excessive tumult of the pressing throng, removed from the hearing of judges. We think it appropriate to record in this work the decrees and statutes agreed in this council by all the bishops as they were publicly declared and received. They are the following:

I. By the authority of blessed Peter, prince of the apostles, and by our own, we utterly forbid churches, ecclesiastical benefices, and honours to be bought or sold. Whoever should be convicted of violating this

---

[4] The late source Thomas of Chesterfield (*Anglia Sacra* i. 434) gives the date of Robert Pecche's death as 22 Aug. 1127. Passion Sunday, the day on which G says Robert was suddenly paralysed, was 28 Mar. in 1126, 20 Mar. in 1127. *Heads*, p. 36, notes the evidence for Hugh de Flori's death in 1126. Both obits could have taken place in 1127 as the preceding events in JW's 1126 annal should be assigned to that year.

clericus quidem, etiamsi canonicus regularis sit uel monachus, ab ordine deponatur; laicus uero exlex et excommunicatus habeatur et eiusdem ecclesie uel beneficii potestate priuetur.

II. *Ordinari quenquam per pecuniam in ecclesia Dei uel promoueri, auctoritate sedis apostolice modis omnibus interdicimus.*

III. *Exactiones certas pecuniarum pro recipiendis canonicis, monachis, et sanctimonialibus, condempnamus.*

IIII. *Nullus in decanum nisi presbyter, nullus in archidiaconatum nisi diaconus constituatur. Quod si quis ad hos honores infra predictos ordines iam designatus est, moneatur ab episcopo ad ordines accedere. Quod si iuxta monitionem episcopi ordinari refugerit, eadem ad quam designatus fuerat careat dignitate.*

V. *Presbiteris, diaconibus, subdiaconibus et omnibus canonicis, contubernia mulierum illicitarum penitus interdicimus. Quod si concubinis, quod absit, uel coniugibus adheserint, ecclesiastico priuentur ordine, honore simul et beneficio. Presbiteros uero parrochiales, si qui tales fuerint, extra chorum eicimus et infames esse decernimus. Archidiaconis uero et ministris, quibus hoc incumbit, auctoritate Dei et nostra precipimus ut omni studio et sollicitudine procurent ab ecclesia Dei hanc perniciem omnino eradicare. Quod si qui in hoc negligentes uel, quod absit, consentientes inuenti fuerint, primo et secundo ab episcopis digne corrigantur, tercio uero canonice seuerius corrigiantur.*

VI. *Concubine uero presbyterorum et canonicorum, nisi ibi legitime nupserint, extra parrochiam expellantur. Quod si postea culpabiles inuente fuerint, in cuiuscunque territorio sint, a ministris ecclesie capiantur. Et sub excommunicatione precipimus ne ab aliqua potestate minore uel maiore* p. 379 *detineantur, sed libere eisdem ministris ecclesie tradantur et ecclesiastice | discipline uel seruituti episcopali iudicio mancipentur.*

VII. *Vt nullus archidiaconus in diuersis episcopatibus diuersos archidia- conatus teneat, sub anathemate prohibemus; immo ei cui prius assignatus est tantum adhereat.*

VIII. *Episcopi, presbiteros, abbates, monachos, priores, subditos firmam tenere inhibeant.*

VIIII. *Decimas, sicut Dei summi dominicas, ex integro reddi pre- cipimus.*

decree, if a cleric, whether a regular canon or a monk, should be deposed from his order, if a layman, should be outlawed and excommunicated, and deprived of the same church and ecclesiastical benefice.

II. By the authority of the apostolic see we utterly forbid the ordination or promotion of anyone in God's church through payment.

III. We condemn the exaction of money for the admission of canons, monks, and nuns.

IV. No one should be made a dean who is not a priest, or an archdeacon who is not a deacon. If anyone should be assigned to these honours who is not in the proper orders, he is to be admonished by the bishop to proceed to the right orders. If he refuses to be ordained as the bishop commands, then he should lose the office to which he had been assigned.

V. We utterly forbid priests, deacons, subdeacons and all canons illicit intercourse with women. If any remain attached to concubines (which God forbid) or wives, then they are to be removed from their ecclesiastical order, honour, and benefice. If any such be parish priests, we expel them from the chancel and declare them infamous. By our authority and by God's we further command archdeacons and officials, charged with this duty, to totally root out with energy and care this evil from the church of God. Those negligent in this task or (which God forbid) acquiescing in the evil when discovered, are to be fittingly corrected by the bishop for the first and second offence, and the third time more severely chastised, according to the canons.

VI. The concubines of priests and canons should be expelled from the parish unless they have contracted a lawful marriage. If they are afterwards found to be guilty, they should be arrested by the officials of the church no matter in whose jurisdiction they might be. And we order, under pain of excommunication, that they should not be protected by any jurisdiction, lower or higher, but that they should be handed over to the officers of the church and suffer ecclesiastical discipline and episcopal judgement.

VII. We utterly forbid an archdeacon to hold different archdeaconries in various bishoprics, but rather let him be attached to that to which he was first appointed.

VIII. Bishops are to prohibit priests, abbots, monks and priors subject to them from receiving rents.

IX. We order tithes to be paid in full, for they are the property of the lord God.

X. *Vt nulla persona ecclesias uel decimas seu quelibet alia ecclesiastica beneficia det uel accipiat sine consensu et auctoritate episcopi, canonica auctoritate uetamus.*

XI.*[l] Nulla abbatissa* uel *sanctimonialis carioribus utatur indumentis quam agninis uel cattinis.*

[m] Rex igitur cum inter hec Lundonie moraretur, auditis concilii gestis assensum prebuit, auctoritate regia et potestate concessit et confirmauit statuta concilii, a Willelmo Cantuuariensi archiepiscopo et sancte Romane ecclesie legato, apud Westmonasterium celebrati.[1]

[n] Hugo quidam nomine de episcopatu Hrofensi abbas institutus, a Willelmo Dorubernie archiepiscopo, in Cicestra, dominico qui fuit .ii. idus Iunii, ad suscepte dignitatis gradum, que est apud Sanctum Augustinum, merito honore promotus est.[2] *[o]* Ricardus Herefordensis episcopus .xviii. kal. Sept., feria .ii., apud suam uillam que uocatur Dydelebyrig *[p]* obiit, cuius corpus Hereford delatum, sepelitur

[(G)]

cum coepiscopis in ecclesia sepelitur.[3]

Comes Flandrensis Karolus prima ebdomada .xl. in ecclesia sancti Donatii in oratione positus a suis iniuste perimitur. Cuius suscepit comitatum Willelmus filius Rodberti comitis Normannorum cum maximo fauore multorum populorum.[4]

Rex Anglorum Henricus mare transiit,

[(G)]

Normanniam adiit, et contra nepotem suum predictum

---

[l] om. *CHLP*   *[m]* paragraph mark here C, (G) resumed its copying of JW here   *[n]* paragraph mark here C   *[o]* paragraph mark here C   *[p]* Ledbery probably over an erasure *H*, Ledeberia *L (G)*, Delebyrig *P*

---

[1] JW is the main source for the legatine council, see Whitelock, Brett, and Brooke, *Councils and Synods*, ii. 743–9, where the canons are printed on pp. 746–9. Brooke in *EHR* lxxii (1957), 690 n. 5 prints the royal writ confirming the council's acts (*Regesta* ii. 1476). *HC* (p. 218) comments on Thurstan's failure to attend. HH *HA* vii. 37 (p. 476) refers to a royal *concilium* on 8 May at London, and to an undated council of Archbishop William at Westminster.

X. We forbid with canonical authority anyone from giving or receiving churches, tithes, or ecclesiastical benefices without the consent and authority of the bishop.

XI. No abbess or nun is to use garments made of material richer than lambswool or catskin.

During this council King Henry had stayed in London. He was informed of the council's proceedings, gave them his consent, and ratified and confirmed by his royal authority the decrees of the council held at Westminster by Archbishop William of Canterbury, legate of the holy Roman see.[1]

One Hugh from the Rochester diocese was appointed abbot, and was raised to the abbacy of St Augustine's with deserved honour at Chichester on Sunday, 12 June, by Archbishop William of Canterbury.[2] On Monday, 15 August, Richard, bishop of Hereford, died at his township of Ledbury whence his body was taken to Hereford for burial

with his fellow bishops in the church.[3]

In the first week of Lent [16–22 February], Charles, count of Flanders, was unjustly slain by his men as he was praying at the church of St Donatian. William, son of Robert, duke of the Normans, received the Flemish county with the full approval of many people.[4]

The English king Henry crossed overseas, went to Normandy, and fought fiercely with his nephew, the

---

[2] The accession of Hugh of Trottiscliffe as abbot of St Augustine's is entered without a specific calendar date in Gervase, *Actus pontificum* (Gervase, ii. 381): see *Heads*, p. 36.

[3] *EEA* vii, p. xxxvi n. 68, reports that Oxford, Bodleian Library, Rawlinson B. 328, fo. 31[v] dates Richard de Capella's death to 16 Aug. 15 Aug. was a Monday in 1127. For the 12th-cent. claim that *Lidebiri* was the original see of the diocese, see *GFL* no. 227.

[4] Charles the Good, count of Flanders, was murdered on 2 Mar., ASC dating it to the 'spring'. See *Histoire du meurtre de Charles le Bon, comte du Flandre (1127–28), par Galbert de Bruges*, ed H. Pirenne (Paris, 1891), c. 15 (p. 24). This murder and Louis VI's grant of the county to William Clito are both in OV *HE* xii. 45 (vi. 370). William Clito's claim was through his grandmother, Matilda, wife of the Conqueror, who was daughter of Baldwin V, count of Flanders 1035–67. ASC and HH *HA* vii. 37 (p. 476) refer both to the murder and to William Clito's acquisition of Flanders.

Willelmum comitem Flandren-
sem magnum conflictum iniit.[5]

Inuentio corporis Sancti
Mathei apostoli in ciuitate
Treuerensi in ecclesia Sancti
Eucharii archiepiscopi, dominica
ante Natale Domini quod Sanctus Ægricius archiepiscopus illuc
attulerat de Constantinopoli,
tempore Constantini senioris, ex
dono Sancte Helene regine tunc
pristine restituuntur.[6]

Rogerius de Berkelaio iunior
.iiii. Kl. Noubr. uita decedens,
ante fores ecclesie Sancti Petri de
Gloecestra sepultus quiescit.[7]

[1128] 1150 Turstanus Eboracensis archiepiscopus, Rotbertum,
quem Alexander rex Scottie ecclesie sancti Andree intruserat,
petente Dauid fratre ac successore Alexandri, in episcopum Eboraci
consecrauit. In quo officio Rannulfum Dunholmensem episcopum et
quendam Radulfum ad Orcadas insulas iam olim episcopum ordinatum, sibi adiutores asciuerat. Qui Radulfus quoniam nec principis
terre, nec cleri, nec plebis electione uel assensu fuerat ordinatus, ab
omnibus refutatus, et in loco pontificis a nemine susceptus erat. Hic
quia nullius episcopus urbis,[a] modo Eboracensi, modo Dunholmensi
adherens ab eis sustentabatur, et uicarius utriusque in episcopalibus
ministeriis habebatur. Ab his itaque Rotbertus consecratus, nullam ut
dicitur professionem de quauis subiectione uel obedientia ecclesie
Eboracensi aut eius pontifici facere permissus a Scottis est, licet
Eboracensis canonicus fuerit.[1]

---

[a] urbis erat (G)

[5] ASC speaks of Henry spending 1128 in Normandy because of William Clito, and HH
HA vii. 37 (p. 476) and *HR* 213 (SD ii. 282) record Henry's crossing in August (26 Aug.
HR) after he had sent his daughter overseas.

[6] The invention took place on 1 Sept. 1127 at the time of Archbishop Meginhard
(Lambert, *Ex inventione et miraculis S Mathiae*, MGH SS viii. 227–34, at p. 229).

[7] *Pipe Roll 31 Henry I*, p. 133, suggests that Robert de Berkeley Junior (II) had died but
recently. He is recorded as a benefactor in the Gloucester Cartulary (*Cart. Gloc.* i. 72, 112).

[1] The consecration of Robert of Nostell, prior of Scone, as bishop of St Andrews had
taken place before 17 July 1127, when, at Roxburgh, and in the presence of King David

said William, count of Flanders.[5]

The invention of the body of St Matthias the apostle in the church of St Eucherius the archbishop in Trier on the Sunday before Christmas [18 December]. The holy archbishop Agricius had brought it there from Constantinople at the time of the elder Constantine. It had been recovered from the earlier gift of the holy queen Helena.[6]

The younger Roger of Berkeley died on 29 October, and was buried outside the front of St Peter's, Gloucester.[7]

[1128] King Alexander of the Scots had forcibly introduced Robert into the see of St Andrew's. At the request of Alexander's brother and successor David, Archbishop Thurstan of York consecrated Robert bishop at York with the assistance of Bishop Ranulf of Durham and one Ralph who had earlier been ordained bishop of the Orkneys. Ralph, however, had been ordained without the election or consent of the lord of the Orkneys nor of the clergy and people, had been universally rejected, and was accepted as bishop by no one. Being bishop of no place, he attached himself now to York, now to Durham, and was supported by them and acted as coadjutor of both in their episcopal ministries. Duly consecrated by these bishops, Robert was not allowed by the Scots, so it is said, to profess submission or obedience to the church of York or to its bishop, even though he was a canon of that church.[1]

and Archbishop Thurstan, he released the priory of Coldingham from the performance of certain dues (A. C. Lawrie, *Early Scottish Charters prior to A.D. 1153* (Glasgow, 1905), no. 73, pp. 59–60). It is recorded in two documents, one of King David's, the other of Archbishop Thurstan's (Lawrie, *Early Scottish Charters*, nos. 75–6, pp. 63–5). Some discussion in *EEA* v. 54. *HC* (p. 52) reports that Ralph Nowell had been elected bishop by the Orcadians. He was consecrated in 1109 x 1114, perhaps c.1112; he appears 'regularly from then on as an assistant to the archbishop, and may never have secured possession of his see' (*HC* (p. 53 n. 4)).

Quidam ecclesie Lugdunensis canonicus, uir probus et grandeuus, electus est ad pontificatum ecclesie Lundoniensis; defunctus siquidem fuerat Ricardus eiusdem ciuitatis antistes, et iste, Gilebertus nomine, cognomine uero Vniuersalis, loco illius a rege Heinrico et Willelmo archiepiscopo annuente clero et populo substitutus erat. Sacratus est autem Cantuuarie ab ipso archiepiscopo in matre ecclesia, .xi. kal. Feb., ^bdie dominica,^b cooperantibus et ministrantibus sibi in hoc officio Seifrido episcopo Cicestrensi et Iohanne Hrofensi, sub presentia abbatum et aliarum magnarum et honestarum personarum pro hoc ipso Cantuuarie conuenientium, suscepta prius ab eo professione ex more antecessorum suorum, quam se illi et omnibus successoribus eius canonicam subiectionem et obedientiam per omnia exhibiturum fore promisit.²

[C³(G)]

^cDe iuramento iam mutato in periurium, in multorum periculum.^c ^dRex Anglorum Heinricus anno regni sui .xxviii.^e, in octauis Pasce quod erat .iii. kal. Maii, indictione .vii.,^f concurrentibus .vii., bissextilibus, epactis .xxv. apud Westmonasterium Lundonie tenuit concilium. Cui presidebant duo metropolitani, Willelmus Dorubernensis, Turstinus Eboracensis, episcopi, abbates, comites, barones, cum totius Anglie primoribus. Vbi de pluribus plurimis tractatis, quis, de medio facto rege et herede carente, in regendi regni statum succedat, communi consilio tractatur. Tandem ad uelle regis consentiunt omnes, ut illius filia, Romanorum imperatoris Heinrici relicta, cum legitimo suo si

^{b–b} om. HL (G)   ^{c–c} om. (G)   ^{d–d} written over an erasure C³, placed at the end of its copy of an earlier version of C³ at 1131 n. f, and then followed by the remainder of the texts interpolated by C³ during its rewriting of 1128–31 (G)   ^e .xxvii. (G)   ^f .vi. (G)

A certain canon of Lyons, a man of quality and advanced years, was elected to the see of London. Bishop Richard of that city was already dead, and this canon, Gilbert, called the Universal, was substituted for him by King Henry and Archbishop William with the agreement of clergy and people. He was consecrated at Canterbury by the archbishop in the mother church on Sunday, 22 January, with the assistance at this ceremony of Seffrid, bishop of Chichester, and John of Rochester, in the presence of many abbots and other great and worthy people gathered at Canterbury for that purpose, having first professed, as his predecessors had done, and promised canonical subjection and complete obedience to the archbishop and his successors.[2]

Concerning the oath now altered through perjury to the peril of many.

In the twenty-eighth year of his reign, in the octave of Easter, that is, 29 April, in the seventh indiction, concurrents seven, a bissextile year, epacts twenty-five, King Henry of the English held a council at Westminster in London, which the two metropolitans, William of Canterbury and Thurstan of York, chaired, and which was attended by bishops, abbots, earls, barons, with the magnates of all England. Among multifarious matters, there was discussed between them all who would succeed as ruler when the king died and an heir was lacking. Finally all agreed to the king's wish that his daughter, the widow of Henry, emperor of the Romans, should receive the

---

[2] This succession is recorded under 1127 in other sources (e.g. HH *HA* vii. 37 (pp. 476–8)), but JW alone gives the day (22 Jan.) of Gilbert the Universal's consecration, which was a Sunday in 1128. Greenway, *Fasti* i. 1, gives *c*. Dec. 1127 as the date of Gilbert's election.

p. 380

habuerit sponso, | in Christi brachio regnum Anglie sustineat; et ut huiusmodi consilium stabile permaneat, ab omnibus ⟨sit⟩*g* iuramentum. Primo omnium iurant *h*archiepiscopi, sicque*h* per ordinem episcopi, Rogero Særesberiensi presule diiudicatore omnium existente. Post episcopos more ecclesiastico, licet omne iuramentum a Domino sit prohibitum, abbatibus foret iurandum. At quoniam a seductis in inuio sepius uilipenditur cucullatus,*3* sequitur ordo preposterus, non necessario sed pro uelle commutatus. Iurat rex Scottorum David; iurans etiam Anglorum regina filie regis que inpresentiarum erat iurate prerogatiue eo pacto assensum dedit, ut si rex in utroque sexu careret herede, [. . . . . .]*i* si uero non in utroque, superstes qui foret regnum hereditaret. Rotbertum regis filium comitem Gloecestrensem ad sinistrum pedem regis sedentem diiudicator allocutus, 'Surge,' inquit, 'surge et pro regio uelle iuramentum effice.' At ille, 'Maior me,' inquit, 'natu prius id agat Stephanus comes Bononiensis, hic ad dextrum pedem regis sedens. Quod et

---

g fit C (G)   *h–h* om. (G)   *i* lacuna here suggested by Michael Winterbottom

---

3 Cf Ps. 106: 40.

English kingdom under Christ's protection with her lawful husband, if she had one, and that all were to swear an oath so that this plan should be firmly implemented. First of all the archbishops took the oath, then the bishops in order, Bishop Roger of Salisbury proposing the oaths to them all. In accordance with ecclesiastical practice, the abbots were to take the oath after the bishops, although all oath-taking is forbidden by the Lord. But because a monk is often held cheaply by those deceived into straying from the road,[3] the order of precedence was reversed wilfully, not out of necessity. David, king of the Scots, then took the oath. Queen Adelaide of the English, also swore for the king's daughter, who was present, and agreed to the sworn formula in such a manner that, if the king did not have an heir of either sex, [. . . . . .], but if he did not lack a survivor of either sex, then the survivor should inherit the kingdom. The regulator of the proceedings spoke to Robert, earl of Gloucester, the king's son, who was sitting to the left of the king, saying, 'Get up, get up, and swear the oath as the king wants!' Robert replied, 'No, rather Stephen, count of Boulogne, was born before me and should do this first, he who is sitting to the right of the king.'

factum est. Iurant postmodum
omnes comites, barones, uicecomites et quique nobiliores milites. Quo facto, diiudicator
exclamat, 'Abbates procedant;
iuramentum faciant.' Tunc exur-
gens uir reuerendus abbas de
Sancto Eadmundo, nomine
Anselmus, respondit pro omnibus, grauiter ferens in se et in
socios preposterum ordinem iur-
amenti factum. 'Ecce,' inquit, 'O
rex, opprobria exprobrantium
nostro ordini ceciderunt super
nos.[4] En contra ius ecclesiasticum
uilipensis abbatum personis, lai-
cales personas etiam nobis homa-
gio subactos tuo iuramento
preposuisti.' [j]Ad hec rex,
'Est quod iam factum, stet,
    sicut cernitis actum.
Fari cessate, mora nulla sit,
    appropiate,
Iuratoteque uos, ut nos iuraui-
    mus, omnes.
Abbates iurant; regem placent
    quia curant.'
Finito concilio, discessum
agentes quique redierunt in sua.
Sed proh dolor, ecce uidemus
iuramentum uersum in periur-
ium. Terrentianum dictum est:
'Obsequium amicos, ueritas
odium parit.'[5] Verum licet hoc
uerum sit, nouit Deus et Chris-
tus eius et utriusque Spiritus: si
non uererer regie maiestati caput

[j-j] om. (G)

[4] Cf. Ps. 68: 10.   [5] *Andria*, I. i. 41.

This was done. Then all the earls, barons, sheriffs, and more noble knights swore. Then the regulator said, 'Let the abbots come forward and swear the oath.' Then the revered abbot of Bury St Edmund's, Anselm, replied for all, seriously complaining of the reversed order of precedence which had been followed against him and his associates. 'Behold,' he said, 'O king, the curses of those who criticize our order have fallen upon us.[4] Look how abbots have been held cheap in contravention of the law of the church, in that you have placed ahead of us in your oath-taking even laymen who are subject to us.' To this the king replied,

'What you see done has been
    done and let it stand.
Stop talking and delaying, but
    come forward
And take the oath as we all
    have done.
The abbots should swear, let
    them appease the king in
    attending to him.'

When the council was over, each one left, and returned home. But alas, behold we see an oath turned into perjury. As Terence says, 'Fawning makes friends, truthfulness hatred.'[5] But although this is true, God and His Christ and the Spirit descending from both, know this: if I were not afraid that the royal majesty

Iohannis condempnari, asser-
erem iuratores omnes periurio
notari. Deus autem rerum cuius
oculis nuda et aperta sunt omnia,
ut bene scit et uniuersis domnis
melius uult, in misericordia et
miserationibus ut optime nouit
cuncta disponat.$^{j\,6}$

Post modicum tempus rex
Anglorum mare transit.^{7}

Anno regni .iii. Leodegarii
Romanorum imperatoris, regis
uero, Anglorum Heinrici
.xxviii., olimpiadis .cccclxx.
anno .ii., indictione .vii., luna
.xxv. existente, .vi. Idus Decembris, sabbato, a mane usque ad
uesperam apparuerunt quasi due
nigre pile infra solis orbitam,
una in superiori parte et erat
maior, altera in inferiori et fuit
minor; eratque utraque directa
contra alteram ^{k}ad huiusmodi
figuram.$^{dkl\,8}$

Vrbanus Glamorgatensis^{m} seu Landauensis episcopus quia de
quarundam rerum^{n} querelis quas anno preterito in generali concilio
super Bernardum episcopum de sancto Dauid promouerat, non
iuste^{o} erga se agi persenserat, emensa festiuitate Purificationis
sancte Marie mare transiit, Romam iuit, apostolico pape causam
itineris certa attestatione suorum intimauit. Cuius idem apostolicus

$^{k-k}$ om. (G) ^{l} Diagram of sunspots placed between two columns of the text it
illustrated in C (see vol. ii, pl. 4) ^{m} Lamorgatensis C ^{n} om. HL, causarum
(G) ^{o} iusta C

---

^{6} Cf. Heb. 4: 13 and Hos. 2: 19.

^{7} ASC speaks of Henry I remaining in Normandy throughout 1128, and there is no
other record of his presence in England nor of his later return to Normandy in this year.
WM's account of the oath-taking in 1127 (HN 452 (pp. 4–5)) shares details with JW's
account of the supposed oath-taking at Easter 1128: namely that Archbishop William swore
first of all, and King David first of the laity, and that the relative precedence of Earl Robert
and Count Stephen was an issue. A renewed oath-taking in 1128 could conceivably have
been advisable in view of Matilda's betrothal to Geoffrey of Anjou in May 1127, but it is
likely that C^{3} erroneously invented a second oath-taking when he came to rewrite the

would harm John's head, I would assert that all oath-takers are guilty of perjury. But may the God of all things to whose eyes everything is open and clear, so that He sees well and wishes all lords to be better, dispose all this in His mercy and compassion, as He knows so well how to do.[6]

Shortly afterwards the king of the English crossed overseas.[7]

In the third year of Lothar, emperor of the Romans, in the twenty-eighth year of King Henry of the English, in the second year of the 470th Olympiad, seventh indiction, twenty-fifth moon, on Saturday, 8 December, there appeared from the morning right up to the evening two black spheres against the sun. The first was in the upper part and large, the second in the lower and small, and each was directly opposite the other as this diagram shows.[8]

Urban, bishop of Glamorgan or Llandaff, thought that he had not been fairly dealt with in a dispute with Bernard, bishop of St David's, which he had raised at the general council the previous year. After the feast of the Purification [2 February], he crossed the sea and went to Rome and explained why he had come, presenting the written support of those in his own diocese. The pope looked

1128–31 annals, and that he incorporated here a newly-acquired account of the 1127 oath-taking, which he had earlier dated to after Christmas 1126. This new account dated the event to Easter, and this may have helped lead JW astray. The elaborate dating of this entry is paralleled in the other interpolation under 1128, that on sunspots (see below, 1128 n. 8). JW's reference to Henry's return to Normandy could equally well have been acquired with the account of this putative oath-taking, or it could simply be duplicating erroneously Henry's return in 1127 (see above, 1127 n. 5). He might also have noted that Henry returned from Normandy in July 1129 (see below, 1129 n. 2).

[8] These sunspots are not recorded elsewhere. It is elaborately dated like the preceding 1128 interpolation.

uotis ac dictis fauit, *et regi* Anglorum Heinrico, et*q* Willelmo arciepiscopo et omnibus Anglie episcopis litteras direxit, omnibus apostolica mandans auctoritate, ut iuste exactioni illius nemo obstaret in aliquo.[9]

[H]

p. 381 Godefridus abbas Seropesber- iensis obiit.

[C³LBP (G)]

Vir uenerandus Godefridus | abbas Seropberiensis, .xi. kal. Aprilis, *feria .iiii.,* obiit.

[(G)]

Successerat iste primus reuer- endo et facundo uiro Fulcheredo eiusdem loci fundatori et rectori primo, qui et uita anno Domin- ice Incarnationis millesimo .cxix. migrauerat Idibus Martii.[10]

[HLBP (G)]

Vir religionis eximie Cantuari- ensis prior, Gausfridus nomine

[C³]

Dorubernensis prior Gausfridus,

rege Scottorum Dauid petente et archiepiscopo Willelmo annuente, abbas eligitur ad locum in Scottia qui Dunfermelin dicitur.

[HLBP (G)]

Ordinatus est autem a Rodberto episcopo ecclesie sancti Andree.[11]

[C³]

Et a Rotberto presule ecclesie sancti Andree ordinatur.[11]

Vrbanus Landauensis episcopus* prospero reditu Angliam reuertitur, regio iussu

[HLBP (G)]

precepta apostolica complentur sicque nunc ille quesitis ex Dei gratia potitur.[12]

De collegio fratrum Seropberie* Deo seruientium unus electus, Herbertus nomine, a Willelmo Dorobernensi archiepiscopo

[C³]

apostolica mandata de eo com- plentur.[12]

Vnus cenobitarum Seropberien- sis ecclesie Herebertus abbas electus, a Willelmo arciepiscopo apud Leawes consecratur.[13]

---

p-p regique *C*   *q om. C*   *r-r om. (G)*   *s* antistes *LBP (G)*
t Scrobbesberie *H*, Seropesberie *(G)*

[9] Bishop Urban of Llandaff's lengthy pursuit of his claims against St David's (which he had raised fruitlessly at the legatine council of 1127 as *LL*, pp. 34–5, 62, testifies) is discussed by Brett, *English Church*, pp. 52–5. The documentation is calendared in Conway Davies, *Episcopal Acts . . . relating to Welsh Dioceses, 1066–1272* (above, 1120 n. 1), ii. L.

favourably on Urban's arguments and statements, wrote to Henry, the English king, Archbishop William, and all the English bishops, and with his apostolic authority commanded them to tolerate no opposition to a single one of Urban's just demands.[9]

Godfrey, abbot of Shrewsbury, died.	The revered abbot of Shrewsbury, Godfrey, died on Wednesday, 22 March. Godfrey had earlier succeeded the founder and first abbot of Shrewsbury, Fulchered, a revered and eloquent man. Fulchered had died in the year of our Lord 1119 on 15 March.[10]
Geoffrey, prior of Canterbury, a most pious man,	The prior of Canterbury, Geoffrey,

was chosen abbot of Dunfermline in Scotland at the request of David, the Scottish king, and with the agreement of Archbishop William.

He was ordained by Bishop Robert of St Andrew's.[11]	And he was ordained by Bishop Robert of St Andrew's.[11]

Bishop Urban of Llandaff returned to England after a successful journey and on King Henry's orders

the apostolic decisions were put into effect, and thus with God's mercy he achieved his aims.[12]	the apostolic commands concerning him were put into effect.[12]
Herbert, a servant of God in the monastery of Shrewsbury, was elected, and was consecrated abbot at Lewes by William,	Herbert, a monk of Shrewsbury, was elected and was consecrated abbot by Archbishop William at Lewes.[13]

49, 50–2 (pp. 622–3), L. 53 (pp. 623–4), L. 55 (p. 624). Urban was in Rome in 1128 and 1129.

[10] VCH *Shropshire*, ii. 37, notes that the charter used to date Fulchered's death before Oct. 1115 at the latest (see *The Cartulary of Shrewsbury Abbey*, ed. U. Rees (2 vols., Aberystwyth, 1975), i. p. xxiii) 'records two assemblies with two different sets of witnesses' and therefore cannot be used against G's dating of Fulchered's death to 15 Mar. 1119. *Heads*, p. 71, notes that 22 Mar. (the day of Godfrey's death, for which JW is the sole source) was a Thursday in 1128.

[11] King David's request to William of Corbeil, archbishop of Canterbury (datable between 25 Jan. 1126, the day of William's appointment as papal legate, and 1128) for a suitable person as abbot of St Andrews is printed in *Regesta regum Scottorum*, i, no. 8.

[12] Brett, *English Church*, p. 53, notes that Henry I probably remained neutral in the affairs of Urban of Llandaff.

[See p. 186 for n. 13]

apud Leauues*u* abbas consecratur, et ecclesie Seropberiensi*v*
abbatis iure preficitur.[13]

[(G)]

Decessit hoc anno reuerendus
Egeneshamnensis ecclesie abbas
Nigellus .vii. Idus Maii, successit
ei Walterus.[14]

Hugo Certesiensis abbas*w* obiit.[15] Comes Flandrensium Willelmus
nomine, Miser cognomine, ab hostibus circumuentus uulneratur, et
ingrauescente*x* dolore,*y* morte cunctis dolenda, .vi. kal. Aug. defungitur et apud sanctum Bertinum sepelitur.[16]

[(G)]

Vrbanus Clamorgatensis episcopus Romam iterum profectus
uita decedens .vii. Kl. Octobr.
inter   corpora   episcoporum
sepultus quiescit.[17]

*z*Dunholmensis episcopus Rannulfus Non. Septembris obiit.[18]

[HLBP (G)]

Gausfridus Rotomagensis archiepiscopus*aa* uita decessit.[19]

[1129] 1151*a* Willelmus Wintoniensis episcopus *b*.viii. kal. Feb.
defunctus*b* Wintonie sepelitur.[1] Mense Iulio rex Anglorum Heinricus
de Normannia Angliam rediit.[2]

[(G)]

Inde *in concilio apud Lundoniam*
congregato in presentia eiusdem

---

u Lewes *LP*, Læwes *B (G)*   *v* Scrobbesberiensi *LBP*, Seropesberiensi
(G)   *w* .xi. Kl. Aug. *add. (G)*   *x* ingrauascente *H, from* ingrauascente
B   *y* monachice religionis habitum suscipiens *add. (G)*   *z* Eodem anno *add.*
(G)   *aa* .iiii. Kl. Decembr. *add. (G)*

a partly erased (G)   *b-b* defunctus .viii. kal. Febr. *HLBP (G)*

---

[13] Gervase, *Actus pontificum* (Gervase, ii. 381) simply records the blessing of Abbot
Herbert without giving the day (see *Heads*, p. 71). OV *HE* xii. 31 (vi. 318-19) speaks of
Herbert, on Godfrey's sudden death, seizing the helm of the abbey ('gubernaculum rudis
abbatiæ usurpauit').

[14] G is the only extant source for the date of Nigel's death. *Heads*, p. 49, notes that his
successor, Walter (I), was present at the translation of St Alban on 2 Aug. in Henry I's 29th
year (*Gesta abbatum S. Albani*, i. 85)

[15] *Heads*, p. 38, notes that an obit in Oxford, Bodleian Library Lat. Liturg. E. 6, fos. 4-
8, gives 20 July as the day of Hugh's death.

archbishop of Canterbury, and
was placed over Shrewsbury
with authority.[13]
                    In this year the revered Abbot of
Eynsham, Nigel, died, on 9 May.
Walter succeeded him.[14]
Abbot Hugh of Chertsey died.[15] William, known as the lesser, count
of Flanders, was ambushed by his enemies and wounded. His pains
grew worse, and he died a universally regretted death on 27 July, and
was buried at St Bertin.[16]
                    Bishop Urban of Glamorgan set-
ting out again for Rome, died on
25 September, and was laid to
rest among the graves of other
bishops.[17]
Bishop Ranulf of Durham died on 5 September.[18]
Geoffrey, archbishop of Rouen,
died.[19]

[1129] Bishop William of Winchester died on 25 January and was
buried at Winchester.[1] In July King Henry of the English returned to
England from Normandy.[2]
                    The feast of the Conception of
the holy mother of God was

[16] ASC reports differently the occasion and the date of William Clito's death as well as
his burial place. OV *HE* xii. 45 (vi. 377), however, dates his death to 28 July. F.
Vercauteren, *Actes des comtes de Flandres 1071–1128* (Brussels, 1938), p. xix and n. 4
suggests that Clito died on 27 or 28 July. G's reference to Clito becoming a monk at St
Bertin is confirmed by ASC and OV *HE* xii. 45 (vi. 378).
  [17] Innocent II's letter to Archbishop William of Canterbury, announcing Urban's death
at Rome, is dated 9 Oct. 1133, or 1134 in the evidence calendared in Conway Davies (ed.),
Episcopal Acts . . . relating to Welsh Dioceses, 1066–1272, ii. 633–34, L. 86, the latter year
being apparently confirmed by HH *HA* vii. 43 (pp. 488–90).
  [18] *HR* (SD ii. 283) confirms the day as do the two Durham obits noted in Greenway,
Fasti ii. 29, which also records that 4 Sept. is in other Durham obits. ASC records his
burial at Durham on 5 Sept.
  [19] OV *HE* xii. 48 (vi. 388) records Geoffrey's death on 26 Nov. 1128.
  [1] ASC E has this obit with 25 Jan. clearly the day of William's burial at Winchester.
C³'s rewritten entry suggests, probably unintentionally, that he died on that day. William
Giffard's death is commemorated on 23 Jan. in a Winchester, and on 24 Jan. in a Durham,
obit (Greenway, *Fasti* ii. 85).
  [2] ASC E reports Henry's return in the autumn. *HR* 214 (SD ii. 283) dates his return to
15 July. *Regesta* ii. 1570 shows that Henry I was still in Normandy on 2 June.

regis Henrici *ex auctoritate*
apostolica confirmata est festiuitas
Conceptionis sancte Dei Genitricis
Marie.[3]

[HLBP (G)]

Henricus Glæstoniensis abbas
nepos regis Henrici ad episcopatum

[C[3]]

Cuius nepos Glestoniensis abbas
Heinricus ad presulatum

Wintoniensis ecclesie mense Octobri electus,

[HLBP (G)]

Wintonie a Willelmo Cantuar-
iense archipresule .xv. kal. Dec.,
die dominico, consecratur episcopus.[4] Rogerus nepos Gausfridi
de Clintun Bukingahamnensis
archidiaconus ad presulatum
Cestrensem[c] electus, .xii. kal.
Ian., sabbato, presbyter ordinatus[d] et die sequenti a Willelmo
Dorobernensi archipresule consecratur episcopus Cantuarie.[e 5]
Honorius papa[f] obiit.

[C[3]]

a Willelmo Cantuuariensi
archiepiscopo .xv. kal. Dec., die
dominica, consecratur episcopus.[4] Rogerus nepos Gausfridi
de Clintun Buccingchamnensis
archidiaconus ad pontificatum
Cestrensem electus .xii. kal.
Ian., presbiter ordinatur et die
sequenti a Willelmo Cantuuariensi archiepiscopo consecratur
episcopus Cantuuarie.[5]

[(G)]

Cui Innocentius qui et Gregorius successit. Inuasit quoque
apostolatum Petrus qui et Anacletus, et facta est tribulatio et
turbatio magna in ecclesia.[6]

[HLBP (G)]

[1130] 1152[a]
[b]Idem Rogerus[b] a Symone
Wigornensi episcopo apud

[C[3]]

(1129 *continued*)

quem postmodum ex precepto
archiepiscopi Simon Wigornen-

---

[c] Couentrensem *L (G)*   [d] ordinatur *BP*   [e] Wintonie *(G)*   [f] uir
magne religionis *add. (G)*

[a] .lii. *in* .mclii. *erased (G)*   [b–b] Predictus Rogerus nouus episcopus *(G)*

---

[3] The italicized words are shared with the Tewkesbury Annals (*Ann. Mon.* i. 45), which,
with G, is the main source for this council's authorization of the celebration of the feast of
the Conception of the Virgin. The council was held from 30 Sept. to 4 Oct. (ASC), and is
described in both ASC and HH *HA* vii. 40 (pp. 482–8), who dates it to 1 Aug. They give

confirmed with apostolic authority in a council held at London
in King Henry's presence.³

Henry, abbot of Glastonbury, King Henry's nephew, was chosen in October to the see of Winchester,	The king's nephew, Henry, abbot of Glastonbury,
and was consecrated bishop at Winchester by William, arch-bishop of Canterbury, on Sunday, 17 November.⁴ Roger, nephew of Geoffrey of Clinton, archdeacon of Buckingham, was elected to the see of Chester, ordained priest on Saturday, 21 December, and the following day was consecrated bishop at Canterbury by William the arch-bishop there.⁵	and was consecrated bishop by Archbishop William of Canter-bury on Sunday, 17 November.⁴ Roger, nephew of Geoffrey of Clinton, archdeacon of Bucking-ham, was elected to the see of Chester, ordained priest on 21 December, and the following day was consecrated bishop at Canterbury by William the arch-bishop there.⁵

Pope Honorius died.

Innocent, also called Gregory,
succeeded him. Peter also
known as Anacletus usurped
the papacy, and there was great
tribulation and disturbance in
the church.⁶

[1130] The same Roger was enthroned bishop at Coventry on Sunday,	**[1129** *continued*] Afterwards he was enthroned bishop of Coventry at the

the putting aside of clerical wives as its main subject of discussion. HH lists those bishops
present. See Whitelock, Brett, and Brooke, *Councils and Synods*, ii. 750–4.

⁴ Like JW ASC gives 17 Nov., which was a Sunday in 1129, as the day of Henry's
consecration. His election, dated 11 Oct. by the Winchcombe Annals (*Ann. Winchcombe*,
p. 126), is said to have taken place at a Winchester assembly (*HR* 214 (SD ii. 283) and
Margam Annals (*Ann. Mon.* i. 12)). The Margam Annals date the nomination to 4 Oct.,
and ASC simply to 'after Michaelmas'.

⁵ 22 Dec. was a Sunday in 1129. *HR* 214 (SD ii. 283) gives the only alternative date of
17 Nov., and assigns Roger of Clinton's consecration to the same day as that of Henry of
Blois. *HR* refers to Roger's purchase of the see for 3000 marks.

⁶ Honorius II died on 13 Feb. 1130. ASC gives 1129 for the pope's death and for the
beginning of the schism. For Honorius' death HH *HA* vii. 41 (p. 486) and WM *HN* 453
(p. 6) have 1130, and OV *HE* xii. 48 (vi. 392) 1131. Innocent II was pope 1130–43 and
Anacletus II antipope 1130–8.

Couentreiam presulari sede inthronizatur .v.*c* idus Ian., dominico.[1]

sis episcopus Couentrei presulari sede inthronizauit.[1]

[C[3]]

[1130][*d*] 1152

[2]Eximie uir religionis Glaucestrensis*e* cenobita Reignoldus nomine,

[HLBP (G)]

abbas est*f* electus ab eodem*g* presule .vi. kal. Feb., die lune, consecratur Wigorne, et sic Eoueshamnensi *h*ecclesie abbatis*h* iure preficitur.[3]

[C[3]]

abbas electus, ab eodem Simone Wigornensi episcopo, .vi. kal. Feb., die lune, ordinatur Wigorne.[3]

[*i*]Qua etiam die quedam memorie digna, meritis Dei genitricis semperque uirginis Marie sanctorumque patronorum nostrorum Oswaldi ac Wlstani diuinitus acta sunt in nostra ecclesia[*j*] diuerso reatu iudiciali sentencie subacti. Duo erant laici et una femina. Hi precedenti die sabbati qua celebrabatur Conuersio Sancti Pauli apostoli, secundum ius ecclesiasticum ignitum portarant ferrum. Ferunt qui oculis perspexerant, mulieris manum intus et foris miro modo igne combustam. *k*Sperantes simul in misericordia Dei Patris et maxime in meritis beati Wlstani pii antistitis, sepulchrum eius frequentant, genua

---

c .ii. *BP*   *d final* .x. *in* .mcxxx. *over erasure C*   *e* Glaocestrensis *C,* Gloecestrensis *(G)*   *f om. BP*   *g* Simone *add. BP*   *h–h om. H* *i–i om. (G)*   *j followed by blank space with erasure C*   *k–k written over an erasure in text, and also scribbled in the upper mg.* C[3]

---

[1] 9 Jan. (JW MSS HLG's date) was a Thursday, and the 12th (JW MSS BP's) a Sunday, in 1130. JW is the sole extant source for the date of this enthronement. C[3]'s omission of the day when rewriting the 1128–31 annals could have been the reason for its failure to start a new annal at this point, and for commencing 1130 with the next entry which is dated 27 Jan. (see below, 1130 n. 2).

9 January by Simon, bishop of Worcester.[1]

command of Simon, bishop of Worcester.[1]

[1130]

[2]The pious Gloucester monk Reginald was elected abbot, and was consecrated on Monday, 27 January, at Worcester by the same bishop there, and thus was placed with abbatial authority over Evesham.[3]

was elected abbot, and was consecrated on Monday, 27 January, by Simon, the bishop there.[3]

On this day certain events worthy of record occurred in our church by the intervention of God and through the merits of the holy Mother of God ever Virgin, and of our patrons Oswald and Wulfstan. Judicial sentences were imposed for different offences. The two sentenced were lay people and one was a woman. On the previous day of the week, when the Conversion of St Paul [25 January] was commemorated, they had to carry the hot iron according to the ecclesiastical judgement. Eyewitnesses are said to have seen the woman's hand dramatically burnt inside and outside by the fire. Trusting at the same time in the mercy of God the Father, and especially in the merits of the pious Bishop blessed Wulfstan, they went to his tomb, knelt, sought intercession,

[2] C[3] starts its annal 1130 (1152) at this point.
[3] JW is the only extant source for the blessing of Reginald Foliot (see *Heads*, p. 47). 27 Jan. was a Monday in 1130.

flectunt, suffragia petunt, et uelut ad excitandum eum in leuamen sui, crebra percussione tumulo palmas imprimunt. Missa celebrata, dum in conspectu totius populi de illis discernendum ^{k} foret iudicium, unius post alterius ostensa manu, immaculata penitus quelibet reperitur. Hinc pro uicissim acta, manuum ostensione trina, cum, 'Te Deum laudamus', signa pulsabantur omnia. ^{i}

[HLBP (G)]

Hugo uenerandus abbas Rædingensis ecclesie ad Rotomagensem archipresulatum eligitur. $^{m\,4}$ Ecclesia Christi Cantuuarie, .iiii. non. Maii, die dominica, a domno Willelmo eiusdem ciuitatis archiepiscopo, dedicata est cum magno honore. Cuius consecrationi interfuere presules hi, ^{n} Iohannes Hrofensis, Gilebertus Lundoniensis, ^{o}Heinricus Wintoniensis, Alexander Lincoliensis, ^{o} Rogerus ^{p}Saeresberiensis, Simon Wigornensis, ^{q}Rogerus^p Couentrensis, ^{q} Godefridus Bathoniensis, Eouerardus Norðuuicensis, Sigefridus Cicestrensis, Bernardus de Sancto Dauid, Audoenus Ebroicensis, Iohannes Sagiensis.

[C³]

^{l}Hugo abbas Rædincgnensis ecclesie ad Rotomagum archiepiscopus eligitur. ^{4} Ecclesia Christi Cantuuarie, .iiii. non. Maii, die dominica, a Willelmo eiusdem ciuitatis pontifice, dedicata est cum honore. Cuius consecrationi interfuere presules hi, Iohannes Hrofensis, Gilebertus Lundoniensis, Heinricus Wintoniensis, Simon Wigornensis, Alexander Lincoliensis, Rogerus Særesberiensis, Godefridus Bathoniensis, Eouerardus Norðuuicensis, Sigefridus Cicestrensis, Bernardus Mewanensis, Audoenus Ebroicensis transmarinus, Iohannes Sagiensis.

[(G)]

Rex Anglorum Henricus huic interfuit dedicationi, abbates multi, populorum innumerabilium sexus uterque omnis conditio.

---

^{l} a new line started here C ^{m} For interpolations by L and B, see Appendices A and B ^{n} hii LP $^{o-o}$ om. P $^{p-p}$ om. (G) $^{q-q}$ om. BP

and, almost as though they hoped to wake him for their own comfort, they often pressed their palms on his tomb. When mass had been said, and the judgement was to be shown to all the people, the hands of first one and then the other were displayed and were found to be completely healed. This was done in sequence, and the hands were displayed three times and all the miracles declared with the singing of 'Te Deum laudamus'.

The venerable abbot of Reading, Hugh, was elected archbishop of Rouen.[4]

On Sunday, 4 May, Christ Church, Canterbury was dedicated with great honour by William, the lord archbishop of the city. At the dedication there were present these prelates, John of Rochester, Gilbert of London, Henry of Winchester, Alexander of Lincoln, Roger of Salisbury, Simon of Worcester, Roger of Coventry, Godfrey of Bath, Everard of Norwich, Seffrid of Chichester, Bernard of St David's, Ouen of Evreux, John of Séez.

Abbot Hugh of Reading was chosen archbishop of Rouen.[4]

On Sunday, 4 May, Christ Church, Canterbury was dedicated with great honour by William, archbishop of the same city. At the dedication there were present these prelates, John of Rochester, Gilbert of London, Henry of Winchester, Simon of Worcester, Alexander of Lincoln, Roger of Salisbury, Godfrey of Bath, Everard of Norwich, Seffrid of Chichester, Bernard of Mevania, Ouen of Evreux across the sea, John of Séez.

The English king Henry, many abbots, and many peoples of either sex and every rank attended this dedication.

[4] Torigni (*Chronicles Stephen, etc.*, iv. 117–18) dates Hugh's consecration to 14 Sept. 1130.

Quarto post hec die, id est non. Mai, presente rege Heinrico, ciuitas Rofensis incendio conflagrauit, dieque*r* sequenti, *s*Dominice Ascensionis,*s* noua ecclesia Sancti Andree consecratur a Willelmo archiepiscopo, suffragantibus sibi in hoc ministerio quibusdam de prefatis antistibus.[5] Religiosus prior de Læwes

[HLBP (G)]	[C³]
Ansgerus Rædingensi ecclesie abbas eligitur Wintonie.[6]	Rædincgensi ecclesie abbas eligitur Wintonie, et postmodum ordinatur.[6]

[(G)]
Magne probitatis homo Vincentius abbas Abbendoniensis ecclesie, hoc anno in uigilia Pasche, .iiii. Kl. Aprilis, decessit hac uita.[7]

Prior etiam Wintoniensis ecclesie, Ingulfus,*t* apud Wudestoke electus*u*

[HLBP (G)]	[C³]
Abbendunensi ecclesie a Rogero Searberiensi presule .vi. idus Iun., die dominica, consecratur Searesbirie.[8]	a Rogero Seresberiensi episcopo Abbandonie abbas ordinatur.[8]
Willelmus Glaornensis *abbas* pre senectute*v* *pastorali cura sponte dimissa,*w* *eiusd*em *ecclesie religiosum cenobitam Walterum nomine cum consensu fratrum pro se abbatem elegit qui a Simone Wigornensi presule .iii. non. Aug., die dominica, consecratur Wigornie.*[9]	Willemus Glaornensis *abbas* pre senectute *pastorali cura sponte dimissa, eiusdem ecclesie religiosum cenobitam Walterum cum consensu fratrum elegit; qui a Simone Wigornensi presule .iii. non. Aug., die dominica, abbas ordinatur Wigornie.*[9]
Eodem mense*x* rex Anglorum Heinricus mare transiit.[10]	

---

r die *H*, et die *L*, die tamen *(G)*   *s-s* que tunc fuit Dominice Ascensionis, id est .viii. Idus Maii *(G)*   *t* nomine *add. HLBP (G)*   *u* eligitur *(G)*   *v* infirmitate *(G)*   *w* absque tamen sui conuentus consensu dimissa *(G)*   *x* anno *H*

---

[5] JW's accounts of the dedications of Canterbury and Rochester Cathedrals, and of the Rochester fire are very close to ASC E's, though G's interpolation is not paralleled there. The list of bishops in HLBP (G) is as in ASC E, with the variants shown.
[6] Reading Annals confirm this date (*UAG*, p. 11): see *Heads*, p. 63.

Four days later, on 7 May, Rochester was destroyed by fire while King Henry was there. On the following day (the feast of the Ascension), a new church of St Andrew was consecrated by Archbishop William, assisted by some of the afore-mentioned bishops.[5] The pious prior of Lewes

| Ansger was chosen abbot of Reading at Winchester.[6] | was chosen abbot of Reading at Winchester, and was afterwards ordained.[6] The abbot of Abingdon, Vincent, a most upright man, died this year on the eve of Easter, 29 March.[7] |

Ingulph, prior of Winchester, was elected abbot at Woodstock

| and was consecrated to the monastery of Abingdon at Salisbury on Sunday, 8 June.[8] William, abbot of Gloucester, laid aside his staff because of age. With the brethren's consent he chose the pious monk Walter as successor in his place. Walter was ordained at Worcester on Sunday, 3 August, by Simon the bishop there.[9] In the same month King Henry of the English crossed overseas.[10] | and was blessed as abbot of Abingdon by Roger, bishop of Salisbury.[8] William, abbot of Gloucester, laid aside his staff because of age. With the brethren's consent he chose the pious monk Walter, and Walter was ordained abbot on Sunday, 3 August, at Worcester by Simon the bishop there.[9] |

[7] *Heads*, p. 25, says that the day of Vincent's death (29 Mar.) is confirmed by an Abingdon obit (Cambridge, University Library Kk. 1. 22, fos. 1ᵛ ff.) and the year by *Pipe Roll 31 Henry I*, p. 123, and by the annals in BL Arundel 326, fo. 21ʳ.

[8] The day of blessing (8 June), which was a Sunday in 1130, is confirmed by the annals in BL Arundel 326, fo. 21ʳ. *Regesta* ii. 1641 (Henry I's grant to Ingulph of Abingdon) suggests that Ingulph was in office between the limiting dates of 29 Mar. and 29 Sept. 1130, limiting dates which were presumably based on JW (see above, n. 7) and HH *HA* (see below, n. 10) respectively.

[9] The italicized words are shared with *Cart. Gloc.* i. 15 and with the presumably derivative account of Gregory of Caerwent (BL Cotton Vespasian A.V fo. 198ʳ): see *Heads*, pp. 52–3.

[10] ASC assigns this crossing to the autumn, HH *HA* vii. 41 (p. 486) to Michaelmas, and the Waverley Annals (*Ann. Mon.* ii. 222) to Sept. Henry was at Le Bec on 8 Sept. and at Rouen on 14 Sept. (Torigni, *Chronicles Stephen, etc.*, iv. 117–18).

[1131] 1153ᵃ   (1130 *continued*)
ᵇEt anno sequentiᵇ mense Iunioᶜ
Angliam rediit.¹

[(G)]
Domnus abbas Wilelmus post
dimissam curam anno uno super-
uiuens .iii. Idus Iulii de hoc seculo
*migrauit ad Dominum.*²

Rodbertus ᵈprior reuerendusᵈ   Serlo quoque Særesberiensis
Lantoniensis ecclesie ad Here-   canonicus ab eodem antistite
fordensem presulatum electus   apud Blockelea uillam episcopa-
est a Willelmo Dorobernie   lem abbas ordinatur et Cirences-
archiepiscopo .iii. kal. Iulii epis- tri ecclesie preficitur.⁴
copus consecratur Oxenefordie.³

Serlo quoque Særesbyriensis   Rotbertus prior reuerendus
canonicus a Symone Wigornen-   Lantoniensis ecclesie ad Heresis pontifice apud Bloccesleaᵉ   fordensem presulatum electus a
episcopalem uillam suam abbas   Willelmo Dorubernie archipre-
consecratur et Cirencestrensi   sule consecratur Oxenofordie.³
ecclesie abbatis iure preficitur.ᶠ⁴

[H]
ᵍVenerandi abbates Reignoldus
Ramesiensis .xiii. kl. Iun. et
Willelmus Glaornensis,

[HBP]
Herueus prius Bancornensis,
postmodum Eliensis primus
episcopus .iii. kl. Sept. obier-
unt.ᵍʰ ⁵

                                    ⁱRex Anglorum Heinricus mare
p. 382   transiit.⁶ |

ᵃ .liii. *in* .mcliii. *erased* G   ᵇ⁻ᵇ Rex Anglorum HL   ᶜ Iulio P   ᵈ⁻
ᵈ reuerendus prior LBP (G)   ᵉ Bloccelea LB, Blokkelea P, Blokeleam (G)
ᶠ L *ended here,* G *completed its copy of an earlier version of* C *at this point, placed* 1128 n. d
here and followed with those other additions of the revised version which it copied, that is, its
1130 nn. j, m, q, s, t, 1131, 1132 *up to* 1132 n. e. *None of these entries was given separate dates*
and so they were assigned to the previously dated annal 1131   ᵍ⁻ᵍ *add. by the scribe later*
H   ʰ obiit P, indictione .ix. *add.* B   ⁱ *paragraph mark here* C

---

¹ ASC dates Henry's return to after 29 June and 'before harvest'. C³ presumably lost
the date of Henry's return in transcribing the erased annals for 1128–31, and this could be
why its new annal does not start here. HH *HA* vii. 41 (p. 486) speaks of Henry returning in

[1131]   (1130 *continued*)
The following year King Henry
came back in June.[1]

The lord abbot William left this
world for the Lord on 13 July a
year after giving up his duties.[2]

The revered prior of Llanthony,   In addition, Serlo, a Salisbury
Robert, was elected bishop of   canon, was blessed as abbot by
Hereford, and consecrated   the same bishop at the episcopal
bishop at Oxford on 29 June,   township, Blockley, and set over
by William, archbishop of Can-   Cirencester.[4]
terbury.[3]

Serlo also, a Salisbury canon,   Robert, the revered prior of
was blessed as abbot by Simon,   Llanthony, was elected to the
bishop of Worcester, at the epis-   bishopric of Hereford, and con-
copal township, Blockley, and set   secrated by William, archbishop
as abbot over Cirencester.[4]   of Canterbury at Oxford.[3]

The revered abbots Reginald and
William of Gloucester died, the
first on 20 May.

Hervey, at first bishop of
Bangor, later the first bishop of
Ely, died on 30 August.[5]

                                         Henry, king of the English,
                                         crossed over the sea.[6]

the summer with his daughter, whilst WM *HN* 455 (p. 10) reports Henry and Matilda's
return in the same year.

  [2] The italicized words are shared with *Cart. Gloc.* i. 15, where William's death is dated
13 July 1131. The derivative Gregory of Caerwent (BL Cotton Vespasian A.V, fo. 198ʳ)
dates William's death at St Paternus, Llanbadarn Fawr, to 3 Feb. 1131.

  [3] HBC gives 28 June, and not JW's 29 June, as the date of Robert de Bethune's
consecration, presumably because it was a Sunday in 1131 (as was noted in *Anglia Sacra*, ii.
307 n.).

  [4] JW is the only extant account of Serlo's blessing (see *Heads*, p. 159).

  [5] JW's date for Reginald of Ramsey's death is apparently confirmed by a 'Libellus de
anniversariis in ecclesie Ramesiensi observatis', which was printed in *Mon.* ii. 566 (see
Heads, p. 62). HH *HA* vii. 41 (p. 488) dates it to 'after Easter' (19 May). G had already
dealt with the death of William of Gloucester (1130 *recte* 1131: see above, 1131 n. 2). JW's
date for Bishop Hervey's death agrees with that in the *LE* ii. 40 (p. 279). HH *HA* vii. 41
(p. 488) assigns it to the beginning of winter, and the Winchcombe Annals (*Ann.
Winchcombe*, p. 126) to 31 Aug.

  [6] 'Mare transiit' usually describes Henry's crossing to Normandy. Having omitted
Henry's return under its 1130 (*recte* 1131) annal (see above, 1131 n. 1) through a possible
error in transcription, C³ may have compounded the original error.

[j](1130 *continued*) 1152[j] [k]Mense Februario, .xvii. die mensis id est
.xiii. kal. Martii, paulo post noctis medium, uisus est a duobus
presbyteris et totidem clericis apud Herefordiam a laudibus nocturnis exeuntibus splendor insolitus ad mensuram unius pertice por-
rectus, in illa celestis spere parte qua sol esse solet circa finem .x.
hore, cum in estiuo solstitio uergit ad occasum. Erat autem corpus
illud unde splendor exibat ille alba tectum nube, et per breuia
temporis interualla sepius a nube prefata quasi exiliens ad superiora
emergebatur, et post breuem moram iterum nubi immergebatur,
quod non sine metu ac stupore cernebatur. Color quoque eius erat
quasi de coloribus plene lune et lucide flamme esset confectus.
Forma uero et quantitas eius sicut breuis piramis, in inferioribus
lata, et in superioribus angusta. Cunque illi qui hec uiderunt
inclamassent, ut plures in hac re testes habere possent, tabula
mediocris in longum erecta stare uisa est super nubem in qua
splendidum corpus illud fuerat, quod super ipsam nubem lumen
ab initio sparserat, et in fine proximas sibi aquilonis partes inferius
magna ex parte tenui luce repleuerat, minus lucida quam locus in
quo stabat. Inter hec uenere quidam qui inclamati fuerant, et mox in
eorum aduentu omnis lux illa penitus est extincta, nisi paucissima
ipsius uestigia que uix in parte aquilonis tenuiter poterant uideri.
Qui autem prius prefatam lucem uidit, duas etiam in initio uisionis
lineas quasi aurorali luce plenas ab equinoctiali solis ortu usque ad
equinoctialem eius occasum porrectas aspexit, sed pro pauore quem
inde incurrit et pro altera de qua dictum est uisione cui totus
intendit, neque quantum ille prefate due linee durauere, neque
quando discessere potuit agnoscere. Visa sunt ista in castello Herefordensi a clericis Sancti Guthlaci. Visa sunt etiam a uigilibus
Brecenæunensis castelli; insuper in pago Herefordensi a pastoribus
in ipsa nocte super gregem suum uigilantibus. [l]Que didici scripsi,
saluet nos gratia Christi.[l] [k]

[m]Heinrico Anglorum regi Normannie moranti, anno regni .xxx.,
etatis uero .lxiiii., miranda in somnis apparuit uisio. [n]Heinricus mira

---

[j-j] C[3] *originally began a new annal here as 1131 (1153) corrected to 1130 (1152). From this
point C(G) were the main witnesses to JW's text though H[2] had some excerpts, starting at 1132
n. e*   [k] Anno precedenti uidelicet millesimo centesimo tricesimo *add. before* Mense
(G)   [l-l] *om.* (G)   [m-m] *written in two columns, each to the right of a pen drawing,
one of a man seated holding a flask and pointing to the second of a sleeping Henry I towered over
by some rustics C, no illustrations (G)*   [n-n] *written around the first two illustrations, and
now mostly illegible in C. The text has been recovered from JW's scribbling of these captions in
the upper mg. of Oxford, Bodleian Library Auct. F.1.9, fo. 20[v], om.* (G)

(**1130** *continued*) Shortly after the middle of the night, on 17 February, that is on 13 Kalends of March, as they were coming out of Lauds, two priests and two clerks at Hereford saw an unusual bright light, about one perch in length, in that part of the heavens where the sun is to be found towards the end of the tenth hour, when it is setting at the summer solstice. The object from which the bright light came was covered with a white cloud. For short periods it would often emerge from the cloud as though it was moving upwards, and then after a short interval it would re-enter the cloud to the fear and amazement of the observers. Its colour was a blend of those of a full moon and of bright flames. In shape and size it was like a small pyramid, broad at the bottom, and narrow at the top. The observers called out so that there could be more witnesses to this matter; they declared that a fairly small plank, stretching upwards a long way was seen to stand on the cloud in which that brilliant object had been—which object had at first shed light on the cloud and had in the end covered with a dim light for the most part from below the northerly parts next to it, a light less bright than the spot in which it stood. Whilst these things were happening, some persons who had been called arrived, and as soon as they had come all that light was completely blotted out except for the faintest trace which could barely be seen on its north side. The person who had seen the earlier light also saw at the beginning of the spectacle two lines seemingly filled with the light of dawn and stretching from the equinoctial sun's rising to its equinoctial setting. However, he was able to establish neither how long the two aforesaid lines lasted nor exactly when they vanished because he felt such fear of the sight and because he was concentrating wholly on the other vision which has been described. This was seen by the clerks of St Guthlac in Hereford castle. It was also seen by the watchmen in Brecon castle as well as in Herefordshire by the shepherds watching their flocks that same night. I have written down what I have heard. May Christ's mercy save us![7]

In the thirtieth year of his reign and in his sixty-fourth year, a marvellous dream appeared in Normandy to Henry, king of England.

---

[7] These aerial phenomena are not reported elsewhere.

rex hec per somnia uidit que medicus Grimbald uigilando per omnia spectat. Prosilit e lecto dum regem uisio terret. Arma capit surgens hominem non uulnerat ullum." *o*Triplex erat uisio et a se diuersa. Prima uisio.*o* Sopore grauatus rex obdormit, et ecce plurimam rusticorum multitudinem cum rusticanis instrumentis propter astare cernit. Omnes in illum diuersis modis seuire, dentibus frendere, et nescio quod ab eo debitum exigere. Somno territus euigilat, nudis fortasse pedibus strato exilit, arma capit, eis quos somnians uiderat uindicta inferre cupit, sed neminem inuenit. Quo uiso, qui regium latus obseruare debuerant fugiunt omnes. O qualis regia dignitas! En rex purpuratus *p*cuius iuxta sententiam Salomonis terror est ut rugitus leonis a rusticis terretur in somnis.[8] Cessa, rex, cessa neminem persequi, ad lectum redi, et ut maiora uideas rursus obdormi.*m* *q*Secunda uisio.*p* Reductus in soporem, conspicit loricis indutam numerosam militum cohortem, galeas capitibus ferentem, lancea⟨s⟩, maceram, tela, sagittas manibus tenentem. Cerneres quisquis adesses, milites per somnium uisos quasi uelle regem occidere et in frusta si ualerent concidere. Nimio rex terrore perculsus in sopore, regiam totam horrendo replet clamore. 'Succurrite,' inquit; 'succurrite.' Sic clamitans, somnum oculis excutit, et prosiliens, gladium
p. 383 arripit, et affectans uulnerare, neminem uulnerat.*q* | *r*Astant pontifices, abbates, necne priores, ceu perquirentes res ecclesie spoliatas.*r* *s*Tertio satisfaciens rex somno, archiepiscoporum, episcoporum, abbatum, decanorum siue priorum aspectat personas, cum baculis pastoralibus astare. Intellectu perspicaci coniceres animum illorum in quendam transisse affectum et uelut ob direptionem rerum ecclesie sue manentem regie misericordie respectum. At persone considerantes terrificum habitum illius et quasi auertentem oculos ab eis minitando plurima, baculorum cuspidibus eum appetere uelle uisi sunt. Hec mira uideos uidit quidam in regie aule secreto angulo latens, scilicet sub nocturno tempore omnia tegit silentio. Erat itaque iste medicine artis peritus, Grimbaldus nomine, qui apud Wincelcumb, me presente et audiente, narrauit hec omnia domno Godefrido eiusdem ecclesie abbati. Summo diluculo regem adhuc lecto

o–o om. (G)　　*p–p* om. (G)　　*q–q* arranged as 1131 n. m, but written in one column between pen-drawings of a man holding a flask and of the sleeping king towered over by some knights C, no illustrations (G)　　*r–r* om. (G)　　*s–s* arranged as 1131 nn. m and q, and written in two columns, each one to the right of a pen-drawing, one of a man holding a wax tablet and the second of a sleeping king towered over by some churchmen C, no illustrations (G)

Asleep King Henry saw these remarkable visions which Grimbald
the doctor fully observed whilst he was awake. He leapt out of bed
whilst the vision frightened the king. Rising and seizing arms, the
king wounded no one. There were three visions, each different from
the other. This was the first vision. Overcome by drowsiness, the
king fell asleep, and behold, he saw a big band of peasants standing
by him with agricultural implements. In different ways they began to
rage, to gnash their teeth, and to demand from him dues which I am
unable to describe. Waking in terror from his sleep, he sprang from
the bed it may be with bare feet and seized his arms, wanting to
punish those whom he had seen in his sleep. But he found no one.
He saw this and saw that those who should watch by the side of kings
had all fled. Such is the dignity of kings! The king dressed in the
purple who inspires fear like a raging lion (as Solomon puts it) is
terrified in his sleep by peasants.[8] King, stop, stop chasing shadows,
go back to bed, so that when asleep you will again see a greater
vision. This was the second vision. Having gone back to sleep, Henry
saw a large band of knights wearing armour, bearing helmets on their
heads, and each of them holding lances, a sword, spears and arrows.
If you were present you could see knights revealed in a dream, all
apparently wanting to kill the king and to cut him into pieces if they
could. Struck by a great fear in his sleep, the king fills the whole
royal chamber with a horrendous cry. 'Help me,' he cries, 'help me'.
Shouting in this way, he shook sleep from his eyes, took up his
sword, and wanting to strike, he found no one to wound. Bishops,
abbots, and priors stand by searching, as it were, for their despoiled
churches. A third time the king sank back into sleep, and saw the
figures of archbishops, bishops, abbots, deans and priors holding
their pastoral staffs. In your mind's eye you might see the churchmen
changing their attitude, and, as it were, their enduring respect for the
king's mercy on account of the plundering of church possessions.
They look at his terrifying countenance and at his eyes almost
averted from them, and with many threats they are seen to want to
attack him with the tips of their staffs. One man secreted in a hidden
corner of the royal chamber, under the cover of the total silence of
the night, saw all these marvellous things. It was that skilled
physician, Grimbald, who related all these matters at Winchcombe
to the lord abbot Godfrey of the church there in my presence and
hearing. The same man approached the king at dawn when he was

[8] Cf. Prov. 28: 2.

cubantem idem uir adit, questionem de his que uiderat cum eo facit. Cui rex cuncta que in somnis pertulerat enarrauit, que ille ut uir illustris prudentie sed iam de medio factus, in uera coniectura exposuit, et ut Nabuchodonosor iuxta consilium Danielis egit, elemosina peccata redimere commonuit.[5][9]

*Actum est post hec in uno dierum rex idem Heinricus Angliam rediturus cum regali curia in nauim ascendit. Et ecce motus magnus factus est in mari, ita ut nauis operiretur fluctibus, erat enim eis uentus contrarius. Proh dolor, Iesus dormiebat omnibus. Veritus rex imminens funus, ut Rex regum in misericordiis euigilet sibique suisque sucurrat,[u] in regno Anglie Danicum tributum .vii. annis non exigi decernit. Votum etiam uouit in orientales partes Anglie se diuersurum, Sancti Eadmundi regis et martyris patrocinia imploraturum, omnemque iustitiam per Angliam seruaturum. *Quo uoto, facta est tranquillitas magna. Angliam ueniens congaudentibus cunctis uota persoluit. Hoc etiam rex Stephanus qui nunc imperat in regali decreto suo promisit, Danicum scilicet tributum se nullatenus exacturum. Verum in Deo odibili periurio, auribus hausi tributum per Angliam exigi. *Hoc nefandum scandalum mouet ueridicum dictum, sicut compositum est.

> Sepe facit reges nummus peruertere leges.[v]
> Si reus es mortis dampnatus ab ore coortis,
> Presenta, da quinque decemue talenta;
> Talia si dederis, quam cito liber eris.[wt] [10]

[1131] (1153)[x] *Annus cycli[z] decennouenalis .iiii. .xiii., cycli solaris .iii., .xiiii., bissextilis .vi. annus .i.,[y] Romanorum imperatoris Lotharii et Anglorum regis Heinrici temporibus, quidam comes erat in partibus Alamannie cui nomen Normannus, potens et diues,

---

[t-t] *written on either side of a pen-drawing of a boat in which the king and his companions appear terrified in a storm* C, *no illustrations* (G)   [u] sucrat C   [v-v] *written in right mg. separately from text on the storm at sea* C   [w-w] *om.* G   [x] *corrected from* 1132 (1154) C[3], (G) *did not start an annal at this point and placed this episode together with* C[3]'s *other interpolations in a block under* 1131, *see above,* 1131 n. f   [y-y] *om.* (G)   [z] *interlin.* C[3]

[9] Cf. Dan. 4: 24. For Grimbald, see C. H. Talbot and E. A. Hammond, *The Medical Practitioners in Medieval England: A Biographical Register* (London, 1965), pp. 67–8, which notes that a Staffordshire gold levy shows that he was alive in 1130, and that he seems to have been continually in the king's household. It is not possible to date John's stay at Winchcombe. JW's source dated the visions to Henry I's 30th year.

[10] This is another example of the chronological confusions caused by C[3]'s rewriting the annals 1128–31. Henry did not return to England in 1130: in that year the only cross-

still in bed, and discussed with him what he had seen. The king told him all he had experienced in his sleep, and the distinguished man of great wisdom, who is now deceased, explained their true interpretation, and, as Nebuchadnezzar did on Daniel's advice, advised him to redeem his sins by alms-giving.[9]

After this the same king Henry one day boarded a ship with the royal household to return to England. And lo, there was a great disturbance at sea so that the ship was covered by waves in the face of a contrary wind. Alas, Jesus was asleep for them all. Fearing an imminent disaster, the king decided that the Danish tax should not be collected in the English kingdom for seven years so that the King of kings would in His mercy be watchful and succour both him and his followers. He also vowed that he would turn aside to the eastern parts of England and ask for the protection of St Edmund, king and martyr, and that he would always preserve justice throughout England. When he had so promised there was a great calm. On his return, to everyone's rejoicing he fulfilled his promise. King Stephen, who now reigns, also promised in a royal decree that he would never collect the Danish tax. We hear that it is now again demanded throughout England by a perjury odious to God. This cursed offence overturned the prophetic pledge just as it had been made.

Love of gain often makes kings pervert laws.
If you are guilty and are condemned to death by the sentence of a judge,
Go forward and give five or ten talents.
If you give such sums you will be quickly set free.[10]

[1131] In the thirteenth year of the fourth nineteen-year cycle, in the fourteenth year of the third solar cycle, the first year of the sixth bissextile, in the times of Lothar, emperor of the Romans, and of Henry, the English king, there was a certain rich and powerful count

---

Channel crossing was made to Normandy 'in the autumn' (ASC E), 'in Aug.' (JW, see above 1130 n. 10). C[3] had, however, already erroneously reported Henry's crossing the channel to Normandy under his 1130 (see above, 1131 n. 6), and the story of the storm had probably accompanied the visions of Henry I in C[3]'s source which could have assigned them to the king's thirtieth year. In 1131 Henry I returned from Normandy after 29 June, and 'before autumn' (ASC E, see above, 1131 n. 1). No other extant source refers to this storm. *Regesta* ii. 1733, a royal act in favour of Bury St Edmund's issued there, could confirm Henry's honouring his oath to suspend the Danegeld. As pointed out by Diana Greenway, HH *HA* x. 3 (p. 704 n. 19), HH's reference to Stephen's promise to abolish Danegeld, which is absent from the king's two 'charters of liberties', is supported by JW's story here.

habitans in oppido Honburch*aa* nomine, habens filiam uocabulo Odiliam a natiuitate cecam. Hanc, cum esset paruula, misit ad quandam uillulam suam longe remotam, ignominiosum ualde reputans, si in eadem uilla qua ipse manebat nutriretur. Que cum adoleuisset, lasciuiam modis omnibus fugiens, in bonis moribus prout poterat | diligentissime Domino seruiebat. Habebat autem fratrem unum, qui eam tenerrime diligens, multotiens patrem ut reuocaretur orabat, sed nullatenus impetrare ualebat. Tandem consilio cum familiaribus suis habito, ignorante patre ubi ipse manebat, profectus, secum reduxit eam, et in quadam domo que curie patris eius erat contigua, commendauit. Quo facto uenit ad patrem, pro reditu sororis sue sicut ante consueuerat deprecatur, sed ille inflexibilis persistens, non acquieuit. Vnde filius ira commotus, ad patrem, 'Velis,' inquit, 'nolis, per me reuocata in proximo mansionem accepit.' His auditis, nimio furore pater accensus, baculo quem manu tenebat filium in capite percussit et occidit. Protinus ad se reuersus, malum quod egerat expauit, paucisque diebus exactis, iuxta ecclesiasticam institutionem penitentiam suscipit agendam. In qua cum modicum tempus exegisset, infirmitate correptus, obiit. At filia eius pro eo quod necdum dimidia penitentia peracta defunctus esset, grauiter afflicta diebus ac noctibus in ieiuniis, uigiliis et orationibus pro redemptione anime Domini misericordiam implorabat. Quod dum ageret, nocte quadam angelus Domini per uisum ei assistens, ait, 'Si diligentius quam facis pro anima patris tui Dominum oraueris, cito ad corpus suum reuertetur, ut iniunctam sibi penitentiam expleat, eaque peracta in bona conuersatione denuo migrabit a corpore.' His dictis, angelica uisio disparuit. Illa autem protinus euigilans, et que per uisionem audierat mente pertractans, cepit modis omnibus quibus poterat, *bb*ieiuniis, uigiliis et precibus Dei misericordiam implorare ut, sicut angelus ei promiserat,*bb* patrem suum recipere mereretur. Quod dum aliquantum temporis in huiusmodi afflictionibus peregisset, ecce die quadam coram omni familia qui defunctus fuerat aulam intrauit, sola indutus camisia, salutatisque omnibus qui aderant ne timerent hortatur. 'Ecce,' inquit, 'Deus omnipotens reddidit mihi uitam, ad peragendam penitentiam.'

p. 384

---

aa Horeburc *(G)*   *bb–bb* satagere ut *(G)*

called Norman in Alemania, who dwelt in the town of Hohenburg. He had a daughter called Odilia who was blind from birth. When she was small, he sent her off to a distant small estate of his since he thought it shameful to have her brought up in the township where he was living. When she reached the age of puberty, she avoided all wantonness, and earnestly served the Lord in an upright manner to the best of her abilities. She had a brother who loved her dearly and who often asked his father to recall her, but he was completely unsuccessful in his request. At length he took counsel with his close followers, and without his father knowing where he was, he set out and brought his sister back with him and put her up in a certain house quite close to her father's household. When he had done this, he went to his father and, as he had done before, begged for his sister's return, but the father did not change his mind, and did not agree. The son was roused to anger, and said to the father, 'Whether you are willing or not, she has been brought back by me and lives in a neighbouring house.' On learning this, the father became exceedingly angry, struck his son on the head with the staff he was holding in his hand, and killed him. Returning straightaway to his house, he was frightened at the ill he had done, and after a few days, he did penance according to ecclesiastical commands. When he had done penance for some time, he became ill and died. His daughter implored God's mercy on his behalf since he had died with only half his penance performed and she assiduously spent her days and nights in fasting, vigils, and prayers for the redemption of his soul. Whilst she was doing these things an angel of the Lord stood by her one night in a dream and said, 'If you will pray to the Lord even more earnestly than you are doing for your father's soul, he will be returned to his body so that he might carry out the penance enjoined on him, and then, when that has been carried out, he will again depart his body after a good way of life.' When these things had been said, the angelic vision vanished. Waking up immediately, Odilia pondered what she had learnt in the dream, and began to try in every possible way to implore God's mercy through fasting, vigils, and prayers that, as the angel had promised her, she might be worthy to welcome her father. When she had continued for some time in this distress, behold, one day he who had died entered the hall in full view of everyone, clad only in a shirt, and, greeting all present, he urged them not to be frightened, saying, 'Behold Almighty God has restored me to life so that I might carry out my penance.' The next

Subsequenti uero die peregrinationem aggressus, postquam legitimam expleuit penitentiam, domum regressus, ecclesiam in honore Sancte Dei genitricis Marie construxit, in qua sanctimonialibus ad seruiendum Deo congregatis, filiam suam Odiliam, iamdudum diuinitus illuminatam, abbatissam constituit. Postmodum domu sua in omnibus ordinate disposita, sicut angelus predixit, in pace quieuit. Camisia uero qua induebatur dum familie sue uiuus apparuit,*cc* in eadem ecclesia ad indicium huius miraculi iuxta principale altare posita seruatur, grauissimo foetore respersa, et ad instar fauille colorata. Hanc si manu palpaueris, nulla ratione poteris ⟨sapere⟩*dd* cuius sit generis aut texture. Denique foetorem eius conuersantes ibidem propter assiduitatem non sentiunt, sed aliunde uenientes statim in ipso ecclesie introitu non sine graui horrore naribus trahunt. Preterea uirgo nobilis Odilia post mortem patris in sancta conuersatione persistens, commanentes sibi bonorum operum informabat exemplis, expletoque dierum suorum curriculo, feliciter iduum Decembrium die, feria .ii., migrauit ad Dominum. In cuius festiuitate que ipso die colitur, biduo ante induitur unus de familia ecclesie camisia supradicta, et ad compunctionem intuentium in medio populi qui ad solennitatem conuenerit, huc illucque deambulat, herbas odoriferas sine intermissione naribus adhibens, ne foetore camisie periclitetur. Is etiam .vii. diebus ante solennitatem ad eundem quem diximus foetorem camisie ⟨mitigandum⟩*dd* omni quo uescitur cibo, crudo utitur allio.[11]

[**1132**] (1154)*a* Eximie uir religionis et reuerentie Wigornensis cenobita, Vhtredus nomine, a beato et cum omni honore nominando Wlstano presule olim temporis cantor constitutus Wigornensis ecclesie, .iiii. non. Aprilis, sabbato ante Palmas, modum fecit huic uite. Et quoniam ex Dei gratia memorie digno fine quieuit, tum pro rogatu fratrum, tum pro dilectione qua me uelut nutritoris uice dilexerat, dignum duxi notitie omnium tradere, qualiter ex Egypto migrauerit. Functus quampluribus annis precentoris officio, omnibus

---

cc fuerat *(G)*   *dd* supplied by editor

a corrected from 1133 (1155) C³, (G) did not begin a new annal at this point and placed the annal up to 1132 n. e together with C³'s other interpolations all under 1131, see above, 1131 n. f

[11] Odilia is said to have lived in the seventh century, though her earliest life is probably tenth century (edited by W. Levison, MGH *Scriptores rerum Merovingicarum*, vi. 24–50).

day, he set out on a journey, and after he had done his due penance, he returned home, and built a church in honour of the Holy Mother of God, where, having assembled nuns for the service of God, he made his daughter Odilia, who had been enlightened by God, abbess. Afterwards having disposed of all things in his house in an orderly fashion, he ended his day in peace, as the angel had predicted. The shirt which he was wearing when he appeared alive to his household, was kept in the same church next to the principal altar as a sign of this miracle, emitting a foul stench, and coloured like ash. If you touched it with your hand, you could not tell what sort of material it was nor feel its texture. In the end those who lived there could not bear its overwhelming smell, and those coming from elsewhere at the very entrance of the church drew breath straightaway with great revulsion. Meanwhile the noble virgin Odilia continued in her holy way of life after her father's death, inspiring those who were with her with the example of good works, completing the cycle of her days, and departed happily to the Lord on Monday, 13 December. Two days before the day kept holy in her memory, one of the church's household put on the aforesaid shirt and went up and down, arousing the sympathy of the onlookers in the middle of the crowd, continually holding sweet smelling herbs to his nostrils lest he be affected by the stench of the shirt and to the compunction of the onlookers in the middle of the crowd who had assembled for the feast. Seven days before the feast this man garnished all his food with raw garlic to counteract the said shirt's stench.[11]

[1132] A most devout and revered Worcester monk called Uhtred died on the Saturday before Palm Sunday, that is, on 2 April. He had earlier been made cantor of the Worcester church by the blessed and ever-honoured Bishop Wulfstan. And because through God's mercy he ended his life in a manner worthy of record, I have thought it appropriate to set down for everyone how he departed this world. I do this both because the brethren have asked me to and because of the affection he showed me almost as a foster-father. For many years he acted as precentor, and acted as everyone's guardian in God's

---

JW's summary with its emphasis on the smelly shirt of Odilia's father is not known elsewhere (see C. Pfister, *Le Duché d'Alsace et la légende de Sainte Odile* (Paris, 1892), pp. 64–5). It is not clear why JW inserted this story with its relatively elaborate introductory dating here. The 13th year in JW's 4th decennovenal cycle was probably 1133. Pertz (MGH SS xiii. 132–3) printed this story.

se uicarium exhibebat in Dei seruitio. Viribus tandem corporis destitutus, paralisis morbo sepius grauabatur. Anno sui decessus singulis fere diebus in spiritu humilitatis ob remissionem peccatorum a .ii. uel a .iii. fratribus crebris et acerrimis uerberibus corpus macerari fecit. Sabbatum predictum illuxerat, quo de seculo migraturus erat. In Domino Deo suo confisus et confortatus, ad missam in choro solito more stabat. Officium 'Liberator meus, Kyrri eleyson' et sequens gradale[b] inchoabat. Lateri eius stans adherebam. Lecto euangelio, offertorium 'Benedictus es, Deus' incepit, et uocatus a Deo paulatim cadere cepit.[c] Quem protinus in dolore cordis excepi manibus. Stupefacti fratres accurrunt. Quos rogat ut poterat, quo in altaris presentia sibi mori liceat. Deportatus denique in domum infirmorum, uespertinali completa synaxi, [d]singulis diebus prius et eodem ipso die[d] corpore et sanguine Domini communicatus, commendat spiritum in manus Creatoris. Humatur crastino a uenerando Wigornensi presule Simone, in conspectu cleri et totius suburbani populi.[1] [e]Stella cometis .viii. idus Octob. fere per .v.[f] dies apparuit.[2]

[1133] (1156)[a] Maxima pars Lundonie ciuitatis [b]cum principali ecclesia beati Pauli apostoli[b] in eptomada Pentecostes, [c]quod erat .ii. idus Maii, igne combusta est.[c][1] Anno .xxxiii. ex quo rex Anglorum Heinricus regnare cepit, feria .iiii., die etiam ipso secundum anni reuolutionem quo frater et predecessor illius, Willelmus, scilicet Rufus rex, interfectus est et ipse Heinricus primo regni sui suscepit gubernacula,[d] tale constat contigisse spectaculum. Cum igitur[e] rex predictus circa maris litus transfretandi causa moraretur, uento sepius ad transfretandum existente secundo, tandem die prefato circa meridiem cum ad mare transiturus perrexisset, suorum ut mos est regibus constipatus militum turmis, subito in aere nubes apparuit, que tamen unius[f] eiusdem[g] quantitatis per uniuersam Angliam non comparuit. In quibusdam enim locis quasi dies obscurus uidebatur, in quibusdam uero tante obscuritatis erat, ut lumine candele ad quodlibet agendum ipsa protecti homines

---

[b] id est responsoris *interlin.* C[3]   [c] -pit *in* cepit *interlin.* C[3]   [d-d] *om.* (G)   [e] *paragraph mark here* C, (G) *started 1132 at this point, having erased .lvi. from its Marianan year .mclvi.,* H[2] *began its extracts from the added annals of* C *at this point, but without a numbered year for this event*   [f] .vii. H

[a] 1133 (1156) *corrected from* 1134 (1157) C[3], 1132 (1153) *add. in the mg. by the continuator* H[2], (G) *had begun its previous annal* (1132) *at* 1132 n. e   [b-b] *om.* H[2]   [c-c] *om.* H[2]   [d] .iiii. N. Aug. *add. by* H[2]   [e] *followed by erasure* C[3]   [f] *interlin. above* eiusdem C[3], *om.* H[2]   [g] eundem H[2]

service. In the end he was deprived of his bodily strength, and was often afflicted by paralysis. In the year of his death his body, in a spirit of humility and for the remission of his sins, used to be struck frequently and sharply almost for whole days by two or three brothers. The aforesaid Saturday came when he would leave this world. Trusting in, and comforted by, the Lord, he stood as usual in the choir at mass. He began the office 'Liberator meus, Kyrie eleison' and the Gradual that followed. I was standing by his side. When the Gospel had been read, he began the Offertory 'Benedictus es, Deus,' and summoned by God, he began to sink little by little. With an anguished heart straight away I took him up in my arms. The astonished brothers rushed forward. He asked that he be allowed, if possible, to die near the altar. In the end he was carried to the infirmary. When Vespers was over, he took the Lord's Body and Blood in communion on that same day as he had on previous days, and commended his soul into his Creator's hands. He was buried the following day by Simon, the revered bishop of Worcester, in the view of the clergy and of all the townspeople.[1] A comet appeared on 8 October for almost five days.[2]

[1133] Most of London including its chief church of St Paul the apostle was burnt down in the week of Pentecost which was on 14 May.[1] In the thirty-third year of the reign of Henry, the English king, on Wednesday, on the same day in the year's cycle when his brother and predecessor, King William Rufus, was slain, and Henry himself first began to rule, a dramatic phenomenon occurred. This was when the said king was at the coast putting off the Channel crossing, even though the wind was more often than not favourable for the transfretation. At length on the aforesaid day at midday the king went down to the sea to cross over, surrounded, as is usual with kings, by bands of knights. Suddenly a cloud appeared in the sky, which was visible throughout England, though of varying size. In some places indeed the day only appeared darkened, but in others it was so dark that men needed the guidance of candlelight to do

---

[1] *Worcester Cartulary*, p. 31, shows that Uhtred was precentor as early as 1092.
[2] This comet is not recorded in other English annals.

[1] This fire seems to have occurred in 1132, see M. Brett, 'The annals of Bermondsey, Southwark and Merton', in *Church and City*, ed. D. Abulafia (Cambridge, 1992), pp. 279–310, at 299, though JW gives a precise date.

indigerent. Vnde rex latusque regium ambientes et alii complures mirantes, et in celum oculos leuantes, solem ad instar noue lune lucere conspexerunt, qui tamen non diu se uno modo habebat. Nam aliquando latior, aliquandiu subtilior, quandoque incuruior, quandoque erectior, nunc solito modo firmus, modo mouens, et ad instar uiui argenti motus et liquidius uidebatur. Asserunt quidam eclypsim solis factam fuisse. Quod si uerum est, tunc *sol erat in capite draconis, et luna in cauda, uel sol in cauda et luna in capite* in .v. signo leonis*ʰ* in .xvii. gradu ipsius signi. Erat autem tunc luna .xxvii.² Eodem etiam die et eadem hora, stelle quamplurime apparuere. Necnon eodem die cum naues ad predicti regis transiturum parate in litore anchoris firmarentur, mari pacatissimo uentoque permodico existente, cuiusdam nauis magne anchore a terra quasi ui aliqua subito auulse sunt, nauisque commota, multis mirantibus eamque tenere nitentibus nec ualentibus, sibi*ⁱ* proximam nauem commouit, et sic .viii. naves ui ignota commote sunt, ut nulla illarum illesa remansisset. Multi quoque dixerunt se eodem die et circa eandem horam in Eboracensi prouincia ecclesias quamplures quasi sudore perualido madefactas. Hec omnia .iiii. non.*ʲ* Aug., .iiii. etiam feria, ut dictum est, contigerunt. *ᵏ*Sexta autem feria eiusdem septimane, scilicet .ii. non. eiusdem mensis, summo mane in pluribus Anglie partibus terremotus factus est magnus. *ˡ*Fuerunt etiam qui dicerent se in subsequenti eptomada, feria .ii., sexto uidelicet idus mensis eiusdem, cum luna foret .iii., ipsam uidisse primam qualis in tali etate esse solet, paruoque interuallo uespere eiusdem se ipsam uidisse magnam, ad modum scuti rotundi, *ᵐ*ualdeque rutilantis.*ᵐ* Dicebant quoque plures se ipsa nocte uidisse duas lunas inter se quasi longitudine haste unius distantes. Rex autem Heinricus mare transiens reliquit Angliam, petit Normanniam, non ulterius uita comite rediturus uel uisurus Angliam.³ Mense Nouembri ciuitas Wigornia, ut crebro solet, incendio conflagrauit.⁴

ʰ *interlin. above* .xvii. C³, *om.* (G), id est leone H²   *ⁱ om.* (G)   *ʲ interlin. by early modern hand* C   *ᵏ paragraph mark here* C   *ˡ paragraph mark here* C   *ᵐ⁻ᵐ written over erasure* C³, et magni (G)

---

² Walter of Malvern's rendering of Petrus Alfonsi, *Sententia de dracone*, published by J. M. Millás Vallicrosa, 'La aportación astronomica de Pedro Alfonso', *Sefarad*, iii (1943), 66–105, at p. 87, which uses the text of Oxford, Bodleian Library Auct. F.1.9, fos. 96ʳ–99ʳ, a manuscript in which the script of both JW and C² appear. As Charles Burnett has pointed out to me, John in using his source here confused the conditions necessary for a solar eclipse with those for a lunar eclipse.
³ These celestial phenomena and the earthquake are variously recorded in English

anything. The king and his followers and many others walked about, marvelling greatly, raised their eyes to heaven, and saw the sun shining as though it were a new moon, though it did not keep the same appearance for long. One moment it was broader, the next it was narrower, now curved, now straight, now steady as usual, now moving, and seemed quivering and liquid like quicksilver. Some claim that an eclipse of the sun had taken place. If this was the case, then the sun was in the head of *Draco* and the moon in the tail or the sun was in the tail and the moon in the head of the fifth sign, *Leo*, in the seventeenth degree of that sign. The moon was twenty-seven days old.[2] At the same day and hour, many stars appeared. That day, when the ships were anchored on the shore in readiness for the king's journey, and the sea was at its calmest and only a slight wind was stirring, all of a sudden one of the ship's big anchors was wrenched, as though by some force, from their moorings, the ship began to move, to the amazement of those trying unsuccessfully to hold it in position. It moved the ship next to it, and in this way eight vessels were shifted by an unknown force so that not one remained undamaged. Many reported that at the same time and on the same day many churches in the diocese of York were sweating as though in a flood of perspiration. It is reported that all these things happened on Wednesday, 2 August. On the Friday of the same week, that is on the fourth of the month, there was a great earthquake at daybreak in many parts of England. Some say that on the Monday of the following week, that is on 8 August, when the moon was three days old, she appeared as she normally does at that age, and then, a little later in the same evening she appeared full like a round and very brilliant shield. Many also say that on the same night two moons were also seen, about a spear's length apart. King Henry crossed overseas, leaving England for Normandy. He was never to return to England or to see it alive.[3] In November Worcester was consumed by fire, a frequent occurrence.[4]

sources under this year, though the Margam and Winchester Annals (*Ann. Mon.* i. 13, ii. 49) assign them to 1132. The darkness and the peculiar appearance of the sun, the precise location of both sun and moon, the age of the moon, and its shield-like aspect are not recorded elsewhere. When they give a date, the chroniclers agree with JW's date for the eclipse (Wednesday, 2 Aug.) though WM *HN* 457 (pp. 11–12) dates Henry's journey to 5 Aug. (which he erroneously says was a Wednesday). 2 Aug. was a Wednesday in 1133. ASC associates a solar eclipse with the death of Henry I two years later in 1135, and, as it has no annals for 1133–4, its 1135 eclipse, which it dates to 2 Aug., must be that referred to in the other chronicles under 1133. The other celestial phenomena are peculiar to JW.

    [4] This fire is not recorded elsewhere.

[1134]*ᵃ* 1157 Rotbertus frater regis Heinrici, quondam comes Normannie sed postmodum ab illo *ᵇ*Normannie morante apud quoddam castrum quod Tenercebrei dicitur*ᵇ* in bello captus, et diu in custodia per Angliam positus, apud Cairdif *ᶜ*defunctus, Glaornamque deportatus, in pauimento ecclesie quod est ante altare, magno cum honore sepelitur.*ᶜ*[1] Godefridus Bathoniensis episcopus*ᵈ* obiit, cui processu temporis successit quidam monachus Rotbertus nomine, Flandrensis genere, sed natus in partibus Anglie.*ᵉ* Ex monacho fit episcopus Rotbertus, sic enim disposuit Wintoniensis episcopus Heinricus,*ᶠ* non tunc sed nunc Romane ecclesie legatus.[2]

Referebant qui bene nouerunt ea tempestate quendam in Apulia fuisse Saracenum, a Christiana fide alienum, impietate plenum, indeficienti philargiria secularibus inhians rebus. Hostili manu fines Christianorum inuadens deuastabat; binos captos baptizatos secum ducens, in magna animi alacritate ad propria remeat. Ferreis uinculis artatos incarcerat. Satisfaciendarum epularum dies illuxerat. Cum nobilibus residens ad mensam Saracenus, ut Christianam fidem illudat, unum de incarceratis ut erat uinculatus adduci et inpresentiarum sistere mandat. Adductus miles Christianus uenit*ᵍ* totus pauidus, in Domino Deo suo totus tamen confisus. Corporis trepidat infirmitas, mentis autem quam habet in Deum solidatur firmitas. Suadetur abnegare Christianitatem. Renuit hoc ille ob nanciscendam regni celestis sullimem dignitatem. Hinc ira succensum diabolicum membrum,*ʰ* mandat ilico monstruosum parari tormentum. In presentia | conuiuantium uermis attrahitur non corpore longus, sed horridus totus, grossus et uelut coluber tortuosus. Astanti Dei seruo ex omni parte nudo monstrum illud nunc sursum, nunc iusum, nunc hac, nunc illac se retorquens morsus infigere querit. At quoniam athleta diuinus lignum erat uergens ad austrum,[3] penitus illum mordere nequit. Fortassis enim quod horridus horreat, in Dei famulo toto Deo signato spectat, quod etiam in sancto corpore

p. 386

ᵃ 1130 *erroneously corrected from* 1135 *C*³, 1134 *H, (G) started* 1133 *at this point* *ᵇ⁻ᵇ om. H*² *ᶜ⁻ᶜ* in Walia defunctus Glauuorne magno cum honore humatur *H* *ᵈ* .xvii. Kl. Sept. *add. (G)* *ᵉ* Normannie *(G)* *ᶠ H ended 1134 at this point* *ᵍ interlin. above* totus *C*³ *ʰ* menbrum *C*

[1] *Cart. Gloc*, i. 15 and Gregory of Caerwent (BL Cotton Vespasian A. V, fo. 197ᵛ) also record Robert Curthose's death (which they date to 3 Feb.) and burial at Gloucester 'coram principali altare'. The wording of the Winchcombe Annals (*Ann. Winchcombe*, p. 127) seems closer to the Gloucester sources than to JW, but omits the day of death. Torigni (*GND* viii. 16 (ii. 232)) dates it to 10 Feb. and places it at Bristol. The Bec Annals record his death on 10 Feb. 1135 (L. Delisle, 'Les courtes annales du Bec', *Notices et documents*

[1134] Robert, King Henry's brother, formerly duke of Normandy, who was later captured by the king in Normandy at a battle near the castle of Tinchebrai, and who had been imprisoned for some time, died at Cardiff, and was taken to Gloucester, where he was buried with due honour before the altar in the church's floor.[1] Bishop Godfrey of Bath died, and was in due course succeeded by a monk called Robert, of Flemish extraction, though he had been born in England. From a monk he was raised to the episcopacy by the action of Bishop Henry of Winchester, who was not at that time, though he is now, legate of the Roman church.[2]

Those who were well informed reported that at that time there was a Saracen in Apulia, unfriendly to Christianity, extremely cruel, and relentlessly covetous of earthly matters. He invaded and devastated Christian territories, and with great joy returned home with two Christian captives, whom he imprisoned, bound with iron chains. A great feast took place. Whilst sitting at the table with his nobles, to make fun of the Christian faith, he ordered one of the prisoners to be brought into their presence, chained as he was. The Christian soldier was brought forward, completely terrified, yet totally confident in the Lord God. His weak body shook whilst his mind strong in its trust in God remained firm. He was asked to renounce Christianity. He refused to do so in order to win the heavenly kingdom's exalted sublimities. Then the limb of Satan, blazing with anger, ordered horrid tortures to be got ready. In front of the guests there was brought forward a snake, not very long, but completely revolting, fat and sinuous like a serpent. This monster tried to bite the upright servant of God, who was quite naked, twisting now up, now down, now here, now there. But since the athlete of God was 'a tree bending to the south',[3] the snake could not bite him. The horrible snake may have bristled, but God's servant

---

publiés par la Société de l'Histoire de France à l'occasion du cinquantième anniversaire de sa fondation (Paris, 1899), pp. 93–9, at 97). Robert had first been imprisoned at Wareham (Winchester Annals (Ann. Mon. ii. 42)) before being guarded at Devizes in the custody of Bishop Roger of Salisbury. ASC 1126 records his transfer to the custody of Robert of Gloucester, who placed him in Bristol, presumably before he was moved to Cardiff. OV HE xii. 46 (vi. 380) says Robert died at Cardiff six years after 1128 and was taken from his prison and buried at Gloucester.

[2] Under its 1135 annal G repeats the death of Bishop Godfrey, assigning it there to 16 Aug. (see below, 1136 n. 5), a date taken over by the Winchcombe Annals. Regesta iii. 46 is Stephen's grant of the bishopric of Bath to Robert of Lewes at Easter (22 Mar.) 1136. JW is the only source for his Flemish origin. On him see GS pp. xxxiv–xl.

[3] Cf. Exod. 26: 18.

morsus omnino negat. Hoc uiso, iussu tiranni uermis absentatur, Dei uero seruus denuo uinculatus incarceratur. Subintroducto*ⁱ* postmodum carceris socio, de neganda fide tyrannicus sermo perorat. Miser ille et miserandus quia lignum uergens ad aquilonem⁴ potius eligit fidem Christi negare quam uermiferum morsum tolerare. Non credens uerbis furor tyrannicus mandat miserum uermi proici dilacerandum; cuius morsibus ilico totus dilaniatur, et de medio factus pro infidelitate tartareis cruciatibus immergitur. Alter uero habitans in adiutorio Altissimi representatur;⁵ ad stipitem tyrannico iudicio ligatur, a teliferis pro fide saggittatur et sic*^j* in martyrii gloriam uita priuatur. *^k*Hec olim exulans Wincelcumbe, ab ore doctissimi uiri abbatis de Sancto Walarico audiui, et huic chronice nostre inserere curaui.*^k* ⁶

[**1135**] (1157)*^a* ⟨R⟩ex Anglorum Heinricus annis .xxxv.*^b* et .iiii. mensibus exactis ex quo regnare cepit, *^c*anno etatis .lxviiii., .iiii. non. Dec. obiit.*^c* Stephanus sororis sue filius electus in regnum Anglie a Willelmo archipresule Dorubernie .xi.*^d* kal. Ian., die dominica, rex consecratur Lundonie, ubi in Dominice Natiuitatis clementi gratia et in regia prerogatiua cum totius Anglie primoribus curiam suam tenuit.¹ *^e*Qua sacrosancta emensa festiuitate, *^f*regis Heinrici nuper defuncti corpori de Normannia*^f*

[**1136**] (1158)*^a* Angliam delato, non modica stipatus nobilium caterua*^b* rex obuiat, et ob amorem auunculi regias scapulas feretro supponens, cum baronibus suis*^c* corpus Rædingum deportari fecit. In missarum celebrationibus et oblationibus diuersis ac pretiosis, in elemosinis pauperum numerose multitudini expensis, exequiis rite celebratis, membris feretro expositis, tumulo ex more composito, in beatissime ac gloriosissime uirginis Marie principali ecclesia, quam ipse rex Heinricus pro remedio anime sue terris, siluis, pratis,

---

ⁱ intro- *interlin.* C, summoto *(G)*   *^j interlin.* C³   *^{k-k} om. (G)*

^a corrected from 1136 (1158) C³, *(G) did not start a new annal at this point*   *^b from* .xxxvi. H², .xxxvi. *(G)*   *^{c-c}* .iiii. Non. Dec. anno etatis .lxix. obiit Normannie H²   *^d corrected from* .xiii. C, .xiii. H² *(G)*   *^e (G) began annal 1134 at this point, omitting the first word* 'qua'   *^{f-f} written over erasure* C³

^a corrected from 1137 (1159). The new annal starts in the middle of a sentence C³, *neither G nor H began a new annal at this point*   *^b* uel turma *interlin.* C³   *^c* Non. Ianuarii *add. (G)*

---

⁴ Cf. Exod. 26: 20.   ⁵ Ps. 90: 1.
⁶ It is not known when either John or the abbot of St Valéry were at Winchcombe. The

seemed marked with the sign of God, and it was unable to bite in any way his holy body. At this the tyrant ordered the snake to be taken away, and God's servant was again incarcerated in chains. Afterwards his fellow prisoner was brought forward, and the tyrant asked him to deny his faith. The poor wretch, because he was 'a tree bending to the north',[4] chose rather to deny his faith in Christ, than to endure the snake's bites. The raging tyrant did not believe his recantation, and ordered the wretched man to be flung to the snake to be torn apart. There and then he was mangled by the snake's bites, and, taken away from their midst, he was cast because of his lack of faith into the tortures of Hell. But his companion was shown as living with the help of God the Highest;[5] he was tied by the tyrant's command to a stake, was shot at by archers for his faith, and thus deprived of his life so as to obtain the glory of martyrdom. I heard this account, when I was once exiled at Winchcombe, from the most learned abbot of St Valéry, and took care to insert it in our chronicle.[6]

[1135] Thirty-five years and four months after he had begun to reign, and in his sixty-ninth year, Henry, king of the English, died on 2 December. Stephen, his sister's son, was elected to the kingship, and was consecrated king at London on Sunday, 22 December, by William, archbishop of Canterbury. There Stephen, with the power of mercy and exercising his royal prerogative, held his court at Christmas in the company of all the greater men of the kingdom.[1] After the holy festival, the body of the recently deceased Henry

[1136] was brought from Normandy to England. The king went to meet it accompanied by a goodly band of nobles, and bearing, through love for his uncle, the bier on his shoulders. With the help of his barons, he brought the body to Reading. Masses were said, various precious offerings made, alms handed out to crowds of the poor, obsequies duly celebrated, Henry's body was exposed on a hearse, and it was placed with great honour in a tomb made according to custom in the principal church of the most holy and blessed Virgin Mary. For the good of his soul King Henry had

story was printed by Pertz (MGH SS xiii. 133), who noted that Lambert was abbot of St Valéry from 1106 to c.1140.

  [1] Henry I died on 1 Dec.: see WM *HN* 457 (p. 12), OV *HE* xiii. 19 (vi. 448–9), or HH *HA* vii. 43 (p. 490). ASC dates his death one day earlier, 30 Nov. WM *HN* 461 (p. 13) and Gervase (i. 94) agree with JW MS C's revised date for Stephen's coronation, which other sources date 15 (OV xiii. 20 (vi. 454)), 19 (*LE* iv. 6 (p. 285)), and 25 Dec. (ASC), and 1 Jan. (John of Hexham, SD ii. 286).

pascuis, ac uariis ditarat ornamentis, ante altare magna honorificentia
regia reconditur gleba.

[C³H²]

*d*Rex hic Heinricus terrenis
   rebus opimus,
Ereptus penis, celi potiatur
   amoenis.*d* 1

Quo sepulto, et Stephano regnante, nec non multo ubique locorum
per Angliam et Normanniam dirupto pacis foedere plurima fit
distirbatio.*e* *f*Quisque in alterum caput eleuat.

[C³H²]

*f*Que oritur discordia in uastando omnia nobilium et ignobi-
lium, alta, magna,*g* ac diuersa
subintrat   moenia.   *f*Quisque
alium rebus spoliat. *f*Potens
impotentem ui opprimit. *f*Ques-
tum super hoc agentem minis
territat. *f*Neci traditur qui resis-
tit. *f*Opulenti regni optimates
diuitiis affluentes minime pro-
curant quam impie tractentur
miseri. Sibi suisque dumtaxat
consulunt. *f*Vite necessariis castella et *h*oppida muniunt;*h* manu
militari *i*cum armis*i* instruunt.
Timent regni mutationem, non
animo supernam perpendentes
dispositionem;   inuestigabiles
enim sunt uie eius.²

Dum autem ob regium terrorem, rugitui leonis comparandum,³
omnia deberent paci cedere, iam in pluribus locis, et maxime in
Walia, depopulatio et depredatio minime cessat.

---

   d-d *rubricated* C, *written in capitals* H²   *e* distirbutio C, distributio
(G)   *f* *paragraph mark* C   *g* *om.* H²   *h-h* *over erasure*
C³   *i-i* *om.* H²

---

¹ JW's 5 Jan. for Henry's burial is confirmed by the Reading Annals (*UAG*, p. 11). As
pointed out in *Reading Abbey Cartularies*, ed. B. W. Kemp (2 vols., Camden Fourth Series,
xxxi, xxxiii; London, 1986–7), i. 14 n. 1, the date usually given (4 Jan.) is Gervase's date

himself endowed this principal church, with lands, woods, meadows
and pastures. and with many ornaments. He was buried before the
altar with all the honour befitting a king.

May this king so rich in earthly
  goods
Rejoice in heaven, freed from
  pains![1]

After Henry's burial, and with Stephen as king, it was not long
before there was much discord throughout England and Normandy,
and the bonds of peace were torn apart. Each man rose against his
fellow.

Conflict arose, infiltrating the
tall, massive, and diverse fortifications of both greater and
lesser alike, and devastating
everything. Each man plundered
the goods of others. The strong
violently oppressed the weak.
They deter with threats any
criticism of their actions. They
kill those who resist. The rich
nobles of the kingdom, in their
affluence and wealth, are not in
the least bothered by the way the
poor are unjustly treated. They
care only for themselves and
theirs. They store castles and
towns with necessary provisions.
They garrison them with armed
followers. They fear any change
in the kingdom, not considering
the divine dispensation: whose
ways are past finding out.[2]

When all should be at peace through fear of the king, who should be
as a roaring lion,[3] there is in many places, particularly in Wales,
depopulation and devastation.

(*Chronica*, Gervase, i. 95) for the bringing of Henry's body to England. For an account of
Henry I's foundation and endowment of Reading Abbey, see *Reading Abbey Cartularies*,
i. 13–19.
  [2] Rom. 11: 33.   [3] Cf. Prov. 20: 2.

[C³H²]

Hinc conicere quis poterit, quod
mediocri prudentia imbecillique
fortitudine, et magis iniustitia
quam iustitia a quibus regi
deberet, regitur Anglia. In
regnante auaritia et in cuiuslibet
honoris ambitione pessima, uix
aliqua intercurrit, que mater est
uirtutum, temperantia.³

ʲRex Anglorum Stephanusᵏ equestri milite et pedestri exercitu
armato Domnaniam penetrat, longi temporis spatio Exancestrense
castellum obsessurus quod Baldwinus de Reduers cognomine contra
regiam maiestatem munierat. At demum his qui intus erant, neces-
sariisˡ deficientibus, dextris datis et acceptis, ipse Baldwinus cum
uxore et filiis exheredatur et Anglia expellitur.⁴

[(G)]

Obierunt uenerabilis Radingensis
abbas ecclesie Ansgerus .vi. K.
Febr., Godefridus Bathoniensis
episcopus, .xvii. K. Sept.⁵
Defuncto rege Henrico .iiii. N.
Decembr., fit statim in K.
Ianuarii graue proelium apud
Guher inter Normannos et
Walenses, ubi quingenti et sede-
cim ex his et ex illis corruerunt.
Corpora uero eorum a lupis
horribiliter per agros discerpta
et deuorata sunt. Facta est exinde
magna nimis Walensium irruptio,
ecclesiarum, uillarum, segetum,

ʲ G started its annal 1135 (1157) at this point   ᵏ om. H²   ˡ uite necessariis
H²

³ This comment on the woes of Stephen's reign like that of GS 8 (p. 14) mentions
disorders in Wales, as do the Margam Annals (Ann. Mon. i. 13–4). GS follows with the
Gower campaign (see below, 1136 n. 6), and Margam mentions the involvement of
Flemings. G's interpolation which follows immediately after the two brief entries on
Baldwin of Redvers' rebellion and two obits (see below, 1136 nn. 4, 5), provides valuable
information on the Welsh campaigns of Stephen's reign. WM HN 465 (p. 20) and ASC

From this anyone can see with how little foresight and with what feeble power, with what injustice rather than with the justice due from rulers, England is governed. Temperance the mother of all virtues is scarcely to be found when greed and the petty search for every kind of honour everywhere rules.[3]

Stephen, the English king, invaded Devon with a mounted and a foot force, and for some time besieged the castle of Exeter which Baldwin de Redvers was defending against royal authority. In the end the garrison became short of provisions, terms of surrender were agreed and Baldwin with his wife and children was disinherited and expelled from England.[4]

Ansger, the revered abbot of Reading, died on 27 January, and Godfrey, bishop of Bath, on 16 August.[5] Immediately after the death of King Henry on 2 December, a fierce battle took place on 1 January in Gower between the Normans and the Welsh in which 516 of both armies died. Their bodies were scattered horribly among the fields and eaten up by wolves. Thereupon the Welsh invaded in force, violently destroyed churches, townships, crops, and

have laments on the miseries of Stephen's reign. On the possible interconnections between these laments, see E. King, 'Introduction', in *The Anarchy of King Stephen's Reign*, ed. E. King (Oxford, 1994), pp. 1–3, though the suggested links between ASC, WM, and JW seem unlikely here. HH *HA* x. 3 (p. 704) refers to Stephen's failure to keep promises.

[4] The fullest account of the rebellion of Baldwin de Redvers, which was mentioned by ASC as the first rebellion against Stephen, is in *GS* 15–21 (pp. 30–44). *Charters of the Redvers Family and the Earldom of Devon, 1090–1217*, ed. R. Bearman (Devon and Cornwall Record Society, n.s. xxxvii, 1994), pp. 5–6, considers this rebellion.

[5] G's year for Ansger's death is confirmed by the Reading Annals (*UAG*, p. 11), and the day by the obit in BL Cotton Vespasian E.V, fo. 11ᵛ (see *Heads*, p. 63). For Godfrey of Bath's death (which G repeats here but with a precise date), see above, 1134 n. 2.

animalium grauissima per eosdem Walenses longe lateque destructio, castellorum seu aliarum munitionum exustio, hominum innumerabilium, diuitum et pauperum, occisio, dispersio, et in exteras terras uenditio.[6] Inter quos nobilis atque amabilis Ricardus Gisleberti filius, eorundem Walensium preuentus insidiis .xvii. K. Maii perimitur, corpusque eius Glaornam delatum, in capitulo fratrum honorifice sepelitur.[7]

[1136] (1158) Subsecutum est hoc anno, bellum aliud grauissimum apud Karadigan, mense Octobrio, ebdomada secunda, in quo tanta hominum strages facta est ut, exceptis uiris in captiuitatem abductis, de mulieribus captiuitatis decies centum decime remanerent, maritis earum cum paruulis innumeris, partim aqua demersis, partim flamma consumptis, partim gladio trucidatis. Eratque ibi magnam uidere miseriam, cum fracto ponte super fluuium Teuwi, fieret huc illucque discursantibus pons humanorum corporum siue equorum inibi dimersorum horrenda congeries.[8]

---

[6] The Gower campaign is undated elsewhere. It was directed by Hywel ap Maredudd and ended with a Welsh victory somewhere between Loughor and Swansea (Gir. Cambr., *Itinerarium*, i. 9 (vi. 78)). It is recorded without a date, but with a description of Welsh destructiveness in *GS* 8 (pp. 14–16), which states that the 516 slain was the total force opposing the Welsh.

[7] Richard fitz Gilbert was the son of Gilbert fitz Clare, and ruler of Cardigan and the honour of Clare. His ambush, which took place at the 'evil pass' of 'Coit Wroneu' (Gir.

beasts far and wide, burnt down castles and other fortifications, slew, scattered, and sold into captivity abroad innumerable men, both rich and poor.[6] Among these the noble and personable Richard fitz Gilbert was ambushed and slain by these same Welshmen on 15 April. His body was taken to Gloucester and honourably buried in the chapter house of the brethren.[7]

[1136] The following year there was another very great battle at Cardigan in the second week of October. There was such slaughter that besides those men taken into captivity there remained 10,000 captive women whose husbands with numberless children were drowned, consumed by flames, or put to the sword. When the bridge over the river Tevi was broken it was piteous to see crowds passing backwards and forwards across a bridge formed by a horrible mass of human corpses and horses drowned in the river.[8]

Cambr., *Itinerarium*, i. 4 (vi. 47–8)) on the borders between Gwent and Brycheiniog, is described also in *GS* 9 (p. 16) and simply recorded *s.a.* 1136 in *AC* (though version C specifically mentions an invasion by Gruffydd ap Rhys which preceded the ambush), and under 1135 (*recte* 1136) in *Brut* Pen., p. 51, Her. pp. 112–13, BS pp. 144–5, 308, and noted by Gir. Cambr., *Itinerarium*, i. 4 (vi. 47–8).

[8] The battle of Crug Mawr, which is again undated elsewhere, was the culmination of a general rising throughout South Wales which followed the earlier Welsh successes. It is named by Gir. Cambr., *Itinerarium*, ii. 118 (vi. 118), and is just north of Cardigan. It is described in *GS* 9 (pp. 16–18), and recorded in *AC*, p. 40 (1136), *Brut* Pen., p. 51, Her. pp. 112–15, BS pp. 144–7 (1135, *recte* 1136), and Gir. Cambr. Both *AC* and *Brut* speak of another Cardigan campaign earlier in the same year. G alone provides dates for the campaign and battle. The Winchcombe Annals (*Ann. Winchcombe*, p. 127) repeat G's Welsh

[C³H²]

ᵐDorubernensis archiepiscopus Willelmus apud uillam suam quandamⁿ defunctus, Cantuuarie sepelitur.⁹

[C³]

ᵒVir magne prudentie, Wido Persorensis abbas, obiit.ᵒ ¹⁰

[(G)]

Dorubernensis archiepiscopus Willelmus .xv. patriarchatus sui anno .xii. Kl. Decembr. Cantuarie decessit.⁹

[(G)]

Vir magne sed mundane prudentie Wido Persorensis abbas .ii. Nonas Aug. obiit.¹⁰

[1137] (1159) Godefridus Wincelcumbensis abbas ecclesie .xvii. prelationis sue anno .ii. Non. Martii, uita decessit.¹¹

Sequenti ebdomada uidelicet idibus Martii magne religionis et castitatis uir Benedictus Theokeberiensis abbas ecclesie .xiiii. prelationis sue anno migrauit ad Dominum.¹²

[C³]

[1137] (1159)ᵃ ᵇMagne religionis et castitatis uir ᶜBenedictus Theodekesberiensis ecclesie abbas obiit.ᵇᶜ ¹

Hic Dei seruus in beatissime ac gloriosissime Virginis Dei genitricis p. 387 seruitio totus erat deuotus. Diatim | nanque horis decantatis aut missam ipse festiue celebrare aut audire solebat in illius honore. Non secus agentem nouimus domnum prioremᵈ Wigornensem.² Et quis sperauit in ea, et desertus est ab ea? Nemo, inquam, nemo. Abbas

---

ᵐ H² started its annal 1136 at this point   ⁿ om. though there is a blank space
H²   ᵒ⁻ᵒ written over erasure C³, uiri religionis eximie et magne prudentie abbatis de Persora Wido Non. Aug. de Wincelcumbe Godefridus, de Teodekesbyrie Benedictus abbas idus Mar. hinc uite modum fecerunt. Exemptis mundo det summus iuiere summo H²

ᵃ corrected from 1138 (1160) C³, H² om. C³'s 1137 text up to 1137 n. h, G started its 1137 (1159) under 1136 above   ᵇ⁻ᵇ placed the death of Benedict of Tewkesbury in a consolidated entry at the end of 1136 H², see 1136 n. o.   ᶜ⁻ᶜ over erasure C³
ᵈ Warinum add. (G)

---

entries, though the Gower campaign is placed last after the ambush, death, and burial of Richard fitz Gilbert. Gregory of Caerwent (BL Cotton Vespasian A. V, fo. 197ʳ) reports

William, archbishop of Canterbury, died at one of his townships and was buried at Canterbury.⁹

Guy, abbot of Pershore, a man of great prudence, died.¹⁰

William, archbishop of Canterbury, died at Canterbury on 20 November in the fifteenth year of his patriarchate.⁹

Guy, abbot of Pershore, a man of great, though worldly, prudence, died on 4 August.¹⁰

[1137] Godfrey, abbot of Winchcombe, died on 6 March, in the seventeenth year of his abbacy.¹¹

The following week on 15 March Abbot Benedict of Tewkesbury, a very devout and chaste man, departed to the Lord in the fourteenth year of his abbacy.¹²

[1137] Abbot Benedict of Tewkesbury, a very devout and chaste man, died.¹

This servant of God was completely devoted to the most blessed and glorious Mother of God. Chanting the hours every day, he would either celebrate on a festival or hear a mass in her honour. We know that the lord prior of Worcester does likewise.² Who has ever put his faith in Mary and been let down by her? No one, I say, no one. As the

---

the ambush and the Gower campaign, but in reverse order, as in the Winchcombe Annals, and under 1137 records Payn fitz John's death and burial (see 1137 n. 7) *before* the battle of Crug Mawr. For these Welsh campaigns, see Lloyd, *History of Wales*, ii. 461–74.

⁹ Canterbury Annals (*UAG*, pp. 5, 80) and Gervase, *Chronica* (i. 99) give 21 Nov. (as do the obits listed in Greenway, *Fasti* ii. 4) against G's 20 Nov. for the day of William's death.

¹⁰ The Tewkesbury Annals (*Ann. Mon.* i. 46) assign Guy's death to 1137 (see *Heads*, p. 59). The JW MSS H (5 Aug.) and G (4 Aug.) alone name the day.

¹¹ Godfrey's death is under 1138 in the Winchcombe Annals (*Ann. Winchcombe*, p. 128), under 1136 in the JW MS H, and under 1137 in G. G's day for his death is also in the Winchcombe Annals (see *Heads*, p. 79).

¹² *Heads*, p. 73, notes obits giving the day of death as 8 and 15 Mar. C inserts his death (without a date) in the next annal (see below 1137 n. 1), as do the Tewkesbury Annals (*Ann. Mon.* i. 46).

¹ G had entered Benedict's death under 1136 (see above, 1136 n. 12).

² Warin as identified by G. On him see *Worcester Cartulary*, p. lvii. Osbert of Clare (*The Letters of Osbert of Clare, Prior of Westminster*, ed. E. W. Williamson (London, 1929), *Ep.* 13) in a letter to Warin refers to an accompanying tract on the Conception.

predictus Sanctissime Marie capellanus dum exitum ageret ex Egypto, alter capellanus apud uillam nostram*e* Linderyche dictam somnium per noctem sumpserat.³ Cui astitit in uisione persona euangelicans ei nuntia bona. 'Surge,' inquit, 'surge; Teodekesberiensis abbas, Sancte Marie capellanus, in proximo modum faciet uite. Et tu capellanus eius es, licet non tanti nec talis meriti.' Hoc tertio factum est. Euigilans ille, illustri cuidam monacho prope quiescenti somnium narrauit. Quod ipse ex Dei et sue dulcissime Matris parte uisum oportere fieri probauit. Moratus ibidem instante necessitate illo die, crastino per Wigorniam adiit Teodekesberiam, sed Virginis Dei capellanum repperit humatum, cuius in manus Creatoris mox commendat spiritum'.

[C³]

De uisione quam de abbate uidit quidam Michael nomine monachus sancte Teodekesberiensis ecclesie.

Nocte dehinc .iii. migrationis eius e seculo, cuidam Theodekesberiensi cenobite Michael uocabulo, quiescenti in stratu talis de illo ostensa est uisio. Visum sibi est uidere se in ecclesia fuisse, ante sanctum altare stetisse, orationi prolixe incubuisse. Qua finita, dum reditum ageret per claustrum, aspicit lumine repletum totum capitulum, in quo erat abbatis sepulcrum. Appropians et introspiciens, uidit plurimam uirginum multitudinem circumsedentem, stolis albis amictam, ardentes lampades manibus tenentem. Et quia cultus iustitie silentium est, non uox aliqua, nec musitatio inter illas audiebatur. Gubernatrix uirginum

aforesaid abbot and chaplain of the most holy Mary was about to depart this world, her other chaplain was asleep at our township at Lindridge.[3] Someone appeared to him in a dream, announcing good news, 'Get up,' this person said, 'get up! The abbot of Tewkesbury and chaplain of St Mary is about to depart this life. You are her chaplain although not worthy of so great or of such an honour.' This happened three times. When he awakened, he told the story of the dream to a well-known monk who lay near to him. He demonstrated that this vision had been brought about through the power of God and of that of His sweetest Mother. That day the prior remained at Lindridge because of pressing duties. Going to Tewkesbury via Worcester the next day, he found that the chaplain of the Virgin of God had been buried and had entrusted his soul into his Creator's hands.

Concerning the vision of the abbot seen by a Tewkesbury monk called Michael.

Three nights after this abbot's death, a vision concerning him was seen by Michael, a Tewkesbury monk, as he lay asleep in bed. In the vision he saw himself standing before the holy altar in the church, rapt in frequent prayers. When he had finished, and was returning through the cloister, he saw that the whole chapter-house, where the abbot lay buried, was filled with light. Approaching and looking into the chapter-house, he saw a throng of many virgins sitting around it, clad in white albs, holding bright lamps in their hands. Because justice is worshipped in silence, no voice, not even a subdued murmur, was heard among them. The

---

[3] Lindridge (Worcs.) had been associated with Worcester since the time of Offa.

illarum sole splendidior uisa est, lucidissimam lampadem in manibus ferens, abbatis loco presidebat. Et forte maris stella fuit hec benedicta puella. Que quia regularis discipline preceptrix est et domna, et bene nouit ordinem quo cenobite cuilibet non licet loqui post completorium, omnino dedignabatur frangere silentium. Signum facit ad proxime sibi dextra leuaque sedentes uirgines, signo mandans, ut surgentes ad sui capellanum tumulum uadant, et quam reuerenter ibidem se res habeat diligenter considerent. Cuius iussis obtemperantes surgunt, locum sepulchri uisitant, leuique motu reuoluto lapide intus aspiciunt, et omnia conuenienter parata conspiciunt. Recluso tumulo, amplexo mento dextera signo[f] nuntiant omnia in summa reuerentia completa de capellano suo. Sic disparuit uisio, et ut credimus Imperatrix reginarum et Saluatrix animarum cum speciosis pedissequis suis summi Regis, beatissime ac dulcissime sue prolis, stellato se recipit solio. [g]Godefridus abbas Wincelcumbensis ecclesie obiit.[4]

---

[f] *letters much spaced out* C   [g] *paragraph mark here* C

---

[4] See above, 1136 n. 11.

leader of the virgins shone more brightly than the sun, holding a very bright lamp in her hands, and presided over them in the abbot's place. And the blessed maiden sparkled as brightly as the star of the sea. As teacher and head of regular discipline she knew well enough the practice by which nuns were not allowed to talk after compline. No one dared in any way break the silence. She raised her right hand to those virgins seated near her, and directed them to get up and go to the tomb of their chaplain, and carefully consider how reverently matters had been arranged. Obeying her orders they went to the burial place, moved the tombstone, and looking inside saw that everything had been fittingly disposed. The stone was put back, and they announced by the gesture of holding their chin with their right hand that everything had been carried out with the greatest reverence for their chaplain. The vision vanished and it is to be believed that the empress of queens and saviour of souls in the company of the distinguished attendants of the most exalted King, and her most blessed and most sweet offspring, were received in the heavenly kingdom. Godfrey, abbot of Winchcombe, died.[4]

*h*Rex Anglorum Stephanus, mense Martio, ante Pasca *i*quod erat .iii. idus Aprilis,*i* mare transiens, in transmarinis partibus moratur.[5]

*j*Rex Walie Griffinus filius Res, dolo coniugis sue circumuentus, defungitur.[6] *k*Walenses in defensione sue natiue terre, non solum a Normannicis diuitibus, sed etiam a Flandrensibus*l* multa perpessi pluribus utrinque peremptis, deuictis tamen *m*ad ultimum*m* Flandrensibus,*n* non cessant in circuitu omnia uastare,*o* uillas ac castella uastando comburere, omnes resistentes sibi simul cum innocentibus et nocentibus neci tradere. Inter quos unus miles, Paganus nomine, uir, ut ferunt, strenuitatis magne, dum predantes Walenses*p* capere uellet et occidere, capite perforatus lancea,

[C³H²]

[(G)]

occubit;

.vi. idus Iulii occubit;

*q*cuius*r* corpus*q* Glaornam delatum in capitulo fratrum sepelitur

a Rodberto Herefordensi episcopo et abbate Walterio, Milone comite et multis aliis astantibus et lamentantibus.[7]

Feria .vi. in epdomada Pentecostes, *s*que erat .vi. idus Iunii,*s* Eboraca ciuitas cum principali monasterio conflagrauit incendio.[8] Non diu post Hrofensis ciuitas igne crematur.[9] *t*Feria ii., que erat [ ],*t* Bathoniensis ecclesia*u* et eodem mense Augusto

Facte sunt hoc anno multorum combustiones ecclesiarum: sancti Petri Eboracensis archiepiscopatus .ii. Non. Iunii, sancte Marie cum domo hospitali in eadem ciuitate die eodem cum aliis .xxxix. ecclesiis. Item ecclesie Sancte Trinitatis in suburbio

h In C a new annal started here, originally as 1139 (1151), and later corrected to 1137 (1149), the announcement of a new year being probably incorrectly prompted by mense Martio in the first entry, H² began its 1137 here, having omitted JW's previous text for that year, no new annal for G, though there is a paragraph mark *i–i* om. H² *j* Hisdem prope diebus add. before Rex (G) *k* paragraph mark here C *l* iussu quondam regis Henrici terram Walie incolentibus add. H² *m–m* in calce H² *n* adiunctis sibi multis ex Anglis predonibus et exheredatis pluribus add. (G) *o* deuastare H² *p* in sequendo add. H² *q–q* om. H² *r* cuiuus C *t–t* om. H², pridie nonas written in the mg. C³ *t–t* feria .v., .iiii. Kl. Aug. H² *u* cum ciuitate tota add. H²

[5] 'Tertia septimana Marcii' (14–20 Mar.) is OV's date for Stephen's crossing (HE xiii. 30 (vi. 481)) and is more precise than 'in Quadragesima' of HH HA x. 5 (p. 708) or 'primo tempore quadragesime' of WM HN 466 (p. 21). OV HE xiii. 30, 32 (vi. 480–6, 490–4) deals with Stephen's activities in Normandy. There is some account of Stephen's activities there in Haskins, Norman Institutions, pp. 124–6.

[6] Gruffydd ap Rhys ap Tewdwr's death is recorded in AC, p. 40, under 1137, and in

In March and before Easter (which was on 11 April), Stephen, king of the English, crossed the channel and remained overseas.[5]

The Welsh king, Gruffydd, son of Rhys, was betrayed by the treachery of his wife, and died.[6] In the defence of their native land, the Welsh were hard pressed not only by the powerful Normans, but also by the Flemings. Many were killed on both sides, but in the end the Flemings were beaten, and the Welsh laid waste all around them, setting fire to townships and castles, killing all who resisted, whether innocent or not. Among those slain was one knight, Payn, a man reputedly of great energy who wanted to take captive and slay the plundering Welsh. His head was pierced by a spear, and

he died.	he died on 10 July.

His body was carried away and buried in the chapter house of the brethren at Gloucester

by Robert, bishop of Hereford, and Abbot Walter in the grieving presence of Earl Miles and many others.[7]

On Friday in Pentecost week (it was on 8 June), York with its chief monastery was destroyed by fire.[8] A little later Rochester was burnt down.[9] On Monday, that is on [. . .] the church at Bath was consumed by fire, and

This year there were many church fires. St Peter's of the archbishops of York was burnt on 4 June, and at the same time St Mary's and the Hospital were burnt with thirty-nine other churches in the same city. A

Brut Pen. p. 52, Her. pp. 116–17, BS pp. 146–7 under 1136 (*recte* 1137), and the Margam Annals (*Ann. Mon.* i. 14), none of which refer to his wife Gwenllian's role. On him, see Lloyd, *History of Wales*, ii. 475.

[7] Payn fitz John had been a chamberlain of Henry I, and was a prominent lord on the Anglo-Welsh border, and had been sheriff of Shropshire and Hereford: see Green, *Government*, pp. 252–3. His Welsh campaign and the manner of his death are described in *GS* 12 (p. 24), though G alone gives the date of death and fills out JW's account of his burial. His death is not reported in Welsh sources, though the campaigns against which he was reacting can be reconstructed retrospectively to some extent (see Lloyd, *History of Wales*, ii. 477–8). Welsh sources mention Flemings among those suffering from the earlier Welsh attacks described in G (see above, 1136 n. 6).

[8] 4 June, G's date and the marginal date in C for the fire at York, is that in the possibly derivative Gervase, *Chronica* (Gervase, i. 100). See J. H. Harvey, 'The fire at York in 1137', *Yorkshire Archaeological Journal*, xli (1965), 365–7. 4 June was on Friday in 1137, whereas C[3]'s original 8 June was a Tuesday.

[9] Gervase, *Chronica* (Gervase, i. 100) dates the Rochester fire to 3 June. The annal in BL Cotton Nero A. VIII (*UAG*, p. 80) is close to Gervase. The Chichester annals mention fires at Rochester in 1137 (*UAG*, p. 95).

ciuitas Leogera igne combuste sunt.[10]

eiusdem ciuitatis modico post tempore.[8] Item ecclesie sancti Andree Rofensis in eodem tempore cum tota ciuitate.[9] Item ecclesie sancti Petri Bathoniensis et totius ciuitatis .vi. Kal. Aug., in eodem mense Augusto ciuitas quoque Leogera igne comburitur.[10]

Vt quorundam ueridico^v relatu agnouimus, apud Windlesoram^w uno dierum stante populo ad celebrationem misse, lux quedam infulserat interioribus ecclesie. Quo attoniti, quidam foras exierunt et eleuatis sursum oculis aspiciunt stellam insolitam celo radiantem. Reuersi, animaduertunt de radiis stelle lucem intus^x descendisse. Miraculum succedit miraculo. ^{y}Que super altare stabat uident plures^z crucem se mouentem et nunc dextra sinistram, nunc sinistra

p. 388   dextram, | more plangentium constringente. Hoc factum est tertio. Crucem dehinc totam tremere, defluenti sudore totam etiam sudare, fere medie hore spatio, postmodum^{aa} in priorem statum reuersam. ^{bb}Apud Suðwællam archiepiscopalem uillam dum in sepulturam cuiusdam pararetur fossa, reliquie quorundam sanctorum, et uitrea ampulla cum limpidissima aqua lateribus surrecta^{cc} uelut a fractura tuentibus eam reperta est. Qua infirmis data et gustata, sanitati pristine restituuntur.

[C^{3}H^2]

Vt aure percepi, precedens miraculum Wintoniensis episcopus Heinricus, sequens^{dd} uero narrauit Eboracensis archiepiscopus^{ee} Turstinus, qui cum Særesbyriensi episcopo Rogero et quibusdam aliis episcopis et regni primoribus concilium tenuerunt^{ff} apud Norðamtoniam, in plurimorum audientiam.[11]

---

^{v} om. H^2 ^{w} over erasure C^3 ^{x} quae uisa est H^2 ^{y} started on new line after a blank space on the previous line C ^{z} om. H^2 ^{aa} uero add. H^2 ^{bb} started on new line with large initial after blank space in previous line C ^{cc} surrectis H^2 ^{dd} subsequens H^2 ^{ee} archipresul H^2 ^{ff} tenuerant H^2

in the same month of August the city of Leicester also.[10]

little later Holy Trinity in the suburb of the same city was burnt down.[8] Also St Andrew's, Rochester was consumed by fire with the whole city.[9] Also St Peter's, Bath, and all the town was consumed by fire on 27 July, and in the same month of August Leicester was also burnt down.[10]

We have learnt from a truthful source that as people were hearing mass one day at Windsor, a light had shone into the interior of the church. In astonishment, some men went outside, and, looking up, saw an unusual star shining in the sky. Returning to the church, they saw that the light from the stellar rays was beaming inside. One wonder was followed by another. Many saw that the cross on the altar was moving from right to left and from left to right in the manner of people in distress. This happened three times. Then for almost half an hour the whole cross moved and was bathed in pouring sweat before taking up its former equilibrium. At the archiepiscopal township of Southwell, a grave was dug for a burial, and there were found the relics of saints and a glass flask with very clear water flowing from its sides as though from cracks. When the water was given to the sick and drunk by them, they were restored to their earlier good health.

I have learnt that Bishop Henry of Winchester narrated the first story, and Thurstan, archbishop of York, the second (both in the hearing of many), when they were attending a council at Northampton with Bishop Roger of Salisbury, some other bishops and leading men of the kingdom.[11]

---

[10] H's 29 July was a Thursday in 1137. The Bath fire is mentioned in the Chichester annals for 1137 (*UAG*, p. 95). *EEA* x. 152 (p. 113) refers to a fire in which a document of the time of Bishop Robert of Bath was lost.

[11] This Northampton meeting presumably took place between 1137 (the date given for the recorded marvels by JW) and 24 June 1139, when Roger was arrested. It might well be the council meeting recorded by JW under 1138 (see below, 1138, n. 8).

[(G)]
Fluctuabat adhuc uiam ab annis
.vii. Romana sedes propter papatum duorum Gregorii scilicet, qui
et Innocentius, et Petri, qui et
Leo.[12]

*gg*Inter Lotharium Romanorum imperatorem et Rogerium Apulie ducem oritur bellum. Diuitiis pleni, ambo hi, unus religione et dignitate superior uel excellentior, alter in confusionem sui auro prestantior. Imperialis tamen sullimitas, ut dignum et iustum est, omni regie dignitati prestat in omnibus. Ambo Rome constituunt episcopos episcoporum, Lotharius Gregorium canonice electum, Rogerus Petro Leoni Romane urbis concessere papatum. Verum hac inter eos dissensione cardinalium auctoritati et prefectorie dignitati displicente, amore pecunie nunc Gregorium in Petri expulsione, nunc Petrum in Gregorii exclusione in apostolicam sedem recipiunt. Constitutus denique a Lothario, Gregorius apostolicam regit sedem. Electus a Rogero uelut alter papa Lateranis sedit antiqui Petri Leonis soboles Petrus Leo, quos utrosque si stimulat dignitatis ambitio, neuter placens Deo. Que enim fiunt in mundo Dei seruantur iudicio, cuius iudicia abyssus multa. Causa tante dissensionis in capite*hh* omnium per orbem ecclesiarum quamplurimis annis habite, communi principum consilio statuitur dies, quo inter Romanos et Apulienses duellium fiat, et Deus omnipotens iudex omnium cui disposuerit uictoriam tribuat. Congregato exercitu fere innumerabili, Lotharius imperator, licet in infirmitate positus, castrametatus est in Apulia. Rogerius multorum milium peditum et equitum multitudine consti-patus occurrit. Pugnatum est utrinque. Deo autem sic disponente, Imperator cum suis uincens triumphat, Rogerus cum suis uictus fugam iniit. Cuius regia corona, quam sibi fecerat ut rex coronaretur, auro *ii*et gemmis pretiosis redimita et regalis lancea auro*ii* prefulgida, insidiose tamen reperta, in donum acceptabile imperatorie traditur excellentie. Qui repatrians, non multo post regnum cum uita amisit.[13]*jj*Ludouuicus rex Francorum obiit,*kk* cui filius suus Philippus*ll* successit.[14]

---

gg H² om. the rest of the annal to 1137*jj*   *hh* uel Roma *interlin. above* capite
C³   *ii–ii* om. (G)   *jj* paragraph mark here C, H² resumed the annal here
kk mense Maio obiit add H²   *ll* uel Luduuuicus *interlin. above* Philippus C³

---

[12] G refers to the schism thrice: at 1129 (see above, 1129 n. 6 above), and here twice, first with this unnecessary interpolation, and then with C's text.

[13] Italian sources do not report Lothar III's campaign against Roger in late 1136 and

For the past seven years the
Roman see was divided between
two popes, between Gregory,
that is Innocent, and Peter, also
known as Leo.[12]

A war started between Lothar, emperor of the Romans, and Roger, duke of Apulia. Both had considerable endowments, one being greater and more praiseworthy in piety and dignity, the other (to his shame) more eminent in wealth. As is right and fitting, the imperial dignity is far greater than the dignity of a king. Both set popes up in Rome, Lothar the canonically elected Gregory, Roger Peter of the Pietro Leoni family of Rome. This dissension between them brought into disrepute the authority of the cardinals and the dignity of the prefect, as through love of gold these men alternately accepted Gregory after expelling Peter, and acknowledged Peter after renouncing Gregory. Finally Gregory, set up by Lothar, ruled the apostolic see. The other pope chosen by Roger, Peter Leo of the Pierleoni, sat at the Lateran. Ambition of power spurred both rivals on, though neither of them pleased God. What they did on earth was reserved for the sentence of God, whose many judgements are deep. As this schism at the head had lasted for many years among all the churches, the princes agreed that a day should be set for battle between the Roman and Apulian supporters, and almighty God, the judge of all things, would grant victory to the side of His choice. Although ill Lothar brought together a large army and camped in Apulia, Roger met him with many thousands of soldiers, both on horseback and on foot. Battle was joined on both sides. By God's disposition the emperor and his army triumphed, Roger and his followers being defeated and put to flight. The royal crown which Roger had made for his coronation, inlaid with gold and precious stones, as well as the royal lance, resplendent with gold (however treacherously obtained), were offered to the emperor, indeed an acceptable gift. Shortly afterwards, Roger went home and lost both his kingdom and his life.[13] Louis, the French king, died, and his son, Philip, succeeded him.[14]

1137 ending in a battle in Apulia, though Otto of Freising, *Chronicon* vii. 20 (MGH SS xx. 258) reports a battle between the two near Bari. That this battle was arranged to end the schism, and that Lothar subsequently acquired a crown and lance are stories JW derived from an unknown source. Lothar III died on 4 Dec. 1137. See F. Chalandon, *Histoire de la domination normande en Italie et en Sicile* (2 vols., Paris, 1907), ii. 1–71.

[14] This is garbled. OV xii. 48 (vi. 390–1) and WM *HN* 455 (p. 10) both note the crowning of Philip as successor, and his death (before that of his father) in 1131.

^{mm}Mense Decembri rex Anglorum Stephanus Angliam rediit, et in Natiuitate Domini apud Dunstapolamⁿⁿ uillam quandam in Bedefordensi prouincia sitam, curiam suam tenuit.¹⁵

[1138]^a   ^bRomanorum .xcviiii. Conradus, ^cdux Bawarorum,^c nepos Heinrici superioris qui habuit in imperatricem filiam regis Anglorum Heinrici regnauit annis ⟨. . .⟩^{d 1}

Olim temporis gens quedam ab aquilonali parte ueniens, Turingiam terram incolendam penetrauit. Cuius terre incole ut ipsius extere terre populus expetiere, haud modicam sui incolatus portionem illi concessere. Creuit populus et multiplicatus est nimis. Longo elapso tempore, debitam Turingis abnegant deditionem. Qua de re cum armis, ut moris est eidem genti, conuenitur utrinque ut debitum exigatur et persoluatur. Id sane semel et iterum sine uulnere tamen agebatur. Tertio sine armis ab utraque^e sub pacis foedere conuenire decernunt.^f Exterorum plurima multitudo sentiens imbecillitatem Turingorum, et nec consilio nec fortitudine bene regi terram illorum conueniunt, statuto die condicto placito se ingerunt, in cautelam et tutelam sui longos cultros inuaginatos in abscondito, secum gerentes. Non in pacis consensu sed in dissensione magna placitatum est. Quid multis? Turingi uincuntur, extera gens et effera triumphat. Nam longorum cultrorum^g iam euaginatorum exercitio, fit in Turingos non modica sanguinis effusio. De terra et de cognatione sua Turingi propelluntur incole in ignominia; fere tota terra illorum cedit quibus ro|talis arriserat fortuna in uictoria. Mutato denique nomine que ad id temporis Turingia, ex longis cultellis sed uictoriosis postmodum uocata est, non Saxonia, sed Anglico elemento Sæxonia.²

^hEmensis festiuis diebus ⁱDominice natiuitatis, rex Anglorum Stephanus,ⁱ ut nominis sui coronam regaliter teneat,³ sicut prius Exanceastre, sic Bedefordense castellum sibi aduersum cum exercitu

p. 389

---

^{mm} H started its 1138 at this point   ⁿⁿ mercionalem added H²

^a originally 1140 with 1161 in the mg., .xxxviii. being substituted for .xl. in .mcxl. C, G started 1138 (1160) here   ^b H² om. C's 1138 text up to 1138 n. h, rubricated heading here De regno Conradi (G)   ^{c–c} interlin. C³   ^d blank space follows with erasure in C, required number is om. (G)   ^e parte add. (G)   ^f decernitur (G) ^g cultorum C   ^h H² resumed its annal 1138 here   ^{i–i} om. H²

---

¹⁵ OV HE xiii. 32 (vi. 494–5) and Torigni (Chronicles Stephen, etc., iv. 133) date Stephen's return to Advent, which began on 28 Nov. in 1137. HH HA x. 5 (p. 708) records Stephen spending Christmas at Dunstable in his second year, presumably 1136. Diana Greenway asked (ibid., p. 708 n. 29) whether Henry had not antedated the Dunstable

In December Stephen, the English king, returned to England, and at Christmas held his court at Dunstable, a township in Bedfordshire.[15]

[1138] Conrad, the ninety-ninth emperor of the Romans, duke of Bavaria, nephew of Henry, who had as his imperial consort the daughter of Henry, the English king, reigned ⟨. . .⟩ years.[1]

In earlier times a tribe migrating from the north came to settle in Thuringia. The inhabitants of that territory granted a sizable portion of their province to these outsiders who came searching for land. The numbers of these people greatly increased and multiplied. After some time had passed they refused to pay the Thuringians their dues. For this reason they took up arms and confronted each other (as that people are accustomed to do) so that the debt might be demanded and handed over. This happened once, and again a second time without anyone being hurt. They agreed to meet a third time unarmed under a mutual guarantee of peace. The mass of new settlers thought the Thuringians weak and claimed their land was poorly governed without good counsel or courage. On the agreed day they came to the said meeting, carrying long knives sheathed and hidden both as a ruse and as a protection. The meeting was not peaceful but very acrimonious. Need more be said? The Thuringians were overcome, the cruel outsiders triumphed. They drew their long knives and shed much Thuringian blood. The native Thuringians were driven in shame from their land and their kin. Almost all their land fell into the hands of those on whom shifting fortune had smiled. The country which until then had been called Thuringia changed its name and was called after the victorious long knives, not Saxony, but as it is put in English, *Sæxonia*.[2]

After the Christmas festival, Stephen, the English king, in order to retain his crown, as befitted a king, and his own name signified,[3] with his army besieged and captured, just as he had done earlier at Exeter,

Christmas by one year. *Regesta* iii, p. xl tabulates charters which could have been issued at Portsmouth ('in transitu meo') and Marlborough (and possibly Woodstock) at the end of 1137.

[1] Conrad III died in 1152, after the ending of JW's chronicle.

[2] J. R. H. Weaver's reference (*The Chronicle of John of Worcester* (Anecdota Oxoniensia, 4th ser. xiii; Oxford, 1908), p. 45) to Widukind, *Rerum gestarum Saxonicarum* (MGH *Scriptores rerum germanicarum in usum scholarum*, lx (Hanover, 1904), i. 4–7), is to a different rendering of this story.

[3] JW refers to the Greek for crown, στέφανος.

obsedit et cepit.⁴ Audito postmodum nuntio de hostium irruptione, terrarum deuastatione, uillarum concrematione, castellorum et oppidorum obsessione, in manu ualida Norðymbriam proficiscitur.ʲ Quo non diu moratus, uix ad uelle suum pro quibus ierat peractis, rediit. Ferunt qui nouerunt a pluribus diuerse gentis hostibus fere .vi. mensibus indicibilem factam irruptionem in Northymbria et per loca longe et prope adiacentia. Capiuntur quamplures, spoliantur, incarcerantur, cruciantur, uiri ecclesiastici pro rebus ecclesie neci traduntur. Numerum occisorum ex nostra uel illorum parte uix quis ualet enumerare.⁵

[C³]	[(G)]
Defuncto apostolico uiro Petro Leone, successit Innocentius,	Defuncto sedis apostolice inuasore Petro Leone anno .ix. inuasoris sue uenerabilis papa Gregorius, qui et Innocentius, sanctam regens ecclesiam

ad satisfactionem ᵏuenientibus cunctisᵏ qui in parte Petri contra eum tenuerant,ˡ et pacificatis in omnibus. Qui, uidelicet apostolicus, die Pascali Rome consecrauit in episcopum Ostiensiᵐ ecclesie Albericum abbatem Verzelliensis ecclesie.⁶

[C³]	[(G)]
Quomodo Zabulus, in dolo malignitatis sue captus, in puerili forma monachus sit factus.	De quodam miraculo in ecclesia Treuerensi facto.

Inter hec fama uolarat per circuitum hoc factum miraculum. In archiepiscopatu Treuerensi cenobium nobile situm est, quodⁿ Prumia dicitur, in honore sanctiᵒ Petri et Pauli dedicatum, antiquis temporibus a Pippino rege Francorum patre Karoli Magni fundatum, in qua talis rei nouitas ab omnibus ibidem conuersantibus accidisse refertur. Quodam mane, cum cellararius eiusdem monasterii cellam uinariam, ut uinum ad altaris sacrificium more solito

---

ʲ H² *ended here*   ᵏ⁻ᵏ uenientos cunctos *(G)*   ˡ suscepit *add. (G)*
ᵐ Ostiensis *(G)*   ⁿ qui *(G)*   ᵒ sanctorum apostolorum *(G)*

---

⁴ OV *HE* xiii. 36 (vi. 510) and *GS* 23 (pp. 46–50) give fuller accounts of the eventually successful siege of Bedford, which *GS* says occurred immediately after Christmas. It was held by Miles de Beauchamp, nephew of Simon de Beauchamp, the greatest tenant-in-chief in Bedfordshire. HH *HA* x. 6 (p. 710) also dates the siege to the Christmas season. OV speaks of Bishop Henry of Winchester's role in the conclusion of the siege. *Regesta* iii. 342 was issued 'apud Giltington in obsidione Beddefordie'.
⁵ Like JW, *GS* 24 (p. 50) places the trouble in the North immediately after the siege of Bedford. JW's reference here to King David's invasion and Stephen's response is a little

Bedford which had held out against him.[4] Learning of an incursion by his enemies, of the devastation of lands, the burning of townships, the siege of castles and towns, he set out with a strong force to Northumbria. He did not stay there long, and returned after barely achieving his aims. Those who are well informed report that for nearly six months an indescribable attack was made on Northumbria, and far and wide on its neighbouring territories by many hostile peoples. Very many were captured, despoiled, imprisoned, and tortured, and ecclesiastics were slain for the sake of their church property. It is scarcely possible to calculate the number of those who were slain on either side.[5]

On the death of the apostolic man Peter Leoni, his successor Innocent

Peter Leoni, usurper of the apostolic see, died in the ninth year of his usurpation, and Pope Gregory, also known as Innocent, then ruling the holy see,

was accepted by all those who had supported Peter against him after they had come to terms. At Easter this pope consecrated Alberic, abbot of Vézelay, bishop of Ostia.[6]

How the devil with his malign guile became a boy-monk.

How a miracle happened in the church of Trier.

At this time report of the following miracle was in general circulation. In the Trier archdiocese there was at Prüm a fine monastery dedicated to SS Peter and Paul, which had been founded of old by the Frankish king Pippin, the father of Charles the Great. Everyone living in the monastery describes an unusual occurrence. One morning, as the monastic cellarer with a servant went into the wine cellar to collect as usual wine for the sacrifice of the altar, he

cryptic. The fullest accounts of the 1138 campaigns in the North are in Richard of Hexham (*Chronicles Stephen, etc.*, iii. 151–71), Aelred of Rievaulx, *Relatio de Standardo* (*Chronicles Stephen, etc.*, iii. 181–99), and John of Hexham (SD ii. 289–95). David's first invasion started with the siege of Wark on 10 Jan. (Richard of Hexham (*Chronicles Stephen, etc.*, iii. 151–2), John of Hexham (SD ii. 289–90)). Stephen's expedition north took place about 2 Feb. (Richard of Hexham (*Chronicles Stephen, etc.*, iii. 155)) and prompted David's retreat. After Stephen's departure at the beginning of Lent (ibid.) David renewed the invasion on 8 Apr. (ibid.), and the battle of the Standard was fought on 22 Aug. JW's vague 'fere sex menses' is too long if it refers to David's first invasion and too brief if it refers to the period from 2 Feb. to 22 Aug. The report of Scottish cruelty is echoed in other sources.

[6] Pierleoni or Anacletus II had been the antipope since 1130, and his death on 25 Jan. 1138 marked the effective end of the schism and the unchallenged papacy of Innocent II (1130–43). Alberic, a former sub-prior of Cluny, was abbot of Vézelay 1131–8. JW's date for his creation as Cardinal-Bishop of Ostia is not known elsewhere.

daret, cum famulo suo intrasset, repperit unam de cupis, quam hesterna die plenam reliquerat, usque ad foramen obicis, qui usitato nomine spina seu pessulum dicitur, euacuatam, et uinum per totum pauimentum diffusum. Qui grauiter de dampno quod acciderat ingemiscens, famulum qui astabat asperrime increpauit, dicens eum preterito uespere minus diligenter obicem firmasse, ideoque dampnum huiusmodi contigisse. Et his dictis sub interminatione precepit ei ne alicui diceret quod acciderat; ueritus ne si abbas hoc animo perciperet, contumeliose eum officio suo priuaret. Facto autem uespere, priusquam fratres irent cubitum, cellarium intrauit, obices uasorum in quibus uinum habebatur diligentissime firmauit, clausoque ostio, lectum petit. Mane autem facto, cum cellarium sicut consueuerat intrasset, uidit aliam cupam usque ad meatum obicis, sicut pridie, uino defluente, uacuatam. Quo uiso, cuius negligentie dampnum hoc imputaret ignorans, grauiter non sine magna ammiratione indoluit, famuloque suo ne cuiquam proderet quod acciderat denuo precipiens, priusquam uespere lectum peteret, omnes obices cuparum diligentia qua potuit muniens, tristis et anxius stratum*p* adiit. Surgensque diluculo, aperto cellario, uidit de tertia cupa pessulum extractum et uinum usque ad foramen effusum. Vnde non immerito super his que acciderant perterritus et diutius commune dampnum silere metuens, ad abbatem festinauit, eiusque pedibus prouolutus, que uiderat per ordinem intimauit. Qui, habito cum fratribus consilio, iussit ut obices uasorum que uinum habebant, aduesperascente die, crismate circumlinirentur: quod et factum est. Illucescente autem die, predictus frater ex more cellarium ingressus, repperit puerulum nigrum mirande paruitatis in uno de pessulis manibus herentem; quem festine comprehendens et ad abbatem deferens, 'En,' ait, 'domine, puerulus iste quem uides, omne dampnum quod in prumptuario pertulimus, nobis intulit.' His dictis, retulit ei qualiter eundem puerulum in obice pendentem inuenit. Abbas autem, eiusdem pueruli qualitatem ultra quam credi potest admiratus, accepto consilio, monachilem habitum ei parare iussit et cum scolaribus puerulis in claustro conuersari. Quo facto, puerulus idem sicut abbas iusserat scolares pueros nocte dieque comitatur, nunquam tamen cibum aut potum sumebat, nulli publice aut priuatim loquebatur; aliis nocturnis aut meridianis horis quiescentibus, ipse in lecto residebat sine intermissione plorans et singultus creberrimos emittens. Inter haec, abbas quidam alterius

p statum *(G)*

found one of the casks, which he had left full the previous day, empty up to the opening which was called a spigot or a tap, with its wine spilled all over the floor. Much dismayed at the loss which had occurred, he sharply rebuked the servant present, saying that the loss had occurred through the latter's carelessness in not plugging the hole the previous evening. With this he ordered him under severe threats to tell no one what had happened, for he was afraid that the abbot would remove him in disgrace from his office if he learnt of it. In the evening before the brothers went to bed, he went into the cellar, firmly closed the taps on the wine casks, shut the door behind him, and went to bed. In the morning when he went as usual to the cellar, he saw another cask emptied as on the previous day up to the bung-hole with the wine flowing out. Seeing this and wondering whose negligence could be blamed for this loss, he was seriously upset and much astonished. He again enjoined his servant not to tell anyone what had happened. Before going to bed in the evening, he firmly closed all the spigots with all his force, and retired anxiously and sadly to rest. Getting up at dawn, and opening the cellar, he saw that the stop had been removed from a third cask, and that the wine was pouring out of the hole. Deservedly terrified by these happenings and fearing to conceal the shared loss any longer, he rushed to the abbot, threw himself at his feet and told him what he had seen. After taking counsel with the brethren, the abbot ordered that the spigots of the wine casks should be anointed with chrism that evening. This was done. At daybreak the said brother went as usual to the cellar and found an amazingly small black boy clinging with his hands to one of the spigots. He quickly seized him and brought him to the abbot. 'See, my lord,' he said, 'this urchin who is before you has caused all the damage which we have suffered in the cellar.' He then explained how he had found the boy clinging to the cask. Struck by the boy's incredible appearance, the abbot took counsel and ordered a monastic habit to be got ready for the boy, who was to be brought up in the cloister with boys of his own age. This was done and the small boy was placed, as the abbot had ordered, night and day in the company of the boy students. However, he neither ate nor drank nor would he converse with them either in public or in private. While the others were resting at night or in the middle of the day, he sat on his bed, crying and sighing deeply and ceaselessly. Meanwhile an abbot from another house came there for prayer

p. 390 ecclesie | orationis gratia *q*uenit ad eundem locum,*q* aliquantis diebus ibidem detentus est: cunque scolares pueri ante eum sepius transirent, ubi cum abbate et maioribus ecclesie eiusdem residebat, puerulus ille paruulus, protensis ad eum manibus, cum lacrimis respiciebat, quasi aliquid petens ab eo. Quod dum sepius ageret, abbas idem paruitatem eius ammirans, sciscitatus est assidentes sibi ut quid tam paruulum puerulum in conuentu uellent habere. Qui subridentes, 'Non est,' inquiunt, 'domine, talis iste puerulus ut estimas'; et narrauerunt ei dampnum quod eis intulerat et qualiter in pessulo cupe herens manibus inuentus sit; seu qualiter se continuerit intrans et exiens inter eos. Quibus auditis, abbas expauit et altius ingemiscens, 'Quantotius', ait, 'eum de monasterio expellite, ne maius dampnum uel grauissimum incurratis periculum: manifeste enim diabolus est in humana latens effigie, sed, Dei misericordia uos protegente per merita sanctorum quorum hic habentur reliquie, non potuit uos amplius nocere.' Protinus ad imperium abbatis eiusdem ecclesie puerulus adductus est et cum eum monachili habitu spoliarent, inter manus eorum ut fumus euanuit.[7]

Rex Anglorum Stephanus, in octauis Pasce quod erat .iiii. idus Aprilis, *r*tenuit concilium Norðamtonie,*r* cui presidebant Eboracensis,*s* episcopi, abbates, comites, barones et nobiles quique per Angliam. In quo etiam concilio, quorundam electione, Exoniensi ecclesie iam pastorali cura destitute de medio facti presulis Willelmi de Warast, archidiaconus nomine Rotbertus pontificali iure preficitur. *t*Due etiam date sunt abbatie, una Wincelcumbe cuidam Cluniacensi monacho, ut ferunt regis propinquo, nomine Rotberto, altera*u* Eboraci*v* cuidam monacho. Vnus eorum, scilicet Wincelcumbensis, electus, die Pentecostes .xi. kal. Iun. a uenerando presule Simundo, abbas Wincelcumbensi ecclesie ordinatur Wigorne.[8] Rex de Norðamtonia mouens castra, diuertit Glaornam;

[C³]

[(G)]

cuius aduentu ciues Glaornenses precognito plus quinque miliariis uenienti cum magno occurrunt gaudio, letumque cum

q-q ad eundem locum ueniens *(G)*   *r-r* over erasure C³   *s* archiepiscopus Turstinus add. *(G)*   *t* paragraph mark here C   *u* sancte Marie add. *(G)* *v* eiusdem ecclesie add. *(G)*

---

[7] This story is also found in Cambridge, Corpus Christi College 111, pp. 51–3, in a selection of extracts used in JW. The text there has G's variants.

and stayed for some days. When the young students often passed before him as he sat with the abbot and the elders of the monastery, the small boy extended his hands towards him, looking upon him tearfully as though asking him for something. He did this often and the abbot, wondering at his small size, asked those who were with him why they kept such a small boy in the monastery. They smilingly replied, 'My lord, this little boy is not what he seems,' and they told the abbot what damage he had caused them and how he had been found with his hands clinging to the spigot of a cask, and how quiet he had been when going in and out among them. On hearing this the abbot was much astonished, and, sighing deeply, said, 'Expel him quickly from the monastery before you suffer even more harm and the most serious danger. He is clearly the devil disguised in human form. By God's mercy and by the relics of the saints which you have here, he has not been able to harm you more.' The abbot ordered that the little boy be brought before him straightaway, and when they took off his monastic habit, he vanished through their hands like smoke.[7]

In the octave of Easter, which was on 3 April, Stephen, king of the English, held a council at Northampton attended by Thurstan archbishop of York, bishops, abbots, earls, barons, and many nobles of England. At this council, Archdeacon Robert was chosen by some and appointed to the bishopric of Exeter which was then vacant through the death of its pastor, William of Warelwast. Two abbeys were also handed over, Winchcombe to Robert, a monk of Cluny, and reportedly a kinsman of the king, and York to a certain monk. One of these abbots, that is of Winchcombe, was chosen and blessed as abbot of Winchcombe on 22 May at Worcester by Simon, its revered bishop.[8] The king moved with his troops from Northampton and went to Gloucester

> at whose coming its citizens met him more than five miles on the road with great joy and conducted the delighted king with

[8] JW is the earliest extant source for this Northampton Council (which may be that referred to under 1137, and which it is just conceivably possible that he attended: see above, 1137 n. 11), for the appointments of Robert to Winchcombe and Savaric (unnamed) to St Mary's York (also unnamed), and for Robert's blessing: see *Heads*, pp. 79, 84. *Ann. Winchcombe*'s (p. 128) record of Robert taking up his abbacy (*s.a.* 1139) might be based on JW. JW is the earliest extant source for the dates of Robert of Warelwast's nomination and consecration (see below, 1138 n. 35).

fauore propriam conducunt ad urbem. Ibique a monachis feria tertia Rogationum cum processionali susceptus honore, anulum suum regium supra sanctum ponit altare, quem die eodem capellani regii, datis pro eo quinquaginta solidis regi reportant. Inde eum Milo, tunc suus constabularius, cum honore regiam conducit ad aulam, ubi ei die sequenti ciues urbis fidelitatem iurant uniuersi. Die tertia, feria scilicet quinta, ad monasterium rex cum suis reuersus, Dominice ascensionis letabundus processionum seu missarum interfuit solemnitati.

ubi fortasse uel prius   Qua peracta festiuitate
audito*w* de castello quod contra illum obfirmabatur Herefordie, illo in expeditione maxima castrametatus est; quo perueniens, fame audite repperit uerisimile. Vnde in eodem loco fere .iiii. uel .v. eptomadarum spatio moratus,

[(G)]

die quoque Pentecostes in ecclesia sancte Dei genitricis Marie coronatus,

mandat per Angliam manus militum uenire sibi in auxilium ad expugnandum omnes regie dignitatis inimicos. Interim in eiusdem regis presentia, ciuitas Herefordensis infra pontem fluminis Wæge comburitur igne. *x*Nec multo post regis et totius curie percutit aures Oxenafordensis ciuitatis dolenda cunctis combustio. *x*Viso et cognito Herefordenses castellani in graui multitudine exercitus regem de se triumphaturum,*y* dextris datis et acceptis regi sese dedebant. Et quoniam ipse rex pietatis et pacis erat, immo quia est, non nociture alicui operam dedit,*z* sed hostes liberos abire permisit.⁹ Oppidum

---

w audito rex *(G)*   *x* paragraph mark here C   *y* triumphantem *(G)*
z uel dat *interlin.* C³

⁹ G's record of Stephen's arrival at Gloucester is detailed, and dates both his stay there, and the subsequent siege of Hereford, the duration of which had been given by John. HH *HA* x. 7 (p. 712) and OV *HE* xiii. 37 (vi. 519) associate the resistance at Hereford with Geoffrey Talbot. Miles of Gloucester was hereditary sheriff of Gloucester, castellan of

honour to their city. There on the third day of Rogations [10 May] he was received in a procession of honour, and he offered his royal ring on the holy altar, which the royal chaplains brought back to him the same day, it having been redeemed for 500 shillings. Thereupon Miles, who was at that time his constable, led him with honour to the royal palace. There the citizens all swore fidelity to him the following day. On the third day, that is on Thursday, the king returned with his followers to the monastery and gladly assisted at processions and masses for the solemn feast of the Lord's Ascension.

where by chance he earlier learnt that Hereford castle was being fortified against him. He pitched camp there with a great force, and found there that what he had heard was true. He stayed there almost four to five weeks, and also on the day of Pentecost [22 May] he wore his crown in the church of the holy Mother of God.

He ordered his troops from all over England to come to his aid and fight those who were opposed to his royal rights. Meanwhile Hereford below the bridge over the river Wye was burnt down in his presence. Shortly afterwards news of the generally lamented conflagration at Oxford reached the ears of the king and his court. The Hereford garrison, seeing and acknowledging that the king with the great strength of his army would triumph over them, made terms and surrendered to him. Since King Stephen was, no rather, is, a pious and peaceable man, he did not injure anyone but allowed his enemies to depart freely.[9] The king also captured the town of Weobley after

Gloucester under Earl Robert, royal constable and royal justice. He was a powerful figure on the Welsh border. See Green, *Government*, pp. 256-7. *Regesta* iii. 383-5, 395 could have been issued during the siege of Hereford. The fire at Oxford is not recorded elsewhere.

insuper Webbeleage nominatum quod Gausfridus de Talebot contra regem tenuerat, illo iam fugam inito, cuius arte et ingenio illis in partibus sub dirumpende pacis foedere regis aduersarii sustinebantur, rex cepit, et illud et predictum Herefordense castellum instructis militibus muniuit.[10]

Inter hec predictus Albericus Ostiensis episcopus, apostolica functus legatione, Angliam uenit, euellere euellenda, destruere destruenda, edificare edificanda, plantare plantanda. Lectis coram rege et primoribus Anglie litteris ab apostolica sede directis, licet non in primis, pro reuerentia tamen apostolice auctoritatis, demum suscipitur. Circumiens Angliam, considerat omnia, conseruat animo uniuersa, prouiso et constituendo concilio corrigenda.[11] *aa*Aliquandiu rex moratus Herefordie, cum suis inde secessit. Orbata regia presentia, ciuitas ipsa die .xvii. kal. Iuliarum, feria .v., ultra flumen predictum Wæge a prefato Gausfrido comburuntur omnia, nullo tamen de nostris, .vii. uero uel .viii. de Walensibus, occisis. Effusionem sanguinis plurimorum de aliis supradictis dicere supersedeo, nam ignoro.*bb*

[C³]

Hoc tamen oro:
*cc*Quisquis Christicola sub
  summa pace quiescat;
Corrigat ista legens offendit
  siqua Iohannes.*cc* 12

[(G)]
Exinde rex instante natiuitate sancti Iohannis, ad Oxinefordiam profectus, audito quod castellum Diuisas nuncupatum contra illum obfirmaretur, missis nuntiis ad eiusdem castelli fundatorem, Selesberiensem episcopum Rogerium, tunc apud Malmesberiam positum, ad

---

aa paragraph mark here C   *bb* ignoratur numerus (G)   *cc–cc* rubricated and extended into mg. C

---

[10] Geoffrey Talbot II is a central figure in GS. Cronne, Reign of Stephen, p. 158, thinks he may have been a stepson of Agnes Talbot (née Lacy). He is best known as a violator of

Geoffrey Talbot (who had held it against him) had fled. Geoffrey's scheming and ability had sustained the king's enemies as they had infringed the peace in those regions. The king garrisoned both Weobley and the afore-mentioned castle at Hereford with his troops.[10]

In the mean time the aforesaid Alberic, bishop of Ostia, came to England as apostolic legate to pluck out and destroy whatever needed plucking and destroying, and to build and plant whatever needed building and planting. The letters sent by the apostolic see to the king and magnates of England were read out, and, after a delay, out of reverence for the apostolic authority, the legate was eventually received. He went round England, noting all things and bearing in mind everything that required correction and setting up a council.[11] The king lingered for a while at Hereford and then left with his army. After the king had departed, the city on the other side of the Wye was burnt down on Thursday, 15 June, by the aforesaid Geoffrey, seven or eight Welshmen being killed, though none of our own men. I omit saying anything of the bloodshed of others since I am ignorant of it.

This however I do entreat:
May every Christian rest in
    total bliss!
Let the reader here correct
    John if he errs![12]

The nativity of John the Baptist [24 June] was approaching, and the king then set out for Oxford. On learning that the castle of Devizes was being held against him, he sent messengers to the castle's founder Roger, bishop of Salisbury, who was then at Malmesbury, ordering him to

churches. He witnessed Stephen's charter to Bath at the 1136 Easter court, Westminster (*Regesta* iii. 46).

[11] The legation of Alberic, cardinal bishop of Ostia, included Scotland; see Whitelock, Brett, and Brooke, *Councils and Synods*, ii. 766–8. In what ways Alberic met resistance 'in primis' is not clear. The fullest accounts of this legation are John of Hexham (SD ii. 297–300) and Richard of Hexham (*Chronicles Stephen, etc.*, iii. 167–72). Alberic reached Carlisle on 26 Sept. and returned south 3 days later.

[12] Presumably this episode is based on local information. The reference to John is one argument for his authorship of the chronicle.

suum iussit uenire colloquium.
Quam ille profectionem, ut
aiunt, nimis inuitus, utpote iam
amplius non reuersurus, aggressus, duos secum nepotes, quos
episcopos Lincoliensem, scilicet,
et Heliensem, cum maximo militum apparatu, armis et equis
multipliciter instructo, adduxit.
Quo uiso, rex proditionem sus-
picatus, suos se armis induere, et
ad sui defensionem, si necesse
esset, paratos iussit adesse.
Interim rege cum episcopis
causas diuersas tractante, inter
utramque militum partem, causa
hospitiorum, tumultus furoris
magnus incanduit: unde regiis
militibus ad arma concurrentibus, fugam ineunt episcopales,
apparatibus suis uniuersis post
terga relictis. Capitur a rege
Selesberiensis episcopus Rogerus
cum Lincoliensi episcopo, et filio
Rogerio, Paupere sensu cognomine; Heliensis elapsus, Diuisas
castellum adiit, muniuit, contra
regem tenuit. Vnde rex, ira
commotus eumque prosecutus,
captos episcopos, unum Rogerium, scilicet, in bostario in boum
presepio, alterum sub uili
tugurio ponit sub custodia,
tertio suspensionis parat suppli-
cium, ni sibi citius reddatur
castellum. Hoc uidens Rogerius,
suo metuens filio, iuramento se
strinxit, nunquam se manduca-
turum siue bibiturum, donec
predictum rex habeat castellum.

come and confer with him. It is said that the bishop set out on this journey with much reluctance, thinking that he would never return. He took with him his two nephews, the bishops of Lincoln and Ely, and a great force of soldiers, mounted and well-armed. When he saw them, the king suspected treachery, and ordered his men to arm themselves and prepare to defend him if this should be necessary. Meanwhile, the king discussed various matters with the bishops, and a big violent quarrel arose between the soldiers of both sides respecting their lodgings. The king's men rushed to arms, the episcopal forces took flight and left all their baggage behind. Roger, bishop of Salisbury, the bishop of Lincoln and Bishop Roger's son, Roger [le Poer], were taken prisoner by the king. The bishop of Ely escaped and went to Devizes and held it fortified against the king. The king became angry, and went to pursue him, and placed the captured bishops under guard: Roger in the crib of a cowshed, the other [Alexander] in a mean hut, and got ready to hang the third [Roger le Poer] unless the castle was handed over to him. Seeing this Roger, fearing for his son, bound himself by an oath to fast and not to drink until the said king gained possession of

Quod et factum est; tribus enim diebus non manducauit neque bibit.[13]

Rex cum regia multitudine*dd* Lundoniam ire perrexit. ⟨G⟩ausfridus autem de Talebot, regem pacis amicum deserens cum suis, ad Glaocestrensis*ee* comitis filium, Brycstouuense castellum contra regem tenentem, diuertit, illius munimini se dedit. Qui uno dierum, uelut cuilibet spatiatui operam daturus, magis autem ut post claruit Bathoniam exploraturus et postmodum inuasurus, cum duobus strenuis militibus | Willelmo Hoset et alio quodam, iter illo direxit. Quo cognito, Bathoniensis episcopus Rotbertus quasi de regis aduersario*ff* triumphaturus, instructo milite sub quadam cautela obuiam procedit. Fugientibus duobus, Gausfridus capitur, custodie mancipatur. Hinc furore*gg* succensi Brycstouuenses castellani cum domno suo comitis filio Bathoniam hostiliter adeunt, post presulem legant, et ni citius commilito suus Gausfridus reddatur, pontifici et suis suspensionis patibulum minantur. Qua de re presul, uice *hh*mercenarii, sibi*hh* suisque timens, educto de custodia Gausfrido et illis reddito, uoluntati illorum cedit. Quod ubi regiis auribus insonuerat, in episcopum uelut in fautorem inimicorum suorum exardescit ira; quem, etiamsi magis discordie quam paci rex ipse cederet, illum pastorali baculo fortasse priuaret. At quoniam presul coactus et inuitus id egerat, rex locum dedit ire, super quam iuxta apostolicam sententiam indignum est ut sol faciat occasum.[14] *ii*Fecit autem rex postmodum quod consilio disposuit, mittens Bathoniam multitudinem exercitus, qui presidio suo ciuitatem muniendo, ab hostium irruptione defenderent.[15]

⟨N⟩on multo post uersus Brycstowam rex mouit exercitum,

[(G)]

ubi hisdem diebus per quendam comitis cognatum, Philippum

---

dd uel manu *interlin.* C³   *ee* Glaocenstrensis C   *ff* uel -iis *interlin.* C³, aduersariis *(G)*   *gg* uel accensi *interlin.* C³   *hh–hh* mercenariis *(G)* *ii paragraph mark C*

[13] G places Stephen's quarrel with the bishops here in its correct calendar sequence (around 24 June) for 1138, but in the wrong year. It is fuller than JW's terse account under 1139 (see n. 5). Fuller accounts are in WM *HN* 469 (pp. 26–7) and *GS* 34–6 (pp. 72–80). Distinctive to G are: that Roger was fortifying Devizes against Stephen; that this was the reason for Stephen's summons (compare *GS* 34 (p. 72), which speaks of Roger fortifying all his castles in readiness to support the Angevin invasion); that Roger was accompanied as he set out by his two nephews; that Stephen was alarmed by the size of the bishops' forces;

the castle. This was done as
Roger neither drank nor ate for
three days.[13]
The king proceeded to London with a large royal force. Geoffrey
Talbot and his followers broke with the peace-loving king, and went
over to the son of the earl of Gloucester, who held Bristol castle
against the king, and applied himself to its defence. One day
pretending to assist a straggler, while clearly, as became obvious
later, wishing to reconnoitre Bath before attacking it, he went there
with two stalwart knights, William Hoset and another. On learning of
this, and hoping to defeat the king's enemies, Robert, bishop of Bath,
gathered a military force, and advanced cautiously against him. Two
of the three fled, but Geoffrey was taken prisoner and placed in
custody. The Bristol garrison was much angered by this and
advanced threateningly to Bath under their lord, the earl's son,
sent messengers to the bishop, and threatened him and his followers
with hanging if their companion-in-arms, Geoffrey, was not freed as
soon as possible. At this, the bishop, fearing, like a hireling, for the
lives of himself and his supporters, freed Geoffrey from custody, and
handed him over to them as they had asked. When the king heard of
this, he raged against the bishop as an accomplice of his enemies. He
would probably have taken away his pastoral staff if he had yielded
more to resentment than to his love of peace. As the bishop had acted
in this way unwillingly and out of fear, the king did not give in to his
wrath, upon which, according to the apostle, it is sinful to 'let the
sun go down'.[14] Afterwards the king did what had been decided in
council, and sent a large army to Bath to strengthen its defences and
defend it against enemy attacks.[15]
A little later the king moved his army to Bristol,
where at that time there had
emerged, as though from Hell,

and that Bishops Roger and Alexander were respectively lodged in a cow shed and in a hut.
Gervase's account (and date) (Gervase, i. 103–4) is taken from a version like G's. ASC
dates the quarrel to 1137.
[14] Cf. Eph. 4: 26.
[15] The account of this episode in GS 27–9 (pp. 56–64) is fuller. GS tells of Geoffrey
Talbot undertaking a full assault on Bath and his being captured when carrying out a
reconnaissance with his relative Gilbert de Lacy; of Bishop Robert being lured by his
enemies with a promise of safe-conduct; and of the besiegers' threat to hang the bishop
alone, not his followers, in Bath. Davis notes (GS, p. xxxvii) that the account there 'is
decidedly partial to the bishop'. A William Hosat was a knight of the bishop of Bath (see
EEA x. 7, 12, 35) and is unlikely to have been opposed to his lord.

Gai nuncupatum, uelut ex inferno emerserunt Neroniana seu Deciana tempora et tormenta. Illo enim agente, coeperunt inibi primitus adinueniri diuersorum acerbitates tormentorum, quem per totam longe lateque disseminate, Angliam uniuersam prope iam ad nichilum redegerunt insulam. Rex igitur uastatisque in circumitu et igne combustis terris ac uillis Glaocestrensis comitis, aliquandiu castellum obsedit. Demum pertesus diutine obsidionis,*ii* ad alia comitis castella, Carif in Dorsetania¹⁶ et Harpetreo in Sumersetania sita, obsidenda diuertit, ibidemque ante castellis extructis et manu militari munitis, discessit,¹⁷ et ad castellum de Duddelæge, quod Radulfus Painel contra illum munierat, cum toto exercitu aggressum egit.*kk* Vbi que in circumitu erant igne combustis, multiplicique preda animalium capta et abducta, ad Seropberiense castellum, quod Willelmus Alani filius aduersatiue tenuerat obsidendum, multitudinem militum secum in mare cepit. Precognito autem regis aduentu, idem Willelmus cum uxore et filiis et quibusdam aliis latenter fugam iniit, relictis in castello qui sibi in non reddendo illo fidelitatem iurauerant. Obsesso pluribus diebus castello, ad id expugnandum, ut ferunt qui nouerunt, talis paratur machina. Congeries non modica lignorum congeritur, adhibetur, castellina fossa iussu regis impletur. Ignis succenditur; fumus in altum se leuat. Omnes infumigat et exfumigat. Regia ui porta aperitur. Decidentes uel derepentes*ll* de castello, fugam misere ineunt omnes; quos insequi et neci tradere regia mandat censura. Quinque ex eis uiri nobiliores suspenduntur. Deuictis hostibus, rex inde discessum egit, et uersus Werham expeditionem mouit. Dextris uero datis et acceptis, Radulfus Paignel cum rege pacificatur ad tempus.¹⁸

---

ii over erasure C³   *kk cepit (G)*   *ll repeated and expunctuated C*

¹⁶ Castle Cary is in Somerset.
¹⁷ The sieges of Castle Cary and Harptree are also described in *GS* 31–2 (pp. 66–70). The first was held by Ralph Luvel, the second by William fitz John (Sanders, *English Baronies*, pp. 27, 64). Both castles belonged to Robert de Bampton, whose early revolt against Stephen had been described in *GS* 14 (pp. 28–30).
¹⁸ The sieges of Dudley and Shrewsbury could well have been in a missing section of

cruelties worthy of the times of
Nero or Decius, and practised by
the earl's kinsman, Philip Gay.
By him various pitiless cruelties
were there first introduced
which were to spread far and
wide throughout England, and
nearly reduce the island to
nothing. The king accordingly
wasting and burning the lands and townships in that area belonging
to the earl of Gloucester, laid siege to the castle for a while. In the
end he tired of the siege, and turned aside to besiege the earl's other
castles, Cary in Dorset,[16] and Harptree in Somerset. He built and
manned castles in front of them, left,[17] and marched with his whole
army to attack Dudley castle, which Ralph Paynell had fortified
against him. Having set fire to the surrounding area, and having
captured and taken away large herds of cattle, he went by water with
a big force to lay siege to Shrewsbury castle, which William fitz Alan
had held against him. William learnt in advance of the king's coming,
and secretly escaped with his wife, children, and some others, leaving
in his castle men who had sworn to be loyal to him and never to
surrender it. After the castle had been besieged for a few days, a
particular siege machine was prepared, according to those who are
well informed. A large structure of wood was put together and
brought forward. At the king's command the castle ditch was filled
in. Fire was started and smoke rose on high. The smoke affected and
smothered all. The gate was forced open by the royal onslaught.
Leaping or crawling out, the castle garrison made a wretched escape.
The king ordered them to be pursued and slain. Five of the higher
rank were hung. With the enemy vanquished, the king departed
thence and moved to attack Wareham. A peace was agreed and Ralph
Paynell was reconciled with the king for a time.[18]

GS. Ralph Paynell was the grandson of Richard fitz Ansculf, the holder of Dudley in
Domesday through his daughter, Beatrice. His father Fulk Paynell died in 1138. His
reconciliation with Stephen is unrecorded elsewhere. OV *HE* xiii. 37 (vi. 520–2) describes
the siege of Shrewsbury, identifies Arnulf of Hesdin, William fitz Alan's uncle, as the
castellan who held out, and reports the hanging of Arnulf and 93 others after the castle's
capture. William fitz Alan is described by OV as a sheriff of Shrewsbury and held lands in
Shropshire. He was the son of Alan fitz Flaald and succeeded him in much of the Bellême
Shropshire inheritance. OV says William held Shrewsbury against the king for a month
before fleeing in Aug. *Regesta* iii. 132 claims to have been issued during the siege of
Shrewsbury. The only indications of the siege's date are OV's statement that William fled

[(G)]

Interim facta coniuratione aduersus regem per predictum Bricstowensem comitem et conestabularium Milonem, abnegata fidelitate quam illi iurauerunt, missis nuntiis Andegauis ciuitatem, accersiunt eximperatricem, Henrici regis filiam, spondentes ei quod infra quinque mensium spatium regnum esset possessura*mm* paratum, sicut ei uiuente patre fuerat iuratum. Initia dolorum hec, hoc discidium grauissimum, immo pene ultimum, omni patrie intulit excidium.[19]

⟨I⟩nterea rex Scottie Dauid in graui multitudine equestrium et pedestrium de uagina finium regni sui iam tertio egressus, circa terminos Norðhymbrie*nn* rura, oppida, et castella cremare et fere totam terram deuastare. Sed iam hac ultima uice, cum usque Eboracum et Humbriam minaretur progressum, Eboracensis arciepiscopus Turstinus colloquium habuit cum omnibus de Eboraca prouincia, fecitque omnes communi consensu et consilio iuramentum in regis fidelitate facere, ut ei resisterent.[20] Inde autem rex Scottie magis irritatus, a nullis dissuadentibus potuit cohiberi, sed ueniens usque Teisam in die .viii. Assumptionis sancte Marie, que feria .ii. euenit, decreuit nostros preoccupare, quia in articulo ipsius diei maxima nebula erat. Et sic ex improuiso se uenturum super ipsos sperans, multas uillas intactas reliquit, nec suos, sicut solebant, ipsa die aliquid ardere permisit. Nostri tamen tarde a quodam armigero premoniti, et pene preoccupati, citissime se armantes et

mm uel adeptura *interlin. (G)*   *nn* cepit *add. (G)*

in Aug. and the implication in G that it was captured about the time of the battle of the Standard (22 Aug.: see below, p. 257). OV *HE* xiii. 37 (vi. 518) says that Robert, son of Alfred of Lincoln (HH *HA* x. 7 (p. 712) 'Robert de Nicole') held Wareham against Stephen. Stephen's move against Wareham is unrecorded elsewhere. G's interpolations on the atrocities of Philip Gai at Bristol, and on the appeal to the empress and to Robert, earl of Gloucester, are peculiar to it at this point. Robert's son, Philip, is described as 'uirum discordiæ, in sævitia primum' in *GS* 93 (pp. 180–1).

In the mean time the aforesaid
earl of Bristol and Miles, the
constable, jointly plotted against
the king, renouncing their loyalty to him, and sending envoys
to Angers to invite the ex-
empress, King Henry's daughter,
promising her that within five
months she would be in control
of her father's realm, in accordance with the oath sworn when
her father was alive. This was
the beginning of despair, the
most grievous, no, the ultimate,
discord, bringing about the
destruction of the kingdom.[19]

While this was happening, David, the Scottish king, invaded for a
third time with a large force, both on horse and on foot, from the
depths of the outermost limits of his kingdom, set fire to fields,
towns, and castles on the frontiers of Northumbria, and laid waste
almost the whole land. At last as he was already threatening to reach
as far as York and the Humber, Thurstan, archbishop of York,
summoned a council of the whole province of York, where after
consultations and the agreement of all, he persuaded all to swear
allegiance to their king and oppose David.[20] The Scottish king was
even more angered by this, and casting aside all counsel to the
contrary, he reached the Tees on the octave of the Assumption [22
August], which was on a Monday, and ordered an attack on our
troops, there being a thick fog at the opening of the day. Hoping to
come upon us unawares, he left many townships untouched, and
would not allow his men on that day to set fire to any place in their
accustomed manner. Our men, forewarned rather late by one of our
squires, were nearly taken by surprise, but they armed themselves

[19] G's description of the summons to the empress is one year too early.
[20] The fullest accounts of the campaign which began with King David's second invasion
around 8 Apr. and which ended with the battle of the Standard on 22 Aug. and the
surrender of Wark around 11 Nov. are in Aelred of Rievaulx, Richard of Hexham, and John
of Hexham (references as above 1138 n. 5). JW's account focuses on the Standard battle
and on the siege of Wark. His 'tertio' presumably refers to King David's previous
invasions, one in 1135 which he did not record, and the other earlier in 1138 (see
above, 1138 n. 5).

ordinantes, sagittarios premiserunt ante primam frontem, a quibus ualde Scottorum exercitus lesus est. Exinde ipsi regii barones cum militibus progressi, qui omnes de equis suis descenderant, et in prima erant acie, manus et arma cum hostibus miscuerunt, et in ipso primo puncto certaminis finem et uictoriam fecerunt, cedentibus sibi Scottis et statim uel cadentibus uel cum maximo timore fugientibus. Nostri autem quia pedites erant, et omnes equos suos longius abduci fecerant, non diu eos insequi potuerunt. Alioquin et ipsum regem et filium eius et omnes qui cum eo erant, uel tenuissent uel morti dedissent.²¹ De ipsius tamen exercitu prope .x. milia in diuersis locis ceciderunt, et ex eius electis usque ad .l., capti sunt. Ipse uero pro maximo timore⁰⁰ et dedecore aufugit deuictus.²² Cancellarius eius Willelmus Cumin a Dunholmensi episcopo tenebatur, sed iam a uinculis solutus gratias agit Deo, exoptans summopere ne unquam p. 392 talem incidat questionem.²³ | Filius autem regis cum uno tantum milite ad Carlor pedes uenit, patre ad Rokesburh per siluas et saltus uix euadente.²⁴ Innumerabilem habuit exercitum tam de Francis quam de Anglis, Scottis, et Galweiensibus et de omnibus insulis que ad se et ad suum dominium pertinebant. De .cc. loricatis militibus quos habuit, non nisi .xviiii. reportarunt loricas, quia prope omnia que habuit^{pp} predam hostibus reliquit. Vnde maxima spolia de exercitu eius, tam de equis et armis et uestibus quam de plurimis rebus, direpta sunt.^{qq 25} Eustachius filius Iohannis cum eo uenit, et eundem cum eo finem inuenit, qui uix cum uita ad castellum suum uulneratus aufugit.²⁶

⁰⁰ coactus *add. (G)*   ^{pp} quisque *add. (G)*   ^{qq} pro certo feruntur *(G)*

---

²¹ In this account of the battle JW differs from other sources in stressing David coming upon the English unawares in a mist at daybreak (though Richard of Hexham (*Chronicles Stephen, etc.*, iii. 162) has the battle begin at 'summo mane'); in ascribing the English army's swift response to the alertness of a squire; in placing the archers before the first line of battle (though most sources speak of archers mixed with knights in the front line and of the damage these archers inflicted on the Scots); in reporting the English failure to pursue their enemies and capture King David and his son (though Richard of Hexham, Aelred of Rievaulx (*Chronicles Stephen, etc.*, iii. 163, 189) and John of Hexham (SD ii. 293) say the English horsemen fought on foot).

²² HH *HA* x. 9 (p. 718) reports 11,000, and Richard of Hexham (*Chronicles Stephen, etc.*, iii. 164) 10,000 men slain. Neither mention the 50 'electi' killed.

and drew themselves in battle formation very quickly, placing archers before them in front, who did much damage to the Scots. Then the king's barons marched forward with their knights. These dismounted and positioned themselves in the front line, and engaged in hand-to-hand fighting with the enemy. At the very first charge they ended the struggle and gained victory. The Scots gave way and immediately they either fell in battle or fled in great terror. Our men were, however, on foot, and had caused all their horses to be taken some distance away, and so were unable to pursue the Scots for long. They would otherwise have either taken prisoner or slain the king and his son and all who were with them.[21] Of the Scottish king's army nearly 10,000 fell in different places, and up to fifty men of standing were captured. The defeated king escaped in flight in the greatest terror and shame.[22] His chancellor, William Cumin, was held by the bishop of Durham, and when he was set free, gave thanks to God, earnestly hoping that he would never again be trapped in such a way.[23] The king's son with only one knight reached Carlisle on foot, and the father barely escaped through woods and defiles to Roxburgh.[24] King David had an extremely large army made up of French and English, Scots and Galwegians, and men of the Isles who belonged to him and his lordship. Only nineteen of his 200 armoured knights returned with their armour, for they had left almost all that they had as booty to the enemy. Great spoil of horses, arms, clothing and many other things were taken from his army.[25] Eustace fitz John had come with him, and suffered a similar fate, having been wounded, and barely escaped alive to his castle.[26]

[23] Richard of Hexham (*Chronicles Stephen, etc.*, iii. 169–70) says Alberic, the papal legate, secured William Cumin's release.

[24] These particular flights are not reported elsewhere.

[25] No other source refers to the number of armed soldiers or to those who lost their armour. The Scottish army was made up of 'Normans, Germans, English, Northumbrians, and Cumbrians, men of Teviotdale and Picts ("qui vulgo Galleweinses dicuntur")' according to Richard of Hexham, and Aelred refers to 'insulani' being in the Scottish third line (*Chronicles Stephen, etc.*, iii. 152, 191)

[26] Eustace fitz John was the lord of Alnwick and Malton. He had been forced into opposition by Stephen's requiring his surrender of Bamburgh (John of Hexham 4 (SD ii. 291)). Richard of Hexham reports the siege of his castle of Malton after the battle of the Standard (*Chronicles Stephen, etc.*, iii. 165). This could be the castle to which he retreated as it was nearer to the battle site than Alnwick. For Eustace fitz John, see Green, *Government*, pp. 250–2, and Paul Dalton, 'Eustace Fitz John and the politics of Anglo-Norman England: the rise and survival of a twelfth-century royal servant', *Speculum*, lxxi (1996), 359–83, at pp. 366–70.

[C³]

"Extiterant isti fortes in nomine Christi: ex Stephani parte regis bellum peragentes," Comes de Albemar, Beornardus de Bailol, et alii plures. Comes tamen ipse multum strenuus in hoc certamine fuit.²⁷

[(G)]

Ex parte regis Stephani in hoc certamine extiterunt strenuissimi comes de Albemar, Bernardus de Bailol cum quibus et plures alii robustissimi quorum nobis non occurrunt nomina.²⁷

Rex Scottie cum reuersus fuisset, ut suos confortaret seque consolaretur, castellum quod prius obsederat unde a comite Mellentino fugatus fuerat, quod Werc uel Carram dicitur, et est Walterii de Spec, omnibus uiribus et multis ingeniis et uariis molitionibus*ˢˢ* obsedit, sed defendentibus se uiriliter et obstinate castellanis, nihil omnino proficere potuit. Exilierunt enim iam sepius de castello, et ingenia eius uel succiderunt uel incenderunt, multos perimentes. Vnde iam *"desperat capi id posse."ᵗᵗ ²⁸*

Septimo die mensis Octobris, luna existente .xxviiii., in crepusculo noctis sexte sabbati, uersus aquilonales*ᵘᵘ* partes uisum est firmamentum totum rubicundum. Radii etiam diuersi coloris uisi sunt, mixtim apparentes et euanescentes. Erant hec forte significantia maximam quam prelibauimus sanguinis effusionem factam per Norðymbriam et in pluribus aliis locis per Angliam.²⁹

[C³]

Magne uir religionis cenobita quidam de cella quadam Ege dicta, Willelmus nomine, iam electus, a Wigornensi presule Simone .xii. kal. Dec., die dominica, abbas Persorensi ecclesie ordinatur Wigorne.³⁰

[(G)]

Peracta Assumptione sancte Marie, huiusmodi fama uictorie ad regem usque peruenit, qui tunc, capto Seresberiensi castello, circa urbem Brucge obsidionem in uigilia sancti Bartholomei gaudens agebat.³¹

ʳʳ⁻ʳʳ rubricated C   ˢˢ rursus add. (G)   ᵗᵗ⁻ᵗᵗ capi id posse, desperans, spe sua frustratus inde discessit (G)   ᵘᵘ aquilonares C

²⁷ Stephen made William Aumale earl of York after the battle (Richard of Hexham (*Chronicles Stephen, etc.*, iii. 165)). Bernard of Balliol and Robert Bruce parleyed in vain with King David (Richard of Hexham (*Chronicles Stephen, etc.*, iii. 161–2)). On Bernard of Balliol, see *History of Northumberland*, ed. E. Bateson et al. (14 vols., Newcastle-upon-Tyne, 1893–1935), vi. 14–26.

²⁸ The siege of Wark on the Tweed apparently occurred twice in 1138, during David's two invasions, once after 10 Jan., and again, from around 8 May to its surrender around 11 Nov. (Richard of Hexham (*Chronicles Stephen, etc.*, iii. 151, 157–8, 165–6) and John of Hexham 4, 5 (SD ii. 289, 291–2)). Walter Espec was lord of Helmsley and of Wark, and was to enter Rievaulx abbey *c.*1153 (Sanders, *English Baronies*, pp. 52, 133, 149). JW alone

These were the brave men who fought in the name of Christ: on King Stephen's side the count of Aumale, Bernard of Balliol, and many others. The count distinguished himself by his great bravery in this battle.[27]

The following were the most valiant men on King Stephen's side: the count of Aumale, Bernard of Balliol with many most stalwart men whose names are not known.[27]

On his return, the Scottish king, hoping to encourage his followers and console himself, laid siege with all his force and many engines and machines to the castle of Wark-on-Tweed or Carham, which belongs to Walter Espec. He had earlier laid siege to it and had been driven back by the earl of Meulan. The Wark garrison defended it vigorously and stoutly and his efforts were of no avail. The garrison often sallied forth from the castle, set fire to or destroyed his engines, and killed many of his men. In the end he gave up hope of taking Wark.[28]

On the seventh day of October, on the twenty-ninth moon, at dusk, on the sixth night of the week, the whole firmament to the north appeared red, and many rays of various colours were seen, blending and disappearing. These signs may have portended the great shedding of blood in Northumbria and many other places in England, of which we have spoken.[29]

William, a man of great piety, from Eye priory, having been chosen, was blessed abbot of Pershore at Worcester on Sunday, 20 November by Simon, bishop of Worcester.[30]

After the Assumption [15 August], the news of this victory reached the king. At that time, Stephen, after having taken Salisbury, was besieging Bridgnorth castle, and he rejoiced on the eve of St Bartholemew [24 August].[31] Whilst there, he gave

mentions Waleran of Meulan's sortie from Wark presumably early in 1138, though John of Hexham 4 (SD ii. 289) mentions an early sortie by Walter's grandson, Jordan of Bussey.

[29] *GS*'s undated account (24 (pp. 50–2)) of a bloody sky is placed after the capture of Bedford and before the Scottish invasions of which it forewarns. JW's date for the phenomenon presumably dictated its position in this annal.

[30] The Tewkesbury Annals (*Ann. Mon.* i. 46) assign the election of William to this year. It is just possible, though probably unlikely, that the unnamed castellan of Eye was Roger, son of William Martel, who is described as constable of Eye in the Snape charter (*The Cartulary of Eye*, ed. V. Brown (2 vols., Suffolk Record Society, xii–xiii; Woodbridge, 1992–4), ii. 26–7), though the evidence associating William with the honour, and Roger with the constabulary, of Eye, is later than 1138.

[31] Stephen was at Shrewsbury in Aug. 1138 (see above, 1138 n. 18). G's Salisbury must be an error for Shrewsbury, and G could be referring here to an otherwise unrecorded siege of Bridgnorth on 23 Aug.

Ibi quoque positus, cuidam monacho de quadam cella Ege dicta, Willelmo nomine, conestabularii eiusdem loci castelli germano, Persorensis ecclesie prelationem concessit. Qui ad suam exinde ueniens sedem a Wigornensi presule Symone .xii. kal. Dec., die dominica, abbas Persorensi ecclesie ordinatur Wigornie.[30]

Rogerius Sereberiensis episcopus, castellorum, murorum, domorum fundator precipuus, pre dolore et tristia infirmatus, et ad finem uite perductus, apud episcopalem sedem, .ii. non. Decembris, defungitur, et in eadem ecclesia sepelitur, infinitam in castellis suis relinquens pecuniam, que non in Dei, sed regis Stephani tota cessit in usum. Sunt qui dicunt plus .xl. milia marcarum argenti ibi fuisse reperta, aurum quoque multum nimis cum uarietate ornamentorum thesaurizauit, et ignorauit cui congregauit ea. Templum in honore sancte Dei genitricis, magnificis decorauit ornamentis.[32]

[C³]
[vv]Ne igitur opus quod Arabica lingua dicitur Ezich quodque uir subtilissime scientie, Elkaurezmus uocabulo, de cursu .vii. planetarum subtilissime composuit et seriatim digessit, obliuioni tradatur, Arabici anni

[vv–vv] *rubricated* C

the abbacy of Pershore to William, monk of the cell of Eye,
brother of the constable of the
same place. William came to his
seat and was blessed as abbot of
Pershore on Sunday, 20 November, at Worcester by its bishop,
Simon.[30]

Roger, bishop of Salisbury, an
eminent builder of castles,
defences, and residences, being
worn out by grief and distress,
came to the end of his life, died
on 4 December at his episcopal
see, and was buried in the
church there. In his castles he
left immense sums of money,
which he bequeathed, not to the
benefit of God, but to King
Stephen. Some say that more
than 40,000 silver marks were
found there, and that he had
stored up a great quantity of
gold and a variety of ornaments.
He did not know for whom he
had assembled this treasure. He
adorned the church of the Holy
Mother of God with magnificent
ornaments.[32]

I set down here the first month
of the Arabic year and the day
and hour with which it began so
that the work which in Arabic is
called 'Ezich' and which the
learned al-Khwārizmī wrote
most carefully on the course of

---

[32] The death of Roger of Salisbury is placed here in its correct calendar sequence for
1138, but in the wrong year (see below, 1139 nn. 14, 18). Both *GS* 46 (pp. 96–8) and WM
HN 481 (pp. 37–9) give accounts of Roger's death and wealth, though G's 40,000 silver
marks is not recorded elsewhere.

primus mensis ubi et qua die uel
qua hora diei incepit notare dis-
posui.*vv*

Annus ab incarnatione Domini .mcxxxviii.

[C³]

secundum Arabes hoc anno incepit .xvi. kal. Octob. et fuit prima
dies Almuharran primi mensis
Arabici, feria .vi., hora diei .vi.,
dominicali littera B existente,
annus autem Arabicorum ex quo
inceptus est Arabicorum dico
collectorum .dxxxvii., planorum*ww* uero .xxii.³³

[C³]

*anno .viiii. pontificatus Innocentii pape, regni uero reg*is *Anglorum Stephan*i *.iii.,*

[(G)]

pontificatus autem domni pape Innocentii anno .ix., regnante nobilissimo *rege Stephano Anglorum, Henrici regis* magni nepote, anno ter*tio regni ipsius*

celebrata est synodus Lundonie in ecclesia beati*ˣˣ Petri apostoli*ʸʸ *apud Westmonasterium mense Decembri, .xiii. die mensis*

[(G)]

ubi post multarum discussionem causarum promulgata sunt hec capitula et ab omnibus confirmata numero .xvi.

Cui*ᶻᶻ prefuit*ᵃᵃᵃ *Albericus Ostiensis episcopus predicti domni pape*ᵇᵇᵇ *in Angliam et Scottiam legatus, cum episcopis diuersarum prouinciarum numero .xvii*i*., et abbatibus circiter .xxx., cum innumera cleri et populi multitudine.*

[(G)]

*Sunt autem hec capitula.*³⁴

[C³]

In dominica que extiterat .xvi.
kal. Ian. *ᶜᶜᶜ*Rotbertus suprano-
minatus consecratur episcopus

---

ww plauorum C   *ˣˣ* sancti *(G)*   *ʸʸ* apostolorum principis *(G)*
ᶻᶻ om. *(G)*   *ᵃᵃᵃ* autem add. *(G)*   *ᵇᵇᵇ* pape Innocentii *(G)*   *ᶜᶜᶜ* paragraph mark here C

the seven planets, and laid out in tables, is not consigned to oblivion.

The year of our Lord 1138 began according to the Arabs on 16 September, and this was the first day of the first Arab month Muharram, on Friday at the sixth hour, the dominical letter being B. I think this is the 537th accumulated year from which the Arab era begins, that is the 22nd simple or plain year.[33]

In the ninth year of Pope Innocent, the third year of King Stephen of the English,

In the ninth year of the lord pope Innocent, in the reign of the most noble King Stephen, nephew of the great King Henry, in the third year of his reign,

a council was held at London at the church of St Peter the Apostle at Westminster on the thirteenth day of December

where after discussion of many matters these canons (sixteen in number) were promulgated, and confirmed by everyone.

Alberic, bishop of Ostia, legate of the afore-mentioned lord pope in England and Scotland, presided over the council, which was attended by eighteen bishops of various dioceses and about thirty abbots with numerous clergy and many people.

These are its canons.[34]

On Sunday, 17 December, the above-mentioned Robert was consecrated bishop of Exeter,

[33] The astronomical tables of al-Khwārizmī in Adelard of Bath's translation are found in a manuscript partly transcribed by JW, Oxford, Bodleian Library Auct. F.1.9, fos. 99ᵛ–159ᵛ. JW would not have found there a ready reckoner for converting AD to AH dates. A.H. year for 1138 was 533 not 537 (which would have begun on 27 July 1142), and the first day of AH 533 would have been 8 Sept. 1138. The collected years were the 30-year intercalary cycles and *anni planorum* the years 1–29 between them. Thus 537 would have been made up of 510 *anni collectorum* and 27 *anni planorum*.

[34] *Acta* of the council edited in Whitelock, Brett, and Brooke, *Councils and Synods*, ii. 774. G provides more phrases than C³ from these *Acta* and twice announces the canons, without reproducing them.

Exoniensi ecclesie, et regis filius Geruasius abbas Westmonasterii ordinatur a legato. De abbatibus tres, abbas scilicet de Bello, abbas de Cruland et de Seropberia, infamati degradantur. *ddd* Eximie uir religionis, abbas Beccensis, Teodbaldus nomine, electus, die Natiuitatis Domini ab eodem legato consecratur archiepiscopus Dorubernie. *ddd* Superuenerat quidam Petrus nomine, et intererat synodo, apostolica deferens nuntia que preceperant ut episcoporum et abbatum persona de Anglia Romam iret et mediante futura .xl. illo ueniret, ad statuta papalia concilia.[35]

[1139] 1161[a]   *Peracta Dominice Natiuitatis solennitate,*

[C³]

communi consilio electi

[(G)]

*et adueniente Sancte genitri*cis *ipsius* Marie Purifica*tione, uenerabilis pater Walterus,* abbas Glaornensis, *anno prelationis sue nono et semis, circa horam diei tertiam, emisit spiritum, sepultusque est a uenerabilibus abbatibus Reinaldo Eoueshamnensi, et Rogerio Theokesheriensi, .vi. Idus Febr. Quo sepulto, duo fratres, propter electum nostrum domnum Gislebertum, ad Cluniacense cenobium destinantur; cui rex Stephanus, audita fama probitatis*

---

ddd paragraph mark here C

a 1139 in the mg. C³, 1141 (1162) in text C, 1139 and .lxi. in .mclxi. over erasure (G)

---

[35] The blessing of Abbot Gervase of Westminster, the degradation of the abbots of Battle and Shrewsbury, and the naming of the second envoy from Rome as Peter are not

and the king's son Gervase was
blessed abbot of Westminster by
the legate. Three abbots, of
Battle, Crowland, and Shrewsbury, were removed from office
and disgraced. Theobald, a man
of great piety and abbot of Bec,
was elected to Canterbury, and
was consecrated archbishop of
Canterbury by the same legate
on Christmas Day. A certain
Peter arrived and attended the
council, bringing with him mes-
sages from the pope asking that
bishops and abbots travel from
England to Rome next Lent and
there attend a papal legislative
council.[35]

[1139] After the Christmas festival
by common agreement

and with the feast of the Purification [2 February] drawing
near, the revered father Walter,
abbot of Gloucester, died at
about the third hour of the day
after holding office for nine and
a half years. He was buried on 8
February by the revered abbots
Reginald of Evesham and Roger
of Tewkesbury. After his burial
two brothers were sent to Cluny
to fetch our abbot-elect, Gilbert.
Hearing of this man's eminence
and probity, Stephen, at the

found in Richard of Hexham's account of the council (Whitelock, Brett, and Brooke,
Councils and Synods ii. 773–9). As pointed out by Brett, JW's 17 Dec. was a Saturday in
1138, and 18 Dec. was the more likely day for the bishop of Exeter's consecration. Note,
however, that JW places a paragraph mark, perhaps erroneously, before the entry on
Robert's consecration, and after the date of 17 Dec. JW was the earliest extant source for
Roger of Warelwast's consecration. Theobald was elected on 24 Dec. 1138, and consecrated
on 8 Jan. 1139.

eius eximie, petente conestabulario suo Milone, apud Lundoniam concesserat prelationem Glaornensis ecclesie.[1]

Teodbaldus Dorubernensis archiepiscopus, Simon Wigornensis, Rogerus Couentrensis, Rotbertus Exoniensis, abbas[b] Reignoldus Eoueshamnensis, a papa iussi tendunt ad limina Petri. Quo uenientes ab apostolica sede magno suscipiuntur honore.

[(G)]

Suscepti concilio interfuerunt Romano, multis retroactis seculis incomparando. Ibi causis suis pro libito peroratis, ad propria cum gaudio reuersi sunt, secum synodalia deferentes decreta longe lateque per Angliam iam conscripta.[2] Reuersi sunt et duo fratres in pace, qui propter adducendum domnum abbatem Gislebertum fuerant destinati, adductumque regi Stephano presentauerunt. A quo susceptus honorifice, sumpto quoque libere dominio Glaornensis ecclesie ab eodem rege, *die solenni Pentecostes, que tunc .iii. Idus Iunii celebra*batur, Wigorniam ueniens, *a* uenerabili presule *Herefordensi Roberto cum magnis ordinatur gaudiis, et diuinis laudibus: indeque sequenti die cum multorum fauore populorum ordinis utriusque, sua* collocatur *in sede*

[b] abbates C

---

[1] The italicized words on the death and burial of Walter and the election of Gilbert Foliot are shared with the fuller account in *Cart. Gloc.* (i. 17–18). Note that the first word in the annal 'peracta', which is that in *Cart. Gloc.* is not JW's more usual 'emensa'. Gregory of Caerwent (BL Cotton Vespasian A. V, fo. 198ᵛ) records Walter's death (on G's date) and the succession at Gloucester. The Worcester Annals (*Ann. Mon.* iv. 378) confirm the succession in this year: see *Heads*, p. 53. On the relationship between JW, G, and the

request of his constable Miles, had given him the abbacy of Gloucester at London.[1]

Theobald, archbishop of Canterbury, Simon of Worcester, Roger of Coventry, Robert of Exeter, and Abbot Reginald of Evesham went on the pope's orders to the court of Peter. The pope received them with great honour on their arrival.

They took their seats at the Roman council. This had not happened for centuries. There they freely discussed their affairs, and returned home joyfully, bringing with them synodal decrees, which are now recorded throughout England.[2] There also returned safely the two brothers who had been sent to lead back the lord abbot Gilbert. They brought him and presented him to King Stephen. Gilbert was honourably received by the king, and by him was freely given rule over the church of Gloucester. Gilbert came to Worcester on Pentecost day, which was on 11 June, and was blessed as abbot with great joy and divine praises by Robert, bishop of Hereford. From there on the following day he was installed in his office with joy and exultation, with the acclamation of many people of

Gloucester chronicle see C. N. L. Brooke, 'St Peter of Gloucester and St Cadog of Llancarfan', in idem, *The Church and the Welsh Border in the Central Middle Ages*, ed. D. N. Dumville and C. N. L. Brooke (Woodbridge, 1986), 50–94, at pp. 77–9, and also above, pp. xxx–xxxi.

[2] Richard of Hexham (*De gestis regis Stephani*, in *Chronicles Stephen, etc.*, iii. 176–7) speaks of four bishops (adding an unnamed Rochester bishop to JW's three) and four abbots accompanying Theobald to attend the Second Lateran Council of 1139. It is possible that C³'s 'abbates' may have been the correct reading and that the names of three abbots have been lost in transcription. Torigni (*Chronicles Stephen, etc.*, iv. 65) shows that Henry of Huntingdon attended the council.

cum letitia et exultatione, ut talem
decuit uirum in Domino.[3]

**ᶜOctauis Pasce, quod erat .ii. kal. Maii, magnificus rex Anglorum
Stephanus regio comitatu Wigorniam ueniens, totius cleri et suburbani populi festiua admittitur processione. Oratione facta et ex
more benedictione data, ad altare rex anulum regium digito extractum offert; qui die crastino communi consilio regie presentie
representatur. | Admirans itaque rex Wigornensis immo Dominici
gregis humilem deuotionem, ut erat adiuratus pro amore sancte Dei
genitricis Marie anulum recipit.

p. 393

Hinc Wigornia rex abscedens, apud Ludelawe castrametatus est.
Vbi in expugnatione castelli quod contra illum erat duobus in locis
extructa munitione forti manu militum instruit. Rediens per Wigorniam, mouit expeditionem uersus Lundoniam. ᵈMinime parcentes
execrande militie, arroganti strenuitate compellente, quidam militum
condixere apud Ludelawe uires probare. In hoc opus perficiendum
non modicus exercitus militum confluere cepit. Vere erat*ᵉ* miseriam
uidere, dum quis in alium hastam uibrans lancea perforaret,*ᶠ* et,
ignorans quod iudicium spiritus subiret,*ᵍ* morti traderet.*ʰ* At rex
Anglorum Stephanus talia molientes minis territat, et Ludelawe per
Wigorniam denuo diuertens,[4] in pacis contubernio omnia sedat, et in
pacifica alacritate Oxenofordiam id est Boum Vadum petit. Quo dum
moraretur, exigente dissensionis causa, Rogerum Særesberiensem
presulem, et nepotem eius Lincoliensem antistitem Alexandrum,
Rogerum quoque suum cancellarium, quasi regie corone insidiatores,
cepit et custodie mancipauit. Quo cognito, Eliensis presul Nigellus,
timens sibi et suis, manu militari ad Diuisas fugit, ut ibi protegeretur.

[(G)]

Quorum causa scriptus superius
est latius propalata que tamen
hoc anno constat actitata.[5]

Habito postmodum consilio, statutum est ut omnia per Angliam
oppida, castella, munitiones queque in quibus secularia solent
exerceri negotia, regis et baronum suorum iuri cedant; ecclesiastici

---

ᶜ *preceded by a blank line and a half* C   ᵈ *paragraph mark here* C   ᵉ uel est
interlin. C³   ᶠ uel -ret *interlin.* C³   ᵍ uel -at *interlin.* C³   ʰ uel -at
interlin. C³

---

3 The arrival of Gilbert Foliot is linked to the return of the bishops from Rome. G gives
the date of his blessing as abbot (see *Heads*, p. 53). Again, as earlier under 1139 (see above,
1139 n. 1), *Cart. Gloc.* i. 18 shares the italicized words with G's text. Gilbert Foliot had

both orders, as befitted such a
man in the Lord.[3]

On the octave of Easter, which was on 30 April, the splendid king
Stephen came to Worcester with a royal retinue and was received by
all the clergy and people of the surrounding area in a festive
procession. When prayers had been said and the accustomed blessing
pronounced, the king took the royal ring off his finger and offered it
on the altar. Next day it was returned to the king by general
agreement. The king wondered at the humility and devotion of the
monks, no, rather of God's flock, at Worcester, and took back the ring
as he had been asked to do for the love of the holy Mother of God.

The king left Worcester and camped at Ludlow. He had forts built
in two places and garrisoned with strong military forces to assault the
castle which was held against him. Returning by way of Worcester,
he moved an army towards London. Some of the soldiers, relentless
in their cursed fighting, and driven by their boastful strength,
decided to try their strength at Ludlow. A large body of soldiers
gathered together for this purpose. It was dire to see one soldier
raising his spear against another and running him through, and
killing him, not caring what judgement his soul would have to
endure. King Stephen checked these activities by his terrifying
threats, and, coming again to Ludlow by way of Worcester, he
settled everything peacefully.[4] He then made his way in peace and
haste to Oxford, that is, the ford of the oxen. Whilst he was there,
some dissension arose, and he seized and placed in custody Roger,
bishop of Salisbury, his nephew Alexander, bishop of Lincoln, and
Roger, his chancellor, for plotting against the crown. On learning of
this, Nigel, bishop of Ely, feared for his safety and for that of his
followers, and fled with an armed band to the security of Devizes.

This episode has been more fully
described above. Its final de-
nouement was in this year.[5]

After discussion in a council it was decided that all towns, castles,
and fortified places throughout England where secular business was
conducted should submit to the jurisdiction of the king and his

---

attended the Lateran Council in the company of his abbot Peter the Venerable (*GFL*, p. 86
n. 1).
  [4] These moves of Stephen are not recorded elsewhere. *Regesta* iii. 964–5 could have
been issued at Worcester at this time.
  [5] See above, pp. 245–9.

uero uiri, uidelicet episcopi, canes, inquam, diuini, in salutem et in defensionem ouium suarum latrare non cessent, ne lupus inuisibilis, malignus scilicet hostis, rapiat et dispergat oues, omnino caueant,[6]

[C³]

in spirituali pugna auxilium Regi
regum prebeant remunerationes
illis quando post uictoriam.[i][7]

Mense Octobri,[j] comes Glaocestrie, Heinrici quondam regis Anglorum filius sed bastardus, cum sorore sua sed ex patre, dudum Romanorum imperatrice, nunc Andegauensi comitissa, cum grandi exercitu [k]mense Octobri[k] Angliam rediit, et apud Portesmuth applicuit

[(G)]

ante festum sancti Petri ad Vincula kal. Aug. rege tunc Merlebergam obsidente.

Cuius aduentus factus est omnibus per Angliam terror immensus. Quo audito, rex Anglorum Stephanus animo mouebatur, et his[l] qui marinos portus uigilanti cura obseruare debuerant indignabatur. Rex est pacis, et o utinam rex rigoris iustitie conterens sub pedibus inimicos, et equa lance iudicii decernens omnia in robore fortitudinis conseruans et corroborans pacis amicos.[8] Vbi autem nouit exreginam apud Arundel eximperatricem cum grandi comitatu suo recepisse, grauiter ferens, illo mouit exercitum. At illa regiam maiestatem uerita, et timens ne dignitatem quam per Angliam habuerat perderet, iureiurando iurat neminem inimicorum suorum per se Angliam petisse, sed, salua dignitate sua, uiris auctoritatis utpote sibi quondam familiaribus hospitium annuisse.

[(G)]

Quo rex audito, illa dimissa, eximperatricem ad castellum Bricstowense conducere fratri suo Wintoniensi episcopo, sicut cognatam suam cum honore, precepit.

---

[i] reddituros *written in the mg.* C³   [j] uero Iulio *(G)*   [k-k] *om. (G)*
[l] *interlin.* C³

[6] Cf. Isa. 56: 10 and John 10: 12.
[7] The council at Oxford to which the bishops were invited is dated 24 June by WM *HN* 469 (p. 26). JW's account of the arrest of the three bishops is much briefer than G's misplaced account under 1138 (see above, 1138 n. 13). G had not referred to a council.

barons; and that churchmen, that is, bishops, or, as I would call them, holy watchdogs, should not stop barking for the safety and defence of their flocks and should be ever watchful lest the unseen wolf, their malevolent enemy, should seize and scatter the sheep.[6] In the spiritual fight let them
give help to the king of kings,
which will bring them rewards
after victory.[7]

In October the earl of Gloucester, the illegitimate son of the former English king Henry, with the ex-empress of the Romans, now countess of Anjou (who was his sister through his father) returned with a large army to England and landed at Portsmouth
before the feast of St Peter ad Vincula, which is on 1 August, when the king was besieging Marlborough.
His arrival filled all England with alarm. When he had heard of this, Stephen, the English king, was much concerned, and was angry with those responsible for watching and guarding the ports. Stephen is the king of peace. If he were only the king of firm justice, crushing his enemies under foot, assessing all things with the balanced lance of judgement, protecting and strengthening with his mighty power the friends of peace.[8] When he learned that the ex-queen had received the ex-empress with her large retinue at Arundel, he was much displeased and moved his army thither. The ex-queen was awed by the king's majesty, and was afraid that she might lose what rank she had in England, and solemnly swore that no enemy of the king had come to England through her doing, but that, saving her dignity, she had provided hospitality to those in authority who were known to her.
When the king heard her explanation he sent her away, and ordered the ex-empress to be led with honour (since she was his cousin) by his brother the bishop of Winchester to the castle of Bristol.

The council held on 29 Aug.–2 Sept. 'pro captione episcoporum' is most fully described in WM *HN* 470–7 (pp. 28–34) and more briefly in *GS* 36 (p. 80). JW's reporting of the distinction between 'secular' and 'ecclesiastical' roles echoes both the arguments made by Stephen's advisers before the arrest of the bishops and the council's ruling (see *GS* 34 (pp. 72–5) and WM *HN* 469 (pp. 25–6)).   [8] Cf. Judith 14: 5 and Rom. 16: 20.

Rex*m* comitem persequitur. Nil autem certi audiens de eo, quedam enim diuerticula ad tempus ille petierat, expeditionem mouit quo disposuit. Milo constabularius regie maiestati redditis fidei sacramentis, ad dominum suum comitem Glaucestrensem cum grandi manu militum se contulit, illi spondens in fide auxilium contra regem exhibiturum.[9]

[(G)]

Iam uero exhinc, ex Bricstowensi scilicet urbe, que mala per totam emerserint Angliam, nullius poterit exprimere scientia uel facundia. Resistentes siquidem sibi, regieue dignitati parentes, quotquot capi poterant capiuntur, uniuersi capti uinculis et tormentis mancipantur horrendis, poenarum diuersitates siue acerbitates exquiruntur, militumque caterue ad hoc opus perditionis exequendum undecunque conducuntur, quibus in stipendium dantur et uenduntur uicorum et uillarum cultores atque habitatores cum rebus suis uniuersis ac substantiis. Consedit itaque ibi domina illa plus duobus mensibus, sumens ab omnibus hominia, et pro libito suo disponens Anglorum regni iura. Inde discedens mense Octobri, .xviii. Kal. Nouembr., Gloecestrensem uenit ad urbem, ciuium et circumiacentium hinc inde finium expetens dominium

---

m Ipse uero *(G)*

[9] Robert, earl of Gloucester, and the empress landed at Arundel (*GS* 41 (p. 86)) on 30 Sept. (WM *HN* 478 (p. 34)). There are differences between JW and G. In G the landing took place in July (JW Oct.) while Stephen was besieging Marlborough, and G mentions the empress's departure to Bristol under Henry of Blois's escort. Fuller and clearer

Stephen went in pursuit of the earl. Hearing nothing certain about his movements (for Robert for some time had been following secondary roads), he moved his army to a pre-arranged place. Miles the constable renounced his allegiance to the royal majesty, and went over to his lord the earl of Gloucester with a large military force, promising him faithful support against the king.[9]

The disasters which spread from this place, Bristol castle, all over England cannot be adequately described by anyone with knowledge and eloquence. As many of those who resisted Miles, or supported the king, as could be captured were seized, and all these were chained and horribly tortured. Many cruel punishments were devised, bands of troops were hired everywhere to carry out this work of perdition. The husbandmen and inhabitants of villages and townships with all their goods and substance were either given or sold to these mercenaries. The ex-empress remained at Bristol for over two months, receiving homage from all sides, and dispensing the laws of the English kingdom as she pleased. She left Bristol in October, and came to Gloucester on 15 October, where she sought to assert her lordship and received the submission of its

accounts are in *GS* 41–2 (pp. 86–90) and WM *HN* 478 (pp. 34–5). Torigni (*Chronicles Stephen, etc.*, iv. 137) dates the landing to Aug., and OV *HE* xiii. 41 (vi. 534) to the autumn. Stephen's siege of Marlborough is unrecorded outside G at this point, as are Stephen's misgivings on the hospitality Matilda received from Queen Adelaide, but G's reference to Bishop Henry's escorting is confirmed by WM *HN* 478 (p. 35), who says Waleran was her second escort. Robert's journey through by-roads is confirmed by *GS* 41 (p. 88). Miles's defection follows close upon Matilda's arrival in Bristol in both *GS* 42 (p. 90) and WM *HN* 478 (p. 35).

et sumens hominium. Hoc uero
agere nolentibus, sed regi potius
fidelitatem custodientibus, Deciana siue Neroniana inferuntur
tormenta cum diuersis mortibus;
fitque urbs, retro anteactis seculis gloriosa, ululatibus dirisque
cruciatibus plena, suisque habitatoribus horrenda. His ita se
miserabiliter habentibus,[10]

Walingafordense castellum sibi aduersum rex obsedit. Obsidionis
diutine pertesus, antecastellis extructis inde profectus, castrametatus
est apud Malmesberiam. Vbi in aduersarios id est in discordie
operarios eadem operatus est.[11]

Inter hec flebile nuntium percutit aures ciuium Wigornensium.
Crebra uolat fama Wigornam, ciuitatem ab hostibus in proximo
deuastandam, rebus spoliandam, igne comburendam. Talia audientes, terrentur ciues Wigornenses. Quid facto opus sit, consulunt.
Quo habito consilio, ad Dei summi Patris et ad beatissime sue
genitricis asylum misericordie confugiunt, et sub patrocinio confes-
sorum sancti Oswaldi et beati Wlstani ciuitatis eiusdem presulum se
et sua diuine tuitioni committunt. Videret qui afforet totam ciuium
suppellectilem deferri in basilicam. O miseriam uidere! Ecce domus
Dei que intranda erat in holocaustis, ubi immolandum erat sacrificium laudis, reddenda uota altissima, uidetur inpresentiarum uelut
suppellectilis casa.[12] Ecce totius episcopatus principale cenobium
factum est ciuium*n* diuersorium et quoddam declamatorium. Armar-
iorum et saccorum plurimorum pre numero, Dei seruis uix locus in
tali nunc diuersorio. Intus psallit clerus, foris uagit infans. Vocibus
p. 394   psallentium resonat uox lactentium, uoxque matrum | lugentium.
Miseria super miseriam uidere. Altare principale stat ornamento
spoliatum. Crux deposita. Imago Sanctissime Dei genitricis Marie
oculis subtracta. Cortine cum palliis, albe cum cappis, stole cum

---

n ciuum C

[10] The account of atrocities at Bristol indicates that G was not a blind supporter of the
empress. Matilda's departure for Gloucester from Bristol on 15 Oct. would have allowed
only the briefest of stays in Bristol if she had arrived at Arundel on 30 Sept. (see Chibnall,
Empress Matilda, p. 83). G gives her a two-months' stay.
[11] Stephen's siege of Wallingford, which was defended by Brien fitz Count, is described
in *GS* 42 (pp. 90–2). WM *HN* 479 (p. 36) shows that Stephen took Marlborough *c.* 21 Oct.

citizens and of those dwelling in
its vicinity. Tortures worthy of
Decius or Nero, and deaths of
various kinds were imposed on
those unwilling to submit to her,
and firm in their allegiance to the
king. The city, which gloried in
its past centuries, was filled with
screams and dire torments, which
were horrendous to its citizens.
Whilst these wretched events
were taking place,[10]
the king besieged Wallingford castle which was held against him.
Tiring of the prolonged blockade, he built forts against it, set out
from there, and camped near Malmesbury. There he set up forts
against his enemies, the traffickers in rebellion.[11]

Meanwhile sad news reached the Worcester citizens. There were
frequent reports that Worcester would soon be devastated by its
enemies, despoiled of its goods, and consumed by fire. Such tidings
terrified the citizens of Worcester, and they took counsel on their
best course of action. After taking advice, they rushed in their
wretchedness to the protection of the most high God the Father
and His most blessed Mother, and to entrust themselves and all
theirs under God's protection to the guardianship of the Worcester
bishops, the confessors St Oswald and the blessed Wulfstan, bishop
of the same city. Then could be seen all the goods of the citizens
carried into the cathedral. Oh what miseries were beheld! Lo, the
house of God into which offerings should be brought, and where the
sacrifice of praise should have been offered, and the most solemn of
vows made, seems now but a furniture storehouse![12] Behold the
principal monastic house of the diocese has become a hostel and
debating chamber for the citizens! There is scarcely any room left for
the servants of God in an inn so filled to abundance with chests and
sacks. Within the clergy chant, outside infants wail. The cries of
sucklings, and of sorrowful mothers mingle with the singing of
choirs. Oh misery of miseries to behold! The high altar is stripped of
its ornaments. Its cross is taken away. The image of Mary, most holy
Mother of God, is removed from view. Curtains and palls, albs and

---

[12] Cf. Ps. 49: 14.

planetis, parietum septis includuntur. In Sanctorum festiuitatibus ad diuinum celebrandum officium desunt decus, honor, omnis solita magnificentia. A timore uel pre timore inimicorum hec disponuntur omnia, ne repente inimicus superueniens tollat cuncta que repperit, et sic in uanitate sua preualeat. [o]In articulo diei incipientis brume, hoc est .vii. idus Nouembris, feria .iii., dum ad laudem diuinam in ecclesia fuimus, et iam primam horam diei decantauimus, ecce quod plurimis ante diebus auribus hausimus, exercitus magnus ualde et fortis ab austro ueniens, e uagina malitie progreditur. Vrbs Glaorna armis militaribus instructa, equestri et pedestri exercitu innumerabili suffulta procedit, ciuitatem Wigornam inuasura, uastatura, igne combustura. Nos autem timentes ornamentis sanctuarii, benignissimi patroni nostri Oswaldi reliquias, albis induti, tota sonante classe cum humili processione foris extulimus, et ob hostium irruptionem de porta ad portam per cimiterium deportauimus. Aduersarii conglobati, accelerando munimen quoddam fortissimum in australi parte ciuitatis propter castellum situm primum impugnant. Nostri fortiter resistere, et uiriliter resistere.[p] Hostes inde repulsi, quoniam olla succensa erant cuius facies aquilonis[q] aquilonalis partis ciuitatis ingressum petunt. Nullo obstante munimine, hostium copiosissima, rabidissima et tota effrenis multitudo intrat, in diuersis locis ignem edibus immittat. Proh dolor, comburitur non modica pars ciuitatis per loca, sed maior pars stando paret inusta. Suppellectilium diuersarum in ciuitate, et in ruribus boum, ouium, animalium, et equorum fit maxima preda. Plurimi per uicos et plateas capiuntur, et uelut in copula canum constringuntur, et miserabiliter abducuntur. Licet habeant, licet non habeant, quantum crudele os illorum censuerit in redemptionem sui iureiurando promittere et reddere compelluntur. Gesta sunt hec die qua intrauit bruma, miseris dubio sine dura, iam predis captis, quampluribus edibus arsis, sic debachata remeant rabidissima castra, in praua cura tali nunquam reditura.

Tricesimo die mensis Nouembris, comes ciuitatis Wigorniam uenit. Combustionem ciuitatis ut uidit, indoluit; ad iniuriam sui, id actum fore persensit. Vnde uindicare se uolens, stipatus manu militum Suðlegiam adiit; audierat enim Iohannem Haroldi filium deserto rege ad Glaocestrensem comitem diuertisse. Vbi quid comes egerit, si queritur, uix memorie tradendum malum pro malo reddidit.

[o] *paragraph mark here C* [p] defendere *interlin.* C^3, ceperunt agere *(G)*
[q] *repeated and deleted, possibly over erasure C*

copes, stoles and chasubles are hidden in the corners of the walls. In the celebration of God's service on the feastdays of the saints all honour, all dignity, all the usual splendour is absent. These things were all put away in terror and through fear of the enemy, lest he should suddenly surprise them, and should take away all that he found, and prevail in his vanity. One morning at the outset of winter, on Tuesday, 7 November, we were engaged in divine service in the church, and had already chanted prime, when behold a large and strong army which we had expected for many days, approached from the south, arriving from the source of all evil. The city of Gloucester had prepared arms and advanced with an enormous force, both on horse and on foot, to assault, lay waste, and set fire to Worcester. Fearful for the sanctuary's treasures, we put on our albs, and, while the bells tolled, carried the relics of our most blessed patron Oswald outside in suppliant procession, and, as the enemy rushed from one gate to another, we bore them to the cemetery. The enemy gathered together in one body and rushed at first to attack a strongpoint in the southern part of the city near the castle. Our men resisted bravely and manfully. The enemy was repulsed here, and as beacons were lit on the northern side of the city, they sought to break through there. There were no defences on that side, and a mass of raging and uncontrolled enemy forces broke through, and set fires to houses in various places. Alas, no small part of the city was burnt down, though the greater part survived unburnt. An enormous booty of chattels from the city, and of oxen, sheep, beasts, and horses from the countryside is carried off. Many are taken prisoner in the streets and in the townships, and led away, coupled like dogs, into wretched captivity. Whether they have the means or not, they are forced to promise on oath to pay whatever ransom the mouthpiece of their captors cruelly fixed. These things, certainly greatly oppressive to the wretched sufferers, happened on the first day of winter. Now the booty is taken away, numerous houses consumed by fire, the rabid and debauched force retreats, never to return on so degraded an enterprise.

On the thirtieth day of November, the earl of the city came to Worcester. Waleran grieved as he saw the firing of the city, and felt as if the damage had been done to himself. Intent on vengeance, he went to Sudeley with a force of soldiers, for he had heard that John fitz Harold had deserted the king and attached himself to the earl of Gloucester. If you ask what the earl did there, the answer is barely worthy of record for he rendered evil for evil. He seized and carried

In hominibus cum rebus eorum et animalibus predam egit et abduxit, et crastino Wigorniam rediit.[13]

[C³]

Rogerus Searesberiensis episcopus mense Decembri apud episcopalem sedem obiit, et in eadem ecclesia sepelitur. Verum quantum pecunie in auro et argento in erario eius repertum fuerit, ʳreticendum arbitror, quia penitus ignoro.ʳ [14]

Post hec rex grandi comitante exercitu de Oxenofordia Wigorniam uenit, cuius de infortunio quod audierat oculis uidit et indoluit. Vbi tribus uel .v. diebus moratus, regii constabulatus honorem Miloni Glaocestrensi suo hosti ablatum

[(G)]

ˢWillelmo filio Walteri de Bello Campo Wigornensi uicecomiti dedit.ˢ [15]

Fama uolante regie maiestati nuntiatur inimicos iurate quidem pacis uiolatores Herefordiam inuasisse, monasterium Sancti Ægeberti regis et martyrisᵗ uelut in castellinum munimen penetrasse.

[(G)]

Agente Gaufrido de Talabot ingressos fuisse, equosque suos in ipsa ecclesia quasi in stabulo collocasse, perque cimiterium fossa transducta fidelium corpora crudeliter effodisse. Hinc eisdem ecclesie pontifex uenerabilis turbatur Rodbertus, turbatur et clerus uniuersus, turbatur quoque rex.

ʳ⁻ʳ *continued into the mg.* C   ˢ⁻ˢ *erased* C   ᵗ *immo Sancti Dei Genitricis* Marie *add.* (G)

---

[13] The source for the events in Worcester must be local. The attack by Miles of Gloucester and the punitive raid by Waleran, neither of whom are named here, are unrecorded elsewhere. John de Sudeley, the son of Harold, the Domesday lord of Sudeley, appears in the 1130 Pipe Roll (*Pipe Roll 31 Henry I*, p. 79). Crouch, *Beaumont Twins*, pp. 39–40, discusses the evidence for Waleran's appointment as earl of Worcester in late 1138.

off a booty of men with their goods and cattle, and returned to Worcester the next day.[13]

Roger, bishop of Salisbury, died at his episcopal seat in December and was buried in his church. I think it best not to say anything (since I am quite ignorant) of the amount of money in gold and silver that was found in his treasury.[14]

After this the king came with a large force from Oxford to Worcester, and, seeing with his own eyes the disasters of which he had heard, he was much grieved. He stayed there three or five days, and deprived his enemy Miles of the royal constabulary and gave it to William, son of William Beauchamp, sheriff of Worcester.[15]

His royal majesty learnt of a report that his enemies, violating their sworn engagements of peace, had attacked Hereford and gone into the minster of St Æthelberht king and martyr as if it had been a stronghold.

Geoffrey Talbot was responsible for this incursion, and had housed his horses in the church as though it were a stable, and in the ditches of the cemetery had cruelly dug up and removed bodies of the faithful. Robert, the church's venerable bishop, all the clergy, and also the king were distressed by this.

[14] The death of Roger of Salisbury on 11 Dec. (see Greenway, *Fasti* iv. 2) is more fully described in WM *HN* 481 (pp. 37–9), and in *GS* 46 (pp. 96–9). Omitted here by G, it is recorded later in the annal at the appropriate chronological point.

[15] JW gives the impression that Stephen returned to Worcester at a later date than Waleran on 30 Nov. This is the only evidence for William of Beauchamp, sheriff of Worcester, being a supporter of Stephen. Crouch, *Beaumont Twins*, p. 47 n. 87, argues that he had been Stephen's supporter and that he had been rewarded, as recorded by G and originally by C, with the office of constable. He was to be made constable of Worcester by Matilda between 25 July and 1 Aug. 1141, and this could be the reason for the erasure in C (see 1139 n. s).

"Vnde rex" illo mouens expeditionem, apud Paruam Herefordiam uel apud Leonis Monasterium castrametatus est. Vbi quidam ex consulto regi fidelitatem iurauerunt. Quidam renuentes, hoc regi intulerunt: 'Si non iuramento, credat rex, si uelit, saltim fidelibus uerbis nostris.' Quoniam uero instabant solennes dies Dominici Aduentus utrinque dextris datis ad tempus, rex Wigorniam rediit.[16] *v*Vbi quidam clericus uir eximie religionis, Mauricius nomine, electus a clero et a populo Pangornensi ecclesie, comitantibus illum presulibus Rotberto Herefordensi et Sigefrido Cicestrensi, in castello regi presentatur, attestantibus illum canonice electum presulatu fore dignum. Quod et rex concessit. Persuasus a pontificibus ut regi fidelitatem faceret, respondit hoc se nullatenus posse facere. 'Vir,' inquit, 'magne religionis apud nos est quem pro spirituali patre teneo, et predecessoris mei Dauid archidiaconus extitit,*w* hoc iuramentum mihi facere inhibuit.' Ad hec

p. 395 illi, 'Quod nos egimus, causa rationis exigit ut agas.' | At ille, 'Et si uos magne auctoritatis uiri hoc egistis, nulla mora sit mihi id idem faciendi.' Iurat et ille fidelitatem regi.[17]

[(G)]

Rogerius Selesberiensis episcopus .ii. non. Dec. hoc uita decessit, cuius obitus anno superiori latius litteris expressus est.[18]

De Wigornia rex Oxenofordiam adiit, indeque cum curia Særesbyriam, ibidem Dominicam Natiuitatem celebraturus, et pro more regio coronam dignitatis portaturus. Ad quem canonici uenientes, optulerunt ei .ii. mille libras, quibus ille dedit omnem libertatem de omnibus geldis suarum terrarum. Insuper ad usus illorum .xx. marcas et .xl. ad cooperiendam ecclesiam. Et si pacem optinuerit, quod dederant ei, restituet.[19]

[1140] (1162)*a* Emensis paucis diebus Dominice Natiuitatis, rex cum curia Rædingum uenit, ubi monet sors humana quanti pendenda sit regum purpura. Ibi, consilio suorum, duas abbatias

---

u–u om. (G)   *v* paragraph mark here C   *w* qui add. G

a 1140 corrected from 1142 and 1163 for its Marianan year C, 1140 started here G, .lxii. in its Marianan year .mclxii. is over an erasure

[16] The capture of Hereford by Geoffrey Talbot is described by GS 44 (pp. 94–6) and more vaguely referred to by WM HN 480 (pp. 36–7), but the information in JW and in G about the campaigns around Hereford and Little Hereford is not found elsewhere.

The king accordingly set out in that direction, and camped at Little Hereford or Leominster. There, taking counsel, some of the inhabitants swore their allegiance to the king while others refused, saying to the king: 'The king may, if he wishes, trust at least in the truth of our words, if not in our oath.' As the holy day of the Lord's Advent [3 December] was approaching, a temporary truce was made between them, and the king went back to Worcester.[16] There Maurice, a clerk of great piety chosen by the clergy and people of Bangor, came to the king's castle, accompanied by bishops Robert of Hereford and Seffrid of Chichester, who attested his canonical election and fitness for the office of bishop. The king confirmed the election. When urged by the bishops to do homage to the king, Maurice answered that he would in no way do this, saying, 'There is among us a man of great piety, whom I look upon as my spiritual father, and who was archdeacon to my predecessor David, who forbade me to take this oath.' They said to him, 'Reason demands that you do as we have done.' And he replied, 'If you who are men of high authority have done this, then I will not put off doing likewise.' He then swore fealty to the king.[17]

Roger, bishop of Salisbury, died on 4 December. His death has been more fully described above.[18]

The king went from Worcester to Oxford, and thence to Salisbury with his court, where he celebrated Christmas, and wore his crown as was the royal custom. The canons approached and gave him £2,000, and he granted them exemption from all taxes on their lands. He further added twenty marks for their own use, and forty for roofing the church. If he should attain a peaceful settlement, he promised that he would restore what they had given him.[19]

[1140] A few days after Christmas the king came with his court to Reading. There the fate of mankind reveals what value there is in royal pomp. There, following the advice of his council, he invested

---

[17] The archdeacon of Bangor was probably Simeon of Clynnog, see Lloyd, *History of Wales*, ii. 469 n. 25, 483.

[18] G inserts the reference to Roger's death at the correct chronological point (see above, under 1139 n. 14).

[19] *GS* 46 (pp. 96–8) speaks of Stephen's distribution of Bishop Roger's wealth. The exemption referred to is in *Regesta* iii. 787, which was issued at Christmas.

Malmesbyriensem et Abbedesberiensem,[b] dum uiueret Rogerus[c] episcopus honore priuatas et suo iuri[d] deditas, propriis pastoribus inuestiuit.

[C[3]]

Viro quidem magne probitatis Iohanni cenobite Malmesberiensem, alteri uero Gosfrido nomine Abbedesberiensem dedit abbatiam.[1]

[(G)]

Malmesberiensem largiendo eiusdem ecclesie cenobite Iohanni uocabulo, sed eodem anno .xiv. kal. Septembris morte prerepto. Abbedesberiensem uero cuidam monacho de sancto Floscello nomine Gaufrido.[1]

Et[e] ut paci satisfaceret, ad sedandum militare negotium, [f]penitus inquam[f] inane, ad Heli mouit expeditionem. Negotium sane deplorandum, quod ad militiam suam in satisfaciendo uane glorie frequentat militum grandis arrogantia. [g]Condicunt, condictis assentiunt, armis se bellicis instruunt. Victor uicti omnia ex auaritie detestando condicto possideat. Et ut ita dicam, comparationem faciens a maiore in minorem, Iuda et Ionatha fratre suo morantibus in terra Galaad, cum Iosepho et Azaria forsitan colloquendo musitant: Faciamus nobis et nos magnum nomen, probando uires in alterum.[2] Mucrone et lancea se inter se uulnerant, minime pensantes quid miseris occisorum animabus proueniat. In rebellatione repugnantium regi plures utrinque uulnerantur, capiuntur, custodie mancipantur. Episcopus Heliensis uidens uirtutem regis et impetum exercituum eius, loco cedit[h] [i]immo uice mercennarii[i] fugam iniit, et in partes Glaornensis pagi diuertens ad comitem Rotbertum secessit. Nec mirum; iam enim quasi manus dextra sibi ceciderat, ubi suus auunculus, Searesberiensis episcopus Rogerius, morti debita soluerat. Rex autem Eliense castellum optinuit, et in eo milites suos posuit.[3] Eboracensis archiepiscopus Turstinus, in ordine [j]uicesimus sextus,[j]

[(G)]

sanctarum elemosinarum sedulus executor, plurimorum monasteriorum, Hagustaldensis scilicet et

---

[b] quas *add. (G)*   [c] Selesberiensis *add. (G)*   [d] tenebat *add. (G)*
[e] Inde rex *(G)*   [f-f] prorsus insanum *(G)*   [g] Siquidem sibi *add. before*
condicunt *(G)*,   [h] cecidit *(G)*   [i-i] om. *(G)*   [j-j] .xvi. *rubricated not*
over an erasure C

two abbeys, Malmesbury and Abbotsbury, with their own abbots. During his lifetime, Bishop Roger had stripped them of their rights and submitted them to his rule.

He gave Malmesbury to John, a monk of great worth, and Abbotsbury to another, Geoffrey.[1]

He gave Malmesbury to John, a monk of the same church, who died the same year on 19 August. He gave Abbotsbury to Geoffrey, a monk of St Floscello.[1]

Then to secure peace and end war he moved his army to Ely, which I think was quite pointless. This move is to be regretted since it much increased the great arrogance of his warriors by satisfying their passion for vainglory. They accept and agree to these terms and put on their arms. The victor should take all from the vanquished in accordance with the hateful dictates of greed. And so if I may compare great things with small, they perhaps whisper to one another as Judah and his brother Jonathan in the land of Gilead to Joseph and Azarias, 'Let us get us a name and fight against the heathen all around us.'[2] They wound each other with sword and spear, caring little for the wretched souls of those whom they killed. In the rebellion of those fighting against the king, many on both sides were wounded, taken captive, and thrown into custody. The bishop of Ely recognized the strength of the king and the power of his army, gave way, no, rather, fled like a hireling, and, turning aside to Gloucestershire, went over to Earl Robert. This is hardly surprising since he had lost his right hand, as it were, when his uncle, Roger, bishop of Salisbury, paid his debt by death. The king took over Ely castle and manned it with his men.[3] Thurstan, the twenty-sixth archbishop of York,

painstaking in his holy alms-giving, the zealous founder or renewer of many monasteries, including Hexham, and of

---

[1] The restoration is also described in WM *HN* 482 (p. 40) and *GS* 46 (p. 98), though the appointment of John as abbot of Malmesbury is not mentioned by *GS*. G is the only extant source for the date of Abbot John's death and for the unidentified origin of Abbot Geoffrey (see *Heads*, pp. 23, 55). Stephen's stay at Reading after spending Christmas at Salisbury is unrecorded elsewhere.   [2] 1 Macc. 5: 55–7.

[3] *GS* 47 (pp. 98–101) also describes Bishop Nigel's rebellion and gives more detail on the siege of Ely. The account in *LE* 62 (pp. 314–15) is 'independent of other known sources'. HH *HA* x. 12 (p. 722) dates the siege to after Christmas 1139.

sanctimonialium in diocesi sua et
Fontium, aliorumque circiter
octo, strenuus fundator siue
renouator

prouecte uir etatis et plenus dierum, deposito uetere homine nouum
induit,[4] dum postpositis rebus apud Punfreit, .xii. kal. Feb., mon-
achicum habitum suscepit et ^{k}nonas Feb.,^{k} in bona senectute uita
decessit, ibidemque humatus requiescit,

[(G)]

anno episcopatus sui .xxvii.
Corpus uero eius post annum et
menses quinque sepulture sue
integrum et odoriferum repertum est.[5]

Milo exconstabularius grandi adunato exercitu, .ii. kal. Feb., feria .v.,
Wincelcumbiam inuadit, maxima ex parte uillam combussit, predam
egit, spoliatos rebus, ob exigendam ab eis, licet iniuste, mammonam
iniquitatis, secum abduxit.[6] Suthleiam inde diuertit, dumque illam
inuadere cupit, regii milites qui in oppido erant resistere, et illum
fugere compulerunt, cesis ut fertur de militibus eius duobus, et .xv.
captis et in custodiam positis.[7] Rex et comes Wigornensis cum grandi
exercitu Wigorniam uenit, et euolutis aliquantis diebus, prius comes,
post rex cum maxima expeditione Paruam adeunt Herefordiam,

[(G)]

^{l}hostes suos hinc inde expugna-
turi.^{l}

Morante itaque rege in illis partibus, comes memor iniuriarum
ciuium suorum, in graui multitudine armatorum Teodekesberiam
inuadit, magnificam domum Glaornensis comitis et omnia que in
circumitu eius erant, quorundam etiam aliorum,^{m} igne combussit,
miliario uno distante^n a Glaorna. ^{o}Victus precibus domni abbatis
Theodekesberiensis et fratrum, rebus illorum pepercit.^{o} Non modica

---

$^{k-k}$ *interlin. above* septimo ab hinc die *which is struck through* C^3 $^{l-l}$ *three-quarters*
of a line erased at this point, though such letters as are visible do not correspond to G's reading
C ^{m} domos cum rebus suis *add. (G)* ^{n} distans *(G)* $^{o-o}$ rebus tantum
Thoekesberiensis uictus abbatis et fratrum precibus pepercit *(G)*

---

[4] Cf. Col. 3: 9–10.
[5] Thurstan was the 26th archbishop of York in JW's *Epis. List* for York, and JW MS
C^3's 16th is impossible on any calculation. John of Hexham (SD ii. 305) dates Thurstan's
reception as a monk to 25 Jan., and his death to 6 Feb., and speaks of his body being lifted
up many years afterwards. An unpublished life of Thurstan (BL Cotton Titus A. XIX) in

                                    convents in his diocese, and of
                                    Fountains,   and   of   around
                                    another eight houses,
a man of advanced years and full of days, putting off the old man,
putting on the new,[4] retired from worldly affairs, and accepted the
monastic habit at Pontefract on 21 January. He died in a good old age
on 5 February and was buried there

                                    in the twenty-seventh year of his
                                    episcopacy. His body was found
                                    to be whole and sweet-smelling
                                    one year and five months after
                                    burial.[5]

Miles, the former constable, put together a large army, and attacked
Winchcombe on Thursday, 31 January, burning much of it down. He
plundered it, and took away with him those whom he had despoiled
so as to demand from them, although this was most unjust, the
Mammon of unrighteousness.[6] He then turned aside to Sudeley, and,
whilst he was thinking of attacking it, the royal garrison there
assaulted him and forced him to flee, killing, it is said, two of his
men, and capturing, and placing in custody, another fifteen.[7] King
Stephen and the earl of Worcester arrived with a large army at
Worcester, and, after a few days, the earl first, and then the king,
advanced with a great force to Little Hereford

                                    in order to drive their enemies
                                    out.

    During the king's stay in those parts, the earl, remembering the
injuries inflicted upon his townsmen, attacked Tewkesbury with a
strong force, burnt down the earl of Gloucester's magnificent house,
and everything in its vicinity as well as some houses belonging to
others, all about a mile from Gloucester. He was persuaded by the
prayers of the lord abbot and brethren of Tewkesbury to spare their
goods. He took much booty, both men and their goods and beasts,

prose and verse by Hugh de Pontefract and Geoffrey de Nottingham (which is referred to
in Raine, *Priory of Hexham*, p. 131 n. f), reads on fo. 55ᵛ: 'corpus post duos annos repertum
est odoriferum et incorruptum'. G's description of Thurstan's fostering of monastic life is
appropriately vague, but for a modern assessment, see Nicholl, *Thurstan*, pp. 111–212.
    [6] *GS* 44 (p. 94) mentions Winchcombe, which it describes as a *ciuitas*, only as an
example of the places captured by Miles.
    [7] Sudeley is mentioned in WM *HN* 483 (p. 42), though in a different context, among
the places, including Harptree and Cerney, reduced by Robert of Gloucester. Waleran had
captured Sudeley in 1139 (see above, 1139 n. 13). *GS* 44 (p. 94) speaks of Miles attacking
Winchcombe and Cerney.

preda capta, tam de hominibus et suppellectili eorum quam de animalibus, respectu mox clementi qui captiui ducebantur a uinculis soluti[p], ad sua redire iussit, et crastino Wigorniam rediit, contestans omnibus se in Normannia nec in Anglia tantam combustionem uix unquam peregisse.[8] Rex autem rediens Wigorniam ire perrexit Oxenofordiam. [q]Supradictus Mauricius Pangornensi et Vhtredus Landauiensi ecclesie presules a Teodbaldo archipresule Dorubernie, presentibus episcopis Herefordensi et Execestrensi, consecrantur.[9] [r]Rex Wintoniam ueniens, consilio baronum suorum, cancellario suo Philippo Searesberiensem presulatum et Henrico cuidam monacho cognato suo Fescamnensem abbatiam dedit. |

p. 395

[C³]	[(G)]
	Sed Philippus a legato et clero non recipitur, unde iam assumptus, Baiocensi ecclesie post aliquantum tempus preficitur.[10]
[s]Eclypsis solis dum caudam luna draconis occupat est facta, caput ipso luce premente.[s] [11]	[t]Eclipsis solis facta est .xi. kal. Aprilis, feria .ii., circa horam diei tertiam.[t] [11]

Consilio baronum regis Francie Philippi et[u] regis Anglie Stephani, factum est ut illius filius Francorum regis sororem acciperet in uxorem. Facta est desponsatio illorum mense Feb., in transmarinis partibus, matre regina Anglorum presente, et quampluribus uiris nobilissimis ex utriusque[v] regni parte coram positis.[12] Miles quidam nomine Rotbertus, cuiusdam nobilis uiri Huberti filius. Hic nec Deum nec homines ueritus, sed totus in suis uiribus confisus, Malmesberiense castellum cum suis doli machinamentis inuasit, regis militibus qui intus erant quibusdam in ecclesiam sancti presulis Aldelmi

---

[p] solutos *(G)*   [q] *paragraph mark here* C   [r] *paragraph mark here* C
[s–s] *rubricated over an erasure which probably contained 1140[t]* C   [t–t] *scribbled in the upper mg., presumably indicating the words to be erased* C³   [u] *petitione add.* (G)   [v] *partibus add.* C

---

[8] This campaign is peculiar to JW.
[9] The identical professions of the two Welsh bishops are in Richter, *Canterbury Professions*, p. 42 (nos. 81–3), and Uhtred's is calendared by Conway Davies (ed.), *Episcopal Acts ... relating to Welsh Dioceses, 1066–1272* (above, 1120, n. 1), ii. 634 (L. 89). *Regesta* iii. 264 in favour of Ely Cathedral could well have been issued during Stephen's stay at Oxford.
[10] The Waverley Annals (*Ann. Mon.* ii. 228) date this council to mid-Lent (*c.*17 Mar). OV *HE* xiii. 42 (vi. 536–7) has a fuller account of this council and of the dispute over the succession at Salisbury. He shows that Bishop Henry of Winchester had hoped that his

and, suddenly overcome by clemency, he ordered the release of the prisoners and their return home. The next day he went back to Worcester, assuring everyone that he had hardly ever caused such a conflagration either in Normandy or in England.[8] The king also returned to Worcester and set out for Oxford. The afore-mentioned Maurice of Bangor and Uhtred of Llandaff were consecrated bishops by Theobald, archbishop of Canterbury, assisted by the bishops of Hereford and Exeter.[9] The king came to Winchester, and, on the advice of his magnates, gave the see of Salisbury to his chancellor, Philip, and the abbacy of Fécamp to a monk Henry who was his kinsman.

Philip, however, was not accepted by the legate and the clergy, and so, already having taken up the rank, he became after a while bishop of the see of Bayeux.[10]

A solar eclipse took place when the moon was in Draco's tail, though its head was illuminated.[11]

A solar eclipse took place on Monday, 22 March, at the third hour.[11]

It was agreed, after the magnates of Philip, king of France, and Stephen, king of England, had been consulted, that Stephen's son should marry the French king's sister. The betrothal took place overseas in February in the presence of the queen-mother of England and of many of the highest nobility of both kingdoms.[12] A certain knight called Robert was the son of Hubert, a noble man. He feared neither God nor man, but trusted completely in his own strength. He attacked the castle of Malmesbury by a cunning ploy. Some of the royal knights in the castle took refuge in the church of the holy

nephew, Henry of Sully, would succeed as bishop of Salisbury, and implies that Stephen gave him the abbey of Fécamp in the same year. Philip of Harcourt became bishop of Bayeux before 18 June 1142 (see Greenway, *Fasti* iii. 8). *Regesta* iii. 991 in favour of St Peter's Hospital, York, could have been issued during Stephen's stay at Winchester.
    [11] The eclipse of the sun is reported in many English sources on 20 Mar. (WM *HN* 484 (pp. 42–3)), ASC, two Canterbury chronicles (*UAG*, pp. 5, 80), and the Reading, Plympton, Battle, Chichester (*UAG*, pp. 11, 28, 53, 95), and Bermondsey Annals (*Ann. Mon.* iii. 436), and on 19 May in the Margam Annals (*Ann. Mon.* i. 14). Some of these annals note stellar phenomena, but none comment on the moon's location at the time, which JW has presumably derived from his reading of Walcher of Malvern's rendering of Petrus Alfonsi, *Sententia de dracone* (see above 1133, n. 2).
    [12] HH *HA* x. 10 (p. 720) mentions this marriage without dating it. JW again mistakenly calls the French king Philip (see above, 1137 n. 14).

uelut in asylum fugientibus. Quos insecutus, quadam die cum suis
armis militaribus constructis*w* capitulum fratrum intrauit. Minis eos
territans, salua tuitione facultatum suarum regie dignitatis uiros cum
equis tradi sibi mandauit. At illi pacem Dei et beati patroni sui
Aldelmi infringere ueriti, iussis huiusmodi consentire renuunt. At
demum licet inuiti quo uesanie illius satisfaciant, reddunt equos.
Diutius illo in castello morante, iam uastatis omnibus in circumitu,
rex cum exercitu superuenit, et fere .viii. diebus castellum obsedit.
Willelm d'Ipre, ut fertur consanguineus ipsius Rotberti, ad red-
dendum castellum utrinque internuntius fuit; idque tandem a rege
optinuit, ut dextris datis et castello reddito, regio iuri omnia cedant.[13]
Quod et factum est. Rotbertus uero ad comitem Glaocestrensem
diuertit, penes illum ad tempus in doli ueneno moraturus. Non
multo post, quia nullatenus uoluit intelligere ut bene ageret, sed ut
sanguine sanguinem tangeret, ignorante comite, cum suis ad Diuisas
se contulit. Vbi, uel prius iam facta conuentione*x* inter se et suos si
castellum optineret, nemini unquam tradendum. Dolo malignitatis
*y*murum ascendit, regiis militibus qui intus erant signum *z*dedit sic
proclamans.*z*

Ex improuiso*y* exteriora castella penetrat, in plures tyrannidem
exercet. Quarta dehinc die, ui et callidate malitiosa turrim inter-
iorem possidendam inuadit; et singulis diebus ac noctibus, in
extollentia cordis ubi*aa* omnia deuastat, et mala que poterat agere
non cessat. Non tandem*bb* ad Iohannem, illustris militie uirum, qui
tunc in regis fidelitate Mællesberiense castellum obseruabat, diuertens, ut suo consilio, immo insilio, consentiat et secum teneat, et non
solum regi sed etiam comiti et quibuscunque poterat, in Satan fiat,
minando postulat. Si nollet, sciret se ex improuiso capite plecten-
dum.

[C³]
*cc*O hominem dementem, uelut
in   multitudine   diuitiarum
suarum sperantem, et in uanitate

---

w instructis *interlin. above* constructis C, instructis *(G)* *x* uel pactione *interlin.* C
y–y ex improuiso murum conscendit regiis militibus qui intus erant signum dedit uictorie.
Hinc *(G)*   *z–z* *over erasure, followed by half a blank line* C
    aa *repeated* C   *bb* *written in mg.* C³   *cc* Invectio in Rotbertum *written in the mg.* C³

---

[13] The capture of Malmesbury by Robert fitz Hubert seems to have taken place in 1139
if the sequence of events in *GS* 43 (pp. 92–4) and WM *HN* 479 (p. 36) is reliable. WM
dates to 7 Oct. Robert's entry into Malmesbury, and records its capture by Stephen within

bishop Aldhelm for sanctuary. Robert pursued them, and one day broke into the chapter-house of the monks at the head of armed men. With terrifying threats, he ordered the brethren to hand over the mighty king's soldiers and their horses if they valued their property. The monks were horrified at the breaking of the peace of God and of their blessed patron, Aldhelm, and refused to do as he asked. In the end, and, unwillingly, they handed the horses over, to appease his wrath. After Robert had remained in the castle for some time and had devastated the surrounding countryside, the king arrived with his army and besieged the castle for almost eight days. William of Ypres, who was said to be a kinsman of the same Robert, was the go-between for the surrender of the castle, and at last gained the king's agreement to a peace settlement and the surrender of the castle with a total submission to the king.[13] And this was done. Robert meanwhile went to the earl of Gloucester, staying with him for some time, brooding treacherous thoughts. A little later, Robert, unwilling to follow what was right, and thirsting for blood, went to Devizes with his men, without the earl's knowledge. There he first agreed with his followers that if he took the castle it would never be surrendered by anyone of them. By treacherous cunning he scaled the wall, and gave the signal of victory to the king's soldiers within.

He took by surprise the outer forts, and acted as a tyrant to many. On the fourth day, by force and evil cunning he took possession of the citadel inside, and, in his vainglory, ravaged everywhere day and night, and did not stop doing all the harm he could. He then turned aside to John, a famous warrior, who was at that time holding Malmesbury castle for the king, and menacingly demanded that he should follow his advice, or rather evil counsel, and carry out his devilish plans not just against the king, but also against the earl and everyone possible. If John were to refuse, he was to know that he would lose his life when he was not expecting it.

Oh the madness of man hoping
to rely on his many riches, and
successful only in his vanity! He

15 days, and refers to Robert's having killed 80 monks in an unnamed church. JW may have decided to consolidate his information on Robert fitz Hubert into his 1140 annal. William Ypres, the natural son of Philip of Loo, and grandson of Robert the Frisian, had claimed the county of Flanders after the murder of his cousin, Charles the Good in 1127. Driven out of Flanders in 1133, he probably provided mercenaries for Stephen's Scottish campaign in 1136, commanded the Flemings for Stephen in Normandy in 1137, and captured Bishop Roger's castle of Devizes in 1139.

sua preualentem. At in abundantia uirtutis sue non saluabitur.
Respondit Iohannes, ^{dd}'In uirtute Dei quenlibet malo capere, quam
ab aliquo capi.' Dixit et mox illum captum in custodiam posuit,
uicemque pro uice reddens, omnia tormentorum genera que in
crudelitate sua prius aliis intulerat, in illum expendi fecit. His
omnibus auditis, comes Glaornensis et Milo exconstabularius cum
pluribus ad predictum Iohannem ueniunt. Cui ipse comes .d. marcas
se daturum spopondit, eo pacto ut sibi Rotbertum ad statutum diem
prestaret, ipseque sibi bonos obsides daret. Iohannes placatus
pecunia promissa^{ee} et obsidibus, tradidit illi Rotbertum eo tenore,
ut infra .xv. dies sibi redderetur. Hac conuentione facta, comes
reuertitur Glaorniam, ducens secum Rotbertum. Conseritur sermo
de reddendo castello apud Diuisas, quod spontaneo uelle sibi tradi
postulat. Abnegat Rotbertus ne iuramentum quod cum suis iurauerat
in non reddendo scilicet castello infringeret. At ubi minis territus in
patibuli suspensione, spondet se cessurum petitis, dummodo periculum euadat mortis. Infra statutum diem conuentionis, ille malignus
Rotbertus ad prefati Iohannis reducitur presentiam, cui nuntiat
comes omnia que gesta sunt, quomodo minis territus Rotbertus
promiserat se redditurum castellum. Rogat etiam denuo Rotbertum
ad Diuisas secum ire permittat, eo pacto, ut si fortassis optinuerit
castellum, iuri Iohannis sub eo subigatur. Annuit Iohannes precibus
comitis, qui protinus cum Rotberto redit ad Diuisas. Interim idem
Iohannes, missis litteris ad eos qui extra uel qui infra castellum erant,
iureiurando iurauit nec se nec comitem aliquid malefacturos Rotberto; hoc dumtaxat agant, ut iuramentum in non tradendo alicui
castello firmiter teneant. Relictis exconstabulario et quodam potenti
uiro Hunfrido et quibusdam aliis,^{ff} comes Glaorniam reuertitur,
mandans omnibus ut si Rotbertus renueret sponte reddere castellum,
suspenderetur.^{gg} ^{14}

---

^{dd} *paragraph mark here* C ^{ee} promissas C ^{ff} apud Diuisas *add.* (G)
^{gg} C *ended imperfectly here* C

---

^{14} The story of Robert fitz Hubert is also found in GS 50–2 (pp. 104–8) and WM HN
485 (pp. 43–4), who dates his capture of Devizes to 26 Mar. 1140. There are some
differences between the two fuller accounts of JW and GS. GS describes John the Marshal
as a loyal supporter of Earl Robert, says that the latter's forces were driven away from
Devizes by Robert fitz Hubert, that John lured and captured Robert by a stratagem, and

will not be saved by his abund-
ant strengths.

John answered, 'By God's help, I would rather seize an evil man than
be taken captive by him.' Saying this he immediately seized Robert
and placed him under guard, where turn for turn he caused every
torture which Robert had formerly inflicted on others to be inflicted
on him. On learning of this, the earl of Gloucester and Miles, the
former constable, came to the said John with many men. The earl
promised him 500 marks if he would agree to hand Robert over on a
fixed day after he had been given valued hostages. John was pleased
by the promise of money and hostages, and handed Robert over to
the earl on condition of his being returned within fifteen days. After
this agreement, the earl returned to Gloucester, taking Robert with
him. They then discussed the surrender of Devizes castle, which the
earl wanted Robert to hand over voluntarily. Robert refused so as not
to break the oath which had been made with his followers that the
castle should never be given up. However, scared by the threat of
hanging on the gallows, he agreed to the request on condition that he
escaped the danger of death. Before the day appointed for the hand-
over, the detestable Robert was led back to the afore-mentioned John,
who was told by the earl all that had happened, and how Robert,
terrified by threats, had agreed to hand over the castle. The earl
again asked that Robert be allowed to come with him to Devizes,
promising that, if by chance he obtained the castle, it would be
surrendered to John under his jurisdiction. John agreed to the earl's
proposal, and the earl straightaway returned to Devizes with Robert.
Meanwhile the same John sent letters to those outside and within the
castle, swearing that neither he nor the earl would harm Robert, and
that they would ensure that the garrison's oath not to hand the castle
over to anyone was firmly kept. The earl went back to Gloucester,
leaving behind the ex-constable, a powerful man Hunfrith, and some
others, and ordering that Robert should be hanged if he refused to
surrender the castle voluntarily.[14]

speaks of Earl Robert hanging Robert fitz Hubert in front of Devizes after John had
handed him over. JW alone gives details of the complicated negotiations between Earl
Robert and John Marshal. WM says that John hanged fitz Hubert. John Marshal, whom
both *GS* and WM describe as cunning, was the son of Gilbert Marshal, had been
Stephen's marshal, is spoken of by the annals of Winchester (*Ann. Mon.* ii. 51) as fortifying
Malmesbury and Ludgershall, and was presumably besieged by Stephen in 1139 (see
above, 1139 n. 9), though JW describes him here as the king's supporter in 1140.

G'S CONTINUATION

(1140 *continued*)

fo. 147ʳ Renuit Rodbertus, renuunt et sui, | ne uiderentur periuri. Quid multis? Vt terror omnibus incuteretur, duobus nepotibus Rodberti prius suspensis, ipse captus suspenditur. Per omnia benedictus Deus qui tradidit impios.[1]

Ante Assumptionem sancte Marie comes Gloecestrie uersus Bathoniam mouit exercitum. At rex exploratores multo ante premiserat ut hostibus insidias tenderent, et fortissima manu se et sua defenderent. Fit itaque progressus et congressus, hinc militum regis inter quos duo milites erant, Iohannes et Rogerius uiri strenui et bellicosi, illinc satellitum comitis. Capiuntur multi, quamplures uulnerantur et occiduntur, quorum unus Gausfridus Talebotus, miles quidem strenuus sed dolosus, nunc enim cum rege, nunc cum comite, omnia agens in dolo, morte tenus uulneratur, quo uulnere defunctus .xi. kal. Septembris, Glaorne sepelitur cum canonicis. Regia uero manus uictoria potitur.[2] Ante Natiuitatem sancte Marie Rodbertus, filius Henrici regis, instinctu Radulfi Painelli, assumptis secum equitibus comitis de Wareuuica, cum his quos de Gloecestria adduxerat, et aliis quampluribus gregariis militibus, inuasit repente urbem Snotingaham et uacuam reperiens bellico apparatu, deuastare cepit, ciuibus undique fugientibus ad ecclesias. Captus est unus ciuium qui locupletior esse dicebatur, et arctius constrictus ductus est ad domum suam, et pecuniam suam prodere coactus. At ille in fo. 147ᵛ subterraneum suum predones nimia seuientes cupiditate | induxit, ubi omnis supellex sua uidebatur esse. Illis itaque circa direptionem rerum intentis, et ostia et seras frangentibus, ille callide elapsus, cameras et deinde aulam egressus, ostia omnia post se clausit, et seris firmauit, et imposito igne domos suas et omnem suppellectilem suam cum ipsis predonibus incendio tradidit. Ferunt autem amplius quam .xxx., qui subterraneum intrauerant, illo incendio tota urbs combustos et dicunt quidam quod de illo incendio concremata sit. Nam milites omnes, omnisque exercitus immunes se ab ipso incendio iureiurando asserunt. Combusta est itaque tota urbs, et qui extra ecclesias capi poterant captiui ducti sunt, quidam etiam usque ad Glaornam. Reliquum uero uulgus, uiri scilicet cum mulieribus et

---

[1] 2 Macc. 1: 17. This sentence concludes the Robert fitz Hubert episode, and must have also been in the mutilated C³.

G'S CONTINUATION

(1140 *continued*)

Both Robert and his followers refused because they did not wish to break their oath. Soon after as a warning to others, first his nephews were hanged, and then he was also taken and hanged. Blessed be God who has delivered up the wicked![1]

Before the feast of the Assumption [15 August], the earl of Gloucester marched against Bath. The king had much earlier sent out scouts to ambush the enemy, and to defend most strongly himself and his followers. An engagement took place. On the one side were the king's soldiers, among whom were two valiant warriors, John and Roger, on the other side the earl's supporters. Many were taken prisoner, others were wounded and slain, among them Geoffrey Talbot, a brave but scheming knight. From time to time he changed sides, always acting treacherously, and he died of his wounds on 22 August, and was buried with the canons at Gloucester. The king's army gained the victory.[2] Before the feast of the Nativity of Mary [8 September], King Henry's son, Robert, urged on by Ralph Paynell, taking knights of the earl of Warwick with him, as well as troops from Gloucester, and many other common soldiers, suddenly attacked Nottingham, and finding it undefended, began to sack it as the citizens fled on all sides to the churches. One of these, who was reputedly wealthier than the rest, was seized and bound, and was led back to his house in the hope that he might be forced to give up his money. This man led his captors, who were overgreedy for loot, into a cellar where all his household goods were supposed to be stored. Whilst they were absorbed in looting and in breaking open doors and locks, he slipped away cleverly, made his way through the chamber and the hall, closing all the doors behind him and locking them with bolts, and set fire to the buildings with all his goods as well as the looters. There were said to have been more than thirty men in the cellar who perished by fire. It is also said that as a result of that fire the whole town was consumed by flames. The knights and the whole army swore that they were not responsible for the fire. The whole town was burnt down, and all who could be captured outside churches were taken into captivity, some of them to as far away as Gloucester. The remainder of the ordinary people, with their

---

[2] An account of Earl Robert's campaign against Bath and of Geoffrey Talbot's death must have been in the folios missing from *GS*.

paruulis, qui ecclesias intrauerant, cum egredi non auderent ne ab hostibus caperentur, seuiente ubique incendio, combustis ecclesiis, pene omnes perierunt. Crudele spectaculum, et ipsis hostibus nimium miserabile, cum uiderent templa Dei igne consumi, quibus etiam paganissimi pepercissent. Itaque destructa est Snotingaham, urbs nobilissima, cum ex quo Normanni Angliam sibi subiugauerant, usque ad hoc tempus, in summa pace et quiete, populosa multitudine et opulentia rerum omnium referta fuisset.³ Cuidam monacho, literis et scientia nobiliter instructo, Petro nomine, data est ab Henrico, Wintoniensis ecclesie episcopo, sancte Romane ecclesie legato, Mal-
fo. 148ʳ mesberiensis | abbatie prelato. Hic apud Cluniacum sumpto habitu religionis, functus est aliquanto tempore prioratu de Caritate. Inde assumptus preficitur monasterio sancti Vrbani pape in diocesi Catalaunensis ecclesie, sed, malis crebrescentibus sibique imminentibus locum illum deserere coactus, suadente prefato Wintoniensi presule, adiit Angliam, predictamque hoc anno suscepit ecclesiam regendam.⁴

[1141] Stephanus rex Anglorum, post diuturnos labores et obsidiones castellorum, quibus pro pace regni .v. annis et .vi. hebdomadibus desudauit, tandem in obsidione Lincoliensis castelli, die Purificationis sancte Marie, dominica die Sexagesime, a Gloecestrensi comite Rodberto, auunculi sui filio, et a Cestrensi comite Rannulfo, iusto Dei iudicio circumuentus et captus, primo ad Glocestrensem dominica Quinquagesima, deinde ad Bricstouuensem urbem abductus et custodie mancipatus est. Capti sunt cum eo quamplures fideles ipsius, uinculisque mancipati.¹ Morabatur interim in urbe Gloecestrensi domina imperatrix, Henrici regis filia, que ob istiusmodi euentum uehementer exhilarata, utpote regnum sibi iuratum, sicut sibi uidebatur, iam adepta, habito cum suis consilio, .v. feria post acceptos Cineres ex urbe secedens,

³ G is the sole known source for this campaign. Davis, *King Stephen*, p. 43, comments that this raid was 'presumably a diversion, but why Nottingham was chosen and why they were aided by knights of the earl of Warwick is a complete mystery'. *GS* 58 (pp. 116–18) implies that Roger de Beaumont, Earl of Warwick (who is described as 'uir mollis'), did not join the empress until after the battle of Lincoln, and it has been assumed that those of his knights who participated in the Nottingham raid did so independently of him. *Regesta* iii. 597 shows, if it is correctly dated, that he was on the empress's side by 2–3 Mar. 1141. On Ralph Paynel see above, 1138 n. 18. He was to witness charters of the empress; see *Regesta* iii. 911, 839, 634, 581, 393–4, 274–5, 111.
⁴ The list in BL Cotton Vitellius A.X, fo. 160, confirms that Peter Moraunt had been a monk at Cluny (see *Heads*, p. 55). *The Letters of Peter the Venerable*, ed. Giles Constable

wives and children, who were inside the churches, dared not emerge because they feared capture by the enemy, and nearly all perished as the fire raged everywhere and the churches were burnt down. It was a cruel sight and most pitiable even to the enemy themselves when God's temples, which even the most fiercely heathen men would have spared, perished in the flames. Thus was Nottingham, the noblest of cities, destroyed, which, from the time the Normans conquered England up to the present, had flourished in the greatest peace and calm, and was famous for its big population and its wealth of all kinds.[3] Peter the monk, who was of great learning and knowledge was made abbot of Malmesbury by Henry, bishop of Winchester, legate of the holy Roman see. He had been a monk at Cluny, and for some time had been prior of La Charité. Thence he became abbot of the monastery of the holy pope Urban in the diocese of Châlons-sur-Marne. When troubles arose and threatened him, he was forced to leave that house, and, at the prompting of the bishop of Winchester, he came to England, and took over the rule of Malmesbury in this year.[4]

[1141] Stephen, king of the English, after endless toil and sieges of castles, which he endured for five years and six weeks for the preservation of the kingdom, was at length by the just judgement of God surrounded and captured at the siege of Lincoln castle by Robert, earl of Gloucester, his uncle's son, and by Earl Ranulf of Chester on the feast of the Purification of St Mary [2 February] which fell on Sexagesima Sunday. He was taken and placed under guard first to Gloucester on Quinquagesima Sunday [9 February] and later to Bristol. Many of his followers were captured with him and thrown into prison.[1] In the mean time the lady empress, King Henry's daughter, who was staying at Gloucester, was ecstatic at this turn of events, having now, as she thought, gained possession of the kingdom, which had been promised to her by oath. Therefore, after taking counsel with her followers, she left the city on the fifth day

(2 vols., Cambridge, Mass., 1967), ii. 298, points out that Abbot Peter of St Urban was unlikely to have been the same man as Prior Peter of La Charité-sur-Loire as they were both in office at the same time, and suggests that the abbot might have been a claustral prior at La Charité. Peter of Malmesbury was among those receiving Matilda at Winchester Cathedral on 3 Mar. 1141.

[1] Fuller accounts of the battle of Lincoln and of Stephen's capture are in HH *HA* x. 13–19 (pp. 724–38), *GS* 54–5 (pp. 110–14), and OV xiii. 43 (vi. 542–6). G alone gives the day of Stephen's arrival at Gloucester.

comitantibus secum duobus episcopis, Bernardo Meneuensi et
fo. 148ᵛ Nigello Eliensi, et Gisleberto abbate | Glaornensi cum baronibus
multis, cum militibus ac ministris, Ciricestrensem adiit ciuitatem, ibi
primum post tantum gaudium habens hospitium simul et eiusdem
ciuitatis sumens dominium. Inde secedens cum appropinquaret ad
ciuitatem Wintonie, occurrunt illam cum gloria et pompa magnifica
presules pene totius Anglie, barones multi, principes plurimi, milites
innumeri, abbates cum suis diuersi, ex eadem urbe duo conuentus
monachorum, tertius sanctimonialium cum processionalibus melodiis
et laudibus, clerus urbis cum ciuibus et populis multis. Traditur
itaque eius imperio urbs nobilissima Wintonie, datur eius dominio
corona regni Anglie. Ab ipso legato maledicuntur qui maledicunt ei,
benedicuntur qui benedicunt ei, excommunicantur contradicentes,
absoluuntur eius iussioni parentes.² A Wintonia egressa cum suis
officialibus domina, adit Wiltoniam ubi ad salutandum eam Cantuariensis affuit archipresul Tedbaldus. Affluxit et tam copiosa populorum frequentia, ut pre multitudine introeuntium uix sufficeret
aditus portarum.³ Inde iam peractis festis paschalibus, ad Radingum
infra Rogationes*ᵃ* ueniens, suscipitur cum honoribus, hinc inde
principibus cum populis ad eius imperium conuolantibus. Conueni-
tur ibi ab eadem de principibus unus, uocabulo Rodbertus de Oleio,
de reddendo Oxenifordensi castello. Quo consentiente, uenit illa,
totiusque ciuitatis et circumiacentis regionis suscepit dominium
atque hominium. Proficiscitur inde cum exultatione magna et
fo. 149ʳ gaudio, et in monasterio sancti Albani | cum processionali suscipitur
honore et iubilo. Adeunt eam ibi ciues multi ex Lundonia, tractatur
ibi sermo multimodus de reddenda ciuitate.⁴ His diebus horrendum
quid in Wigornensi contigit diocesi, quod relatu dignum iudicauimus. Siquidem quarta feria ante octauam Ascensionis Dominice circa
nonam diei horam, apud uillam que Walesburna dicitur, distans ab

---

ᵃ negationes *(G)*

---

² Matilda's progress to Winchester is outlined in *GS* 58 (pp. 116–18), and in WM *HN*
491 (pp. 50–1). WM dates to 2 Mar. a meeting between the empress and Bishop Henry on
an open plain outside Winchester (at Wherwell monastery according to *Regesta* iii. 343),
and to the following day the reception of the empress in Winchester cathedral in
ceremonial procession. By the agreement Henry promised her his allegiance in exchange
for his control of ecclesiastical appointments. This meeting may have been planned on 16
Feb., when envoys were sent to Bishop Henry by the empress (WM (ibid.)). G omits much
but is alone in dating the empress's departure from Gloucester, in identifying her
companions, and in recording her stay at Cirencester.
³ The meeting with Theobald at Wilton 'paucis post diebus' after 3 Mar. is confirmed

after Ash Wednesday [17 February], accompanied by two bishops, Bernard of St David's, and Nigel of Ely, and by Gilbert, abbot of Gloucester, many nobles, knights and officials, and approached Cirencester. There after learning such good news, she first received hospitality, and then imposed her rule. Leaving Cirencester, she approached Winchester, and there the bishops of almost all England, many nobles, the chief magnates, innumerable knights, different abbots with their monks, from the same city monks from two houses, nuns from a third house, chanting in procession hymns and thanksgivings, and the clergy of the city with the citizens and crowds of people, all came to meet her in great state and pomp. Then the most famous city of Winchester was handed over to her, and the crown of the English kingdom was given to her rule. The legate cursed all who cursed her, blessed those who blessed her, excommunicated those who were against her, and absolved those who submitted to her.[2] Matilda left Winchester with her officials, and went to Wilton where Theobald, archbishop of Canterbury, came to greet her. Here there were such crowds to meet her that the town gates were hardly wide enough to let them in.[3] After celebrating Easter [30 March] there, she came in the Rogation days [6–8 May] to Reading, where she was received with honour, the chief men and the people flocking to submit to her. There Matilda sounded out one of these leaders, Robert d'Oilli, on the surrender of Oxford castle. When he agreed, she came to Oxford, and received the submission and homage of the whole city and of the surrounding region. From there she proceeded further joyfully and in high spirits, and was received at the monastery of St Albans with processions, honour, and rejoicing. Many of London's citizens approached there and discussed in detail the surrender of their city.[4] We think it worth relating the horrible occurrence which took place at this time in the diocese of Worcester. On Wednesday before the octave of the Ascension [15 May] at about the ninth hour, at a township called Wellesbourne

by WM *HN* 491 (p. 51), which says that Theobald delayed his change of allegiance until he had obtained the king's agreement.

   [4] WM (ibid.) says that the empress spent Easter at Oxford, and H. W. C. Davis, 'Some documents of the Anarchy', in *Essays in History presented to R. L. Poole*, ed. H. W. C. Davis (Oxford, 1927), pp. 168–89 at p. 182, suggested that G's account could be reconciled with WM's by placing its sentence 'inde, iam peractis . . . conuolantibus' after 'dominium atque hominium'. WM gives a lengthy account of a legatine council held on 31 Mar.–3 Apr. to recommend the empress's succession. WM and *GS* 58 (p. 116) also record Robert d'Oilli's recognition of Matilda. G alone speaks of her stay at St Albans. Davis, *King Stephen*, p. 55, and Chibnall, *Empress Matilda*, p. 102, point out that the empress's route to London avoided Windsor.

Hamtonia, episcopi Wigornensis uilla, miliario uno, uentus turbinis uehemens exortus est, et caligo teterrima, pertingens a terra usque ad celum, et concutiens domum presbiteri cui nomen Leouredus, et officinas eius, omnes solo*b* tenus prostrauit et minutatim confregit, tectum quoque ecclesie abstulit, et ultra Auenam flumen proiecit. Domus etiam rusticorum fere quinquaginta simili modo deiciens, inutiles reddidit. Grando quoque ad magnitudinem oui columbini*c* cecidit cuius ictibus percussa quedam femina occubuit. Hoc uiso, qui affuerunt admodum exterriti fuerunt et conturbati.[5] Imperatrix, *d*ut prediximus, habito*d* tractatu cum Lundoniensibus, comitantibus secum presulibus multis et principibus, secura properauit ad urbem, et apud Westmonasterium cum processionali suscipitur honorificentia, ibique aliquantis diebus de regni statu dispositura resedit. Et primo quidem, quod*e* decuit sancte Dei ecclesie, iuxta bonorum consilium, consulere procurauit. Dedit itaque Lundoniensis presulatum ecclesie cuidam Radingensi monacho uiro uenerabili, Rodberto nomine, presente et iubente reuerendo abbate suo Ædwardo. Hoc itaque Dei peracto negotio, interpellauit dominam

fo. 149ᵛ Anglorum regina, pro domino | suo rege capto et custodie et uinculis mancipato. Interpellata quoque est pro eadem causa et a maioribus seu primoribus Anglie, obsidibus multis, castellis et diuitiis magnis sue dicioni tradendis, si rex absolutus, non regno sed sue tantum redderetur libertati. Se enim*f* ei suasuros spoponderunt, quatinus regno dimisso, Deo soli, siue monachus siue peregrinus, exinde deseruiret. At illa non exaudiuit eos; interpellata est et ab episcopo Wintoniensi ut consulatus qui fuerat sui fratris nepoti sue daretur, scilicet filio eiusdem regis Stephani; nec hec exaudiuit. Domina interpellata est a ciuibus, ut leges eis regis Ædwardi obseruare liceret, quia optime erant, non patris sui Henrici, quia graues erant. Verum illa non bono usa consilio pre nimia austeritate non adquieuit eis, unde et motus magnus factus est in urbe. Et facta coniuratione aduersus eam, quam honore susceperunt cum dedecore conprehendere statuerunt. At illa a quodam ciuium premunita ignominiosam cum suis arripuit fugam, omni sua suorumque suppellictili post tergum relicta.[6] Quo uiso, presul Wintonie qui et legatus

---

b sole *(G)*   *c* occumbini *(G)*   *d–d* bis *(G)*   *e* quid *(G)*   *f* enim se *(G)*

[5] This is not recorded elsewhere and could have been part of the lost text of C³. Wellesbourne Hastings and Wellesbourne Mountford are both one mile away from Hampton Lucy (Warwicks.), which was an estate belonging to the bishop of Worcester.

about one mile from the bishop of Worcester's estate at Hampton, there arose a violent whirlwind, together with a terrifying darkness, stretching from earth to heaven. This struck the house of Leofrith, a priest, and its outbuildings, levelled everything to the ground, and broke them into pieces. It also tore off the roof of the church and carried it across the Avon. Nearly fifty houses of the villagers were cast down and ruined in the same way. Hailstones as large as a pigeon's egg fell down and one hit and killed a woman. All were frightened and apprehensive when they saw this.[5] As we have already said, the empress had had discussions with the Londoners, and hastened in impunity to the city, accompanied by many bishops and nobles, and was received with a magnificent procession at Westminster, where she remained some days deciding how to set the affairs of the kingdom in order, but first, following good counsel, she took measures for the benefit of God's holy church. She gave the see of London to Robert, a venerable man and Reading monk, in the presence and at the urging of his abbot Edward. God's affairs being dealt with in this way, the queen of England interceded with the empress on behalf of her king, who was a prisoner under guard and in chains. She was also implored on his behalf by the chief men and highest nobles of England, who offered to give her many hostages, castles, and great riches, if the king were to be set free and allowed to recover his liberty, though not his crown. They promised to persuade him to give up the crown, and thereafter live devoted to God alone as a monk or pilgrim. She would not listen to them nor would she hear the bishop of Winchester's plea that the earldom which belonged to his brother should be given to his nephew, the king's son. The lady was asked by the Londoners that they might be allowed to live under the excellent laws of king Edward, and not the oppressive ones of her father, Henry. She did not listen to good advice but harshly rejected their petition, and there was great disorder in the city. A plot was made against her, and the Londoners who had received her with honour now tried to seize her with indignity. She was forewarned by some of them, and escaped shamefully with her followers, abandoning her goods and those of her men.[6] On seeing this, the bishop of

---

[6] Fuller accounts of Matilda's stay in Westminster are in WM *HN* 497 (pp. 58–9) and in *GS* 61–2 (pp. 122–5). *HN* dates her arrival to a few days before the nativity of John the Baptist. G alone describes the consecration of Robert de Sigillo as bishop of London and the Londoners' request for the laws/customs of Edward the Confessor not those of Henry I. The honour of Boulogne was the earldom claimed for Eustace.

sancte Romane ecclesie ad deliberationem fratris sui mentem apposuit, atque adhuc peragendum Lundoniensium sibi animos uirtutemque applicuit. Porro fugiens domina per Oxenefordiam uenit ad
Glaorniam, ubi cum Milone exconstabulario consilio inito statim
cum eodem ad Oxinefordense reuertitur urbem, ibi prestolatura seu
recuperata suum dispersum militarem numerum. Et quia eiusdem
fo. 150ʳ Milonis precipue fruebatur consilio et fouebatur | auxilio, utpote que
eatenus nec unius diei uictum nec mense ipsius apparatum aliunde
quam ex ipsius munificentia siue prouidentia acceperat; sicut ex
ipsius Milonis ore audiuimus ut eum suo arctius uinciret ministerio
comitatum ei Herefordensem tunc ibi posita pro magne remunerationis contulit premio.[7] Inde iam militum uirtute roborata et
numero appropinquante[g] festiuitate sancti Petri, que dicitur ad
Vincula, ignorante fratre suo comite Bricstouuensi, Wintoniensem
uenit ad urbem, sed eam a se iam alienatam inueniens, in castello
suscepit hospitium.[8] Cuius inopinatum aduentum ciuitatis eiusdem
episcopus Henricus miratus, indeque uehementer turbatus, per aliam
egrediens portam, sese tunc et deinceps conspectibus eius absentauit.[9] Hinc iam discordiis in alterutrum prorumpentibus, ciuitas
opulenta et multis retro ante seculis gloriosa et omnibus terris nota
atque famosa, repentina obsidione parentibus secum ad inuicem
compugnantibus, circumdatur, rebus et hominibus exinanitur, militibus gregariis et conducticiis in hoc spirantibus et furibunde hinc
inde conuolantibus. Nec hoc solum pontificis ire potuit sufficere
quin insuper ob terrorem siue horrorem illis incutiendum, immisso
igne urbem totam conburere, furore cogente decreuit. Quod et fecit.
Siquidem secunda die mensis Augusti ignis ciuitati inmissus monasterium sanctimonialium cum suis edificiis, ecclesias plus .xl. cum
fo. 150ᵛ maiori seu meliori parte ciuitatis postremo cenobium monachorum, |
Deo et sancto Grimbaldo famulantium cum suis edibus redegit in
cineres. Erat in hac ecclesia sancti Grimbaldi crux magna, crux

---

[g] appropinpinquante *(G)*

---

[7] Miles was made Earl of Hereford on 25 July 1141 (*Regesta* iii. 393). G alone describes
Matilda's movements before her return to Oxford. The growing estrangement between
legate and empress, the alliances between legate and queen, and legate and Londoners are
indicated in *GS* 63 (p. 126) and WM *HN* 497–8 (pp. 56–7).

[8] 31 July is *LVH*'s date for Matilda and Robert's arrival at Winchester. It is unlikely that
Robert was unaware of Matilda's plans. WM *HN* 500 (p. 61) dates Robert's arrival to 'a
few days before 15 August'. Matilda presumably occupied the castle in the south-west of
Winchester.

Winchester, who was also legate of the holy Roman see, began to think of setting free his brother, and to this end won over the minds and support of the Londoners. The fugitive lady came to Gloucester by way of Oxford, and after consulting the ex-constable Miles there she returned with him to Oxford, hoping to stay there while she equipped and reassembled her dispersed troops. She had had the counsel, and enjoyed the support, of this Miles to such an extent that (as he himself told us) she would not for even one day or one month have had provisions nor have had her table served without his munificence and stewardship. It was for this reason that, while she was there, she gave him the earldom of Hereford to bind him the more closely to her service and as an outstanding reward for it.[7] Her forces increased in numbers and strength, and, before the feast of St Peter ad Vincula [1 August], she went to Winchester without informing her brother the earl of Bristol. She found Winchester opposed to her, and made her home in the castle.[8] Henry, bishop of that city, was amazed at her unexpected arrival, and much troubled as a result. He left by another gate, and withdrew there and then from view.[9] The opulent city, for ages glorious and whose renown was famous in all lands, was from now on dislocated by internal strife, placed all of a sudden in a state of siege, with kinsmen engaged in mutual hostilities, its inhabitants and their belongings being destroyed by common soldiers and mercenaries, who rampaged furiously everywhere. This was not enough to assuage the bishop's rage, for urged on by his fury, and in order to strike terror and fear into the citizens, he decided to set fire to Winchester and raze it to the ground. This he accomplished. On 2 August, he set fire to the city, and reduced to ashes the convent of the nuns with its buildings, more than forty churches together with the largest and best part of the city, and finally the monastery of monks devoted to the service of God and St Grimbald with its buildings. In the church of St Grimbald there was a large and holy cross, which long ago had

---

[9] GS 63 (p. 126) agrees that Henry of Blois left by another gate, and says that the empress ordered the investment of the bishop's *castellum* and of 'domum illius, quam ad instar castelli fortiter et inexpugnabiliter', which are now taken to be respectively the royal palace in the centre of the city and the palace at Wolvesey (see Davis, *King Stephen*, p. 59 n. 24, and M. Biddle and D. J. Keene, 'Winchester in the eleventh and twelfth centuries', *Winchester in the early Middle Ages*, ed. M. Biddle (Winchester Studies, i; Oxford, 1976), pp. 325–7)). GS 65 (pp. 128–30) implies that the bishop remained outside the town, reports the arrival there of the queen's forces, and of those of Stephen's supporters, and names some of the leaders on both sides.

sancta, iussu regis Kanuti dudum fabricata, et ab eodem auro et argento, gemmis et lapidibus preciosis decentissime adornata. Hec iam sibi approximante incendio, quod mirum dictum est, quasi imminens sibi presentiens periculum, intuentibus qui aderant fratribus, cepit sudare, nigrescere immo comburentium nigredinem exprimere. Sed et in ipso concremationis eius momento fragor horrisonus tonitrui magni tribus uicibus intonuit quasi de celo. Hoc itaque incendio combusta ciuitate interius, et ab hostibus obsessa exterius dixisse fertur episcopus comiti Norðamtoniensi, 'En comes, ego iussi, tu ista radere stude.' Quibus dictis, patuerunt intima cordis dicentis.[10] Septem igitur septimanis in obsidione transcurrens, tandem episcopus tam diutine tribulationis pertesus, aduesperascente die que festiuitatem Exaltationis sancte Crucis precedebat, iussit per urbem pacem predicari, portas ciuitatis aperiri. Iamque domina imperatrix conscenderat equum, comitante seque conducente fratre suo Reinaldo, relictis ob excubias plus ducentis militibus cum comite Bricstowense eisdem presidente, cum ecce subito presul, ad arma suos consurgere et in hostes ilico uiolenter iussit insurgere, quotquot poterant uiriliter comprehendere. Comprehenduntur itaque multi, perimuntur hinc et inde plurimi, inter quos quidam miles, uocabulo Wilelmus de Curcel, cum militibus sex neci datus, et apud sanctum Grimbaldum est tumulatus.[11] Hec fo. 151ʳ audiens domina, uehementer exterrita | atque turbata, ad castellum quo tendebat de Ludekereshala tristis ac dolens aduenit, sed ibi locum tutum quiescendi, propter metum episcopi, non inuenit. Vnde hortantibus suis, equo iterum usu masculino supposita, atque ad Diuisas perducta, cum nec ibi secure se tutari posse ob insequentes formidaret, iam pene exanimis feretro inuecta, et funibus quasi cadauer circumligata, equis deferentibus, sat ignominiose ad

---

[10] *LVH* (p. 2) agrees with G's date for the firing of Winchester. WM *HN* 499 (p. 59) reports, and *GS* 65 (p. 130) implies, that Nunnaminster was among the places affected, and *LVH* (p. 2) speaks of many churches being burnt in a fire which must have extended outside the city. WM *HN* 499 (pp. 59–60) briefly reports the burning at Hyde Abbey of Cnut's cross, which was made of gold, silver, and precious stones. Simon of Senlis, earl of Northampton, was a staunch supporter of the queen.

[11] Bishop Henry's proclamation of peace on 13 Sept., which is not mentioned elsewhere, is to some extent confirmed by WM's date of 14 Sept. (*HN* 500 (p. 61)) for the departure of the empress's supporters from Winchester. G's '7 weeks' for the duration of the siege seems a little too long even if it began on 1 Aug. (which was G's date for its start). Both WM and *GS* stress the opposing forces' efforts to control the supply route to Winchester from the west. The queen's forces burnt down Andover (WM *HN* 499 (p. 59)), and Matilda's tried to establish a castle at Wherwell (*GS* 65 (pp. 130–2)). The empress's

been made on King Cnut's orders, and beautifully enriched by him
with gold and silver, gems, and precious stones. Marvellous to tell,
the cross, as the fire drew nearer, and almost as though it was aware
of the approaching danger, began to sweat and blacken before the
eyes of the brethren present, and to convey the blackness of the
incendiaries. Then just as it caught fire, three dreadful claps of loud
thunder sounded as though from heaven. The city was in this way
burnt from within and attacked by its enemies from outside, and
the bishop is reported to have said to the earl of Northampton,
'Behold, earl, you have my orders, concentrate on razing the city to
the ground.' These words show the speaker's innermost feelings.[10]
The siege had taken seven weeks. At length the bishop tired of the
protracted suffering, ordered the proclamation of peace throughout
the city, and the opening of its gates on the evening of the day
before the feast of the Exaltation of the Cross [14 September]. The
lady empress had already mounted her horse, being accompanied
and guided by her brother Reginald, more than 200 knights being
left as a rearguard under the earl of Bristol, when the bishop
suddenly ordered his men to take up arms, assault the enemy
forcefully and take captive energetically as many as possible. Many
were captured, many were killed here and there, among them the
knight, William de Curcel, together with six soldiers, and he was
buried at St Grimbald's.[11] On learning this, Matilda was very much
terrified and troubled, and reached Ludgershall castle for which she
was making, both sad and grieving. She found it offered no safe
resting place because of the fear of the bishop. As a result on the
advice of her companions, she again mounted her horse, male-
fashion, and was led to Devizes. When even there she feared that
she would not be safe from her pursuers, she was placed, almost
half-alive, upon a litter, which was borne by horses, and bound with
cords, as though she was a corpse, and carried ignominiously

leading supporters are listed by WM *HN* (ibid.), John of Hexham 13 (SD ii. 310–11), and
GS 64 (p. 128), the latter's list including Reginald, earl of Cornwall. Reginald, one of
Henry I's illegitimate sons, and the son-in-law of William, son of Richard fitz Turold, is
recorded rebelling with his father-in-law against Stephen early in 1140 in Cornwall. The
capture of the empress's supporters and the death of William de Curcel are not recorded
elsewhere. A 12th-c. marginal addition to *LVH* (p. 41) commemorates the death of William
de Curcella on 6 Aug., as pointed out independently by S. Keynes, *The Liber Vitae of the
New Minster and Hyde Abbey, Winchester* (Early English Manuscripts in Facsimile, xxvi;
Copenhagen, 1995), p. 92. The Hyde obit dates William's death before 14 Sept., which is
WM's date for the withdrawal from Winchester.

ciuitatem deportatur Glaornensem.[12] Porro frater suus, comes Bricstouuensi Rodbertus, per aliam uiam egressus, ab insequentibus
oppressus est, atque in loco qui Stolibrycge dicitur, a Flammensibus
cum comite Warennensi captus, et regine in urbe residenti presenta-
tus, Willelmo de Ipre eius iussu commendatur, et in ciuitate Rofensi
custodie mancipatur. Comes quoque Herefordensis Milo, ab hostibus
circumseptus, ab eorum manibus et iaculis mirabiliter elapsus,
abiecta sua arma tam cum suppellictili uniuersa, de sola uita letus
ad Glaornam cum dedecore fugiendo peruenit lassus, solus, et pene
nudus.[13] Iohannem etiam, fautorem eorum, ad monasterium Ware-
wellense fugientem milites episcopi persequentes, cum eum exinde
nullo modo expellere ualuissent, in ipsa die festiuitatis Exaltationis
sancte Crucis, immisso igne ipsam ecclesiam sancte Crucis cum
sanctimonialium rebus et domibus cremauerunt, indumentis earum
et libris cum ornamentis inclementer ablatis, sanguine quoque
plurimo coram sancto altari humano horribiliter effuso. Predictum
tamen Iohannem nec capere nec expellere ut diximus potuerunt. Hoc
fo. 151ᵛ | monasterium, regnante glorioso Anglorum rege Ædgaro, Alfryða
uxor eius, compuncta priuigni sui nece, edificauit in honore sancte
Crucis.[14] His ita gestis, presul Henricus, ira quantulumcumque
sedata sed cupiditate admodum dilatata, suggerente priore Noui
Monasterii nuperrime conflagrati, tulit ex combusta cruce quingen-
tas argenti libras, auri quoque marcas triginta, diademata tria cum
totidem scabellis ex auro Arabico purissimo, et lapidibus pretiosissi-
mis undique operta, opere pulcherrimo et mirifico facta, eaque in
suis recondidit thesauris.[15] Seruabantur interea rex et comes sub
custodia, uerum regina nimium satagente pro rege, et uicecomitissa

---

[12] Rosalind Hill, 'The battle of Stockbridge 1141', *Studies in Medieval History presented
to R. Allen Brown*, ed. C. Harper-Bill, C. Holdsworth, and J. L. Nelson (Woodbridge,
1989), pp. 173–7, is the most recent discussion of the departure of the empress's forces
from Winchester. There is a brief reference to her escape to Devizes in *GS* 66 (p. 134), but
G alone gives the details of her retreat, though its description of her riding astride her
horse is confirmed by *Histoire de Guillaume le Maréchal, comte de Strigil et de Pembroke*, ed.
P. Meyer (3 vols., Société de l'Histoire de France; Paris, 1891–1901), i. 9 (ll. 214–15).

[13] Both WM *HN* and *GS* report the empress's forces' retreat from Winchester as one
body with Robert of Gloucester as its rearguard, as well as his capture. Neither identifies
Robert's captors, the battle site, or the place of his final custody. G may be mistaken in
dividing up the retreating forces into two, each following a different route. In that case, the
death of William de Curcel and others (though for the date of William's death see above,
1141 n. 11), and the narrow escape of Miles of Gloucester, which are unique to G, could
have occurred during Robert's rearguard action. WM *HN* 500 (p. 61) dates Robert's
capture to 14 Sept. William of Warenne (III), earl of Surrey, was a consistent supporter of
Stephen.

enough to Gloucester.[12] Robert, the earl of Bristol, her brother, escaping by another route, was hard pressed by his pursuers, taken prisoner at Stockbridge by the Flemings with Earl Warenne, and offered to the queen who was staying in the city. On her orders he was entrusted to William d'Ypres, and confined at Rochester. Miles, earl of Hereford, being hemmed in by the enemy, miraculously escaping their clutches and their spears, cast off his arms and their furnishings, and, glad to escape with his life, fled with dishonour to Gloucester, which he reached, exhausted, tired, and half-naked.[13] The bishop's soldiers also pursued John, their enemies' abettor, who had fled to the monastery of Wherwell. They were not able to expel him thence, and, on the same day of the feast of the Exaltation of the Holy Cross [14 September], they set fire to the church of the Holy Cross with the nuns' goods and buildings, and, after spilling much blood horribly before the sacred altar, rudely took away their clothes, books, and ornaments. As we have said they were able neither to take or to expel John. In the reign of the glorious King Edgar, his wife Ælfthryth, in remorse for her stepson's murder, built this house in honour of the Holy Cross.[14] After these events, Bishop Henry's anger was slightly appeased, though his greed knew no limits, and at the suggestion of the prior of the recently-burned down New Minster, recovered from the ashes of the burnt cross fifty pounds of silver, thirty marks of gold, three crowns with the same number of footstools of the purest Arabian gold, adorned all over with precious stones, of beautiful and amazing workmanship.[15] In the mean time the king and the earl were kept under guard. The queen worked hard on the king's behalf, and the countess of

[14] The burning of Wherwell is reported by WM *HN* 499 (p. 60) (by William of Ypres) and by *GS* 65 (p. 132) (in response to an abortive building of a castle there by the empress's forces), and the role of John fitz Gilbert in the diversion to Wherwell is confirmed later by *Histoire de Guillaume de Maréchal,* i. 8, 9 (ll. 197–9, 212). John of Hexham 13 (SD ii. 310) reported that John fitz Gilbert and Robert with a force of 200 had emerged before the final withdrawal from Winchester in an attempt to break the queen's blockade, and that it had been pursued to Wherwell by William of Ypres and his force: this is difficult to reconcile with G's account. G's date of 14 Sept. for the burning of Wherwell seems early, though the first attacks on John fitz Gilbert at Wherwell could have been made by forces approaching from Andover some time before the burning of the nunnery, which might have occurred at roughly the same time as the battle of Stockbridge.

[15] The burning of Cnut's cross is also reported by WM *HN* 499 (p. 60) who speaks of 300 marks of silver and 30 of gold being available from the cinders of the cross for largesse to knights, not as additions to Henry of Blois's treasury. See discussion in Keynes, *The Liber Vitae of the New Minster and Hyde Abbey,* pp. 35–6.

ualde desudante pro comite, multis internuntiis et amicis fidelibus hinc inde discursantibus, amborum deliberationis talis prouideretur conditio, ut rex suo restitutus regno, et comes sub eo totius Anglie sublimatus dominio, fierent ambo regni et patrie iusti moderatores et pacis recuperatores, sicut totius dissensionis et tribulationis[h] extiterant incentores atque auctores. At comite id agere renuente absque consensu imperatricis, sororis sue, conuenta de hoc illa omnino contradixit, omnem pacem et concordiam erga regem penitus abnegauit. Vnde factum est, ut ab inuicem impacificati discederent, per totum annum deinceps omne regnum cum patria rapinis pauperum, cedibus hominum, uiolationibus ecclesiarum crudeliter . . .[16]

---

[h] uel turbationis *interlin.* (G)

---

[16] WM *HN* 500 (pp. 61–2) and *GS* 68 (pp. 136–7) both deal with the negotiations for the exchange of Stephen and Earl Robert.

Gloucester on the earl's, many messengers and reliable friends
going to and fro. It was finally agreed on both sides that the king
should be restored to the royal dignity, and the earl should be raised
to the government of England under the king, that both should be
just rulers and restorers of peace just as they had been instigators
and authors of dissension and upheaval. The earl refused to carry
this out without the consent of his sister, the empress, repudiated
all that had been agreed, and utterly rejected all terms of peace and
accord with the king. Thus it happened that the negotiators left
without coming to terms, and for a whole year all over the kingdom
and country the poor were pillaged, men were slaughtered, and
churches cruelly violated . . .[16]

APPENDIX A
THE ABINGDON INTERPOLATIONS

These Abingdon additions are found in L, the Abingdon witness of JW, and partly in marginal additions in the hybrid witness P. Here L is the base text, with P's few variants shown in parentheses. The source of many of these interpolations is the Abingdon Chronicle, and recourse has also been had to one of the two manuscripts of this chronicle, BL Cotton Claudius C. IX (siglum A).

1071[c]

Aldredus etiam abbas Abbendonie *apud castellum Walingafordense in captione* ponitur, sed *aliquanto post tempore* inde *eductus in manus Wintoniensi episcopi Walchelini seruandus committitur apud quem mansit quoad uixit.* Cui in abbatiam successit Athelelmus *de monasterio Gemmetico monachus.* (*Chronicon de Abingdon,* i. 486, 494; A, fos. 135ᵛ, 136ʳ)

1084[c]

⟨A⟩bbas Athelelmus (Adelmus *P*) Abbendonensis ecclesie obiit, cui successit Rainoldus et ipse monachus Gemmeticensis (Gemmeticiensis *P*) ecclesie. (ibid., ii. 15; A, fo. 138ᵛ)

1097[d]

Decessit etiam domnus Rainaldus abbas Abbendonie.

1100[c]

et abbatiam Abbendonie et alias plures

1100[g]

Quarto itaque mense regis illius, die Omnium Sanctorum, per manum episcopi Lincoliensis Rotberti domnum Faricium, ex Malmesbiriensi cenobio monachum Abbendoniam direxit, et ut debitam illi subiectionem deferrent monachis mandauit, utiliorem eis fore nusquam, ut rebatur, posse se prouidere patronum contestans. Hic itaque genere Italicus *seculari prudentia cautissimus, litterarum adprime scientia optime eruditus, medic*ine peritia adeo exercitatus, *ut eius solius antidotum confectionibus rex ipse se crederet sepe medendum.* Erat et Romane ecclesie notus cum et in ea tum multis et in aliis ecclesiis per ausonias oras diu deguerit. *Quare tante opinionis personam, arciepiscopo Anselmo ab hac uita migrato, parasset rex substituere nisi norma equitatis eius*

308 APPENDIX A

inflexibilis, quibusdam maioris ordinis ecclesiastici suspecta, ipsorum factione id tum perturbaretur. (ibid., ii. 44, 48; A, fos. 144^r, 146^r)

1117^d

Vir etiam *laudabilis* domnus *Faricius* abbas Abbendonensis ecclesie cum eius *industria opes illius ecclesie multiplicate de die in diem augmentarentur, decidit in egritudinem, qua ex* hac *luce subtractus a laboribus suis beato fine quieuit .xvii. uidelicet regiminis, .vii. Kl. Martii.* (ibid., ii. 158; A, fo. 164)

1121^d

Rex etiam *optimatum suorum consilio* Abbendonensi ecclesie prefecit *in pastorem quendam bone fame uirum, nomine Vincentium, ex Gemmeticensi ecclesia monachum, cunctis qui aderant id laudantibus. Erat* enim *ualde benignus ac pietatis gratia plenus. Omnibus compatiebatur, omnes pie affectu diligebat.* (ibid., ii. 161–2; A, fo. 164)

1130^m

Venerabilis abbas Abbendonie domnus Vincentius *decimo anno sui regiminis* .iiii. Kal. Aprilis ex hac uita decessit. (ibid., ii. 172; A, fo. 168)

APPENDIX B
THE BURY ST EDMUNDS
INTERPOLATIONS

The Bury additions and interpolations are found in the Bury manuscript, Oxford, Bodleian Library, Bodley 297 (siglum B). They were the work of various hands, which are distinguished below.

1071

ᵃB added at the opening
Domnus abbas Baldwinus cum consilio et auxilio regis Willelmi profectus est Romam domnumque Alexandrum papam secundum in sede beati Petri principantem inuenit. A quo benigne et diligenter susceptus maximo honori et uenerationi habitus insigne priuilegium, ᵃut prelabiuimus,ᵃ 1 ad gloriam et laudem beati regis et martyris Eadmundi optinuit, cuius premunitione ᵇeadem ecclesiaᵇ usque ad finem seculi in maxima libertate Deo protegente perseuerabit.ᶜ

ᵇ⁻ᵇB's substituted text
Lanfrancus, ut supra diximus, *Cadomensis cenobii abbas, uir strenuus et in diuinis atque humanis rebus excellenti scientia preditus, Angliam ex precepto domni pape Alexandri et predicti regis* Willelmi *aduenit, et pauco post tempore,* ut prelibauimus, *archiepiscopatum Cantuuariensem regendum suscepit. Sacratus est autem in ipsa metropoli sede, .iiii. kl. Septemb., a cunctis ferme episcopis Anglie. Hic Romam pro debito sibi pallio iens, Thomam archiepiscopum Eboracensem, quem ipse facta sibi de subiectione sua canonica professione Cantuuarie consecrauerat, et Remigium Lincoliensemᵈ episcopum, comites itineris habuit. Qui Romam simul peruenientes urbane suscepti sunt honore singulis congruo. Postque statuto die pater Lanfrancus apostolice sedis pontifici Alexandro presentatur. Cui quod Romanam scientibus consuetudinem forte mirum uideatur, ipse papa ad se intranti assurgens eum ut gressum figeret dulciter ortatus est. Ac deinde subdens, 'Honorem', inquit, 'exhibuimus non quem archiepiscopatui tuo, sed quem magistro cuius studio sumus in illis quem scimus imbuti debuimus. Hinc quod ad te pertinet ob reuerentiam beati Petri te exequi par est.' Residenti igitur illo, Lanfrancus progressus humiliat se ad pedes eius, sed mox ab eo erigitur ad osculum eius. Consident et lete inter eos agitur dies ille. Sequenti luce cum iam diuersa negotia in medium ducerentur, calumniatus*

ᵃ⁻ᵃ *struck through*   ᵇ⁻ᵇ *corrected from* eandem ecclesiam   ᶜ *corrected from* perseveraverit   ᵈ *corrected from* Lindicoliensem

1 The information in this addition could well have been derived from an earlier addition in B (see vol. ii. 647–8).

est coram papa memoratus Thomas cum prefato Remigio quod neuter illorum iure fuerit promotus ad pontificatum. Primus ea scilicet re quod sacri canones filios presbiterorum quos religionis ordo non ornat a sacrorum ordinum promotione remoueant. Sequens uero pro eo quod facta conuentione illum a Willelmo post rege facto emerit officio uidelicet quo ei in excidium Anglie properanti multifaria intentione ac multiplicibus impensis deseruierat. Ad hec illi nullam qua excusari possent probabilem causam habentes, redditis baculis et anulis cum cura pontificali ad petendam misericordiam conuersi sunt. Quorum precibus sese Lanfrancus medium iniciens, sicut erat uir pietate ac sapientia pollens eos multarum rerum scientia fultos, nouo regi in nouis regni dispositionibus per necessarios, multis prestare oratoria facultate ostendit. Quibus auditis, pontifex summus conuersus ad eum, 'Tu uideris,' inquit, 'pater es patrie illius, ac per hoc industria tua consideret quid expediat. Virge pastorales quas reddiderunt, ecce hic sunt. Accipe illas atque dispensa prout utilius Christianitati regionis illius agnoscere poteris.' At ille, susceptis eis, ilico in presentia pape reuestiuit prefatos uiros, quemque sua. Dein Lanfrancus stola summi pontificatus a papa suscepta, in iter reuersus Angliam cum sociis alacer aduectus est. Et a Cantuuaritis debita reuerentia receptus, primas totius Britannie confirmatus est. Post hec euoluto breui temporis spatio, fama nominis eius et magnitudo prudentie eius *quaque insonuit eumque apud hominum mentes clarum fecit atque spectabilem. Is inter alios—immo pre aliis erat—memorato regi Willelmo acceptus, et Dei rebus in cunctis non mediocri cura intentus. Quapropter magno semper operam dabat* quatinus *et regem Deo deuotum efficeret, et religionem morum bonorum in cunctis ordinibus hominum per totum regnum illius renouaret. Nec priuatus est desiderio suo. Multum enim instantia illius atque doctrina per totam illam terram religio aucta est, et ubique noua monasteriorum edificia sicut hodie apparet constructa. Quorum edificiorum constructoribus ipse primum exemplum prebens ecclesiam Christi Cantuuariensem cum omnibus officinis que infra murum ipsius curie sunt cum ipso muro edificatum.*[2]

1081

[a]B added two texts at the opening

(i) Finitis placitis, calumniis et querimoniis, quas Arfastus episcopus faciebat Balduuino abbati, uidelicet de ecclesia sancti Eadmundi et de uilla in qua sanctus martyr requiescit, die pridie kl. Iunii, apud Wintoniam coram rege et principibus terre dedit rex Willelmus glorioso regi et martyri Eadmundo hoc priuilegium:

Pax! Willelmus rex Anglorum, princeps Normannorum atque Cynomannensium archiepiscopis, episcopis, abbatibus, comitibus et ceteris suis fidelibus. Quoniam nos ad regni fastigia Dei miseratione prouectos esse credimus opportet ut de prospera stabilitate plebis nobis subiecte et maxime eorum qui in Domini seruitio die ac nocte desudant uigilare curemus. Igitur notum facimus fidelibus regni nostri presentibus et futuris quod Arfastus

---

[2] Eadmer, *HN* i (pp. 10–12).

episcopus ecclesiam beati Eadmundi in qua ipse uenerabilis rex et martyr incorrupto corpore diem expectat beate resurrectionis suam episcopalem debere esse sedem nobis et multis aliis referebat. Vnde inter Balduuinum abbatem predicte ecclesie et ipsum episcopum per multum temporis facta quam maxima altercatione consilio archiepiscoporum, episcoporum et aliorum multorum nobis fidelium ut utrorumque super his ratio in nostra discuteretur curia dignum censuimus. Qui dum die statuto coram adessent episcopus suum satis facunde fecit clamorem, sed scriptis et testimoniis omnimodo uacuum. Abbas uero e contra, quomodo Canutus rex a predicta ecclesia cum communi consilio archiepiscoporum, episcoporum et optimatum suorum presbiteros qui inibi inordinate uiuebant eiecerit et monachos posuerit quoadque post modum ipsam ecclesiam Ailnodus archiepiscopus Cantuariensis iussu prelibati regis dedicauerit atque primum abbatem loci illius episcopus Lundoniensis secundum episcopus Wintoniensis, ipsum etiam Balduuinum qui tercius est abbas archiepiscopus Cantuuariensis sacrauerit, et quia per .liii. annos siue alicuius iam dicti Arfasti antecessoris contradictione monachi predicti loci a quibus uoluerunt episcopis ordines susceperint ex ordine luculenter enarrauit. Ostendit denique et precepta uidelicet Canuti regis atque gloriosissimi regis Eaduuardi in quibus ab omni dominatione omnium episcoporum comitatus illius funditus sepe dictam ecclesiam liberam perpetualiter ipsi reges esse concesserunt. Quod Cantuuariensis archiepiscopus Lanfrancus et Thomas Eboracensis archiepiscopus et Odo Baiocensis episcopus frater meus et comes Cantie et plerique alii episcopi Rotbertusque filius meus atque ceteri principes regni nostri qui aderant audientes censuerunt tanti loci tantam auctoritatem inuiolatam usque in finem seculi debere permanere. Quorum inrefutabili iudicio prout dignum fuit assensi et consensum prebeo. Placuit etiam nobis consilio archiepiscoporum, episcoporum, comitum aliorumque multorum nobis fidelium atque digna petitioni Balduuini abbatis qui nostram humiliter requisiuit serenitatem antecessorum nostrorum Anglorum regum, scilicet Eadmundi, Canuti, Hardecanuti, atque illustris Eadwardi cuius miseratione Domini genere et dono in regno sumus heredes precepta que iam sepe nominate ecclesie contulerunt nostro roborare precepto ex hoc ut ab Arfasto episcopi omniumque sibi per tempora succedentium episcoporum dominatione ipsa ecclesia et uilla in qua sita est eadem ecclesia sit libera. Et ut hec auctoritatis nostris et futuris temporibus circa ipsum sanctum locum perhenniter firma et inuiolata permaneat manus nostre subscriptione cartam hanc decreuimus roborare et sigilli nostri impressione firmare.

+ Ego Willelmus Dei gratia Anglorum rex hoc preceptum iussi scribere et scriptum cum signo Dominice crucis confirmando impressi.

+ Ego Mathildis regina corroboraui.

+ Ego Lanfrancus Cantuuariensis archiepiscopus confirmaui.

+ Ego Thomas archiepiscopus Eboracensis roboraui.

+ Ego Odo Baiocensis episcopus assensum dedi.
+ Ego Gosfridus Constantiensis episcopus consignaui.
+ Ego Hugo Lundoniensis episcopus consensi.
+ Ego Walquelinus Wintoniensis episcopus conclusi.
+ Ego Wlstanus Wigornensis episcopus assensum probaui.
+ Ego Remigius Lindisfarnensis episcopus non renui.
+ Ego Stigandus Bathoniensis episcopus affirmaui.
+ Ego Osbertus Axoniensis episcopus assensum dedi.
+ Ego Petrus Cestrensis episcopus consensi.
+ Ego Arfastus Theodfordensis episcopus collaudaui.
+ Ego Gundulfus Rofensis episcopus laudaui.
+ Ego Osmundus Searuberiensis episcopus roboraui.
+ Ego Rodbertus Herefordensis episcopus consensi.
+ Ego Rodbertus regis filius assensum dedi.
+ Ego Willelmus filius regis collaudaui.
+ Ego Heinricus filius regis confirmaui.
+ Ego Mauritius regis cancellarius relegi et sigillaui.
+ Ego Bernardus capellanus regis.
+ Ego Scollandus sancti Augustini abbas.
+ Ego Wlfwoldus Certesiensis abbas.
+ Ego Vitalis abbas de Westmonasterio.
+ Ego Ægelnothus Glastoniensis abbas.
+ Ego Ægeluuinus Eoueshamensis abbas.
+ Ego Ægelsinus Ramesiensis abbas.
+ Ego Turoldus Burgensis abbas.
+ Ego Rogerius comes de Monte Gumerici.
+ Ego Hugo comes Cestrensis.
+ Ego Alanus comes Orientalium Anglorum.
+ Ego Albericus comes Nordanhymbrorum.
+ Ego Rodbertus de Bellomonte.
+ Ego Hugo de Monteforta.
+ Ego Ricardus Gisleberti comitis filius consignaui.
+ Ego Balduuinus frater eius.
+ Ego Heinricus de Ferrariis.
+ Ego Hugo de Grentemaisnilo.
+ Ego Walterus Giffardus.
Data pridie kl. Iunii anno .xv. regnante Willelmo rege gloriosissimo ab incarnatione autem Domini anno .MLXXXI., indictione .iiii. Actum apud Wintoniam in palatio regio. In Dei nomine feliciter. Amen.[3]

[3] D. C. Douglas, *Feudal Documents from the Abbey of Bury St Edmunds* (London, 1932), pp. 50–2, which uses two 11th-c. witnesses. Douglas's tentative argument in favour of the diploma's authenticity (pp. xxxii–xxxiv) has been rightly challenged by A. Gransden, 'Baldwin, abbot of Bury St Edmunds, 1065–1097', *ANS*, iv (1981), 64–76, at p. 71.

(ii) Littere regis quas ipse misit cum sigillo suo ad comitem et ad uicecomitem.

Willelmus rex Anglorum Rogerio Bigoto ceterisque omnibusque fidelibus suis salutem. Sciatis quod de calumnia et querimonia quam Arfastus episcopus faciebat Balduuino abbati uidelicet de ecclesia sancti Eadmundi et de uilla in qua est sita meo precepto coram me archiepiscopi et episcopi, abbates et comites, aliique mei proceres iudicium inter episcopum et abbatem tenuerunt et iuste iudicauerunt et assensuerunt unanimiter quod Arfastus episcopus predictam ecclesiam et uillam iniuste requirebat. Et abbas ea iuste habere debebat. Et quod Arfastus episcopus neque successor eius in prefata ecclesia et uilla nichil reclamare debebat. Quod sic stare et firmiter inuiolatum manere a modo precipio. Valete.[4]

1087
ᵃB¹ added in the margin with signe
Sanctus Nicolaus archipresul translatus est a Mirrea metropoli Grecorum ad Barium ciuitatem Apulie, die dominica, hora uespertina, .vii. id. Mai., susceptus est cum magno gaudio in basilica Sancti Benedicti ipsius ciuitatis abbatiam apud domnum Heliam uenerabilem abbatem monasterii eiusdem egri et statim diuersis languoribus oppressi quas ex omnibus partibus ciuitatis concurrentes populi cum magnis deuotionibus secum in idem monasterium detulerant sanitati sunt restituti. Ex quibus nocte illa et .ii. feria sanifacti sunt .xl. et .vii. homines diuersi sexus et etatis qui omnes erant habitatores eiusdem ciuitatis Bari, et uicinis locis qui festinanter uenerant in illa die. Cottidie undecumque ad suas fideliter concurrentibus reliquias quacumque infirmitate grauitatis idem Dei confessor inuisibiliter obuians in uiis uel plateis seu siluis atque ruribus immo ciuitatibus eorum ac oppidis celerem prestare dignatur sanitatem et quanti infirmi cotidie in amissam conualescunt sanitatem iam innumerabiles esse uidentur.[5]

1088
ᵈB added in the text
Sed et Rotbertus filius Balduuini de Eaxanceastra depredauit regionem illam circa Domnaniam. Similiter Hugo de Grentemaisnilo circa se in pago Leogerceastrensi et Northamtunensi et in illis partibus depredauit et occidit homines et feminas simulque infantes et multos in captiuitate secum duxit ad castellum suum. Rogerus Bigot etiam apud Orientales

---

[4] This writ is printed from an 11th-c. copy in Douglas, *Feudal Documents of Bury St Edmunds*, pp. 55–6.

[5] OV *HE* vii. 12 (iv. 54–70) gives a full account of the translation, which is based on *De translatione* of John, archdeacon of Bari (BHL 6190). B's very summary note shares with the narrative of Nicephorus, a clerk of Bari who was a monk of La Cava, the number (47) of those initially healed (BHL 6179).

Anglos maximas depredationes fecit, depredauit etiam Suthberiam et alias nonnullas uillas.[6]

ᵉB⁴ added in the lower margin with signes
Hoc etiam anno, id est secundo regis Willelmi secundi, Herebertus, prior Fiscamnensis ecclesie de rebus monasterii sui emit abbatiam Ramesiensem, sed post aliquot annos dimisit eam, et emit episcopatum orientali*ᵉ* Anglie mille nongentis libris argenti a rege Willelmo secundo.[7]

1093
ᵃHand not found elsewhere added in lower margin with signe
Circa istum annum dominice incarnationis obiit Alanus comes Brittannie et constructa nobilis cenobii sancte Marie extra urbem Eboracam sed aput sanctum Ædmundum cuius ecclesie multorum bonorum impensor exstiterat ab abbate Baldewino iuxta australe ostium ecclesie primo sepultus est, sed succedente tempore infra ecclesiam supplicatione monachorum Eboracensium et parentum suorum in opposito loco prioris tumulationis conditus est cuius nobilitatem exornat epythahfium quod super eum sic scriptum monstratur:

> Stella ruit regni; comitis caro marcet Alani;
> Precepto legum, nitet ortus sanguine regum;
> Vixit nobilium prefulgens stirpe Brittonum.
> Anglia turbatur satraparum flos cineratur.*ᶠ*
> Dux uiguit summus, rutilans a rege secundus;
> Ia⟨m⟩, Brito, flos regum, modo marcor in ordine rerum.
> Hunc cernens plora; requies *ᵍ* sibi sit, sic Deus. Ora.[8]

ᵉ changed from orientis   *ᶠchanged from* cinerarat   *ᵍ* uel m *interlineated*

---

[6] The activities of Hugh of Grandmesnil and of Roger Bigod are reported in ASC, which does not, however, mention Sudbury. B is the only known source for Robert fitz Baldwin's ravaging of Devon.

[7] The 14th-c. Ramsey annals (*Chronicon abbatiae Rameseiensis*, ed. W. D. Macray (RS lxxxiii; London, 1886) date Herbert's election to Ramsey to 1087. JW (see above, *s.a.* 1094 n. 1) had reported his purchase of the see of Thetford (Norwich) for 1000 pounds. He was elected and consecrated bishop 1090 x 1091.

[8] Alan the Red (Rufus) was one of the 'companions' of the Conqueror, and the greatest magnate in the north of England (see J. F. A. Mason, 'The "Honour of Richmond" in 1086', *EHR* lxxviii (1963), 703–4). The date of his death is uncertain. B's date, *c.* 1093, may be too early if Anselm's two letters to Gunnhildr, the Wilton nun Alan Rufus had abducted (Schmitt, *Anselmi opera omnia*, iv. 43–50, nos. 168–9), are considered. They could not have been written until after his consecration on 4 Dec. 1093, and the first implies that Alan Rufus was still alive at the time. Alan Rufus and his brother Alan Niger (who is named in Anselm's second letter) were commemorated at York on 4 August (see C. T. Clay, *Early Yorkshire Charters*, iv. *The Honour of Richmond*, 2 pts. (Yorkshire Archaeological Society Record Series. Extra Series i–ii (Wakefield, 1935–6), i. 86n). See Barlow, *William Rufus*, pp. 313–14.

*d–d*B *substituted this text*

Acta sunt hec anno dominice incarnationis millesimo nonagesimo tercio, pridie nonas Martii, prima dominica Quadragesime. Precepit itaque rex ut sine dilatione ac diminutione inuestiretur de omnibus ad archiepiscopatum pertinentibus intus et extra, atque ut ciuitas Cantuaria, quam Lanfrancus suo tempore in beneficio a rege tenebat, et abbatia sancti Albani, quam non solum Lanfrancus sed et antecessores eius habuisse noscuntur, in alodium ecclesie Christi Cantuariensis pro redemptione anime sue perpetuo iure transirent.[9]

*f*B *added here*

Duo tamen episcopi Vigornensis uidelicet et Exoniensis, infirmitate detenti, huic consecrationi interesse non ualuerunt, sed nuntiis apicibusque directis, absentiam suam coepiscoporum suorum presentie hac in causa presentem et consentaneam fore denuntiauerunt. Verum cum ante ordinandi pontificis examinationem Walchelinus Wentanus episcopus rogatu Mauricii episcopi Lundoniensis, cuius hoc officium est ecclesiastico more electionem scriptam legeret, mox in primo uersu Thomas Eboracensis, grauiter offensus, eam non iure factam conquestus est. Nam cum diceretur, 'Fratres et coepiscopi mei, uestre fraternitati est cognitum quantum temporis est ex quo accidentibus uariis euentibus, hec Dorobernensis ecclesia, totius Brittannie metropolitana suo sit uiduata pastore', subintulit dicens, 'Totius Brittanie metropolitana? Si totius Brittanie metropolitana, ecclesia Eboracensis que metropolitana esse scitur metropolitana non est. Et quidem ecclesiam Cantuuariensem primatem totius Britannie esse scimus, non metropolitanam'. Quod auditum, ratione subnixum esse quod dicebat intellectum est. Tunc statim scriptura ipsa mutata est, et pro 'totius Britannie metropolitana' 'totius Britannice primas' scriptum est, et omnis controuersia conquieuit. Itaque sacrauit illum ut Britannie totius primatem. Cum igitur inter sacrandum pro ritu ecclesie textus euangelii super eum ab episcopis apertus, tentus et peracta consecratione, fuisset inspectus. Hec in summitate pagine sententia reperta est, 'Vocauit multos, et misit seruum suum hora cene dicere inuitatis ut uenirent quia iam parata sunt omnia. Et ceperunt simul omnes excusare.'[10]

1095

*a*Scribe not found elsewhere wrote this text in the margin with signes. The margin has been clipped and some letters are worn away

Religiosus prior sancti Eadmundi Benedictus, qui et Saxo dicebatur, circa hunc annum obiit .v. id. Aprilis, et in capitulo fratrum tunc temporis sepultus est. Erat enim primitus capellanus Eadighe regine Eadwardi regis, et tali honore a rege habitus est, ut [si] ei cure esset pontificales honor[es] [pro]fecto adeptus fuisset. Post ipsos au[tem ui]ta extractos religiose conuersatus est cum canonicis qui habitabant apud sanctum Iohannem

---

[9] Eadmer, *HN* i (p. 37).
[10] Luke 14: 17–18. Eadmer, *HN* i (pp. 42–3).

316 APPENDIX B

Beuerlegcensem ubi et fa[ctus] est eorum decanus. Exinde abbate Baldwino inuitante apud sanctum Eadmundum monachus et deinde prior loci effectus p[ri]mos annos in sancta conuersatione uita transegens. Cuius uita quantum fuit Deo accepta satis claruit, dum post plus[quam] .xxx. annos tempore abbatis Ans[elmi] in loco quo prius fuerat capit[ulum] pararetur claustrum infirm[orum] placeret remouere eum et iu[xta] parietem ecclesie recondere. Et [cum in remo]tione sarcofagi cooperculum motum esset apparuit ipse iacens pene incorruptus, et cuculla eius pene to[ta] atque tanta suauitas [ama]bilis odoris de corpore eius [. . .]uit ac si illic [. . .] odorum genera congesta fui[. . .], et sic post multorum conspectum in loco quo decretum fuit conditus est.¹¹

ᵇScribe not found elsewhere added in the lower margins with signes
Venerabilis abbas Baldwinus monasterii sancti Eadmundi destructa ecclesia quam condiderat gloriosus rex Cnutus et eius regina Emma, *simplici facta scemate*, nec *sic artificiali*ter *ut quedam construuntur hoc tempore, monitu* senioris *regis Willelmi artifici*orem et pulcriorem *iactis fundamentis inchoa*uit, columnari, *testudinali*, marmorali opere fabrefacta qua multi qui uiderunt *speciorem* et delectabiliorem *nunquam se uidisse* testati sunt. Et ut perducta sunt ad perfectum edificia presbiterii, *anno ab incarnatione Domini millesimo nonagesimo quinto a passione* sancti Æadmundi *ducentesimo uicesimo quinto .iii. kl. Mai.* presente iam dicto abbate Baldwino, et monachis eius disponentibus digno cum honore beatus martir *die dominica transfertur* a *Walchelin*o *Wintoniensi* episcopo et a *Ranulf*o tunc *regis capellan*o postea Dunhelmensi episcopo in preparatam sibi basilicam, astante innumerabili caterua cleri populique et retro magnum altareʰ decenter reconditur.¹² Tunc, cum *tanta* esset *aeris siccitas ut uredo et aurugo solis inclementia germinantia queque pessundederat* et pene tota *periclitaretur* Anglia populus ab episcopo monitus quatinus Deum per sanctum suum inuocaret sibi misereri *tertia* supplicatione *Kirrie eleison*; statimque exaudit uiderent pluuiarum copia terram madefacere, atque deinde sic temporaneam fuisse ut *premarcida sata uirerent* et quod minitabatur in germine non expleretur in propagine, quia super multorum annorum tunc *frugum incrementa* prouenirent. Cuiusdam etiam militis *brachium* in exitu illisum parieti ui multitudinis ut *abrasis carnibus* pene *nuda facies os*sis *pat*eret et indumento circumductum statim *sanum* et incolume est repertum *sola cicatrice ad testimonium uirtutis permanente.*¹³ Translati sunt nichilominus cum rege beatissimo et reliquiis multis sanctorum corpora duorum sanctorum uidelicet Botulphiⁱ episcopi et Iurmini clitonis Christi amboque ut percipimus illo delati sunt tempore

ʰ *erasure followed*   ⁱ *erasure followed, probably of* Orientalis Anglorum

¹¹ Printed in *Memorials St Edmund's*, i. 351.
¹² Hermann, *De miraculis Sancti Eadmundi* (*Memorials St Edmund's* i. 84–91).
¹³ Ibid., i. 158–60.

Lefstani abbatis. Corpus namque beati Botulphi episcopi primitus*j* aput quandam uillam Grundesburc nominatam humatum est, cuius translatio cum obscura nocte fieret columna lucis super feretrum eius ad depellendas tenebras protendi celitas uisa est. Corpus uero beati Iurmini similiter aput uillam quandam Blihæburc primum iacuit in cuius plumbea theca in qua delatus est tale ephithaphium inscriptum continebatur. *k*Ego Iurminus commendo in nomine Trinitatis sancte ut nulla persona audeat depredare locum sepulture usque in diem resurrectionis; sin autem remotum se sciat a sorte sanctorum.[14]

1097
aIn the margin angular hand not found elsewhere wrote
[A]nnos triginta duos a sumpta abbatia [etatis] ut putabantur plusquam octoginta.

1100
eB¹ added in the lower margin with signes
Deditque ipso die consecrationis sue abbatiam sancti Eadmundi Rotberto Hugonis Cestrensis comitis filio, et abbatiam Elgensem Ricardo Ricardi filii Gisleberti comitis filio.[15]

1101
aB added in the text
Anselmus archiepiscopus a rege *mandatur Wintoniam uadit. Vbi episcopis terreque principibus sub uno coactis, communi* assensu *apud Anselmum actum est quatinus nuntii prioribus excellentiores ex utraque parte Romam mitterentur. Romano pontifici uiua uoce exposituri, illum aut a sententia necessaria discessurum, aut, Anselmo cum suis extra Angliam pulso, totius regni subiectionem, et commodum quod inde singulis annis habere solebat, perditurum. Ab archiepiscopo igitur missi sunt monachi duo,l scilicet Balduuinus Beccensis et Alexander Cantuariensis, non quidem ut eorum instinctu Romanus pontifex rigorem iusticie causa Anselmi* illo *modo exiret, sed partim ut curialibus minis testimonium cui papa incunctanter crederet ferrent, partim ut de negotio certam apostolice sedis sententiam Anselmo referrent. Ad ipsum uero negotio conficiendum directi a rege sunt tres episcopi, Girardus uidelicetm Herefordensis nuper factus archiepiscopus Eboracensis, Herebertus Tydfordensis, Rotbertus Cestrensis. Sed horum episcoporum duos sua quoque causa Romam agebat, Girardum scilicet adeptio pallii, et*

---

j erasure of two letters followed *k change of hand* *l gap with erasure followed* *m gap with erasure followed*

---

[14] Printed in *Memorials St Edmund's*, i. 351–2.
[15] Printed in *Memorials St Edmund's*, i. 353. *Heads*, p. 32, refers to Bury annals which confirm the year for Robert I's appointment.

Herebertum non equa cupido dominandi *super abbatiam* beati *Eadmundi.* Eadem quippe abbatia ex quo primum fundata fuit, *salua primatis obedientia,* semper a *subiectione* omnis episcopi libera fuit, libertatem ipsam quasi a beati martyris iure trahens qui loco in quo situ est regali potentia presidens, speciali quadam eum, inibi corporaliter dum uiueret degens, libertate *ⁿdonauerat.* Hanc quoque libertatem*ⁿ* cum priuilegia Romanorum pontificum, tum instituta et sanctiones principum ipsi regi in regnum Anglie succedentium, tum nichilominus decreta et confirmationes celebrate astipulationibus generalium conciliorum annuerunt, roborauerunt et inconuulsa manere constituerunt, solius primatis nutum in sacramentis et consecrationibus ecclesiasticis abbatiam ipsam expectaturam in commune decernentium. *Hic itaque Herebertus, cum, relictis sociis, uenisset, et partes Lugdunensis prouincie impiger attigisset, comprehensus a quodam Guidone uiro prepotente ac fero est, et quod episcopus de Anglia esset, quodque pro damno domni sui Anselmi Cantuuariorum archiepiscopi Romam iret, ab eodem calumniatus. Negat ille, nec ei creditur. Instat negando et deierando sed nequiquam. Tandem prolatis sanctorum reliquiis super eas iurare cogitur et asseuerare, se nulla omnino ratione Rome quid scienter acturum, quod aut honori aut uoluntati patris Anselmi uideri posset obnoxium.* Quo facto, *ut pace ac securitate uiri comitatus uie* redimeretur⁰ *ferme quadraginta, sicut fertur, marcas argenti ei non grata largitate reliquit, quas suo negotio* contra *ecclesiam sancti Eadmundi Rome adminiculaturas Angliam egrediens mage putauit. Emensa dehinc longitudine uie, nuncii Romam una ueniunt, sui aduentus causam pro eo quem preferebat tenore apostolicis auribus, suggerunt, tanti mali dirimendi consilium proni deposcunt. Audit ille que feruntur, et non inuenit uerba quibus exprimat quantum inde miretur. Cum tamen magno ab episcopis opere precaretur suis rebus precauere ac definite predecessoris sui sententie rigorem ut undique pax esset temperare, asseruit se nec pro capitis sui redemptione hoc facturum; 'decreta', dicens indignando, 'et institutiones sanctorum patrum minis actus unius hominis dissiparem?' Finierat in istis. Super hec scriptas epistolas regi et Anselmo, cuique suam, destinauit; regi, inter alia, ecclesiarum inuestituras iudicio Sancti Spiritus interdicens, et Anselmum ut que agebat ageret, et que loquebatur perloquerentur affectuose deprecans, firmata et apostolice sedis auctoritate roborata in omnibus sui primatus dignitate.*[16]

1102
ʰ⁻ʰB substituted this text
multa ecclesiastice discipline necessaria seruari Anselmus instituit, que postmodum sedis apostolice pontifex sua auctoritate confirmauit. Cuius concilii seriem, sicut ab eodem Anselmo descripta est, huic operi inserere non incongruum existimauimus. Scribit itaque sic.

ⁿ⁻ⁿ added in the inner margin   ⁰ *originally* reddimeretur

---

[16] Eadmer, *HN* (pp. 132–4). Printed in *Memorials St Edmund's,* i. 353–4.

Anno dominice incarnationis millesimo centesimo secundo, quarto autem presulatus Pascalis summi pontificis, tercio Heinrici gloriosi regis Anglorum, ipso annuente, communi consensu episcoporum et abbatum ex principum totius regni, celebratum est concilium in ecclesia beati Petri in occidentali parte iuxta Lundoniam sita. In quo presedit Anselmus archiepiscopus Dorobernensis et primas totius Britannie, considentibus uenerabilibus uiris Gerardo Eboracensi archiepiscopo, Mauricio Lundoniensi episcopo, Guilielmo Wentonie electo episcopo, aliisque tam episcopis quam abbatibus. Huic conuentui affuerunt, Anselmo archiepiscopo petente a rege, primates regni, quatinus quicquid eiusdem concilii auctoritate decerneretur, utriusque ordinis concordi cura et sollicitudine ratum seruaretur. Sic enim necesse erat, quoniam multis retro annis sinodali cultura cessante uitiorum uepribus succrescentibus christiane religionis feruor in Anglia nimis refrixerat.

Primum itaque ex auctoritate sanctorum patrum symoniace heresis surreptio in eodem concilio damnata est. In qua culpa inuenti depositi sunt Wido abbas de Perscore et Wimundus de Tauestoc et Ealdwinus de Ramesei, et alii nondum sacrati remoti ab abbatis, scilicet Godricus de Burgo, Haimo de Cernel, Ægelricus de Middeltune. Absque symonia uero remoti sunt ab abbatiis pro sua quisque causa, Ricardus de Heli, et Robertus de sancto Eadmundo, et qui erat apud Micelenei.

Statutum quoque est ne episcopi secularium placitorum officium suscipiant et ut non sicut laici sed ut religiosas personas decet ordinatis uestes habeant et ut semper et ubique honestas personas testes habeant sue conuersationis.

Vt etiam archidiaconatus non dentur ad firmam.

Vt archidiaconi sint diaconi.

Vt nullus archidiaconi, presbiter, diaconus, canonicus uxorem ducat aut ductam retineat. Subdiaconus uero quilibet qui canonicus non est, si post professionem castitatis uxorem duxit, eadem regula constringatur.

Vt presbiter quamdiu illicitam conuersationem mulieris habuerit, non sit legalis, nec missam celebret, nec, si celebrauerit, eius missa audiatur.

Vt nullus ad subdiaconatum aut supra ordinetur sine professione castitatis.

Vt filii presbiterorum non sint heredes ecclesiarum patrum suorum.

Ne quilibet clerici sint secularium prepositi uel procuratores aut iudices sanguinis.

Vt presbiteri non eant ad potationes nec ad pinnas bibant.

Vt uestes clericorum sint unius coloris, et calciamenta ordinata.

Vt monachi uel clerici qui ordinem suum abiecerunt aut redeant aut excommunicentur.

Vt clerici patentes coronas habeant.

Vt decime non nisi ecclesiis dentur.

Ne ecclesie aut prebenda emantur.

Ne noue capelle fiant sine consensu episcopi.

Ne ecclesia sacretur donec prouideantur necessaria et presbitero et ^{p} ecclesie.

^{p} gap with erasure followed

Ne abbates facient milites; et ut in eadem domo cum monachis suis manducent et dormiant, nisi necessitate aliqua prohibente.

Ne monachi penitentiam cuiuis iniungant sine permissu abbatis sui; et quod abbates eis licentiam de hoc dare non possunt nisi de eis quorum animarum curam gerunt.

Non monachi compatres uel monache commatres fiant.

Ne monachi teneant uillas ad firmam.

Ne monachi ecclesias nisi per episcopos accipiant neque sibi datas ita expolient suis redditibus, ut presbiteri ibi seruientes in iis que sibi et ecclesiis necessaria sunt penuriam patiantur.

Vt fides inter uirum et mulierem occulte et sine testibus de coniugio data, si ab alterutro negata fuerit irrita habeatur.

Vt criniti sic tondeantur ut pars aurium appareat et oculi non tegantur.

Ne cognati usque ad septimam generationem ad coniugium copulentur uel copulati simul permaneant; et si quis huius incestus conscius fuerit et non ostenderit eiusdem criminis se participem esse cognoscat.

Ne corpora defunctorum extra parrochiam suam sepelienda portentur ut presbiter parrochie perdat quod inde illi iuste debetur.

Ne quis temeraria nouitate corporibus mortuorum aut fontibus aut aliis rebus quod contigisse cognouimus sine episcopali auctoritate reuerentiam sanctitatis exhibeat.

Ne quis illud nefarium negotium quo hactenus homines in Anglia solebant uelut bruta animalia uenundari deinceps ullatenus facere presumat.

Sodomiticum flagitium facientes et eos in hoc uoluntarie iuuantes in eodem concilio graui anathemate damnati sunt donec penitentia et confessione absolutionem mereantur. Qui uero in hoc crimine publicatus fuerit statutum est, siquidem fuerit persona religiosi ordinis, ut ad nullam amplius gradum promoueatur, et siquem habet ab illo deponatur. Si autem laicus, ut in toto regno Anglie legali sue conditionis dignitate priuetur. Et, ne huius criminis absolutionem iis qui se sub regula uiuere non uouerunt aliquis nisi episcopus deinceps facere presumat. Statutum quoque est ut per totam Angliam in omnibus ecclesiis et in omnibus Dominicis diebus excommunicatio prefata renouetur.

Et hic quidem Lundoniensis concilii textus est qui post non multos institutionis^q sue dies multos sui transgressores in omni hominum genere fecit. Sane quod ultimum de renouanda excommunicatione Dominicis diebus statutum fuit ipsemet Anselmus rationabili dispensatione usus postponi concessit.[17]

^j*B*⁴ *added in the lower margins with signe indicating its addition at the end of 1102*^h *above*

Anno eodem et in eodem concilio, id est .iii. Henrici regis anno, Herebertus episcopus Norwicensis proposuit calumniam satis facunde de subiectione

^q *corrected from* institutiones

[17] Eadmer, *HN*, iii (pp. 142–4). Printed in *Memorials St Edmund's*, i. 354–5.

ecclesie[r] sancti Ædmundi multisque de causis iustam ac necessariam ibi fore suam prelationem. Sed causa diligenter uentilata, calumpniam ipsius irritam esse debere comprobauit ac decreuit uniuersa sinodus, quia episcopi quamplures et abbates necnon duces regii considentes affirmauerunt se interfuisse causis Arfasti episcopi et Baldwini abbatis, ipsumque, Arfastum a causa cecidisse, abbatem uero Baldwinum per legitimos testes comprobasse se ac suam abbatiam per quinquaginta tres annos liberam et quietam ac sine calumnia fuisse ab omnibus antecessoribus ipsius Arfasti. Demonstrasse quoque testati sunt predictum abbatem suum monasterium dedicatum ab archiepiscopo Agelnotho Doroberensi seque postea abbatem consecratum fuisse a metropolitano eiusdem sedis, antecessorum etiam ipsius, alterum ab episcopo Lundoniensi, alterum a presule Wintoniensi ordinatos monachos quoque sui monasterii a quibuslibet episcopis ad diuersos ordines promotos[s] sine contradictione Tetfordensis episcopi eleganti testimonio comprobasse. Discussa tandem causa calumniaque prefati Herberti honestis rationibus refutata per dccretum uniuersalis concilii ne mutire quidem ausus est deinceps contra ecclesiam sancti Eadmundi quoad uixerat.[18]

1107
[g]?B[1] *added in lower margin with a signe*
Deposito canonice per concilium Rotberto, filio Hugonis comitis Cestrensis, eo quod inuaserat ecclesiam sancti Eadmundi martiris sine electione monachorum eiusdem loci, [t]Rotbertus prior Westmonasterii electus est abbas ab ipsis fratribus et iussu Henrici regis ab Anselmo archiepiscopo consecratus die Assumptionis sancte Marie. In cuius ordinatione presente Rannulfo episcopo Dunholmensi et Halgoto abbate ecclesie sancte Audoeni Rotomagensis atque pluribus religiosis uiris, fratres premisse ecclesie sancti Eadmundi probabili auctoritate demonstrauerunt ipsum abbatem consecrari debere sine professione facta metropolitano aut cuilibet alii episcoporum Anglie. Quod et factum est dum constabat antecessorum eius, alterum, id est Wium, ordinatum fuisse ab episcopo Lundoniensi, alterum, hoc est, Leofstanum a presule Wintoniensi et Baldwinum, qui tertius successit duobus prioribus ab archiepiscopo Dorobernensi nec quemlibet posse demonstrare ipsos tres abbates professionem fecisse alicui episcoporum uel metropolitano.

[u]Cui quidem ecclesie ante consecrationem amplius quam .iiii. annis iure abbatis prefuerat, capitulo tamen, nisi uocatus a fratribus aliqua utilitatis

---

[r] ecclesia B   [s] permotos B   [t] *the third hand of the addition on pp. 72–3 (see above, vol. ii. p. l) added in margin for insertion here* tamen plene per tres annos sibi vendicarat   [u] *change of hand and subject*

[18] Printed in Whitelock, Brett, and Brooke, *Councils and Synods*, ii., 681–2, and in *Memorials St Edmund's*, i. 355.

322 APPENDIX B

causa reuerenter abstinens. Et inter cetera bona interim claustrum, capitulum, refectorium, dormitorium et cameram suam edificari fecerat. Sed non nisi .iiii. ebdomadas et totidem dies post consecrationem superuiuens oleo sacro unctus et^v [. . .]ione [. . .] dormi[. . .] munitus .xvi. kl. Octob., feria .ii., uiam patrum ingressus est. Qui quidem inter omnes abbates optime custoditor et adquisitor terrarum laudatur^v amplius fuisset ad maximam terrarum et rerum. [19]

^{i} *B^1? added in the margin of p. 408a text on Roger Bigod and his burial, which is now mutilated*
Rogerus Bigod [ ]ndo quandam terram [ ]retur die quo [ ]unt cum abbate [ ]a Rodberto deo [ ] caute causam [ ] sui subita [ ]perisse inuentus est Norwicum ibi ab episcopo sepultus est.[20]

1115
^{a}*B added in text*
Conuentus monasterii sancti Eadmundi elegerunt Alboldum priorem sancti Nicasii Meldensis ecclesie sibi abbatem. Qui consecratus est in festiuitate Omnium Sanctorum ab archiepiscopo Cantuariensi Radulfo sine professione conscripta iuxta predictam rationem legitime a monachis confirmatam in presentia Anselmi archiepiscopi, quando ordinatus est domnus Rotbertus predecessor ipsius Alboldi.[21]

1119
^{d}*B interlineated addition*
et Albold abbas ecclesie sancti Eadmundi die kl. Martii.[22]

1130
^{m} *B^1? marginal addition in lower margin with signe*
Hoc etiam anno sepius celum uisum est habere sanguineam sperem quo nichil terribilius mortalium timori est, incendium cadens inde ad terras. Anno illo et sequenti secuta est mortalitas hominum et animalium.[23]

^{v} *text after these words was lost through clipping of the page*

---

[19] Printed in *Memorials St Edmund's*, i. 355–6. See *Heads*, p. 32, for evidence confirming B's dates for Robert II's election, blessing, and death.
[20] Roger I Bigod, sheriff of Norfolk and Suffolk, steward of Henry I, died in 1107 and was buried at Norwich.
[21] *Heads*, p. 32, reports the evidence for Aldebold of Jerusalem's election on 16 August (ASC H) and blessing on 1 Nov. 1114 (Eadmer, *HN* v (p. 226)).
[22] *Heads*, p. 32, for the Bury annals' confirmation of this date.
[23] ASC reports a fiery sky on 11 Jan. 1131, and a great mortality of cattle in that year.

1131

Two additions in a thirteenth-century hand at the end of the chronicle

(i) Miraculum de cipho Sancti Ædmundi.

Anno gratie .mc. nonagesimo .viii. uoluit gloriosus martyr Eadmundus *terrere conuentum* suum *et docere, ut corpus eius reuerentius et diligentius custodiretur. Erat quidam ligneus tabulatus inter feretrum et magnum altare, super quem duo cerei solebant* stare et ardere. Solebant quia sepius cerei cereis noui ueteribus turpiter inferi et *indecenter coniungi. Erant sub tabulatu illo multa* superflua *reposita*[w] . . . *hostio et parietibus ferreis existentibus. Cum ergo dormirent custodes noc*tis translationis *Sancte Eteldrethe, cecidit, ut credimus, pars cerei*[x] *iam combusti super predictum tabulatum pannis opertum, et cepit omnia proxima que supra et subtus erant accendere, ita quod parietes ferrei omnino igne candescerent. Et ecce furor Domini sed non sine misericordia, iuxta illud, 'cum iratus fueris, misericordie recordaberis'.*[24] *Eadem enim hora cecidit horologium ante horas matutinas, surgensque magister uestiarii, hec percipiens et intuens, cucurrit quantocius et, percussa tabula tanquam pro mortuo, sublimi uoce clamauit dicens feretrum esse conbustum. Nos autem omnes accurrentes flammam inuenimus incredibiliter seuientem, et totum feretrum amplectentem, et non longe a trabibus ecclesie ascendentem. Iuuenes ergo nostri propter aquam currentes, quidam ad puteum, quidam ad horologium, quidam cucullis suis impetum ignis cum magna difficultate extinxerunt, et sanctuaria quedam prius diripuerunt. Cumque frigida aqua super frontem feretri funderetur, ceciderunt preciosi lapides et quasi in puluerem redacti sunt. Claui autem, quibus lamine argentee configebantur feretro, exilebant a ligno combusto ad spissitudinem digiti mei, et pendebant lamine sine clauis una ex altera. Aurea quidem maiestas in fronte feretri cum quibusdam lapidibus remansit, firma et intacta, et pulcrior post ignem quam ante, quia tota aurea fuit.*

Contigit etiam, uolente Altissimo, tunc temporis magnam trabem, que solebat esse ultra altare, sublatam esse, ut noua sculptura repararetur. Contigit et crucem et Mariolam et Iohannem et loculum cum camisia Sancti Eadmundi, *et philateria cum reliquiis, que ab eadem trabe pendere solebant, et alia sanctuaria que super trabem steterant, omnia prius sublata esse. Alioquin omnia combusta essent, ut credimus, sicut pannus depictus combustus fuit, qui in loco trabis pendebat. Sed quid fieret si cortinata esset ecclesia? Cum ergo securi essemus quod ignis in nullo loco perforasset feretrum, rimas et foramina, si qua essent, attentissime inuestigantes, et omnia frigida esse percipientes, mitigatus est in parte dolor noster. Et ecce, clamauerunt quidam ex fratribus cum magno eiulato ciphum Sancti* Eadmundi *esse combustum. Cumque plures hinc et inde quererent lapides et laminas inter carbones et cineres, extraxerunt chipum omnino inuiolatum, iacentem in medio magnorum carbonum, qui iam extincti erant, et inuenerunt*

---

[w] *Five lines of erasure follow*   [x] reclutati *erased after* cerei

[24] Hab. 3: 2.

eundem inuolutum panno lineo, sed semiusto. Pixis uero quercina, in qua chiphus de more ponebatur, combusta erat in puluerem et sole ligature ferree et sera ferrea inuente sunt. Viso itaque miraculo, omnes lacrimati sumus pre gaudio. Maiorem ergo partem frontis feretri excrustratam uidentes, et turpitudinem combustiones aborrentes, de communi consilio, accersito clam aurifabro, laminas coniungi fecimus et feretro apponi, sine omni dilacione, propter scandalum. Vestigia uero combustionis, uel cera uel alio modo cooperiri fecimus. Sed teste euangelista, 'Nihil opertum quod reuelabitur.'[25] *Venientes summo mane peregrini oblaturi, nichil tale quid perceperunt. Quidam tamen circumcirca intuentes querebant, ubi fuit ignis quem circa feretrum fuisse iam audierant. Cumque ergo omnino celari non potuit, responsum est querentibus, candelam cecidisse et manutergia tria combusta esse, et ad ignis* ardorem *lapides quosdam in fronte feretri deperisse. Fingebat tamen fama mendax caput sancti esse combustum. Quidam dicebant capillos tantum esse combustos, sed cognita postmodum ueritate, opstructum est os loquentium iniqua.*[26]

(ii) Qualiter Abbas Samson uidit corpus Sancti Ædmundi.

Audite celi,[27] *que loquar, audiat terra fact*a *Samson abbatis. Igitur appropinquante festo Sancti* Eadmundi, *politi sunt lapides marmorei et parata sunt omnia ad eleuacionem feretri. Celebrato igitur die festi, sexta feria, sequente die dominica, indictum est triduanum ieiunium populo, et ostensa est eis publice causa ieiunii. Abbas autem predixit conuentui ut se prepararent ad transferendum corpus nocte proxima post feriam secundam, et ad transferendum feretrum et consistendum super magnum altare, donec machina cementaria perficeretur, et tempus et modum prefixit ad tale opus. Cum ergo uenissemus illa nocte ad horas matutinas, stetit magnum feretrum super altare, uacuum intus, ornatum coriis albis ceruinis, sursum et deorsum et circumcirca, que affigebantur ligno clauis argenteis, et panellus unus stetit deorsum iuxta columpnam ecclesie, et sanctum corpus adhuc iacebat, ubi iacere solebat. Percantatis laudibus, omnes accessimus ad disciplinas suscipiendas. Quo facto, uestiti sunt albi dominus abbas et quidam cum eo, accedentes reuerenter, sicut decebat, festinabant detergere loculum. Erat autem pannus lineus exterius, qui loculum et omnia cetera includebat, qui quibusdam ligamentis suis desuper ligatus inuentus fuit. Postea quidam pannus sericus, et postea alter lineus pannus, et postea tertius, et ita tandem discoopertus est loculus stans super ligneum alueolum, ne ipse loculus possit ledi a lapide marmoreo. Iacuit super pectus martyris, affixus loculo exterius, angelus aureus ad longitudinem pedis humani, habens ensem aureum in una manu, et uexillum in altera, et subtus erat foramen in operculo, ubi antiqui custodes martyris solebant manus imponere ad tangendum sanctum corpus. Et erat uersus suprascriptus imagini, 'Martyris ecce zoma Michaelis agalma'. Erantque anuli ferrei ad duo capita loculi ad* portam, *dum* sicut solet *fieri in cista Norensi. Subleuantes ergo*

[26] Ps. 63: 11. *The Chronicle of Jocelin of Brakelond*, ed. H. E. Butler (NMT, 1949), pp. 106–9.   [27] Isa. 1: 2.

loculum cum corpore, portabant usque ad altare, et apposui manum meam peccatricem in auxilium ad portandum, licet abbas precepisset, ne aliquis accederet, nisi uocatus. Et inclusus est loculus in feretro, panello apposito et coniuncto. Putabamus omnes quod abbas uellet loculum ostendere populo in octauis festi et reportare sanctum corpus coram omnibus, sed male seducti sumus, sicut sequentia docebunt. Feria quarta, canente conuentu completorium, locutus est abbas cum sacrista et Waltero medico, et initum est consilium, ut duodecim fratres uocarentur, qui fortes essent ad portandos panellos feretri, et prudentes essent ad eos coniungendos et disiungendos. Dixitque abbas se habere in uotis uidere patronum suum, et se uelle sibi associari sacristam et Walterum medicum ad inspectionem. Et nominati sunt duo capellani abbatis et duo custodes feretri, et duo magistri de uestiario, et alii sex, sacrista Hugo, Walterus medicus, Augustinus, Willelmus de Disce, Robertus, Ricardus. Dormiente ergo conuentu, uestiti sunt illi duodecim albis, et extraentes loculum de feretro portauerunt illum, et ponentes super tabulam iuxta antiquum locum feretri, parauerunt se ad disiungendum operculum, quod coniunctum et confixum erat loculo sexdecim clauis ferreis longissimis. Quod cum difficultate fecissent iussi sunt omnes longius abire, preter duos socios prenominatos. Eratque loculus ita repletus sancto corpore et in longitudine et in latitudine, quod uix posset acus interponi inter caput et lignum, uel inter pedes et lignum, et iacebat caput unitum corpori aliquantum leuatum paruo ceruicali. Abbas ergo intuens cominus, inuenit prius pannum sericum uelantem totum corpus, et postea pannum lineum miri candoris, et super caput pannum paruum lineum, et postea alium pannum paruum sericum et subtilem, tanquam hoc esset uelum alicuius sanctimonialis femine. Et postea inuenerunt corpus inuolutum lineo panno, et tunc demum patuerunt omnia lineamenta sancti corporis. Hic restitit abbas, dicens se non esse ausum procedere ultra ut sanctum carnem nudam uideret. Accipiens ergo caput inter manus suas, gemendo ait, 'Gloriose martyr, sancte Eadmunde, benedicta sit illa hora qua natus fuisti. Gloriose martyr, ne uertas mihi in perdicionem audaciam meam, quod te tango, peccator et miser. Tu scis deuocionem et intencionem meam.' Et procedens tetigit oculos et nasum ualde grossum et ualde eminentem, et postea tetigit pectus et brachia, et subleuans manum sinistram digitos tetigit, et digitos suos posuit inter digitos sanctos. Et procedens inuenit pedes rigide erectos tanquam hominis hodie mortui, et digitos pedum tetigit, et tangendo numerauit. Datumque est consilium, ut ceteri fratres uocarentur et miracula uiderent, et uenerunt sex uocati et sex alii fratres cum illis qui se intruserunt sine assensu [ab]batis[y] et uidebant sanctum corpus, scilicet, Walterus [de Sancto][y] Albano, et Hugo infirmarius, et Gilbert[us frater pri]oris[y] et Ricardus de Hehingham, et Jocellus celerarius, et Turstanus Paruus, qui solus manum apposuit et pedes sancti tetigit et genua. Et ut esset copia testium, disponente Altissimo, unus ex nostris fratribus Iohannes de Disce sedens supra testudinem[z] ecclesie, cum seruientibus de uestiario, omnia ista euidenter uidebat. His factis, affigebatur operculum loculo

---

[y] *manuscript mutilated* [z] *from* testitudinem

eisdem clauis et totidem, et simili modo, ut prius, cooperto martyre eisdem pannis et eodem ordine, sicut prius inuentus fuit. Et postea collocatus est loculus in loco solito, et positus est super loculum, iuxta angelum, furulus quidam sericus, in quo reposita fuit scedula Anglice scripta, continens quasdam salutaciones Ailwini monachi, ut creditur, que scedula prius fuit inuenta iuxta angelum aureum quando loculus detegebatur. Et iubente abbate, statim scriptum fuit et aliud breue, et in eodem furulo reconditum, sub hac forma uerborum 'Anno ab incarnatione Domini .mc. nonagesimo octauo, abbas Samson, tractus deuocione, corpus sancti Eadmundi uidit et tetigit, nocte proxima post festum sancte Katarine, his testibus—' et subscripta sunt nomina monachorum .xviii. Inuoluerunt autem fratres totum loculum panno lineo satis apto, et posuerunt desuper pannum sericum preciosum et nouum, quem Hubertus archiepiscopus Cantuariensis eodem anno optulerat et quendam pannum lineum dupplicatum ad longitudinem loculi posuerunt proximum lapidi, ne loculus uel alueolus eius posset ledi a lapide. Et postea portati sunt panelli et decenter coniuncti in feretro. Cum autem ueniret conuentus ad matutinas cantandas, et ista perciperet, doluerunt omnes qui hec non uiderant, intra se dicentes quod 'male seducti sumus'. Cantatis autem horis matutinis, conuocauit abbas conuentum ante magnum altare et ostendens eis breuiter rem gestam allegabat quod non debuit nec patuit omnes uocare ad talia. Quibus auditis, 'Te Deum laudamus', cantauimus, et ad campanas[aa] in coro resonandas properauimus.

Quarto die sequente, custodes feretri, et custodem sancti Botulfi, deposuit abbas, nouos substituens, et leges eis proponens, ut sanctuaria honestius et diligentius custodirent. Magnumque altare, quod prius concauum erat ubi sepius quedam indecenter reponebantur, et spacium illud quod erat inter feretrum et altare, solidari fecit lapide et cemento, ne aliquod ignis periculum fieri possit per negligentiam custodum, sicut prius, iuxta dictum sapientis, 'Felix, quem faciunt aliena pericula cautum'.[28]

[aa] *from* campandas

[28] *The Chronicle of Jocelin of Brakelond*, ed. H. E. Butler (NMT, 1949), pp. 111–16.

INDEX OF QUOTATIONS AND ALLUSIONS

A. BIBLICAL ALLUSIONS

B. ALLUSIONS TO CLASSICAL WRITERS

CONCORDANCES

(i) With *Florentii Wigorniensis Monachi Chronicon ex Chronicis*, ed. B. Thorpe (English Historical Society; 2 vols., London, 1848–9).

Thorpe, ii	This edition	Thorpe, ii	This edition	Thorpe, ii	This edition
1	4	43	88–90	85	166–8
2	4–6	44	90–2	86	168–70
3	6–8	45	92	87	170
4	8–10	46	92–4	88	170–2
5	10–12	47	94–6	89	174–6
6	12–14	48	96–8	90	182–6
7	14–16	49	98–100	91	186–92
8	16–18	50	100–2	92	192–6
9	18–20	51	102	93	196, 208–10
10	20–4	52	102–4	94	210–12
11	24–6	53	104–6	95	212, 214–16
12	26–30	54	106–8	96	216–18
13	30–2	55	108–10	97	218–20
14	32–4	56	110–12	98	220–2, 228–30
15	34–6	57	112–14	99	230–2
16	36–8	58	114–16	100	232–4
17	38–40	59	116–18	101	234
18	42–4	60	118–20	102	234–6
19	44	61	120–2	103	236–8
20	44–6	62	122	104	238–40
21	46–8	63	122–4	105	240–2
22	48–50	64	124–6, 130	106	242–4
23	50–2	65	130–2	107	244–6
24	52–4	66	132–4	108	246–8
25	54	67	134–6	109	248–50
26	54–6	68	136–8	110	250–2
27	56–8	69	138–40	111	252–4
28	58–60	70	140–2	112	254–6
29	60–2	71	142	113	256–8
30	62–4	72	142–4	114	258–64
31	64–6	73	144–6	115	264–6
32	66–8	74	146–8	116	266–8
33	68–70	75	148–50	117	268–70
34	70–2	76	150	118	270–2
35	72–4	77	150–2	119	272–4
36	74	78	152–6	120	274–6
37	74–6	79	156–8	121	276–8
38	76–8	80	158–60	122	278–80
39	78, 82	81	160–2	123	280–2
40	82–4	82	162	124	282–4
41	84–6	83	162–4	125	284–6
42	86–8	84	164–6	126	286–8

Thorpe, ii	This edition	Thorpe, ii	This edition	Thorpe, ii	This edition
127	288–90	131	294–6	134	300–2
128	290–2	132	296–8	135	302
129	292	133	298–300	136	302–4
130	292–4				

(ii) With *The Chronicle of John of Worcester 1118–40*, ed. J. R. H. Weaver (Anecdota Oxoniensia, 4th ser., xiii; Oxford, 1908).

Weaver	This edition	Weaver	This edition	Weaver	This edition
13	142–4	30	190–4	47	238–40
14	144–6	31	194–8	48	240–2
15	146–8	32	198–200	49	242–4, 248
16	148–50	33	200–2	50	248–50
17	150–4	34	202–4	51	250–4
18	154–8	35	204–6	52	254–6
19	158–60	36	206–8	53	258–62
20	160–2	37	208–10	54	262–4, 266
21	162–4	38	210–12	55	266–8
22	164–6	39	212–14	56	270, 272
23	166–8	40	214–18	57	272–6
24	168–70	41	218, 222–4	58	276–8
25	170–4	42	224–8	59	278–80
26	174–6	43	228–30	60	280–4
27	176–80	44	230–2	61	284–6
28	180–4	45	232–4	62	286–8
29	184–90	46	234–8	63	288

GENERAL INDEX

Cumbrians 255 n. 25
Cuthbert, St, translation of xxix, 106–7
Cycles:
532-year cycle 22–3

Danegeld 202–3
Danish fleet 8–9, 10–11, 14–15, 26 n. 10
David, bishop of Bangor 146–7, 150–1,
158–9, 160–1, 168–9
dispute with see of Glamorgan 184–5
David, king of Scotland 154–5, 174–5,
178–9, 236–7
invasion of 1138 xxxviii, 252–7
devil, appears at time of William II's
death 92–3
Devizes:
Gregory Gréne ordained at 150–1
Duke Robert imprisoned at 212 n. 1
capture of 244–9, 266–7
Robert Fitz Hubert and 286–9
Matilda escapes to 300–1
Devon 8–9, 218–19, 313
Diarmait mac Máel na mBó, king of
Leinster 8 n. 2
Divizo, cardinal of St Martin 122–3
Dol, siege 28–9
Dolfin 62–3
Domesday survey xxii, 44–5
Dominic, prior of Evesham 160–1
Donald Bane, king of Scotland xxiii,
66–7, 72–3, 84–5
Dorchester 4–5
bishop of, see Wulfwig
Duncan, son of Malcolm III, king of
Scotland xxiii, 48–9, 66–9, 72–3
Dunfermline 67 n. 7
abbots of, see Geoffrey
Dublin, bishops of, see Gregory
Dudley 250–1
Dunstable, court at 234–5
Durham:
Liulf retires to 32–3
burial place 82–3
bishop consecrated at 90–1
bishops of, see Æthelric, Æthelwine,
Walcher, William, Ranulf Flambard
priors of, see Turgot

Eadmer, Historia Novorum:
use by John of Worcester xxvi–xxvii
Eadnoth the Staller 6–7
Eadric, son of Ælfric, called Silvaticus
xxi, 4–5, 14–15, 20–1

Ealdred, abbot of Abingdon 307
Ealdred, archbishop of York xxi, 6–7,
8–9, 12–13, 14–17
Earcongota 126–7
earthquakes 36–7, 56–7, 58–9, 118–19,
140–3, 144–5, 210–11
East Angles, bishops of, see Thetford
Ecgfrith, abbot of St Albans 14 n. 4
Ecgwine, bishop of Worcester 78–9
Edgar the Atheling:
in Scotland xxii, 6–7, 22–3, 59 n. 5
and William I xxiv, 4–5, 22–3
helps invade England 8–9
goes to Apulia 44–5
expelled from Normandy 58–9
brokers peace between William II and
Malcolm III 60–1
returns to Normandy 62–3
invades Scotland 84–5
Edgar, king of Scotland xxiii, 84–5,
110–11
Edith, queen 26–7
Edmund, Harold II's son 6–7
Edward, Malcolm III's son 66–7
Edwin, earl 4–5, 18–21
Elmham, bishops of, see Æthelmær, Herfast
Elster 37 n. 2
Ely 14 n. 5, 20–1, 102–3, 280–1
abbey changed to bishopric 118–19,
128–31
foundation and early history 126–31
abbesses, see Æthelthryth, Seaxburg,
Eormenhild
abbots, see Brihtnoth, Richard
bishops of, see Hervey
Eormenhild, abbess of Ely 126–7
Ermenfrid, bishop of Sion, papal legate
10–11, 12–15
Ernulf, abbot of Peterborough, bishop of
Rochester 112 n. 6, 134–5, 138–9,
148–9, 156–7
Eu, county of 58–9, 70–1
Eustace II, count of Boulogne xxix, 50–1,
82–3, 96–7, 102–3
Eustace, count of Boulogne, Stephen's
son 284–5, 296–7
Eustace Fitz John 254–5
Everard, bishop of Norwich 150–1,
158–9, 168–9, 192–3
Evesham xxix
mother house of Odense 44–5
foundation 78–9

Gilbert Foliot, abbot of Gloucester xxxi
n.47, xliv, 262–3, 264–6, 294–5
Gilbert the Universal, bishop of London
176–7, 192–3
Giso, bishop of Wells 14–15, 56–7
Glamorgan, bishops of, *see* Urban
Glasgow, bishops of, *see* John
Glastonbury:
incident at xxix, 38–41
abbots of, *see* Seffrid
Gloucester xxix
court at 42–3, 152–3
in 1088 rebellion 52–3
William II at 64–5
foundation 80–1
dedication of church 92–3
fires xxxi, 96–7, 152–3
burial place 174–5, 212–13, 220–1,
228–9, 290–1
Stephen at xliv, 240–3
summons and reception of Gilbert
Foliot xliv, 262–7
Matilda at 270–3, 292–5, 298–9, 302–3
army from, at Worcester 274–5
Robert Fitz Hubert taken to 288–9
Stephen taken to 292–3
chronicle and John of Worcester xxx–
xxxi
abbots of, *see* Serlo, William, Walter,
Gilbert Foliot
Gloucester and MS G:
annals written by G² xl–l
annals for 1128–31 xli
G²'s use of John xlii–xliii
G²'s additional information xliii–xliv
G²'s merging of different sources xliv–
xlv
G² and *Gesta Stephani* xliv
G²'s dating of annals 1128–40 xlv–xlvii
annals 1140–1 in G xlviii–l
Gloucestershire 145 n.4
Godfrey, abbot of Shrewsbury 184–5
Godfrey, abbot of Winchcombe 160–1,
200–1, 222–3, 224–5, 226–7
Godfrey, bishop of Bath xliv, xlv
consecrated 154–5
at Bishop Simon of Worcester's consecration 158–9
escorts abbot of Tewkesbury in procession 160–1
at council of Westminster (1127) 168–9
at dedication of Christ Church, Canterbury 192–3

death xliv–xlv, 212–13, 218–19
Godfrey, count 120–1
Godfrey, duke of Lorraine 82–3, 90–1,
98–9
Godric, abbot of Peterborough 102–3,
319
Godric, abbot of Winchcombe 14 n.4
Godwine, Harold II's son 6–7
Gospatric xxii, 6–7
Gower, campaign in xlv, 218–21
Gregory (VIII), antipope, bishop of Braga
142–3, 150–1
Gregory, bishop of Terracina 132–3
Gregory, cardinal of St Chrysogonus
122–3
Gregory, cardinal of SS Peter and Paul
122–3
Gregory VII, pope xxiv, 22–5, 26–7,
28–31, 36–7, 38–9, 40–1
Gregory Gréne, bishop of Dublin 150–1
Grimbald, doctor 198–203
Grimbald the Fleming 18–19
Gruffydd ap Cynan ap Iago, king of
Gwynedd 135 n.7, 146–7
Gruffydd ap Rhys ap Tewdwr xxxi n.50,
138–9, 220 n.7, 228–9
Gundulf, bishop of Rochester 18–19,
92–3, 102–3, 112–13, 312
Gunnhildr, Wilton nun 314 n.8
Guy, abbot of Pershore 102–3, 160–1,
222–3, 319
Guy, abbot of St Augustine's 64–5
Guy, bishop of Vienne, *see* Calixtus II
Gyrontinus, bishop of 132–3
Gytha, Harold II's mother xxi, 6–7

Haimo, abbot of Cerne 102–3, 319
Hampton, near Leominster 154–5
Hampton Lucy, Warwickshire 154–5,
296–7
Harold II's sons, invasion of 8–9
Harold, king, son of Swein Estrithson
8–9, 28–9
Harptree 250–1, 283 n.7
Hastings 68–71, 98–9
Helena, empress 174–5
Henry of Sully, abbot of Fécamp 284–5
Henry, archdeacon of Huntingdon xxiii,
xxix, 265 n.2
Henry of Blois, bishop of Winchester:
elected and consecrated 188–9
at dedication of Christ Church 192–3
papal legate 212–13